*Milton Cross*

MORE STORIES

OF THE

GREAT OPERAS

# Milton Cross

## MORE STORIES
## OF THE
## GREAT OPERAS

---

*Milton Cross and Karl Kohrs*

Doubleday & Company, Inc.
GARDEN CITY, NEW YORK

Library of Congress Catalog Card Number 77–132495
Copyright © 1971 by Doubleday & Company, Inc.
Copyright 1947, 1952 by Milton J. Cross
All Rights Reserved
Printed in the United States of America

# CONTENTS

PART II

## The Concert Operas

# FOREWORD

In the fifteen years since the second edition of *Complete Stories of the Great Operas* came off the press, opera as an art form has undergone the most profound and radical changes in its four-hundred-year-old history. Modern composers have brushed aside romantic conventions, eschewed melody for its own sake and—taking the cue from modern playwrights—aimed for stark and uncompromising realism in their choice of subject matter. In that respect, contemporary opera reflects the nervous, restless temper of the times—a universal mood of questioning, rebellion, skepticism and defiance of tradition.

At the same time, the lure of stage pageantry, the sensuous appeal of music as communicated by the human voice, and the fascination of the world of make-believe—those concomitants which have made opera what it is—draw the public to opera in greater numbers than ever before. Thus, classic and modern works emerge side by side in the mainstream of opera today.

With the objective of reflecting the trend of operatic repertoire during the past decade, as well as presenting works which have appeared as revivals or as new and original productions, the present volume offers thirty classic and contemporary operas, plus fifteen which have had successful presentations in concert form. By way of further orientation to the operatic scene, there are the following sections: biographical data on approximately six hundred leading singers of the past and present; "Opera Today," a brief survey; a glossary of operatic terms; a bibliography; a survey of contemporary opera; and a representative list of opera organizations in the United States.

It is hoped that the expanded scope of the present volume will in turn expand the knowledge about opera for those who treasure this art form—whether in classic or modern idiom—as an enduring source of inspiration and pleasure.

# ACKNOWLEDGMENTS

The authors wish to acknowledge with grateful thanks the invaluable assistance of those who made available the research material—in the form of opera scores, opera programs, miscellaneous subject matter from official or personal files, and so on—needed to confirm the authenticity of the information contained in this book.

Those who co-operated in providing such services include: Francis Robinson, assistant manager of the Metropolitan Opera; Mrs. John Dewitt Peltz, Metropolitan Opera archivist; Frank Paola, Metropolitan company manager and musical secretary; Miss Anne Gordon and David Reuben, of the Metropolitan press department; Miss Ruth Heider, assistant to the director of the New York City Opera; Allen Sven Oxenburg, director of the American Opera Society, and his staff; Thomas Scherman, music director of The Little Orchestra Society, Inc., and his staff; David Griffith, of National Educational Television, and his staff; Mrs. Lynda La Russo, librarian, Port Chester, New York, Library; Mrs. Vivian Farrell, New York City; Miss Hildegarde Becher, Harrison, New York; and Mrs. Kathryn Kohrs, Port Chester, New York.

# PART I

---

## THE STORIES OF
## THE GREAT OPERAS

# Adriana Lecouvreur

## *by* FRANCESCO CILÈA

### (1866–1950)

### *Libretto by*
#### ARTURO COLAUTTI

Adapted from the play *Adrienne Lecouvreur,* by the French dramatists Augustin Eugène Scribe and Ernest Wilfried Legouvé

#### CHARACTERS

| | |
|---|---|
| Adriana Lecouvreur, leading actress of the Comédie Française | Soprano |
| Maurizio, Count of Saxony | Tenor |
| Michonnet, stage manager of the Comédie | Baritone |
| Prince de Bouillon | Bass |
| Princess de Bouillon | Mezzo-soprano |
| Abbé de Chazeuil | Tenor |
| Quinault | Bass |
| Poisson | Tenor |
| Mlle. Jouvenot   members of the Comédie | Soprano |
| Mlle. Dangeville | Mezzo-soprano |
| Major-domo | Tenor |
| Lady's maid | Mezzo-soprano |

Ladies and gentlemen, actors, stagehands, servants

#### CHARACTERS IN THE BALLET

Paris, Mercury, Juno, Pallas, Venus

*Place:* Paris
*Time:* March 1730
*First performance:* Teatro Lirico, Milan, November 6, 1902
*Original language:* Italian

---

*Adriana Lecouvreur* is the fourth of five operas composed by Cilèa, a contemporary of Puccini, Leoncavallo and Mascagni and one of the leading Italian musicians of his day. The opera is based on incidents in the lives of actual people prominent in the theatrical world of eighteenth-century Paris. It is the story of the tragic love affair between Adrienne Lecouvreur, the leading actress of the Comédie Française during the earlier years of Louis XV (1710–74), and Count Maurice de Saxe, who later became Marshal of France.

*Adriana* and *L'Arlesiana,* Cilèa's third opera, are the only two of the composer's works which have survived in the repertoire. The 1907–8 season of the Metropolitan Opera in New York opened with *Adriana.* In the cast were Caruso, Cavalieri, Scotti, and Journet. In 1963 the opera was revived at the Met for Renata Tebaldi. She also sang the leading role (opposite Franco Corelli) at the opening performance of the Metropolitan Opera's 1968–69 season on September 16, 1968.

Like his contemporaries, Cilèa was a melodist, and *Adriana* is outstanding for its lyrical qualities. It has been pointed out, however, that the composer has a tendency to repeat melodic themes associated with the individual characters, which makes for a certain monotony. Yet this fault is compensated for by the richness and beauty not only of the arias but of the concerted numbers as well.

There is no overture. The curtain rises immediately.

## ACT I

The Green Room of the Comédie Française, where two plays are about to be performed: Racine's tragedy *Bajazet,* and Régnard's comedy *Les Folies Amoureuses.* Mlle. Jouvenot, Mlle. Dangeville, Quinault and Poisson are putting on their costumes and giving last-minute touches to their makeup. Meanwhile they are driving Michonnet, the stage manager, nearly frantic with their demands for attention. Their voices blend in a spirited ensemble ("Michonnet, della biacca!") which reflects the backstage tension at curtain time.

In a lively refrain ("Michonnet su! Michonnet giù!") the stage manager complains about his lot. Worse than a lackey's, he grumbles —listening to griping actors, running their errands, trying to keep peace backstage. . . . He would give it all up if it weren't for the hope of becoming a *sociétaire* ("di socio proprietario"), a full-fledged member of the Comédie, and retiring on a pension—plus the fact that his job keeps him near that glorious creature Adriana, with whom he is hopelessly in love.

He is jolted out of his reflections as Quinault, practicing gestures with a scimitar he uses in his role, almost runs him through. The ensemble becomes more agitated as tension rises and the players begin snapping at each other.

They are interrupted by the entrance of the Prince de Bouillon and the Abbé de Chazeuil. As the two are announced by Michonnet, Poisson observes that the Prince is the current heart interest of La Duclos (Adriana's stage rival) and a dabbler in chemistry as well as in love ("di chimica dilettante e d'amore")—a significant remark in the light of later events.

In a continuation of the ensemble, the Prince and Chazeuil fatuously compliment the players, who respond in kind. In a brief duet, the visitors, with spurious gallantry, commend the two actresses for their irresistible charm. Then, as they both turn to leave, they ask Michonnet where La Duclos is. Dressing, Michonnet answers, to which Jouvenot and Dangeville spitefully remark that "undressing" would be more accurate. Ignoring this sally, the Abbé remarks that the theater is packed. Michonnet tells him that is to be expected when Adriana and La Duclos are to appear in the same play. This brings more ribald comment from the two envious supporting players.

At this point, to the accompaniment of an imposing chord in the orchestra, Adriana appears. She is costumed in oriental fashion for the role of Roxane in *Bajazet* and is wearing a magnificent necklace, a gift from the Queen.[1] Oblivious to everyone, Adriana declaims the lines of her role over sustained chords in the orchestra: "Del sultano Amuratte m'arrendo all'imper." Dissatisfied with her reading, she repeats the passage.

When the Abbé and Bouillon exclaim loudly in admiration, Adriana responds in the first of the opera's well-known arias—"Io son l'umile ancella." She is nothing more than the humble servant of that glorious art which can touch the heart of mankind, she sings, merely the instrument which gives voice to poetry. Her name is Sincerity. Her voice itself is but a fragile breath which will die away. The aria ends on a high pianissimo note.

Bouillon, impressed, asks what more she would seek. Truth alone, Adriana replies simply. She adds that she has learned nothing

[1] Queen Marie of France. Born Marie Leszczynska, daughter of Stanislas I Leszczynski, King of Poland (1677–1766). She was married to Louis XV when he was fifteen years old. He had become King at the age of five.

about her art from anyone—except from her faithful friend and adviser Michonnet ("Umile cor devoto"). Michonnet, brought close to tears, protests that no credit is due him.

The stage callboy interrupts the scene and the actors prepare to go on. There is an excited murmur of voices in the background, signaling that the play is about to begin. As the Abbé and Bouillon leave, they again ask about La Duclos. Michonnet tells them she is in her dressing room hastily writing a letter. Bouillon asks sharply: "To whom?" Jouvenot and Dangeville break in to remark flippantly that the note is certainly not for him, because La Duclos knows he already is here. When Bouillon and the Abbé are alone, the Prince, with a meaningful look at the Abbé, declares he must have that letter. The Abbé asks how he is to get it. Handing him a purse, Bouillon curtly tells him to proceed. They leave.

During a brief orchestral interlude Adriana, absorbed in her role, continues studying her lines while Michonnet stares at her longingly, trying to get up enough courage to speak his mind. "At last we are alone," he murmurs ("Eccoci soli, alfin!"), and this phrase introduces a touching musical dialogue in quasi-recitative.

For five long years, he sings, he has been tormented by his love for Adriana. She is young and beautiful—while for him, alas, the Maytime of life is past. Shall he confess his love now, or wait until tomorrow? But then it will be a day later still. This thought propels him to a decision.

Hesitantly, he begins by telling Adriana that he has good news: His uncle, the pharmacist in Carcassonne, had died and left him a legacy of ten thousand francs. Half amused, Adriana is duly impressed. Then, in mock seriousness, she commiserates with him ("Tanto peggio") as he wonders what he is to do with all that money. In any case, Michonnet goes on rather desperately, this stroke of fortune has given him an extraordinary idea: to get married. "Excellent!" Adriana exclaims, adding somewhat wistfully that she wishes she could ("Ah, se potessi anch'io!").

Beside himself with joy, Michonnet murmurs that now he must tell her ("Allora, glielo dico"). But before he can speak Adriana remarks, with a troubled expression, that she seems to be losing her touch—as last night's performance of *Phèdre* proved. She was too concerned over the fact that there had been no further news following the report of the battle in Courland. "News of whom?" Michonnet asks. "The man I love," Adriana answers ("Il mio cavalier").

Michonnet's joy turns to despair as she goes on to explain (mistakenly) that her beloved is a lieutenant of Count de Saxe ("Era unsemplice alfiere").[2] He has been at the front in Courland, where a battle has been raging. There had been no word of him for a long time, Adriana says, but yesterday she saw him. And tonight, she adds joyfully, he will see her as Roxane. Then, with touching concern, she asks Michonnet about his own plans for romance and a wedding. "That can wait," he answers bitterly. He leaves as three knocks are heard—the traditional signal in French theaters for the raising of the curtain.

Adriana watches him go, then turns again to the study of her role. Suddenly there is an excited burst of music, then the voice of Maurizio calling Adriana's name. The lovers rush into each other's arms to the accompaniment of an impassioned theme in the orchestra. Impetuously Maurizio tells Adriana that he could no longer wait for her appearance, and so made his way backstage. When Adriana chides him for being reckless he launches into the well-known aria "La dolcissima effigie," in which he extravagantly acclaims her as his soul's inspiration.

In ensuing dialogue, Adriana asks if he has spoken to the Count de Saxe about his promotion. Maurizio evasively replies that the Count promises—but does nothing. When Adriana says she will somehow contrive to speak to the Count on this matter, Maurizio warns her that Saxe is a dangerous man, a devil with women ("È un uom pericoloso").

Adriana turns to go onstage and Maurizio protests that she is deserting him. Repeating the theme of his aria, Adriana assures him that tonight she will act for him alone. Their voices blend as they repeat their avowals. As they are leaving, Maurizio tells her he will be in the "third box on the right." Adriana gives him a bunch of violets as a token of her love.

Prince de Bouillon and the Abbé now reappear. The Abbé hands Bouillon a letter with the remark "Corpus delicti!" This introduces a musical colloquy in which the two plan the strategy that is to entrap the clandestine lovers. The Abbé explains that he got the letter (written by La Duclos in her dressing room) by the simple expedient of bribing her maid with one hundred louis. In spoken recitative, the Abbé reads the message aloud to the infuriated Prince: "Stasera alle undici, laggiù nel solito villino, presso

2 Maurice, Count of Saxony (Maurizio), was the son of Stanislas II Augustus (1732-98), Elector of Saxony and King of Poland. The Count had pretensions to both thrones.

la Senna . . . per un affare d'alta politica"—"Tonight at eleven, at
the villa near the Seine, on a matter of political importance." His
very own villa, the Prince rages. What is worse, the letter is signed
"Constancy," the nickname he himself gave to Duclos. The Abbé
relishes the irony.

Examining the address—"third box on the right"—the Abbé suddenly recalls that he saw Maurice de Saxe enter it. Quite obviously, the two men agree, Saxe is the secret lover. Forthwith,
they begin plotting to trap the guilty pair ("Un gaio festino").
Meanwhile, unknown to the two men, Jouvenot, Dangeville,
Quinault and Poisson return to the Green Room, hide in the
background and overhear the entire plot, which is revealed in the
continuation of the duet.

The Prince will invite the entire cast to a gay supper party at
his villa. There the lovers will be surprised in their "nest," and the
next day all Paris will smack its lips over the scandal. The Prince
orders a servant to take the letter to "Box Three—confidential."
At this point an ensemble builds up as the four players comment
on the situation ("Quanto è burlevole!") and incidentally disclose
additional information about the intrigues at the villa.

It seems that, while La Duclos has the Prince as her "patron,"
she has another ally—the Princess herself. The conniving actress has
given the key to the love nest to the Princess, who brazenly entertains her own lover there. And now, an anonymous letter
("Ma già una lettera") making an appointment at the villa, written
for the Princess by La Duclos, has been sold by the actress' maid
to the Prince. The ensemble (calling to mind the quintet in *Carmen*) comes to a crackling finish as the players maliciously speculate on what will happen, while the Prince and the Abbé discuss
their plot to bring the guilty lovers together. The scene comes to
an end as Michonnet orders them to take their places in the wings
for their next cues.

Stationing himself in the wings where he can watch Adriana,
Michonnet listens enthralled to the monologue of Roxane. He
fumes at the audience for not applauding louder for his idol's
divine performance. In a plaintive refrain, "E dir che così bene,"
he laments that her superb acting is for someone else, not for
himself. But, even so, when he listens to her voice he forgets.
. . . Even the props, he gasps suddenly, striking his forehead. Frantically he begins looking for the letter which Jouvenot, in the role
of Zatime, must hand to Adriana in the next scene.

At that moment, Maurizio strides in cursing because some "political matter" ("Maledetta politica!")—as stated in the letter just

handed to him in his box—will prevent his seeing Adriana after the performance. Over an agitated orchestral accompaniment, the byplay involving the prop letter now follows. Maurizio reflects that his being summoned to the villa means that the Princess has mentioned his political plans to the Cardinal. Now he is torn between love and duty. He decides to wait for Adriana's exit.

Michonnet, at last finding the prop letter—a blank piece of paper —lays it on a table and, when Quinault walks by, asks the actor to give it to Jouvenot. Quinault, unco-operative as usual, ignores the request. Maurizio snatches up the paper and scribbles a message to Adriana. When Jouvenot rushes in calling for her prop letter, he hands her the piece of paper with a bow. Highly pleased with his improvised strategy, Maurizio sings in an impassioned refrain ("Adriana avrà due mie") that Adriana will know why they cannot meet as planned—ruefully adding that this is what Courland has cost him. His voice blends in a ringing phrase with that of Michonnet, who enthuses over Adriana's fabulous art as she plays the letter scene. Adriana's genuine shock and dismay at reading Maurizio's message in the prop letter brings thunderous applause from the unsuspecting audience at the closing curtain.

A brief ensemble follows as the actors troop into the Green Room, followed by Bouillon, the Abbé and other members of the audience. The players, though furiously jealous of Adriana's triumph, join in hailing her as she enters ("Ad Adriana onor!"). Pale and distraught, she is on the verge of collapse. As Michonnet revives her with smelling salts she murmurs brokenly that she saw Maurizio in the theater.

Bouillon invites all to the midnight supper party in honor of Adriana's success. She at first declines but decides to go when the Prince tells her that the Count of Saxony will be there. With that he hands her the key to the villa. Aside, Adriana sings that she will speak to the Count about Maurizio. In a choral phrase, all on stage voice their pleasure over the revelry in store at the midnight party. The curtain falls.

## ACT II

A small salon in the villa La Grange Batelière on the banks of the Seine not far from Paris. From the terrace a flight of steps leads to a broad esplanade extending to the river's edge.

In the salon the Princess de Bouillon is waiting for her lover. A brief pulsating theme in the orchestra underscores her anxiety and impatience. In one of the opera's most dramatic arias, "Acerba voluttà, dolce tortura," she gives voice to her conflicting emotions of love, anguish and fear. A clock strikes in the distance. The Princess springs to her feet and listens intently. Every echo, every shadow of night mocks a lover's impatience, she sings ("Ogn'eco, ogn'ombra").

Finally she goes to the doors at the back, flings them open and stares at the starry sky. In the brilliant climax of the aria she implores the wandering Star of the East never to set until she is in her lover's arms ("O vagabonda stella d'Oriente"). As the music dies away on a serene phrase the Princess sinks down on a divan.

A moment later Maurizio bounds in through the doors at the back and kneels before the Princess. She greets him somewhat irritably. Maurizio explains that he was delayed because he was trying to elude two mysterious men following him. Glancing at the bunch of violets pinned to his uniform, the Princess pointedly asks if a certain sweet-scented posy might not have been the reason for his being late ("Il ritardo cagionato"). With a courtly gesture, Maurizio instantly hands her the flowers.

A long duet then ensues as the Princess informs Maurizio that she plead his cause (as Pretender) so fervently that Her Majesty was moved to tears ("Con la Regina a lungo favellai"). The Cardinal,[3] however, is still undecided. She goes on to warn the Count that he has enemies. Maurizio sharply interjects that he has never yet been vanquished, adding that he will flee the country rather than risk imprisonment in the Bastille as royal Pretender and plotter.

At that the Princess upbraids him for daring even to think of casting her love aside and deserting her ("Ed io dovrei lasciarvi"). When Maurizio protests that he must put royal duty before love, the Princess becomes suspicious. In jealous fury she accuses him of being in love with someone else. Admitting as much, Maurizio tries to assure her that he still is devoted to her. When he flatly refuses to name her rival, the Princess warns him she will tear the mask from the woman's face.

Then, in a ringing aria, "L'anima ho stanca," Maurizio implores her (somewhat fatuously) to show him mercy instead of hatred in this hour of his anguish. Even though love is ended, their friendship must last forever. In rage and scorn the Princess cries that love is flame, friendship ashes ("Amore è fiamma, e cener l'amistà").

[3] André Hercule de Fleury (1653–1743), French cardinal and statesman.

Suddenly the two are startled by the sound of carriage wheels outside. Panic-stricken, the Princess rushes to the door, then gasps that her husband is stepping out of his carriage. Maurizio, promising to save her, pushes her into an adjoining room.

An instant later, Bouillon and the Abbé burst in and confront Maurizio, gloating over the success of their plot. As the dialogue continues in trio form over a crackling orchestral accompaniment, they gleefully inform him that they caught a glimpse of the lady— a slim-waisted creature all in white. With a shrug, Maurizio answers that there was no such person present. Bouillon retorts that he knows everything. Losing his temper, Maurizio promptly challenges the Prince to a duel. The latter immediately backs down, remarking that it was all a joke. The Prince, says the Abbé, is in the Count's debt. "La Duclos," adds Bouillon in explanation. He has grown tired of her, he goes on, and now that the Count is her lover, he himself is free.

Suddenly everything becomes clear. Maurizio realizes—to his vast relief—that Bouillon and the Abbé assumed they were trapping him in a rendezvous with La Duclos, not the Princess. The Prince holds out his hand and the Count takes it gladly.

Adriana now appears and Bouillon hurries to welcome her. Leading her into the room he introduces her as "the great Sultana" to the Count de Saxe. The Abbé dryly comments that one merely need say "Adriana." A theme associated with Adriana sounds prominently in the orchestra at this point. As Adriana, in stunned surprise, stammers Maurizio's name, the Count, aside, warns her not to betray herself. Bouillon pompously announces that this great actress wishes to speak to the Count de Saxe about a certain young officer. Adriana quietly observes that, under the circumstances, the young officer no longer is in need of her assistance.

The Prince abruptly reminds the Abbé that he is to make preparations for the midnight supper party. Aside, he tells the Abbé that their prey is in the trap, and there she will stay. As the Abbé leaves, the Prince declares that no one is to leave the villa until daylight. He then leaves to search the grounds.

One of the opera's finest duets ("Eri degno d'un trono") now follows as Adriana and Maurizio confront each other. Still incredulous, she asks him if he really is the renowned Count de Saxe. In the opening phrases of the duet she sings that even as "lieutenant" he was worthy of a throne. In an answering refrain ("Tu sei la mia vittoria") Maurizio apostrophizes her as his victory and his crown. In each other's arms, their voices blend in the passionate climax of the duet.

Hearing voices outside, Maurizio frees himself from Adriana's embrace. A moment later Michonnet enters with the Abbé. He is trying to get permission to leave the villa, contrary to the Prince's orders. He has urgent businesss with La Duclos, he explains—he must ask her if she will consent to play a certain new role ("Per una parte nuova").

With an affable leer, the Abbé tells Michonnet there is no need to go to fetch her, because she already is at the villa. Adriana gasps in surprise. Enjoying the effect, the Abbé, in a phrase insinuatingly sung on one note, explains in mythological terms ("questa è Citera") that here in "Cytherea,[4] Venus has arranged a tryst with Mars."

Adriana askes if the Abbé means the Count. Despite Maurizio's angry command to keep quiet, the Abbé obstinately insists that La Duclos is in the other room. Adriana starts for the door but Maurizio bars her way. In a flash, Michonnet enters the door and slams it behind him. In an ensuing refrain ("Adriana, ascolta") Maurizio explains that he came to the villa solely for political reasons. He swears on his honor that it is not La Duclos who is hiding in the room. Then he asks Adriana to stand guard at the door and under no circumstances allow the Abbé to enter. Moreover, she herself must promise not to attempt to find out who the lady really is. Adriana promises. Maurizio rushes away. Adriana sings ("Sull'onor suo giurò") that, as he swore on his honor and cannot lie, so she too will keep her word.

Suddenly Michonnet emerges from the room completely bewildered and stammers to Adriana and the Abbé: "What a blunder! It is not Duclos after all!" ("Che granchio!"). This introduces a dialogue in trio form, in 6/8 waltz tempo, which underscores the seriocomic mood of the scene. When the two ask Michonnet who *is* in the room, he sheepishly admits that he never saw her.

It was pitch-dark in there, he complains ("tenebre peste"), and as he groped about, a needle pricked his hand. In a falsetto imitation of a woman's voice Michonnet relates that a voice asked who he was and whom he was seeking ("Chi siete?"). The "unknown" told him she was not the one, then offered to make it worth his while if he helped her to escape secretly.

Adriana and the Abbé laughingly ask Michonnet what happened next. Nothing to do but leave, says Michonnet with a shrug. Thereupon the Abbé picks up a candelabra from the table and starts for

---

[4] The Greek island near which, according to mythology, the goddess Venus rose from the sea.

the door of the room. Adriana, resolutely barring his way, pointedly reminds him that this is someone else's secret ("È d'altri un segreto"). The Abbé asks slyly: "The Count's secret . . . or the Prince's?" With a knowing laugh, Adriana replies that the Prince's friend is innocent ("La bella è innocente"). Saying he will so inform the Prince, the Abbé leaves to the accompaniment of a descending chromatic figure in the orchestra.

A brief colloquy follows over sustained chords in the orchestra. Michonnet asks Adriana what she intends to do. Save the person in that room, she answers. Michonnet vainly tries to dissuade her, then is made even more unhappy when she says she is taking the risk not on his behalf but to keep her promise to the Count. Resignedly, Michonnet agrees to stand guard at the door.

As a slow waltz rhythm begins in the orchestra, Adriana blows out the candles one by one until the salon is in almost complete darkness. Going to the door, she knocks three times. When there is no answer she calls out: "Open, Madame, in the name of Maurizio!" ("Apritemi, Signora, nel nome di Maurizio!"). This marks the beginning of the dramatic duet which concludes the act.

Slowly the door opens and the figure of the Princess clad in white becomes dimly visible. She asks Adriana why she has come. To save you, Adriana replies. When the other tells her that all escape has been cut off, Adriana hands her the key previously given her by Bouillon. This, she says, will unlock the garden gate. She warns that she cannot give explicit directions because this house is unfamiliar to her. "I know it well," the Princess says. "There is a secret panel here."

After a moment's search she finds the panel and pushes it open. But before making her escape she insists that she must see her rescuer's face. Adriana curtly warns her not to try. Growing suspicious, the Princess, aside, murmurs that she has heard that voice before ("Ma questa voce l'udii sovente").

Here a rather menacing theme in the orchestra reflects the mounting tension of the scene as the Princess demands to know the identity of the person who is so vitally concerned with her fate at this point. Someone who trusts her, Adriana answers with simple candor. Instantly the Princess realizes that it is Maurizio. The duet surges to a powerful climax as the two women, both claiming the love of the same man, pour out their jealous rage and scorn.

At the height of the quarrel servants bearing torches are seen outside. When the Princess cries that her husband is coming, Adriana contemptuously dares her to stay. Going toward the door, she shouts to the servants to bring in the lights. Terror-stricken, the Princess rushes to the secret panel and vanishes through its opening.

Adriana turns, finds her rival gone. In wild anger she cries that the coward has fled ("Fuggita! Vile!"). As the orchestra blares out the closing theme of the duet, Bouillon, the Abbé and the players from the Comédie pass along the terrace at the back. Suddenly Michonnet rushes in holding a bracelet which the Princess dropped as she fled. This he hands to Adriana, at the same time trying to comfort her. Tormented by the thought that Maurizio probably fled the villa with her rival, Adriana collapses in despair.[5]

## ACT III

The grand ballroom of the Prince de Bouillon's palace. At one side is a small stage. At the Abbé's direction, servants are completing preparations for the Princess' reception. After a spirited orchestral introduction, during which the Abbé officiously orders the servants about, the Princess enters costumed for the ball. In an ensuing monologue ("Ah! quella donna!") she moodily ponders how to learn the identity of her rival—she who came to her rescue and yet is stealing away her lover. In tones of suppressed fury she recalls the sound of the rival's voice—caressing yet menacing ("Oh quella voce che carezza").

Her reflections are interrupted by the Abbé, who fawns on her and comments extravagantly on her beauty—with particular reference to her voluptuous bosom. She acknowledges the compliment with amused sarcasm. In a brief, mocking refrain ("Dite che il dio d'amore") the Abbé sings that even though the god of love has given her a heart of marble, he will gladly play Pygmalion to her Galatea.[6]

---

[5] This detail of the plot is not explained in the stage action of the abridged version of the opera. In another version Bouillon and the Abbé enter shortly after Adriana has sung her final phrase. The Abbé takes the Prince into the room to prove to him that La Duclos was not hiding there. Michonnet then enters, gives Adriana the bracelet and tells her he saw the Count leave with the "unknown." Bouillon and the Abbé re-enter. La Duclos was not in the room and the Prince is satisfied. At his invitation, all leave for the supper party in another part of the villa. Only Adriana remains.

[6] In the Sonzogno score, the Princess, unimpressed by the Abbé's flattery, remarks that he would serve her better by finding out who Maurizio's new light-o'-love is. This the Abbé promises to do.

The Princess, though amused, dismisses his madrigal as nonsense, and says that the Prince has no use for mythology. The Abbé significantly remarks that Bouillon prefers chemistry ("Un chimico, s'intende"). This banter is interrupted by the entrance of the Prince himself, followed by servants. At that moment the Princess asks the Abbé to bring her a box of powder. He hands her one of several the Prince has just placed on a nearby table, explaining —for some reason—that he was obliged to move the boxes out of his laboratory.

With a startled exclamation, the Prince snatches the box away from the Abbé, saying that the powder is deadly poison. He describes its properties in a sardonic refrain ("Candida lieve, come la neve"). That glittering, snow-white poison, he sings, is a favorite with traitors bent on revenge, or of heirs impatiently waiting for a bequest. A bit of it sprinkled on a ring or a glove, or dropped in tea or wine, achieves lethal results.

The Princess shows intense interest. Can it be, she asks, the famous *poudre de succession?* It is, says the Prince, adding that he has been asked by the Cardinal de Fleury to analyze it. "As a renowned chemist, of course," the Abbé puts in fawningly. The Prince sternly refuses to allow the Princess to examine the box, which he then carries out of the room.

In a brief byplay, the Princess, with deliberate emphasis, asks the Abbé if he really believes this mysterious powder has the deadly qualities attributed to it. Smirking, the Abbé replies that he has another kind of poison in mind—and she alone can cure him of its effects. The Princess abruptly changes the subject.

She has made a wager, she declares, and wishes the Abbé to help her win it. She must find out the name of the Count de Saxe's new love. La Duclos, of course . . . the Prince was certain, the Abbé lies. Knowingly, the Princess observes that the Abbé is much too clever to believe that.

At that point the Prince returns with Michonnet, who thanks Bouillon for having extended a "favor" to Mlle. Lecouvreur. In angry suspicion the Princess wonders, in an aside, what that "favor" might consist of—money? . . . diamonds? . . . The Prince and Michonnet leave to get ready for the party.

The Princess tells the Abbé that this very night she will win her wager. She challenges him to guess who among her acquaintances is likely to be the mysterious rival. At this juncture the Major-domo announces the Duchess d'Aumont. Aside, the Abbé murmurs that *she* is the woman. The Princess quickly whispers: "Make her say one phrase—'Someone who tells me all'" ("Chi mi confida tutto"). Then, with elegant courtesy, she greets the Duchess.

The other guests now crowd in and an ensemble develops as greetings are exchanged. It is announced that there is to be a ballet, *The Judgment of Paris,* and that La Lecouvreur will recite. The ladies exclaim with pleasure when the Prince announces that the hero of the hour, the Count de Saxe, will be present.

Feigning surprise, the Princess asks if he is not still in the Bastille, imprisoned for gambling debts.[7] Somebody must have paid them, the Prince declares, adding that there is talk of a love affair. In any case, he goes on, the Count is free and already has fought a duel with the man who betrayed him—a certain Count Kalkreutz.

The Major-domo now announces Mlle. Lecouvreur, who is welcomed with great dignity by the Prince ("Venite. D'ammirar più da presso"). As Adriana modestly acknowledges his fulsome greeting ("Io son confuso") there is a startled exclamation from the Princess, to whom the actress' voice has a vaguely familiar sound. She notes with satisfaction that Adriana is not wearing the diamond necklace given her by the Queen.

The scene continues mainly in the form of a duet between Adriana and the Princess. While Adriana expresses her gratitude for the homage paid her by so brilliant an assemblage, the Princess comments in spiteful asides, waiting for the right moment to discover the identity of her rival ("Io lo saprò"). The Prince announces that the entertainment is to wait until Maurizio arrives. Staring intently at Adriana, the Princess remarks that they may wait in vain: It is reported that Maurizio has been badly wounded in the duel with Count Kalkreutz. With a gasp of horror, Adriana collapses fainting on a divan. Revived by Michonnet, she stammers that she was suddenly overcome by the heat and the glaring lights. Yet even in her confusion she notes the icy look on the face of the Princess ("il gelo di quello sguardo").

There is a stir of excitement as Maurizio is announced. Adriana, about to rush to him, is restrained by Michonnet, who warns her not to betray herself. Welcoming the hero, Bouillon tells him of

[7] Maurizio's imprisonment, and the reasons for it, are never satisfactorily explained. As far as can be deduced from the three versions of the libretto, his imprisonment occurred after the scenes at La Grange Batelière—ostensibly for the gambling debt he owed Prince Bouillon. However, the duel he fought with "the man who betrayed him" implies political reasons for his arrest. That leaves unexplained how Adriana's settlement of the gambling debt with the aid of the diamond necklace could have effected his release.

the report that he had been wounded in the duel with Kalkreutz. With a careless laugh, Maurizio answers that he disarmed him with the first sword stroke.

The ensuing dialogue consists mostly of asides sung to the accompaniment of a graceful waltz tempo. Maurizio tells the Princess he returned only to see her ("Per voi qui venni"), but says he cannot accept her help in paying his gambling debts (a favor he mistakenly gives her credit for). Adriana, seeing the two whispering together, wonders fretfully if the "unknown" could have been the Princess. Maurizio, becoming aware of Adriana's presence, greets her casually. Bouillon interrupts to ask him to tell the guests about his military triumphs in Courland—particularly the story of the assault on Mittau ("non ci narraste ancora").

Protesting that he has forgotten all about his exploits, the Count promptly launches into the story to the accompaniment of a vigorous martial theme ("Il russo Mèncikoff"). He tells how the Russian commander Menchikov led an assault on his palace. The defenders were outnumbered fifteen to one, but—like Charles XII at Bendera—he did not pause to count friend or foe. After three days of siege the attackers were ready to put the palace to the torch. Maurizio himself rolled out a barrel of gunpowder, lit the fuse and pushed it toward the oncoming horde. One hundred Cossacks were blown sky-high and the battle was over.[8] The assemblage hails the hero in a choral phrase.

The Prince then announces the performance of the ballet, *The Judgment of Paris.* To the accompaniment of elegant, pastoral music, the story is told in dance with choral interludes. Paris, attired as a shepherd, is given one of the golden apples of the Hesperides by the god Mercury, with instructions to bestow it upon the most beautiful of the goddesses. Juno, Pallas Athene and Venus—jealous rivals for the prize—each try to convince Paris of their rightful claim to the prize. When Venus flings aside her cloak and reveals her beauty, Paris rises to confer the trophy upon her.

But at this point the ballet myth departs from the original. Paris approaches the Princess de Bouillon and, kneeling at her

[8] A fictionalized account of an actual event. Charles XII of Sweden, defeated at Poltava in 1790, found asylum in the palace of a Turkish potentate at Bender (or Bendera) and spent several years there in exile. Relations between host and guest, however, apparently deteriorated, and at one point the Turks besieged Charles's headquarters. He defended his refuge as described by Maurizio in the operatic version.

feet, presents her with the golden apple. The three goddesses pay
their tribute to her, then dance away with the nymphs.

The musical dialogue, with occasional ensemble passages, now
continues over a graceful orchestral accompaniment. At the same
time there is a sharp exchange between Adriana and the Princess.
First, the Abbé points to one of the ladies and whispers that she
is the mysterious rival. The Princess disdainfully rejects his assertion. Turning to Adriana, she remarks that perhaps Mademoiselle
knows the name of Count de Saxe's beloved ("La bella del Conte").
At court, she continues, there was some gossip about an actress.
At the theater, Adriana retorts, the talk was about an amorous
noblewoman. To the huge enjoyment of the other women, the
sparring goes on about a "secret midnight rendezvous."

At this point the Abbé brings matters to a head by asking for
proof. The Princess mentions a charming posy given a certain hero;
Adriana tells of a beautiful bracelet lost by someone in hasty
flight. Both women try to conceal their discomfiture at these revela-
tions. In chorus, the onlookers exclaim that the situation is as
delightful as a Chinese puzzle or a Spanish romance.

"Not so," Adriana cries; "the situation is typically French" ("No,
la vita francese!"). Showing the bracelet around, she explains that
it was recently handed to her. As the women admire it in chorus,
the Princess glares at Adriana. The Prince comes forward, examines
the bracelet and exclaims that it belongs to his wife. There is
general consternation. In a brief choral passage the guests take
due note of the furious glances exchanged between Adriana and
the Princess.[9]

Adriana and the Princess now are convinced of each other's
identity. With forced politeness the Princess invites Adriana to
recite. The actress flares up angrily at her patronizing tone, but
controls herself at a word of caution from Michonnet. With deliberate malice the Princess suggests she recite the monologue
from *Ariadne abbandonata* (*Ariadne Forsaken*).[10]

Stung by the implied insult in the play's title, Adriana glares
at the Princess. The Prince hastily suggests that she recite the
great speech from *Phèdre,* the role in which the actress scored one
of her greatest triumphs.[11] Suddenly deciding, Adriana answers:

[9] In the Sonzogno edition (1903).
[10] Probably from the play *Ariana* by Thomas Corneille (1625–1709), brother
of the renowned French dramatist Pierre Corneille (1606–84).
[11] The play by the French dramatist Jean Baptiste Racine (1639–99),
based on Greek mythology.

"E *Fedra* sia!" Over a dark, sinister theme in the orchestra, Adriana declaims, in spoken tones, the passage in which the legendary Phèdre, wife of Theseus, voices her remorse for her illicit love for her stepson Hippolyte ("Giusto Cielo! che feci in tal giorno?"). With loathing and dread she anticipates the moment when her husband will return to his home, where his wife and his son are guilty lovers.

Adriana notices that the Princess and Maurizio are whispering together, and her voice rises in anger and intensity. Almost losing control, she speaks the final lines of furious denunciation directly to the Princess: "So il turpe mio . . . nè compormi potrei comme fanno le audicissime impure, cui gioia è tradir una fronte di gel, che mai debba arrossir!" ("I know my own infamy, but I cannot face it calmly, as do shameless women who glory in treachery while they display an icy countenance that cannot blush!").

Her final accusation rings out in a majestic climax. Shaken with fury, Adriana stands glaring at the Princess, who contemptuously joins the guests in their shouts of "Brava!" In an aside to the dumfounded Michonnet, Adriana murmurs fiercely that now she has had her revenge ("Son vendicata"). She asks leave of the Prince, who escorts her to the door. Gazing after her malevolently, the Princess, aside, says she will pay out her rival. Seeing Maurizio start for the door, she harshly orders him to remain. As Adriana passes, he manages to whisper: "Tomorrow." The curtain falls.

## ACT IV

A small sitting room adjoining the bedroom in Adriana's house. It is late afternoon in March. There is a brief prelude on a melancholy theme (strikingly similar to the introduction to the fourth act of *La Traviata*). Michonnet is shown in by Adriana's maid, who whispers that Adriana is still sleeping. In recitative ("So ch'ella dorme") Michonnet observes wryly that Adriana wouldn't be an actress if she weren't asleep while the rest of the world is awake. "When she does awake," he tells the maid, "tell her I am here."

Then, in a melodious aria, "Taci, mio vecchio cuor" (recalling Colline's farewell to his overcoat in *La Bohème*), he melodramatically bids his poor old heart to beat no more with hopeless passion. Let it be like this faithful friend, he goes on, looking at his watch, which also has grown tired of ticking. As for Adriana, she is not sleeping. She is sick. Her sickness is love, the same malady which has afflicted him—but too late. Michonnet scribbles a note and hands it to the maid when she reappears. This, he says, is the medicine Adriana needs.

A few moments later Adriana enters. Her demeanor is one of utter dejection and defeat, but she greets Michonnet with obvious pleasure ("Amico mio!"). This marks the beginning of a moving duet in which the two commiserate with each other about the pangs of unrequited love.

Adriana complains that she cannot sleep. Nothing matters now —the theater, fame, a career—all are illusions. Gazing at her tenderly, Michonnet asks: "But what about the one who loves you?" When Adriana asks who that could be, Michonnet blurts out that it is he himself. Seeing her startled expression, he loses courage and adds lamely that he means merely that he loves her like a father.

Touched by his devotion, Adriana looks at him in mingled tenderness and pity. But suddenly she is haunted by the memory of her encounter with the Princess at the ball. She can remember only the look of hatred on the Princess' face, she cries, as she listened to the closing lines from *Phèdre* ("che mai debba arrossir!"). Then, as though demented, Adriana seizes a shawl, throws it around her shoulders and rushes toward the door, shouting that she must have revenge on this courtesan who has stolen her beloved. Michonnet bars her path, then gently forces her into a chair. Adriana bursts into hysterical sobs. Although she refuses to take a sedative he offers her, she gradually grows calmer.

Michonnet reminds her that she is not alone in her suffering. He too, he says, has endured the pain of unrequited love ("Non soffri sola"), but in any case he did not die from it. In the closing phrases of the duet they agree that love is madness, a worse torture than burning or freezing—but one survives somehow.

There is an abrupt change of mood as Adriana's four fellow players come to pay her a surprise visit in honor of her birthday ("La vostra festa"). Adriana greets them in delighted astonishment. Laughing and joking, they hand her their presents—candy, a portrait, a bit of lace. Looking on, Michonnet mutters that there is something more to this than simply a birthday party. Then he announces he has a present of his own, and hands Adriana a small case. She opens it and gasps in surprise. In the case is her diamond necklace, the Queen's gift. Adriana had given it to Prince de Bouillon as "ransom" to free Maurizio from the Bastille. The players exclaim admiringly over its beauty. In answer to Adriana's question, Michonnet shyly explains that he redeemed the gems from Prince de Bouillon with the legacy left him by his uncle. Profoundly moved, Adriana takes both his hands in a gesture of gratitude ("Nobile cor!"). Michonnet furtively wipes away a tear.

With exaggerated solemnity, Quinault and Poisson announce that they have a request to make ("Di tutti i soci") in behalf of all the members of the Comédie Française. In unison the two men, Jouvenot and Dangeville sing the titles of Adriana's four celebrated roles—Phèdre, Roxane, Chimène, Mira—and ask her to return to the stage as queen of her art.

As though suddenly inspired, Adriana replies in a ringing aria ("Si, tornerò!") that she will indeed return. The sacred fire still burns within her heart. Through the high calling of her art she will show that he who loses as a lover can triumph as an artist. Her companions applaud her vociferously. Eagerly Adriana asks for backstage news of the theater. With great relish the players inform her that La Duclos has left the Prince, then elaborate upon the situation in an impudent quartet ("Una volta c'era un Principe").

There was, it seems, a certain elderly Prince who sought to win a young lady's hand by guile and trickery. But she paid him back in his own false coin by having a romance behind his back with a young, handsome lover. The moral of the story (expressed in a pianissimo phrase which ends the quartet) is that false coin can only buy false love ("A fals'oro falso amor").

The general merriment is interrupted by the entrance of the maid, who brings in a small casket covered with crimson velvet. With it is a note. Adriana, reading it quickly, murmurs that it is from Maurizio. In an aside, she asks Michonnet to get the others out of the room. He invites them into the adjoining room for a drink, ushers them out, then returns.

Adriana opens the casket, then suddenly staggers back as though overcome. She gasps that a strange odor rose from the casket—almost like the cold mist of death. Michonnet scoffs at this grim fancy, then asks what is in the casket. Adriana takes from it a faded bunch of violets. She cries out in dismay as she recognizes the posy she gave to Maurizio ("I fiori offerti"). In a brief refrain ("Oh, crudeltà . . . L'avesse negletto") she voices her anguish. If he had even crushed the flowers under his foot, she sobs, it would have been kinder than adding insult to injury by sending them back.

Michonnet tries to comfort her by saying that Maurizio never would do such a thing—this is a woman's trick. Taking up the flowers again, Adriana pours out her grief in one of the loveliest arias in the opera, "Poveri fiori." Yesterday, she sings, these poor flowers bloomed in all their beauty. Today they are withered and dead—like the vows of a faithless lover. And now she will give them one last kiss of love and death, Adriana goes on, raising the posy to her lips. Thus, everything is ended ("Tutto è finito"). Crushed by despair, she throws the flowers into the fireplace.

It is not the end, Michonnet protests, because Maurizio will come to her—perhaps even in the next few moments. He then confesses that he himself wrote Maurizio and told him the whole story . . . he hopes he did not do the wrong thing. Adriana is overwhelmed by his kindness and loyalty. At that moment, Maurizio's voice is heard outside. Adriana cries out that this must be a dream, and rushes to the door. Watching her in sadness and resignation, Michonnet murmurs ironically: "To think that I myself brought my rival here!" ("E dir ch'io stesso chiamato ho il mio rivale!"). He leaves to join the players in the other room.

In the next moment Maurizio bursts into the room. Adriana first tries to hide her emotions under an assumed air of indifference. She asks him coldly why he has come ("Che mai qui vi sprona"). This marks the beginning of the concluding duet of the opera.

Imploring her forgiveness ("Perdona l'oblio d'un istante"), Maurizio tells her he was misled by lies and trickery, but now he knows Adriana alone rules his heart. But Adriana bitterly tells him to go back to the woman he really loves. Maurizio responds that he has learned the price of this woman's treachery, and despises her.

Unrelenting, Adriana tells him that now it is too late. In a phrase repeating the love theme of the opera, Maurizio tells her it was her hand alone that rescued him—and now he offers his own hand and his royal name in marriage. Shaken and bewildered, Adriana replies that her head is not worthy of a royal crown ("No, la mia fronte"). She can wear only the motley of the stage.

In a passionate refrain ("No, più nobile") Maurizio sings that she is more regal than any queen because, through her art, she rules over the hearts of mankind. Adriana rushes into his arms. They bring the duet to a blazing climax, singing that not even death can destroy their golden dream ("vince la morte nel sogno d'or"). They stand locked in each other's arms as the love theme dies away in the orchestra.

Suddenly Adriana reels back as though about to faint. As Maurizio steadies her, she gasps that she has been made ill by the odor of the flowers he sent her. To his utter confusion she goes on to say she threw the flowers into the fire because they had died—

just as his love for her had died. She clutches her side in a paroxysm of pain, then begins raving in delirium. Staring at Maurizio, she asks him who he is. She imagines she sees him in his box at the theater with her rival. For a moment her reason returns, then she collapses in a faint. Maurizio calls distractedly for help.

Michonnet comes rushing in and together the men manage to revive Adriana. When Michonnet asks what brought on this seizure, Maurizio tells him Adriana apparently became delirious as the result of smelling the flowers ("Fiutò dei fior"). In a horrified whisper Michonnet voices his suspicion that the flowers had been sprinkled with the poisonous powder by her rival ("Un velen . . . Quella rivale?"). Maurizio cries out in despair as the terrible realization dawns upon him.

Bending over Adriana, he sobs that her eyes are glazing over in death. As he desperately calls her name she opens her eyes. Summoning her ebbing strength, she implores Maurizio to save her ("Salvatemi!"). She does not want to die, she sings in an exultant phrase, because the one she loves has claimed her as his bride. Then, convulsed by pain, she gasps that a serpent is gnawing at her heart.

In wild delirium she starts up and begins declaiming as though in the theater. Imperiously she commands the "profane ones" to stand aside, for she is the goddess Melpomene ("Scostatevi, profani, Melpòmene son io"). Over a poignant theme high in the strings, Adriana sings that she is winging her way like a tired white dove to the Light ("Esso la Luce"), the purifying light of love. Before her is the gate to immortality—the portal which opens to joy eternal. Adriana's voice dies away in a sigh and she falls back lifeless into the arms of Maurizio and Michonnet. In wild despair Maurizio cries out: "Adriana! Mortal" The curtain falls.

# Antony and Cleopatra

*by* SAMUEL BARBER

(1910–     )

*Libretto by*
FRANCO ZEFFIRELLI

Adapted from William Shakespeare's play of the same name

### CHARACTERS

| | |
|---|---|
| Cleopatra, Queen of Egypt | Soprano |
| Octavia, sister of Caesar and Antony's second wife | Lyric soprano |
| Charmian ⎫ Cleopatra's attendants | ⎧ Mezzo-soprano |
| Iras ⎭ | ⎩ Contralto |
| Antony, triumvir of Rome | Bass |
| Caesar, triumvir of Rome | Tenor |
| Agrippa ⎫ | ⎧ Bass |
| Lepidus ⎬ Roman senators | ⎨ Tenore buffo |
| Maecenas ⎭ | ⎩ Baritone |
| Enobarbus, Antony's companion in arms | Bass |
| Eros, armor-bearer to Antony (Young Man's Voice) | Tenor or high baritone |
| Dolabella, friend to Caesar | Baritone |
| Thidias, ambassador from Caesar | Tenor or high baritone |
| Canidius ⎫ | ⎧ Baritone |
| Demetrius ⎪ | ⎪ Low tenor |
| Scarus ⎬ Officers to Antony | ⎨ Bass |
| Decretas ⎭ | ⎩ Bass |
| Mardian, a eunuch | High tenor |
| A Rustic | Baritone or bass |
| Messenger | Tenor |
| Soothsayer | Bass |
| Alexas, attendant on Cleopatra | Bass |
| A soldier of Antony | Tenor |
| A captain of Antony | Tenor |
| A soldier of Antony | Baritone or bass |
| Three guards in Antony's camp ⎫ | |
| Two watchmen ⎭ | Basses |

People of the Empire, attendants on Cleopatra, senators, guards, watchmen, soldiers

*Place:* Alexandria in Egypt, and Rome
*Time:* Circa 30 B.C.
*First performance:* Opening of the new Metropolitan Opera House, Lincoln Center, New York City, September 16, 1966
*Original language:* English

---

The world premiere of *Antony and Cleopatra* marked one of the most significant events in the modern history of opera: the opening of the new forty-five-million-dollar Metropolitan Opera House in Lincoln Center, New York City. Samuel Barber, the American composer, was commissioned by the Metropolitan Opera Association to write the work for the opening. The commission was under a grant from the Ford Foundation and the production was made possible by a gift from Francis Goelet, of New York City, a patron of the opera.

This spectacular production was staged by the Italian director Franco Zeffirelli, who also adapted the text of Shakespeare's play for the libretto and designed the sets and costumes. Mr. Zeffirelli had previously staged Verdi's *Falstaff* for the Metropolitan in 1964 with outstanding success.

*Antony and Cleopatra* is Samuel Barber's second opera. His first, *Vanessa,* with a libretto by Gian-Carlo Menotti, was premiered at the old Metropolitan in 1958 and won a Pulitzer Prize. Mr. Barber wrote the role of Cleopatra specifically for the American soprano Leontyne Price. "Every vowel," said Mr. Barber, "was placed with Leontyne Price in mind."

Although given a brilliant production with a huge cast, the opera was not an unqualified success. It was given only eight performances during the 1966–67 season of the Metropolitan. Critics found it skillfully wrought and occasionally interesting, but with the music subordinate to the staging. It is atonal and difficult to sing —as the composer himself concedes. While there are echoes of Wagner and Mahler, the vocal line is angular and quasi-recitative. There are no arias in the conventional sense of the term. All the scenes are bridged by instrumental interludes.

There is no overture. The curtain rises immediately.

## ACT ONE

[*Scene One*] Rome. Milling around a huge symbolic golden pyramid is a shouting, jeering throng of Romans, Greeks, Jews, Persians, Africans and soldiers. In a harshly dissonant chorus ("From Alexandria this is the news") they voice their anger over the reports of Antony's wild revels with Cleopatra in Alexandria —to the utter neglect of his duties as one of the triumvirate of Rome. In a furious chant they repeat: "Let his shames drive him quickly to Rome." The chorus rises to a climax as the mob shouts: "Antony, leave thy lascivious wassails."

The mood of the scene momentarily changes as the people, in insinuating tones, express the hope that Cleopatra will treacherously enslave Antony with her seductive charms and rob him of his honor as the price of his libertinage ("Salt Cleopatra, soften thy wan lips"). In the next moment, the denunciations break out again, rising to a feverish pitch on the repetition of the phrase "Leave thy lascivious wassails."

At this point the sides of the golden pryamid unfold like the petals of an enormous flower, disclosing Antony and Enobarbus in Cleopatra's palace in Alexandria.

[*Scene Two*] The dialogue ensues in quasi-recitative. Antony declares that he must free himself once for all from Cleopatra's spell and leave Alexandria. In leaving, Enobarbus observes brusquely, we kill our women, who cannot endure separation. When Cleopatra hears of this, he goes on, she will certainly die. Cynically he adds that she seems to have a penchant for dying. Antony is momentarily bemused by thoughts of Cleopatra but abruptly shakes off the spell and reiterates his decision to leave. Enobarbus exits.

Heralded by a chorus of attendants, Cleopatra enters with Charmian, her lady in waiting. She is so overcome by the realization that Antony is determined to leave her that she calls on Charmian to support her. When Antony approaches to help her she repulses him, telling him to make his farewell and go, for now it is too late for words. Gazing passionately at her, Antony reminds her of the bliss of their love, which was like eternity—never ending. Cleopatra replies in poignant phrases that without Antony there is only oblivion. Though still resolved to leave, Antony sings that for them there can be no parting.

[*Scene Three*] The Senate in Rome. In the chamber are Caesar, Lepidus, Agrippa, Maecenas, Antony, Enobarbus and other senators. There is a fanfare of trumpets as the Senate convenes. The senators hail Antony. In an ironic byplay, he and Caesar, observing protocol, invite each other to be seated first. The two immediately plunge into matters of state. Antony rather arrogantly remarks that Caesar seems unduly concerned about certain happenings in Alexandria. Caesar angrily upbraids him for breaking his promise of assistance with arms.

As tempers rise, Maecenas, Enobarbus and the other senators try to placate the two triumvirs, but Antony sharply warns them not to interfere. He even lashes out at Enobarbus when he objects to the wrangling. Finally controlling himself, he tells Caesar he will try to make amends. Caesar, in turn, declares that he would go to the ends of the earth to find a way to patch up their differences.

Suddenly Agrippa steps forward with an extraordinary suggestion for settling the problem. If Octavia, Caesar's sister, will marry Antony, the union will provide a bond between the two triumvirs. Caesar is taken aback, but Antony expresses interest in the idea. The senators, shaking their heads, leave the chamber during a brief musical interlude. A rhythmic theme in the bass bridges to the next scene.

[*Scene Four*] Cleopatra's palace. With the Queen are Charmian, Iras and Mardian, a eunuch. An oboe solo, languorous yet plaintive, sets the mood. Cleopatra, thinking of Antony, calls for music to calm her restless thoughts. Two ballerinas are escorted in by Mardian. He dutifully tries to entertain the Queen with an inane ditty ("Now the master's gone away") and then dances with the ballerinas. They play Egyptian cymbals, antique clappers and tambourines. Cleopatra, bored to distraction, first suggests a game of billiards, then decides she will go fishing ("Give me my angle, we'll to the river").

She and Charmian fall to musing about the happy days spent with Antony, fishing and drinking and making love. Cleopatra recalls how she playfully mde him wear her crown and mantle while she buckled on his sword. Beguiled by these thoughts, she asks Charmian to give her mandragora[1] to drink so that she can fall asleep and dream of her lover. Under the influence of the potion she abandons herself to thoughts of Antony. "O Charmian,

---

[1] A narcotic plant.

where think'st that he is now?" At the conclusion of the brief but passionate refrain the dancers carry the Queen out on her luxurious couch.

[*Scene Five*] Caesar's palace in Rome. Caesar, Antony, Octavia, Maecenas, Enobarbus and people of the court.

In a recitative passage, Antony assures Caesar of his loyalty and co-operation. Caesar leads Octavia, his widowed sister, forward and presents her to Antony. In lyrical phrases he sings that he bequeaths to Antony a sister who, as his bride, will unite their kingdoms and their hearts. Gazing fondly at Octavia, Antony sings that "the April's in her eyes."

Octavia suddenly turns and whispers mysteriously into Caesar's ear. In answer, he assures her that he still will be with her in his thoughts, even though they now will be parted as brother and sister. He leaves her and Antony together. Antony tells Octavia that, to his regret, his military duties sometimes will take him away from her side. In his absence, Octavia replies, she will pray to the gods for his safety. The court, looking on, murmurs with a certain ironic effect: "Happily, amen." Rather sententiously, Antony asks Octavia not to hold his past faults against him. Henceforth, he says, everything will be "done by the rule." Enobarbus, watching him, repeats with heightened irony the phrase sung by the chorus: "Happily, amen."

[*Scene Six*] Cleopatra's palace in Alexandria. With her are Iras, Charmian, ladies of the court and attendants. Standing before her is the Messenger who brings the news of Antony's marriage to Octavia. The scene is introduced by a rising chromatic phrase that explodes in the orchestra to underscore Cleopatra's fury. She greets the Messenger with a curse, lashes at him with a whip, then threatens him with even worse punishment.

Cowering under her blows, the Messenger protests that, after all, it was not he who arranged the marriage. In a capricious change of mood Cleopatra offers the Messenger an entire province if he will say that the report of the marriage is not true. When the hapless man truthfully replies, "He's married," the Queen lunges at him with a knife. The Messenger dodges out of reach and crouches in a corner of the room. At this point Charmian intercedes, reminding Cleopatra that the Messenger has done no wrong.

Controlling herself for the moment, Cleopatra commands the Messenger to come forward, then resumes her inquisition. Calm and enraged by turns, she demands details—and the Messenger tells her exactly what she wants to hear: Octavia is unattractively short, her voice is unpleasantly low, she does not walk—she creeps —she was a widow, she is about thirty, with a plain round face, brown hair and a low forehead.

In an amusing ensemble, the ladies of the court parrot the Messenger's answers. Finally appeased, Cleopatra tosses the man a bag of gold and dismisses him. Exhausted by her outbursts of jealous fury, the Queen asks Charmian to help her to her chamber. The music subsides into silence. The brief interlude bridging into the next scene rises to a feverish pitch, symbolizing Cleopatra's frustrated, passionate desire for Antony.

[Scene Seven] Aboard a Roman galley. Drinking and talking at a table at the very front of the stage are Caesar, Antony, Lepidus, Dolabella, Maecenas and Enobarbus. Torchbearers light up the scene as Roman soldiers, half drunk, make their way aboard. With them come dancers and slave girls. A rhythmic "stick dance" begins in which the dancers strike the deck in a steady drumbeat which continues to throb throughout the entire scene. The music and the action gradually crescendo to an orgiastic pitch.

At its height, a remarkable musical dialogue ensues among the company drinking at the table. Over the pounding rhythm of the stick dance the singers improvise their own sung recitative. Befogged with wine, Lepidus, Antony and Maecenas fall into a discussion about the crocodile. This serpent of the Nile, Lepidus begins, is bred out of mud by the sun. Thereupon Antony launches into a solemn, nonsensical discourse on the crocodile, which, he explains, is as broad as its breadth, high as its height, moves with its own motion and transmigrates its soul when it dies. Plied with more wine by Maecenas, Lepidus listens until he collapses in a drunken stupor. A servant carries him away. While Antony is holding forth about the crocodile, a mysterious offstage voice sings an invocatory phrase to Cleopatra: "Salt Cleopatra, soften thy lips."

As the drinking continues, Enobarbus urges the company to join the bacchanalian dance. Antony jumps up on the table and sings the drinking song, "Come thou monarch of the vine." All the men on the stage join in the refrain in a two-part chorus: "In thy vats our cares be drowned." Caesar, though unsteady on his feet, calls a halt to the revelry, reminding the others that serious business waits to be done. He bids them goodnight and leaves. The men settle down at the table, where Antony already is fast asleep.

Enobarbus, Dolabella and Maecenas begin speculating about Antony and Cleopatra. When Dolabella insists that Octavia's beauty has captured Antony's heart. Enobarbus flatly contradicts him. Antony, says he, will go back to his "Egyptian dish," then adds in Shakespeare's trenchant phrase: "Age cannot wither her, nor custom stale her infinite variety." Enobarbus then describes the first meeting of the two on the Queen's resplendent barge with its poop of beaten gold and its purple, perfumed sails. This refrain ("When she first met Mark Antony") is one of the few passages in the opera resembling the conventional aria.

Now begins the fantastic dream sequence. As an offstage chorus softly repeats Enobarbus' words, Cleopatra's barge materializes in the background. The music takes on an otherworldly, Debussyan quality. In sensuous phrases against a flowing choral background, Cleopatra sings of her longing for Antony ("Where's my serpent of old Nile?"). As the music rises to a climax, the barge slowly recedes. Antony, suddenly awakening, stares at the phantom ship. In a passionate outburst he sings that he will go to Egypt, for there his "pleasure lies." He rushes toward the vision with outstretched arms as the curtain falls.

## ACT TWO

[*Scene One*] Caesar's palace in Rome. With him are Octavia, senators and military officers. The music begins with a repetition of the figure heard at the opening of Act One. Caesar is furiously denouncing Antony for disgracing Rome by enthroning himself in Alexandria with Cleopatra at his side. There he made her Absolute Queen of Syria, Cyprus and Lydia. The chorus comments in a running accompaniment.

Octavia, refusing to believe this report, insists that Antony is in Athens on a mission of state. Caesar informs her that on the contrary, he is indeed with Cleopatra, again enslaved by her wit, charm and beguiling companionship. Octavia cries out in despair. The Romans, in an intensely dramatic choral passage ("He hath given up his empire"), enumerate the kings whom Antony has enlisted to make war on Rome. Octavia laments that now her heart is torn between two friends turned enemies.

Touched by her grief, Caesar sings that the gods themselves will see to it that justice is done. Overhearing him, the crowd screams: "Justice! Justice!" In a violent outburst, Caesar rages against Antony's insulting treatment of his beloved sister and his arrogant usurpation of power. He calls on his forces to fight to the last ditch. The music crescendos into a blazing fanfare of trumpets which bridges into the next scene.

[*Scene Two*] Cleopatra's palace garden in Alexandria. Charmian and Iras, who are there with Mardian, tell the servant Alexas to bring in the Soothsayer to tell their fortunes. The ensuing dialogue is mostly in trio form, set off by a striking figure in the bass—repeated ascending quadruplets in an insistent rhythm. The Soothsayer's auguries meet with mocking banter from Charmian and Iras. The scene ends with the two women cynically offering up a prayer to the goddess Isis in behalf of their fortunes. Mardian suddenly warns them that Antony and Cleopatra are approaching. The women leave with the Soothsayer.

To a sensuously flowing accompaniment, Antony and Cleopatra are talking of love. Their avowals are interrupted by Enobarbus, who rushes in with the news that Caesar has captured Toryne.[2] Antony expresses shocked surprise that Caesar has advanced so rapidly. Then in a ringing phrase ("tomorrow, soldier") he declares to Enobarbus that he will fight by land or sea—or redeem his honor with his own blood. With that he rushes away to prepare for battle.

No sooner has he gone than Cleopatra whirls on Enobarbus and upbraids him for trying to prevent her from joining Antony on the battlefield. But in a further effort to dissuade her, Enobarbus says her presence might distract Antony from his military problems. Even now, he adds, there is trouble enough. Antony's reckless conduct is the talk of Rome. There, in fact, it is being gossiped that the war is being waged by a eunuch and the women of Cleopatra's court. Stung to fury by this insult, Cleopatra curses Rome ("Sink Rome, and their tongues rot") and vows to join Antony as Enobarbus protests in vain. She storms out of the room followed by Enobarbus as the music continues in a martial tempo. It subsides into a tranquil theme as the scene changes.

[*Scene Three*] Antony's camp at night. A company of soldiers stands guard. The entire scene is in the form of an ensemble as the soldiers converse about the coming battle and about the sound of ghostly music that seems to be coming out of the ground and filling the air. It is a sign, one soldier says, that the god Hercules, Antony's mentor, is abandoning him to his own fate. In awed tones the soldiers comment on the mysterious sounds as they withdraw to the accompaniment of a foreboding chromatic passage.

[*Scene Four*] Antony's tent. He and Cleopatra are seen inside. It is dawn. Antony, declining Cleopatra's suggestion to sleep a little

[2] Presumably a town in ancient Greece. Its exact location is untraceable.

longer, calls to Eros, his armor-bearer, to bring his battle dress. Cleopatra laughingly helps him buckle on his armor. In an aside, she reflects that if Antony and Caesar could decide this war in a single fight, then Antony . . . She leaves the rest of the thought unspoken and instead salutes Antony as her "brave lord." He exultantly hails the dawning day of battle.

There is a fanfare of trumpets as Antony's officers, Canidius, Demetrius and Scarus, enter with a group of soldiers. They express alarm as Antony announces his decision to fight by sea. The officers warn that his ships are unseaworthy and manned by "muleteers." It will be no disgrace, they assure him, to refuse to fight Caesar with a fleet. But Antony, urged on by Cleopatra, obstinately repeats that he will fight by sea. Enobarbus joins the others in trying to turn him from this rash course ("Trust not in rotten planks"). The army, he declares, is trained to fight and conquer on land. Cleopatra steps forward and cries that she has "sixty sails," a fleet better than Caesar's.

At this point the soldiers, swayed by Antony and Cleopatra and defying their officers, burst into a challenging chorus, "By sea, we will fight by sea!" Taking Cleopatra in his arms, Antony kisses her in farewell, then cries exultingly: "What-e'er becomes of me, this is a soldier's kiss!" A stormy orchestral interlude follows, during which the scene changes to the battlefield at Actium. The Egyptian army is seen in battle formation at the feet of the towering figure of the Sphinx.

[*Scene Five*] In a rousing chorus ("On to our ships") the Egyptians hail the order to go aboard and man the galleys. At the conclusion of the chorus, which ends on an "open fifth" chord with stunning effect, the army rushes into battle. A moment later comes the din of the sea battle. The clamor is heard over a striking pianissimo passage in the orchestra, punctuated by the clangor of metal on metal. In the distance, Cleopatra's fleet can be seen in full flight, headed for Alexandria.

Enobarbus suddenly staggers in, crying in despair that he can no longer bear to watch the sixty ships of Cleopatra's demoralized fleet sail away in defeat. He is joined by Canidius, Decretas, Scarus and Demetrius. In an ensuing ensemble ("Cleopatra, in the midst of the fight") they rage against this shameful debacle. Worst of all, Antony broke off the battle at its height and followed after Cleopatra in disgraceful panic. Shaken by the disaster, the officers turn to Enobarbus with the despairing question: "What shall we do?" Enobarbus can only answer: "Think, and die!" They wander aimlessly out of sight.

An ominous drumbeat begins in the orchestra, building up to a climax of harsh, dissonant chords. As the drumbeat continues, Antony approaches with Eros and a group of wounded soldiers. Surveying the desolation of the battlefield, he voices his despair in a bitter refrain: "The land bids me tread no more upon it." In shame and anger he sings that now he, who once did as he pleased with half the world, must grovel before the upstart Caesar. There is nothing left, he tells the weeping Eros, but death. Plunged in gloom, he bids his wounded soldiers farewell.

A moment later Caesar enters with his triumphant army. Antony, he proclaims harshly, can expect nothing from him. As for Cleopatra, he will grant her pleas—providing she will either banish Antony from Egypt or put him to death. Commanding his soldiers to carry this message to his vanquished rivals, Caesar dismisses his army. An interlude of martial music follows as the soldiers leave.

[*Scene Six*] Cleopatra's palace in Alexandria, where Thidias, a wily and experienced diplomat, has come to lay down Caesar's terms of surrender. With Cleopatra as she meets the ambassador are Charmian and Iras. The Queen tells Thidias to inform Caesar that she is ready to surrender her crown to the conqueror. Following his orders to win Cleopatra over by flattery, Thidias requests the privilege of kissing her hand. Cleopatra offers it with a knowing smile, remarking that Caesar's father himself had rained kisses upon it when he came to ask for kingdoms.

Just at that moment Antony strides in with a number of his soldiers. Seeing Thidias in the act of kissing the Queen's hand, he flies into a rage and orders the ambassador to be whipped for his insolence. The soldiers drag Thidias away.

When Cleopatra placatingly asks Antony why he is angry with her, he turns on her in furious denunciation. Let her go to Caesar, he shouts, who can show her to the mob in Rome like a victor's trophy. And then let Octavia take a wronged wife's revenge by raking her rival's face with her nails. Accusing the Queen of selling him to Caesar, the "Roman boy," Antony rushes from the room.

On the verge of collapse, Cleopatra gasps for help. Charmian and Iras counsel her to lock herself in her monument (her tomb), then send word to Antony that she has died. At once the Queen prepares to go. She orders Mardian to tell Antony that she has killed herself and that her last word was "Antony." Then Mardian is to report back to her how Antony reacted to the news. She quickly leaves with the two women.

[*Scene Seven*] The battlefield. It is night. Enobarbus is seen standing alone, staring up at the sky. He is stricken with remorse for having deserted Antony and gone over to Caesar after Antony's defeat at the Battle of Actium. In a moving soliloquy, "O bear witness, night," he calls on the moon to mark how bitterly he repents his perfidious actions. A soldier interrupts to tell him that Antony, in a gesture of forgiveness, not only has sent back the treasures Enobarbus had left behind but has added gifts of his own. When Enobarbus sardonically offers the soldier the entire store of treasures, the latter reminds him that Antony still is a "Jove" despite his ruin.

Turning away, Enobarbus resumes his self-accusation ("O sov'reign mistress of true melancholy"). Let the moon distill the poison damp of night upon him . . . let his heart shatter itself upon the flinty hardness of his crime. He will seek a ditch in which to die. Enobarbus' outpouring of grief and remorse comes to a climax in a poignant refrain, "I am alone the villain," which is particularly striking for its melodic line. He asks only for Antony's forgiveness, let the world condemn him as it will. The refrain ends on a lyrical phrase: "O Antony, Antony!" The quiet closing measures of the accompaniment underscore Enobarbus' sorrow.

[*Scene Eight*] Antony's ruined tent on the battlefield. It is night. Antony is seen with Mardian and Eros. The dialogue ensues over a somber, brooding figure in the bass. Mardian brings the news of Cleopatra's death, then leaves. Antony quietly resolves to "overtake" the Queen in death, and the scene that now follows is one of the most gripping in the opera.

Antony asks the unsuspecting Eros if he remembers the oath he swore when he was made a freedman: to slay his master if ordered to do so. Realizing what Antony means, Eros recoils in terror. But the fatal command comes. Instantly, Eros makes a decision. Drawing his sword, he asks Antony to turn his face away. Then, crying out, "Thus do I escape the sorrow of Antony's death," he kills himself. Antony gazes at the boy's body in sorrow and utter despair, then falls on his own sword—but fails in his attempt to die.

In his agony, he calls on his guards to strike him dead, but not one of them will obey his command. Suddenly Alexas dashes in asking for Antony. When the guards point to him, Alexas cries that Cleopatra sent him. Antony gasps in stunned disbelief. Though fatally wounded, he orders the guards to carry him to Cleopatra's monument—the last service they will be asked to perform for him. Offstage a men's chorus comments in a brief unison phrase that "the star has fallen." The curtain falls.


## ACT THREE

Cleopatra's monument (the tomb in the shape of a pyramid). She is seated on a throne at the top. Near her on either side are Charmian and Iras. The scene opens with a brief trio passage in which the women declare that they will never leave the monument. Alexas enters to tell them that Antony, dying, is being brought to the monument by his guards. When he appears, Cleopatra greets him in mingled exultation and sorrow—"O Antony, my man of men!" She asks the women to help Antony up the steps to her— she herself does not dare to leave the throne for fear of capture.

But Antony stops them with an imperious gesture. Quietly he sings that he is asking death to wait only until he can imprint the last of many thousand kisses upon Cleopatra's lips. When she again desperately entreats the women to help him, Antony himself urges them to hurry. Momentarily deranged by her frenzy, Cleopatra mocks Antony's struggle in the grip of death. To the accompaniment of an upward-rushing chromatic theme in the orchestra, the onlookers finally lift Antony into the Queen's arms. Their voices blend in a phrase of triumph, with Antony crying out: "My old serpent of the Nile!"

Now within moments of death, Antony asks for wine. Reviving briefly, he tells Cleopatra not to lament, for he has lived out his life as the greatest prince of the world. He will die nobly— a Roman vanquished only by a Roman. Then, as Cleopatra looks on in horror, Antony falls back dead.

Wild with grief, the Queen cries out: "Noblest of men, woo't die? Hast thou no care of me?" This marks the beginning of a powerful trio in which Cleopatra, Charmian and Iras lament the death of Antony. It concludes with a softly sung phrase: "Noblest of men, past the size of dreaming."

For a long moment the three women, numbed with grief, sit staring into space. A flourish of trumpets breaks the silence, then Caesar enters with his train. Cleopatra kneels before him, but Caesar at once asks her to rise. She replies that the gods have willed that she should make obeisance before the "sole sire of the world." Caesar magnanimously assures her that her wishes as

Queen will be respected, but sternly warns her not to take Antony's course.

The two take each other's measure. When Caesar, with elaborate courtesy, says he will take his leave, Cleopatra remarks with subtle irony: "And may through the world—'tis yours!"

As guards carry Antony's body away, Caesar takes the dead man's sword in his outstretched hands and delivers his sorrowful eulogy—"The breaking of so great a thing." He grieves that a malign fate has divided him from his friend and companion in arms. He and his court then leave the scene in a stately procession. One of his emissaries, Dolabella, remains behind.

At this point a brief but significant dialogue ensues. As though divining Caesar's intention to take Cleopatra to Rome as a prize of war, the three women make a pact to die together and thus cheat him of his triumph. Cleopatra contemptuously observes that the conqueror plies her with words ("He words me, girls"). She whispers her own decision to Charmian as Iras murmurs that their day has come to its end. They will die gloriously, after the fashion of the Romans, the Queen adds ironically.

Dolabella speaks up and confirms Cleopatra's suspicions that Caesar indeed intends to lead her as his captive to Rome. She thanks Dolabella for warning her. Then in an impassioned refrain ("Nay, 'tis most certain") she voices her anger and disdain at Caesar's effrontery in assuming that he could lead proud Egyptians through the streets like strumpets for the amusement of the Romans. Imperiously calling for her royal robes and her crown, she sings that she sees herself again on her royal barge, welcoming Antony.

A guard now brings in an old farmer, who has been admitted to the monument by prearrangement. Alone with him, the Queen indicates the basket of figs he is carrying and asks him if it also contains the "pretty worm of the Nile." He has it, the old man answers, adding that it has already killed many men and women. Only yesterday a woman died of its bite. She spoke very highly of the worm, the old man says. He sets down the basket and leaves as Cleopatra dismisses him.

As Iras brings in her robe and crown the Queen begins her dramatic farewell—"Give me my robe, put on my crown." She hears Antony call, she sings, and must hurry. Calling Charmian and Iras to her, she kisses them in farewell. Iras collapses and mysteriously dies. Cleopatra, looking down at her tenderly, murmurs: "Have I the aspic on my lips? Dost fall?" The Queen muses that death is like a lover's pinch, which hurts but is desired. Charmian, crouched beside her, gives expression to her grief in a poignant phrase. Cleopatra takes an asp from the basket and holds it to her breast, then takes another and applies it to her arm. In mingled pain and exaltation she cries out, "O Antony," and falls back dead.

Charmian, gazing into Cleopatra's face, sings softly that death now has possessed a woman without peer in the world. Tenderly she straightens the crown on the Queen's head. A guardsman enters saying that Caesar has sent for the Queen. Charmian holds an asp to her breast and gasps that Caesar's messenger was too slow. Her voice soaring over a chorus which now begins offstage ("She looks like sleep"), Charmian sings that this day's work has been well done—"fitting for a princess descended of so many royal kings." Then she dies.

Soldiers and townspeople crowd upon the stage and the chorus swells to a majestic climax. The words they sing are actually from Caesar's final speech in Shakespeare's play:

> . . . she looks like sleep,
> As she would catch another Antony
> In her strong toil of grace. . . .
> . . . Take up her bed,
> And bear her women from the monument:
> She shall be buried by her Antony:
> No grave upon the earth shall clip in it
> A pair so famous. . . .
> . . . Our army shall
> In solemn show attend this funeral,
> And then to Rome.

# The Ballad of Baby Doe

*by* DOUGLAS MOORE

(1893–1968)

*Libretto by*
JOHN LATOUCHE

### CHARACTERS

| | |
|---|---|
| Horace Tabor, mayor of Leadville | Baritone |
| Augusta, wife of Horace Tabor | Mezzo-soprano |
| Mrs. Elizabeth (Baby) Doe, a miner's wife | Lyric soprano |
| Mama McCourt, Baby Doe's mother | Contralto |
| William J. Bryan, candidate for President | Bass-baritone |
| Chester A. Arthur, President of the United States | Tenor |
| Father Chapelle, priest at the wedding | Tenor |
| An old silver miner | Tenor |
| A clerk at the Clarendon Hotel | Tenor |
| Mayor of Leadville | Tenor |
| Stage doorman at the Tabor Grand | Tenor |
| Bouncer | Baritone |
| Albert, a bellboy | Baritone |
| A footman | Baritone |
| A Denver politician | Baritone |
| Sarah, Mary, Emily, Effie, old friends of Augusta | Two sopranos, two mezzo-sopranos |
| Sam, Bushy, Barney, Jacob, cronies and associates of Tabor | Two tenors, two baritones |
| Four Washington dandies | Two tenors, two baritones |
| Kate, dance hall entertainer | Soprano |
| Elizabeth, aged twelve | soprano part |
| Silver Dollar, aged seven | silent part |
| children of Horace and Baby Doe | |
| Meg, dance hall entertainer | Mezzo-soprano |
| Silver Dollar (grown-up) | Mezzo-soprano |
| Samantha, a maid | Mezzo-soprano |

Dance hall girls, Baby Doe's family and foreign diplomats at the wedding, miners and their wives.

*Place:* Leadville, Colorado; Denver; Washington, D.C.
*Time:* 1880 to 1899
*First performance:* Central City Opera House, Central City,
Colorado, July 1956
*Original language:* English

---

This opera by the late contemporary composer Douglas Moore has
established itself in the repertoire as a truly American opera. Its
characters are drawn from American history. It is the drama of an
ambitious young American, the two women who dominated his life
and a silver mine that made him fabulously rich—and ruined him.

Horace Tabor trekked from Vermont to Colorado in the 1890s
with his young wife Augusta, there discovered the "Matchless
Mine" and then met and fell in love with Baby Doe, the wife of
a miner. At the pinnacle of his success, the U. S. Government
abandoned the silver standard, and his fortune vanished. Before he
died in 1899, Tabor asked Baby Doe to promise that she would
never sell the Matchless Mine. Baby Doe kept that promise—until
the day in 1935 when she was found frozen to death at the entrance
to the abandoned mine.

The music of *The Ballad of Baby Doe,* though in the contemporary idiom, is not atonal. Richly melodic, with strong rhythmic
patterns, it ranges from sentimental folk tunes of the Victorian era
to passages of striking dramatic power in the best tradition of grand
opera.

## ACT I

[*Scene one*] Outside Tabor Opera House, Leadville, Colorado,
1880. At left, the Clarendon Hotel; at right, a saloon. The curtain
rises after a brief orchestral introduction. Shouts and laughter are
heard in the saloon, then a pistol shot. Suddenly an old miner
comes lurching out of the saloon, propelled by a kick from the
Bouncer. He picks himself up and begins singing about finding a
silver mine—the "Matchless Mine," he calls it—which is why he is
celebrating.

The Bouncer comes out and warns the miner to be quiet—there
is to be a concert at Tabor's new opera house next door. Continuing in a catchy, impudent refrain, the miner sings that Horace

Tabor wants to buy his mine. The saloon girls, followed by the Bouncer, come out and join the miner in a mocking chorus of praise of Tabor and his "opry house." The Bouncer vainly tries to quiet them. Catching hold of the drunken miner, they whirl him around from one to the other until he finally lurches away, still bawling about his Matchless Mine. Shrieking with laughter, the girls follow the Bouncer into the saloon.

A moment later Tabor comes out of the opera house followed by four of his cronies. In a vigorous refrain ("It's a bang-up job") he sings boastfully about his opera house, its glittering chandeliers, brass and mahogany trim, and tapestries from Europe. Fawning around him, his four cronies—Sam, Bushy, Barney and Jacob—comment in chorus.

Tabor sings that his wife Augusta deserves credit for the opera house because she was determined to bring "culture" to Leadville. He and his cronies josh each other about still being "pay dirt" miners at heart even though they are dressed in swallow-tailed coats and top hats. A colorful scene follows as the girls troop out of the saloon, join the chorus and dance with Tabor and the miners. In a lusty ensemble they sing, "Gophers, dig them holes! Dig away to save your souls!"

At the height of their capers, the doors of the opera house swing open and Augusta comes out with her friends—the wives of Tabor's four cronies. For a moment they stand in shocked surprise at the antics of the miners and the saloon girls. Then Augusta launches into a tirade against Tabor for allowing this undignified behavior, exclaiming: "Horace, have you taken leave of your senses?"

She berates Tabor and the miners for leaving the opera house in the middle of the concert and thus embarrassing the ladies. Their uncouth behavior, Augusta storms, has made a mockery of her efforts to bring some refinement to this money-grubbing town.

Tabor tries to placate her—reminding her, incidentally, that the money from the saloon helped build the opera house. Meanwhile, the saloon girls, somewhat abashed, quietly go back into the saloon. A bell signaling the end of the intermission puts an end to the argument. Augusta, followed obediently by the ladies, stalks back into the opera house. Tabor stands looking after her.

As a graceful waltz theme begins, Baby Doe, followed by a Welsh servant, enters and approaches Tabor. She asks if he can direct her to the Clarendon Hotel—she has just come from Central City and is a stranger in town. With a bow, Tabor introduces himself, points in the direction of the Clarendon and gallantly welcomes her to Leadville. Their dialogue continues over the waltz music.

With another courtly bow, Tabor says he hopes they will meet again. At that moment, Augusta calls to him from the door of the opera house. As he goes inside with her, Baby Doe sings in a climactic phrase, "Indeed, we'll meet again!" The waltz theme goes on in the orchestra as the curtain slowly falls.

[*Scene Two*] Without interruption, the rhythm of the music changes and the curtain goes up. The scene is outside the Clarendon Hotel later that evening. Augusta and her friends and Tabor and his cronies enter on their way to the hotel following the concert. They are in the formal dress of the 1890s. In a brief chorus ("What a lovely evening!") they comment in stilted, poetic phrases on the music. The friends leave. Augusta and Tabor thank them and bid them goodnight. When they are alone, Augusta remarks that the evening has been tiring—although Adelina Patti "sang divinely." She goes inside. Tabor sits down on the hotel steps and lights a cigar.

Kate and Meg, two saloon girls, enter. They do not see Tabor, half hidden in the shadows. In a short duet, they gossip about Baby Doe, with catty comments about the airs she gives herself. Their conversation reveals to Tabor that Baby Doe has a husband —"Harvey Doe, up in Central City." The girls' voices, repeating Baby Doe's name, fade as they go on their way. Tabor, looking after them, reflectively murmurs Baby Doe's name.

Then the light comes up in the large front window of the hotel to reveal Baby Doe seated at the piano. Here she sings the aria "Willow, where we met together," a plaintive song, embellished with coloratura passages, about a lover who has gone, leaving his beloved alone and weeping.

As Baby Doe finishes the aria on a high, soaring phrase, Tabor, still sitting in the shadows, applauds. Baby Doe comes to the window and exclaims in surprise. The two look at each other, both deeply moved and now aware of their destiny. Tabor says that "Baby Doe" is the prettiest name he has ever heard. Baby Doe answers: "The fabulous Horace Tabor . . . eyes afire with dreaming." Then Tabor sings to her in an ardent refrain, "Warm as the autumn light." He tells her that her singing has brought back the memory of all the beautiful things in life he had forgotten as the years went by. The aria rises to a passionate climax as he repeats her name, then tenderly kisses her hand.

A harsh dissonance in the orchestra breaks the spell, and then comes the voice of Augusta calling to Tabor from an upstairs window. Tabor, his eyes still on Baby Doe, answers quietly, "Anything you say," then turns and goes into the hotel.

[*Scene Three*] The living room of the Tabor apartment in the hotel. Augusta stands at the window looking out at the deepening twilight. Samantha, the maid, is lighting the lamps. She and Augusta converse in quasi-recitative. Augusta admonishes Samantha to be more careful about dusting, wonders why Tabor has not arrived, then fusses over the messy state of his desk.

Shuffling through the papers there, she suddenly finds a check. She exclaims in irritation as she sees it is made out to Jake Sands to buy another mine. Pocketing the check, Augusta continues shuffling through the papers and suddenly comes upon a pair of white lace gloves. She examines them in puzzled surprise. A gift from her husband, of course, but why? Their wedding anniversary? No . . . that is not until next April . . . and they will have been married twenty-seven years.

Samantha picks up a card which has fallen from between the gloves and hands it to Augusta. As the music echoes the theme of Tabor's song to Baby Doe, Augusta reads the card. It is a tender love note—"I send these lacy nothings." Augusta turns the card over and reads: "Baby Doe." A violent orchestral passage underscores Augusta's fury and dismay. She asks Samantha if she has seen this woman . . . she is young and pretty, no doubt? The maid nods, then quietly leaves the room.

Augusta, staring at her hands, gives way to her grief and anguish in a wild outburst—"Look at these hands!" Age and toil have wrinkled them and made them ugly, she cries, and all for Tabor's sake. She has worked at his side through the years to build a life together. No, Augusta sobs, these hands are not pretty now . . . not like hers.

Tabor suddenly enters, goes to his desk and starts rummaging through his papers. Watching him with icy calm, Augusta asks him what he is looking for. Now follows a long, bitter scene of accusation and recrimination. Tabor furiously accuses Augusta of prying into his personal affairs. Augusta retorts that indeed she would like to know more about his personal affairs. He shouts that she is nagging him, holding him back, trying to make him "knuckle under."

But Augusta has been waiting for her moment of revenge, and now it has come. With a sneer she asks Tabor if he would prefer that she whisper "sweet nothings" the way some brazen women do, Baby Doe, for instance. With that she holds up the pair of white gloves.

Beside himself with rage, Tabor demands the gloves. Augusta, now aware that she has the upper hand, pours out her contempt, deriding him for making a fool of himself over a young girl. Tabor retorts that this girl is generous and kind, and has given him the tenderness that his coldhearted wife has denied him. Stung by this accusation of coldness, Augusta warns her husband that she will drive "that woman" out of town. Tabor, alarmed by her threat in spite of his rage, entreats her not to ruin both their lives by a senseless act of revenge. As Augusta storms out of the room, the duet ends in a violent, climactic phrase, underscored by a harsh orchestral fanfare.

[*Scene Four*] The lobby of the Clarendon Hotel, where the clerk is seen busy at his desk. There is a brief orchestral introduction in a perky, nervous rhythm. Then Baby Doe appears, carrying a hatbox, followed by a bellboy with her bags. She tells the clerk she has decided to go to Oshkosh, Wisconsin, to visit with her family. Ignoring the clerk's look of startled surprise, Baby Doe goes over to a writing desk in a corner of the lobby. In an aside, the clerk tells the bellboy to find Horace Tabor at once and tell him that Baby Doe is leaving town. And that, he adds, means trouble.

In a poignant aria, Baby Doe sings the words of the letter she is writing to her mother—"Dearest Mama, I am writing." She relates that her husband Harvey has left her and that she is alone in Leadville. But, after all, she never loved him. They weren't suited to each other.

She recalls that her mother once told her that someday she would meet a man who would treat her like a princess and give her the things her beauty deserved. Now, she writes, she has met that man. They both know they are meant for each other . . . but this is not to be. And so they must part forever. As the tender letter theme is reiterated by the orchestra, Baby Doe reads what she has written, then signs her name.

To the accompaniment of a somber theme in the bass, Augusta suddenly appears. The two women confront each other and a long and dramatic colloquy ensues. Augusta warns Baby Doe that there will be serious trouble if she does not end her affair with Horace Tabor. As a waltz theme begins in the orchestra, Baby Doe answers with quiet candor—"I knew it was wrong." Horace Tabor stood by her when she was in trouble, Baby Doe sings, and gave her help when she needed it most. They did nothing to be ashamed of. He is a kind man, she goes on, and a strong man—and above all an unusual man. And unusual men have unusual ways, she observes. She tells Augusta that she is leaving, then pleads with her to try to understand this man. It is a privilege to serve him—but at the same time he must not be denied his freedom.

Balked by Baby Doe's calm reasonableness, Augusta resorts to sneering that Tabor is nothing more than an overgrown child and a weakling. All his success, she says, was pure luck. The mine that he found by mere chance was so rich that even he, wastrel that he is, could not have spent all the money it made. It was she—Augusta—who saw to it that all the profit was not wasted on drinking and carousing. Condescendingly, she remarks that she is glad Baby Doe has come to her senses at last and has decided to leave. With that she says goodbye and sweeps out of the room as a mockingly heroic theme sounds in the orchestra.

No sooner has she left than Tabor appears. He and Baby Doe rush into each other's arms, Tabor crying out, "You're not going, my heart!" In a passionate duet they pledge their devotion to each other, then go up the stairs together as the curtain falls.

[Scene Five] Augusta's parlor in Denver, a year later. She herself is in conversation with her four women friends, all seething with righteous indignation. An ensemble follows in which the five women gossip maliciously. The women ask Augusta what she intends to do about Tabor and "that woman" who flouts all standards of decency. Augusta only keeps reiterating "nothing at all" in almost identical musical phrases with the sinister effect of a fate motive. One juicy bit of gossip is that Tabor secretly is trying to get a divorce with the help of a corrupt judge. With remorseless determination, Augusta vows that she will never let Tabor out of her grasp.

Like a chorus of witches, the four friends urge her to revenge ("tell the truth . . . shout the scandal from the housetops"). They repeat this in minor thirds with baleful effect as the curtain falls.

[Scene Six] A suite in the Willard Hotel in Washington, D.C., 1883. On a table heaped with flowers and gifts there towers a wedding bell of white roses surmounted by a heart of red roses pierced by an arrow of violets. Mama McCourt, Baby Doe's mother, is fussing with the decorations. Her husband, sons and another daughter are sitting stiffly on gilt chairs. At one side are four dandies, stylishly dressed, mincing young men. Everyone is waiting for the bridal couple—Horace Tabor (now Senator) and his new wife Baby Doe.

A lively ensemble follows over a restive orchestral accompaniment in alternating 7/8 and 4/4 tempo which paces the give-and-take of the dialogue. Mama McCourt flutters about, telling everybody how beautiful Baby Doe is and inviting the guests to help themselves to champagne. In brief choral passages, the four dandies comment superciliously on the proceedings or express their opinions about "high protective tariff rates." Mama McCourt brags about her "little Lizzie's" wedding gown, which cost Horace Tabor more than seven thousand dollars. The four dandies snobbishly turn their backs on Mama, remarking that nobody of any importance showed up at the wedding.

The priest who officiated at the wedding appears and is tearfully greeted by Mama. He unctuously comforts her with the usual banalities, observing that she has not lost a daughter but has gained a son. Suddenly there is a stir of excitement as a footman announces Senator and Mrs. Horace Tabor. They are saluted with a mock-operatic *maestoso* chorus.

Tabor, beaming and pompous, with Baby Doe on his arm, urges everyone to join the celebration. Greeting the dandies, he asks what the latest news is from Capitol Hill. "Bimetallism," they reply in chorus. Mama, overhearing, says she thinks that would be fun and innocently asks if the ladies can try it.

At this point the four dandies sound the first warning note of future disaster as they tell Tabor that the "silver standard is doomed." When they add that gold is the coming thing, Tabor flares up angrily. Quieting him with a gesture, Baby Doe launches into a rather florid aria in which she compares the worth of silver and gold ("Gold is a fine thing"). While gold is the sun, she sings, silver is the moon—and she herself is a child of the moon. Silver, she exults in a soaring phrase, is the stuff of dreams.

Tabor then boastfully shows the guests a case of glittering jewelry—the very ones, he says, which Queen Isabella of Spain pawned to finance Columbus' discovery of America. These, he proclaims, are what silver can buy. The onlookers gasp in admiration, while Mama McCourt fatuously expresses the wish that Harvey Doe could be present now. When the priest casually asks who Harvey Doe is, Mama then and there blunders into the damaging disclosure that both Tabor and Baby Doe have been divorced. In icy tones the priest asserts that he was not told of this, then stalks out of the room. In suppressed excitement, the guests whisper, "Scandal!" They repeat the word in a dramatic crescendo passage.

Just as they start to leave, the footman announces the arrival of the President of the United States, Chester A. Arthur. He toasts the bride, with the guests joining in a brief waltz chorus which closes the act.

## ACT II

[*Scene One*] A balcony off the ballroom of the Windsor Hotel in Denver. It is the evening of the Governor's Ball in 1893, ten years after the marriage of Tabor and Baby Doe in Washington. After a brief introduction in waltz tempo, the curtain rises to show the dancers through the windows of the hotel.

Augusta's four friends come out and an ensemble ensues which is joined later by the four cronies. The women first gossip in their usual spiteful fashion about Baby Doe, then express their sympathy for Augusta, now rejected and alone. The cronies come out and begin to argue with their wives. They try to defend Tabor and Baby but the women scorn their arguments. With malicious assurance they predict that Baby will leave Tabor "when something better comes along."

As a waltz tempo begins in the orchestra, Baby Doe and her mother come out, fanning themselves. Seeing the four women and their husbands, Baby Doe greets them cordially. Without a word, the four women turn their backs and go inside, followed by their shamefaced husbands. Baby ironically remarks on the sudden chill in the air, but Mama fumes over the insolent behavior of the wives.

Then in a long and moving aria Baby Doe compares her own happiness with the wretched frustration of those who scorn and criticize her. Their lives are bleak and empty, she sings, because they do not know what love is. Her own life is precious and warm because she is enveloped by a love that will last forever. And this, Baby sings in a triumphant climax, is something "they will never, never know."

Suddenly a butler appears and hands her a calling card on a tray. In suppressed excitement she sends her mother to find Tabor. A moment later she turns to face Augusta, a forbidding figure in a black ball gown. Augusta is strangely humble as she explains that she has come only to say something that must now be said. Baby Doe, she goes on, has been too happy for her own good. It has made other people hateful and jealous because it has made their own loveless lives more unbearable by contrast.

Baby, at first suspicious, feels a sudden rush of pity for this lonely, despairing woman and expresses regret for any wrong she has done her. Augusta absolves her of any blame, then discloses her real reason for coming. It is to warn her that Horace Tabor faces certain ruin. Tomorrow the President of the United States will sign a bill devaluating silver—and that means that Tabor's fortune will vanish.

Baby Doe refuses to believe her and cries that Horace knows what is best and that nothing can harm him. Vainly Augusta tries to convince her that, with the price of silver steadily diminishing, Horace's wealth is a thing of the past. But he is blind to everything but his love of silver, she goes on, which is like his love for Baby Doe. In the ringing climax of her pleading, Augusta begs Baby to persuade Tabor to sell his Matchless Mine.

At that moment Horace enters. Confronting Augusta, he accuses her of trying to turn Baby Doe against him—as she has half the town. Both Baby and Augusta try to reason with him but he storms that this talk of ruin is a lie. Crying that Tabor will never see her again, Augusta rushes out of the room. As Baby starts to follow, Tabor takes her in his arms and begs her not to desert him. The Matchless Mine will never fail them, he cries.

In a touching gesture of faith, Baby takes off her necklace and ring, thrusts them into his hands and tells him to bet her treasures on the Matchless Mine. Inspired by her confidence in him, Tabor asks her to promise always to hold onto the mine. Baby Doe resolutely replies: "Always, I promise!"

[Scene Two] A club room in Denver, 1895. Tabor's four cronies are playing poker. In dialogue partly spoken and partly sung, they discuss Tabor—how he keeps harping on silver and won't change with the times. They comment disparagingly on his chances in the coming election.

The four fall silent as Tabor enters to join the game. He announces he has a proposition to offer them and asks their support against McKinley and the anti-silver gang. If they will back him up, he continues, he will risk everything he has to win the fight. But the cronies only eye him silently and shake their heads. Tabor's pleading becomes desperate. The wind is sure to blow their way again, he cries, because a great champion of humanity and free silver is on their side—William Jennings Bryan. Thereupon the cronies denounce Bryan as a faker and ridicule Tabor for his faith in him.

Goaded to fury, Tabor accuses his erstwhile companions of

deserting him ("turn tail and run then!"). Let them forget that silver made them what they are, he roars, and let them crawl before their new masters. There still are free men who will stand their ground and fight. With an angry shout, he sends cards and chips flying from the table with a sweep of his hand, then strides out.

[*Scene Three*] Matchless Mine, 1896. Miners' wives are decorating a speaker's stand in front of the mine entrance. On the stand is a lectern and a huge photograph of Bryan. As the women work, they wordlessly sing a brisk marching tune. Baby Doe enters with her two children. She explains to them that flags are flying and people are shouting because the great William Jennings Bryan is coming to make a speech. He is a very great man, she says, a man who can charm the birds off the trees.

The martial music grows louder and soon a parade appears, led by Tabor. Mounting the platform, he exhorts the crowd to vote for Bryan and the silver standard. The crowd responds with a cheering chorus, "We want Bryan!" The mayor then tries to introduce Bryan, but his voice is lost in the clamor. Bryan finally silences the throng with an imperious gesture, then launches into a flowery speech on the theme historically associated with his name: "Never shall we worship before the Calf of Gold!"

He goes on in resounding, cliché-laden phrases, praising the pioneer spirit of the silver miners and Horace Tabor in particular. As he speaks, Tabor's little daughter, carrying a bunch of roses, pulls at his coattails. Finally taking notice of her, Bryan interrupts his speech to take her in his arms and thank her for the tribute. Reaching into one of the bags of silver ore banked around the lectern, he sprinkles some of it on the child's head and christens her "Silver Dollar." Then to the accompaniment of massive orchestral chords he brings his speech to a fervid climax—"Renew the ancient covenant between man and God!" Cheering him wildly, the crowd forms a procession. Several men lift Bryan to their shoulders and lead the parade away.

[*Scene Four*] Augusta's parlor, November 1896. She is standing at the window listening to the voices of newsboys shouting: "Republican landslide . . . Bryan defeated." Augusta cringes at the sound.

Samantha brings in Mama McCourt. The ensuing dialogue reveals the extent of the disaster which has befallen Tabor. With Bryan's defeat and the abandonment of the silver standard Tabor has lost everything. When Mama appeals to Augusta for help—for the sake of the children—Augusta coldly reminds her of Tabor's words: "I want nothing from her." Mama implores her to forgive Tabor, now a ruined man, but Augusta relentlessly refuses to help. Defeated and hopeless, Mama leaves.

Alone, Augusta gives way to her despair in a deeply moving soliloquy, "Augusta, how can you turn away?" Memories of her life with Tabor come back in a flood of anguish. She sings that she cannot understand why—now when he needs her most—she cannot bring herself to help him. In a descending phrase of complete desolation she murmurs, "But—I cannot go."

[*Scene Five*] The stage of the Tabor Grand Theater, April 1899. The curtain rises as a plaintive melody sounds in the orchestra. Tabor, in workman's clothes, walks slowly out on the stage, ignoring the stage doorman, who tries to stop him. Quietly Tabor identifies himself and the doorman apologizes for not having recognized him. Here begins the fantasy which brings the opera to its poignant climax.

Staring trancelike into the gloom of the deserted theater, Tabor begins: "I wanted to take a long, long look around." He recalls how he built the opera house, repeating the musical phrases he sang in Act I when he boasted to his cronies about his accomplishment. Suddenly a spotlight reveals the pompous figure of a man holding a glittering watch fob. Tabor hears the speaker's voice—"the citizens of Denver present this watch fob of purest gold." It should have been silver, Tabor murmurs, not gold. The doorman stares at him in alarm, then mutters that he must go for help. The figure of the speaker vanishes.

Tabor stands lost in his fantasy of the past. He sees again the green hills of the Vermont farm where he was born, hears a woman call to him in shrill, querulous tones. In his dream he confuses this voice with Augusta's. An ominous hooded figure appears. Tabor rushes toward it with a happy cry of "Maw!" The apparition slaps him violently, then berates him for being a worthless no-account "like your Paw."

Reeling from the blow, Tabor still tries to embrace the woman, who suddenly throws back her hood. It is Augusta, now as a young girl. Tabor recalls the days of his courtship of the girl who was named for Augusta, Maine. He was an ambitious young man then, working for Augusta's father and determined to "be somebody." A ghostly chorus chants: "To be somebody, marry the boss's daughter."

The fantasy continues with Tabor's vision of his journey to the West with his bride . . . he and his four cronies digging for silver . . . Augusta forcing him to sign "the pledge" . . . saloon girls . . . the wild life in Leadville . . . the discovery of the fabulous silver mine that made him rich . . . Tabor, the leading citizen of Leadville . . . builder of the opry house, monument to Tabor. . . . The music swells to a blazing fanfare of trumpets.

Suddenly it subsides into dark, foreboding chords as Augusta's voice intones, "You are goin' to die, Horace Tabor, and you die a failure." Remorseless, accusing, the voice foretells his doom, but Tabor shouts defiantly that Baby Doe will save him. Augusta answers that even his own children will repudiate him. Instantly Tabor is confronted with a vision of Silver Dollar as a half-naked, drunken cabaret girl raucously singing. The music rises to a frenzied climax as Tabor, with Augusta glaring at him malevolently, utters an agonized cry for help. The vision of Augusta fades. Tabor stands dazed and exhausted.

The doorman comes in followed by Baby Doe, who rushes to Tabor and takes him in her arms. She wears a black cloak with a hood covering her hair. Shaken by his terrible dream, Tabor at first does not realize it is Baby Doe. He puts his hands to her face and murmurs that he can feel tears. Thinking it is Augusta, he gasps defiantly: "You cannot divide us."

Baby Doe gently reassures him. His life ebbing away, Tabor sinks to the floor. Baby Doe kneels beside him and covers him with her cloak. As the light gradually fades, Tabor's body is enveloped in darkness. Baby Doe begins the aria which ends the opera: "Always through the changing of sun and shadow." Singing that she and her love will walk through eternity together, she slowly pushes back her hood, revealing her hair. It is snow-white.

The light comes up, bringing the shaft of the Matchless Mine into view. Baby Doe's final words die away on a serene major chord. The curtain falls.

# Capriccio

*"A conversation piece for music in one act"*

*by* RICHARD STRAUSS

(1864–1949)

*Libretto by*
CLEMENS KRAUSS and RICHARD STRAUSS

Based on the libretto of an old Italian "opera parody" by Abate Giovanni Battista Casti (1724–1803), with music by Antonio Salieri

### CHARACTERS

| | |
|---|---|
| The Countess Madeleine | Soprano |
| The Count, her brother | Baritone |
| Flamand, a composer | Tenor |
| Olivier, a poet | Baritone |
| La Roche, the theater director | Bass |
| Clairon, an actress | Contralto |
| Monsieur Taupe, the prompter | Tenor |
| An Italian singer | Soprano |
| An Italian tenor | |
| A young dancer | |
| Major-domo | Bass |
| Eight servants | Four tenors, four basses |

Three musicians

*Place:* A château near Paris
*Time:* About 1775—during the period when the German composer Christoph Willibald von Gluck began his reform of opera
*First performance:* Munich, October 28, 1942
*Original language:* German

---

*Capriccio* is not an opera—the composer himself did not call it that. As his subtitle indicates, it has to do with a musical conversation among a group of witty and sophisticated artists in a

fashionable eighteenth-century salon near Paris, and as such it has
no plot. It is a blend of solos, ensembles and spoken dialogue in
the Singspiel pattern.

The salon discussion centers on the rather esoteric question of
the relative importance of words and music, and the participants
eventually come to the conclusion that this problem is solved only
when words and music are given their respective values in the
creation of a work of art. But it is by no means a pretentious
intellectual exercise. With superb artistry, Strauss has presented
his "conversation" with deep human feeling and enchanting lyricism.

*Capriccio* is Strauss's fifteenth and last work written for the
stage. What is called his "last opera"—written in conventional
form—is *Die Liebe der Danaë,* which he completed some three
years prior to *Capriccio*.

It was during that period, in fact, that Strauss read the libretto
of Casti's "opera parody," which had been sent him by the German
writer Stefan Zweig. But Strauss decided he did not want to write
simply another opera—he was interested in "something unusual, a
treatise on dramaturgy, a theatrical fugue." Accordingly, he discussed his plan with Clemens Krauss, director of the Munich State
Opera. The upshot of it was that the two men fashioned *Capriccio*
from the Casti libretto. It was given its premiere under Krauss's
direction.

Since then it has been in the repertoire of most of the important
opera houses in Europe, where it has enjoyed great popularity.
While it has been performed less frequently in America, it has
always met with success. Its first performance in this country was
given by a cast of graduate students of the Juilliard School of
Music in New York City in May 1954. Its first professional performance was given by the New York City Opera Company on
October 27, 1965.

Although the work is scored for a fairly large orchestra, its full
volume is reserved for a few climactic moments in the action, with
voices and accompaniment always kept in dynamic relationship.
The overture itself is played by a string sextet; it states the leading musical themes heard later throughout the work.

The entire action takes place in the salon of the young widowed
Countess Madeleine. At the rear, tall glass doors lead to the
terrace, beyond which is a park. At one side is a door leading to
the dining room; another door downstage leads to the Countess'

chamber. At the other side, a door leads to the stage of the private theater. In the salon, chairs and divans are casually arranged. Candles in wall sconces light the scene.

[*Scene One*] It is early afternoon on the Countess' birthday. Flamand, a composer, and Olivier, a poet, are standing near the door listening to the string sextet which Flamand composed for the occasion, and which serves as the "overture." (Throughout the action, the music continues without interruption from scene to scene.) Near the center of the room, La Roche, the theater director, is asleep in an armchair.

Flamand comments that the Countess looks enchanting as she listens from her room with eyes closed. Olivier, nodding toward La Roche, asks if he too is "enchanted." The two men speculate as to whether the Countess is charmed by words or by music, and in the process they both disclose that they are in love with her.

Olivier insists that words come first, then music: "prima le parole —dopo la musica." Flamand argues the contrary. They sing the Italian in echoing phrases. Finally they compromise: It is a matter of words *and* music.

As the music of the sextet dies away, La Roche wakes up and remarks that one sleeps best to soft harmonies. Half in mockery, Olivier wonders why an artist's fate must be in the hands of a man like this—pity poor Gluck! La Roche retorts that, without a theater director, an artist's creations are nothing but paper ("Ohne mich sind eure Werke totes Papier"). At the mention of Gluck, a brief phrase from his *Iphigenia in Aulis* sounds in the orchestra.

An argument ensues in trio form. Flamand and Olivier champion Gluck's reforms leading to emphasis on subject matter, while La Roche insists that nothing surpasses Italian opera, with its glorification of vocal art.

When Flamand and Olivier deride the bad librettos of the old Italian school, La Roche cites the successes of Piccini and Goldoni.[1] The latter, he says, once remarked that the new operas were "heaven for the eyes, but hell for the ears." The argument grows more heated as Flamand and Olivier ridicule the trivial farces performed for the masses. La Roche insists that the people want flesh-and-blood human beings, spectacular scenery and beautiful women on the stage—not static figures out of the dead past.

The mention of women brings up the name of the actress

[1] Niccolò Piccini (1728–1800), Italian composer and Gluck's rival. Carlo Goldoni (1707–93), Italian dramatist and librettist.

Clairon, who is expected at the rehearsal of La Roche's play. The controversy over aesthetics is forgotten as the three discuss the beauty and talent of this famous actress.[2] It is brought out that Olivier is currently her admirer—but now the Count seems destined to take his place. La Roche suddenly notices that the Countess is leaving her room, and now the stage must be prepared for the rehearsal. The three hurry into the theater.

[*Scene Two*] Countess Madeleine enters with her brother, the Count. They converse in one of the principal duets of the opera, which begins as the Countess sings that the flood of musical sounds transported her to an enchanted land ("Der Strom der Töne"). In the ensuing dialogue, they discuss music versus poetry, the Countess' romantic interest in the poet and the composer and the Count's probable adventure with Clairon. The duet comes to a richly melodious climax as the two sing that truth, beauty and happiness—the greatest treasures in life—are easily lost, but as eaily won ("Leicht zu verlieren").

[*Scene Three*] La Roche comes back with Flamand and Olivier to announce that the program in honor of Madeleine's birthday is about to begin. First, he says, there will be a symphony by Flamand, then a play by himself and finally a dazzling production by the entire company—which will include singers from the Italian opera. This is greeted with disparaging remarks from Flamand and Olivier about the probable quality of that portion of the performance.

Any further argument, however, is interrupted by the arrival of the actress Clairon. Her carriage is seen through the doors of the terrace, and the Count hurries out to meet her. The Countess remarks that the renowned tragedienne is dressed in ordinary traveling costume. Olivier compliments La Roche on having persuaded Clairon to appear in the play; Flamand remarks that if she could sing she would be completely irresistible.

[*Scene Four*] The Count brings in Clairon, whom he presents to the Countess with suave formality. The Countess greets her with studied courtesy, while La Roche melodramatically acclaims her as the embodiment of "Andromaque, Phèdre, Medea, Roxane." Clairon modestly acknowledges the compliment, then asks

[2] Mlle. Clairon (1723–1803). Real name, Claire Josèphe Hippolyte Léris de la Tude.

Olivier if he has finished the drama she and the Count are to enact. He answers that only this morning he was inspired to write a beautiful sonnet. The Count then shows her the poet's manuscript, and the two begin reading their lines in spoken dialogue. It is a highly dramatic scene in which two lovers bid each other farewell before the lover departs for the battlefield. Its climax is the sonnet, which is read by the Count ("Kein Andres, das mir so im Herzen loht").[3]

At the conclusion of the reading, Clairon enthusiastically commends the Count on his histrionic talent. Then she ceremoniously hands the manuscript to La Roche and commands him to produce the drama on the spot. La Roche tells her that the theater is ready, then turns to go. When Olivier starts to follow, the director advises him to wait—he is too tenderhearted to allow the author to be present while his work is being prepared for the stage. With that La Roche goes into the theater, followed by Clairon and the Count.

The Countess watches her brother with a knowing smile. Turning to Olivier, she says that the lover in his play expressed himself ardently indeed. The words, Olivier answers, were addressed to the wrong person—and he will now correct that error. He thereupon fervently repeats the sonnet to the Countess herself. As she listens, Flamand goes to the clavichord and begins to improvise a melody to fit the words of the sonnet over a graceful waltz theme ("Und trüg ich's fünfmal hundert tausend").

Saying that so lovely an avowal should not be proclaimed publicly, the Countess takes the manuscript from Olivier. Flamand, exclaiming that he already can hear the music which the words inspire, takes the manuscript from the Countess and rushes into the adjoining room to compose.

[*Scene Five*] Olivier protests that now Flamand will ruin the sonnet with his music. Perhaps the music will make the words more beautiful, the Countess says, then provocatively asks the poet if he has anything to say to her in prose—now that they are alone.

A lyrical colloquy in an elegant waltz tempo follows as Olivier declares his love ("Meine Prosa verstummt") and the Countess responds. When Olivier entreats her to affirm her position on the issue of "words or music," she answers that she cannot decide.

[3] In reality, the German translation of a poem by Pierre de Ronsard (1524–85), a French lyric poet.

Music enchants her, she explains, but she also cherishes the intellectual beauty of words. Well then, Olivier sings, concluding the duet, name the victor. At that moment, Flamand rushes in with a sheet of music in his hand, hears Olivier's words, and cries: "Here he is!"

[*Scene Six*] Sitting down at the clavichord, Flamand sings the sonnet in one of the opera's most beautiful arias, "Kein Andres, das mir so im Herzen loht." This in turn leads into a magnificent trio as the Countess and Olivier express their reaction. The Countess ponders whether words give birth to music or music gives life to words. Olivier laments that the composer's "ear-tickling" sounds have robbed his verses of their symmetry. The poet's words, then, are merely the steps on which the composer climbs to victory.

At the end of the trio Olivier demands to know to whom the sonnet now belongs: to himself or to Flamand. "If you will allow me," the Countess answers graciously, taking the music from Flamand's hand, "it is mine."

At this point, La Roche comes in and says he needs Olivier's help in making certain cuts in his play. He and the poet go back into the theater.

[*Scene Seven*] Now it is Flamand's turn to declare his love for the Countess. First he asks her to decide which will win the prize: music or poetry. Then he pours out his love in an impassioned aria, "Diese Liebe, plötzlich geboren."

He describes how, this very afternoon, love suddenly awakened as he watched her reading a book in the library, where he had entered unobserved. When she left, he had picked up the book she had put down opened and had read the words of Pascal: "In love, silence is better than speech" ("In der Liebe ist Schweigen besser").[4] For a long while he had sat there in the deepening twilight, and in that silence he became a changed man. Now, he sings, he asks only one word from her to crown his rapture. The Countess promises that he will have his answer in the library at eleven o'clock tomorrow morning. Exultantly singing her name, Flamand impetuously kisses her arm and rushes away.

During an orchestral interlude, the Countess, deeply moved, reflects on Flamand's avowals. From the theater come the sounds of the rehearsal, punctuated by occasional laughter. Stirred out of her reverie, the Countess rings and orders her Major-domo to serve chocolate.

[4] Blaise Pascal (1623–62), French philosopher.

[*Scene Eight*] The Count enters, full of enthusiasm over Clairon's acting—and her praise of his own performance. But he scoffs at the Countess' implication that he is falling victim to Clairon's charms. Her own situation, says the Countess, is more serious: Both Olivier and Flamand already have made violent declarations of love to her. It all came about after Flamand had set Olivier's sonnet to music—and what is more, the Countess adds, half in jest, the net result of all this may even be an opera. The Count mockingly compliments her on her role as the Muse. As for himself, he says, he prefers words to music. With equal mockery, his sister wishes him luck with Clairon.

[*Scene Nine*] Clairon, La Roche and Olivier enter from the theater and are joined a moment later by Flamand. After a brief discussion about the progress of the rehearsal, La Roche announces that there now will be a variation in the day's entertainment—by way of a dancer and two Italian singers. At a sign from him, the entertainers come in followed by three musicians with violin, cello and cembalo. First on the program is the ballet dancer, who performs three dances—a passepied, gigue and gavotte. The musical dialogue of the onlookers continues throughout the dances.

As they watch the passepied, La Roche informs the Count (who is obviously fascinated) that the beautiful dancer is his latest discovery, for whom he predicts a brilliant career. During the gigue, Clairon and Olivier, in a private quarrel, break off their love affair once for all. At the end of the gavotte, the company applauds the dancer, who goes back into the theater. La Roche remarks to Flamand that in the realm of the dance, at least, music is not the primary element, merely a contribution. Flamand dryly retorts that without music nobody would lift a leg.

This exchange leads into a remarkable section called the Fugue, which is virtually the climax of the opera and which embodies the philosophical concepts underlying the "words versus music" controversy. The section is subtitled "Discussion on the theme: Words or Music." It is a striking example of Strauss's ability to fuse the rhythms of words and music. The fugal theme which dominates the entire section takes its rhythm from the pulse of the opening phrase, "Tanz and Musik stehn im Bann des Rhythmus" ("Words and music are governed by rhythm").

One by one, those in the salon expound their theories. Flamand and Olivier each asserts that his art is supreme, while La Roche insists that music and poetry are nothing more than servants of the stage. He elaborates on his theory in a vigorous refrain in which he declares that the theater's ruling goddess is Fantasy, and all arts serve her. The Countess and Clairon champion the director's viewpoint.

Flamand sings (like the Composer in *Ariadne*) that music is the most sublime of the arts. Olivier argues that words alone can express pain—music is powerless to do so. At that point the Countess brings the debate up short by asking the poet how he can believe that to be true at a time when a "genius" (Gluck) has demonstrated that it is possible to write a "musical tragedy."

Thereupon the Count remarks sardonically that with one more step they will be standing on the edge of the abyss: opera! To derisive comments about the silly conventions of classical opera, the Count adds that opera is an absurdity ("Eine Oper ist ein absurdes Ding").

As the Count speaks these words there is an extraordinary musical effect. The key suddenly changes to A-flat major to introduce an intermezzo in Strauss's most ingratiating musical vein. The melody has its source in the last song of a set of twelve written by Strauss in 1918 and published (1918) in a limited edition of 120 copies under the title *Krämerspiegel* (*Shopkeeper's Mirror*).[5] The talk continues about the trend of opera, the boring recitatives and the deafening racket of the orchestra, which drowns out not only the words but the singers themselves.

Finally, La Roche cries dramatically that *bel canto* is at death's door. Thereupon the Countess suggests that he bring in the Italian singers so that the company may hear an example of the dying Italian vocal art. La Roche promptly calls in the Italian soprano and the tenor, and announces that they will sing a duet from an Italian opera with words by Metastasio.[6]

The two singers launch into a duet ("Addio, mia vita"), a parody of the florid, overblown operatics of the pre-Gluck Italian school. While the words have to do with parting and death, the gay, lighthearted accompaniment points up the superficiality of this musical form.

Bored with the performance, the Countess invites the singers to have something to eat. The servants seat them at a small table to the rear of the salon, where the two eat ravenously.

[5] Mentioned in the introductory essay by E. Roth (© 1959) to the Angel recording (35669–70–71) of *Capriccio*.

[6] Pietro Antonio Domenico Bonaventura Metastasio (1698–1782), celebrated Italian poet and librettist.

Meanwhile, the Count asks Clairon if he may accompany her back to Paris. She gives him permission. The Countess asks La Roche finally to reveal the details of his spectacular production in honor of her birthday.

The director announces that his stupendous "azione teatrale" will be divided into two parts. The first presentation will be *The Birth of Pallas Athene.* This is greeted by the company with sarcastic comments which build up into the first part of an octet, called the "Laughing Ensemble." La Roche and his production become the targets of their ridicule. Meanwhile, the two Italians, stuffing themselves with food, watch the scene and at the same time notice that the director is beginning to lose his temper. While the tenor frets about collecting their fee, the soprano helps herself to the Spanish wine and gradually becomes tipsy.

The Countess, realizing the situation is getting out of hand, tells La Roche that his grandiose production is far beyond the capabilities of the ordinary stage. She begs him not to take the criticism of his productions too seriously. And now, she asks, what is the second part of his show to be?

It will be *The Fall of Carthage,* La Roche informs her, and then goes on to describe this great drama, with its realistic scenery, crowds of actors, lightning, thunderbolts, and a real ship sinking in flames. This sets off the second part of the octet, called the "Quarreling Ensemble." Flamand and Olivier rail at La Roche for offering tawdry theatricals instead of real drama. They warn him that the day of cheap melodrama is over, and they will have nothing more to do with his fraudulent arts.

The Count, enjoying the squabble, comments that now the protagonists of the "noble arts" are quarreling among themselves, with the hapless La Roche—the traditionalist—caught in the cross fire of their attacks. The Countess expresses alarm over the scathing criticism leveled at the director and implores Flamand and Olivier to desist. La Roche protests that he is being judged unfairly and demands a chance to defend his principles.

The voices of the Italian singers blend with the ensemble in a comic parody of their "Addio" duet, in which they sing farewell to their chances of collecting their fee ("Addio mio dolce acconto"). Clairon assures the two that the director will make good his word. He is a man of action, accustomed to fighting for his rights. When his adversaries have talked themselves out, he will have his revenge.

Then, as though in proof of her warning, La Roche turns on

Flamand and Olivier in furious denunciation. His outburst, part recitative and part aria, is the longest individual number in the opera. He launches into his diatribe by asking how these "champions of the Muses" ("ihr Streiter in Apoll") dare to mock a leading authority in the theater. He sneers at their amateur attempts at poetry and music, branding it too superficial to touch the human heart. It is men like himself, he goes on, who uphold the sacred tradition of the theater, who have discovered the talent that brings splendor and majesty to the stage.

La Roche climaxes his peroration in a powerful refrain in which he declares that, because he has given his life for the glory of the theater, he will become one of its immortals ("Ich streite für die Schönheit"). And on his tombstone men will read the epitaph: "Here lies La Roche, the unforgettable" ("Heir ruht La Roche, der unvergessliche").

Overwhelmed by his eloquence, the others burst into applause. Clairon impetuously throws her arms around his neck and kisses his cheek. The Italian soprano, now completely befuddled with wine and overcome with emotion, bursts into tears. In comical exasperation, the tenor, reminding her that the director is not dead yet, upbraids her for making a scene, then drags her away. Shaking with laughter, the Count shouts, "Bravo!"

The Countess steps forward and in a solo passage ("Verlasst die Irrewege") declares that it is now the duty of the poet and the composer to combine their talents in a work of art which will be worthy of the director and his eloquent defense of his theater. In an aside to Clairon, the Count murmurs that his sister is (perish the thought) commissioning an opera.

In a theatrical gesture, Clairon takes the hands of Flamand and Olivier and leads the men to the Countess to pay her homage as the "Goddess of Harmony." The Countess gravely acknowledges the tribute. Sustaining Clairon's ceremonial mood, Flamand, Olivier and La Roche join with her in the "Homage Quartet" ("Was hebt sich götterlich").

The only dissenting voice is that of the Count, who cynically observes that, willy-nilly, he is about to be afflicted with an opera. The Countess explains that her brother's musical tastes run to triumphal marches and that in his opinion opera composers are nothing but "word killers."

La Roche officiously orders the project to begin and announces the rules of procedure: There is to be no meddling with the aria; the singers must be heard over the accompaniment; verses must be repeated so that they can be understood. Flamand scoffs at these conventional restrictions on creative effort and calls for new ideas. La Roche tartly advises him not to exaggerate his own importance, then says they must first decide on a subject. Olivier and Flamand in turn suggest *Ariadne auf Naxos* and *Daphne;* themes from Strauss's own operas on these subjects are heard in the orchestra. Fuming impatiently that this is "mythology" all over again, La Roche insists on a subject that involves human beings—in short, themselves.

Thereupon the Count says he has an extraordinary suggestion: Write down the events that have occurred in this château this very day, set them to music, and there you have a contemporary opera. They themselves will be the characters in the drama. The novelty of the idea takes the others completely by surprise, and an animated discussion follows in an ensemble in quasi-recitative. All finally express their enthusiasm for the plan.

The discussion ends as Clairon says she must return to Paris. She takes leave of the Countess, who retires to her room. Flamand and Oliver accompany her to the door and remain standing there in the same positions as in Scene One.

[*Scene Ten*] La Roche brings the two Italian singers from the theater and escorts them out. On the way, he promises the tenor that he will be paid his fee tomorrow. Clairon and the Count leave together. Flamand turns to Olivier and with grave courtesy sings an inversion of the phrase heard at the beginning of the action: "prima le parole, dopo la musica." With equal chivalry, Olivier responds: "No, first the music—but born of the words."

Staring at the Countess' door, the composer and the poet give voice to their thoughts in brief, quiet phrases over a variation of the theme heard at the beginning of the first scene. Each one is thinking of his secret rendezvous with the Countess in her library at eleven o'clock the following morning. It is then that they will learn which has won her heart: the music (and thus Flamand) or the words (and thus Olivier). Their reflections are interrupted when La Roche comes bustling in saying they must leave for Paris at once. As before, he plies them with advice on how to write the opera. The three leave together.

[*Scene Eleven*] This scene consists of a delightful ensemble in which eight servants, who enter to put the salon in order, comment on the day's events. In subdued tones they discuss the behavior of the Countess and her guests—who all talked at once and made a wonderful lot of noise ("Das war ein schöner Lärm").

The Italian singer, says one servant, had a tremendous appetite —she gobbled up all the cake. Another wonders what the director's long oration was about. It is duly explained that the director is trying to reform the theater, and hopes to do so before he dies. They are all mad, the servants sing together, and they are all play acting. But behind the scenes the servants know what is going on: The Count is having a new love affair, while the Countess herself cannot decide which one of two men she is in love with. To settle the matter, a servant goes on to say, she is having them write an opera for her. Several of the others argue that there is nothing to be learned from opera because nobody ever understands the words. They insist that it is much more interesting to watch tightrope dancers or a marionette show. One of the servants suggests they entertain the Countess with a pantomime of their own.

Their chatter is interrupted by the Major-domo, who comes in and orders them to get on with their work. They are to set the table for supper, after which they will be free for the evening. In great good humor the servants conclude the ensemble, softly singing that an evening without guests will be a pleasure ("Welch Vergnügen, ein Abend ohne Gäste!"). When they leave, the Major-domo lights a candelabra. Suddenly he hears a quavering voice from the theater calling, "Director!"

[*Scene Twelve*] A gnomelike figure emerges from the shadows. Staring in surprise, the Major-domo asks him who he is. The wizened little man replies that he is the invisible ruler of a magical kingdom underground. Impatiently reminding him that he is quite visible at the moment, the Major-domo asks him his name. "I am Monsieur Taupe, the prompter," the other answers finally. He is a man of importance in the theater, he goes on, and rules this realm from his box. When he falls asleep, the actors stop talking and the public wakes up. It logically follows, then, that it is sleep that makes him indispensable to the theater.

But this time, he whimpers, he slept too long and now his director has gone back to Paris without him. Amused but sympathetic, the Major-domo invites Monsieur Taupe to the kitchen and assures him that he will arrange to have a carriage ready to take him to Paris. As the prompter thanks the Major-domo and follows him out, the music softly subsides into the lyrical theme of Strauss's *Krämerspiegel* song heard earlier as the Count commented on the absurdity of opera.

[*Scene Thirteen*] As the intermezzo continues, the deserted salon darkens and moonlight floods the terrace outside. After a few moments the Countess, elegantly gowned, enters the steps out on the terrace, where she stands in deep thought. The Major-domo and two servants enter and light the candles. The Countess comes in from the terrace and asks where her brother is. He escorted Mlle. Clairon to Paris, the Major-domo replies, and will not return this evening. She will dine alone, the Countess says. She reflects for a moment on the Count's romantic dalliance, then asks the Major-domo if there are any other matters.

He informs her that Olivier will visit her tomorrow to learn how the opera he and Flamand are writing is to end. With a start of surprise, the Countess asks, "Tomorrow . . . when and where?" In the library at eleven o'clock, the Major-domo answers. He bows and leaves.

The Countess smothers a gasp of dismay as she realizes that she asked Flamand to meet her at the same place at the same time. This, she murmurs, will be a disaster ("Es ist ein Verhängnis"). The phrase introduces the great monologue-aria which concludes *Capriccio*. The sonnet, Madeleine sings, has made poet and composer inseparable—although Flamand will be surprised to see Olivier in the library instead of herself. But now . . . how is the opera to end? Will music or words prevail—or, to put it another way, which lover will she choose?

Placing the music on the stand, she seats herself at her harp and begins singing the sonnet as Flamand sang it to her ("Kein Andres, das mir so im Herzen loht"). After several verses she breaks off to exclaim that the love of poet and composer has caught her in a trap from which there is no escape. Then she sings the sonnet to its conclusion. At this point a theme from Flamand's sextet, heard in the overture, sounds in the orchestra.

Suddenly Madeleine catches sight of her image in the mirror. Half in mockery, she entreats the reflection to tell her what her heart has decided. In a sudden, passionate outburst, she cries that she wants an answer—not this ironic glance ("Ich will eine Antwort, und nicht deinen prüfenden Blick!"). Then, recovering her composure, Madeleine, in the soaring climax of the aria, implores the image of herself—a woman ardently in love with poet and composer—to help her find an ending for their opera. Is there, she sings softly but with passionate intensity, one that would have meaning?

As themes of Flamand's sextet again sound in the orchestra, Madeleine smiles mischievously at her reflection, waves her fan flirtatiously, then makes an elaborate curtsy. She turns and walks into the dining room past the Major-domo, who had entered a moment earlier to announce supper. He stares at Madeleine, looks back at the mirror, then shakes his head in utter bewilderment. A horn call echoes softly and mysteriously in the orchestra. The curtain falls.

# Le Coq d'Or
## (*The Golden Cockerel*)

*by* NIKOLAI ANDREYEVITCH RIMSKY-KORSAKOV

(1844–1908)

*Libretto by*
VLADIMIR BIELSKY

*Based on a fairy tale by Pushkin*

### CHARACTERS

| | |
|---|---|
| The Astrologer | Tenor |
| King Dodon | Bass |
| Prince Guidon ⎱ sons of King Dodon | ⎰ Tenor |
| Prince Aphron ⎰ | ⎱ Baritone |
| General Polkan, commander-in-chief of the King's armies | Bass |
| Amelfa, the royal housekeeper | Contralto |
| The Queen of Chemakha | Soprano |

Boyars, townspeople, soldiers, slaves, dancers

*Place:* Mythical
*Time:* Legendary
*First performance:* Zimin's Theater, Moscow, September 24, 1909
*Original language:* Russian

---

*Le Coq d'Or*, the last of some fifteen operas by Rimsky-Korsakov, is a delightful mixture of fantasy, symbolism, and political satire. The fact that it portrays a monarch as a lazy, capricious individual is said to have provoked the disapproval of the censor, who banned the production until certain changes had been made. The first performance did not take place until after the composer's death. Besides making extraordinary demands on the vocal resources of the artists, the opera requires singers who can dance and dancers who can sing. In some presentations it is given with the singers seated at the sides of the stage, while dancers pantomime the action.

There is a brief prelude in which we hear the musical phrase imitating the crowing of the Golden Cockerel and the theme characterizing the Queen of Chemakha.

## PROLOGUE

The Astrologer, holding a magic key, appears before the curtain and addresses the audience ("Ya, koldoon. Naookoy taynoy"). As a magician endowed with extraordinary gifts of enchantment, he declares, he is about to conjure up an ancient fairy tale. None of it is true, he says, but it contains a lesson that is worth remembering. With these words the Astrologer disappears.

## ACT ONE

The council hall of King Dodon's palace. Dodon is seated on a magnificent throne and at his side are his two sons, Prince Guidon and Prince Aphron. Before the King, seated in a semicircle, are the boyars[1] and General Polkan, commander of the King's armies. The soldiers who are posted as guards are sound asleep. Dodon, who appears troubled and anxious, complains of his arduous duties as ruler of the kingdom ("Ya vas sdyes zatem sozval"). Just as he has decided to take a rest from the cares of state, a neighboring king takes up arms against him. No sooner has he dispelled the threat of invasion from the north and south than the enemy strikes from the coast. It is all very disheartening, Dodon wails, and he could weep with anger. Now, he declares, he wants some constructive advice from his councilors.

Guidon at once rises to say that he has been thinking about the problem all night long and has finally arrived at a solution ("Noch vsew doomal do zari"). The trouble is, he says, that their own soldiers are too close to the enemy—they are face to face with the foe across the border. Withdraw the troops, he advises, post them around the capital, and lay in plentiful supplies of food and wine. While the enemy is expending himself in destroying the surrounding villages, their own troops can make good use of the time by training. When the enemy has finally exhausted his power in comparatively minor depredations, Dodon's forces can annihilate him in a surprise assault. The boyars loudly hail Guidon's superior strategical wisdom, but the Prince modestly deprecates their praises.

[1] Privileged members of Russian aristocracy, next to the ruling princes. The class was abolished by Peter the Great (1682–1725).

The only dissenter is General Polkan, who growls that there is a possibility the enemy may attack the capital first. Imagine what would happen, he remarks, if their beloved sovereign should get in the way of a bullet. There is general consternation. Dodon angrily declares that Polkan should be jailed for such treasonable utterances. The King then calls on Prince Aphron for suggestions.

As usual, Aphron begins, his brother is completely wrong about everything. At those words Guidon advances menacingly on Aphron, while Dodon implores the two not to waste time quarreling. Aphron then explains *his* plan ("Chto lookavit"), which, he says, is naturally the only logical one. Dismiss the troops, he counsels, and send them home. This will lull the enemy into a false sense of security. Then, exactly a month before the day on which the foe will make an assault on the capital, the army is to be quickly called up again to deliver a surprise attack which will catch the foe off his guard and put him to rout. Dodon, overjoyed at this magnificent display of military reasoning on the part of his youngest son, fervently embraces him, while the boyars acclaim his genius.

But Polkan again protests. As the enemy is notorious for his lack of consideration, he observes sardonically, he probably will neglect to notify the King as to the day on which he proposes to attack the capital. Dodon and the entire court turn on poor Polkan and denounce him for his miserable, unsoldierly objections, after which they ignore him completely.

When the King asks for further advice on the problem, one of the boyars remarks that it is a pity that some of the official fortunetellers of the kingdom have gone to their reward. A violent argument develops as to the best method of foretelling the future —counting beans, reading the dregs of a cup of kvass, or divining the stars. When the dispute is at its height, the Astrologer comes in. An impressive figure in a white shako and a long blue robe decorated with stars, he carries an astrolabe and a bag. As the boyars stare at him openmouthed, the Astrologer walks over to the throne and bows respectfully to King Dodon.

In an ensuing aria ("Slaven bood velikiy tsar") he explains the purpose of his visit. He has heard of the King's dilemma and has brought with him a fabulous bird which will protect the King and his realm from all harm. It is a Golden Cockerel. Placed upon a high perch, the Cockerel will stand guard day and night and crow a warning when danger threatens. The moment the foe appears, the Cockerel will shake his golden comb, turn in the direction from which the enemy is approaching, and utter his warning cry, "Kiricoo-cool"

As the boyars crowd around, the Astrologer reaches into his bag and brings forth the Golden Cockerel, which flaps its wings, crows, and proclaims that it will stand guard. Beside himself with joy, Dodon orders the bird to be placed on the highest perch available and then asks the Astrologer how he can reward him for this priceless boon. He need only ask, Dodon exclaims, and it will be granted. The Astrologer replies that worldly treasures do not interest him ("Mudretczam dari nye lestni"). All he desires is Dodon's promise in writing that he may have anything he asks. Bridling at this implied reflection on the value of his word, Dodon refuses, loudly assuring the Astrologer of his good faith. Bowing, the Astrologer leaves. Dodon dismisses the boyars.

As the Cockerel crows and exhorts the King to take his ease, Dodon settles down to pleasant reflections ("To to stchastye! Rooki slojha"). How convenient it will be, he muses, to take a nap whenever he pleases and rule his kingdom without lifting a finger. Meanwhile he will enjoy himself with music and dancing. Descending from his throne, he goes to the open door of the council chamber and stretches himself out in the sun.

The housekeeper, Amelfa, enters, urges the monarch to banish all cares of state, and offers him a variety of delicacies. Nibbling away at them, Dodon tells Amelfa to see to it that he does not fall asleep sitting up. She is to awaken him later if it becomes absolutely necessary. He then decides that he wants his parrot. After talking to the bird for a few moments he becomes bored, and Amelfa takes the parrot away. At her command the servants bring in an enormous bed made of ivory and covered with luxurious furs. Dodon lies down on it and immediately falls asleep, while Amelfa sits at his side and brushes the flies away from his face. The atmosphere of slumber gradually pervades the entire palace. Amelfa herself finally falls asleep at the side of the bed. The Cockerel crows softly, while an unseen chorus sings in brief, drowsy phrases.

The silence is shattered a few moments later by the shrill warning crow of the Cockerel. Pandemonium breaks loose as panic-stricken people storm into the palace, shouting that the enemy is at the gates of the capital. Polkan dashes in, arouses Dodon, and finally makes him understand that danger is threatening. Dodon jumps up and begins haranguing the crowd, appealing to them in the name of patriotism to put all their treasures and goods at the disposal of the army ("Noo, rebyatushki, voyna!")

Guidon and Aphron rush in. The King embraces his sons and urges them to hurry off to battle. They plead for a little more time to prepare, however, saying that the soldiers can do the fighting in the meanwhile. Polkan fumes that the Cockerel is making the air hideous with his crowing and is spinning madly about on his perch. Now he stops and faces eastward, Polkan wails, and in that sector the defenses are the weakest. He then advises sending all the old men as well into battle.

Dodon calls excitedly for his armor and his great red shield. The servants drag in the rusty, dust-covered armor and laboriously try to help the King put it on. He frets about its being too tight for him. His shield is eaten through with rust, he complains; the sword is too heavy; he cannot get his breath. He calls for a horse —a gentle one. When it is led forth, the servants, by dint of much pushing and tugging, finally get him into the saddle. At intervals the shrill warning of the Cockerel cuts through the din.

Ordering Polkan to go before him, Dodon starts off to war. Amelfa, much distressed, calls after him that he has forgotten to eat. The King answers that he can eat on the way. As Dodon rides away with Polkan the people hail him as their glorious leader and warn him not to go too near the enemy. The curtain falls.

## ACT TWO

A narrow pass in a desolate mountain region. Lying everywhere are the bodies of hundreds of warriors killed in battle. Black carrion birds are perched on the corpses, among which are those of Guidon and Aphron. Their two horses stand with heads lowered over the bodies of their masters. A gray mist swirls over the scene and a cold wind is blowing. It is night.

The remnants of King Dodon's army, marching in double file across the battlefield, comment on the grisly scene in a mournful chorus ("Shepchet strakhi noch nemaya"). They speak of the evil birds of prey sitting on the corpses in the ghostly light of the moon, and of the icy wind that walks among the dead, sorrowing over their fate.

The soldiers stand silently as King Dodon and Polkan ride up. Suddenly they come upon the slain princes. Dismounting, King Dodon throws himself on the bodies of his sons and gives way to his grief and anguish in a poignant refrain ("Chto za strashnaya cartina"). He sobs that his two beloved sons lie here on ground soaked with their own blood, each slain by the other's sword in the confusion of battle. Crying that both his brave falcons have been snared, Dodon raises his arms and calls upon the mountains and valleys to weep with him in his sorrow. The soldiers utter phrases of lamentation. Dodon cries that henceforth he himself will lead his armies into battle so that the lives of young men will not be needlessly sacrificed.

Polkan, philosophically observing that what is done is done, announces to the soldiers that they must now annihilate the enemy to avenge King Dodon's misfortune. The soldiers swear that they will fight—as soon as they find the enemy. Pacing up and down, Dodon rages that the treacherous blackguards who inflicted this loss upon him must be run down and destroyed.

Meanwhile the rising sun dispels the mists and brings into view a large, brilliantly colored tent. Peering at it, Polkan declares that it is probably the tent of the enemy commander-in-chief and orders his soldiers to attack it at once. Unwilling to do any more fighting, the soldiers hang back, reluctantly loading their weapons. The cannoneers suggest that it would be safer first to fire from a distance. Polkan agrees, and then the cannoneers wheel an absurd-looking cannon into position, load it, and aim.

Just as Polkan is about to give the order to fire, a ravishingly beautiful young woman emerges from the tent, followed by four slaves carrying musical instruments. She is resplendently gowned and wears a white turban with a long feather. Turning toward the sun, she raises her arms in a gesture of invocation and sings the beautiful *Hymn to the Sun* ("Otvet mnye zorkoye svetilo"). In phrases of exotic beauty she implores the sun to tell her of her native land. She asks if the roses and the lilies still bloom in all their loveliness, if the maidens still go down to the river's edge at dusk to sing of the forbidden delights of love, and if they still go to meet their lovers in the cool, soft darkness with tender promises and warm kisses on their lips. The aria dies away on a lovely minor strain.

Dodon, who has been listening as though spellbound, pokes Polkan in the ribs and tells him to take due note of the lady's beautiful singing. The general suggests with a wink that if she invites them to stay and rest awhile they certainly should accept. The two walk hesitantly toward the young woman. When Dodon asks her name she answers in alluring phrases that she is the Queen of Chemakha and that she is on her way to conquer his nation ("V svoey vole ya devitcza"). The idea, says Dodon, is rather quaint, for in order to fight a war one must have an army. The Queen replies that she does not need an army—she conquers with beauty alone. She claps her hands, and two slaves bring wine for Dodon and Polkan. Dodon warily invites her to drink first. Looking at him seductively, the Queen asks if he could possibly imagine

that anyone as beautiful as she would poison him. Greatly embarrassed, Dodon drinks and Polkan does likewise.

The slaves bring out a carpet and arrange seats of pillows for
the Queen's guests. At a signal from Polkan the soldiers retire and
begin dragging the bodies from the battlefield in the background.
After a moment of uncomfortable silence Polkan clumsily attempts
to make conversation by asking the Queen if she slept well. She
assures Polkan that she slept soundly but adds that she was awakened at dawn by the sound of someone sighing passionately. The air
was heavy with a choking perfume, and then she heard a voice tenderly calling to her. With a crude attempt at humor Polkan asks if
she looked under the bed.

The Queen tartly answers that it was dark and then goes on
musing over the mysterious nocturnal visitor. Polkan's persistent
scoffing over what he calls romantic nonsense finally arouses the
Queen's ire, and she requests Dodon to send this annoying boor
away. Dodon angrily orders Polkan to sit behind the tent. The
general hurriedly obeys. He is seen occasionally sticking his head
out in an effort to hear what is being said.

Moving close to Dodon, the Queen murmurs in his ear that she
wishes to talk to him privately about several matters ("Oo menya
k tebe yest dyelo"). This marks the beginning of a long colloquy
that is carried on to the accompaniment of a flood of sensuous and
exotic music. Dodon begins to show some alarm over the Queen's
provocative looks and gestures. She begins by remarking that she
often wonders if she is really as beautiful as people say she is. When
she asks Dodon his opinion he can only stammer incoherently. It is
a pity, says the Queen, that he must look upon her when her beauty
is hidden by her garments. In a voluptuous melody ("Sbroshoo
choporniya tkani") she describes how, when she retires, she lets
her robes fall from her and gazes at herself in the mirror to see
if perhaps any blemish mars her loveliness. Then she removes her
combs, and her hair streams over her body in a black torrent. So
that she may enjoy refreshing sleep, the Queen continues, she
bathes herself in dew. She concludes with a more detailed description of her charms, all of which leaves Dodon gasping and a
little pale. When the Queen asks him if he is ill he controls himself
with an effort and mutters that it is merely his liver.

Deliberately tantalizing him, the Queen sings a song which concludes with an invitation to enter her tent. Perhaps the old man
would at least like to look inside, she murmurs. Dodon hastily
assures her that he really is not as old as he looks. In caressing tones
the Queen says that she has tired herself with singing and asks

Dodon to favor her with a song. If he has ever been in love, she sighs, he surely must have sung. Assuring her that his repertoire is endless, the fatuous Dodon strikes up a ridiculous ditty—fortunately very brief ("Boodoo vek tebya loobit"). The Queen applauds him in cynical merriment.

As the conversation continues the Queen's mood of ironic mockery gives way to melancholy, and in another sensuous refrain she voices her longing for her homeland ("Da, doyedesh do vostoka"). As though seeing a vision, she describes an enchanted island, where her white palace gleams through the cypress trees. There on her throne she reigns in solitary splendor. No one is near, and yet, by means of her magic power, she can summon a host of young friends who will amuse her with laughter and gaiety. But then everything fades into the shadows, and she is left to weep alone in her palace on that fabled and mysterious island.

Lamenting over these painful memories, the Queen cries that she can no longer bear her grief and loneliness. She longs for a man who will put an end to the aimlessness of her existence by possessing her and ruling her life. Thereupon Dodon loudly declares that her troubles are over, for he is the very man who is qualified to be her lord and master.

Pretending to be delighted with the idea, the Queen asks him to dance with her by way of celebration. Dodon protests that he is out of practice, but the Queen continues to coax. She makes him look more ridiculous than ever by draping a scarf around his shoulders and placing a fan in his hands. But Dodon, noticing the soldiers looking on, refuses point-blank to make a fool of himself in front of his army. When the Queen, however, threatens to dance with Polkan, Dodon changes his mind and begins prancing about in an awkward attempt at dancing.

Slave girls come out of the tent and begin a slow, sinuous dance, in which the Queen joins. Weaving and swaying before the posturing Dodon, the Queen mocks and gibes at his clumsiness. The King is oblivious to her taunts, however, as he begins whirling madly about to keep pace with the quickening tempo of the music. Laughing hysterically, the Queen finally sits down to watch his foolish antics.

At length Dodon falls exhausted at her feet. After a moment he rises and, completely under her spell, offers his entire kingdom, including himself. He implores her to come with him, saying that he will spare nothing to make her happy. They will lie at their ease all day long, he promises, with nothing to do but eat sweetmeats and listen to fairy tales. The Queen answers that she will go, pro-

vided that boor of a general is given a sound beating for his insolence. Dodon prompty offers to have him beheaded.

The Queen immediately prepares to depart. At her call the
slaves hurry out of the tent, dress her for the journey, and bring
out all her belongings. The soldiers also prepare to march. Dodon
calls for the Queen's golden chariot. As he and the Queen seat
themselves in it the Queen ironically commands her slaves to
sing the praises of the royal bridegroom.

The procession at last moves off, with the slaves chanting a
mocking chorus of praise in which they hail Dodon as a sorry
humbug with the gait of a camel and the features of an ape
("Sestry kto khromayet ryadom"). As soldiers and slaves join in
shouts of acclaim, the curtain falls.


## ACT THREE

The capital of Dodon's realm, with the palace in the background.
Although the sun is blazing down, black thunderclouds loom on the
horizon. An ominous, oppressive calm pervades the streets. The
Golden Cockerel is seen perched motionless on his spire. People
are crowded in the street in front of the palace, gaping at the
couriers who rush in and out. There is an air of intense excitement
as the city awaits the royal procession.

In an agitated chorus ("Strashno, bratiki") the people talk among
themselves. Some take heart from the fact that the Golden Cockerel
is silent on his perch, while others murmur in frightened tones
about the sullen clouds on the horizon and warn that a violent
storm will soon strike the city.

Amelfa appears on the steps of the palace. Crowding around her,
the people anxiously inquire if there is any news of the King. At
first she impatiently orders them to be off, but finally, to quiet
their clamor, she tells them what has happened ("Vot kackye
vesti"). Their monarch, she proclaims, has sent word that he has
conquered four kings—named Hearts, Spades, Clubs, and Diamonds,
respectively—and has saved a beautiful princess from the jaws of a
dragon. He is bringing her to the city to be their Queen.

Someone asks about Guidon and Aphron. They were put in irons
and executed by their father, Amelfa replies. The crowd asks why
they were put to death. They quarreled, Amelfa tells the people,
adding contemptuously that their own heads may be lopped off
next. As the people bow and scrape before her a fanfare is heard
in the distance. Looking down at the throng, Amelfa sardonically

exhorts all to caper and dance about for joy over the King's return. They needn't, however, expect any favors or mercy, she adds.

There is a tremendous uproar as the procession appears, led by the strutting warriors. Then comes Queen Chemakha's fantastic retinue, made up of a grotesque array of freaks—dwarfs, giants, horned people, some with dog heads, people with a single eye in their foreheads, and so on. They are followed by male and female slaves carrying enormous quantities of treasure.

Finally the golden chariot appears with Dodon and the Queen. Dodon has lost his air of fatuous pride and seems apprehensive. He keeps looking at the Queen, who ignores him and gazes disdainfully at the crowd. The people greet their monarch with a rousing chorus ("Dolgo jhit tebe, Oorral"), in which they assure him that they will stand on their heads, if necessary, to amuse him. It was only to serve him that they were born at all, they shout.

Just as Dodon is about to descend from the chariot the Astrologer appears. He walks slowly toward the chariot, the crowd respectfully making way before him, while the Queen stares at him as though hypnotized. Dodon greets him cordially and asks what he wants. With his eyes on the Queen the Astrologer replies to Dodon's greeting and then suggests that they now settle their bargain ("Tsar velikiy yeto ya! Razotchemsya kack droozya"). He reminds Dodon that he promised him anything he desired in return for bringing him the Golden Cockerel. Now, says the Astrologer, he desires Queen Chemakha.

Dodon promptly flies into a rage, shouting that he has no patience with such silly requests. Why—of all things—should he ask for the Queen? The Astrologer quietly replies that he desires to know the delights of love and wishes to marry. Dodon fumes that he may have anything else—knighthood, a horse from the royal stables, half his kingdom—but not the Queen. When the Astrologer repeats request Dodon loses his temper completely and orders the guards to take the Astrologer to prison. When he turns back to protest this injustice, Dodon, in a burst of rage, strikes him dead with his sword. There is a terrific clap of thunder as the Astrologer falls. Laughing sardonically, the Queen observes that such is the fate of all disobedient serfs.

Looking down at the body, Dodon wonders if this bloodshed will bring misfortune on their marriage. Nothing more than an argument at the wedding feast, perhaps, says the Queen casually. Reassured, Dodon tries to kiss her, whereupon she pushes him away and denounces him as a miserable, doddering fool whom the very earth itself detests. She warns him that his own doom is not far off.

Smiling vacantly, Dodon remarks that she is joking. There has already been one jest, the Queen says grimly.

As they descend from the chariot the Golden Cockerel flies from its perch. Crowing harshly, it hovers over Dodon, crying that it will peck the King's head. The people cower in fear. Suddenly the Cockerel hurtles downward and kills Dodon with a blow of its beak. There is a tremendous crash of thunder and the scene is plunged into darkness. Out of the blackness comes the Queen's malicious laughter. When the light returns, both the Queen and the Cockerel have vanished.

In astonishment and stupefaction the people look at the body of King Dodon. Falling to their knees, they break into a dramatic chorus of lamentation ("Oomer tsar. Oobit serdechniy"). The King is dead, they cry, their happy, fearless King—wisest of monarchs, who ruled while he lay at his ease in his palace. When angered by his subjects, he punished sternly but justly, and when his anger passed he smiled on all, and his smile was like the sunlight. In hopeless despair the people ask each other how they will live without a king. As they bow to the ground, shaken by sobs, the curtain falls.

## EPILOGUE

The Astrologer steps once more before the curtain. The story, he says, is ended ("Vot chem konchilasya skazka"). The spectators, however, need not take its tragic conclusion too much to heart, for the truth of the matter is that of all the people in the play only the Queen and he himself were real. The others were mere phantoms. So saying, he vanishes.

# The Crucible

*by* ROBERT WARD

( 1917–    )

*Libretto by*
BERNARD STAMBLER

*Based on the play of the same name by Arthur Miller*

### CHARACTERS

| | |
|---|---|
| Betty Parris | Mezzo-soprano |
| Reverend Samuel Parris | Tenor |
| Tituba | Contralto |
| Abigail Williams | Soprano |
| Ann Putnam | Soprano |
| Thomas Putnam | Baritone |
| Rebecca Nurse | Contralto |
| Francis Nurse | Bass |
| Giles Corey | Tenor |
| John Proctor | Baritone |
| Reverend John Hale | Bass |
| Elizabeth Proctor | Mezzo-soprano |
| Mary Warren | Soprano |
| Ezekiel Cheever | Tenor |
| Judge Danforth | Tenor |
| Sarah Good | Soprano |

Chorus of girls: Betty Parris (mezzo-soprano), Ruth Putnam (coloratura), Susanna Walcott (contralto), Mercy Lewis (contralto), Martha Sheldon (soprano), Bridget Booth (soprano)

*Place:* Salem, Massachusetts
*Time:* 1692
*First performance:* New York City Opera Company, New York, October 26, 1961
*Original language:* English

---

As the work of three contemporary Americans, as well as in the locale of its plot, *The Crucible* is a native American opera in

every sense of the word. It began as a play written by the dramatist Arthur Miller and successfully produced on Broadway. Its
composer, born in Cleveland, Ohio, studied and taught at the Eastman School of Music and the Juilliard School of Music. The librettist, a native New Yorker, holds a doctorate in comparative literature at Cornell University, is an authority on Dante and is head
of the Academic Department of Juilliard.

Sung by a cast of young American singing actors, *The Crucible*
was unanimously acclaimed by critics as a milestone in the annals
of American opera. At the close of the 1961–62 season it was
awarded the Pulitzer Prize for Music and the New York Music
Critics Citation.

The plot of this opera is based on a bizarre chapter in American
history—the infamous witchcraft trials in the Puritan settlement of
Salem, Massachusetts. A powerful mixture of religion and sex, it
is a story about innocent people trapped by accusations made by
individuals temporarily deranged by mass hysteria. The demonic
quality of Robert Ward's music reflects the madness which obsessed
the impressionable young women whose screaming charges of witchcraft doomed their neighbors.

The score, in the modern idiom, is atonal, but a melodic line
predominates. There are no arias in the conventional sense, although certain passages begin as arias and lose their identity as
such when they merge with the ensemble. There is no overture.
The curtain rises immediately.

## ACT I

A spring morning in 1692. The house of The Reverend Parris in
Salem. He is kneeling at the bed, on which his daughter Betty is
lying motionless, scarcely breathing. Parris watches her silently
as a keening, sinister figure sounds high in the strings. The
servant Tituba, a Negress, enters and anxiously asks if her Betty
is going to die. Parris angrily orders her out of the room, then in
panic-stricken tones implores his daughter to awaken. She does
not move.

As he bends over her, Abigail, his niece, bursts into the room.
She tells Parris that a neighbor girl, Susanna Walcott, has come
from the doctor with the message that he is unable to prescribe
a cure for Betty. In an ominous, unaccompanied phrase, Abigail
adds that the doctor advises looking for "unnatural causes."

When Parris flares up at this, Abigail, in growing excitement, warns him that the townsfolk are gossiping about witches . . . and perhaps he'd better go out and explain. "Explain that I found my daughter and my niece dancing in the forest like pagans," Parris breaks in wrathfully. His outburst is underscored by a remarkable orchestral effect—an ascending unison passage interspersed with harsh open fourths.

Under Parris' relentless questioning Abigail admits that she and Betty danced under the trees, with Tituba making strange gestures over the fire. But she vehemently denies the preacher's accusation that they danced naked. Over the pulsating 12/8 rhythm of the accompaniment, Parris demands an explanation. For three years, he says, he has tried to win his stubborn congregation over to reason and respect. Now she—Abigail—has made a mockery of his efforts through her folly. His future is at stake. There is one thing he must know: Why did Elizabeth Proctor discharge her as a servant? What is more, why is it that Mrs. Proctor no longer comes to church, giving as the reason that she does not want to sit next to "something soiled"?

Abigail retorts that Goody Proctor is bitter because she—Abigail —refuses to work for her as a slave. If she wants a slave, the girl goes on, let her send to Barbados for one. In rising anger Abigail cries that her name is as good as any woman's in Salem. Elizabeth Proctor, she screams over a descending chromatic passage, is a liar.

There is a knock at the door. Parris, ordering Abigail to stay at Betty's bedside, goes to the door to greet Ann and Thomas Putnam. They ask about Betty, then, over dark, sustained chords in the orchestra, they tell Parris that their daughter Ruth is suffering from the same affliction. But it is not a sickness, Ann says, it is the devil's touch: Ruth's eyes are open but she sees nothing . . . she walks, she eats . . . She has been robbed of her soul.

It is witchcraft, Putnam cries, then tells Parris he has sent to Beverly for the Reverend Hale, who knows how to deal with witches. Parris, outraged at the suspicion that he is harboring witchcraft in his own house, asks the Putnams if they would have him howled out of Salem. Ann hysterically wails that once the devil took only babies—now he takes young women. Putnam sobs that Ruth, the last of their eight children, is dying before their eyes and not even the doctor can help.

At that moment, Rebecca and Francis Nurse enter, followed by Giles Corey. They too inquire about Betty. Before Parris can answer, Ann tells them that their daughter Ruth also has been stricken and that it is the devil's work. Parris says quickly that no

one knows the cause of the illness. Putnam reminds him that
he has sent to Beverly for the Reverend Hale. Giles sarcastically
observes that perhaps the Reverend Hale will make Betty fly
again—the way neighbor Collis saw her soar like a bird over the
treetops.

Putnam turns on him angrily for jesting at a time like this, then
pompously quotes the Bible to the effect that witches must not
be suffered to live—and there are witches this moment in Salem.
His words are underscored by an equally pompous fanfare in the
orchestra.

Yes . . . call them witches and hang them all, Giles sneers.
Then Thomas Putnam can take over their land. Putnam turns on
Corey in fury and a violent quarrel breaks out as he threatens
to bring Corey before the law for slander. This is the devil's work,
Putnam says, and the Bible will bear him out. Corey retorts that
even the devil can quote Scripture to his purpose. Thereupon
Putnam accuses Giles of twisting the Scriptures—the way John
Proctor does.

"Twisting, that's the word for you," Giles bursts out in a dramatic
refrain. He reminds Putnam that his own father stole half his
neighbor's land and called it his Christian duty. And now his son
cries "witch" so he can steal the rest of it. As for John Proctor,
he is an honest, upright man whose reputation is safe from the
likes of Thomas Putnam.

At this point, Rebecca Nurse sharply intervenes. Quarreling
will not help, she sings. This introduces an aria in which Rebecca
tries to dispel the bitterness that is alienating the neighbors. The
bustling music subsides into a serene melodic line as she reassures
the parents that the girls will recover. As the mother of eleven
children and twenty-six times a grandmother, she observes, she
understands the silly games children sometimes play. One of them
in an ancient sport: "Bedevil the old ones." But the "old ones"
must be patient. As Rebecca sings, John Proctor enters unnoticed
and listens intently.

Thomas Putnam impatiently interrupts Rebecca, fuming that
there is no time for all this nonsense. None at all, Rebecca agrees
gravely. In a flowing, Puccinilike melody she sings that love alone
is the cure for this childhood malady. A child is a runaway thing,
and love is the only lure that can bring the runaway home.

As the aria ends on a quiet phrase, John Proctor steps forward
with a word of approbation. The others voice surprise at seeing
him. Meanwhile, Abigail, who has been in Betty's bedroom on the

floor above during this scene, comes forward as she hears Proctor's voice. Unnoticed by those below, she stares down at Proctor, then begins pacing back and forth in feverish excitement.

Now the quarreling breaks out again. Proctor sharply asks Putnam why he sent for Reverend Hale without official permission of the congregation. Because it was necessary, Putnam snaps. Rebecca again intervenes, exhorting all to trust in prayer rather than in Reverend Hale. Here an ensemble builds up as Putnam, Proctor, Giles and Parris—ignoring Rebecca—lash out at each other with bitter recriminations. As the quarrel rages, Abigail, watching from the floor above, grows wilder and more abandoned in her movements. Her body undulates as though goaded by passionate desire.

In towering fury, Proctor roars that neither Parris nor Putnam will be allowed to bring ruin to Salem with their threats of hell-fire and damnation. He, John Proctor, will see to it that all the townspeople have an equal voice in deciding between right and wrong. Whirling on Putnam, Proctor cries out: "You wear no halo!" Parris screams: "Blasphemy!"

Rebecca, thrusting herself between the men, fiercely commands them to stop quarreling. Their feuding will "tear the town apart," she warns. This brings the men to their senses and the dispute subsides. Parris unctuously asks all to forget their differences and join in singing a psalm. Proctor, growling that soul searching is more important than psalm singing, stalks out of the room, with Giles Corey following.

Parris announces the grim Puritan hymn: "Jesus, my consolation." He is lustily joined by Ann Putnam, Rebecca, Thomas Putnam and Francis Nurse. Abigail, now quieter, comes to the head of the stairs and sings with them until she notices that Betty is beginning to writhe and moan on the bed.

At this point, separate action continues simultaneously in two scenes—one in the bedroom, the other in the parlor below. The orchestral accompaniment is so divided that each scene has its own music. While the elders roar out the psalm, Betty's movements become more violent. Abigail vainly implores her to be quiet and tries to hold her down.

Suddenly, with a wild shriek, Betty tears herself free and dashes to the window with her arms spread in a flying motion. Abigail screams for help. A rising chromatic passage in the orchestra accentuates the terror of the moment.

The psalm singing breaks off abruptly and the singers scramble up the stairs. The men clumsily try to quiet Betty. Rebecca pushes them aside, takes the hysterical girl in her arms, and calms her with a soothing gesture. During the uproar, Reverend Hale enters and goes upstairs. He carries a heavy book. Going to the bed, he begins asking questions with a ponderous air of authority. Ann Putnam whimpers that Betty is possessed and cannot hear the Lord's name. Not only that, she tried to fly—fearsome proof of the devil's work. Parris, with a desperate look at Hale, declares that one cannot be certain of this. Hale solemnly agrees.

In an ensuing refrain, "For much in the world seems devil's work," Hale pontificates on the mysteries of witchcraft. It is all revealed here, he sings as he opens his book—all the evil secrets of the demon world. This book is the weapon which will crush Satan, once he has been hunted down, Hale goes on with fanatical fervor. He raises Betty to a sitting position and in caressing tones commands her to awaken. When the girl gives no sign of hearing, he releases her and begins to question the elders about what happened. Ann tells him Betty was stricken after she, Ruth and Abigail danced secretly in the forest. Tituba was there—and Tituba knows conjuring. Parris insists that no one can be sure about such things.

But *she* can be sure, Ann Putnam bursts out. That is why she sent Ruth to Tituba—to find out from her who murdered Ruth's seven sisters. There is a gasp of horror from the listeners. When Rebecca protests against implicating Tituba in this terrible crime, Ann answers that it is for God alone to judge the guilty. Hale orders Tituba to be brought before him, then questions Abigail. She admits that she and the girls were dancing but again denies Parris' insinuation that they were naked. When Parris interjects a question about "toads in a kettle," Abigail mischievously explains that a little frog jumped in. At that Hale bluntly asks her if she made a compact with the devil. Suddenly fear-stricken, Abigail screams a denial.

Then, over a sinuous, rhythmic theme in the orchestra, Abigail accuses Tituba of bewitching her and the other girls. Tituba, bewildered and confused, denies the accusations. This introduces a dramatic ensemble as Ann, Parris, Putnam and Hale express reactions of terror and revulsion. Abigail, reveling in the havoc she is causing, now changes her story and describes how Tituba came to her as she was lying naked and tempted her with pagan songs. Ann wails that the Negress surely is the devil's own because she made the girls drink the witches brew of babies' blood. Rebecca, who alone is untouched by the frenzy, sings that it is God, not the devil, who can help them now, and that they are dealing with hysterical girls, not witches.

Parris and Putnam, convinced that the girls are possessed, implore Hale to remove the curse. Aside, Nurse voices his suspicions of Hale's motives, and his own conviction that this is a matter of dealing with poor, silly girls who need only "love and charity" to cure them of their illness.

The ensemble is sung over a rising and falling harmonic figure in the orchestra, accentuated with eerie effect by one chromatic passage high in the strings. At the climax of the ensemble the orchestral pattern changes to a succession of powerful chords rising in half tones with increasing intensity. The sinuous, flowing rhythm takes over again as Hale continues questioning Tituba. He demands to know if she spoke with the devil and threatens to whip her if she does not tell the truth. Tituba defiantly protests her innocence. With malicious insistence, Parris and the Putnams urge Hale to make her confess.

Tituba, in her panic and fear, has a momentary vision of the gibbet to which she is being condemned. During this, the triplet figure in the orchestra continues as remorselessly as the inquisition by Hale and Parris. At last, cornered and desperate, the woman lashes out at her tormentors. In a dramatic refrain ("Oh, how many times, Mister Parris") she sings that the devil has told her many times to cut Parris' throat—and the Putnams' as well. But she refused to kill even though the devil tempted her with offers of a new dress, "big black wings," and a chance to fly back to Barbados—and freedom. For a moment Tituba is lost in her fantasy, then her mood abruptly changes.

In menacing phrases of rising octave intervals she sings that the devil told her that white people as well as black are in his power. Then she saw the witchlike figure of an old woman. Ann Putnam asks excitedly: "Were it Sarah Good?" Tituba obediently answers: "It were Sarah Good." Ann gives a wild cry of triumph, then babbles that Sarah Good was a midwife to her and seven babies died in her arms. Reverend Hale sings that Tituba's confession has broken Lucifer's power. Betty sits up slowly on the bed as all in the room watch her in surprise and relief. They join in singing "Jesus, my consolation" as a hymn of thanksgiving.

Abigail's voice rises in an obbligato over the ensemble as she gives way to her mingled sexual and religious ecstasy. While these neighbors piously rejoice because Tituba's soul is saved, Abigail sings that she herself drank the devil's brew, danced before him naked and became his bride. In a soaring phrase she beseeches God to forgive her sin as the hymn comes to a roaring climax. The curtain falls.


## ACT II

The kitchen of John Proctor's house eight days later. Doors up-stage center and left, fireplace right. A musket hangs above the fireplace. Prominent on the mantelpiece is a poppet, a small rag doll. The curtain rises after a brief orchestral introduction. Eliza-beth Proctor is preparing dinner.

John Proctor enters and a long musical dialogue ensues, begin-ning with Elizabeth's greeting: "What keeps you so late?" John answers that he has been busy with his planting. He is grateful for the return of spring and tells Elizabeth that on Sunday they will walk through their fields and enjoy the flowers. But he be-comes aware that his wife is preoccupied and moody, listening absently to what he is saying. She curtly informs him that Mary Warren insisted on going to Salem, where, she said, she was to be an "official of the court." This is Deputy Governor Danforth's court, Elizabeth goes on. He is a ruthless judge, and will hang anyone who is charged with witchcraft and does not confess.

When Proctor scoffs at the idea of hanging, Elizabeth tells him that Abigail foments hysteria—real or pretended—among the other girls. If they fall into a fit when a suspect is brought into court their victim is promptly flung into jail. Elizabeth begs John to go to court and expose this vicious fraud—he must testify that Abigail herself confessed the fraud to him in his own house.

Hesitatingly, Proctor says he will think it over. Elizabeth pointedly asks him if he would scruple if Abigail were not in-volved. Thereupon Proctor launches into an angry tirade ("Let you not judge me"). He has had quite enough of her jealous suspicions, he sings, and it is useless to try to reason with her. Then, unwittingly betraying himself, Proctor goes on to say that if he accuses Abigail of fraud, she will retaliate by branding him an adulterer. He adds that he could not prove in court that she con-fessed to fraud because they were alone when she admitted it. Elizabeth gasps in dismay at this startling revelation. In anger and shame, Proctor storms at her not to judge him.

Elizabeth answers in one of the principal arias in the opera, "I do not judge you, John." In sustained, melodic phrases she sings that only his heart can judge him, then recalls the love they had for each other before their dreams were shattered. With increasing emotion she declares that Abigail will not dare accuse him of adultery for fear of damning herself. She bids him think of the innocent people who will be doomed if he keeps silent. Let Abigail dream of a promise made in bed—where promises are easily made. In the climax of the aria Elizabeth exhorts Proctor to break that promise and tear Abigail out of his heart. This he must do, she cries in passion and despair, for she has vowed to be his only wife—"or no wife at all!"

Shaken by her violent outburst, John goes to Elizabeth with outstretched arms in a conciliating gesture, but she recoils and turns away. Plunged into despair, Proctor sits down at the supper table, stares dejectedly at the food before him, then pushes it aside. Dark, heavy chords reverberate in the orchestra during this action.

The brooding silence is broken by the entrance of Mary Warren, who tries to sneak up the stairs to her room without being seen. A staccato phrase in the orchestra signals her presence. Suddenly noticing her, John angrily asks why she went to Salem without his permission. When he threatens to whip her she bursts into tears. Between her sobs she tells the couple that not fourteen but thirty-nine women have been thrown into jail and that Judge Danforth has sentenced Goody Osborn to the gallows. Then follows an eerie recital of what happened in court.

Sarah Good won't hang, Mary explains, because she confessed she was in league with the devil. Then poor Goody Osborn was brought in. She was such a sorry sight, Mary goes on, that at first she could not bring herself to accuse the old woman. But when Goody kept on denying her guilt, Mary says her scalp began to tingle and she heard a voice scream. And that voice was her own, Mary cries half deliriously. Grating dissonances in the orchestra underscore the tinge of madness in her story.

Aghast at this senseless folly, Proctor thunders that Mary is never to go back to court again to help hang innocent women. Mary whimpers that they will not hang if they confess. It is God's work—if the devil is in Salem he will be driven out. Proctor snatches a whip from the wall and lunges toward the girl, who cowers in terror.

Pointing to Elizabeth, Mary cries that she saved her life. Instantly realizing what she means, Elizabeth demands to know who accused her. Mary refuses to answer. Convinced that it was Abigail, Elizabeth desperately entreats Proctor to go to Salem.

At that moment there is a loud knock on the door. Proctor opens it to admit Ezekiel Cheever, Reverend Hale and a group of townspeople, all carrying muskets. Hale announces that they have a warrant for Goody Proctor. In a recitative passage, Cheever reads the charge sworn out by Abigail Williams: While she was at supper with Judge Danforth, Reverend Hale and Uncle Parris she felt a stab of pain. Examining her, Parris found a needle stuck into her belly. A voice whispered that Elizabeth Proctor had done this with the help of her witch's poppet.

Over repeated phrases in descending chromatics, Elizabeth protests that she has no poppet, whereupon Hale declares that puts an end to the matter. But Cheever, with vindictive relish, points to the poppet on the mantelpiece. He takes it down, examines it and exclaims that a needle is stuck in the doll's belly. Utterly bewildered, Elizabeth asks what that means. "Your murder of Abigail Williams," Cheever replies gloatingly.

Elizabeth bursts out that Abigail herself is a murderess who should be "ripped out of this world." In savage triumph Cheever repeats her words, declaring that the court must hear of this threat. Shouting that he will give Cheever something to tell the court, Proctor drags Mary forward. In answer to his question, the fear-stricken girl admits the poppet is hers, that she stuck the needle into the doll's belly and that Abigail saw her do it.

Hale, realizing that the witch hunt has taken a sinister turn, gravely tells Elizabeth that she must answer in court to the charge. He assures her that Judge Danforth, though stern, will see that justice is done. Proctor, wild with anger, storms that he will not let Elizabeth go, then tries to drive the men out of the house. Restraining him, Elizabeth resolutely tells him she must go. Quietly she orders Mary to take care of the house in her absence, then in a poignant phrase asks John to "bring her home soon." The men lead her away.

Proctor whirls on Mary, glares at her for a moment, then snatches his musket from over the mantelpiece. For one terrible moment he seems ready to kill her on the spot. Controlling himself, he slowly lowers the gun and speaks with cold ferocity. The ensuing refrain ("You will go to that court with me"), with its clamorous dissonances punctuated by Mary's terror-stricken protests, builds up to the violent climax of the act.

When Mary cries that if she tells her story of the poppet Abigail will kill her and ruin his life with her disclosure of adultery, Procter answers that then they will slide down together into their own hell. But whatever happens, the innocent Elizabeth will not be allowed to die for him. On the verge of madness, he seizes Mary by the throat and hurls her to the floor, shouting that God's icy wind will blow upon them as they walk naked in their sin. As staccato chords crash like hammer blows, the curtain falls.


## ACT III

[*Scene One*] Early morning, two days later. A moonlit clearing in the forest, with a corner of Parris' house visible. A brief orchestral introduction sounds a romantic theme with a sinister undertone. Abigail, with a cloak thrown provocatively over her nightgown, enters with Proctor. The entire scene which follows is in the form of a musical dialogue, beginning with Abigail's languorous phrase: "John, I knew you'd come back to me."

Thrusting herself into his unwilling embrace, she amorously sings that she has been waiting for him night after night, and that now at last they are free to be lovers again. Roughly pushing her away, Proctor answers that indeed they are *not* free: Elizabeth is in jail, accused by Abigail herself, and Salem is under Abigail's curse. It is *they* who must be freed.

At that Abigail craftily changes her tactics as an impudent theme ripples in the orchestra. With her mystical powers, she sings, she freed these "psalm-singing hypocrites"—who said she danced for the devil—from their own corruption. And someday they will thank her for it. Outraged, Proctor curses her and threatens to whip her.

By way of answer, Abigail, in a voluptuous gesture, lets the cloak drop from her shoulders, presses her body to Proctor's and gazes avidly up into his face. In a passionate refrain ("I look only for John Proctor") she entreats him to leave his sickly wife so that together they can do God's holy work of ridding Salem of corruption. Proctor scorns her as a fraud and warns that he will expose her trickery. Wild with anger, Abigail sneers that he can do as he likes, then adds venomously that if Elizabeth dies it will be her own husband who killed her. Snatching up her cloak, she rushes away.

[*Scene Two*] The next morning. The town meetinghouse, now used as a courtroom. Townspeople are seated; Cheever, the court clerk, is at his desk. During an orchestral interlude Giles Corey and Francis Nurse enter together, then Mary Warren and John Proctor. The crowd makes way as Abigail leads the other girl accusers into the courtroom. Cheever rises and declares the court in session. To a fanfare, Judge Danforth enters with Thomas Putnam and Reverend Hale. The people rise respectfully and stand with bowed heads as Danforth gives the invocation: "Open Thou my lips, O Lord." It begins as a simple hymn tune but grows in dignity and power as the Judge asks the Lord's help in purging the land of the festering plague of witchcraft.

As the business of the court begins, Giles Corey is called to the witness stand. Cheever, in recitative over an ascending chromatic passage, reads Corey's deposition. It sets forth that Thomas Putnam prevailed on his daughter Ruth to "cry witch" on Rebecca Nurse and Martha Corey for the sole purpose of taking over the property to which the two women held title. Putnam indignantly denies this. Corey interjects that if his wife is guilty she will of course hang and her property will be forfeit. But who, he asks, has the money to buy? Nobody but Putnam.

Judge Danforth demands proof. Giles thereupon testifies that when Putnam told Ruth to accuse Martha Corey he said that this would bring him Martha's property as a gift—and three townsmen heard him say it. When Danforth orders Giles to name them he defiantly refuses. They would rot in jail like the others, he says. Danforth rebukes Corey for daring to criticize the court. Putnam unctuously remarks that only a man in league with the devil would withhold information. Thereupon Danforth orders Corey arrested for contempt. The court is in a fever of excitement.

Giles, wild with fury, leaps at Putnam and seizes him by the throat. The others pull him off as Danforth pounds his gavel to restore order. In harsh tones he orders Corey to be taken to a cell and tortured by "pressing" until he reveals the names of the townsmen. There is a gasp of horror from the crowd at the brutality of the sentence.

As Corey is led away, Parris rises to say that John Proctor has brought a statement from Mary Warren. From this point on the dialogue continues over a steady 6/8 rhythm which seems to reflect the inexorable progress toward doom to be meted out to those enmeshed in the charges of witchcraft.

Over Parris' protests, Proctor bluntly tells Danforth that the girls have nothing to do with witchcraft and that their so-called supernatural powers are fraudulent. Parris and Putnam angrily contradict him. Asked for proof, John says Mary will swear that she and the girls are faking—and Mary promptly does so. Taken aback, Danforth berates her for telling lies in his court. Mary responds in a mystical phrase, singing that she can lie no more, for she is "with God."

The Judge begins to question Abigail about Mary's statement that she, Abigail, saw her stick the needle into the poppet as a hex symbol of murder. Skillfully avoiding a trap, Abigail replies that Mary is lying. When Proctor denies this, Danforth sharply asks if he is trying to involve "this child" in murder. She is no child, John answers vehemently. Disturbed, the Judge turns again to Mary, drawing from her the admission that the girls all pretended to be possessed when they made accusations of witchcraft, and that she herself never saw any "spirits." Confronting Abigail, Danforth, warning that those who trifle with human lives risk the terrible vengeance of the Lord, asks her if she saw these "spirits."

Assuming an air of outraged innocence, Abigail cries out that her only reward for trying to rout the devil and his crew is to be vilified in this court. With malevolent emphasis, she warns Danforth that he himself may fall victim to the demons.

In the next instant she stares upward with a look of horror, hugs her arms together and begins singing in a wailing voice— "a wind . . . I freeze . . . and cold winds blow"—then turns to glare at Mary. This introduces a brief ensemble passage as the other girls, picking up their cue, repeat the phrase like an incantation. Abigail, playing her role to the hilt, kneels in prayer. John strides over to her and pulls her to her feet by her hair. She shrieks in terror.

The court erupts in pandemonium as Proctor brands her a whore and confesses his adultery with her. Now you know, he shouts, why Elizabeth is accused—because he turned this girl out of his house as a harlot. Danforth abruptly orders Parris to bring in Elizabeth Proctor, then directs Abigail and John not to face the witness. Brought before the Judge, Elizabeth looks distractedly about. Danforth brusquely commands her to look only at him and tell him why she discharged Abigail. Insisting that it was because the girl was a bad servant, Elizabeth resolutely refuses to confirm that her husband committed adultery. The Judge impatiently orders her to be removed. Turning to face her, John shouts that he has confessed and implores her to tell the truth. Elizabeth cries out in despair as she is led away. The court is in an uproar.

Only Reverend Hale comes to John's defense, begging Danforth not to condemn another innocent victim. He himself, he goes on remorsefully, is haunted by the fact that he signed Rebecca Nurse's death warrant. As for this trial, he says, it is solely a matter of private revenge. Hale reiterates his belief in Proctor's confession and denounces Abigail as a fraud.

Here begins the demonic scene which builds into the closing ensemble of the act. Abigail, realizing she is cornered, abandons herself to a simulated frenzy, crying, "Yellow bird, begone." Mary stares at her in panic, while Proctor shouts to Danforth that the girls are shamming again. The contagion quickly spreads not only to the other girls but to Ann, Danforth, Parris and Putnam. Gaping upward, they sing meaninglessly about the "bird coming down, down, down." Mary, losing all control, joins Abigail in a hysterical wailing obbligato.

Proctor, Hale and Francis Nurse, trying to make themselves heard above the din, vainly protest that this exhibition of witch-craft is a monstrous lie. Proctor rushes over to Mary and tries to restrain her. Dodging out of his reach, she launches into a wild tirade, accusing him of being "the devil's man." He came to her the other night, she sings, clawed at her back with his icy fingers and forced her to sign the devil's book. But now, she screams, she loves God and will no longer obey John Proctor.

At that the throng in the courtroom, caught up in mob hysteria, bursts into a frenzied shout of "Allelujah!" Mary, sobbing uncontrollably, throws herself into Abigail's protecting arms. The two are joined by Ann Putnam in their witch's chant. Abigail, Mary and Ann and Reverend Hale and Francis Nurse stand apart as the spectators turn on John Proctor, howling: "He's the devil's man, beware." At the climax of the chorus, Hale and Nurse, overcome with horror at the scene, rush away. The curtain falls.

## ACT IV

The fall of 1692. A large, gloomy room in the Salem jail. Tituba and Sarah Good, awaiting execution, are sitting huddled together in the light of flickering torches on the wall. The Negress sings a plaintive refrain, like a spiritual: "The Devil say he's a-comin' to set his people free." Sarah Good chimes in with a mournful, wordless obbligato. The devil will give them big black wings, Tituba chants, and then they'll fly to Barbados, where there's singing and feasting all night long.

As her chant dies away, Cheever lurches in carrying a lantern and a bottle. He pushes the two women out of the room, giving Sarah the bottle as she reaches for it. A moment later, Abigail, wearing a hooded cloak, enters and gives Cheever a bag of money. He walks over to the heavily barred door of John Proctor's dungeon cell, calls to the prisoner, unlocks the door and leaves it ajar. As he staggers out, Proctor appears. He is gaunt and haggard from months of torture. Abigail steps swiftly to the door. In suppressed excitement she shows him clothing and money and tells him that now he is free. Proctor remains motionless, staring into space. Abigail desperately implores him to hurry—a boat is waiting at the Salem dock and there is no time to lose. In a passionate phrase she sings that they will sail away to a sunny land where they will be lovers forever.

Without a word, Proctor closes the cell door and drags himself back into the darkness. Abigail reels back in stunned surprise, then with a gesture of resignation turns to leave. Cheever, leering at her, attempts to embrace her as she passes. Fighting him off, Abigail rushes away sobbing. Cheever breaks into satanic laughter.

At his call Tituba and Sarah Good again emerge from the shadows. Cheever snatches back his bottle and drinks. Tituba, in a mournful reprise of her chant, sings that the devil has broken his promise—he is going to let them rot and die in Salem town.

Suddenly there is a loud drum roll. Danforth and Reverend Hale enter. As the Judge orders Cheever to bring in Elizabeth Proctor, Hale agitatedly warns him that trouble is brewing. The town of Beverly, revolted by the witch trials, has thrown out the court. Orphans of those executed wander about the streets; farms are left unattended and even the cattle roam wild. No one in the terror-stricken community is safe from the vicious attacks of the witch-ridden girls.

At that point Parris bursts in crying that Abigail has disappeared after rifling his money box. When Hale says that now the case against the Proctors has collapsed, Danforth angrily declares that they will either confess or hang. The fear-stricken Parris protests that the townspeople will not tolerate these hangings —only this morning he found a dagger thrust into his door as a warning of impending revenge.

Hale implores the Judge to postpone the hangings. With remorseless emphasis Danforth retorts that to smash a rebellion he would hang and quarter ten thousand men. He will not be thwarted in carrying out God's law. Elizabeth is brought in and Danforth gestures to Hale to speak to her. Warning her that her husband is doomed to die at sunrise, Hale pleads with Elizabeth to persuade him to confess to witchcraft to save his life—even if he lies to do it. Elizabeth quietly replies that she can promise nothing, but that she will speak with him. Puzzled and infuriated by her calm defiance, Danforth snarls that this woman is beyond understanding: In the face of disaster she sheds no tears.

As somber chords reverberate in the orchestra, Proctor is brought in. Danforth, Hale and Parris move away as Elizabeth and John face each other and speak over a tender, lyrical theme. John inquires about the children. Mary Warren brought her word that they are well, Elizabeth says. She goes on to tell him about the trials: A hundred or move have confessed—but not Rebecca Nurse or Giles Corey. Giles spoke only two words to the torturers who piled the crushing stones on his chest: "More weight." Shaken with horror, Proctor asks Elizabeth if she would forgive him if he lied to save his life.

She answers that it was her own lie that doomed him—and her own failure as a wife that drove him to adultery. Now, she cries in a passionate outburst, she will abide by his decision and share his fate, whatever it may be. Crushing Elizabeth in his embrace, Proctor triumphantly shouts to Danforth: "I want my life!" The Judge and the others rush forward exultingly hailing his decision. Their voices blend briefly with a backstage chorus.

But suddenly the mood of the scene changes. Danforth hands John a pen and a written confession and asks him to sign. As Proctor stares at it in bewilderment, Rebecca Nurse is brought in. She totters forward, catches sight of the document and gasps in dismay. Danforth tells her Proctor has confessed and urges her to do the same. "It is a lie," Rebecca answers without hesitation.

Thereupon Danforth treacherously attempts to trick John into implicating Rebecca and other accused women in his confession. John curtly answers that he can only be responsible for his own sins. Hale hands him the pen and beseeches him to sign, while Danforth in vindictive fury demands a signed confession so that the village will have proof. In a majestic refrain, "God does not need my name nailed upon a church door," Proctor hurls his final defiance. He has confessed, he sings, and that is enough. He will not stain the name of his sons with his own black sins. He has forfeited his soul, but he will not forfeit his good name.

Beside himself with fury, Danforth thrusts the document into Proctor's hands with a final warning. Proctor, ignoring the distracted pleading of Hale and Parris, tears the confession to shreds. Now at last, he shouts, he sees some goodness in John Proctor.

As Elizabeth rushes into his arms, he exhorts her not to quail before these tormentors but to show "a stony heart that will sink them." He kisses her in farewell.

To the strains of a funeral march, the gates of the blockhouse slowly open, showing the gallows outside. Supporting Rebecca, Proctor begins his walk to the scaffold as Danforth screams for the hanging. The chorus of villagers, "Weep for them," rises in a great surge of sound. As it dies away, the voice of Elizabeth soars in a phrase of anguish and triumph: "He has his goodness now. God forbid I take it from him."

The blockhouse gates close to a thunderous drum roll. Reverend Hale falls to his knees sobbing a prayer. Elizabeth stands motionless, the rising sun flooding her upturned face. The curtain falls.

# Ernani

*by* GIUSEPPE VERDI
(1813–1901)

## *Libretto by*
FRANCESCO MARIA PIAVE

*Based on Victor Hugo's drama*
HERNANI

### CHARACTERS

| | |
|---|---:|
| Ernani, an outlaw (Don Juan of Aragon) | Tenor |
| Elvira, niece and ward of | |
| Don Ruy Gomez de Silva | Soprano |
| Don Carlo, King of Spain | Baritone |
| Giovanna, waiting woman to Elvira | Mezzo-soprano |
| Don Ruy Gomez de Silva, grandee of Spain | Bass |
| Don Riccardo, lieutenant to Don Carlo | Tenor |
| Iago, esquire to Don Ruy | Bass |

Outlaws, knights, ladies, courtiers, women in waiting

*Place:* Aragon and Castile in Spain; Aix-la-Chapelle in France
*Time:* About 1519
*First performance:* Teatro La Fenice, Venice, March 9, 1844
*Original language:* Italian

---

This opera has as its theme the revolt against the tyranny of Charles V of Spain (1500–58; Holy Roman Emperor 1519–56), which was the core of Victor Hugo's revolutionary drama. The theme of the uprising stirred the Italian people to patriotic fervor in their own mid-nineteenth-century rebellion against the tyranny of the Hapsburgs.

Hugo, in his *Hernani* (written in 1830), had expressed what the censors considered dangerously subversive sentiments—not to mention his exploiting the idea of conspiracies against a reigning monarch. This aroused the anger of the Austrian authorities, particularly because they were having their hands full trying to keep the Italian populace quiet during the occupation of Venice.

In *Ernani*, Verdi had woven the conspiratorial elements of Hugo's drama into his own plot.

A scene in the original libretto brought down on the composer's head the wrath of the Austrian chief of police, who demanded that the scene be withdrawn. Verdi and his librettist finally placated the censors by toning down the conspiratorial implications.

But the revolutionary spirit still pervaded *Ernani* and aroused audiences to violent political demonstrations. The Venetians, for example, considered the great chorus in Act III, "Si ridesti il Leon di Castiglia" ("Rise up, Lion of Castile"), a patriotic tribute to the city they loved. All over Italy that chorus came to symbolize the sufferings of a nation under the heel of the hated Austrians. On more than one occasion it touched off clamorous demonstrations.

At the first performance of *Ernani* in Rome in 1849, the audience, joining in another great Act III chorus, "A Carlo Quinto sia gloriae onor" ("Glory and honor to Charles V"), substituted the words "Glory and honor to Pio Nono," a reference to Pope Pius IX, who was Pope from 1846 to 1878. The popular belief was that this new Pope would lead a movement for unification of Italy. Thus the volatile Italians turned a night at the opera into a political free-for-all.

After its premiere in Venice, *Ernani* became an operatic sensation, and within nine months was taken up by fifteen other theaters. It was the first Verdi opera to be heard in London, and was the first grand opera ever to be heard in San Francisco, where it was given by an Italian troupe about 1851. The San Francisco Opera gave its own premiere of the opera on September 13, 1968.

The role of Elvira was a favorite with such legendary prima donnas as Adelina Patti and Marcella Sembrich. Mme. Sembrich sang the role for the first time in the first Metropolitan performance on January 28, 1902, with Antonio Scotti and Édouard de Reszke. Although given infrequently thereafter, *Ernani* was revived in 1921 and remained in the Metropolitan repertoire for three successive seasons. Recent Metropolitan revivals include performances in 1965, when it proved popular with opera audiences. The opera was scheduled for the opening performance of the Metropolitan Opera's 1970–71 season.

As the composer's fifth opera, *Ernani* belongs to his "first period." The four acts bear the subtitles "The Bandit," "The Guest," "Clemency," and "The Masker."

There is a brief prelude which states two important themes heard later in the opera.

## ACT I
### (*The Bandit*)

[*Scene One*] A rugged, wild region in the mountains of Aragon, the hideout of the fugitive bandit Ernani—in reality Don Juan of Aragon—and his followers. The rebel mountaineers and bandits are seen eating, drinking, playing cards or cleaning their weapons. They sing a lusty drinking song in praise of their wild, free life in the mountains.

Ernani appears and silently watches them. He is moody and preoccupied. Noticing him, his comrades ask him why he is so sad, and then try to cheer him by assuring him of their loyalty. In an aria, "Come rugiada al cespite," preceded by a brief recitative, Ernani tells them what is troubling him. Elvira, the woman he loves, is being held a virtual prisoner in a neighboring castle by her uncle, Don Ruy Gomez de Silva—who, Ernani says, "will drag her to the altar." In a striking staccato chorus, "Quando notte il cielo," the bandits promise to help him abduct Elvira. Cheered by their comradely spirit, Ernani sings that reunion with Elvira will make him forget the bitterness of his exile. As the chorus comes to a rousing close, he leads his men toward the castle.

[*Scene Two*] Elvira's apartment in Silva's castle. It is night. Restless and troubled, Elvira, in recitative ("Sorta è la notte"), expresses her loathing of Silva, who relentlessly pursues her, imploring her to marry him. But the more Silva insists, the more she thinks of Ernani and the deeper her love for him grows. In the brilliant aria "Ernani, involami," she voices her longing for him. If Ernani could take her away from Silva's hated caresses, she sings, they could both be happy—even in an alien land. Her aria is interrrupted by a chorus of her women in waiting, who come in with wedding gifts. Ironically, they sing that many a girl in Spain envies Elvira as the bride-to-be of Silva.

In spite of herself, Elvira is touched by their naïveté, but she sings that without Ernani any thought of love is a mockery. Not even the most priceless jewel could banish the hatred of Silva from her heart. Elvira brings the aria to a dazzling finish over the accompaniment of the chorus, then she and the women leave the room.

Suddenly Don Carlo enters, in disguise, followed by Giovanna. He curtly orders her to tell Elvira that he is waiting to see her. Alone, he laments that Elvira spurns his love in spite of all his devotion and kingly power—and all because of a common bandit who is his rival. Yet, he murmurs, he will try once more to win her. At that moment Elvira returns, and a dramatic duet follows, beginning with Elvira's angry exclamation: "Sire!—fia ver? Voi stesso."

Although Don Carlo, in a passionate outburst ("da quel dì che t'ho veduta"), begs for her love, Elvira furiously orders him to leave her. Royal pomp and splendor mean nothing to her, she cries, and she will never yield. In rising anger, Don Carlo seizes her arm and tries to force her to come with him. At that Elvira snatches Don Carlo's dagger from his belt, then warns him that if he does not leave her instantly she will plunge the dagger into his heart and into her own ("Mi lasciate, o d'ambo il core").

Staggering back in horror, Don Carlo shouts for his henchmen. But instead of their appearance, a secret door in the chamber is flung open and Ernani strides in, announcing sardonically: "As one of your henchmen, here I am" ("Fra quei fidi io pur qui sto"). This signals the beginning of a fiery trio. The two men recognize each other instantly. Confronting his archenemy, Don Carlo rages that he, as King of Spain, could doom Ernani as a rebel, but out of sheer pity for so despicable an outlaw he will give him a chance to flee for his life.

"So you know me," Ernani retorts. "You whose father killed my father and robbed me of all I own!" Now, he goes on, he despises this King more than ever, because he is also his rival in love. With that, Ernani draws his sword and Don Carlo draws his.

Instantly, Elvira steps between the two men with dagger upraised. She bitterly rebukes both men for their effrontery in claiming her for themselves. One more word, she cries, and she will plunge the dagger into her heart—she belongs neither to the King nor to the lover. These words and Ernani's defiance blend in a striking unison passage, and then Don Carlo's voice joins to bring the trio to a ringing climax.

As the three stand glaring at each other, Silva comes in followed by Giovanna and lords and ladies of the court. In fury he demands to know what these two interlopers are doing in his home —and, what is worse, in the same room with his bride-to-be. Turning to the onlookers, he rages that they can see for themselves how the sanctity of his home has been violated.

Then in a moving aria, "Infelice! e tuo credevi," he accuses Elvira of betraying his trust and his love . . . old age and death itself would be better than this cruel disgrace. In a sudden change of mood he whirls on Don Carlo and Ernani, crying out that this insult must be avenged. He calls for his sword. Continuing the aria in a vigorous martial tempo ("Infin che un brando vindice"), Silva sings that there is one weapon left to him—his sword, which alone can wipe out infamy. Although his soul recoils from this monstrous disgrace, he will meet it bravely. The lords and ladies of the court, commenting on Silva's courage, bring this cabaletta to a stormy climax.

Ernani and Don Carlo try to speak, but Silva cuts them short, saying swords alone can answer. And the first to answer, he adds, glowering at the King, will be Don Carlo.

At that moment Iago, esquire to Silva, enters and announces Riccardo, standard-bearer to the King. The members of the court, suddenly realizing that the King of Spain is standing before them, express their surprise in a tremendous choral outburst: "Oh cielo! è desso il Re!"

Then follows a typically Verdian ensemble in which all on-stage give voice to their thoughts at the same time. It also serves to move the plot forward. The chorus begins in a hushed undertone, unaccompanied. Don Carlo bids Riccardo notice how Silva has suddenly restrained his anger in the presence of his King, and this observation is echoed by the chorus. Elvira and Ernani voice fears for each other's safety. Ernani implores her to flee with him; she sings that now she can only choose between him and the dagger she holds. Silva himself sings that in the presence of his King he cannot harbor suspicions of betrayal.

At the thunderous conclusion of the ensemble Silva kneels before the King and asks pardon for his inhospitable actions. Don Carlo instantly grants it. Silva then asks him why he entered the castle in disguise. The wily Don Carlo, in an aside to him, answers that he had come to ask Silva's advice about a successor to the Holy Roman Emperor Maximilian, who recently had died. The truth is, of course, that Don Carlo himself wants to win Elvira.

He asks the unsuspecting Silva if he may stay as a guest, and Silva readily assents. At this Elvira and Ernani exclaim in dismay, realizing that both Silva and the King now can thwart their plans to escape. But Don Carlo, who wants Ernani out of the way, uses his kingly prerogative to order him out of the castle. In reply, Ernani defiantly accuses the King of plotting his father's death and warns that he, Ernani, will exact vengeance for the deed.

Elvira implores him to flee—"Fuggi, Ernani, ti serba al mio amore!" This marks the beginning of the great ensemble which closes the act. At its end, Don Carlo angrily motions Ernani to leave. He goes with a gesture of farewell to Elvira, who looks at him despairingly, then goes to her apartments. Silva escorts Don Carlo from the room.

## ACT II
### (*The Guest*)

The great hall of the castle of Don Ruy Gomez de Silva. Family portraits in richly carved frames hang on the walls. The hall is thronged with nobles, knights and ladies gathered for the nuptial ceremony of Silva and Elvira. The scene opens with a chorus hailing the bridal pair, "Esultiamo! Letizia ne inondi!"

The massive central door opens and Silva, in the magnificent robes of a grandee of Spain, is ushered in by Don Iago. He tells his esquire that he will grant an audience to a pilgrim who has just come to the castle gates. Ernani is led in, disguised in the rough garb of a monk, the hood partially hiding his features. In recitative, Silva tells the stranger that he is welcome—that here "the guest is lord."

Elvira, in her bridal finery, enters with her attendants. In an hour, Silva announces proudly, this beautiful woman will be his bride. Ernani gasps in surprise, then throws back his pilgrim's hood and reveals his identity. He will be the first, he storms, to offer a bridal gift—his own head.

As Elvira watches in stunned disbelief, Ernani turns furiously on Silva, shouting that he is Ernani, a dispossessed nobleman now hunted down like a beast of prey. Yet it is his hatred of his enemies that gives him courage to go on. Elvira sings distractedly that he will be doomed ("Ohimè, si perde"), and then the music continues in trio form. Ernani sings that even his own men would be accused of treason if they dared protect him. Elvira reiterates her warning of doom. Silva vainly tries to assure Ernani that as a guest the ancient law of hospitality will protect him here in the castle ("In queste mura ogni ospite").

As proof, Silva calls for his halberdiers to man the castle walls and ensure the safety of his guests. He leaves with his retinue and Elvira follows. At the entrance she pauses and turns to Ernani with a pleading look. Ernani, glaring at her, calls her a traitress ("Tu . . . perfida!"). Elvira begs him not to question her fidelity, for she had been told Ernani had been slain. Snatching up the dagger she had taken from the King earlier, she cries that she would have used this dagger at the altar to prove she had kept faith with the man she loves. Moved by this avowal, Ernani takes Elvira in his arms and together they pledge their love ("Ah morir potessi adesso!").

As their duet ends in a quiet, passionate phrase, Silva enters. He halts for a moment in shocked surprise, then advances on the couple with drawn sword. At that moment Iago enters and announces that Don Carlo and his troops are at the castle gates demanding entrance. Sheathing his sword, Silva orders the gates to be opened. Ernani exultantly cries that fate has spared him, but Silva warns that proper vengence will be forthcoming at the time of his own choosing. In a powerful unison passage ("La vendetta più tremenda"), Elvira and Ernani sing that death will be better than parting. Their voices blend with Silva's in the trio which brings the scene to a close.

Silva strides to a portrait of himself on the wall, thrusts it aside to reveal a secret door. He motions Ernani to enter, closes the panel, then stands waiting for Don Carlo. Elvira leaves, weeping. Don Carlo enters with Riccardo, his lieutenant, and a group of knights, and a dramatic dialogue ensues in quasi-recitative. The King demands to know why the castle is so heavily guarded. Without waiting for a reply, he goes on to say that he suspects certain noblemen of plotting against the regime—and they will be dealt with accordingly. Silva protests that he is loyal. In rising anger, the King fumes that even though an incipient rebellion has been headed off, the bandit Ernani still hides in this castle. Give him up, Don Carlo shouts, or he will order his soldiers to level "all eleven towers" of this castle to the ground.

Silva calmly asks if the King expects him to betray a poor pilgrim who came asking only shelter for the night. "Yet you would dare betray your King," Don Carlo thunders. The Silvas, Don Ruy answers in cold scorn, are not betrayers. Don Carlo rages that now it will be either Silva's or Ernani's. Quietly Silva replies: Take mine. Ordering Riccardo to take Silva's sword, the King commands his soldiers to search the castle. Aside, Silva murmurs that his castle—like himself—will keep faith with his guest.

Face to face, Silva and Don Carlo express their thoughts in a powerful duet "Lo vedremo, o veglio audace." Don Carlo sings that now it will be shown how long Silva's defiance will last—

when the issue is his life or Ernani's. Don Ruy, pointing to his portrait, sings that never will men look at it and say that *this* Silva was a betrayer.

The colloquy ends when the King's soldiers return, swords in hand. In a staccato chorus, "Fu esplorata del castello" (a foreshadowing of the "Zitti, zitti" chorus in *Rigoletto*), they report that they found no trace of the bandit. Pointing to Silva, they urge the King to punish him for shielding this outlaw. Don Carlo ominously responds that perhaps torture will bring the desired results.

At this point, Elvira enters and, overhearing the King's threat, throws herself at his feet and begs for mercy. Don Carlo, taken aback at her anguished plea, suddenly turns to Silva. In menacing tones he delivers his ultimatum: Either give up Elvira to him or surrender Ernani. Staggering toward the portrait which hides the secret panel, Silva asks the King to kill him then and there rather than force him into betrayal. Relentlessly, Don Carlo repeats his ultimatum. In mingled despair and triumph, Silva leads Elvira to the King, then cries out that he still has kept faith with his guest.

Here begins another of the opera's dramatic ensembles, blending the voices of Don Carlo, Silva, Elvira, Riccardo and Giovanna. The soldiers, looking on, sing that they will carry out the King's commands. Don Carlo declares his love for Elvira ("Ah! vieni meco, sol di rose"). Silva swears vengeance. Riccardo assures Elvira that now her sorrow will turn to happiness. Giovanna laments Elvira's misfortune, while Elvira herself sings that now all hope is gone.

At the conclusion of the ensemble, Don Carlo leads Elvira away, with the King's soldiers and members of the court following. All leave except Silva, who for a long moment stands motionless, arms folded. Then, breaking from his reverie, he sings that only heaven can protect the King from the hatred he bears him ("Vigili pure il ciel sempre su te"). Striding over to one of the suits of armor ranged along the wall, he snatches up two swords, measures them one against the other. With both in one hand he steps quickly to the secret portrait panel and presses a spring. The panel flies open, revealing Ernani.

Then and there, Silva challenges Ernani to a duel. When Ernani protests that he will not fight a man of Silva's years, the old man furiously demands that he cross swords. Ernani replies that he would gladly fight—and die—if he could see Elvira once

more. Silva tells him he is doomed, because Don Carlo has taken
Elvira away as hostage. No, not as hostage, Ernani cries out, for
Don Carlo really wants Elvira for himself—he is their rival in love.
He implores Silva to allow him to share his revenge on the King.
But Silva, beside himself with rage, shouts that Ernani must be
the first to die.

Well then, Ernani says, if there is no other way, he will die, but
not now. He takes his hunting horn from his belt and hands it
to Silva, saying that if Silva still claims the life of Ernani after
they have accomplished their revenge, he will return to pay the
forfeit at the sound of the hunting horn. With terrible intensity
he sings the fateful words: "Ecco il pegno: nel momento in che
Ernani vorrai spento, se uno squillo intenderà tosto Ernani, morirà"
("When the horn sounds, Ernani will forfeit his life"). This he
swears on the memory of his dead father. Both men then repeat
the oath in ringing phrases ("Iddio m'ascolti, e vindice").

Silva summons his cavaliers, who rush in and pledge their
allegiance. Together, Silva and Ernani order them to mount their
horses and dash in pursuit of the fugitive King and Elvira ("In
arcion, cavalieri"). The cavaliers join the two men in the stirring
chorus of vengeance which concludes the act ("Per te spirano,
sangue, vendetta").

# ACT III
## (Clemency)

The tomb of the Emperor Charlemagne in Aix-la-Chapelle, the
city where the Electors are gathered to choose the new Holy
Roman Emperor. Don Carlo and Riccardo are seen in front of the
tomb. In recitative, Don Carlo reveals that he has learned of a
plot to kill him and he has decided to hide in the tomb itself
to find out the identity of the conspirators when they gather here
for their rendezvous. He orders Riccardo to report the decision
of the Electors. If they choose Don Carlo as Emperor, Riccardo
is to signal their choice with three cannon salvos and then return
—bringing Elvira with him.

Alone before the tomb, Don Carlo invokes the spirit of Charlemagne in an impressive soliloquy, "Gran Dio! costor sui sepolcrali
marmi." He broods on the futility of striving for honor, power and
possessions. All these are nothing ("Con voi nel nulla"). And yet,
he sings in the ensuing cavatina ("Oh de' verd' anni miei"),
he knows that destiny has accorded him one moment of godlike

power. Don Carlo turns, unlocks the door of the tomb and slowly enters.

To the accompaniment of a staccato theme in the orchestra the conspirators enter, muffled in cloaks and carrying torches. They are led by Silva, Ernani and Iago. In hushed tones they sing that here at the tomb of the great Charlemagne they will uphold the cause of the Catholic League and save Spain from the usurper ("Per la lega santo ardor"). In a dramatic gesture they throw down their torches, plunging the scene into darkness as they sing that they need no light to guide their blows for freedom.

Silva announces that Don Carlo's assassin will be chosen by lot. At his command the plotters write their names on slips of paper and place them on top of a nearby tomb. When all have signed, Silva picks up one of the slips and reads the name: Ernani. In a ringing phrase Ernani exults over his good fortune and the soldiers shout that if he fails in his mission they will avenge him.

But Silva calls on Ernani to yield the assassin's task to him, saying that in return he will release Ernani from the pledge to forfeit his life at the sound of the hunting horn. Ernani resolutely refuses, crying out that first his own thirst for revenge must be satisfied. Brandishing their swords, the soldiers burst into the famous unison chorus "Si ridesti il Leon di Castiglia." Hailing the heroic spirit of the Lion of Castile, they sing that, just as Spain once rose up against the Moorish oppressors, so they will fight for freedom to the last man. At the fiery conclusion of the chorus, a cannon shot booms out. The conspirators stand transfixed. Then there is a second shot, and the door of Charlemagne's tomb is flung open. A third shot—and Don Carlo strides forth, crying in a thunderous voice: "Carlo Quinto, o traditor!" ("Traitors! It is Charles the Fifth!").

As the conspirators shrink back in fear and confusion a huge crowd emerges from the tomb, led by the Electors. They are followed by pages carrying the crown, scepter and other imperial insignia. Seen among the throng are Elvira and Giovanna. Don Carlo peremptorily orders the nobles among the conspirators to be executed, the others imprisoned. Thereupon Ernani steps forward, identifies himself as Don Juan of Aragon and claims his right to stand with the nobles ("Io son conte").

As Don Carlo glares at him, Elvira rushes forward, throws herself at the King's feet and begs for mercy ("Ah, Signor, se t'è concesso"). Don Carlo looks down at her for a moment in furious anger. Then, restraining himself, he turns his gaze to the tomb of Charlemagne and begins the great aria "Oh sommo Carlo." In majestic phrases he sings that, as successor to the mighty Emperor, he will emulate the monarch and pardon those who plotted to destroy him. As a crowning gesture he leads Elvira to Ernani and gives them both his blessing as lovers. This introduces the stirring ensemble which closes the act, "A Carlo Quinto sia gloria e onor," in which all hail the magnanimity of the new Emperor.

## ACT IV
### (*The Masker*)

The scene is a masked ball at the palace of Don Juan of Aragon (Ernani). During a gay chorus a mysterious masked figure in domino costume enters, looks around as though searching for someone, then leaves. As the guests also leave, Elvira and Ernani enter. For a brief moment they sing of their happiness in a duet which ends in a phrase of passionate intensity, "Fino al sospiro estremo."

But in the next instant the mood is shattered by the distant sound of a hunting horn. Ernani, knowing what it means, recoils in horror. As Elvira anxiously asks what is wrong, the horn sounds again, nearer this time. Momentarily losing control, Ernani imagines he sees the face of a devil grinning mockingly at him. Recovering, he tells Elvira that it was only the pain of an old wound returning and asks her to go for a doctor. When she leaves he murmurs that the specter of the grinning devil was only a figment of his imagination. He starts to leave—and comes face to face with the masked figure.

In menacing tones the stranger repeats the words of Ernani's pledge—the pledge which dooms him: "Ecco il pegno: nel momento in che Ernani vorrai spento, se uno squillo intenderà tosto Ernani morirà." With that he tears off his mask. It is Silva.

Despairingly Ernani begs for a reprieve. In reply, Silva offers him the choice of a dagger or a cup of poison. In hopeless resignation Ernani reaches for the dagger just as Elvira rushes in. Here begins the fiery trio which brings the opera to its close, "Ferma, crudele, estinguere."

Elvira desperately pleads for mercy. Ernani cries that her pleas will be in vain and that now all he needs is the courage to die. Silva remorselessly demands fulfillment of the pledge. Wildly calling Elvira's name, Ernani stabs himself. Elvira falls fainting over his body. Looking down at them, Silva, in ferocious triumph, sings that the demon of revenge has done his work well. The curtain falls.

# La Fanciulla del West
## (*The Girl of the Golden West*)
### *by* GIACOMO PUCCINI
### (1858–1924)

*Libretto by*
CARLO ZANGARINI and GUELFO CIVININI

Based on David Belasco's drama
THE GIRL OF THE GOLDEN WEST

CHARACTERS

| | |
|---|---|
| Minnie | Soprano |
| Jack Rance, sheriff | Baritone |
| Dick Johnson (the outlaw Ramerrez) | Tenor |
| Nick, bartender at the Polka saloon | Tenor |
| Ashby, a Wells Fargo agent | Bass |
| Sonora ⎫ | Baritone |
| Trin ⎪ | Tenor |
| Sid ⎪ | Baritone |
| Handsome ⎬ Miners | Baritone |
| Harry ⎪ | Tenor |
| Joe ⎪ | Tenor |
| Happy ⎪ | Baritone |
| Larkens ⎭ | Bass |
| Billy Jackrabbit, an Indian | Bass |
| Wowkle, Billy's squaw | Mezzo-soprano |
| José Castro, a Mexican from Ramerrez's gang | Bass |
| Jake Wallace, a wandering folk singer | Bass |
| A post rider | Tenor |

Men of the California mining camp

*Place*: At the foot of the Cloudy Mountains in California
*Time*: 1849–50
*First performance*: Metropolitan Opera House, New York City, December 10, 1910
*Original language*: Italian

On a visit to New York in 1907, Puccini saw David Belasco's Broadway production of *The Girl of the Golden West*. Impressed by its dramatic power, the composer invited Belasco—whose *Madama Butterfly* had formed the basis of Puccini's previous opera—to collaborate on an operatic version of the melodrama of the forty-niners.

The opera was given one of the most memorable premieres in the history of the Metropolitan, with Enrico Caruso, Emmy Destinn and Pasquale Amato in the cast, Arturo Toscanini conducting, and Puccini and Belasco standing in the wings. Despite its brilliant premiere, the opera lasted only four seasons at the Metropolitan, a "weak libretto" being blamed for its indifferent success. It has been revived periodically, however, to considerable acclaim.

In its use of recitative and in the symphonic quality of the orchestral accompaniment, *Fanciulla* represents somewhat of a departure from Puccini's earlier style of composing.

There is a brief but dramatic orchestral introduction, which states one of the romantic themes of the opera.

## ACT ONE

The interior of the Polka saloon. It is sunset and the room is partially in darkness. Sheriff Jack Rance, smoking a cigar, is sitting near the fireplace. Larkens, a young miner, is seated on a cask, his head in his hands. He takes an envelope from his pocket, walks over to the counter, puts a stamp on the envelope and drops it into the mailbox. Then he sits down again dejectedly.

From outside come the voices of miners calling to each other, then snatches of a song, "Là lontano, là lontan." Nick the bartender starts lighting the lamps and then, during a brief orchestral passage, the miners come trooping in from camp.

There is noisy byplay as they josh each other, call for drinks, and sit down to play cards. Someone asks about Minnie, the proprietress of the saloon. During all the talk and banter, Larkens continues to brood. Glancing at him, Rance asks Nick what is wrong with the boy. "Homesick—as usual," says Nick. "He's dreaming of his mother in Cornwall." Somberly, Rance remarks that the boy is cursed with gold fever in this godforsaken country ("Che terra maledetta"). Then with a gesture of impatience he asks why Minnie has not appeared. Nick shrugs in answer. Frowning, Rance walks into the adjoining dance hall.

Meanwhile, the miners go on with their card games. Billy Jackrabbit, the Indian, sidles up to the counter, steals some cigars and scurries out. Nick bawls that anybody who wants to dance can go into the dance hall, which adjoins the bar. The miners jeer good-naturedly because there are no women to dance with.

When Nick comes by with cigars, Sonora, aside, asks if there is any message from Minnie. "Yes," Nick tells him slyly, "she says *you* are her favorite." Overjoyed, the gullible Sonora passes out cigars. A moment later Nick tells Trin exactly the same story, whereupon Trin calls for drinks all around.

Suddenly above the barroom clamor comes the sound of a plantive song, "Che faranno i vecchi miei." The men pause and listen. As Nick calls out that the singer is Jake Wallace, the men become strangely quiet, moved by the homesickness expressed in this refrain, in which the singer muses about his aged parents far away, hoping and longing for their son's return. Strumming his banjo, Jake enters singing. He stops in surprise at the faces turned toward him in silence. Softly the miners echo a phrase of his song. And here begins one of the most affecting choruses in the opera—"Al telaio tesserà." Moved close to tears by memories of home, the miners express their feelings in phrases of simple tenderness, in sharp contrast to their raucous behavior of a few moments before. As the song dies away into anguished silence, Larkens, bursting into tears, gets to his feet. In abject despair he cries that he wants to go home ("Non reggo più"), that he is sick to death of this brutal existence. He begs for help to get back home. The miners promptly take up a collection and pour the money into his hands. Larken sobs his thanks and then leaves as the miners hum the closing phrases of the chorus.

As some of the miners resume their game of faro, there is a sudden burst of violent action. Handsome accuses Sid of cheating. Crowding around him, the miners, in a staccato chorus ("Al laccio il ladro"), shout that they will hang the scoundrel then and there. Sid whines for mercy.

At that moment, Rance strides in from the dance hall and restrains the miners with a contemptuous gesture. Coldly he asks why death should seem so terrible ("Cos'è la morte?"), then adds that he knows of a worse penalty. He calls for Sid's cheating card, and a miner hands him the two of spades. Pinning it above Sid's heart, the sheriff sneers that he will wear it like a flower. And if he dare take it off, Rance growls, hang him. With bellows of rage, the miners brutally kick Sid out of the barroom. Then, as though nothing had happened, Rance and the others go back to their card game.

At this point Ashby, the Wells Fargo agent, enters. First calling for whisky and asking about Minnie, he announces that he is finally closing in on the bandit he has been hunting for three months. This fellow, he warns, is at the head of a dangerous band of thieves ("La banda di ladri"), and the miners should be on their guard. With that, Ashby, groaning that he is dead tired, flings himself down on a bunk in the corner of the room and covers himself with a cloak.

The men drink a toast to Minnie. With an arrogant smile Rance murmurs, "Missis Rance, quite soon" ("Mistress Rance, fra poco"), a remark which sets off a brief but violent quarrel. Sonora taunts Rance that Minnie is only making a fool of him. The sheriff warns Sonora that he will take no insults from a drunken miner ("è il whisky che lavora"). Sonora whips out his pistol, whereupon Rance rushes at him and the two start fighting.

Before the miners can intervene, Minnie bursts into the room, thrusts the two men apart and snatches Sonora's pistol away from him. The others step back. There is a sudden silence, then they hail Minnie with a shout. Confronting Sonora, Minnie angrily berates him for causing trouble. He, and the other men as well, shuffle in embarrassment. Rance sulkily retreats to a corner. Minnie sharply warns the men that if there is any more of this nonsense she will discontinue her school. Like guilty schoolboys, the miners clumsily try to placate her by offering her flowers, a length of ribbon and a silk handkerchief. Minnie's anger melts away as she smiles her thanks.

Ashby now joins the group and clinks glasses with the lady. The dialogue continues in a kind of quasi-recitative. Ashby plays the gallant for Minnie's benefit. Noticing Rance sitting alone, she favors him with a greeting. She settles Sonora's barroom bill as he pays off with a bag of gold. Ashby, talking to Rance, expresses concern because so much of the miners' gold is kept unguarded in the saloon when there are so many outlaws around. He recommends the security of the Wells Fargo bank.

At length Minnie takes a Bible out of a box at the end of the bar, then sits down with the miners to continue their "Scripture lesson." A droll and charming scene underscored with striking musical ingenuity ensues as she asks: "Dove eravamo?" ("Now, where were we?"). Opening the Bible to the "Fifty-first Psalm of David," she asks her pupils to recite. The burly miners respond like schoolboys.

First, Harry describes King David ("Era un re dei tempi antichi") as a "reg'lar hero" who slew a giant with the jawbone of an ass.

In the "second lesson" Minnie explains to the mystified Joe that hyssop, a plant that grows in the Orient, also can grow in men's hearts. Then in a simple but moving refrain she reads the familiar verses beginning "Wash me and I shall be whiter than snow," and explains its message: In all the world there is not one sinner who cannot be redeemed through love.

The calm mood of the scene suddenly is broken by the sound of hoofbeats outside. It is the post rider bringing the mail—along with a warning that an outlaw has been seen in the neighborhood. The rider hands a letter to Ashby, who reads it with astonishment. He asks the messenger if he knows a certain Nina Micheltorena. Before he can answer, Minnie, with noticeable relish, declares that this Nina is a Spanish hussy ("È una finta spagnuola") who spends all her time flirting with the men. Ask them, she adds mischievously, looking at the miners. They shrug in embarrassment.

Aside in recitative, Ashby tells Rance that he will have the outlaw Ramerrez swinging at the end of a rope by nightfall. He explains that Nina Micheltorena will lure him to the Palmetto saloon at midnight, and then . . .

A brief choral interlude follows in which the miners, reading their letters, express their reactions to the news from home: Handsome's girl, Kitty, has married the old clockmaker . . . Happy's parrot died calling his name . . . Harry reads about wars and other disasters . . . Joe howls in grief because his grandmother has died. As the others try to comfort him he wipes away his tears and calls for whisky. The miners drink and then go into the dance hall. Only Rance remains, his eyes on Minnie.

Nick comes in to say that a stranger—a San Franciscan, he thinks—is at the door asking for whisky and water. Minnie, amused at this unusual drinking order, tells Nick to bring the stranger in. As the bartender goes out, Rance impulsively tries to embrace Minnie, then asks her to marry him. She bluntly tells him that she is not interested in his proposal. When he persists in his attentions she warns him away by brandishing her pistol. Rance controls himself with an effort, then sits down at a table and picks up a deck of cards.

In a curious change of mood, Minnie asks him why he is angry with her—when she has given him an honest answer to his proposal. Rance replies in a melodious refrain, yet in words of despair and self-mockery. When he left home, he sings ("Minnie, dalla mia casa son partito"), no one cared—he left unloved and unloving. He was born with a gambler's poisoned heart, and gold alone gave him what he was looking for. And now, he adds sardonically, he will give a fortune for a kiss.

Minnie remarks that real love is very different, then goes on in a predominantly minor refrain ("Laggiù nel Soledad") to recall her own luckless childhood in Soledad, where her father kept an inn. There he dealt cards at the gaming tables while her mother cooked and tended bar. Sometimes, when both parents sat at the card table heaped with money, Minnie would creep under the table looking for stray coins. There she would notice her mother's pretty feet snuggled up to her father's. And now, Minnie concludes in a soaring phrase, remembering how deeply her mother loved her father, she herself will never marry a man unless she truly loves him.

The scene is interrupted as Nick enters followed by Dick Johnson (who is really the outlaw Ramerrez), who tosses his saddle into a corner and then announces that he is the man who asked for whisky and water. Face to face, he and Minnie instantly realize that they have met before. Both try to hide their mutual astonishment.

Rance, with deliberate malice, asks Johnson if by any chance he might be looking for a certain Nina Micheltorena. Johnson brushes the question aside and simply identifies himself as "Johnson from Sacramento." Rance, fuming with rage, strides to the other side of the room.

In a brief colloquy in quasi-recitative ("Vi ricordate di me?"), Minnie and Johnson recall how they met on the road to Monterey. As they talk affectionately, Rance, beside himself with jealous fury, walks up to the bar and knocks Johnson's glass off it with a sweep of his hand. Again he demands to know why Johnson has come to the camp, but the latter merely looks at him in contemptuous silence.

Rance rushes to the entrance of the dance hall and calls the miners into the barroom, telling them that the stranger refuses to explain his business. When the men threaten Johnson Minnie intervenes, saying she will vouch for him. The miners promptly start shaking hands with him while Rance, pale with anger, walks away.

As a waltz rhythm begins in the orchestra, Johnson offers his arm to Minnie to escort her into the dance hall. Minnie demurs, saying she has never danced, but the men urge her on. They all join in a wordless, lilting waltz tune, stamping their feet and clapping their hands in time to the music. All of them leave except Sonora, Trin, Handsome, Harry and Rance.

Nick enters and asks for Minnie. A moment later Ashby and a group of miners burst in, pushing José Castro, one of Johnson's gang. Kicking him to the floor, they tie him up and then shout for a hanging. The music of the waltz continues as an ironic accompaniment to their violent outcries. Castro, catching sight of Johnson's saddle, thinks his leader has been captured. Desperately playing for time, Castro tells the men that he knows where Ramerrez is and can lead them to him.

After a brief discussion the men storm out to saddle their horses. Johnson comes out of the dance hall and Castro manages to tell him that he allowed himself to be captured to throw the pursuers off the trail. The gang is hiding close by, he says, and will soon give a signal, a whistle. If all is ready, Johnson is to whistle in return. Rance and several of the men come back in. Glaring at Johnson, who watches with assumed indifference, the sheriff orders the men to untie Castro and take him away.

Nick starts closing the saloon, putting out the lights. Minnie enters from the dance hall as Nick leaves the barroom. The agitation of the music gradually subsides into serene chords as Johnson and Minnie stand facing each other. Here, *andante sustenuto*, begins the duet "Mister Johnson, siete rimasto." Johnson, touched by Minnie's charming naïveté, comments that it is strange to find her in a place where anyone could walk in and rob her—even of a kiss. Minnie replies that she has handled that kind of a situation before—and still can. With growing interest, Johnson asks her more about her life, remarking that she deserves something better than this. Minnie answers that she wants nothing better ("Mi contento, a me basta"). She lives alone, goes her own way and is afraid of nobody. With disarming candor she tells Johnson that she feels quite safe with him.

In ringing phrases Johnson sings that, even though he is a stranger to himself, he too has enjoyed his solitary life to the fullest. Yet somehow he knows that here is a woman who has still to enjoy all that life has to offer.

Minnie, strangely disturbed, answers ("Io non son che una povera fanciulla") that he is talking to her—a common good-for-nothing—in a new and beautiful language she does not understand. To a surging orchestral accompaniment, Johnson cries that her heart understands it and that now they both know it is the language of love.

There is a sudden interruption as Nick enters to warn that an outlaw gang is skulking around the camp. A moment later a shrill whistle sounds outside. Johnson realizes it is the signal. Minnie makes an involuntary move toward him, as though seeking his protection.

As the action continues from this point, the music again takes up the symphonic pattern of the duet. Minnie says her fears now are only for the safety of the keg which contains a fortune in the miners' hard-won gold. The miners usually take turns in guarding it, but tonight they are on the trail of the outlaw. Whoever wants that gold, Minnie exclaims, will have to kill her to get it. When Johnson asks why she would risk her life for someone else's gold, she tells him.

These poor men ("Povera gente"), she says, have left home, wives and children to live here like dogs, to wrest the gold from the earth with backbreaking labor, then send it home to support their families. It is for such men, Minnie declares, that she would die guarding the contents of that keg.

Deeply moved, Johnson swears he will protect her and the gold. But now, he says, he must go. He asks if he may come to her cabin for one more goodbye. Yes, Minnie answers . . . and then perhaps he can explain to her what she, a good-for-nothing "with thirty dollars' worth of education," might have been. She tries to laugh, but breaks down sobbing.

As the closing love theme of the duet soars through the orchestra, Johnson tenderly comforts her ("No, Minnie, non piangete").[1] Nothing matters, he says, but goodness of heart. Looking into her eyes, he sings quietly, "e avete un viso d'angelo" ("you have the face of an angel").

Johnson abruptly turns away, picks up his saddle and rushes out of the door. The music stops and there is a profound silence. Nick tiptoes in and puts out all the lights except one, which dimly lights the room. As though in a dream, Minnie murmurs softly: "Un viso d'angelo!" The curtain falls slowly.

## ACT II

Minnie's cabin on the mountainside. The cutaway stage set shows the loft above the single room. Toward the rear of the room is a canopied bed; at one side is a fireplace. Wowkle, the Indian girl, is seated cross-legged on the floor with her papoose cradled on her back in typical Indian fashion. Rocking back and forth, she sings a plaintive lullaby, "Il mio bimbo." Billy Jackrabbit enters, greets Wowkle with an Indian grunt, then goes over to the table,

---

[1] To heighten the effect here, Puccini added a chorus humming the theme backstage.

on which there are glasses and a plate of cream cakes. When he reaches for the cakes, Wowkle sharply tells him not to touch them.

The two begin talking about getting married, and about the baby. Tomorrow, Billy says, they will go to church and sing. Nestling close to him, Wowkle begins singing a doleful hymn tune, "Come fil d'erba"—the grim text from the fortieth chapter of the Book of Isaiah. Billy chimes in, then irreverently remarks that they will get married and have plenty of beads and whisky.

Suddenly Minnie enters carrying a lantern. Hurrying about excitedly, she straightens out the room and gives orders to the Indians. She begins dressing up for Johnson's visit, first trying on a pair of slippers only to discover that they are too tight. As she is primping in front of the mirror, there is a knock on the door. Johnson enters, bundled in a fur coat. In charming confusion, Minnie stammers a welcome. Johnson gallantly compliments her on her appearance, then tries to embrace her. Annoyed by his familiarity, Minnie fends him off. A swift chromatic passage played by the flutes underscores her momentary irritation.

Taken aback, Johnson begs to be forgiven, but teasingly adds that he is not the slightest bit sorry. Minnie's annoyance vanishes. Then, rather pensively, she asks him why he came to the Polka —did he perhaps take the wrong road, thinking he was going to see Micheltorena? Anxious to change the subject, Johnson again tries to embrace her and again she rebuffs him. Looking around the room, Johnson remarks that it is curious that she should prefer to live alone like this in the mountains.

In a lilting refrain ("Oh, se sapeste"), Minnie describes how exciting her life really is—galloping through the fragrant meadows on her pinto or drifting in her boat down the river past banks of wildflowers, then home again to her Sierras—so high they seem to touch the hand of God. In the winter she is busy teaching at the "Academy," her school for the miners. Over a rhythmic, flowing accompaniment, the two philosophize about literature, love and men and women in general.

Under the spell of Minnie's charm, Johnson impulsively asks for a kiss, but she adroitly keeps him at a distance. Outside, the blizzard howls furiously. Minnie dismisses Wowkle, telling her she may stay in the barn for the night. Alone in the cabin, Minnie and Johnson passionately embrace as the music storms to a climax. A violent gust of wind tears the door open and snow swirls into the room. Oblivious to the storm, the lovers remain locked in each other's arms.

The clock strikes, breaking the spell. Relinquishing their embrace, the two stare at each other as though hypnotized. In a sudden change of mood, Johnson harshly warns Minnie not to listen to anything he says. Bewildered, Minnie exclaims that she gave her heart to him the first moment they met. Johnson abruptly says goodbye and starts to leave.

Warning him that it will be impossible to get through the snow, Minnie urges him to stay. At that moment three shots ring out. Johnson is alarmed, but Minnie merely shrugs. Perhaps they have caught the outlaw Ramerrez . . . what does it matter . . . Gazing at Johnson passionately, she cries, "Resta! È destino!" Then, in the great unison duet "io non ti lascio più," Minnie and Johnson sing that they belong to each other and will live and die together.

Freeing herself from Johnson's arms, Minnie says that now they must say goodnight. Johnson stretches out on the bed, Minnie wraps herself in a bearskin robe and lies down in front of the fireplace. After a few moments she breaks the silence with a question: "Did you ever know Nina Micheltorena?" From behind the bed curtains: "Never." Then, "Buona notte," and silence again.

They are roused by a knock on the door and Nick's voice is heard outside. Johnson, pistol in hand, faces the door. As Nick calls out that Ramerrez is on the trail, Minnie forces Johnson to hide behind the bed curtains. In the next moment Nick, Rance, Ashby and Sonora burst into the room, and, in recitative, they break the news to Minnie: Mister Johnson, her gallant partner from Sacramento, is really the outlaw Ramerrez. He came to rob the Polka. Minnie furiously denies his intention, then demands to know who told them that Johnson is Ramerrez.

Rance, with malicious enjoyment, answers: "Nina Micheltorena." He is her lover, the sheriff goes on, and when she was questioned at the Palmetto she showed the men his picture to prove it. With that he hands Johnson's picture to Minnie. With a forced laugh, she remarks that Johnson keeps charming company.

Recovering her composure, she thanks the men and bids them goodnight. As they leave, Rance, with a sneer, warns her to be on her guard. In a voice edged with fury and contempt, Minnie orders Johnson to come out. Stricken with shame, he admits he came to rob the Polka, but when he saw who his victim would be . . . Minnie cuts him short, branding him a liar and a thief. Struggling to hold back her tears of rage, she orders him out.

Johnson desperately begs her to allow him at least one word before he goes ("Una parola sola"). This is the beginning of the magnificent aria in which Johnson discloses his dark and bitter past—the wretched life that made him an outlaw. Yes, he says, he is indeed Ramerrez and he has been living under a curse. When his father died the only heritage he left his family was a gang of murderous outlaws. To escape this miserable existence, he left home for a life of banditry. Then destiny led him to Minnie. At that moment, inspired by love, he resolved to make a new start in life—to turn from crime to honest work. His only prayer was that Minnie would never know about his past. But this prayer God has not answered, Johnson says somberly as the aria ends in a minor key.

In bitter despair Minnie answers that she can forgive him everything except his betrayal with a kiss—her first kiss of love. Now nothing matters. Go, she cries. Johnson walks out like a man going to his execution.

A moment later a shot cracks out, then there is the thud of a body falling against the door. Minnie frantically tears the door open, and Johnson, holding his side, staggers in. He makes a weak effort to go outside again, but Minnie forces him to climb the ladder to the loft and hide.

As he falls there exhausted, Minnie takes away the ladder and runs to answer a knock on the door. Rance, brandishing a pistol, strides in. Minnie feigns surprise when he shouts that Johnson is in the house, and sarcastically urges him on when he begins searching. In baffled fury Rance stops looking, then suddenly and violently catches Minnie in his arms, shouting that he is madly in love with her. Wrenching free, Minnie snatches up a whisky bottle and raises it to strike.

Rance staggers back. Stretching out his hand, he cries that he knows she loves Ramerrez, but he will never have her. A drop of blood falls on his hand. Rance looks up at the ceiling with a ferocious cry. Minnie desperately tries to divert his attention, but is foiled when the blood keeps dripping down on the handkerchief with which Rance is wiping his hand.

Spying the ladder, Rance places it under the trap door, draws his pistol and orders Johnson to come down. Minnie begs him not to shoot. Johnson climbs slowly down the ladder and with Minnie's help drags himself to the table. There he sinks into a chair and, fainting from loss of blood, slumps forward with his head on his arms. Watching him, Rance sardonically asks if he would like to play poker—he can have his choice: the gallows or the pistol.

Outraged at the sheriff's cruelty, Minnie entreats him to stop tormenting his victim ("Basta, uomo d'inferno!"). Then suddenly she has an inspiration. To a sinister rhythm in the orchestra, she

makes a deal with Rance. We are three of a kind, she tells him—
he a gambler, Johnson a thief, she herself the owner of a gambling
house. Well then, they will settle matters in the way they know
best: in a game of poker. If Rance wins, Minnie and Johnson will
be at his mercy. If Minnie wins, Johnson belongs to her. The best
two hands out of three will win.

Rance, crying that he is sure to win, gazes avidly at Minnie.
Here the famous card game begins, to the accompaniment of an
ominous theme which continues throughout. Unseen by Rance,
Minnie slips several cards into her stocking. She wins the first
hand, Rance the second. They cut cards for the final hand. Stalling
for time, Minnie tells the sheriff she is sorry for what she said in
anger. Rance gloats over the prize which will soon be his.

Suddenly Minnie gasps that she feels faint and asks Rance to
bring her a drink. When he goes to a shelf for the bottle and a
glass, Minnie hides the losing hand in her bodice, then takes the
winning cards from her stocking. By the time Rance comes back
to the table Minnie is waving the cards and screaming that she
has won with "three aces and a pair" ("Tre assi e un paio!").
Rance slams his cards on the table, glares at her for a moment,
then stalks out of the cabin in cold fury.

Over a surging orchestral climax, Minnie bursts into hysterical
laughter. Seeing Johnson still unconscious at the table, she bends
over him sobbing as the curtain falls.


## ACT III

A forest clearing in the Sierras, the rendezvous of the Wells
Fargo posse which is pursuing Johnson. It is dawn. Rance, Ashby
and Nick are huddled near the campfire. Nick and Rance curse the
day Johnson crossed their path. The sheriff bitterly regrets his
bargain with Minnie—and also that he kept his word and did not
reveal Johnson's hiding place to the posse. Nick ironically compliments him on behaving like a gentleman.

Rance moodily wonders what attracts Minnie to an upstart
scoundrel like Johnson. In a comically melodramatic phrase
("Amore! Paradiso ed inferno"), Nick observes that love alone is
the cause of all the trouble. It is heaven and hell. It is a disease
that afflicts the whole world—and Minnie worst of all.

The scene is interrupted by the sound of shouting in the distance.
Ashby leaps to his feet, unties his horse and starts toward the trail
in the background. As the babble of voices sounds nearer, an

agitated chromatic passage sweeps through the orchestra like a portent of fateful events. Looking down the trail, Ashby shouts that the outlaw will not escape this time.

The posse comes running in armed with pistols, knives and clubs. There is a tremendous uproar. The orchestral accompaniment changes to a sinuous theme in the bass. Led by Ashby, the posse rushes away to continue the search. Rance and Nick remain. Glaring in the direction of Minnie's cabin, Rance sings that now it will be her turn to weep—just as he did when she mocked at his love ("Or piangi tu, o Minnie"). From the distance come the voices of the miners in brief echoing phrases, almost like a wail.

Some of the miners now come by shouting that the outlaw is surrounded. Rance mutters that even though Johnson has the devil on his side, he—Sheriff Rance—will pay him out. The miners come storming back with the news that Johnson was captured but escaped. From this point on, the scene builds into the climactic ensemble of the opera. The voices of the individual miners—Joe, Handsome, Happy and Sonora—describing the progress of the chase to Rance blend with those of the other miners as they ask for news. At one point, Billy Jackrabbit appears with a rope, which he slings experimentally over a branch.

Watching him, several miners sing that they will teach the outlaw to dance at the end of a rope ("Lo faremo ballare"), then break into the familiar refrain "Dooda, dooda, day!" Rance sings despairingly that even though he himself kept his bargain with Minnie, his word of honor will not save Johnson now. Almost unnoticed in the confusion, Nick drags Billy Jackrabbit to one side. Thrusting some gold into the Indian's hands, Nick orders him not to make the noose until he is told. No tricks now, Nick warns, pointing his pistol at Billy's head.

A moment later Johnson is dragged in by the cursing, yelling miners. He is pale and disheveled, but still defiant. Ashby turns the prisoner over to Sheriff Rance, pompously declaring that justice must be done. The agent rides off, ironically wishing Johnson luck. The men now gather around Johnson in kangaroo court formation and the trial begins. It is set forth in musical terms in one of the most remarkable ensembles in opera, opening as Rance, savoring his moment of revenge, lights a cigar, blows a cloud of smoke in Johnson's face and says: "E così, Mister Johnson, come va?"

Johnson contemptuously tells him to get on with the hanging. Inflamed by Rance, the miners burst into a chorus of vituperation, accusing Johnson of robbery, plunder and murder. They lay all the crimes of the region at his feet—the killing of a post rider, the massacre of a squadron in Monterey. But worst of all, they shout, was the crime of stealing Minnie away from them. Now they will make him pay for his caresses.

Johnson replies that while he has been a thief, he is not a murderer. He is not afraid of death, he cries, and offers to cut his own throat to prove it. He asks only to say one more word—one word about the woman he loves. The men are surprised into momentary silence. Rance lunges at Johnson, checks himself, looks at his watch and says he will give the prisoner two more minutes. Sonora steps forward to quiet the crowd, insisting that Johnson has the right to speak.

Johnson thanks him and then makes his plea in the great aria "Ch'ella mi creda." He asks his captors never to let Minnie know how he died, but to tell her instead that Johnson has gone far away to lead the better life she taught him how to live. He will never return, he sings, but he will never forget Minnie, the one and only flower of his life.

As he finishes, Rance again lunges at Johnson and this time strikes him brutally in the face, an act which brings a mutter of angry protest from the miners. Johnson gets up and strides toward the tree where Billy Jackrabbit is standing with the noose in his hands. The crowd follows in awed silence. Six men, pistols drawn, range themselves on either side of the tree.

Suddenly from the distance comes a piercing shout and the sound of hoofbeats. Everyone stops in his tracks and stares down the trail. Then there is a tremendous shout: "Minnie!" Rance, screaming like a madman, rushes forward to go on with the hanging. Minnie, brandishing a pistol, rides up followed by Nick. Leaping from her horse, she rushes over to Johnson and defies Rance and the crowd to touch him. Rance tries to goad the miners on, but as they press closer Minnie screams that she will kill Johnson and herself if they move one step nearer.

Sonora, throwing himself between Minnie and the crowd, shouts at the men to leave her alone. Livid with rage, Minnie denounces them for turning against her ("Non vi fu mai chi disse"). Bitterly she reminds them that not one of them ever said "Stop" when she made sacrifices in their behalf, patched up their quarrels and helped them when they needed help. Now, she goes on, she claims as her own another man she has helped—to whom she has shown the way to a new life. The robber he once was has died. They cannot kill this man again.

Sonora interrupts to say that it is not the theft of gold that matters, but the theft of her heart. Instantly Minnie's anger vanishes and she thanks Sonora for being the first to forgive. Then, as the miners shuffle guiltily, she approaches them one by one, recalling how she tried to teach them that love and forgiveness could redeem the very worst of sinners. As a gesture of faith and trust, Minnie tosses away her pistol. Some of the miners weep unashamedly. Finally won over, the men sing that Minnie deserves their mercy ("Minnie merita tutto").

Speaking for all, Sonora says that Minnie's words have come from God Himself ("Le tue parole sono di Dio"). With that he cuts the rope binding Johnson's hands and helps him to his feet. He leads him over to Minnie, then turns away, choking back a sob.

The lovers slowly leave the scene as the farewell chorus of the opera begins—"Addio, mia dolce terra." Weeping, the miners watch them until they are out of sight, singing *sotto voce* that they will never return. From the distance the voices of Minnie and Johnson drift back like an echo . . . "Addio, mia California." The curtain slowly falls.

# Die Frau ohne Schatten
## (*The Woman Without a Shadow*)

*by* RICHARD STRAUSS

(1864–1949)

*Libretto by*
HUGO VON HOFMANNSTHAL

### CHARACTERS

| | |
|---|---|
| Emperor of the Southeastern Islands | Tenor |
| Empress | High dramatic soprano |
| Nurse | Dramatic mezzo-soprano |
| Spirit Messenger | High baritone |
| Guardian of the Temple Threshold | Soprano or falsetto singer |
| Apparition of a Young Man | High tenor |
| Voice of the Falcon | Soprano |
| A Voice | Alto |
| Barak the Dyer | Bass-baritone |
| His Wife | High dramatic soprano |
| One-eyed brother ⎫ | ⎧ High bass |
| One-armed brother ⎬ Brothers of Barak | ⎨ Bass |
| Hunchback ⎭ | ⎩ High tenor |
| Voices of six children | Three sopranos, three altos |
| Voices of the Watchmen | Three high basses |

Royal servants, beggar children, slave girls, attendant spirits, voices of spirits

*Place:* The legendary Empire of the Southeastern Islands
*Time:* Universal
*First performance:* Vienna Opera, October 10, 1919
*Original language:* German

---

This operatic amalgam of fantasy and reality is a product of Richard Strauss's later period as a composer. Although overblown and pretentious to a certain degree, with a libretto burdened with abstract symbolism and somewhat confusing allegory, the opera contains some of Strauss's finest music. In its use of leitmotivs it is Wagnerian, and in the scope of its music and drama it is truly a "superopera." The "woman without a shadow" is a woman without children—the woman who repudiates motherhood. The central theme of the opera is that through true marriage, love and sacrifice the shadowless woman can be brought to the fulfillment of her destiny: the giving of life.

The premiere marked the first great evening of the post-World War I Vienna Opera.

Although given frequently in Europe, *Die Frau ohne Schatten* did not achieve immediate popularity in the United States. It was given its American premiere at the San Francisco Opera on September 18, 1959. Its next presentation in this country, however, made history. It was performed on October 2, 1966, at the new Metropolitan Opera House in Lincoln Center, New York City, in one of the most elaborate productions in the annals of the Metropolitan. Received with tremendous acclaim, it played to sold-out houses during the 1966–67 and 1968–69 seasons.

There is no overture. The curtain goes up immediately.

## ACT I

[*Scene One*] A terrace overlooking the imperial gardens of the Emperor's palace. At one side, dimly lit, is the entrance to the royal bedroom, where the Emperor and the Empress are sleeping. The Nurse, crouching in the shadows, is guarding the bedroom.

A powerful three-note theme sounds in the orchestra. Then the Nurse sings that a light is rising over the lake ("Licht über'm See"), and wonders if it heralds the approach of Keikobad, the all-powerful monarch of the shadowless spirit world. She sings that she has been watching all night long in pain and sorrow over his child, the Empress.

The Spirit Messenger steps out of the shadows. Clad in armor, he is bathed in a ghostly bluish light. It is not Keikobad, he announces ("Keikobad nicht"), but his Messenger. Here begins a long musical dialogue in which the significance of the shadow is made clear. The Messenger reminds the Nurse that he is the twelfth to have visited her in a year to ask the fateful question: Does the Empress cast a shadow?" ("Wirft sei einen Schatten?")

A single note, repeated in sextuplets, underscores his question. If so, the Messenger goes on, the Nurse and everyone else are doomed.

In suppressed triumph the Nurse answers that there is no shadow—the light passes through the Empress' body as though she were made of glass. The Messenger berates her for her carelessness in allowing the girl to fall, as a human being, into the hands of the Emperor.

Trying to defend her actions, the Nurse says that the girl inherited from her own mother a longing to be human. And it was her own father who gave her the power to transform herself into a gazelle, which the Emperor then captured. How could she, the Nurse asks tartly, pursue a gazelle?

Abruptly the Messenger asks to see the Empress. Shaking her head, the Nurse replies that the Emperor is with her. To the accompaniment of the "Huntsman" theme in the orchestra, she explains that the Emperor is a hunter and a lover—but nothing more. Although he has been with his wife for twelve months, at dawn he is off to the hunt and does not come back until nightfall. His nights are her days; his days are her nights.

After twelve long months, the Messenger declares, the Emperor now has only three short days left to be with the Empress. Then she must return to her father Keikobad. "And I with her," the Nurse exclaims joyfully. In a foreboding phrase foretelling the fate of the Emperor the Messenger says: "He will be turned to stone!" ("Er wird zu Stein!"). But she herself will meet Keikobad, the Nurse says, and will bow before him. Warning her to remain on guard for the fateful three days, the Messenger vanishes.

The Emperor, dressed for the hunt, comes in and calls to the Nurse. The Empress is sleeping, he says, and the Nurse is to answer her call when she awakes. Then in a long dramatic monologue ("Heute streif ich bis an die Mondberg") he sings that today he will go hunting in the moon mountains—where he first found the Empress. She was in the form of a gazelle and cast no shadow. Her beauty set his heart on fire.

Now if he could only find his red Falcon, the Emperor cries— the Falcon who caught his gazelle. As she bounded away, the Falcon swooped down and struck her between the eyes. She fell. The Emperor leaped toward her with his spear poised for the kill. At that instant the gazelle was transformed into a woman —and he held his beloved in his arms. Yet in this feverish moment, the Emperor continues, he was shaken with fury because the

Falcon had struck down his bride. He hurled his dagger at the bird and wounded it. The Falcon's look haunts him still.

Casually the Nurse asks him how long he will be away on the hunt. Probably three days, the Emperor answers. Tell the Empress, he goes on in a fiery refrain ("wenn ich jage, es ist um sie"), that when he goes hunting it is for her sake alone, for she is the prize of all prizes. He rushes away.

The Nurse dismisses the servants who had come in with the Emperor, and a moment later the Empress comes out of her room. She asks if her beloved has gone ("Ist mein Liebster dahin?"). This marks the beginning of a brilliant aria. Had she not awakened, she sings, she might have dreamed herself back into the body of a bird or a gazelle. She laments that she has lost the talisman that could transform her, because she gladly again would be the quarry to be hunted down by the Emperor's Falcon.

Suddenly she looks up, sees the red Falcon, and exclaims joyfully over his return. Then in alarm she cries that blood is dripping from his wounded wing and tears are gushing from his eyes. Anxiously she asks the Falcon why he weeps.

The Falcon theme, repeated on a single note accented by appoggiaturas, strikingly imitates the call of a bird. "Why should I not weep?" the unseen Falcon sings ("Wie soll ich denn nicht weinen?"). "The Empress casts no shadow, and so the Emperor must be turned to stone." Terrified, the Empress recalls that on the lost talisman a curse was engraved. The voices of the Empress and the Falcon blend as they reiterate these thoughts.

In desperation the Empress asks the Nurse where she can find a shadow ("wo find' ich den Schatten?"). A long musical dialogue now ensues. The Nurse sternly answers that the Emperor has failed to accomplish what had been decreed: He has not given the Empress a child and she casts no shadow. For this failure he must pay the penalty. As the Empress begs the Nurse to help her find a shadow the Nurse relentlessly reminds her of the terms of the contract. Moreover, if the Empress wants a shadow, she herself must go and get it. And to find it, the Nurse adds softly, but with malevolent emphasis, she must go down into the world of mankind ("Bei den Menschen").

The harsh "Mankind" theme sounds in the orchestra in minor thirds as the Nurse goes on to say that the breath of man is the breath of death. Its very purity reeks of corruption. And now they must descend from their own realm among the stars to mingle with these vile earthly creatures and endure their stupidity for the sake of finding a shadow.

The Empress cries that she must have that shadow and demands to be led down to earth. Still trying to dissuade her, the Nurse warns that dawn is breaking—the human dawn. The light is the earth's sun, which these wretched beings use to cast their shadows. Thus the day dawns over this monstrous realm where mindless hordes with blank faces and unseeing eyes struggle for survival. Does the Empress still wish to go to this loathsome place—or shall they relinquish the shadow?

Undaunted, the Empress replies that she must go—there is an overpowering urge within her that makes her do the very thing that fills her with horror. Well then, says the Nurse, go they will ("Hinab denn mit uns"). From this point the dialogue continues in duet form as the two plan their journey. At its conclusion the curtain falls, while the orchestra continues with a vivid musical description of the descent of the Empress and the Nurse to the earth. A number of leitmotivs are interwoven, including the cry of the Falcon and the "Mankind" theme. The interlude goes on without pause into the next scene.

[*Scene Two*] Barak the Dyer's house, which also serves as his workshop. The Dyer's three brothers—One-eyed, One-armed, and Hunchback—are quarreling savagely. Underscoring their imprecations is the "Mankind" theme. Suddenly the Dyer's Wife rushes in and stops the quarrel by dousing the three with a bucket of water. The brothers turn on her in violent denunciation, railing at her for being a meddling outsider. Once there were thirteen children in this family, they shout, but even then there was always something to eat for any hungry beggar who came to the door. And yet this "upstart beauty" dares abuse the members of the family.

At the height of the altercation the Dyer appears in the doorway. Turning on him in fury, the Wife screams at him to get the brothers out of the house—either they go or she goes. Driving them out, Barak orders them to prepare the animal skins he has brought home to take to market.

Trying to placate his wife, Barak reminds her that these brothers once were healthy children without deformities. This is their home, as it has always been. Where else should they go? When the Wife makes a spiteful reference to the "thirteen children" and their platefuls of food, Barak declares that if they had thirteen children of their own he would see to it that they too had enough to eat. Now, as her husband, he demands to know when she will give him children. Impulsively, Barak touches her shoulder in a tender gesture of affection.

Rudely shaking him off, the Wife sneers that she knows what "husband" means—it means that she has been bought for the sole purpose of being a slave to him and his house. But now, she adds harshly, there is an end to it—she will be slave no longer.

The argument continues in duet form. The Dyer recalls that the godmothers, according to custom, spoke incantations over the Wife's body to assure her fruitfulness—and he has reason to be grateful for these portents of good fortune. The Wife retorts that spells muttered by bleary-eyed hags have no power over her.

Oblivious to her ill temper, Barak kneels before the pile of skins he brought in and begins sorting them over. There is a brief orchestral interlude based on the theme of "Barak's Goodness." Watching him contemptuously, the Wife sings that for two and a half years she has been his wife ("Dritthalb Jahr bin ich dein Weib") and still he has not made her a mother. Now she has lost interest in motherhood, and he himself can put his desire for her out of his mind.

Barak recoils at her cruel words but patiently explains that he is not angry with her. He will wait for the blessings which are sure to come. Here the theme of "Barak's Patience" gives orchestral emphasis to his words. The Wife gibes angrily that no "blessings" will come to this house. Rather, they will shake the dust of this wretched place from their feet. Ignoring her bitterness, Barak picks up the bundle of skins and leaves for the market place.

A moment later there is a flash of light which reveals the Nurse, in a robe of black and white patches, and the Empress, dressed as a servant girl. The Wife stares at them in bewilderment. Kneeling before her and kissing her foot, the Nurse launches into mocking flattery of the Wife's matchless beauty ("Schönheit ohne Gleichen"). Addressing her as "Princess," she asks if the fellow who just left with a pack on his back is one of her lackeys.

"The man is a dyer and my husband," the Wife tells the Nurse coldly, "and that you know as well as I do." Unabashed, the Nurse continues her outrageous blandishments, saying that the Wife's body is "as slender as a palm tree." The Empress breaks in to exclaim that she will kiss the shadow this charmer casts. The Nurse pretends to be distressed because the Wife must languish here alone and bear children. Stung by their mockery, the Wife sobs that they are making a fool of her before God and man.

Playing out her evil masquerade, the Nurse begins to lead the Empress away, exclaiming that the Wife knows the "secret" and is only making fun of her visitors. Completely bewildered, the Wife asks what she means. The "secret," the Nurse answers, is her shadow—which she can sell for whatever price she asks. But who, murmurs the Wife, would buy a poor crooked shadow like hers?

In a dramatic refrain ("Alles, du Benedeite") the Nurse tells her that eager buyers will give her anything she wants if only she will surrender her shadow. She can have slaves, silken garments, palaces, throngs of lovers, imperishable beauty. With that she snatches a jeweled tiara out of the air and places it upon the Wife's head. The latter wails that she does not even have a mirror to see her own image.

The Nurse puts her hands over the Wife's eyes, then the two women vanish. The scene changes at once into a luxurious boudoir, with a bevy of beautiful slave girls waiting to attend their mistress. They hail her as princess in a flowing, wordless chorus sung with the effect of gentle laughter.

As it fades away, the Nurse leads in the Wife, now wearing a loose wrap, with the tiara glittering in her hair. She sits down in front of a large mirror and gasps in delighted astonishment as she sees her image. The voice of the Empress is heard asking the Wife if she will give up her shadow for this image. Before she can answer, the voice of a Young Man sings that for such an image he would give up his life and his soul into the bargain. Lost in wonder, the Wife sings that this is all a waking dream.

The scene suddenly changes back to the Dyer's house. The Wife, once more in her tattered clothes, clings to the Nurse in terror. How, she asks, can she cast off her shadow and give it away? The Nurse, exchanging a significant glance with the Empress, sitting nearby, craftily leads the Wife into admitting that she is satiated with the idea of motherhood without ever having been a mother. Henceforth, she declares, she will deny her husband his wish to have children. The Nurse has now won her point.

In a long aria beginning with the "Renunciation of Children" theme ("Abzutun Mutterschaft") the Nurse commends the Wife on her decision. For this renunciation she will be glorified among women. Then the Nurse explains how she and the Empress will help the Wife in her resolve to thwart her husband. For three days they will stay in the Dyer's house as servants and deliberately upset the routine of domesticity. For this service, the Wife will give them her shadow. Then she will be free to enjoy the dream of delight they showed her before—the slave girls, a palace garden, tons of gold.

The Wife warns that Barak is coming home and will want his supper—and his bed, which she will deny him. Tomorrow, then, the Nurse says, she and the Empress will arrive at noon disguised as poor relations. She is to greet them only after midnight, then permit them to leave secretly for a while. Now, the Nurse announces briskly, there is work to do.

With that she conjures up a fantastic array of legerdemain. As a gust of wind sweeps through the room, five fishes come flying through the air and land in the frying pan, under which the fire blazes up. Half the double bed breaks away and becomes a single cot. The Nurse and the Empress disappear. As the Wife stares uncomprehendingly, children's voices are heard as though issuing from the frying pan. Plaintively they beg to be let in. Here the music states the "Unborn Children" theme. The Wife fumes over the whining voices coming from the fire and looks around for water to douse the flames. The voices, chiding her for her hard-heartedness, die away.

To the accompaniment of the theme of "Barak's Suffering," the Dyer enters bent under the weight of a huge basket. He sniffs the odor of frying fish and asks the Wife why she does not sit down to eat. "Here is your dinner," she snaps. "I am going to sleep." Pointing to the single cot, she tells him there is his bed. Barak looks at it in dismayed surprise. In spoken phrases, the Wife then announces that tomorrow her two cousins will move in. They will sleep at her feet and will work here as her maids. So be it.

Shaking his head sadly, Barak sits down on the floor and begins eating a slice of bread. He muses that he had been forewarned that at first his wife would act strangely—but this behavior is hard to bear. Now he cannot even enjoy his meal.

Then from the outside comes the chorus of the Watchmen, sung in unison over a majestic choralelike accompaniment. In ironic contrast to the bitter mood of the foregoing scene, they exhort husbands and wives ("Ihr Gatten in den Häusern dieser Stadt") to hold marriage sacred, for they are entrusted with the seed of life. Gazing at his sleeping wife, Barak softly asks if she can hear the Watchmen. He listens intently as they sing that husbands and wives are the bridge over which the dead cross the abyss to return to life. With a deep sigh of resignation, Barak lies down to sleep. The curtain falls.

## ACT II

[*Scene One*] Barak's house. The Empress, in her role as servant girl, helps Barak pack up his load of skins, then urges him to return home quickly to the Wife who cannot bear his absence. At the moment, the Wife is sitting to one side, still wearing the tiara. The Empress goes over to her, kneels before her and holds up a mirror; the Wife admires her image. When Barak leaves, the Nurse goes to the Wife and asks if she is to call the "one who is now expected"—the one for whom she has adorned herself ("Wie ruf ich den, der nun herein soll?").

When the Wife replies that she adorns herself for no one but the image in the mirror, the Nurse deliberately tempts her with a romantic description of a youth who is burning with desire for her. At first skeptical, the Wife recalls that one day a young man did indeed come toward her in a crowd . . . but she does not remember the street where it happened, much less his name.

The Nurse, stealthily picking up a broom and using it as a wand, mutters an incantation and commands the Wife to close her eyes. Here the "Phantom Lover" theme echoes in the orchestra. When the Empress exclaims in shocked amazement over this trickery the Nurse assures her that it is all to her advantage. Are men really so corrupt, the Empress asks. Men, replies the Nurse sardonically, are monsters.

Eyes closed, the Wife muses over the youth, whom she recalls as in a dream, thus betraying her secret desires. Then suddenly, at the Nurse's command, the Young Man materializes as the "Phantom Lover" theme again sounds insinuatingly in the orchestra. Apparently a lifeless dummy, he is supported by two small dark creatures, who vanish immediately. Opening her eyes, the Wife murmurs that he is the young man she met . . . and yet he is not. The Phantom appears to come to life and approaches her. She shrinks back from his touch, crying that she wants only to run away and hide.

Excitedly the Nurse urges the two to take advantage of this magic moment. Her words are echoed by a ghostly chorus. The Empress laments because these two meet—the love thief and the housewife—one with a heart and the other without. In sudden alarm, the Nurse warns that Barak is approaching. She throws her cloak over the Phantom, who disappears.

Barak and his brothers come storming in, followed by a crowd of beggar children. The Dyer is carrying a huge bowl; One-eyed is playing a bagpipe; Hunchback, with a wreath on his head, drags in a cask; One-armed carries in another large dish. The four are in high spirits, and Barak jovially greets his wife as "Princess" and invites her to the feast. She turns her back on him.

The three brothers strike up a lusty refrain in praise of their successful shopping spree on this lucky day ("O Tag des Glücks"). The beggar children, crowding in the doorway, echo their phrases. But the gay mood of the scene is suddenly shattered as the Wife bursts out in a venomous diatribe against Barak ("Wahrlich, es ist angelegt"). All this merrymaking, she sings, is a coarse insult to sensitive feelings. He who hungers for bread is given a stone . . . he who longs to taste the food of dreams is thrown the leavings from the table of the rich. There is nothing left to him but his tears. Here the "Discontent" theme is heard briefly in the strings. Overcome by rage and self-pity, the Wife sits down sobbing in a corner, burying her face in her hands.

Trying to ignore her outburst, the genial Barak invites all to enjoy the feast. He observes that, although the Wife has a sharp tongue and a bad temper, she still is blessed because of her pure heart and her youth. Then he orders the servant girl (the Empress) to offer the Wife some delicacies. As she obeys, the Wife screams at her to keep away. Again she sobs about her cruel misfortune.

At this point a long ensemble begins with a trio passage sung by the three brothers ("Wer achtet ein Weib"). While no one heeds a wailing woman, they sing, they realize that she always has been a long-suffering wife. Then they sing again about their lucky shopping day and the feast that is being prepared. When Barak invites everyone to share, the beggar children join the chorus to praise his generosity. Meanwhile, the Wife continues her lamentations. This chorus, in which variations of the themes of "Bitterness and Mockery" and "Barak's Suffering" are briefly intermingled, brings the scene to a close. The music continues in an interlude in which the theme of "Barak's Suffering" is again heard, then the notes of the Falcon's call.

[Scene Two] Outside the Emperor's falcon house deep in the forest. Moonlight shines through the trees. The Emperor rides up on his horse, dismounts and hides behind a tree from where he can see the door of the house. This entire scene is given over to the Emperor's intensely dramatic monologue "Falke, du wiedergefundener," sung over a symphonic accompaniment. The Emperor implores the Falcon to tell him why he has been led to this place. The letter from his wife explained that she would be secluded

here for three days—but the house is empty. The Emperor wonders if the Falcon has misled him.

Then he sees the Nurse and the Empress come stealing through
the trees and into the house. Watching in dismay, the Emperor
cries that the scent of mankind clings to the Empress. Certain
that he has been betrayed, he resolves to kill her. He draws an
arrow from his quiver, then unsheathes his sword. But unable to
drive himself to murder, he moans despairingly, "Du bist nicht,
der sie töten darf" ("It is not for you to kill her"). Begging the
Falcon to lead him from this accursed place, the Emperor rushes
into the forest with an anguished cry as the music storms to a
climax, ending suddenly with the Falcon's call. The next scene
follows without pause.

[*Scene Three*] Barak's house, where he is at work over his
skins, with the Wife and the Nurse watching him impatiently. The
Wife—as usual—complains because Barak will be late getting to
market. He replies that he has been working hard since morning
without much to show for it. When he asks the Wife to bring him a
drink she snarls that there are servants here to do that.

The Nurse pours a drink and slips a drug into it, and Barak
gulps it down. A few moments later he says he is sleepy, whereupon the Wife resumes her remorseless nagging. Mumbling that
he will take his goods to market later on, Barak falls fast asleep
on the floor. The Wife's bad temper now begins to annoy even the
Nurse. Sharply ordering her to be quiet, she informs her that
Barak has been given a sleeping potion. Panic-stricken, the Wife
tries in vain to rouse her husband.

He will sleep until morning, the Nurse says casually, adding
that in the meantime many happy hours are in store. She offers to
bring the person for whom the Wife is waiting. Angry and suspicious, the Wife spurns all the Nurse's suggestions. She goes on
talking mysteriously about a person of her own choosing who will
come to her from a strange place without any help from the Nurse.

Despite her objections, the Nurse again summons the Apparition
of the young man. The dialogue continues in trio form as the Young
Man, the Wife and the Nurse talk in abstract terms about death
and unrequited love. Suddenly the Young Man falls to the floor as
though in a faint. As the Wife bends over him he tries to seize
her hand. She shrinks back in terror. Seeing the Nurse and the
Empress stealing toward the door, the Wife screams at them to
help her. "If the dead are living," she wails, looking from the Young
Man to Barak, "then the sleepers may well be dead." She manages

then to awaken Barak. The Nurse turns back and throws the cloak of invisibility over the Young Man, remarking that when the wind changes she will recall him.

A long colloquy now ensues between the Wife and Barak. She berates him for falling asleep instead of guarding his home and his wife from intruders. Alarmed, he calls to his brothers for help, while the Wife continues her torrent of abuse. Gathering his tools together, Barak murmurs that something is happening to him that he does not understand . . . his best mortar is broken . . . he wonders if he no longer understands his trade.

There is one "trade" he never has understood, the Wife remarks sarcastically. Thinking of how she resisted the temptations of the Phantom Lover, she adds that if Barak knew what had happened he would scarcely dare move for fear of shattering so precious a treasure as her faithfulness. Barak, utterly bewildered, mutters that he hears but cannot understand.

This is not the first time she has spoken and he has not understood, the Wife sneers. But the day will come, she goes on ominously, when she will leave this house and never return. She is, after all, not a captive bird in a cage. For her, home will be somewhere else.

During an ensuing orchestral interlude in which the theme of "Bitterness and Mockery" is prominent, the Wife leaves with the Nurse while the Empress gathers up the rest of the scattered tools. Barak sits staring blankly into space. Then, as if in a dream, he asks: "Who's there?" The Empress answers: "Your servant, my lord."

The scene curtain falls and, after an agitated orchestral interlude, rises on the Emperor's bedroom in the falcon house. On the bed the Empress is tossing restlessly in her sleep. The Nurse is asleep at the foot of the bed. In her sleep the Empress murmurs that the man's eyes have a tormented look before which even cherubim would quail. Suddenly sitting bolt upright, she cries: "Barak, I have sinned against you!" ("Dir, Barak, bin ich mich schuldig!"). Still in sleep, she falls back.

During an orchestral passage her dream materializes. One wall of the room disappears. In its place is a huge cave with a bronze door in one side. Tombstones show up in the flickering light of torches. From the distance comes the call of the Falcon. The Emperor enters, as though following the bird, and passes in front of the bronze door. There is a sound of rushing water. An unseen chorus intones: "To the water of life . . . to the brink of death . . . beware!" Then comes the voice of the Falcon calling that the woman casts no shadow and so the Emperor must be turned to stone ("Die Frau wirft keinen Schatten"). The Emperor leaves through the bronze door and the cave disappears.

The Empress awakes, still in the grip of her dream. She cries that the Emperor's body is stiffening . . . he can no longer speak. Everything is her fault, she wails, and she has even destroyed Barak . . . whatever she touches she kills . . . if only she herself could be turned to stone.

During a brief orchestral interlude the scene changes to Barak's house. He is sitting on the floor. As the room gradually darkens the three brothers enter, murmuing in awe that something strange is happening. The Nurse, who has returned with the Wife, warns that some supernatural power is at work here. But she assures the Wife that what she desires will come to pass.

This introduces a long ensemble sung by the Wife, the Nurse, the Empress, the three brothers and Barak. The Wife sings ("Wie ertrag ich dies Haus") that she cannot endure a house where darkness falls in the middle of the day and even the dogs howl in fright. The Empress muses on the behavior of the "sons of Adam" and expresses guilt over the fact that her presence among humans only adds to their troubles. Yet she is thankful that destiny has led her to the Dyer, whose sterling qualities as a man have made her visitation worthwhile. The three brothers sing that the sun darkens and the waters of the river stand still—strange things are happening that they do not understand. Barak wonders why some mysterious dark power seems to hold him in its grip. The Nurse continues to promise the Wife that her desires will be fulfilled.

The ensemble is interrupted as the Wife, enraged by Barak's outwardly calm demeanor, launches into a furious tirade ("Es gibt derer, die bleiben immer gelassen") underscored by the "Bitterness and Mockery" theme. There are some people, she storms, who face life with a calm that nothing can disturb. Glaring at Barak, she rages that such people are beneath contempt.

She goes on to taunt her trusting husband with her infidelity. While he went to market, she tells him, she entertained a stranger. At first the thought of her husband spoiled her pleasure, but then she found a way to thrust him out of her mind. Once for all, she has rejected her unborn children—his and any other man's as well. To seal this act she has sold her shadow—and for a magnificent price.

Barak leaps to his feet and stares at her in horror. In spoken tones he gasps that this woman has gone mad, then orders the brothers to stir up the fire so that he can look into her face. As the flames rise, the brothers scream that the Wife casts no shadow.

At this point the ensemble is resumed. The Nurse calls to the Empress to seize the shadow for herself. Now the deed is done, she adds maliciously. Finally roused to fury, Barak shouts that he will drown this brazen wench. The Empress cries that she does not want the shadow because it is stained with blood. Trying to restrain the raging Barak, the brothers warn that there must be no blood on his hands. They curse the Wife and implore Barak to chase her out of the house. The Nurse cries triumphantly that at last the shadow is theirs—and now, he who calls for blood must have a sword. At this instant Barak raises his arm in a gesture of swearing an oath of vengeance. A glittering sword flies through the air and into his outstretched hand. He lunges at his wife as the brothers desperately try to hold him back.

For a moment, the Wife stands paralyzed with fear. Then with an anguished cry she flings herself toward Barak, sobbing that her faithlessness was a lie and that her own lips betrayed her. Here and now, she goes on, she sees a man she never saw before—Barak, a stern judge and a noble husband. If she must die for something that never happened, then let him kill her quickly.

Shaking off the brothers, Barak raises the sword to strike. It flies out of his hand. A moment later the room splits apart and Barak and his Wife disappear into a yawning gulf. Water roars into the room through great cracks in the walls. The brothers flee through the open door to escape the torrent, while the Nurse drags herself and the Empress to a place of refuge. The scene is plunged into darkness. To a fanfare of trumpets the Nurse invokes the infernal powers. The curtain falls.

## ACT III

A subterranean vault divided by a thick wall. Barak sits on one side, his wife on the other, with neither aware of the other's presence. The wailing theme of the "Unborn Children" sounds in the orchestra. Begging the voices to be quiet, the Wife expresses her remorse in a touching monologue which begins as she again denies she deceived her husband ("Ich hab' es nicht getan!"). She longs desperately to see him again, to make him understand that although she enticed her would-be lover into her house she did not violate the sanctity of marriage. In despairing tones she calls out Barak's name.

On the other side of the wall, Barak sings of his love for his

Wife, whose young heart has been entrusted to his care. The voices of the two then blend in a tender duet ("Mir anvertraut"). It ends in a swift change of mood as Barak recalls the terrible moment when he was about to murder his wife. Now all he desires, he sings in pianissimo phrases, is to tell her: "Do not be afraid." This passage brings to mind the love duet in *Tristan und Isolde*.

A sudden shaft of light pierces Barak's cell and lights up a staircase at the back. As a rising major chord passage sweeps through the orchestra, a Voice commands the Dyer to climb. When he does so, the Wife implores him in ringing phrases ("Komm zu mir") to come to her. To see him once more she would gladly die by his sword. Then, commanded by the Voice, she also hurries up the stairs.

During a surging orchestral interlude marked by a series of ascending chords, the scene changes to a stone terrace rising above a river. Steps lead up to a bronze door where Keikobad's Messenger is waiting with attendant spirits. Moored at the foot of the steps is a boat in which the Empress lies sleeping, with the Nurse seated beside her. As the Messenger and attendant spirits disappear through the bronze door the Nurse rouses the Empress. A long dialogue follows. In angry impatience the Nurse urges the Empress to leave this accursed place ("Fort von hier").

When the Empress protests that the boat will not move, the Nurse tells her to climb out so that they may take the road that leads away from this evil region. But the Empress, looking up, exclaims that she sees a gateway—one she has seen before. From somewhere on the mountain comes a trumpet call sounding the "Keikobad" theme. In great excitement the Empress sings that this is a summons from her father. She will go to him to intercede for her husband the Emperor, who now stands before the judgment seat.

Craftily the Nurse tries to dissuade the Empress from entering the gateway—which leads to Keikobad's temple—promising her a shadow ("Ich schaff dir den Schatten"). She reminds her that the light still can be seen through her childless body, even though the Wife's miserable shadow clings to her. The Nurse says she even will help the Empress find the one she loves—the Emperor— if only she will come away from this fearsome threshold. To cross it, she warns, is worse than death.[1] When the Empress demands

---

[1] It may be noted that at this point the plot of the opera moves into the realm of symbolism. Actions and utterances of the characters cannot be explained in terms of everyday reality.

to know what lies beyond the threshold, the Nurse replies, "The water of life." No, the Empress cries, it leads to the brink of death. Then she angrily accuses the Nurse of deliberately misleading her and keeping from her the meaning of supernatural mysteries. But for herself, the Empress declares, everything is clear: She must and will go to her husband. As though in a trance, she sings that she must taste of this water of life. Is it, perhaps, blood from human veins? As she moves toward the portal, the Nurse throws herself in front of her, crying out that the water of life is a monstrous delusion. Whoever drinks of it is doomed to unspeakable disaster.

Desperately the Nurse begs the Empress to heed her warning. Though Keikobad is her father, he is a heartless tyrant who will punish her horribly for falling in love with a mortal. To him, there is no fouler crime than trafficking with the accursed creatures of earth.

The Empress answers in one of the most brilliant arias in the opera—"Aus unsern Taten steigt ein Gericht"—introduced by a blazing fanfare of trumpets. We will be judged by our deeds alone, she sings, and we must obey only the call of the heart. And now she and the Nurse will part forever, because the Nurse knows too little of what is in men's hearts. They pay a terrible price for their guilt—but, phoenixlike, they rise out of death into life. She belongs to them, the Empress sings. Looking at the Nurse in mingled contempt and pity, she adds, "You are not my kind!" With that she turns toward the temple door, which opens to admit her, then closes. The Nurse, beside herself with anger and frustration, screams a curse on all mankind.

Now the voices of Barak and his Wife are heard. They are wandering over the mountain searching for each other. In an ensuing trio, the Nurse continues her maledictions, while Barak and his Wife despairingly cry out for each other. Suddenly Barak comes upon the Nurse and asks her if she has seen his Wife. With deliberate malice, the Nurse points in the wrong direction—then does the same thing when she meets the Wife a few moments later. To add to their confusion, she first tells Barak to avenge himself because his Wife is cursing him, then tells the Wife that her husband is about to murder her. In helpless confusion, Barak and his Wife wander away.

The Nurse, as though suddenly transfixed by a vision, cries out for her "child"—the Empress. She sees her drinking the lethal golden liquid, the water of life, and hears the scream of agony torn from her throat. Wild with fear, the Nurse flings herself on the temple door, screaming "Keikobad!" Her cry is echoed by unseen voices. In answer, Keikobad's Messenger appears and harshly orders her to leave the threshold—at once and forever.

On the verge of madness, the Nurse protests that it was the Messenger himself who gave the Empress into her care ("Mir anvertraut"). She followed instructions, but the Empress rejected her. Keikobad must believe this. The Messenger cuts her short, saying that the Empress is now with Keikobad. As for her—the Nurse—no one needs her.

The scene darkens and a violent thunderstorm breaks. At this point an ensemble begins. The Nurse wildly implores Keikobad to listen to his faithful servant ("Deine Dienerin schreit zu dir"). The voices of Barak and his Wife again are heard as they call to each other. The Messenger denounces the Nurse for daring to utter the name of Keikobad. As punishment for her failure and her arrogance she will be banished to the world of men which she so despises. With that the Messenger pushes her violently into the boat, which drifts away. Screaming a final, savage imprecation ("Fressendes Feuer in ihr Gebein"—"May fire devour their bones"), the Nurse vanishes.

As the wailing voices of Barak and his Wife are heard once more over a brief interlude dominated by the "Retribution" theme, the scene changes to a templelike hall. At the back is a curtained niche. The Empress enters, and attendant spirits go to meet her, bidding her to meet her destiny with courage. To the accompaniment of a solo violin the Empress walks slowly to the niche and calls to her father—"Vater, bist du's?" This introduces the beautiful aria in which the Empress confesses that though she surrendered herself to human love, she did not buy a shadow. Now she asks where she can find a shadow of her own.

As though in reply, a fountain of golden water gushes up near her. Gazing at it thoughtfully, the Empress sings that she does not need the water of life, for she has something stronger to sustain her: love. The Guardian of the Threshold appears and beseeches her to drink. Then the shadow of the Wife will be hers. Refusing, the Empress asks what then will happen to the Wife.

Suddenly she hears Barak calling to his Wife. Excitedly the Empress exclaims that this human being also is a symbol of her failure, because to protect herself from mortal guilt, she invoked supernatural powers. As for the water of life, it is stained with blood, and she will not drink. To a swirling harp glissando, the fountain subsides.

In ringing phrases the Empress proclaims that she belongs to

the world of men ("Mein Platz ist hier in dieser Welt"). There is
her guilt, there she will remain. She calls on her father to pass
sentence. The light in the niche grows brighter, finally revealing
the Emperor turned to stone, with only his eyes showing any sign
of life. As variations of the "Empress" theme flare in the orchestra,
the Empress calls out in spoken phrases that the curse has struck—
thus the Emperor has been punished for her sins. In imitation of
the Falcon's cry, foreboding voices intone that the woman casts
no shadow; therefore the Emperor has been turned to stone. With
a cry of anguish, the Empress falls to the ground.

The golden fountain bubbles up again. The Guardian of the
Threshold reappears and, bending over the Empress, again tempts
her to drink. One sip . . . and then not only will the Wife's
shadow be hers forever, but the Emperor will return alive to her
arms. From the distance come the plaintive voices of Barak and
his Wife pleading for mercy—for if the Empress now drinks of
the water of life their doom will be sealed. Struggling against her
desire to drink the life-giving water, the Empress begs Keikobad
to let her die rather than tempt her further. As the voices of
Barak and his Wife fade away, the Empress raises herself to her
knees beside the fountain and utters a final tormented cry: "Ich
will nicht!"

The fountain disappears. As light begins to flood the scene, a
shadow appears on the ground in front of the Empress. The
Emperor, now restored to life, rises from his throne. In an ensuing
aria ("Wenn das Herz aus Kristall zerbricht") he explains the
miracle that has taken place. When a crystal heart is shattered
by a plea for mercy, unborn children hasten to receive the gift of
life. Man and wife are redeemed and can now fulfill their destiny.
This he learned, the Emperor sings, when he was in the grip of the
deathly spell which turned him into stone.

From the distance come the voices of the unborn children calling
to "Father and Mother." As the Emperor and the Empress comment on their happiness their voices blend with those of the
children in a triumphant chorus. At its conclusion the scene
changes, during an orchestral interlude, to a sunlit landscape
through which a golden torrent flows. The Emperor and the Empress gaze on the scene from a height.

The Dyer's Wife now appears, singing that if she cannot find her
beloved husband she wants only the sentence of his sword. Barak,
on the other side of the stream, calls out that he will protect her
forever. In the next moment they catch sight of each other and
Barak exclaims that he sees his wife's shadow. Magically, the

shadow becomes a golden bridge upon which the two rush into each other's arms. The chorus of unborn children hails their reunion.

Jubilantly Barak sings that now, inspired by the promise of future children, he will work as no one ever worked before ("Nun will ich jubeln"). This marks the beginning of the magnificent quartet which concludes the opera. The Emperor sings that the sound of children's voices is the sound of humanity. The Empress and the Dyer's Wife rejoice in the fact that they both have shadows because they have been rewarded the gift of humanity after a trial by fire. The unborn children sing that all trials are over and that happiness reigns supreme. After a soaring climax the music subsides into a serene major chord as the curtain falls.

# Les Huguenots

## *by* GIACOMO MEYERBEER
### (1791–1864)

### *Libretto by*
#### EUGENE SCRIBE *and* EMILE DESCHAMPS

### CHARACTERS

| | |
|---|---|
| Count de Nevers, a young Catholic nobleman | Baritone |
| Tavannes | Tenor |
| Cossé | Tenor |
| Méru — Catholics, friends of Nevers | Bass |
| Retz | Bass |
| Thoré | Bass |
| Raoul de Nangis, a Huguenot nobleman | Tenor |
| Marcel, a soldier and Raoul's servant | Bass |
| A servant of Count de Nevers | Tenor |
| Urbain, page to Marguerite de Valois | Mezzo-soprano |
| Marguerite de Valois, Queen of France, espoused to Henry IV of Navarre | Soprano |
| Valentine, daughter of Count de St. Bris and betrothed to Count de Nevers | Soprano |
| Count de St. Bris, a leader of the Catholics | Baritone |
| Bois-Rosé, a Huguenot soldier | Tenor |
| Maurevert, a Catholic nobleman | Bass |

Catholics, Huguenots, soldiers, ladies and gentlemen of the court, students, townspeople, monks, gypsies, dancers

*Place:* Touraine and Paris
*Time:* August 1572
*First performance:* Grand Opéra, Paris, February 29, 1836
*Original language:* French

---

*Les Huguenots,* which was spectacularly successful and which established Meyerbeer as the foremost operatic composer of his day, deals with the violent and bloody struggle between the Catholics and Protestants in France during the sixteenth century. It is based on events leading up to the St. Bartholomew's Day massacre, around which the climax of the opera is built. Like *L'Africaine,* it is usually sung in Italian, its title being *Gli Ugonotti.*

The prelude is dominated by the powerful theme of the great Lutheran chorale, *Ein' feste Burg* (*A Mighty Fortress*). It continues through several variations of rhythm and harmony, after which the music leads directly into the first act.

## ACT ONE

The banquet hall in the castle of Court de Nevers, a prominent Catholic party leader, in Touraine, where Nevers has gathered a group of his friends—Tavannes, Cossé, Méru, Retz, Thoré, and other noblemen—for an evening of gay entertainment. The banquet has not yet begun. Greeting his friends, Nevers strikes up a refrain of careless gaiety ("Ne bei di di giovinezza"—"Des beaux jours de la jeunesse"), hailing the days of youth and folly. The others join him in a lusty chorus. Tavannes approaches him and asks why the banquet is being delayed. Nevers explains that he is awaiting another guest, a young nobleman who has recently received a commission in the Lancers through the aid of Admiral Coligny (head of the Huguenot party). This news brings a scornful exclamation of "Huguenot!" from the guests.

Nevers, however, entreats the noblemen to look upon the newcomer as a brother, thus following the example recently set by the rulers of France. He reminds them that the Protestant Admiral Coligny and Catherine de' Medici, the Catholic Queen Mother, have agreed to forget their differences and live in eternal peace. The noblemen comment sardonically on the probable implication of the word "eternal." As they are discussing the matter Cossé exclaims that a stranger is approaching. Saying that he is Raoul de Nangis, Nevers hurries to meet him. The others meanwhile make cynical references to the visitor's solemn "Calvinist" demeanor.

Raoul answers Nevers's greeting in a dignified refrain ("Sotto il bel ciel della Turrena"—"Sous le beau ciel de la Touraine"), in which he voices his appreciation of the fact that he, a humble soldier, is privileged to meet the nobles of Touraine. He bears himself with such gallantry and forthrightness that he wins the grudging approval of the noblemen. After introducing him to the others, Nevers invites all to the banquet table. As the feasting begins the men sing a long and vigorous chorus in praise of youth, wine, and merrymaking ("Piacer della mensa"—"Bonheur de la table").

After the chorus Nevers, seated next to Raoul, remarks on the latter's preoccupied manner and suggests that perhaps he is in love.

He himself, Nevers reveals, is to be married the next day. In a mock-tragic tone he laments that now he must forsake all the adoring court beauties who have besieged him with their attentions. Thereupon Tavannes suggests that all the guests tell the stories of their amours. Nevers invites Raoul, as the guest of honor, to begin the round of stories. The noblemen are vastly amused when Raoul admits that though he is very much in love he knows neither the name nor the title of the lady whom he adores.

Raoul recounts how one day, when he was riding near Amboise, he saw a crowd of rough students about to attack the occupant of a luxurious equipage. He rushed up, quickly routed them, and then was rewarded with a dazzling smile of thanks from the enchanting creature whom he had rescued. From that moment, he exclaims, he has been her slave. Raoul voices his ardor in the graceful aria, "Bianca al par hermine"—"Plus blanche que la blanche hermine." He recalls that as he gazed on this lovely being, fair as a lily, he murmured that even if he were never to see her again he would carry her image forever in his heart. Her smile, he continues in ecstasy, seemed to speak of love. The noblemen voice their approval of his romantic sentiments in a choral phrase.

The conversation is interrupted by the entrance of Marcel, Raoul's servant and a fanatical Huguenot. Striding to his master, he chides him for consorting with Catholic infidels and excitedly urges him to leave their evil presence. Raoul tries to calm him and then apologetically explains that Marcel is a rough old soldier who is as brave as he is religious. He was reared, says Raoul, according to the stern laws of Luther and taught to hate the Pope, and he never loses an opportunity to express himself on the subject. Quietly ordering Marcel to keep silent, Raoul turns back to the table. Nevers proposes a toast. Just as they are about to drink, Marcel, muttering that he must protect his master from damnation, roars out the Lutheran chorale *Ein' feste Burg* ("O tu, che ognor in guardia stai"—"Seigneur, rempart et seul soutien").

More amused than annoyed at the interruption, Nevers asks Raoul the meaning of the song. Raoul, greatly embarrassed, explains that it is a chant sung by the Huguenots to ward off evil. The noblemen good-naturedly allow Marcel to finish his hymn, after which Cossé remarks that the old soldier reminds him of an adversary he encountered during the Battle of Rochelle. He remembers that meeting well, he goes on, fingering a sword cut on his cheek. Looking at him, Marcel admits it was he who inflicted the wound. Raoul is alarmed over Marcel's lack of diplomacy, but

Cossé gaily laughs the matter off and invites Marcel to drink with him.

Marcel, of course, refuses, whereupon Nevers suggests that if he will not drink perhaps he will sing. Marcel replies that he will oblige the company with the battle song of the Protestants at Rochelle—a song against Papists, bigots, and women—one that was sung to the accompaniment of the "piff, paff, piff, paff" of bullets. He then sings the famous *chanson huguenote* ("Finita è per frati" —"Pour les couvents c'est fini"), describing how the Protestants will put monks and priests to rout, strike them down without mercy, and destroy their altars. The second stanza concerns itself with the punishment to be meted out to women. They, too, must perish by sword and gun, so that their evil charms will no longer ensnare honest men. As Marcel sings the recurring "piff, paff" phrases he pantomimes the motions of firing a gun. The song ends in a fierce crescendo.

As the noblemen applaud Marcel's song a servant approaches Nevers and informs him that a very beautiful lady is waiting in the garden to see him. Nevers, remarking that he would not leave his drinking if the King himself were to summon him, casually asks if the visitor is one of the ladies of the court. The servant replies that she is a stranger. In that case, says Nevers to his guests, who have been listening avidly, he will go at once, for this may mean a new conquest. Urging the noblemen to continue the banquet, he tells them he will return shortly with full details about the fair stranger.

In a lively ensemble ("L'avventura è singolare"—"L'aventure est singulière") the guests speculate on this newest adventure of Nevers's and comment on his consistent good fortune with the ladies. Tavannes suggests that they go quietly to the windows at the back, which overlook the garden, and spy on Nevers during his interview. All rush to the windows except Raoul and Marcel, who withdraw to one side of the room and speak quietly together. Noticing that Raoul has not joined the group at the window, Méru approaches him and jestingly asks if his stern Huguenot principles do not permit him to look at a pretty face. Smiling, Raoul answers that he will oblige him by looking.

He gazes outside and then recoils with an exclamation of dismay. Excitedly he tells Marcel that Nevers's visitor is the very lady whom he rescued from the students. Disillusioned at finding the woman he idealizes in a rendezvous with so notorious a cavalier as Nevers, Raoul declares that his love for her has turned to hate.

The noblemen derisively comment that another trusting lover has been deceived. Raoul tries to rush out but is restrained by the other guests.

They cease their conversation when Méru warns that Nevers is returning. Nevers comes back into the room and, as the guests talk among themselves, he reveals, in an aside, what has transpired. The visitor was Valentine, his betrothed, lady-in-waiting to Queen Marguerite. At the request of the Queen, she came to ask that their nuptials be canceled. Nevers adds that though he courteously acquiesced, as any cavalier would, he is burning with rage over the matter. Meanwhile the noblemen come forward and, in a mocking chorus ("Al gran conquistator"—"Bonheur au conquérant"), acclaim Nevers as an irresistible conqueror of womankind.

At the conclusion of the chorus Urbain, Queen Marguerite's young page, appears. When Nevers asks whom he seeks, Urbain replies in the florid cavatina "Lieti Signor, salute!"—"Nobles Seigneurs, salut!"[1] He informs the noblemen that a gracious and beautiful lady has sent him with a message for one of them. Never has any cavalier been so highly favored, he avows. Ending the aria in a brilliant cadenza, Urbain brings forth the letter.

Taking it for granted that the letter is for him, Nevers reaches for it, remarking that it is rather boring to be constantly importuned by adoring ladies. He is considerably taken aback when the page informs him that the letter is for a certain Raoul de Nangis. Raoul, equally astonished, takes the letter and reads it aloud. It informs him that a royal carriage will shortly be waiting for him. He is to permit himself to be blindfolded and conducted to the carriage, which will bring him to the writer of the letter.

Looking at Nevers and the other noblemen, Raoul observes that this is undoubtedly an attempt to have some sport at his expense. He adds that he will see the adventure through and then casually hands the letter to Nevers. Examining it, Nevers exclaims that it bears the seal of the Queen. His manner toward Raoul instantly changes from condescension to almost fawning respect. He assures Raoul of his firm friendship, saying that he has his best interests at heart ("Voi sapete ch'io sono"—"Vous savez si je suis un ami"). This introduces the finale of the act. The other noblemen crowd around Raoul with effusive congratulations and declarations of friendship.

Urbain also comments on the kind fate which has bestowed such

[1] This cavatina is also known by the phrase which follows the opening cadenza—"Nobil donna e tanto onesta," or "Une dame noble et sage."

good fortune on Raoul, who still does not know what to make of the sudden change in attitude on the part of his host and the noblemen. Marcel expresses his happiness by roaring out several bars of a *Te Deum* and by proclaiming that Samson has overcome the Philistines. After the thunderous climax of the chorus, Raoul is led away by Urbain and the curtain falls.

## ACT TWO

The garden of the castle of Marguerite de Valois at Chenonceaux. Queen Marguerite is seated in her pavilion, attended by Urbain and her maids of honor. In a long and brilliant aria ("Ovago suol della Turrena"—"O beau pays de la Touraine") she reflects happily on the beauties of Touraine. Here among the plashing fountains, the lovely flowers, and the pleasant woodland glades all care is cast aside and thoughts of love fill every heart. The maids of honor echo her sentiments in a graceful chorus. In the last part of the aria Marguerite declares that she would be content to relinquish her regal power and preside only over this peaceful retreat.

At the conclusion of the aria Valentine approaches. Urbain, who is in love not only with all the maids of honor but with the Queen and Valentine as well, breathes an amorous comment on Valentine's beauty. When the Queen asks her about Nevers, Valentine replies that he readily agreed to release her from the nuptial contract. Marguerite tells her that she has already arranged another alliance. Raoul de Nangis, she says, will be here today. When Valentine expresses some reticence in meeting him, Marguerite says that she herself will see him first.

The maids ask the Queen's permission to bathe in the nearby stream. When permission is given they sing a melodious chorus about the joys of bathing in the cool and sparkling waters ("Giovin beltà su questa riva"—"Jeunes beautés sous le feuillage") and then retire to the bank of the stream. Noticing Urbain stealing close to watch them, Marguerite reprimands him and sends him away. In a few moments, however, he returns. The Queen is about to rebuke him again for his amorous spying when he announces that a cavalier is approaching. As the maids exclaim in fright over the possibility of being seen at their bath, Urbain assures them that all is well, for the cavalier is blindfolded. Marguerite announces that it is Raoul. Valentine protests that she cannot stay, and leaves despite Marguerite's request that she remain.

While the Queen is waiting for Raoul, Urbain sings a gay cavatina

("No, caso egual giammai"—"Non, vous n'avez jamais, je gage")
in which he recalls his thrilling adventure of escorting a handsome,
blindfolded cavalier through the streets of the village to the castle.
Crowds followed them, while the village girls, all agog, strewed
flowers in the stranger's path. The maids of honor, having finished
their bathing, crowd around Urbain and chatter in excited wonder
over his remarkable story.

As the page ends the cavatina with a flashing cadenza, the
maids see Raoul approaching and sing admiringly of him in a lively
chorus ("Desso à qua"—"Le voilà!"). Dismissed by the Queen, the
maids and Urbain withdraw, with many a backward glance at the
mysterious cavalier.

When Marguerite and Raoul are finally alone she commends
him for keeping the appointment and tells him he may remove
the blindfold. Complying, Raoul utters an exclamation of wonder
over the beauty of the woman before him. A long, florid duet
ensues as Raoul, unaware that she is the Queen of France, addresses her in phrases of extravagant praise ("Beltà divina, incanta-
trice"—"Beauté divine, enchanteresse"). He cries that he is burning
with a desire to serve her. Smiling, Marguerite says that she will
require some proof of his sincerity. Kneeling at her feet, Raoul
swears that his sword and his very life are hers to command.
Moved by his ardor, Marguerite reflects, aside, that if she were
so minded she could make a conquest at this moment. She resolves, however, to keep faith with Valentine. The duet continues
to a thrilling climax as Raoul reiterates his pledge of devotion,
while Marguerite declares that she will deny herself the pleasure
of a romantic conquest for the sake of Valentine's future happiness.

At the conclusion of the duet Urbain once more appears. He
informs Marguerite that the ladies and gentlemen of the court
have come to pay their respects to their Queen. Raoul is surprised and embarrassed when he realizes that he had been pouring
out his heart to the Queen of France herself, but Marguerite reassures him with a smile. She then tells him of her plan to arrange
a marriage between him and Valentine, daughter of Count de
St. Bris, a leader of the Catholics, for the purpose of uniting the
Catholics and the Huguenots and putting an end to their bloody
strife. When Raoul consents, Marguerite declares that he will henceforth be a member of her court. Urbain plaintively murmurs that
the Queen bestows favors on everyone but himself.

During the playing of a minuet the people of the court appear,
led by St. Bris and Nevers. Catholics and Huguenots separate
into two groups. Marguerite announces that they are to witness a

nuptial union which she herself has arranged and then introduces Raoul. The people acclaim the Queen in a brief choral passage, during which a courier arrives and hands her several messages. Reading them, Marguerite informs St. Bris and Nevers that her brother, King Charles IX, requires their presence in Paris at once on important state business. Before they go, however, Marguerite adds, all noblemen—Catholics and Huguenots alike—must swear by the marriage that is soon to take place that they will forever keep the peace. Surrounding the Queen, St. Bris, Nevers, Raoul, and the nobles, holding forth their hands, take the oath in a tremendous chorus ("Per la fè, per l'onor"—"Par l'honneur, par le nom"). They swear by the King, their swords, and their faith that they will keep sacred the vows of peace. In a brief, unaccompanied quartet sung by Raoul, Nevers, St. Bris, and Marcel, the first three ask the blessing of Heaven on the peace that has now been established. Marcel, however, ignores the vow and confines himself to praying that his master may be protected from these infidels. Marguerite and the others then add their prayers for peace.

At a sign from the Queen, St. Bris leaves to bring Valentine. A moment later, as Marguerite announces that the bride will be presented, St. Bris comes forward escorting Valentine, whom he leads toward Raoul. Seeing her, Raoul staggers back in astonishment, recognizing her as the lady whom he saw with Nevers in the garden on the night of the banquet. Crying out that he has been betrayed and deceived, Raoul furiously declares that he will never marry her.

The reactions of the court to Raoul's outburst are expressed in a powerful ensemble ("Oh delir, oh demenza"—"O transport, ô délire"). Marguerite, Urbain, St. Bris, Nevers, and the Catholic faction denounce him for his outrageous insult to Valentine, who laments that he has rejected her without reason. Marcel commends his master's courage, his sentiments being echoed by the Huguenots. Raoul himself declares bitterly that neither Valentine's smiles nor tears will ever deceive him again.

In an interlude Marguerite implores Raoul to explain his actions. It is a matter of honor, Raoul answers, adding that the reason is his secret. Turning on him in fury, St. Bris and Nevers swear revenge. They draw their swords, whereupon Raoul draws his. Marguerite signals a guardsman to disarm Raoul and then angrily reminds St. Bris and Nevers that they have no time to waste in quarreling, for the King expects them in Paris today. When Raoul declares that he will go with them, St. Bris sneers that the scoundrel who can thus win the Queen's favor is indeed fortunate. Marguerite sternly silences him, while Raoul retorts that it is St. Bris whom the Queen is protecting. If he had not been deprived of his sword, Raoul threatens, St. Bris would already have paid for his insults with his life.

The ensemble continues to its great climax with St. Bris, Nevers, and Raoul hurling denunciations, while Catholics and Huguenots threaten each other with dire vengeance. Occasionally the stentorian voice of Marcel is heard in the phrases of the Lutheran chorale. At the conclusion of the chorus St. Bris and Nevers carry away the fainting Valentine. Raoul tries to follow them but is restrained by guardsmen. There is great uproar and confusion as the curtain falls.

## ACT THREE

The Pré-aux-Clercs, an open space on the banks of the Seine in Paris. At one side is a tavern. At the other, the entrance to a chapel. It is a holiday, and a crowd of townspeople sing a chorus about the joys of feasting and taking their ease ("Quest' è giorno de festa"— "C'est le jour du dimanche"). A company of boisterous Huguenot soldiers, drinking at the tavern, then strike up the well-known *Rataplan* chorus, clapping their hands to simulate drumbeats. They are led by the soldier Bois-Rosé, who first sounds a note of defiance to the Catholic foes and then voices a pledge of allegiance to the Calvinist cause. The rest of the chorus is devoted to praise of the embattled Huguenot warriors and is climaxed by a shout of acclaim for the Protestant leader Admiral Coligny.

Preceded by a group of Catholic women chanting an *Ave Maria*, St. Bris, Nevers, Valentine, and the people of the court appear in a nuptial procession moving toward the chapel. Having been spurned by Raoul, Valentine is to marry Nevers. As the procession passes, Marcel strides up and asks if St. Bris is there. The townspeople warn him that he must not try to speak to the count and must bow as a sign of respect. Marcel retorts that he makes obeisance only to God. The Huguenot soldiers shout their approval of his sentiments and break out again with their defiant *Rataplan*. The enraged townspeople denounce them for their disloyalty and lack of respect. Signs of a brawl gradually develop.

Just as soldiers and citizens advance threateningly toward each other, a gypsy troupe comes along and changes the mood of the scene with a gay chorus ("Da me chi vien"—"Venez! Venez!"). They move about among the throng, trying to sell their wares and offering to tell fortunes, after which they entertain the crowd with a gypsy dance. At the conclusion of the dancing the crowd settles down to feasting and drinking.

Nevers, emerging from the chapel with St. Bris and Maurevert, another nobleman, says that Valentine will remain in the chapel to pray for a while. He will return later and escort her as his bride to his castle. St. Bris remarks that this marriage will compensate him for Raoul's insult to his daughter. As Nevers leaves, Marcel approaches St. Bris with a letter from Raoul. The soldier explains that the Queen and Raoul—as well as himself—came from Touraine to Paris this morning. St. Bris exclaims in surprise as he reads the letter, in which Raoul challenges the count to meet him on the meadow of Pré-aux-Clercs at nightfall. Marcel leaves when St. Bris assures him that he will be at the appointed place. The count tells Maurevert that he will keep the meeting a secret from Nevers, for his son-in-law is not to risk his life. Declaring that there is no need for St. Bris to risk his own, Maurevert tells the count that there are other ways to punish this miscreant. The two men go back into the chapel to discuss plans for dealing with Raoul.

With the ringing of the curfew, the people gradually disperse. After they have gone St. Bris and Maurevert reappear from the chapel, having made arrangements for ambushing Raoul. As they leave, Maurevert assures St. Bris that his friends will be near to aid him. No sooner have they gone than Valentine rushes out of the chapel. In great agitation, she exclaims that she has heard her father and Maurevert plotting Raoul's murder. She must save him, not only for the sake of her love for him, but for the sake of her father's honor.

As she is wondering how she can warn Raoul, Marcel appears, saying to himself that he will remain here to share his master's fate. A long and dramatic duet ensues ("Nella notte io sol qui veglio"–"Dans la nuit où seul je veille"). Peering through the gloom, Marcel declares that he will keep watch all night for the enemies who will surely be gathering here. Valentine, heavily veiled, approaches him with an entreaty for help. Marcel draws his sword, but sheathes it again when she speaks Raoul's name. Valentine then tells him what he already knows—that Raoul is to fight a duel in the meadow with St. Bris. But she adds the warning that he must not come alone, for there is a plot against his life. Though he has scorned her, she says sadly, she still loves him and would gladly die for him.

Marcel fears it is too late to warn Raoul, for he has already left

his home to go to the scene of the duel. Marcel prays for his
safety, while Valentine gives way to despair, lamenting that she
is torn between her love for Raoul and her duty toward her father.
Marcel exhorts her to have courage, assuring her that her devotion
will be well rewarded. Reiterating these sentiments at great
length, they finally bring the duet to a close. Valentine goes back
inside the chapel, while Marcel stands guard outside.

Raoul and St. Bris now arrive with their seconds. Marcel warns
his master that there is a plot against his life, but Raoul scoffs
at the thought. The six principals—Raoul, St. Bris, Cossé, Tavannes,
Retz, and Méru—then sing a ringing sextet in which they swear
to abide by the rules of honorable dueling ("De'dritti miei ho
l'alma accessa"—"En mon bon droit j'ai confiance"). They prepare
to fight, while Marcel voices his despair over the fact that he can
do nothing to save his master from the treachery that will strike
him down. In the continuation of the ensemble the principals
declare that no one is to enter the field except the combatants
and that the victor will show no mercy to the vanquished. At its
conclusion Raoul and St. Bris raise their swords but are stopped
by a warning cry from Marcel.

Drawing his sword, he rushes toward the back, shouting that
intruders are lurking near by. Thereupon Maurevert and two
armed men appear. Maurevert accuses the treacherous Huguenots
of appearing in force to aid Raoul, while Marcel calls down the
wrath of Heaven on the perfidious Catholics for the same reason.
At that moment he hears the voices of the Huguenot soldiers in
the tavern, singing their *Rataplan* chorus. Dashing to the tavern,
he pounds on the door, crying, "Coligny! Coligny!" This brings the
soldiers streaming out of the tavern. St. Bris and his adherents
meanwhile shout for the Catholic students, who rush out of another
part of the tavern. Huguenot and Catholic women appear suddenly and join the men of their respective factions.

The two groups insult and defy each other in a roaring chorus
("Siamo qui"—"Nous voilà"), and then fierce fighting begins. The
uproar is brought to a sudden halt by the appearance of Marguerite on horseback, attended by her retinue and guardsmen. With
majestic anger she denounces the two groups for breaking the
peace they swore to keep. When she asks who is to blame for starting the quarrel, St. Bris and Raoul hotly accuse each other of
treachery. Marcel interrupts to declare that a lady informed him
that the noblemen had plotted to assassinate Raoul when he arrived to fight St. Bris. There is the lady, he announces dramatically, as a veiled figure comes slowly out of the chapel.

Rushing up to her, St. Bris tears aside her veil, recoiling in horror as he recognizes his daughter. As he upbraids her for betraying him, Valentine implores the Queen for mercy. Turning to the Queen, Raoul, utterly bewildered, asks the meaning of Valentine's secret interview with Nevers. Marguerite explains that she met the nobleman only to break off her engagement to him at the request of her Queen.

She is interrupted by St. Bris, who insists that Valentine is to be the bride of Count de Nevers. There are expressions of consternation from the crowd. Looking toward the river, St. Bris calls attention to the approach of a gaily decorated nuptial barge bringing Nevers and the bridal party. In a ringing refrain ("Ma che! ascolta te, del sposa triofante"—"Mais écoutez de l'époux triomphant") St. Bris exults that the glorious houses of Nevers and St. Bris will now be united.

Nevers comes ashore, approaches Valentine and ardently greets her, saying that everything is in readiness for the nuptials. Hostilities are momentarily forgotten as the gypsies appear, dance about Valentine and Nevers, and offer gifts and flowers. They join the people of the court in singing a bridal chorus ("Il destin che dal ciel"—"Au banquet où le ciel"). Lighting torches, the gypsies then escort the bridal party to the barge. The gay chorus continues, underscored, however, by the ominous theme of the ensemble sung by the Huguenots, who reiterate their warnings of vengeance.

Valentine laments that she is bound in marriage to a man she hates, while Raoul cries in fury and despair that the woman he loves has been given to his detested rival. Marcel tries to comfort him. As he and Raoul sadly watch the glittering barge move away, the curtain falls.

## ACT FOUR

A hall in the castle of Count de Nevers. At the back is a large window overlooking the street. At one side is a door leading to Valentine's room. It is St. Bartholomew's Day, August 25, 1572. Valentine comes in. Overwhelmed by sorrow and haunted by thoughts of Raoul, she voices her grief in a tender aria ("In preda al duol"—"Parmi les pleurs"). She sings that the realization of Raoul's love for her is her only solace. Her reflections are interrupted when Raoul suddenly enters the room. He has come, he says, to see her once again before he dies. Valentine warns that

St. Bris and Nevers are on their way here at this very moment. Distractedly she urges Raoul to flee, but he replies that he will have it out with his foes here and now. Finally she persuades him to conceal himself behind the curtains of a window at the rear.

St. Bris, Nevers, and the gentlemen of the court come in. St. Bris announces that the time has come to reveal the plot which Catherine, the Queen Mother, has ordered to be put into effect against the Huguenots. Turning to Valentine, he asks her to leave the room, but Nevers requests that she be allowed to remain. Her devotion to the cause, he says, gives her the right to share the secrets of state.

In a vigorous refrain ("Di guai crescenti ognor"—"Des troubles renaissants") St. Bris asks assurances of the nobles that they will aid in delivering the country out of the hands of the Huguenots. When they reply, he explains the royal decree: the Huguenots are to be put to the sword at once—this very day. Nevers asks who has condemned them. Heaven itself, St. Bris replies. And who, Nevers inquires, is to strike the first blow? In answer, St. Bris points to Nevers and the other noblemen. There is a rousing choral interlude as the noblemen, led by St. Bris, call on Heaven to aid them in destroying their foes ("D'un sacro zel l'ardore"—"Pour cette cause sainte").

Only Nevers is silent. When St. Bris asks him why he does not join in the pledge of devotion to the cause, Nevers replies that he will not stain his father's sword with contemptible murder. Defying St. Bris, he breaks his sword across his knee and hurls the pieces at the count's feet. Valentine steps quickly to his side, commends his bravery, and urges him to leave with her. But St. Bris, declaring that Nevers obviously has repudiated the Catholic cause, orders him taken into custody. As Nevers is led away, Valentine, at a sign from her father, goes to her room.

St. Bris then gives the orders: The Catholics are to station themselves at strategic points throughout the city. Some are to meet outside the Hôtel de Nesle, where the Huguenots will be gathered to celebrate the nuptials of Queen Marguerite and the Huguenot Henry of Navarre. Coligny is to die first. At the first sound of the bell of St. Germain the Catholics are to poise for the attack. When the bell tolls the second time they are to fling themselves upon the Huguenots and put them to the sword. Valentine, reappearing at the back of the room and hearing her father's words, wails in despair that though Raoul now knows of the plot he cannot make his way out of the castle in time to warn his friends.

While St. Bris is speaking three monks come in carrying baskets of white scarves. Now follows the famous scene which is known as the *Benediction of the Swords*. The men draw their weapons and hold them aloft. In a powerful unison refrain St. Bris leads the monks in blessing the swords and the cause in which they are drawn ("Nobili acciar, nobili e santi"—"Glaives pieux, saintes epées"). The noblemen answer in a tremendous burst of sound. As they ferociously cry that they will show no mercy in striking down the infidels, St. Bris gives each man a white scarf stamped with a cross, which is to serve as an identifying badge in the combat. After rising to a blazing climax, the voices sink to a dramatic whisper as the men caution each other to keep silent. The music dies away on ominous chords and not a sound is heard as the nobles and monks steal out of the room.

When all have gone, Raoul emerges cautiously from his hiding place, looks around, and then rushes to the door. He finds it locked. At that moment Valentine comes back through the door leading to her room. Now there ensues the famous duet, "O ciel! dove vai tu?"—"Oh ciel, où courez-vous?" one of the most magnificent numbers in the opera.

Valentine asks him where he will flee. Raoul says he will not flee but will go to warn his friends that assassins are near. Valentine cries that among his enemies are her father and her husband. Justice must be done, Raoul answers grimly. But the attack is being made at Heaven's command, Valentine avers. With bitter scorn Raoul asks if the faith to which she confesses requires men to murder their brothers. He is about to leave, exclaiming that the hour of the attack is almost at hand. Valentine implores him not to go for the sake of his own safety.

Desperately clinging to him, Valentine finally cries out that she cannot let him go because she loves him. Despite his anxiety and agitation, Raoul greets her confession of love with feverish ecstasy. Passionately he entreats her to flee with him, but Valentine begs him to stay and save his life. Suddenly the bell of St. Germain tolls the signal for the alert. Tearing himself from Valentine's arms, Raoul cries that he cannot stay while death is poised to strike down his friends. In terror and despair, Valentine continues her entreaties, while Raoul conjures up visions of streets running red with the blood of the Huguenots.

Then the bell tolls the second time, signaling the beginning of the massacre. Raoul draws Valentine to the window and opens it to let her look down on the fearful slaughter taking place in the streets below. Valentine faints in his arms. Placing her gently in a chair, Raoul utters a despairing prayer for her protection and then leaps out of the window. Reviving momentarily, Valentine opens her eyes and sees him. She collapses as the curtain falls.[2]

## ACT FIVE

[*Scene One*] The Great Ballroom of the Hôtel de Nesle, where the Huguenots are celebrating the marriage of Queen Marguerite and Henry of Navarre. There is an interlude of ballet. The tolling of the signal bell is heard faintly above the sound of the music. The festivities come to an abrupt halt as Raoul, disheveled, his clothing drenched with blood, rushes in shouting the terrible news of the massacre. Frenziedly he calls the Huguenots to arms ("All'-arme, amici miei"—"Aux armes, mes amis") telling them that the Catholics have put the Protestant churches to the torch, murdered Coligny, and plundered his home. The Huguenots respond in a fiery chorus ("L'armi impugnamo"—"Courons aux armes") in which they swear to avenge their dead. At its conclusion the men draw their weapons and prepare to follow Raoul. There is wild disorder as the curtain falls.

[*Scene Two*] The cloister of a Huguenot church, partially in ruins as the result of the fighting, where many Huguenots have taken refuge. Shouts and gunfire sound in the distance. Marcel, Raoul, and Valentine appear. Raoul exclaims over Marcel's wounds. The old soldier says that the church is surrounded by their foes and there is nothing left but to die. Raoul turns to leave, saying that he must go back to the fighting, but Valentine restrains him.

She suggests that he tie a white scarf around his arm and go with her to the Louvre, where he will be safe under the protection of the Queen. When Raoul asks what he must do to save his life, Valentine answers that he must turn Catholic. Then, she says, she can freely give him her love. Flatly refusing to betray his faith, Raoul asks about Nevers. Valentine tells him that her husband has been slain. Again Valentine implores Raoul to go with her, but a quiet word from Marcel strengthens his resolve not to yield. In a dramatic and poignant refrain ("Così, io ti vedro perir"—"Ainsi je te verrai périr") Valentine makes her final plea. So great is her love, she cries to Raoul, that she will risk eternal damnation by renouncing her faith for his. After the aria she asks

---

[2] In some versions the opera ends at this point.

Marcel to consecrate their union with his blessing. As they kneel before him and he raises his hands, the Huguenots softly intone the Lutheran chorale. In a brief trio ("Nell'unir vostre man"— "Savez-vous qu'en joignant") Marcel asks the lovers if they will remain true to their vows. Valentine and Raoul devoutly respond.

The tender and tragic mood of the scene is shattered by the harsh voices of the oncoming Catholic soldiers, calling on the Huguenots in the church to yield or die. From within the dark recesses come answers of defiance. There are sounds of a brief but fierce encounter, followed by a terrible silence. Listening, Marcel murmurs that the Huguenots will never sing again.

An impressive trio follows ("Ah, vedete il ciel"—"Ah! voyez! le ciel") as Marcel, Valentine, and Raoul, inspired by the heroic defiance of their people, join in expressions of religious ecstasy over a vision of heaven and bid farewell to earth. The Catholic soldiers finally burst in and call on them to recant or die. Oblivious to everything in their joy, Valentine, Marcel, and Raoul sing the phrases of the chorale and then, in ringing tones, hurl their defiance at the soldiers. As they are dragged away the curtain falls.

[*Scene Three*] A street in Paris. A crowd of Catholic soldiers stampedes by, shouting for revenge. As they go on their way Marcel and Valentine appear, supporting Raoul. They have managed to escape their captors, but, in fleeing, Raoul has been mortally wounded. St. Bris approaches through the darkness at the head of his soldiers. When he demands that the three identify themselves, Raoul, despite Valentine's desperate efforts to keep him quiet, shouts, "Huguenots." St. Bris gives the order to fire. Rushing over to the group as they fall, St. Bris cries out in anguish as he recognizes his daughter. Gasping that she will pray for him in heaven, Valentine falls dead beside the bodies of Marcel and Raoul.

As the soldiers gather around, savagely clamoring for further revenge, Marguerite's equipage appears. She is returning from the nuptial ball and is on her way to the Louvre. Transfixed with horror, she gazes upon the bodies and then tries vainly to silence the bloodthirsty shouts of the soldiers as the curtain falls.

# Jenufa
## (*Her Ward—Její Pastorkyně*)
### *by* LEOŠ JANÁČEK
### (1854–1928)

### *Libretto by the composer*

*Based on the drama of the same name by Gabriella Preissova*

#### CHARACTERS

| | |
|---|---|
| Grandmother Buryjovka, housekeeper at the mill | Alto |
| Laca Klemen ⎰ stepbrothers, Buryjovka's grandsons | ⎰ Tenor |
| Steve Buryja ⎱ | ⎱ Tenor |
| Kostelnitchka Buryjovka, a widow, Buryjovka's daughter | Soprano |
| Jenufa, Kostelnitchka's stepdaughter | Soprano |
| The Miller | Baritone |
| The Mayor | Bass |
| His wife | Mezzo-soprano |
| Charlotte, their daughter | Mezzo-soprano |
| Maidservant | Mezzo-soprano |
| Barena, servant girl at the mill | Soprano |
| Jano, a cowherd | Soprano |
| A woman | Alto |

Villagers, musicians, young people

*Place:* A village in eastern Moravia
*Time:* Early nineteenth century
*First performance:* Czech National Theater, Brno (Brünn),
Moravia, January 21, 1904
*Original language:* Czech

----

The Moravian composer Leoš Janáček, along with Antonin Dvořák and Bedřich Smetana, formed the historic triumvirate of artists who expressed in music the intensely nationalistic spirit of the Czechoslovakian people. Janáček himself was a specialist in folk music and developed specific theories about the effect of national speech rhythms on musical expression. He employed these theories in his operas—notably *Jenufa*—to infuse them with rugged peasant vitality that gives voice to elemental emotions in uninhibited flow of melody.

*Jenufa* is essentially an example of Czech *verismo*. The drama on which it is based had its source in an actual occurrence described in court records—a fact which recalls the origin of Leoncavallo's *Pagliacci*. Janáček spent ten years writing *Jenufa*, never losing faith in its worth as an expression of the true Czech spirit. He dedicated it to the memory of his daughter, Olga, whose illness and death at the age of twenty-one shadowed the years of his work on the opera.

The third of the composer's ten operas, *Jenufa* at first was slow in finding favor with the public. After its premiere in 1904 it virtually disappeared from the repertoire, but following its revival in Prague in 1916, *Jenufa* brought Janáček international fame. Translated into German, it was given in Vienna in 1918 with Maria Jeritza in the title role.

Its first performance in America was at the Metropolitan, also with Jeritza. There was little interest in the work at the time and it was dropped from the repertoire. Subsequently, it was performed by the Chicago Lyric Opera Company in 1959, then in 1966 by Thomas Scherman and the Little Orchestra Society in New York in concert form.

A recent performance of *Jenufa* in this country was that given by the Hamburg State Opera Company at the Metropolitan, Lincoln Center, New York, on June 26, 1967. The leading male role of Laca was sung by the American tenor Richard Cassily, formerly a member of the New York City Opera Company.

There is a brief but vigorous overture dominated by a broad, sweeping theme in 6/4 tempo over a pizzicato in the basses. A xylophone obbligato gives the effect of the clacking of the mill wheel, which is part of the background of the opening scene.

## ACT ONE

A rustic mill in an isolated section of eastern Moravia. In front of the mill is a footbridge over the millstream. At right a peasant hut with a porch; at left another hut. There are bushes about, and a number of fallen trees. Jenufa stands near the millstream, looking off into the distance; Grandmother sits on the porch peeling potatoes. Laca, seated on a tree trunk, is carving a whip handle out of a branch.

Jenufa, waiting for Steve, her lover, frets because he has not returned, and sings that last night she was haunted by terrible fears ("Uz se večer chyh"). Overcome by anxiety, she kneels and prays to the Virgin Mary ("O panno Maria"), at the same time revealing her agonizing secret: If Steve is called up for military service, they cannot be married—and thus her shame will become known. She is soon to have a child by Steve. Jenufa ends her prayer with a plea for mercy.

Grandmother breaks in to complain that Jenufa is idling instead of helping an old woman whose eyesight is failing. With that, Laca comments in an ironic refrain ("Vy starenko"), sung over a repeated triplet figure in the orchestra. With some bitterness he remarks that there are many things Grandmother no longer can see—she mistakes him for the Miller, for one thing.

He is well aware, he goes on accusingly, that he is not her grandson. She always ignored him and favored Steve when they were children. But all he wants now, Laca sings, is his inheritance of twelve hundred gulden, and then he will go where he pleases.

Jenufa's voice blends with Laca's as she chides him for his disrespect toward Grandmother. In jealous irritation, Laca says that no one can expect Jenufa to keep her mind on her work when all her thoughts are on Steve. Wincing at his resentful look, Jenufa turns to Grandmother and tries to placate her. In a tender, melodic passage ("Stařenko, nehněvejte se!") she sings that she will make amends for Laca's rudeness.

Going toward the porch, she happens to notice that her rosemary plant is withering and needs watering. With a sigh, Jenufa sings that if it should wither, all the luck in the world would wither with it ("A kdyby mi uschla"). This meditative phrase, softly dying away, emotionally foreshadows Jenufa's tragedy. It is a striking illustration of how Janáček used the repetition of words or brief phrases—typical of Czech folk music—to produce a psychological effect.

Jenufa's thoughts are interrupted by a shout from Jano, the young cowherd, who rushes in excitedly waving a piece of paper. He exclaims that he has learned how to read, and entreats Jenufa to write out another lesson for him. She promises to do so, and also to teach him how to write. Jano skips happily away. Grandmother commends Jenufa for helping the villagers, adding that she has a man's head on her shoulders and should have been a teacher.

Jenufa answers ruefully that, as for her poor head, she lost it long ago.

An ensemble scene now follows. The Miller enters and notices Laca trying to carve out his whip handle. When Laca complains that the knife is dull, the Miller takes a whetstone from his pocket and offers to sharpen it. Laca meanwhile teases Jenufa by flicking her scarf from her head with his stick. When she remonstrates, he sneers that she would not mind if Steve did the same thing. Exasperated, Jenufa runs into the house.

Gazing longingly after her, Laca admires her beauty and the Miller adds his words of approval. With malicious satisfaction, Laca says that he deliberately put worms in the flowerpot to wither the rosemary—just the way Jenufa's marriage to Steve will wither away. The Miller upbraids him angrily for his spitefulness, then taunts him for being in love with the girl. Laca scoffs at this. At any rate, he says, if Steve was drafted today, that will end everything between him and Jenufa.

But Steve was not drafted, the Miller declares. Jenufa, who at that moment has come out of the house, overhears and gives a cry of joy. The scene continues briefly in quartet form as the four express their reactions. Jenufa rejoices; Grandmother and the Miller comment on Steve's never-failing good luck; Laca fumes over the "injustice" of the situation. Kostelnitchka appears, is told the news about Steve, then goes into the mill. The Miller hands Laca his knife, saying he is unable to sharpen it. He leaves.

Now from the distance come the voices of the recruits singing to the music of the band. In a boisterous chorus ("Všecí ženija") they sing that only those who want to marry are afraid of war. He who has money can stay home; he who has none must go. The recruits swarm in, along with a shouting throng of mill hands and small boys. Finally Steve appears, followed by four fiddlers. Jenufa joyously greets him.

Celebrating his escape from the draft, Steve is roaring drunk. When Jenufa reproaches him, he answers in a blustering refrain ("Já napily? To ty mně, Jenufa?"). How could she dare accuse Steve Buryja, who owns a mill and a farm, and who is a prime favorite of all the girls? One even gave him a bouquet, Steve boasts, showing Jenufa the flowers, then tossing them away. Turning to the fiddlers, he throws money to them with both hands and orders them to play Jenufa's favorite song—"It's a long way to Nove Zamky" ("Daleko široko"). This chorus is one of the finest examples of Janáček's technique in the use of native folk song, combining music with the basic rhythms of speech.

The chorus has to do with a legendary tower built of young men. It was crowned, symbolically, with the body of the girl's lover transformed into a golden dome. When the dome tumbled down, the lover's sweetheart caught it in her lap. The chorus is interrupted at intervals by a wild peasant dance called the "odzemek." Steve, seizing Jenufa around the waist, drunkenly tries to dance with her.

Suddenly Kostelnitchka stalks grimly through the crowd and silences the musicians with a wave of her hand. She turns on Jenufa with a torrent of reproof ("A tak bychom slí celým životem") for wasting her time collecting "cast-off coins." She climaxes her diatribe with a stern warning that she will prevent Jenufa's marriage unless Steve promises to stay sober for one year.

The recruits, staring at her in awe, comment on her stern visage. Kostelnitchka, ignoring them, threatens Jenufa that if she heeds Steve instead of her stepmother, God Himself will punish her. Grandmother tries to intercede on Steve's behalf, while Laca contemptuously looks on, secretly relishing the discomfiture of his stepbrother and rival.

As Kostelnitchka leaves, she drops her shawl. Laca, with exaggerated courtesy, snatches it up and hands it to her. She coldly acknowledges the gesture. The festive atmosphere of the scene evaporates as Grandmother orders the musicians and the recruits to leave. In a kindlier tone she advises the crestfallen Steve to go home and sleep off the effects of his drunken brawling. Then she turns to comfort the sobbing Jenufa in a phrase which introduces a lyrical quartet in a minor key—"Every young couple must endure some sorrow" ("Každý párek si musi"). The voices of the others—the Miller, Jenufa and Laca—blend with Grandmother's in the theme of consolation. The mill hands, also repeating the words, sing a melodious choral accompaniment as they follow the others from the scene.

Jenufa and Steve are left alone, and a dramatic colloquy ensues in quasi-recitative. Quietly, but with desperate earnestness, Jenufa implores Steve to show decent concern for her plight and warns him not to provoke her stepmother any further. Things will be bad enough, she cries, when the birth of the child will reveal her sin. Now that he has been released from the draft, Steve must marry her.

Resorting to bluster to hide his fright, Steve retorts that Kostelnitchka is hounding him unjustly . . . she is mean and suspicious. His intentions are honorable, he insists. After all, he adds boastfully, he is Steve Buryja, the prime favorite of all the girls.

Infuriated by his arrogance, Jenufa seizes him by the shoulders and storms that she alone has claim upon him. If he fails her now, she warns, she will commit suicide. Alarmed by this threat, Steve promises Jenufa that he will never desert her ("Však tě snad nenechám tak"). Grandmother, who has been listening to the two young people arguing, urges them to desist. Again she advises Steve to go home and rest. Making the most of the situation, Steve melodramatically sings that Jenufa is the most beautiful of all girls, then strides away. Grandmother goes into the house; Jenufa sits down on the porch and takes up her work, her head bowed in despair.

Laca enters. With an angry gesture he tosses his stick away and stands for a moment looking at Jenufa. Here begins the duet which leads into the ensemble concluding the act. With his knife still in his hand, Laca moves closer to Jenufa and gloatingly comments that Steve's courage deserted him in the face of Kostelnitchka's anger ("Jak rázem všecko"). Even so, Jenufa retorts, he is a hundred times the better man. Stung by this thrust, Laca picks up the bouquet Steve had thrown away and reminds Jenufa that it came from one of the girls who had smiled at her lover. Jenufa answers that she is proud to have even this token of his love ("Takovou kytkou"). For a moment, Laca stares at her in disbelief. Then in jealous fury he shouts that Steve, the lover she considers "a hundred times the better man," is interested only in her rosy cheeks.

Suddenly Laca looks at the knife in his hand. In an ominously quiet phrase, he murmurs that it could make those same cheeks rosier still. A xylophone passage in the orchestra gives a macabre emphasis to his words. With the knife in one hand and the bouquet in the other, Laca stalks toward Jenufa, who shrinks back in terror. At that moment, Barena, the servant girl, appears and watches the scene, paralyzed with fear.

Laca, raging, asks Jenufa what price she is willing to pay for this gift of flowers. He seizes her in a violent embrace. With a scream of terror, she struggles to escape. Trying to restrain her, Laca gashes her cheek with his knife. The action continues to the thunderous accompaniment of rising and descending sextuplet figures.

Gasping in pain, Jenufa holds her apron to her wounded cheek as Barena stands by helplessly wringing her hands. Laca, shaken by remorse and despair, takes Jenufa in his arms, crying that he has loved her since they were children. Jenufa wrenches herself free and stumbles blindly into the house.

The screaming and confusion bring Grandmother and the Miller rushing to the scene. Barena hysterically tells them what has happened. The Miller dashes into the house, then emerges shouting that Kostelnitchka must be summoned to dress Jenufa's wound. Laca, numbed with horror for a moment, rouses himself and walks slowly away. The Miller roars after him: "You madman, you did this deliberately!" The curtain falls.

## ACT TWO

There is a brief orchestral prelude with an undulating theme in a minor key. The curtain rises on the living room of Kostelnitchka's farmhouse, six months later. Jenufa, her face disfigured by a livid scar, sits at a table sewing. She is pale and obviously despondent.

Kostelnitchka, who has been sitting nearby, opens the door to the adjoining room to let in more warmth. Looking concernedly at Jenufa, she asks why she spends so much time praying to the Virigin Mother. For help in her misery, Jenufa answers sadly. In a quasi-recitative passage, Kostelnitchka reflects on the events of the past months ("Už od té chvile"). When Jenufa finally confessed that she was carrying Steve's child, her stepmother brought her to her own house, where she kept Jenufa hidden until the child was born. To explain her absence for six months, Kostelnitchka told the neighbors that Jenufa had gone to visit relatives in Vienna.

As for Steve, Kostelnitchka says bitterly, he shows not the slightest interest in his child. Jenufa interrupts to hurry to the door of the adjoining room, exclaiming that she heard the child cry. Her tender solicitude is reflected in the gentle, flowing theme which sounds in the orchestra.

Kostelnitchka upbraids Jenufa for making a fuss over the child, saying it would be more to the point if she prayed to be relieved of this unwelcome burden. When Jenufa protests that her baby has not cried once since he was born. Kostelnitchka snaps that the child's constant whimpering is driving her to distraction. She turns on Jenufa with a flood of ill-tempered reproach.

Exhausted by the bickering, Jenufa murmurs that she wishes to go to bed. With a sinister glance at her, Kostelnitchka pours out a drink from a small pan on the stove and hands it to Jenufa, saying it will help her sleep. To the accompaniment of a lyrical theme in the orchestra, Jenufa drinks the potion, bids her stepmother goodnight and walks slowly into the other room. Kostelnitchka closes the door behind her as the music dies away.

Alone, Kostelnitchka gives way to her pent-up anger and hatred in a dramatic soliloquy ("Ba, ta tvoje okenička"). For twenty weeks, she fumes, this gallant lover of her daughter has not dared come near the house. But today he will be here, because she made him promise to come, and so the matter will be settled once for all. And then there is this child, a pale, helpless wretch like his father . . . she hates the one as much as the other.

In harsh, disjointed phrases, Kostelnitchka sings that she prayed the child never would be born. Her prayers were in vain—the child is a week old and still alive. In suppressed fury she murmurs that now she must face the humiliation of begging Steve to marry Jenufa.

There is a knock at the door. Kostelnitchka quickly locks the door of Jenufa's room, then admits Steve. Eyeing her suspiciously, he asks her why she has sent for him. In answer, Kostelnitchka points to the door of Jenufa's room. Alarmed, Steve asks if something has happened to her. Telling him that Jenufa and the child are well, Kostelnitchka angrily berates him for neglecting his son. Steve whines that he often thought of the baby, but stayed away because he did not want to face Kostelnitchka's accusations. And besides, he adds callously, Jenufa has lost her beauty—and for that he is not to blame.

Kostelnitchka flings open the door of Jenufa's room and points inside. "There is your son," she cries. "His name is Steve . . . I christened him myself!" Momentarily overcome by pity and affection, Steve then and there offers to support the baby and Jenufa on the condition that his fatherhood is kept secret.

Thereupon Kostelnitchka turns on him in furious denunciation ("Odivej se také na ni") for bringing shame upon Jenufa, then deserting her like a coward. Her anger changes to desperate entreaty as she falls to her knees and begs him not to abandon those who belong to him by the sacred law of parenthood. Momentarily overcome, Steve buries his face in his hands.

But suddenly he tears himself away from Kostelnitchka, crying that marriage would only bring tragedy both to Jenufa and himself. Puzzled, Kostelnitchka asks why. Steve's answer, in an agitated refrain ("Proto, že se ji bojim"), is deliberately evasive until he finally blurts out the truth. First he insists he is afraid of Jenufa because she has changed from a gay young girl into a sad and unfriendly creature. Besides, the disfiguring wound on her cheek completely banished his love for her.

Then, to Kostelnitchka's consternation, he tells her he also is afraid of her. She seems like a witch who is constantly spying on him. But in any case, he goes on with brash candor, he cannot marry Jenufa because he is engaged to the Mayor's daughter, Charlotte. Kostelnitchka recoils with a scream of fury as Steve dashes out of the door.

As she glares after him, Jenufa's voice is heard from her room in an eerie wail over an insistently repeated note in the orchestra. Tormented by a dream, Jenufa cries that a huge rock is falling on her. Kostelnitchka listens, realizes that Jenufa is still asleep, then again abandons herself to the torturing thoughts of Steve's treachery. She rages that she longs to throw the body of Steve's wretched offspring at his feet and force him to acknowledge it as a symbol of his guilt. Her baleful outburst is given emphasis by a piercing dissonance high in the strings. Then, spent by her fury, she murmurs desolately: "Now who will save her?"

At that moment, Laca enters unobserved and overhears her. For a moment he is taken aback. Quickly recovering, he comes forward and casually asks Kostelnitchka if Steve and Jenufa have made their plans for marriage. They did not even talk together, the stepmother replies gloomily. Laca, in sudden excitement, asks her if she now will give Jenufa to him—as she had promised. He swears he will never leave her.

Thereupon Kostelnitchka tells him the grim truth: Jenufa never went to Vienna, but was hidden here in this house while she gave birth to Steve's son. Although stunned by this disclosure, Laca asks if he now will be obliged to take both Jenufa and the child. The child is dead, Kostelnitchka replies. Steve knows, she adds, and she will have revenge upon him for his perfidy. As though the thought suddenly occurred to her, Kostelnitchka asks Laca to leave immediately to find out when Steve and Charlotte are to be married. As she virtually pushes him out of the room, Laca promises to "be back in a moment."

Now follows Kostelnitchka's great soliloquy, one of the climactic moments in the opera, in which she plans the murder of Jenufa's child ("Co chvila . . . a ja si mán"). In hushed, fear-stricken tones she sings that the "moment" in which Laca said he would return will be for her an eternity of agony. Feverishly she tries to decide on a course of action. Shall she hide the baby? No . . . alive, it soon would be discovered—and her daughter's shame still would live on. Suddenly she comes to a decision: She will give the child back to God ("Já Pánubohu chlapce zanesu"). The phrase is sung to the accompaniment of a semiquaver figure in the orchestra which musically reflects her growing dementia. In spring, when the ice melts, there will be no trace of the body, Kostelnitchka babbles, thinking of the millstream. And so, this sinless child will go back to heaven. . . .

Half crazed by her sense of guilt, Kostelnitchka imagines she sees accusing eyes staring at her. She stabs a forefinger into the air, crying that this is how they will point to Kostelnitchka when they learn of her monstrous crime. Then with insane cunning she steals into Jenufa's room, picks up the child and wraps him in her shawl. As a menacing theme thunders in the orchestra, she pauses and looks down at the baby. Dementedly she cries: "He was born in sin—like the black soul of Steve!" Clasping the child to her breast, Kostelnitchka rushes out of the house, locking the door from the outside.

A moment later Jenufa enters and begins the scene which brings the opera to the peak of tragedy. Still under the influence of the drug given her by Kostelnitchka, she calls dazedly for her stepmother ("Mamičko, mám těžkou hlavu") and stares vacantly around the room. Like a sleepwalker she goes to the window, opens the shutters and gazes up at the sky. In disjointed phrases she sings about the stars and the moon, and then her thoughts turn to Steve. If only he would come to see his little blue-eyed boy . . .

The thought of her baby sends her rushing back into her room with a cry of alarm. In a frenzy she tears away the bedclothes, searching for the child. Momentarily deranged, she implores unseen neighbors not to harm the boy, and sobs that she and Steve alone are guilty. With a wild scream of terror she rushes to the door and tries to tear it open.

At that moment her reason partially returns and she becomes calm. Making a supreme effort to collect her thoughts, Jenufa tells herself that ". . . this is Mother's room . . . the door is locked . . . Mother has taken little Steve to the mill to see his father . . . but now I must pray for him. . . ." Kneeling before a picture of the Virgin Mary, she sings the beautiful prayer "Zdrávas královno" ("We greet thee, O Queen"). She concludes the prayer with a feverish plea for the safe return of her baby.

Suddenly the door bursts open and Kostelnitchka staggers in. She is haggard and shivering with cold. Jenufa eagerly asks if Steve has seen his child and if he will bring the boy back and stay with her. In answer, Kostelnitchka tells the girl that she has been out of her mind with fever for the past two days, and during that time the baby died.

Jenufa crumples to her knees and buries her face in her stepmother's lap. A theme of indescribable sorrow sweeps through the orchestra as she sobs in her anguish: "Mother, my heart is breaking" ("Mamičko, srdce mi bolí"). It is one of the most profoundly moving moments in the opera.

Unmoved by her grief, Kostelnitchka coldly tells her to thank God for being free of her burden at last. Jenufa asks her if she has sent for Steve, as she had promised. The scoundrel deserves nothing but curses, Kostelnitchka replies fiercely. When he finally came to see his son, she goes on, she begged on her knees for his help—but his only answer was to offer money. In frantic self-justification, Kostelnitchka repeats Steve's words: He was afraid of Jenufa because of her scar, afraid of Kostelnitchka because she was a witch . . . . and now he is going to marry Charlotte, the Mayor's daughter. There is a striking musical effect here as Jenufa, in repeated phrases almost like an obbligato to her stepmother's theme of accusation, sings a prayer asking forgiveness for Steve.

Kostelnitchka, now aware that Jenufa no longer has any strength left to resist, urges her to bestow her affections on Laca, a decent young man who can be trusted. Seeing him approaching at that moment, she adds hastily that he knows the entire story and is willing to forgive.

In response to Laca's affectionate greeting, Jenufa thanks him warmly for his kind thoughts of her ("Děkuji ti, Laco"). From this point the dialogue continues in duet and trio form. When Jenufa mournfully says that she has reached the end of her life, Laca asks her point-blank if she will marry him. Kostelnitchka, trembling with excitement, entreats Jenufa to accept his proposal.

Chiding her stepmother for her presumption, Jenufa reminds Laca that now she is a woman without money and without honor . . . a woman unworthy of pure love. Does he then, she asks, still want her as his wife?

In answer, Laca takes her in his arms and passionately declares his love. Jenufa, overcome with happiness, responds in a lyrical phrase that now they can face the good and bad in life together. Kostelnitchka gives them her blessing.

But as she does so, a sinister theme begins to sound in the orchestra. It continues with increasing intensity as Kostelnitchka launches into a denunciation of Steve as the cause of all the past misfortune. Losing all control, she curses Steve, the woman he will marry and herself. As she collapses in a chair, a violent gust of wind wrenches a window open. Over a descending chromatic passage in the orchestra, Kostelnitchka, mad with fear, wails that she hears a howling from the river. She throws herself into Laca's arms. Jenufa, slamming the window shut, exclaims that the wind is icy. In a phrase which rises to a maniacal scream, then drops to a gasp of horror, Kostelnitchka cries: ". . . As though Death is trying to enter here!" The curtain falls to a clamorous fanfare.

## ACT THREE

Kostelnitchka's room, as in Act Two. A white tablecloth is spread over the table, on which is a pot of rosemary, a bottle of wine, glasses and a plate of cakes. Jenufa, in her Sunday dress, is seated at the table, prayer book in hand; a maidservant is arranging her shawl. Laca is standing nearby. Also in the room are Grandmother and Kostelnitchka, who is restlessly pacing back and forth. She is pale and worn.

A scene in quasi-recitative follows as the Mayor and his wife arrive for the wedding festivities and are greeted by Jenufa, Laca and Kostelnitchka. As greetings are exchanged, Kostelnitchka grows more excited and distraught, and acts irrationally. One moment she exclaims that today Jenufa will be betrothed to a good and upright man; in the next, she presses her hands to her head and wails that she has not been able to sleep. When Jenufa assures her that she soon will be well again, Kostelnitchka hysterically protests that a long life would be a horror. Staring wildly, she cries: "What then?" Abruptly coming to her senses, she quietly wishes Jenufa well on her wedding day.

A lively discussion now ensues about Jenufa's wedding dress, which the Mayor's wife considers much too simple and severe for the occasion. When Kostelnitchka remarks rather tartly that even royal brides prefer to dress simply these days, the Mayor's wife sniffs that she would never think of going to the altar in anything but her best finery. The discussion ends when Kostelnitchka invites everyone into Jenufa's room to look at the trousseau—which, the stepmother says proudly, she herself made.

Jenufa and Laca, remaining behind, exchange confidences in an ensuing duet which begins when Jenufa remarks wryly on the comments about her wedding costume. Laca shyly hands her a bouquet, which she pins to her jacket, murmuring that Laca deserves a better bride than she. Brushing aside her self-denigration, he assures her that his only wish is to atone for all the sorrow he has caused her. He confesses he was jealous and envious of Steve, but because of her love he has banished these evil thoughts. In fact, Laca says, he has invited Steve and his bride-to-be to the wedding.

At that moment Steve and Charlotte arrive and the scene continues briefly in quartet form. Steve is ill at ease, and Charlotte speaks for him in a brief refrain ("Pánbůh rač dát dobrý den"). It is Steve's fault they are late, she explains. Today they will only be onlookers, but their turn at the altar will come. She wishes the bridal couple luck, and Steve self-consciously joins her. At Jenufa's urging, the two young men shake hands.

The four continue chatting until the others re-enter, which leads into a short ensemble passage. While the Mayor complains good-naturedly about the ordeal of inspecting the trousseau, Kostelnitchka, in an aside to Laca, says that it was only because of him that she consented to Steve's presence at the wedding. It was Jenufa's wish too, Laca replies quietly.

Meanwhile, Barena and a group of village girls come by to extend their good wishes, which they do in a spirited chorus ("Nepozvali jste nás"). They sing that even though they weren't invited, they want to add some merrymaking to the occasion. They follow with a typical peasant folk song ("Ej mamko, maměnko moja!"). Its theme is a lighthearted conversation between a mother and daughter—about marriage, of course. At its conclusion, Barena hands Janufa a bouquet. She thanks the girls warmly as they leave.

Laca warns that the wedding party must be at the church promptly at nine o'clock. The Mayor announces that it is now time for the nuptial blessing. Laca and Jenufa kneel before Grandmother. She intones the blessing ("Tož já vám zehnám") over a hushed minor theme in the orchestra expressed in a repeated chromatic figure. At its conclusion, Grandmother adds softly to Laca: "Remember me with love."

The Mayor then calls on Kostelnitchka to give her blessing, remarking banteringly that she probably "will do it like a parson." But just as she raises her hands, there is a babble of voices outside, with shouts of ". . . some beast has murdered the child!" Kostelnitchka gasps in terror. This marks the beginning of the opera's powerful climax.

Jano bursts in with the news that a child's body has been found in the millstream by the men who were cutting ice. He begs the Mayor to look at the body. The Mayor rushes out, followed by all but Steve, Kostelnitchka and Grandmother. Over the accompaniment of a driving figure in descending chromatics, Kostelnitchka frantically calls for Jenufa to help her. Grandmother tries to calm her. Steve, panic-stricken, dashes for the door, but is met by Charlotte, who sends him sprawling back inside. Jenufa is heard outside, screaming that the child is her son. Laca drags her into the house and tries desperately to quiet her. The Mayor follows, holding the baby's blanket and red cap, which were found with the body. Staring at them, Jenufa, mad with grief, wails that her poor child does not even have a coffin or a wreath.

The townspeople, shouting that Jenufa has killed her child and should be stoned to death, crowd threateningly into the room. Jenufa implores Steve to flee. As the Mayor stands irresolute, Laca confronts the throng and roars that he will kill anyone who touches Jenufa. Awed by his furious defiance, the people stare at him in sudden silence.

Kostelnitchka drags herself to her feet and in dramatic, unaccompanied phrases begins her terrible confession. As her listeners gasp in horror, she tells how, to save her daughter's honor, she kept Jenufa in her house until the baby was born, so that no one would know. She explained Jenufa's absence by saying the girl was in Vienna. Then one night she gave Jenufa a sleeping potion, took her sleeping child to the millstream and pushed him under the ice. And from that moment on, she knew she was a murderess. In stricken tones, Kostelnitchka adds that she told Jenufa her baby had died while she lay unconscious from fever.

Jenufa bursts out in a wild cry of rage. Charlotte, who has been listening stunned with horror, whirls on Steve and cries that he is to blame for this disaster. Hysterically she runs to her mother and demands to be taken home, saying she would rather die than marry Steve. He himself buries his face in his hands and stumbles blindly away.

Laca, in agonized self-accusation, moans that it is he who is to blame because he disfigured Jenufa and caused Steve to reject her. With dramatic suddenness, to the sound of a serene major chord in the orchestra, Jenufa steps forward. Lifting Kostelnitchka to her feet, she says quietly that now there has been enough of shame and disgrace. Kostelnitchka, screaming that she will kill herself before the police come for her, rushes toward the adjoining room. But she stops abruptly, muttering that the police would hold Jenufa responsible for her death.

In ringing phrases, Jenufa sings that at this moment she understands everything. Turning to the crowd, she entreats them not to condemn. They must forgive this woman, because the Redeemer Himself will not deny her mercy. Laca is outraged at Jenufa's magnanimity. In a final dramatic entreaty ("Odpust' mi jenom ty"), Kostelnitchka implores forgiveness. She loved herself more than her daughter, she sings, and is no longer worthy to be called "Mother." Yet now she receives strength from the very one whose life she has ruined—strength to face the ordeal of expiation. Turning to the Mayor, she orders him to take her away. As he does so, and the others follow, Jenufa murmurs: "God be with you."

Facing Laca, Jenufa calmly tells him that all the others have gone and now he too must go ("Odešli . . . Jdi také!"). This marks the beginning of the magnificent duet which concludes the opera. Jenufa sings that, after what has happened, marriage would be impossible. She blesses Laca, adding that he is the best man she ever has known. She long ago forgave him the senseless crime of slashing her face. Like herself, she says, he sinned because he loved.

Laca's answer is a question ("Ty odejdeš do světa"): Will she go in search of a new life without taking him with her? Jenufa warns that she will have to testify in court and bare her shame to the world. Laca passionately declares that for her love he will endure anything—nothing matters so long as they have each other. As Jenufa ecstatically sings his name, he enfolds her in his arms. The music surges to a lyrical climax as the curtain falls.

# La Juive

*by* JACQUES HALÉVY

(1799–1862)

*Libretto by*
EUGENE SCRIBE

### CHARACTERS

| | |
|---|---|
| Eleazar, a wealthy Jewish goldsmith | Tenor |
| Rachel, his daughter | Soprano |
| Albert, sergeant at arms of the Emperor's archers | Baritone |
| Prince Léopold | Tenor |
| Ruggiero, provost of the city of Constance | Bass |
| Town Crier | Baritone |
| Cardinal Brogni | Bass |
| Princess Eudoxia, niece of the Emperor and wife of Prince Léopold | Soprano |

Townspeople, soldiers, Jews, ladies and gentlemen of the court, dancers, an officer, a major-domo

*Place:* The city of Constance
*Time:* 1414
*First performance:* Grand Opéra, Paris, February 23, 1835
*Original language:* French

---

Although Halévy was somewhat overshadowed by Meyerbeer, his contemporary, he was an eminent musician in his own right and was highly respected by other composers of his day. Halévy composed more than thirty operas, but *La Juive*, which established his fame, is the only one which has survived in modern operatic repertoire.

There is an elaborate overture, which states several important themes of the opera—principally the strongly contrasting themes symbolic of Eleazar's steadfast loyalty to his faith, and the power of the Christian church.

## ACT ONE

A square in the city of Constance. At one side is the entrance
of a large church. Opposite is the shop and home of Eleazar, the
goldsmith, and his daughter Rachel. The doors of the church are
open, and a number of people unable to get inside are kneeling
at the entrance and on the steps. Inside the church the choir is
heard chanting a *Te Deum*. One of the worshipers outside looks
across the square at Eleazar's shop and angrily remarks that the
Jew is working on a Christian festival day.

As the others murmur against this desecration in a brief choral
phrase, Eleazar appears at the door of his shop and gazes defiantly
at the throng. Rachel appears at his side and entreats him to return
inside so that he will not further provoke the crowd. As the Jew
and his daughter retire, the concluding phrases of the *Te Deum*
peal forth.

Unnoticed by the people at the church, a man in a long cloak
strides across the square. He encounters Albert, sergeant at arms
of the Emperor's archers, who recognizes him as Prince Léopold
and expresses astonishment at seeing the Prince on what is apparently a secret visit to the city. The Prince cautions him to be
silent, saying that Emperor Sigismond must be kept in ignorance of
his presence in the city at least until nightfall.

Léopold then asks the reason for the great crowd at the church
and the general air of festivity. Albert explains that the Emperor
has called together the council of nobles and prelates, following
the defeat of the heretic John Huss and his adherents. The Emperor's aim, says Albert, is to rally all Christians under the
banner of one faith, the better to stem the onslaught of all
infidels throughout the world. Now that the Hussites have fallen,
Albert continues, Emperor Sigismond has ordered the people to
give thanks. Albert and Léopold then leave the square. The people
raise their voices in an exultant chorus of thanks for the victory
("Hosanna, plaisir, ivresse").

At the conclusion of the chorus, Ruggiero, provost of Constance,
announces that a royal edict will be read by the Town Crier. In
dramatic recitative ("Monseigneur Léopold, avec l'aide de Dieu")
the Crier proclaims that Prince Léopold, with God's help, has put
down the Hussite rebellion. In recognition of the victory, the
Emperor and Cardinal Brogni declare this a day of Christian
festivity and thanksgiving in the churches. Wine shall flow from
the fountains in the square and the people are to rejoice. The

crowd acclaims the beneficence of the Emperor and the Cardinal in powerful choral phrases.

During a moment of silence the sound of hammering is heard. When Ruggiero asks who dares work on this sacred day some of the people in the crowd tell him that the offender is Eleazar, the rich goldsmith. Thereupon Ruggiero orders his guard to bring Eleazar before him, declaring that the Jew must be punished for his insolent disregard of proprieties. With Rachel clinging to his arm, Eleazar is dragged from his shop by the guardsmen. When Rachel distractedly asks what her father has done to deserve punishment Ruggiero denounces Eleazar for working on a church festival day. Eleazar retorts that he is an Israelite and owes no respect to the God of the Christians. He has every reason to hate them, he shouts, for it was the Christians who burned his two sons at the stake before his very eyes. Ruggiero, infuriated by Eleazar's defiance, tells him that he will suffer the same fate, for the Emperor has decreed death for heretics.

The proceedings are interrupted by the approach of Cardinal Brogni. Bowing obsequiously before him, Ruggiero informs him that he has arrested two heretics for profaning the festival day by working. The Cardinal asks the Jew his name. When Eleazar replies, Brogni remarks that the name seems familiar. Eleazar recalls that when Brogni was in Rome, before he took holy orders, he had a wife and daughter. Brogni sharply orders him to be silent, murmuring that their loss was a tragedy he wishes to forget. Now, he says, he lives only to serve God.

Eleazar, still angry and defiant, asks the Cardinal if he remembers banishing him from Rome. As Ruggiero fumes over the Jew's audacity Brogni quietly asks Eleazar's pardon, tells him he is to go free, and expresses the hope that they will henceforth be friends.

In a majestic refrain ("Si la rigeur et la vengeance") Brogni, addressing the crowd before him, declares that hatred and bitterness must give way to compassion and mercy. An ensemble develops as Rachel voices her relief at hearing the Cardinal's plea for tolerance, while the people praise his kindness. Eleazar, however, grimly resolves that he will never allow himself to be drawn into friendship with the Christians. Ruggiero, gazing at him in scorn and contempt, asserts that goodness is the refuge of the weak and that the soul triumphs by the sword alone. Brogni concludes by exhorting the people to remember the admonition of the Holy Scriptures: Forgive your enemies.

The Cardinal and Ruggiero retire, Eleazar and Rachel return to their home, and the crowd disperses. When the square is quiet Léopold appears and looks cautiously around. Stepping quickly into the shadow of the balcony of Eleazar's house, he sings a tender serenade ("Loin de son amie vivre sans plaisirs"), in which he expresses the joy of being reunited with his beloved after a long absence. In the second stanza he sings that the charms of other scenes were lost upon him because the one he loved was not at his side. He thought only of the day when he could return to her arms. After his serenade Rachel comes out on the balcony. Her song blends with Léopold's as she sings of the happiness of hearing his voice again, while he rejoices over returning to her.

Leaving the balcony and coming out of the house, Rachel eagerly greets Léopold, addressing him as "Samuel." (For the sake of carrying on his romance Léopold has taken the name of Samuel and has told Rachel that he is a Jewish artist.) Léopold tenderly asks Rachel if she still loves him. She fervently reassures him, saying that she is happy in her love, for they have the same religion and the same God. Samuel's art, she goes on, means more to her than all her father's treasures. Eagerly Léopold asks when he may see her again. Tonight, at the Feast of the Passover, Rachel answers, because at that rite all Israelites are welcome at her father's house. With that she sends Léopold away and hurries inside.

In a few moments the people crowd into the square, eager to begin the feasting and drinking. Surrounding the fountains, which shortly begin to flow with wine as promised in the royal proclamation, they begin the chorus introducing the magnificent finale of the act ("Hâtons-nous, car l'heure s'avance"). Urging each other to make the most of this joyous occasion, they drink to the Emperor, the Cardinal, and the members of the council, and then dance around the fountains to the rhythm of a spirited waltz. The dancing stops when the royal procession is seen approaching, and the people hail the dignitaries in a continuation of the chorus.

Eleazar and Rachel thread their way through the jostling throng toward the steps of the church, from which vantage point they hope to watch the procession, which is being held to celebrate Prince Léopold's victory over the Hussites. Just as they reach the steps they are espied by Ruggiero, who promptly calls the attention of the crowd to the fact that Jews have dared to profane the steps of the church by their presence. In an angry chorus ("Au lac, oui, plongeons dans le lac") the people shout that they will throw the Jews into the lake as punishment for their impiety. Eleazar pours out his scorn and contempt for their threats, while Rachel vainly

tries to quiet him. At the height of the altercation Albert rides up
and orders Eleazar and Rachel to be seized.

Léopold suddenly appears. At a sign from him Albert calls off
his soldiers, who, on seeing the Prince, draw back respectfully.
Rachel is dumfounded at seeing the man she knows as Samuel, an
artist and a Jew, wielding unquestioned authority over the royal
soldiers. As he rushes to her she entreats him not to intervene lest
he fall victim to the fury of the mob. Meanwhile the attention of
the people has been distracted by the approaching procession.
They acclaim the glittering pageant of cavaliers, warriors, and
dignitaries of Church and State in a vigorous chorus ("Le cortège,
le voici, plaçons-nous").

The voices of Rachel, Eleazar, Léopold, and Albert are heard in
interludes as they express their reactions to the situation. Rachel
prays that it may be made clear to her why Samuel has suddenly
appeared as a powerful leader of the Christian forces. Clinging to
his daughter, Eleazar implores her to flee with him from the
scene of their persecution and shame. Léopold confides to Albert
that Rachel must never learn the mystery of his dual identity, saying that if she were to learn the truth it would shatter her love
for him.

As the Emperor and the Cardinal appear, followed by their
retinues, the chorus swells to a thunderous climax, a *Te Deum*
mingling with shouts of acclaim for the Emperor. Léopold suddenly
pushes through the crowd and then vanishes. Utterly bewildered,
Rachel watches him go. Eleazar, standing at her side, scornfully
regards the throng, which moves by, singing and shouting, as the
curtain falls.

## ACT TWO

A room in Eleazar's home, where the Feast of the Passover is
being celebrated. Eleazar, Rachel, and Léopold are seated with a
group of Eleazar's friends around a large table. Led by Eleazar and
Rachel, the Jews chant the ritual prayer ("O Dieu, Dieu de nos
pères"). In an impressive refrain ("Si trahison ou perfide") Eleazar
prays that the wrath of the Hebrew God may fall on all traitors to
the faith. He then calls on all to partake of the unleavened bread.
As it is being distributed Eleazar offers another eloquent prayer
for guidance and strength ("Dieu, que ma voix tremblante"),
in which he asks that the enemies of Zion may be confounded.

To her surprise and dismay Rachel sees Léopold secretly throw

away the bread which has been given him. Her attention is
diverted at that moment by a knock at the door. Men's voices
demand admittance in the name of the Emperor. At Eleazar's
command the ritual vessels and candles are hurriedly concealed
and the table taken away, after which the Jews leave through a
door at the rear of the room.

Léopold is about to go into an adjoining room with Rachel
when Eleazar detains him, saying he may need his help. Rachel
goes into the other room, while Léopold takes his place before an
easel standing at the rear, keeping his back to the entrance door
of the house. When all is in order Eleazar opens the door to find
a woman standing there. Motioning her servants to withdraw, she
enters, glances at the man standing before the easel, and asks
who he is. Recognizing the voice of his wife Eudoxia, Léopold
utters a suppressed exclamation of consternation and dismay.
Eleazar quietly answers that the man is an artist in his employ. He
will be dismissed if the lady so desires, the Jew adds. Smiling,
Eudoxia says that there is nothing secret about her visit. She
then identifies herself as the niece of the Emperor, whereupon
Eleazar kneels respectfully. Ordering him to rise, Eudoxia says
that she has been told that he has a rare piece of jewelry ("Tu
possèdes, diton, un joyau magnifique"). This marks the beginning
of a long dialogue in trio form. Eleazar replies that the jewelry in
question is a costly gold chain set with precious stones which was
once worn by the Emperor Constantine himself.

Eudoxia tells him that she wishes to purchase it as a gift for
her husband, Prince Léopold, who won the glorious victory over
the Hussites. He returns today, she goes on, and then ecstatically
reflects on the bliss of being reunited with him. At these words
Léopold gives way to remorse over the thought that he is destroying the happiness of two women through his faithlessness and
deception. Eleazar murmurs that though he has cursed the Christians there is much solace in the prospect of adding to his wealth
through the sale of the desired gift.

At length he brings forth the chain, and Eudoxia admires its
magnificent workmanship. She readily agrees to pay the price
Eleazar asks—thirty thousand florins—saying that the person for
whom it is intended is well worthy of so superb a gift. Eleazar
increases Léopold's discomfiture by murmuring to him, aside, that
those in love greatly bnefit those who sell. Eudoxia orders Eleazar
to engrave the chain with Prince Léopold's coat of arms and her
own and tells him to deliver it without fail the next day. Eleazar
promises to do so.

The trio is concluded as Eudoxia repeats her expressions of happiness over Prince Léopold's home-coming, and Léopold bitterly reproaches himself for his duplicity. Eleazar mingles expressions of contempt for the Christians with rejoicing over his good fortune. As the ensemble ends with a brilliant flourish, Eleazar escorts Eudoxia to the door and goes out with her.

Rachel, who has not heard the foregoing conversation, reappears from the other room and takes this opportunity to ask Léopold to explain his strange actions before the church and at the Passover feast. Warning that her father is returning, Léopold promises to tell her later. Eleazar re-enters, sees the two whispering together, and suspiciously asks what is troubling them. Without waiting for a reply he tells Léopold to go to his home and orders Rachel to join him at evening prayers. A brief trio follows ("Si trahison ou perfide"), in which Eleazar and Rachel repeat the sentiments expressed during the Passover feast, while Léopold muses over the punishment that may be visited upon him for his treachery.

After Léopold leaves and Eleazar goes into the other room to begin his prayers Rachel voices her fear and confusion in the dramatic aria, "Il va venir! et d'effroi . . . je me sens frémir." She awaits her lover's return with foreboding, not happiness, because distrust and uncertainty envelop her like a dark cloud. Even though she may deceive her father, she reflects, the eyes of God see all her sinful actions. Despairingly she cries that though she should flee to avoid this fateful meeting her strength has failed her.

At the conclusion of the aria Léopold returns. Noticing his look of unhappiness and guilt, she upbraids him for his mysterious and suspicious behavior. To her surprise and horror, her lover confesses that he is a Christian. A dramatic duet follows as Rachel turns on him in anger and scorn ("Lorsqu'à toi je me suis donnée"). In bitter despair she reproaches herself for dishonoring her father by yielding to the love of a Christian. Léopold cries that he has risked his honor and his fortune for her sake. When Rachel reminds him that they can never marry, for the penalty is death, Léopold passionately entreats her to flee with him. They will forget that they are Jew and Christian and will live only for their love.

Rachel recoils at the thought of leaving her father and struggles against Léopold's feverish entreaties. Finally, overwhelmed by her passion for him, she joins him in rapturous expressions of love and devotion. As they declare that the same destiny awaits them both, Eleazar comes unnoticed from the other room and overhears them.

When they turn to leave the house he strides forward and bars their way. In grim tones he asks Rachel where she would go to escape a father's curse. A stormy trio now ensues ("Je vois son front coupable") as Eleazar declares that their guilt is written in their faces and that they will be relentlessly punished for the sin of loving without a father's blessing. Rachel and Léopold voice their terror over his wrath. Turning on Léopold, Eleazar denounces his perfidy, shouting that if he were not of his own race he would strike him dead. Thereupon Léopold tells him to strike the blow, for he is a Christian.

Wild with rage, Eleazar rushes toward Léopold with upraised dagger. Rachel interposes herself between the two men, crying that she is as guilty as Léopold. With poignant eloquence she implores her father to forgive them and to pronounce his blessing on their love. Moved by her pleas, Eleazar finally tells Léopold that he may take Rachel as his bride.

Léopold now confesses that he cannot marry her. Horror-stricken, Rachel and Eleazar ask him why he refuses, to which Léopold answers that the laws of heaven and earth forbid him to marry. Eleazar wildly curses him for his treachery. Rachel, desperate and bewildered by his refusal, vows that she will yet find out his secret. Léopold can only repeat his expressions of remorse and self-reproach. After the trio comes to a stirring climax Léopold hurries away. Eleazar sinks sobbing into a chair. Snatching up the cloak which Léopold has left, Rachel throws it around her shoulders and rushes out to follow him as the curtain falls.

## ACT THREE

[*Scene One*[1]] A room in the Emperor's palace. It is the day of the fete in honor of Prince Léopold's return. Eudoxia enters and, in joyous reflection over the return of her hero, expresses her emotions in a long and fervent aria ("Assez longtemps la crainte et la triste"). At its conclusion a major-domo announces that a pale and distraught young woman is waiting outside and earnestly requests to see the Princess.

The visitor proves to be Rachel, who, determined to learn the secret of Léopold's refusal to marry her, has trailed him to the palace. She is still unaware, however, of his actual identity. With revenge in mind, she asks Eudoxia to allow her to serve as slave in her court for one day—the day of the fete. Startled at the

[1] In some versions this scene is omitted, Act Three beginning with the scene of the fete.

bizarre request, Eudoxia at first refuses, then finally gives her consent. Their voices blend as Rachel sings that Eudoxia's kindness has given her a measure of solace, while the Princess comments to herself that Rachel seems to be buoyed by a strange new hope.

After Rachel leaves, Léopold appears. Noting his anxious, preoccupied air, Eudoxia tries to cheer him by singing a gay and alluring bolero ("Mon doux seigneur et maître"). As she concludes the song a fanfare is heard without. Léopold asks why the trumpets are sounding. Eudoxia informs him that it is the signal for the opening of the fete honoring him as conqueror of the Hussites.

[Scene Two] The gardens of the Emperor's palace, where the royal fete is in progress. The Emperor is seated under a canopy with Cardinal Brogni, Eudoxia, and Léopold. After an opening chorus sung by the people hailing the festal day ("O jour mémorable"), the major-domo announces that there will be a presentation of the ballet pantomime, The Enchanted Tower. The pantomime depicts the assault on an enchanted Moorish castle by cavaliers. In a picturesque struggle the cavaliers strike down the wicked Moors, rush inside, and shortly emerge escorting a group of beautiful ladies whom they have rescued from captivity. During the performance the Emperor and his retinue leave.

Following the ballet, the people sing a vigorous chorus in homage to Prince Léopold ("Sonnez, clairons, que vos chants de victoire"), over which Eudoxia sings a brilliant obbligato by way of expressing her own happiness as the wife of the illustrious hero.

At the conclusion of the chorus, Eleazar, accompanied by Rachel, is escorted to the dais, carrying a golden casket containing the jewel-encrusted chain. Seeing Léopold at Eudoxia's side, Rachel starts back in surprise. Eudoxia takes the chain from the casket and proudly presents it to Léopold, saying that, as his royal wife, she confers the gift in the name of the Emperor.

Revelation of the fact that Léopold is the husband of Eudoxia brings a cry of tragic rage from Eleazar and Rachel. Rushing up on the dais, Rachel tears the chain out of Léopold's hands and gives it back to Eudoxia, storming that he is unworthy of the honor. She denounces him as the vilest of betrayers—one who has committed a crime for which the Christian law demands death. He has given his love to a Jewess, and that Jewess, she cries dramatically, is herself. Léopold cries out in terror and despair, and his words mark the beginning of a powerful ensemble ("Je frissonne et succombe"). All join in expressions of incredulous horror, while

Rachel begs to be allowed to share Léopold's fate. Brogni and Ruggiero, who has meanwhile appeared at the Cardinal's side, ask each other in dismay if the law must inflict its punishment even on their Prince. Eleazar resigns himself to death. The onlookers, calling on God in terror and bewilderment, lament this day of impiety and evil.

Supporting Rachel, Eleazar turns to the royal group on the dais and asks them to prepare the scaffold. In sneering defiance he demands to know if the miscreant is to be spared because of his royal station. Rising, Brogni looks at Léopold, who stands with bowed head. His silence, the Cardinal declares after a moment, is evidence of his guilt. Stretching his hands toward the Prince, Rachel, and Eleazar, Brogni pronounces upon them the terrible anathema of the Church ("Vous qui du Dieu vivant outragez la puissance"). Cursing them, Brogni turns to Léopold and proclaims that he is banished from the church and will be denied absolution. The bodies of the criminals will be left unburied, and no prayers will be said over them. Against them the doors of heaven are shut forever. In a continuation of the chorus the people comment on the grim words of doom. Eudoxia and Rachel both cry out that they would gladly die in Léopold's stead. Eleazar furiously dares Brogni to do his worst, while Léopold implores the Cardinal to spare the Jews. The people grimly intone that the guilty ones must pay the supreme penalty for their impious crime. As the ensemble concludes in a tremendous flood of sound the curtain falls.

## ACT FOUR

A gloomy Gothic room which serves as antechamber to the council room. Guardsmen are stationed about. Eudoxia comes in and hands one of the guards a slip of paper, saying that it is a writ from the Cardinal giving her permission to speak to Rachel. As the guards go to bring Rachel, Eudoxia murmurs that she still loves the Prince and is determined to save him even at the cost of her own life. Rachel is brought in and the two women stand face to face. The guards retire. A long and dramatic dialogue follows, during which the voices of the women blend in duet interludes. As Rachel gazes at Eudoxia with proud contempt, the Princess tells her that the judges have condemned Léopold. Rachel alone can save him now, Eudoxia says. The Jewess sardonically comments on the justice dispensed by the Christian tribunal.

The Princess desperately entreats Rachel to testify that Léo-

pold is innocent and thus save his life. Rachel scornfully rejects
the plea, declaring that her heart is broken and that her only wish
is to die with the man who betrayed her. Though he has ruined
her life, she says, she still loves him. Footsteps sound outside, and
Eudoxia cringes in terror, crying that Léopold is being led before
the council to hear the death sentence. Rachel exclaims in horror,
and then the two voices blend in dramatic phrases of prayer
("Dieu tutélaire"), which bring their conversation to a close. Both
conclude with passionate declarations of love for the Prince.

Cardinal Brogni appears, followed by guards who are to take
Rachel before the council. Eudoxia leaves. When Brogni informs
Rachel that she is about to face her judges she tells him that she
will make a confession which will save the man she loves. Brogni
asks if the confession will save her own life as well. Her life is
forfeit, Rachel answers, adding that she has only one desire—to
save Léopold. As guards lead her away Brogni grieves over the
fact that one so young must die ("Mourir, mourir si jeune!"). This
is the introductory phrase of the long duet which ensues as Eleazar
is brought before him. Just before Eleazar appears, Brogni murmurs that the father may yet be persuaded to save his daughter
from death.

When Eleazar is led in Brogni warns him that Rachel is now
before the council and tells him that he can save her by repudiating his faith. Eleazar retorts that he would rather die than bow
to the will of the Christian God. Brogni says that the God of
Christian judgment is stern and implacable, to which Eleazar
replies that there is no God but the God of Jacob. But He has
deserted His people, Brogni observes. Though some fall in the
strife, Eleazar answers firmly, the God who led the Maccabees will
still lead His people in triumph. Thus, then, says Brogni resignedly,
Eleazar prefers to die.

Yes, Eleazar replies, but before he dies he will have his revenge
on *one* Christian. With that he points a shaking finger at the
Cardinal. As Brogni stares in surprise, Eleazar recalls to him the
sacking of Rome, years before, when Brogni's wife and daughter
fell victims to the mob and his palace was burned. Brogni asks
him not to speak of that terrible day when everything he held
dear was lost.

Not everything, Eleazar remarks grimly. A certain Jew, he goes
on, saved Brogni's daughter from the flames and brought her up
as his own child. This Jew he knows well, Eleazar says. In
anguished phrases ("Ah! j'implore en tremblant") Brogni entreats
him to tell him the name of the man who has his child. In a

repetition of the musical theme Eleazar asks with savage irony by what right Brogni begs mercy of his victim ("Et de quel droit viens-tu?"). In the fiery conclusion of the duet Eleazar shouts that the secret will die with him on the scaffold, while Brogni, frenzied by the Jew's refusal to impart his secret, abjectly begs Eleazar to take pity on him. Shaken by anguish, Brogni staggers to the door of the council chamber and goes inside.

Alone, Eleazar gives way to conflicting emotions of triumph and despair in the magnificent aria, "J'ai fait peser sur toi mon éternelle haine." Now that he has doomed his archenemy to eternal, tormenting grief, he muses, he is willing to die. But it is Rachel, after all, who will pay with her life for the satisfaction of his revenge, for if he revealed his secret to Brogni the Cardinal would most certainly free her. In a tender strain ("Rachel, quand du Seigneur la grâce tutélair") he reflects on his love for his daughter. It is as if he heard the voice of Rachel herself—Rachel, so young and lovely—beseeching him to save her. Reflecting that he has only to speak one word to save her, he resolves to forego his revenge.

At that moment he hears the harsh voices of the throng outside, demanding death for the Jews. Goaded to fury and defiance by their taunts, Eleazar cries that Rachel must not be allowed to live her life among these vile Christians who howl for his death. In feverish exultation he calls on his God to give him strength to take his daughter with him to his doom ("Dieu m'éclaire, fille chére"). In the final phrases of his soliloquy he prays that God may pardon him when He gives his daughter the martyr's crown. As the guards appear to conduct him to the council the curtain falls.

## ACT FIVE

A large square in another part of Constance, where the accused are to be put to death. In the foreground is a huge tent, from which the nobles and prelates are to witness the executions. Beyond, at one side of the square, is an enormous caldron filled with boiling water. The crowds packed on all sides of the square sing a rather macabre chorus, the burden of which is that they are looking forward to the day's entertainment—the spectacle of Jews being boiled alive ("Quel plaisir! quelle joie! contre eux que l'on déploie"). After the chorus, Brogni, Ruggiero, and dignitaries of Church and State march in solemn procession to the tent to the accompaniment of a majestic *marche funèbre*. A group of penitents leads in Eleazar and Rachel.

Ruggiero proclaims that Eleazar and Rachel must die. Léopold, through the Emperor's intervention, will suffer not death but banishment. When Eleazar comments sardonically on this example of Christian justice, Ruggiero declares that Léopold's life was saved by the testimony of a witness that he was innocent.

Eleazar asks who gave this testimony. Stepping forward, Rachel answers that it was she. Eleazar is stunned by her words. At Ruggiero's command she turns to the populace and in a firm voice asserts that she swore falsely to Léopold's guilt ("Devant Dieu qui connaît"). The throng shouts savagely for her death. Ruggiero denounces the two Jews for conspiring against the Prince.

As the Cardinal and the people intone a prayer for the souls of the condemned, Rachel cowers in her father's arms. Torn by anguish, Eleazar, looking from his daughter to Brogni, tries to decide if he should allow Rachel to go to her death or abandon her to the Christians. Coming close to Eleazar, Brogni once more implores him to tell his secret. Without answering, Eleazar turns away. Suddenly the executioner gives the death signal and Rachel is led toward the platform above the boiling caldron. Frantically Eleazar calls to Rachel, who stops and faces him. Going close to her, he asks if she wishes to live. Calmly and dispassionately Rachel asks how that can be. By renouncing her faith and embracing Christianity, Eleazar answers. Pointing toward the caldron, Rachel quietly says that her God awaits her there. In a brief, exultant phrase ("C'est le ciel qui m'inspire") Rachel and Eleazar welcome death and the martyr's crown. The prayers of the people sound softly.

As Rachel mounts the platform Brogni again approaches Eleazar and in tones of desperate entreaty asks if his daughter, saved from the flaming ruins in Rome, still lives. Glancing at Rachel, Eleazar answers yes. In feverish joy Brogni asks where she is. "There!" Eleazar cries in a terrible voice, and at that instant the executioner hurls Rachel into the caldron. Groaning in agony, Brogni sinks to his knees, burying his face in his hands. With a look of sardonic triumph on his face Eleazar goes to his death. As the people exult that at last they have been revenged on the Jews, the curtain falls.

# Khovanchina
## (*The Khovanskys*)

*by* MODEST PETROVICH MOUSSORGSKY

(1839–81)

*Libretto by the composer
and Vladimir Vasilyevich Stassov*

*Based on the drama of the same name by Aleksandr Pushkin*

### CHARACTERS

| | |
|---|---|
| Prince Ivan Khovansky, commander of the Streltsy (Archers) | Bass |
| Prince Andrei, his son | Tenor |
| Prince Vassily Golitsin | Tenor |
| The Boyar Shaklovity | Baritone |
| Dossifé, patriarch of the Old Believers | Bass |
| Marfa, a young widow, member of the Old Believers | Mezzo-soprano |
| Scribe | Tenor |
| Emma, a young girl from the German quarter of Moscow | Soprano |
| Varsonoviev, henchman of Golitsin | Baritone |
| Kouzka, a Streltsy | Bass |
| First | Bass |
| Second } Streltsy | Tenor |
| Third | Tenor |
| Streshniev, a herald of the Czar's guards | Tenor |
| Susanna, an older woman, member of the Old Believers | Soprano |

Archers, Old Believers, ladies in waiting and Persian slaves in the court of Ivan Khovansky; bodyguards of Peter the Great; the populace

*Place:* Moscow, and on the estate of Prince Khovansky, near the city
*Time:* 1682
*First performance:* Kononov Theater, St. Petersburg, February 21, 1886 (amateur production). Official premiere given at the Maryinsky Theater, St. Petersburg, November 7, 1911
*Original language:* Russian

*Khovanchina* (variously spelled *Khovanstchina, Khovantschina, Chovantchina*) was Moussorgsky's last opera (1885) and the successor to *Boris Godunof*. Although the composer's work on this immense drama was cut short by his death, he left an almost complete vocal score. The opera was revised for stage performance and orchestrated by Moussorgsky's friend Nikolai Rimsky-Korsakov.

There is a marked difference in musical style between this opera and *Boris*. For example, the conventional form of recitative in *Boris* is replaced in *Khovanchina* by broad, intensely melodic passages. Moussorgsky regarded this elaboration as his own discovery, which he called "melody justified by meaning." In the opera's great choruses—particularly those sung by the Old Believers—he utilized some of the liturgical melodies of the ancient Russian Church. They were adapted from manuscripts of masses dating back to the Middle Ages.

The action of *Khovanchina* has its roots in the history of Old Russia; it deals with the struggle between the ancient beliefs and the radical influences of Peter the Great (1682–1725). It was Moussorgsky's idea to dramatize this turbulent period in Russia's history—to portray the clash between the old regime and the new, the conflict of Eastern and Western ideas, the confrontation of orthodoxy and iconoclasm.

In the opera, Old Russia is represented by Prince Ivan Khovansky and his son Andrei, along with their followers (the Streltsy), and by Dossifé, leader of the Old Believers (the orthodox adherents of the Old Russian Church), and his disciple, Marfa. The radicals are represented by Prince Golitsin and his henchman, Varsonoviev, both of whom were identified with the faction of Czar Peter the Great. That monarch, by the way, gave the opera its title: He coined "Khovanchina" as a term of contempt for the Khovansky princes who hatched a revolt against him.

Actually, the central figures in the action are Marfa and Dossifé. Moussorgsky presents Marfa in basically human terms—a woman torn between overpowering sensuality and religious fervor. Dossifé symbolizes the fanatical mysticism of Old Russia. These two people embody the three fundamental ideas of *Khovanchina:* the Russian soul and its torment, the history of Russia and the problem of sin and its expiation.

Yet in the larger sense *Khovanchina* is an opera of the Russian people—as Moussorgsky said: "It is the Russian people I want to paint." The hero is not a person, but a nation. In the music itself, the composer revealed where his sympathies lay. The sectarians and the serfs, for example, are given rich, sweeping melodies in their choral utterances. The non-Russian Western elements are delineated in a deliberately gauche, superficial style. With the soul of the Russian people as its protagonist, *Khovanchina*—like *Boris*—is a genuine musical folk drama.

Although *Khovanchina* was heard infrequently during the years following its premiere, it was eventually given in major opera houses all over the world. Probably the most widely known music from the score is that of the two orchestral excerpts—the Prelude to Act One and the Entr'acte preceding Act Four, both of which are in the symphonic repertoire.

The opera's American premiere, in Russian, took place at the Hammerstein Metropolitan Opera House in Philadelphia on April 18, 1928. Its first hearing in New York was on March 7, 1931, at the Mecca Temple (later the City Center), where it was presented by a company called The Art of Musical Russia. The opera was given its first performance at the Metropolitan Opera House in New York on February 16, 1950. It was sung in English by a cast including Risë Stevens (Marfa), Lawrence Tibbett (Khovansky), Charles Kullman (Golitsin) and Jerome Hines (Dossifé). The role of Dossifé was created at the opera's premiere in St. Petersburg by the great Russian basso Feodor Chaliapin. The work is often sung in Italian and in French.

During the past several years *Khovanchina* seems to have enjoyed a revival of interest, and it reappeared in some of the principal opera houses in Europe. The Bolshoi Opera, in Moscow, presented a televised production on March 20, 1969, and that same year it was sung in Turin, Lausanne and East Berlin. In America, the Chicago Lyric Opera opened its 1969 season with a new production of *Khovanchina*.

The Prelude, during which the curtain rises slowly, was entitled "Dawn on the Moskva River" by the composer and is a musical landscape painting of Moscow at sunrise. It is dominated by a typically Russian melody which is heard in five variations—much in the manner of traditional Russian singers, who vary the melody with each succeeding stanza.

## ACT ONE

Red Square, Moscow. At one side is a stone pillar on which is a brass plate with an inscription; a chain fastened to the pillar stretches across the square. On the other side of the square is the Scribe's hut. Kouzka, a Streltsy (archer), is sleeping near the pillar. It is dawn.

There is a sound of church bells mingled with a fanfare of trumpets. A detachment of Streltsy, coming from night guard duty, crosses the square, and the men awaken Kouzka. In a robust unison chorus ("Je marche sur Ivangorod"–"Me ne andrò verso Ivangorod"), they boast of their exploits in defending a portion of the city.

As they mill about, the Scribe emerges from his hut, sharpening his quill. The Streltsy bow in mock solemnity, hailing him as "Worshipful Writer to the Council." Laughing derisively, they then go on their way. The Scribe, shaking his head, laments the evil days that have fallen on Russia, but in the next breath murmurs that, for himself, business is not bad.

Shaklovity enters and calls to the Scribe; dialogue in quasi-recitative follows. The Boyar orders the old man to write a letter he is about to dictate, warning him beforehand of fearsome torture if he ever dare reveal its contents ("Si tu braves tous les tourments"–"Si ti regge il cuore a soffrir"). The Scribe is momentarily terrified but forgets his fear when Shaklovity hands him a purse. As he begins the letter, a passage in the orchestra suggests the motion of the writer's hands. It is similar to that heard in *Boris* when the monk Pimen is writing in his cell.

The letter, addressed to "mighty Czars, Grand Dukes and Princes" ("Aux tsars souverains"–"A gli imperatori"), states that Prince Ivan Khovansky and his son Andrei are plotting a rebellion against the Empire. As the Scribe reads back what he has written, a group of Russians passes by. In a brief mocking chorus ("Il etait une commère"–"C'era una comare") the peasants comment slyly on the connivery that is afoot.

After they leave, Shaklovity continues dictating the details of the Khovansky plot ("l'effroi sur la Russie"–"chiamare per l'immensa Russia") over a descriptively sinuous accompaniment: The traitor means to incite peasants and soldiers alike against the Czar, enlist the aid of the Old Believers,[1] then place his son, Prince Andrei, on the throne.

Suddenly the Streltsy are heard returning. Shaklovity wraps himself in his cloak and conceals himself while the Scribe, wailing in

---

[1] The fanatical sect which clung to traditional beliefs and refused to accept the reforms of Patriarch Nikon in 1654. They broke away from the Orthodox Church when a revision of the Bible was introduced.

terror, stuffs the letter in his pocket. The Streltsy, roaring out a unison chorus of dire threats against their enemies, pass through the back of Red Square.

Shaklovity emerges and dictates the conclusion of the letter, which states that when peace is restored the writer's name will be revealed. Taking the letter, he again brusquely warns the Scribe to keep silence. The latter, irritated by the Boyar's insolent manner, turns on him angrily. Shaklovity, though somewhat taken aback by the outburst, advises the Scribe never to try to learn the name of the writer of the letter. Curiosity, he adds pointedly, is the devil's work. With that he glides away.

Gazing after him, the old Scribe sardonically wishes him a pleasant journey ("Douce soit ta route!"—"Facile ti sia la via!"). In the ensuing refrain he sings that his own wits are more than a match for this fellow who gives himself such high and mighty airs. Accordingly, he has signed the incriminating document with the name of Ananiev. He is dead—and the dead can feel no disgrace.

The people and the Streltsy now crowd into the square to hail Prince Ivan Khovansky, singing the first of the great choruses for which the opera is famous: "Gloire au grand prince Ivan"—"Gloria al padre e onor!" This powerful number, with its phrases in open fifths giving the effect of raw peasant vitality, is sometimes called the "White Swan" ensemble. The peasants hail Khovansky by that title ("au blanc cygne"—"al cigno candido").[2]

In an unaccompanied phrase, the Streltsy command the populace to listen to His Highness the Prince. Arrogant and proud, Ivan strides forward and addresses the throng in the form of a rhetorical question ("Vous, mes enfants"—"O figli miei"): Is it not true that the treacherous boyars[3] are spreading ruin not only in Moscow, but in all of Russia? Have we not pledged ourselves to destroy the enemies of the people? In answer, the peasants and soldiers again sing the "White Swan" chorus. After its thundering climax, the crowd follows Khovansky and his soldiers from the scene, the voices dying away in the distance.

Suddenly an agitated theme breaks out in the orchestra, and Emma comes rushing in pursued by Prince Andrei, who tries to embrace her. Fending him off, she distractedly implores him to

[2] Adapted by Moussorgsky from a traditional Russian wedding song.

[3] Also spelled "boyard." They were privileged members of the Russian aristocracy, next to the ruling princes. The class was abolished by Peter the Great.

leave her alone ("Grâce, trop faible"—"Grazia! Lasciate mi"). When
he leers that the dove can never escape the falcon, she furiously
denounces him as the villain who murdered her father, drove her
lover into exile and scorned her mother's pleas for mercy. In
desperation, Emma begs Andrei to kill her. But her protestations
only inflame his desire, and he passionately entreats her to yield
to him.

As Emma struggles to elude the Prince, Marfa steals behind a
pillar and watches the scene. She ironically repeats the Prince's
amorous phrases. In complete panic, Emma screams for help.
With that Marfa comes forward and throws herself between the
girl and Andrei, who staggers back in surprise.

With majestic dignity, Marfa turns on the hapless Prince with
a flood of denunciation. So this, she begins ("Ah! oui, prince"—
"Ah, tal fede, mio principe"), is how you repay me for my devotion . . . has a noble Prince nothing better to do than dally
with the affections of an innocent maiden?

Andrei furiously orders Marfa to leave. Turning to Emma, he
tells her to ignore this meddling strumpet ("Ignores tu, ma chère
enfant"—"Udisti mai, bellezza mia") and listen instead to the
story about a handsome young man and the mistress he no longer
loves. He solved the problem of getting rid of her in a very
practical manner.

Thereupon Andrei springs at Marfa with an upraised dagger.
Quick as a flash, she draws a dagger from underneath her cloak
and parries the blow. In an unaccompanied phrase, she sings
quietly that two can play at this game. In any case, she goes on,
this is not the way in which a certain Prince will meet his fate—
it will not be her hand that will send him to his doom.

Marfa's voice blends with Emma's and the Prince's in a trio
passage. The Prince curses that the devil himself sent Marfa to
torment him. Emma bewails the fact that while Marfa saved her
life, she is powerless to save Marfa's. Marfa herself, as though in a
trance, sings that she hears the voice of Fate and can see the
shining portals of the blessed.

At this point Ivan Khovansky returns with the Streltsy and the
people, who sing a reprise of the "White Swan" chorus. Over the
ensemble, the voice of Emma is heard in a brief but anguished
prayer for help. Ivan catches sight of Prince Andrei with Emma
and exclaims in surprise. Struck by Emma's beauty, Khovansky
orders his bodyguards to take her to his palace. Thereupon Andrei
plants himself in front of the girl and defies his father to take
her away from him. Furious at the Prince's defiance, Ivan bellows

to his guards to take the girl. Andrei, with equal fury, commands them not to touch her. In helpless confusion, the men ask whom they are to obey.

As Ivan and Andrei rage at each other with increasing violence, Dossifé appears with a group of Old Believers. With commanding authority he strides between the two men and demands to know the reason for their frenzy ("Possédés du diable"—"Ravvedervi!"). As the two recoil in surprise, Emma throws herself at Dossifé's. feet and implores him to save her. He turns to Marfa and orders her to take the terror-stricken girl home.

Whirling on the two Princes, the patriarch pours out his wrath in brief but dynamic aria, "Le regne des ténèbres s'étend"—"La tenebra impera trionfa." He accuses them of bringing the Church of Russia to disaster through their pride, treachery and unbelief. Turning to the Old Believers, he exhorts them to cling to their orthodoxy even if it means martyrdom. Humbly, but with intense conviction, Dossifé calls on all true believers to hold fast to their faith ("Orthodoxes, soyez notre appui!"—"Ortodossi, aiutatetci!").

Wild with fury over Dossifé's accusations, Prince Ivan orders the Streltsy to place the patriarch and the Old Believers under arrest and imprison them in the Kremlin. To a fanfare of trumpets he then proclaims Andrei as the head of the Streltsy. As he leaves with his guards, the people stare in utter bewilderment. Andrei, still shaken by the quarrel with his father, follows slowly. As the Old Believers are led away, Dossifé leads them in a beautiful prayer, "O Seigneur! Que la Force enemie"—"Dio Signor! Non far prevaler." They respond with an unaccompanied choral refrain, the so-called "Aeolian Chorus"[4]: "Dieu délivre nous"—"Dio possente." Their hymn dies away in the distance as the curtain falls.


## ACT TWO

The summer home of Prince Golitsin[5] in Moscow. The Prince is sitting at a candlelit desk reading a love letter from the Czarevna, his royal mistress. Before the rise of the curtain there is a brief introduction in a foreboding minor key. This theme

---

[4] Aeolian: Refers to one of the ancient systems of musical scales. Another used in this opera is the Phrygian, in the brief chorus of the Old Believers in the last act.

[5] Counselor (and lover) of the Czarevna Sophia. He is representative of Western-oriented Russia—as opposed to the Khovanskys, symbolic of feudalism, and Dossifé, symbolic of mystical Russia.

accompanies Golitsin's aria as he reads the letter ("Tendre frère Vassienka"—"Mio diletto Vassienka").

Although the letter is full of impassioned phrases, the Prince is wary of the Czarevna's avowals ("Doit-on croire au serment d'une femme"—"Credere devo al giuro di donna"). He reflects that she is ambitious and capricious—and if he suddenly fell out of favor with her it might well cost him his head. Be careful, Prince, he murmurs softly as the aria ends.

Golitsin's thoughts are interrupted by the entrance of his hench-man, Varsonoviev, who tells him that the "sorceress" he sent for has arrived. When the Prince angrily upbraids him for calling the woman a sorceress, Varsonoviev servilely apologizes for this slip of the tongue.

He then brings in Marfa, who looks around cautiously as she approaches Golitsin. She remarks that the suspicious glances of the servants aroused her fears of an ambush. Golitsin says ap-prehensively that in these dangerous times no one knows what disaster the future may bring. Marfa then reveals that she is well aware of Golitsin's reason for summoning her: She has a reputa-tion as a seeress, and she is to tell his fortune.

Marfa asks for a bowl of water. It is set before her, and then begins the Divination Scene, with Marfa's great aria, "Forces mystérieuses"—"Forze recondite," one of the most memorable scenes in the opera. The aria is introduced by a strangely dissonant passage which heightens the effect of superstitious dread.

In quasi-recitative, Marfa invokes the spirits of dead mariners to lift the dark veil of the Prince's future. Staring into the bowl, she intones that now the vision becomes clearer: She sees the Prince hemmed in by treacherous "friends" who smile as they plot his doom. Then she launches into the prophecy itself ("Bientot va venir in disgrace"—"T'incombe funesto il bando"). It is de-claimed in a minor key, in the steady rhythmic pattern of a typical Russian folk song.[6]

The Prince's destiny, Marfa sings somberly, is disgrace and exile. His fate is sealed—and neither his wit nor his wisdom will save him. Stripped of wealth and honor, he will suffer deprivation. In lonely, bitter exile he finally will learn the truth.

Listening in mingled horror and anger, Golitsin bursts out: "Go!" With a baleful glance at him, Marfa slowly withdraws, again

---

[6] The tune of the prophecy reappears in an orchestral variation when Golitsin is taken into exile; also when Marfa warns Andrei, in the final scene, that death is near.

searching with her eyes every corner of the room. Varsonoviev glides in. Golitsin, *sotto voce*, orders him to see to it that the woman is drowned in the nearby lake. Marfa, at the door, overhears this and rushes away.

Alone, Golistsin gives way to his despair in the great soliloquy "Et voilá mon avenir fatal"—"Ecco il giudizio del destino mio!" He broods over the ruin of all his hopes and ambitions for a better Russia. He had won the confidence of the boyars and had strengthened Russia's ties with other nations. His victory over the Poles had inspired foreign respect. Finally, he had restored to his people the lands torn from them by greedy invaders. And now his reward is oblivion. In an agonized phrase ("La rouille des Tatars" —"Addentro t'ha la ruggin tartara") he cries that the shadow of the Tatar lies long over this holy land.

As he sits staring into space, Ivan Khovansky enters without being announced. Golitsin looks up. For a moment the two leaders of the opposing factions in Russia—sworn enemies—face each other. Then Golitsin curtly invites his visitor to be seated. With a sneer, Khovansky remarks that, under the circumstances, taking a seat presents a problem ("M'asseoir! Le pourrais-je!"—"Seder! Che problema!"). This introduces a long and bitter dispute between the two men, carried on over a powerfully stated unison passage in the orchestra.

It begins as Ivan Khovansky, with mocking courtesy, asks where he is to sit—now that Prince Golitsin, with his treacherous scheming, has reduced the Khovanskys to the level of serfs ("Maintenant nous avons plus de place"—"Privi siam dei nostri posti orinai"). Perhaps his place is on the door mat, he adds sardonically.

It is strange, Golitsin retorts sarcastically, that the rich and powerful Khovansky should suddenly be concerned about the fortunes of other nobles. Be that as it may, Ivan answers, Prince Golitsin, in his ruthless disregard of the honor of the boyars, no doubt is following the precept of the Tatars themselves: "All men are created equal." That being the case, heads may be lopped off indiscriminately. Infuriated by this sally, Golitsin flares up momentarily, then controls himself with an effort.

In a calmer tone he goes on to say that he was forced to adopt harsh measures with the boyars ("J'ai pu blesser les boyars"— "Ho forse offessi boiardi"), but those measures were necessary. At the same time, no punishment was meted out to Ivan Khovansky, leader of the Guards and the most powerful man in Moscow, before whom all must bow their heads. And now this grandee complains of being slighted!

Goaded to fury by Golitsin's stinging sarcasm, Khovansky roars that he will listen to no more slanderous accusations ("Arrête, prince!"—"Ah, basta al fin"). At that moment Dossifé enters and stands listening, his eyes fixed on Khovansky. Golitsin, noticing the patriarch, bows ironically to Prince Ivan. Oblivious to everything in his rage, Khovansky goes on to remind the other that he is of royal Tatar blood and need not submit to contempt and insult. Moreover, he asks, how can Golitsin boast of his generalship when half his army died of privation even before his latest campaign began.

This thrust rouses Golitsin himself to violent anger, and the two men advance threateningly toward each other. But once more Dossifé steps forward in the role of peacemaker, exhorting the raging noblemen to calm themselves ("O princes, calmez vous"—"Ponete all' ira il fren"). The scene continues in trio form over reverberating chords in the orchestra. Dossifé tells the princes that their personal quarreling will never save Russia. They must turn to God for help and put their trust in the ancient faith.

Khovansky falls silent but Golitsin obstinately argues with the patriarch. When the latter insists that the people must be taught according to the traditional customs and beliefs, Golitsin scornfully says he has no use for the old ways. Dossifé cries that this attitude is the result of insidious foreign influence. The radicals and reformers have so terrorized the people that they are fleeing their homes and hiding in the forests.

At this point Khovansky unctuously remarks that time and again he has tried to reason with this headstrong Prince to convince him that he must return to the old ways. In spite of his efforts, he adds, Golitsin destroyed the repository of ancient wisdom, *The Book of Pedigrees*.

Before Golitsin can reply, the voices of the Old Believers are heard in the distance chanting that they have triumphed over heresy ("L'hérése nous l'avons flétrie"—"Vinta abbiamo l'eresia"). The conversation of the three men continues over the chorus. A moment later the Old Believers and a crowd of townspeople, carrying lighted tapers, pass by outside, singing as they go.

Scowling at them, Golitsin asks who these people are. They are men of deeds—not words, Dossifé replies pointedly. They have remained true to their old faith. With angry contempt, Golitsin brands them ineffectual dissenters. Khovansky, relishing the other's discomfiture, remarks that the traditionalists may yet save Russia.

Suddenly Marfa bursts into the room, falls on her knees before Golitsin and begs him to save her life. The Prince curses her as a witch. As the others stare in consternation, Marfa turns to Dossifé and tells him what has happened ("Au jour tombant je sortais"—"Me ne tornavo"). When she left the Prince's house at dusk a serf followed her. As she passed the "Marsh" near Belgorod the man seized her, saying he had been ordered by Prince Golitsin to drown her. Just then a group of Petrovsky, the Czar's personal guards, came by and saved her.[7] The realization that the Czar's troops are in Moscow brings expressions of alarm and dismay from Ivan and Golitsin, as well as from Dossifé. In the general confusion Marfa and her accusations are forgotten.

Excitement flares as Varsonoviev comes charging in, crying that the Boyar Shaklovity is at the door. Striding forward, Shaklovity announces that the Czarevna has issued a proclamation accusing the Khovanskys of conspiring against the Empire ("Seigneurs! la tsarevna vous fait"—"O principi! La tsarevna ordine"). Dossifé tells Ivan that now all hope is lost. Turning to Shaklovity, he asks what the Czar's own reaction is to the plot. With obvious relish, the Boyar answers: "He calls it 'Khovanchina.'"[8] There is general consternation as the orchestra thunders out the theme heard in the five variations in the Prelude. The curtain falls.


## ACT THREE

The massively timbered barracks of the Streltsy in a suburb of Moscow. Opposite is the home of Prince Ivan Khovansky. As the curtain rises, the chorus of the Old Believers is heard in the distance, again chanting their hymn of triumph over the heretics. It swells to a great crescendo as the procession passes through the Streltsy quarter, then gradually dies away as the Old Believers move out of sight.

One of the last in the procession is Marfa, who unobtrusively remains behind. As the bass theme associated with the Old Believers continues in the orchestra, she sits down on an embankment near Prince Andrei's house. There, in one of the opera's most beautiful arias, "Moi, jeunette, j'ai parcouru"—"Ha percorsi la gió-vane," she sings of her love for the Prince. This aria, actually a Russian folk tune, is introduced by a tender phrase in descending

[7] The motive of the Prelude, describing the peaceful dawn in Moscow, is heard during Marfa's story. It is here symbolic of her relief at being saved.

[8] Thus the Czar contemptuously characterized the treason of the Khovanskys.

triads. The folk melody is sustained throughout the aria in a throbbing 6/4 tempo.

The song portrays Marfa's passionate longing for her lover in the symbolic terms of a love-smitten maiden stumbling through brook and briar in the night to the home of her beloved. But there she knocks in vain. Her faithless lover has deserted her. Ending the aria on a menacing phrase, Marfa sings that she will avenge herself on her lover for his cruelty ("sa vengeance éclatante et cruelle!" —"or ti resta la gretta settaria!").[9]

But while Marfa is giving expression to her amorous longings, Susanna, one of the Old Believers, steals in and listens to her song. A stern, self-righteous member of the sect, she warns Marfa that she will be damned eternally for her carnal thoughts ("Blasphéme! Point de pardon"—"Grave peccato inespiabil fai"). This introduces a long and dramatic duet.

The old woman, shocked and outraged, upbraids Marfa for her "shameless singing." Tormented by memories of her love affair with Prince Andrei, Marfa answers that she will not hide the truth about the past. If Susanna had ever known a man's ardent kiss, Marfa goes on, she would not now presume to condemn another woman for yielding to the soul-consuming fire of love ("Si tu comprenais" —"Ah, se intender mai pottesi"). Susanna grows almost hysterical as Marfa's words stir to life her own long-suppressed desires ("Est-ce le diable qui me trouble?"—"O che li demonia sé mi trae?").

In a passionate frenzy Marfa turns toward Prince Andrei's house and implores him not to forget her ("Rappelletoi ma chère âme" —"Pensa, ricordi, diletto mio"). Losing all control, Susanna furiously accuses Marfa of corrupting her with visions of carnal love ("Tu as voulu me tenter"—"Tu m'hai tentata"). For this she will denounce her to the Old Believers and have her burned at the stake.

As the old woman hurls her imprecations, Dossifé comes out of Andrei's house and Marfa bows low before him. Quietly she tells him that Susanna is condemning her because she has told the truth about her sinful past. Dossifé sternly rebukes Susanna for her self-righteous cruelty toward an unfortunate sister. When she defies him, the patriarch loses his temper and roars that she is the devil's own offspring ("Belial s'empare de ton esprit"—"Belial é il solo

---

[9] This aria is built upon three themes: Two refer to Marfa's despairing love for Andrei. The third is associated with her prophecy in the Divination Scene.

tuo Signor!"). Wrathfully he orders her out of his sight. Susanna scurries away in terror.[10]

A moving duet ensues as Dossifé turns to Marfa with words of comfort and encouragement ("Ah! mon enfant si chère"—"Ah, creatura mia!"). Marfa reveals that Prince Andrei has betrayed and abandoned her, but she confesses that her tormenting desire for him gives her no respite. If it is wrong to love, she cries in despair, then let her be put to death so that her soul may be saved.

Dossifé, profoundly moved by her anguish, tells her he himself has sinned and is in need of forgiveness. Trust in God's mercy, he counsels her, and do not be afraid of loving. With that the patriarch gently leads her away.

The Boyar Shaklovity now appears. Though notorious as a scoundrel and a plotter, he is haunted by a premonition of Russia's doom. He expresses his forebodings in one of the opera's principal arias, "Ah, malheureuse Russie"—"Ah, che destino maligna." He ponders whether the Empire will at last fall victim to her enemies. She has survived the depredations of the Germans, as well as the tyranny of the Tatars—but she is still the prey of other evil forces. Shaklovity climaxes his aria with a prayer for Russia's deliverance from the clutches of merciless enemies ("des mains de mercenaries, arrache la Russie!"—"O Dio, ribenedici questo suol, esaudimi!").

As he stands for a moment plunged in gloom he hears the sound of a brawling chorus of the Streltsy in the distance. Let the "Khovansky lambs" sing while they may, he murmurs sardonically, for their song soon will be ended. He turns and disappears.

The Streltsy, some of them still drunk after a night of carousing, come stampeding in and roar out a mighty chorus—mostly about their prowess in drinking and fighting. One of the most stirring numbers in the opera, it is in the best tradition of Russian male ensembles.

At the climax of the chorus they are interrupted by an excited crowd of women—most of them the wives of the Streltsy themselves. The men fall back as the women, in a shrill ensemble ("Ah! les vauriens maudits"—"Ah, maledetti beoni"), rail at them for behaving like drunken brutes. Hurling insults at each other, the men and women bring the chorus to a turbulent conclusion.

The uproar comes to a sudden stop as the Scribe comes rushing

---

[10] In some productions the character of Susanna does not appear. Then the next scene between Marfa and Dossifé follows immediately after Marfa's aria.

in, obviously beside himself with terror. The Streltsy crowd around him, trying to find the reason for his panic ("Quelle espèce d'âne!" —"Che ti piglia, scemo?"). Over an agitated theme in the orchestra, the Scribe finally tells the incredulous Streltsy that while he was busy at his letter writing in the suburb of Kitaigorod ("J'étais au travail près de Kitaigorod"—"A Kitaigorod ero per ufficio") he heard mounted troops approaching. When they came to the Streltsy quarter, he goes on, the troops began to attack women and children.

Ignoring the jeering disbelief of the Streltsy, the Scribe reports that suddenly the Petrovsky joined the troops in the attack and routed the Streltsy, who were defending their quarter. At this news there are outcries of terror from the women and the Streltsy. The Scribe makes his getaway unnoticed.

Kouzka comes forward to urge the others to ask Prince Ivan Khovansky if this alarming report is true, or if the miserable Scribe is lying for reasons of his own. Thereupon the women and men surge toward the Prince's house and make their plea in a brief chorus ("Père, montre toi!"—"Padre, vien a noi"). When Khovansky comes out of his house with a paternal greeting, the Streltsy implore him to lead them in a counterattack against the Petrovsky.

But the Prince's reply ("Qu'il vous souviene du temps"—"Vi ricordate, o figli") takes them by surprise. Recalling how they once fought a bloody battle to drive the traitors out of Moscow, Ivan declares that now things have changed: They must submit to the will of the Czar Peter. With a pompous "farewell," Khovansky goes back into the house.

Fear-stricken and completely bewildered, the Streltsy and their women pray for deliverance from their enemies ("Que l'enemi s'éloigne"—"Ci guarda dai nemici"). The curtain falls slowly.

## ACT FOUR
### (Part I)

The luxuriously furnished dining hall in the house of Prince Ivan Khovansky outside Moscow. The Prince, seated with guests at his banquet table, is listening to the song of his serving girls ("Sur la verdoyante rive"—"Su la riva del ruscello me"). Their song, a typial Russian folk tune in a minor key, is about a young lover who bathed in the brook before he went to meet his sweetheart.

Khovansky interrupts the singing, complaining that the song is much too sad for this festive occasion. At his prompting the girls strike up a lively ditty ("Tard au soir quand tout sommeille" —"Vigilavo a tarda sera") which they call "Haiduchok."[11] The chorus is interrupted by the entrance of Varsonoviev, who warns Prince Ivan that his life is in danger.

Khovansky scornfully rejects the possibility that he could be attacked on his own estate. He curtly dismisses Varsonoviev, then calls for his Persian dancers, who entertain him and his guests with the "Dance of the Persians," familiar as a concert number.

A few moments after the dancers leave the scene, Shaklovity enters and obsequiously approaches Prince Ivan. He informs the Prince that the Czarevna is calling a meeting of the Guard Council to discuss the crucial state of affairs in Russia, and she urgently requests the Prince to be present. Ivan at first flatly refuses to go, but Shaklovity, playing upon the Prince's exalted opinion of his own statesmanship, persuades him to attend.

Calling for his most resplendent robe of state and his jewel-encrusted staff, Khovansky commands his serving maids to sing in his honor. They oblige with a stately chorus ("Il nage fier le cygne blanc"—"In contro al cigno"). In resounding unison phrases —interspersed with the salutation "Ladou," almost like an incantation—they hail him as the glorious White Swan who now goes to meet his snowy mate.[12] The irony of this paean becomes violently apparent in the next few moments. As Prince Ivan turns and strides majestically toward the door, Shaklovity plunges his dagger into his back. Khovansky, with a terrible cry, falls dead. The serving maids rush away screaming in terror.

Shaklovity, glaring down at the Prince's body, repeats with savage mockery the refrain of the serving maids: "Aye, all glory to the snow-white swan, Ladou, Ladou!" The curtain falls.

## ACT FOUR
### (Part II)

The square in front of the Cathedral of Vassily Blyenye (St. Basil) in Moscow, where a crowd is gathered. A troop of cavalry, armed with sabers, rides in and forms ranks in front of the church, their backs to the entrance. The people quickly move to the

[11] A name once given to the Hungarian infantry. The song itself has the rhythm and character of the czardas.

[12] This chorus was described by Oskar von Riesemann, Moussorgsky's biographer, as "almost the only example of continuous 17/4 time (6/4+5/4+6/4) time in music."

opposite side of the square. Soon a carriage escorted by soldiers passes through the square; the onlookers, craning their necks, chatter excitedly. In the carriage is Prince Golitsin, on his way to exile. As the procession moves out of sight, the people slowly follow with heads bowed. In a brief choral phrase ("Que le Sauveur t'absolve"—"Iddio ti dia perdon!") they implore God's mercy on the departing Prince.[13]

For several moments the square is empty. Then Dossifé appears with Marfa, to whom he describes the succession of tragic events which have shaken Russia: Prince Golitsin exiled, Prince Ivan Khovansky murdered, the destiny of Prince Andrei hanging in the balance—in Moscow certain factions even have hailed him as Czar. The patriarch relates these events in a recitative passage ("Tel du Destin l'ârret s'est accompli"—"Compiuto s'e il giudizio de destin").

Marfa herself has news of further disaster. The Grand Council has ordered "foreign troops" to slaughter the Old Believers. In fanatical excitement, Dossifé cries that the hour has come for the final immolation of the faithful. He exhorts Marfa to win Prince Andrei to the faith, so that he may die with them and save his soul. Assuring her that she will receive a crown in heaven as her reward, Dossifé hurries away. Alone, Marfa, in a transport of religious fervor, exults in the expectation of martyrdom.

To the accompaniment of a quivering theme in the orchestra, Prince Andrei bursts in and angrily demands to know where Emma has been kept hidden. Marfa tells him that the girl is now far away from Moscow—and probably reunited with the man from whom Andrei himself had once separated her. Wild with rage, Andrei curses Marfa as a witch and shouts that he will call his guards and have her executed on the spot.

In quiet defiance, Marfa answers him in one of the most intensely dramatic passages in the entire opera, "Tu ne comprends guère, prince"—"Né presagio, sire," sung in a variation of the theme of her prophecy. Over the steady beat of a single note accentuated by a harsh, open-interval figure in the bass, she warns Andrei that he is sealing his own doom by ignoring the call of his destiny. But Andrei, his thoughts still on Emma, pays little heed.

Marfa goes on to remind him that the corpse of his father, murdered by traitors, still lies stark and unburied in his home,

[13] This phrase is sung over an orchestral variation of the theme of Marfa's prophecy about Golitsin.

with wind and wolves for a deathwatch. Meanwhile, these selfsame traitors are hunting down his son.

But Andrei, now beside himself with fury, refuses to believe her ("Non, je ne tu crois pas"—"Non, vo' credere a te") and accuses her of trying to destroy him with her witchcraft. One word from him, he rages, will bring his guards to lead her to the stake.

"Call your guards," Marfa says quietly. Staring incredulously at her for a moment, the Prince sounds his horn. Suddenly the great bell of the cathedral begins tolling, and then a bizarre procession comes into view. The Streltsy, carrying axes and blocks for their own beheading, march in followed by their wives—who now, strangely enough, apparently have turned against them.

There is a gasp of horror from Andrei, who abjectly begs Marfa to save him from sharing the fate of the Streltsy. Assuring him of safety, she leads him away. Meanwhile, the women, in a frenzied chorus ("Non, pas de grâce"—"Morte, a gli empi, morte!"), scream for death without mercy for the hapless Streltsy, who kneel in prayer before their execution blocks.

But the scheduled execution is thwarted by the arrival (in a fantastic turn of the plot) of the Czar's guards (the Preobajensky), who enter to a blazing fanfare followed by a majestic, hymnlike march.[14] They are led by the herald, Streshniev, who proclaims that the Czars Ivan and Peter have pardoned the Streltsy. They are to go in peace to their homes and pray that the glorious Empire may continue to prosper. In honor of this royal gesture of magnanimity, the Preobajensky are to parade before the Kremlin.

The Streltsy, stunned by their reprieve, rise silently and watch the Czar's men leave to the accompaniment of the march tune. The curtain falls.

## ACT FIVE

The hermitage of the Old Believers in a pine forest not far from Moscow. A bright moon glimmers through the trees. Dossifé enters slowly to the accompaniment of a serene unison passage in ascending and descending eighth-note patterns, descriptive of the sighing of the wind through the pines. In one of the opera's most impressive arias, "Là, en cet endroit"—"Qui in questo luogo," he reflects that here in this peaceful spot the Old Believers will meet

[14] This march tune is the same as that of the familiar hymn "Glorious Things of Thee Are Spoken," by Franz Josef Haydn.

their final doom. He recalls how he has struggled to keep his flock unwavering in its faith. The way has been hard, but now the time is at hand for their eternal reward. He prays that their unshakable devotion will inspire men for ages to come. Sinking to his knees, Dossifé ends the aria in a quiet invocatory phrase.

One by one the Old Believers appear, Marfa among them. In dolorous tones, Dossifé tells them that their cause is lost ("Perdu est notre cause"—"Perduta è la causa"). They are now at the mercy of their enemies. Prince Ivan Khovansky is murdered, Prince Golitsin banished, Prince Andrei himself is hiding in the hermitage to escape those who have marked him for death. Now the Antichrist has come among them, but they must be prepared to die rather than yield. In a brief choral phrase the Old Believers reassure the patriarch of their steadfastness.

Dossifé bids them put on their white ceremonial robes, light their tapers and wait for the hour of immolation. As the bell of the hermitage begins to toll, the Old Believers defy the power of the Antichrist and hail their redemption "by flame and fire." After the chorus they return to the hermitage with Dossifé, while Marfa remains alone.

She gives way to her anguish over Andrei's treachery toward her, but prays that she may have the strength to save his soul through her abiding love. As though mocking her agony of spirit, she hears Andrei's voice in the distance singing of his longing for Emma ("Où donc est ma liberté?"—"Dove sei, o libertà?"). But when he appears a moment later, calling Emma's name, Marfa rushes to his side. She pours out her love in a sweeping aria ("Souviens-toi des jours"—"Ah, fa che ti souvenga") in which she gives expression to her mingled feelings of religious ecstasy and sensual desire. Offering Andrei her last embrace, she ends the aria with a fervid "Alleluia!"[15]

Dossifé, clad in a ceremonial shroud, emerges from the shadow of the pines proclaiming that the trumpet of doom has sounded. The fanfare of the approaching Poteshny guards is heard in the distance. For the second time, Andrei beseeches Marfa to save him.

Over the sound of a funeral march, Marfa replies ("Entends monter"—"Non odi tu") that the troops—the executioners—are upon them, and now there is no place to hide. Destiny has decreed that they are to be forever united in death. As she thus pronounces

---

[15] This scene, which Moussorgsky called the "requiem of love," was said to be one of the things in the opera that pleased him most.

Andrei's doom, the Old Believers, carrying their tapers, assemble and begin building a pyre. Taking Andrei by the hand, Marfa leads him up to the pyre. Repeating the passionate avowal expressed in her aria ("Souviens-toi des jours de notre amour"—"Ah, fa che ti souvenga l'ora dell'amor"), she sings that now they will rekindle the fire of their love in the devouring flames.

They both then mount the pyre, followed by the Old Believers, who sing the invocatory "Phrygian Chorus," "O Dieu de gloire" —"Dio della gloria." In a solo over a descending chromatic passage in the brass, Dossifé exhorts the faithful to have courage, for they shall see God. Snatching a taper, Marfa ignites the pyre. The harsh fanfare of the Czar's guards comes nearer.

As the flames billow upward, the doomed victims join in a mighty plea for pardon of their sins ("O Maitre, toi mon aide"—"O Signor! Nostro padre").[16] Soaring over the chorus comes Marfa's final passionate entreaty to Andrei, "Remember our moments of bliss!" But Andrei, engulfed with the others in the flames, cries out: "Emma!"

To a clamorous fanfare, the Czar's guards rush in, then stagger back in horror at the holocaust. As the theme associated with the Poteshny resounds in the orchestra, the curtain slowly falls.

[16] This final chorus was composed by Nikolai Rimsky-Korsakov from Moussorgsky's rough draft of the scene.

# The Last Savage
## (*L'Ultimo Selvaggio—Le Dernier Sauvage*)
### *by* GIAN-CARLO MENOTTI
### (1911–    )

#### *Libretto by the composer*

##### CHARACTERS

| | |
|---|---|
| The Maharajah of Rajaputana | Bass |
| The Maharanee | Contralto |
| Kodanda, the Prince, their supposed son | Tenor |
| Sardula, a servant girl | Soprano |
| Abdul, a peasant | Baritone |
| Mr. Scattergood, an American millionaire | Bass-baritone |
| Kitty, his daughter | Soprano |
| Two Indian scholars | Tenors |
| Two American tailors | Tenor, baritone |
| An English tailor | Tenor |
| A Roman Catholic priest | Bass |
| A Protestant minister (a Negro) | Baritone |
| A rabbi | Tenor |
| A Greek Orthodox priest | Tenor |
| A philosopher | Baritone |
| A physician | Baritone |
| A painter | Tenor |
| A poet | Tenor |
| A scientist | Tenor |
| A composer | Baritone |
| A concert singer | Soprano |
| A businesswoman | Soprano |

In India: Hunters, Indian nobility, ladies in waiting, attendants

In Chicago: Journalists, military and civil authorities, politicians, society women, debutantes, various guests

*Place:* In India and Chicago, U.S.A.
*Time:* Present
*First performance:* Opéra-Comique, Paris, October 22, 1963, in French, as *Le Dernier Sauvage*
*Original language:* Italian

*The Last Savage,* Gian-Carlo Menotti's ninth opera, was his first full-length work in *opera buffa* form. He had been fairly successful in this form with his first opera, the one-act *Amelia Goes to the Ball* (1934), and again wanted to try his hand at comedy. Accordingly, in about 1947 he began sketching out a plot for an opera. First called *The Last Superman,* it was about a young American girl, a student of anthropology at Vassar, who went to the Himalayas in search of a cave man as a research subject. There she found her "primitive," brought him to Chicago to expose him to civilization, then ended up by marrying him and living with him in a cave in India—complete with refrigerator and television.

The opera is a penetrating but good-natured satire on the foibles and pretensions of modern society, as contrasted to the serenity of life close to nature which mankind has sacrificed for the sake of becoming "civilized." Menotti, of course, gives the simple life the best of it. Accordingly, he eschewed harsh dissonances and other "far-out" musical elements, writing out of the conviction that there is in people an instinctive desire for, and sensitivity to, simple melody. He preferred, as he said, to adhere to the lyric tradition of Rossini, Donizetti and Cimarosa. The score abounds in melody and bubbles with humor. It is eclectic—but the artistry which infuses the music is Menotti's own.

Menotti wrote the libretto in Italian, and it was given in its original form as *L'Ultimo Selvaggio* in Venice on May 15, 1964. The first American performance, in an English translation by George Mead, was given at the Metropolitan on January 23, 1964.

There is a lively overture in a brisk tempo, which mingles jazz and conventional rhythms. Opening with a C-major chord, it states several leading themes of the opera.

## ACT ONE

[*Scene One*] A room in the palace of the Maharajah in the foothills of the Himalayas. The Indian potentate and Mr. Scattergood are examining various documents. A long musical dialogue takes place in which the two discuss the possibility of marriage between the Maharajah's son, Kodanda, the Crown Prince, and Scattergood's daughter, Kitty. They begin by enumerating their respective possessions—motor cars, airplanes and wives ("How many motor cars?"—"Quante automobili?").

The Maharajah piles up an impressive total—twenty-two cars,

thirty-two airplanes, twenty-seven wives (one official), ninety-six little cities and six big ones. Scattergood can boast of a paltry six cars, three airplanes, one wife (all the law allows), châteaux, chalets and villas in Europe and Peru, a ranch in Arizona, six buildings and eight skyscrapers in Chicago and New York. All this is sung in quasi-recitative over an accompaniment in a rollicking tempo.

Having duly taken inventory, the two conclude that marriage between their two children would be a commendable idea. The only obstacle is that Kitty and the Crown Prince are stubborn and flatly refuse to get married. Scattergood suggests that the Maharanee might be helpful. She is too stupid for that, the Maharajah snorts, adding that the one thing to her credit is that she bore him his only son.

"What!" Scattergood exclaims. "Only one son from twenty-seven wives!" In a brief refrain ("It seems rather improbable"—"E già, pare impossibile") the Maharajah blandly explains that twenty-six of the wives turned out to be sterile, but the Maharanee vindicated his manhood by bearing him a son without delay. The boy, he says, is blue-eyed and fair-haired (doesn't resemble his father) and it may well be that one of his ancestors was pure Anglo-Saxon.

At this point the Maharanee herself appears. Enormously fat, she waddles in supported by Sardula and another servant girl, sinks into a heap of cushions and begins munching almonds.

Looking at her with casual contempt, the Maharajah observes that she is pear-shaped, but at least she gave him an heir. He goes on to describe her in derisive terms in a hilarious aria, "Look her over"—"Ma la guarde." This is a mountain of a woman, he sings, a Rock of Gibraltar, a tuba, an entire band. Yet she is as logical as the dome on the nave of a cathedral. She neither reads nor writes, never walks and seldom talks. Her favorite diversion, next to stuffing herself with sweets, is playing the stock market. Scattergood, fascinated, murmurs that she is obviously a smart woman.

Asking her advice, says the Maharajah, is a waste of time, but he invites Scattergood to go ahead. Awed by the woman's vast bulk, he timidly approaches and with a nervous stammer asks what she thinks of the marriage plans. Like a massive idol, she stares at him for a long moment, then replies in sepulchral tones. Her advice is brief and to the point: If he will see to his daughter, they will do the same with their son. Both Scattergood and the Maharajah hail this solution as a stroke of genius.

Scattergood starts to leave, saying he must find his daughter. The Maharajah protests his going in the heat of the day and leads him back to his chair. With a clap of his hands he summons servants, whom he orders to call the Crown Prince and to tell the American girl that her father wishes to see her.

An orchestral interlude in 5/4 time follows, during which several masons, working with lightning speed, erect a wall separating the Maharajah and Scattergood and dividing the stage into two parts. After the masons have left, Crown Prince Kodanda enters and announces that he knows why he has been called ("Father dear, I already know"—"Padre mio, indovino perché").

This introduces a remarkable ensemble which blends the voices of the characters on either side of the wall (in the manner of the *Rigoletto* quartet). Kodanda at once declares he will have nothing to do with the marriage proposals. His father denounces him as an ungrateful son. A family argument develops briefly as the Maharanee blames her husband for spoiling the Crown Prince. Kodanda implores his parents to spare him the fate of marriage to the American girl. Arguing in pantomime, the three move upstage.

On the other side of the wall, where Scattergood is sitting staring into space, Kitty enters. She is dressed in an explorer's costume. Noting her father's woebegone expression, she asks what is troubling him ("Papa, what's wrong?"—"Papa, che c'è?"). Musical dialogue ensues. Scattergood's explanation is that times are bad and that his ulcer is bothering him. But Kitty, realizing what really is on his mind, warns him—just as Kodanda did on the other side of the wall—that she will have nothing to do with any plans for marriage.

Then in a kind of parody of an operatic *secco* recitative ("I have traveled here to India"—"Siam venuti appasta in India") she says she has come to India for the sole purpose of finding the "last primitive cave man." As this is to be the subject of her Ph.D. thesis, she does not intend to interrupt her scientific studies by getting married. She is convinced that this prehistoric man has survived and is somewhere in India—and she will be the one to find him.

Kitty and her father withdraw upstage and the scene shifts back to the other side of the wall. From this point on the ensemble continues in sextet form involving the four principals plus Sardula and the Maharanee. It begins as the Maharajah and Scattergood, in echoing phrases, entreat their offspring to heed parental advice. Kodanda reiterates that he is not interested in American women —their skins are too white. He would much prefer a girl like Sardula. The Maharanee gasps in dismay at the idea of his marrying a servant girl.

Sardula herself chimes in to advise Kodanda that his wife should be an American girl with oil wells. Half jestingly, the Crown Prince ticks off other marital possibilities—German, French, Greek, Italian. The women reject them out of hand for various reasons. They have only one suggestion, which they repeat in thirds like a chant: "But this American girl fits to perfection"— "L'Americana in vice è perfetta").

The three now withdraw as Kitty and Scattergood move into the scene. Insisting that she will not marry until she finds her "wild man," Kitty assures her father that this discovery will make her famous. This is her destiny, she sings, and to accomplish her mission she will stay in India "forever." For want of a better answer, Scattergood plaintively remarks that the future is uncertain and that all he asks is to die in peace. Kitty climaxes her part of the argument on a high coloratura phrase.

Kodanda, Sardula and the Maharanee now resume the battle. Again the women insist he must marry a rich girl. Again they reject Kodanda's candidates: English or French (too mannish and too clannish, respectively). In the identical musical phrase sung before, they repeat their chant: "But this American girl fits to perfection."

Kodanda thereupon launches into a discourse on the relative wifely qualifications of American and Indian women. He does not deny that American women are attractive, but they complain too much. He prefers a simple, tenderhearted native girl—the kind of woman he can understand. He concludes his discourse on a lyrical phrase.

At this point the Maharajah steps in to upbraid his son for being somewhat stupid: After all, this is to be a marriage of convenience. This introduces a new phase of the discussion on both sides of the wall. In a last-ditch effort to win the battle, the Maharajah and Scattergood call attention to the deplorable state of world affairs. In India—reformers, constitutions, revolutions! In America—billion-dollar budgets, Democrats, taxes, Senate investigations! Under the circumstances it is difficult to amass another million. Kitty and Kodanda must not miss their golden opportunity, the fathers declare. They must marry *now*. The upshot of all this is that the two suddenly agree to be married. The parents and Sardula shout a joyful "Bravo!"

But in the next instant their hopes are dashed. Kodanda says

he will marry only if Kitty gives up anthropology. Kitty announces
she will marry only after her mission is completed. Kodanda points
out that it would be a disgrace for an Indian Crown Prince to
marry a girl hunting an ape man. Kitty asks her father how he
could reasonably expect her to face Vassar without a scientific
trophy. And so the question remains: What is to be done? The
others shrug helplessly.

At this point there begins a brilliantly contrived concerted
number, introduced by the phrase "Now, another question"—"Senta
che furba è questo," in which the six principals ponder the
situation. The parents and Sardula sing that, under the conditions
as stated, their problem is to find this prehistoric man. Kitty
declares she would do anything to please dear Papa—but it must
be done her way. She is not interested in being a rich man's wife
and is determined to dedicate her life to science.

Kodanda observes that he knows any number of charming women
who are mad about him—he does not have to waste his time on
a conceited Vassar girl. In any case, he adds, his only true love
is Sardula. The sextet ends with a flourish on the phrase "That
is the problem as of now"—"Il gran problema è tutto qua." Kitty
and Kodanda leave by their separate exits.

The Maharajah claps his hands to recall the masons and orders
them to remove the wall immediately. This they do as quickly as
they built it, while the music that accompanied the building is
played backward. Face to face again, the Maharajah and Scattergood gloomily admit their plans have failed. The dilemma is
unchanged: no wild man, no marriage. The men decide once more
to ask the Maharanee's counsel. In her usual oracular fashion she
delivers her answer: If a genuine savage cannot be found, they
will have to invent one. The men applaud her ingenuity.

Thereupon Sardula edges forward and says she knows of someone
who could play the role to perfection. As the others stare in
surprise she explains that this likely prospect is a handsome
young peasant from the hills who has been courting her for the
past two years. As it happens, he is here at this very moment
because today is her birthday and he came to bring her a present.
The Maharanee orders her to bring him in at once.

As Sardula runs off there is a brief byplay between the Maharanee and Scattergood which has an important bearing on the
plot later on. Looking at him intently, the Maharanee asks if they
have ever met before. When Scattergood says no, she insists his
face is familiar. The matter is dropped as Sardula reappears, pushing her young man ahead of her. A majestic fanfare accompanies

his entrance. Awed by his physique, the parents stare at him. Self-conscious and embarrassed, he stares back.

In answer to the Maharajah's question, he says his name is Abdul. An ensemble then follows in which Abdul is persuaded to play the role of a prehistoric savage and is instructed on how to carry out the masquerade. When he protests he knows nothing about acting, the others assure him he is perfect for the part. Sardula impatiently urges him to accept. The Maharajah explains what he is to do. He is to let his hair and beard grow and hide in the jungle like a wild man. When he finally is "discovered," he is not to speak, but only to emit ferocious, apelike growls. To illustrate, the Maharajah thumps his chest and imitates a Tarzan howl. With an understanding nod, Abdul says: "Like Hollywood." The Maharajah beams approvingly.

Then Abdul is told that after he is taken to the jungle he is to allow himself to be captured by a "lady from Chicago." He then will be exhibited in public for two or three weeks as a prize specimen of prehistoric man. For this caper he will be well paid—the American will take care of that, the Maharajah adds complacently. Scattergood gasps. His Highness looks at him expectantly.

Afraid to refuse, Scattergood offers one thousand dollars. Mistaking Abdul's bewilderment for dissatisfaction with the offer, Scattergood raises it to ten thousand. Abdul, in helpless confusion, protests that it is not a question of money—and furthermore, he is not interested in being an actor. Scattergood offers fifty thousand. The Maharajah generously suggests making it an even hundred thousand. As Scattergood groans over the figure, the Maharajah leads Abdul to a table, scribbles out a contract, then reads it in spoken words. It stipulates that Abdul is to receive one dollar in advance, ninety-nine thousand, nine hundred and ninety-nine dollars when the job is finished.

The ensemble continues in quasi-recitative interspersed with concerted passages. Unable to reason with his determined benefactors, Abdul turns to Sardula with a pleading look. She, of course, tells him to be practical and not to refuse all this "lovely money" which is being thrust into his hands. The parents are aghast at the thought of anyone refusing to accept one hundred thousand dollars.

Losing his temper completely, Abdul furiously rejects the whole idea. At that point, Sardula resorts to her ultimate weapon: tears. If he cannot support her, she wails, how can they be married? Sardula, of course, wins the day—with the help of the others, who loudly berate Abdul for being a coldhearted monster. Abdul consents to sign the contract if Sardula will promise to marry him. Instantly her demeanor changes to passionate affection. The Maharajah and the Maharanee compliment Abdul on his decision and assure him that once he signs the contract he can live like a king for the rest of his life. Reiterating these various sentiments, the principals bring the scene to a close.

[*Scene Two*] There is a long orchestral introduction dominated by a sinuous rhythmic figure. It is late afternoon in the court of the palace. The Maharanee is dozing in a corner as Sardula reads her the latest stock market quotations. From the distance comes the sound of a women's chorus ("O my hunter, far away"—"Dove erri, O cacciator"). They sing about the hunter whose sweetheart assures him that she will be waiting for him with her lamp to light his way safely home.

As the refrain dies softly away, Sardula stops reading, sees that the Maharanee is fast asleep and starts to tiptoe out of the room. Suddenly Kodanda appears, blocks her way and tries to embrace her. A brief scene in quasi-recitative follows. Struggling to free herself, Sardula angrily reminds Kodanda that she is engaged to another man—and, what is more, he himself is engaged to that American girl.

Kodanda contemptuously dismisses the thought of marrying "that anthropologist" and tells Sardula that he is madly in love with her. Sardula retorts that he will marry the anthropologist whether he likes it or not. It is all arranged—even if she doesn't find the primitive man. But Kodanda only becomes more ardent and vows he will tame her. She defies him, which only serves to make him more persistent. The theme of conquest and resistance continues in duet form. It reaches a climax when Sardula tears herself from Kodanda's arms, then slaps his face and runs away. Crestfallen, Kodanda stares after her.

A moment later there is a distant fanfare of hunting horns. This awakens the Maharanee, who orders Kodanda to assemble the court. As the fanfare swells, a great throng crowds upon the scene—men and women of the court, visiting princes and their retinues, a band of hunters, porters carrying the spoils of the chase. Then come the Maharajah, Scattergood and Kitty, all in hunting costume. Finally, four porters carry in a huge cage. In it sits Abdul disguised as a savage.

In a delightful spoof of the conventional operatic "triumphal chorus," the crowd hails the success of the hunt ("These are the mighty hunters"—"Che i cacciatori"). The focus of attention, of course, is the strange creature in the cage. The crowd speculates as to whether he is a demon from the moon, half man or half beast, or a Hollywood star. The chorus rises to a mighty crescendo of wild guesses, with one and all finally wondering if this captive could be the Abominable Snowman.

Kitty steps forward and, in recitative, orders her trophy to be exhibited as evidence that she has not been chasing phantoms at her father's expense. In an ensuing aria, the first in the opera ("Just look at him"—"Guardatelo"), she triumphantly declares that here is living proof that she has discovered the surviving member of a prehistoric race. She bids the crowd to take note of his muscular build, but warns them not to come too close. Kitty says she is convinced that beneath that savage exterior is a human being of true nobility who will respond to kindness and patient understanding. She herself will teach him the arts of civilization, and the world of science will honor her for her accomplishment. The crowd acclaims her vociferously, while Kodanda laments that now he is fated to marry her.

The Maharajah, calling for silence, commands the scholars of his court to come forward and render a scientific opinion about this fabulous creature. Aside, he warns them that any adverse remarks will cost them their heads.

An amusing colloquy follows as the First and Second Scholars discuss the prehistoric specimen in pompous, pseudoscientific terms. They begin by agreeing that he obviously is not oriental, then experimentally address him in German, English, French and Italian. Abdul roars obligingly. They decide that he belongs to an unknown race—possibly a direct descendant of Pithecanthropus erectus. Their final conclusion is that his speech is monosyllabic and a trifle unrefined.

The Maharajah, bored with their chatter, curtly dismisses them. As the crowd again acclaims this scientific wonder, Scattergood steps forward and urges Kitty and Kodanda to set the wedding date. Thereupon Kitty causes general consternation by disclosing the next step in her anthropological research. This specimen, she explains, will require intensive study. Accordingly, she proposes to tame him, then take him to the zoological gardens in New York.

At this there are expressions of dismay from the parents and Sardula, while the onlookers voice their approval of Kitty's decision. This introduces an ensemble. Scattergood fumes that Kitty's plan is outright treason; she denies any ulterior motive. Sardula wonders how far this bizarre experiment will go. Kodanda sees a ray of hope—perhaps this turn of events will free him of the obligation to marry Kitty. The Maharajah and the Maharanee resign themselves to letting Kitty have her way, thus wrecking their hopes for marriage.

At this point it is agreed that there must be an official answer to Kitty's proposal, and the crowd calls on the Maharajah to decide. He steps forward, calls for silence, then pauses uncertainly. The Maharanee whispers in his ear, whereupon his harassed expression gives way to a happy smile. Turning to Kitty and Kodanda, he proclaims that their problem has been solved: They are to remain engaged, but the wedding will be postponed for six months. The two young people enthusiastically agree to the plan. The Maharajah promptly invites everyone to a banquet in honor of Kitty. It will be a magnificent feast, he promises, with dandelion soup for the Indians and toasted lions for the Christians. During a brief interlude of martial music all follow the Maharajah into the palace.

The Maharanee detains Scattergood for a moment. In a repetition of the musical phrase she sang in Scene One, she repeats her mysterious question—this time asking if he has ever been in Singapore. As puzzled as before, Scattergood answers no. And also as before, the Maharanee murmurs that his face is so familiar. They both go into the palace.

Abdul, alone in his cage in the deepening twilight, gives way to his gloomy forebodings in a long dramatic soliloquy preceded by a recitative ("Ah, see where my love for her has brought me" —"Guard un po in che guaio me son messo"). Here he is, he reflects bitterly, a captive slave in a cage, trapped by love. What is worse, he probably will be taken to America. Ruefully he admits he alone is to blame for his predicament because he allowed a woman to make up his mind for him.

In the ensuing aria, "Only for you"—"Solo per te," he laments that for Sardula's love and the lure of money he bargained away his freedom and his happiness. In the dramatic climax of the aria he bids farewell to the forests, fields and mountains of his beloved native land—these treasures which money cannot buy. A thunderous phrase in the orchestra underscores his despair. The aria is a fine example of Menotti's gift for simple, classic melody.

Abdul's melancholy reflections are interrupted by Sardula, who tiptoes in carrying a lantern. He greets her by complaining bitterly about his fate. She tries to soothe his feelings by telling him she has brought him something to eat, along with bandages and disinfectant for his cuts and bruises. When he fumes about being taken to America she offers him some practical advice: Get civilized in a hurry, collect your fee, then come back and marry Sardula.

With that she cautiously enters the cage and sits down next to Abdul. In a charming duet ("My handsome hunter") the two plan their future life together. Thanks to that beautiful money, it will be one long, glorious holiday . . . wining and dining like kings . . . servants by the score . . . no boring household duties. Perhaps they will raise a family, twenty children or so . . . there will always be music and dancing . . . nothing as dull as farming for them. Enchanted by their dream of affluence, they climax the duet with an ardent declaration of love. A noise outside puts an end to their tryst. Sardula snatches up the lantern and scampers away. The curtain falls.

## ACT TWO

[*Scene One*] Kitty's boudoir in her father's penthouse in Chicago a few months later. Lounging on a sofa, she is talking on the telephone. Abdul, still in his cave man costume with his hands chained together, is having his measurements taken by three tailors. An ensemble in quartet form follows as Kitty describes Abdul to a friend over the telephone, while the tailors argue about the proper attire for him. Kitty is inviting "all Chicago" to a party —"artists, scientists, and the clergy"—where she will present her primitive man to society.

The tailors, gasping at Abdul's chest measurement—fifty inches —wrangle over the color of his suits. By the time they have discussed the relative merits of zippers versus buttons and are caviling about the sartorial tastes of American versus British tailors, Kitty has completed her telephoning. Driven to distraction by the squabbling, Abdul explodes. Denouncing them as stupid clowns, he bellows at them to leave him alone. In uproarious confusion, the tailors snatch up their materials and scramble for the door. When one of them turns and sticks out his tongue, Abdul lunges at him with a roar of anger. Kitty seizes a whip and cracks it like a lion tamer. Abdul stops in his tracks and glares at her.

Ordering him to lock the door, Kitty informs him that the next step in his education will be a lesson in the art of love. Stepping back suspiciously, Abdul asks what she means by "love." A complicated subject with a complicated object, Kitty explains casually. Abdul tells her curtly he will have none of it, whereupon Kitty lashes at him with the whip. Abdul begs for mercy. Then, to the accompaniment of a languorous theme (somewhat like the love motive in *Tristan*), she gives him his first lesson in the art of kissing, going into seductive detail. After the first try, she concedes that, for a primitive, he is quite adept at this esoteric art. Getting into the spirit of the "lesson," Abdul assures her that he can do even better.

Realizing that the situation may get out of hand, Kitty hastens to explain that "civilized" love is another matter: It demands more poetry. Nevertheless, she continues with the next lesson—the art of embracing. For best results, she informs Abdul, there must be soft lights, sweet music and whisky. With that she leads him to the sofa, stretches out voluptuously and pulls him down beside her. For a moment, Abdul is repelled by this brazen exercise in civilized love-making, but then he surrenders to her embrace. They remain in each other's arms as the scene fades.

The romantic mood is sustained by the orchestral interlude which continues without pause.

[*Scene Two*] The garden of the Maharajah's palace, where Kodanda is discovered alone. Like Abdul, he is brooding over his uncertain future. In recitative, he reflects on his life as an only son and heir to a throne. And now, he muses, Sardula is beginning to fall in love with him—which complicates matters still more. Committed as he is to marry Kitty, what can he offer Sardula?

Kodanda ponders this question in one of the most melodious arias in the opera, "No, I dare not ask"—"Chiedere non so." His reasoning is that, so long as he does not know how she would answer his declaration of love, he still can live in hope. But if she answered no, he would not care to live. In the dramatic concluding phrases of the aria he sings that this doubt is both a torment and a pleasure.

[*Scene Three*] The living room of Scattergood's penthouse. On a platform at one end of the room is a large table. Before it, chairs are arranged as for a lecture. Abdul, impressive in a dark blue suit, stands at the window gazing at the Chicago skyline. It is five o'clock in the afternoon.

To the accompaniment of an agitated theme in the orchestra, Scattergood comes hurrying in. Dialogue in recitative follows. Scattergood informs Abdul that after tonight's reception his job will be finished, and he can go back to India. Handing him his plane ticket, Scattergood adds that his chauffeur will rush him to the airport immediately after the party. As to his fee, he says, showing Abdul a huge roll of bills, it's much too bulky to carry around, but he will find it in his pocket when he leaves.

Abdul mutters that he will be happy to go back to India. Scattergood dryly observes that he will be equally happy, because he was beginning to be concerned about these long "private lessons" with his daughter. Stung by the insinuation, Abdul bursts out that this "tutoring" has torn him apart emotionally and left him in a state of complete confusion.

With a placating gesture, Scattergood launches into one of the principal baritone arias of the opera, "You are free now"—"Tu mi piaci." Sung in a vigorous tempo, it is a brilliant example of Menotti's skill in fusing words and music. It is Scattergood's sardonic litany of the multiple blessings of civilization, of which he, as one of its products, is a helpless victim. With cynical relish he enumerates them: from dictaphones to doctors, from stenographers to sleeping pills. He urges Abdul to make his escape from civilization while he still is free—free from lunches, conventions, stock market fluctuations, "those damned initials, P.T.A., UN, NATO," insurance men, politicians, pensions, and contributions to Spoleto.[1] Scattergood concludes this spectacular aria with a dramatic reiteration of his warning: "Save yourself today!"—"Tu salvati che puoi!"

Kitty, wearing a cocktail gown, now enters and asks her father what is delaying the party—the guests are getting impatient. Let them in, Scattergood says, sarcastically cautioning his daughter not to make any high-flown speeches because these "leeches" are interested exclusively in drinking. Kitty peremptorily orders Abdul to the platform, then opens the doors. The guests, most of them brandishing cocktail glasses, burst in on a wave of senseless chatter. Ahead of them is a frenzied group of photographers, who lunge toward Abdul aiming their cameras. The crowd enters during a descriptively discordant orchestral interlude as Scattergood, at the door, does his best to maintain his dignity as a welcoming host.

What follows is a devastating satire, set to music, on the exhibitionistic tomfoolery of the typical "intellectual" cocktail party. When the guests finally seat themselves and the uproar momentarily dies down, Kitty addresses the assemblage in a deliberately flamboyant aria, "Let me present to you"—"Io vi presento." Beginning with a coloratura phrase ("Ladies and gentlemen"), it is a

[1] Menotti's private joke about the Festival of Arts in Spoleto, Italy, which he founded.

mocking imitation of the conventional operatic aria, complete with recitative and cantabile.

Kitty solemnly bids her audience to look upon this man who only six weeks ago was a savage prowling the jungle. Because of her knowledge of Freudian psychology, anthropology, parabiology and philology (plus a few flicks of the whip), she was able to tame and train this creature. Today he is as civilized as any member of the audience. He has faultless manners, knows the value of a dollar and is not afraid of television. All this goes to prove, Kitty declares, that she is unquestionably the world's greatest anthropologist. The audience wildly applauds her.

From this point on the scene builds into a long and complex choral ensemble. The guests express their admiration for Kitty's achievement and marvel that this erstwhile primitive's manners are as impeccable as their own. Abdul fumes that the behavior of these representatives of civilized society is more than he can bear. Kitty repeats the concluding phrases of her aria in a coloratura obbligato to the chorus. The score calls for an ending on a high E-flat.

Scattergood, pounding a gavel in true board chairman style, pompously calls upon the various distinguished groups present to come forward and identify themselves for Abdul's benefit, to give him some idea of how an enlightened society functions. First he calls on the clergy.

The members of the ministerial group, vociferously contradicting each other, begin explaining who God is. The Philosopher chimes in to assure Abdul that God does not exist—and neither does he. The Physician elbows close to warn Abdul about the fatal effects of tobacco. A fluttering covey of ladies presses forward to gaze at Abdul admiringly and invite him to dine with them—individually. Members of the working press, representing the newspapers, radio and television, demand to know what he thinks of Chicago, the U.S.A., and American women. The hapless Abdul only stares impassively at the clamoring mob. When some protest, in a brief concerted passage, that he is acting like a temperamental Hollywood star, Kitty entreats them to be patient with him.

Next, a chorus of debutantes approaches with the information that they are out to capture rich husbands. They need not be clever—merely rich; if not rich, perhaps they will serve as lovers. The debutantes are elbowed out of the way by the politicians, who bellow that Abdul's salvation lies in voting, respectively, for communism, Democrats, Republicans, Conservatives, a dictator and a king. Each politician warns Abdul not to believe the others. They are all liars.

Then it is the turn of the military officers and city officials. The military threatens Abdul with arrest if he tries to escape; the civic authorities remind him that the local law requires every savage to have an elementary school education.

Abdul next is favored with an exhibition of the creative talents of an avant-garde painter, a poet and a composer. The painter produces a masterpiece on the spot by splashing his canvas with multicolored paint squirted from an iron tube. There is a burst of frenzied applause. The poet recites an incomprehensible bit of free verse entitled "I." More applause.

The composer, carrying a tape recorder, steps forward with three instrumentalists and a soprano, who are to perform his latest opus. He first explains he has succeeded in creating "lots of sound" while avoiding anything that would make musical sense. Announcing he will demonstrate a "perfect example of the new electrododecaphonic style," he turns on the tape recorder and gives the cue to the instrumentalists and the singer. For this perform-ance Menotti has written some eleven measures of excruciating dissonances (he once described this as "my first dodecaphonic composition"), over which the soprano screeches a two-line ballad in German: "Tag ohne Schmerzen/ Ist wie Nacht ohne Kerzen."[2] This brings more hysterical applause from the guests, who embrace the composer.

The final display in this extravaganza is provided by the scientist, who exhibits a boxlike contrivance bristling with push buttons, dials and knobs. This clever invention, he announces, has won him the Nobel Prize and it represents the ultimate solution to all cosmic problems. Simply by pushing a button, one can destroy the universe.

Again the audience madly applauds. Abdul despairingly asks Kitty how she can endure this lunacy. It simply shows, she re-plies imperturbably, how complicated and exciting life can be.

At this point the reception explodes into headlong pandemo-nium, with each guest bellowing louder than the others for Abdul's attention. A "career woman" pushes a contract under his nose, shrieking at him to endorse a new perfume called "Essence of Wild Man." With the others reiterating their own claims and de-mands, the ensemble surges to a frenzied climax.

[2] Roughly translated: "Day without pain is like night without candles."

Suddenly Abdul, losing control of himself, bursts out in a wild scream of rage. The guests stare at him in stunned silence. Turning to Kitty, he cries that although he loves her he cannot endure this maniacal civilization of which she is a part. In rising anger he denounces her for deceiving him and tells her to find another victim for her selfish adventures. Let her keep her idols, he roars, he will end his life as a self-respecting peasant. With that he springs from the platform and fights his way to the door, bowling over everyone in his path and tearing down a mobile hanging from the ceiling as he goes. As it comes crashing down, the panic-stricken guests scream in terror. The curtain falls to the accompaniment of a thunderous orchestral climax. This scene has been compared to the famous brawl in Act Two of *Die Meistersinger*.

## ACT THREE

A month later, in a clearing deep in the Indian jungle. At one side, almost hidden by foliage, is the entrance to a cave. Abdul, clad in a leopard skin, is sprawled under a tree.

In a spoken soliloquy, he reflects on the incredible train of events of the past months, trying to fathom the reason for the fantastic behavior of the "civilized" people he encountered. They talked endlessly about freedom, love and money . . . yet they seemed to long desperately for the serenity he himself is enjoying at this moment in the jungle.

He lacks only one thing, he muses: love. His thoughts turn amorously to Kitty, but he slaps himself in the face to end this reverie. When he again lapses into thinking about Kitty's kisses, a monkey in the tree above him shatters that dream by pelting him with coconuts. Rubbing his head, he mutters that he has paid the penalty for wasting his time daydreaming. Hearing a sudden noise in the jungle, Abdul vanishes into the cave.

After a brief orchestral interlude, a company of servants and soldiers of the Maharajah straggles into the clearing carrying picnic baskets, suitcases and other gear. They are part of the searching party organized by the Maharajah to hunt down and recapture Abdul.

In a doleful, minor chant ("Long is the journey"—"Lungo è il cammino") they complain about the endless journey they are forced to make at the whim of rich people. They are followed by Kitty and Scattergood in hunting costume. A passage in recitative ensues. Scattergood fumes that they have been hunting this wretch Abdul for three weeks all in vain. He blames Kitty for the entire fiasco and denounces Abdul as a brazen fraud.

If she will forget him, Scattergood says beseechingly, it not only will make her poor father happy but will save him from paying this savage the ninety-nine thousand, nine hundred and ninety-nine dollars he still owes him. But Kitty obstinately insists that she must find Abdul and learn the truth from his own lips. She will not believe he deliberately deceived her, she adds, bursting into tears. The servants and soldiers again break out in their lugubrious refrain, chanting that death lurks behind the green mask of the forest.

Heralded by an orchestral interlude in a stately martial tempo, the Maharajah arrives followed by the Maharanee, Sardula, Kodanda and the rest of the royal entourage. Showing impatience with the general air of gloom, he commands everyone to join him at lunch in the tent which servants are setting up. Then His Highness rasps out an order to the soldiers to continue the search for Abdul until they find him. If they do not find the fugitive immediately, he warns, he will execute them all for a crime against the state. With that he stalks into his tent, followed by the crowd.

Meanwhile, some distance away, Sardula is reclining under a tree. Kodanda steals up behind her and closes his hands over her eyes. She gently frees herself and then they kiss passionately. A brief colloquy follows. Kodanda says he has come to a decision: He will marry Sardula if she will have him. Taken by surprise, she asks what is to be done about Abdul. Forget him, is Kodanda's succinct advice—if a tiger hasn't eaten him, "our little Kitty" will. Sardula giggles at this, then reminds Kodanda that his father is waiting for him. He goes into the tent.

Alone, Sardula gives expression to her perplexing thoughts about Abdul in the aria "How shall my lips deny it?"—"Che gli dirai quel giorno?" The theme of it is that she does not know how she can find the words to tell Abdul she no longer loves him. At the conclusion of the aria she walks slowly into the tent.

A moment later Scattergood comes bustling out with the Maharanee waddling after him. The two sit down on stools placed under a tree by a servant. The scene which follows in recitative unravels the plot of the opera in terms of high comedy. The Maharanee begins by reiterating her apparently pointless question: "Where have I seen you before?" This time she mentions Egypt. Scattergood casually answers that he had traveled there. With a startled shriek, the Maharanee babbles that now it all comes back to her: Scattergood was the handsome young tourist ("you looked like Rudolph Valentino") who made love to her in the shadow of the pyramids beside the Nile. With that she throws herself into his arms, crying that she is about to faint. Staggering under her weight, Scattergood groans in dismay.

To his utter consternation she reveals that there was a sequel to their romantic adventure—a sequel in the person of Kodanda, who is their own son. Then, Scattergood stammers incredulously, his daughter Kitty is Kodanda's sister. In a brief "patter" duet, they sing that this love match they have been promoting actually would be an incestuous relationship which must be broken off at all costs.

The Maharanee promises to head off the marriage on the condition that the Maharajah never will find out about his wife's indiscretion. As Scattergood swears eternal silence—and sighs in relief—she frightens him out of his wits by hinting, with ponderous coquetry, that perhaps it is not too late to revive their romance.

He is rescued from the Maharanee's amorous clutches by the entrance of a group of servants who have dragged Abdul out of his cave at the end of a rope. In a brief chorus ("See what we've got"—"Eccoli, l'hanno acchiappato") they describe how they fought to subdue this dangerous savage. Abdul struggles furiously to free himself and the servants finally untie him.

The Maharajah, Kodanda and Kitty come rushing out of the tent. Abdul falls to his knees and in a dramatic refrain ("Won't you hear me"—"Ascoltatemi vi prego") implores them to give him his freedom. He has kept his part of the bargain, he cries, and now he asks only to be left in peace. In chorus, all the others assure him they do not mean to harm him—they have come simply to pay him the rest of his fee, as per agreement. Holding out a huge roll of bills, Scattergood declares in a recitative passage that as an honest American he will now pay Abdul the balance still owed him.

From this point, the scene continues in a succession of ensembles, duets and arias to the finale of the opera. When Abdul, as before, protests that he has no use for money, his would-be benefactors exclaim that this is impossible. But Kitty comes to his defense, praising him as a "superman" who is above any such crass considerations as money. Impulsively throwing her arms around his neck, she declares that all she wants is his love.

Abdul tries to restrain her ardor, reminding her that he is still engaged to Sardula. He and Kitty turn to her questioningly. With simple candor Sardula confesses she no longer loves Abdul because her heart has changed. With that she bursts into tears. In a brief ensemble the others try to comfort her, while Abdul tells her that his heart too has changed. Hearing this, Kitty again impetuously embraces him. Suddenly the Maharajah, who has been staring at these bizarre goings-on as though hypnotized, bursts out in exasperation to demand what it all means. Scattergood's efforts to explain only irritate him more, and he roundly berates the millionaire for condoning all this nonsense. But he is somewhat mollified when he hears Abdul try to convince Kitty that, though he loves her madly, nothing could drag him back to face those "fiends of hell" in Chicago whom she calls her friends.

Thereupon Kitty, in mock-heroic phrases underscored by a majestic cantabile in waltz tempo, proclaims that for his love she will renounce civilization and live with him in a cave. She tells the others they may as well go home, because she has decided to live in the jungle with the man she loves. Her resolve ("And I shall stay"—"Io restero") is sung in a ringing dramatic phrase which soars to a high D sharp. (The comparison here with the scene between Radames and the High Priest Ramfis at the third-act curtain in *Aida* is irresistible.)

There is a bellow of rage from the Maharajah, who demands immediate action from Scattergood on his daughter's about-face. Prompted by an approving glance from the Maharanee, he answers that he is in favor of Kitty's decision and will not stand in her way. Furiously reminding Scattergood that their investment is at stake, the Maharajah growls that this is what happens when one deals with Americans.

To make matters worse, Kodanda, leading Sardula, kneels before him and asks his paternal blessing. His Highness roars that he will have him shot for his impudence. The Maharanee intervenes, advising her husband not to stand in the way of true love. The others add their entreaties, reminding him that love has nothing to do with logic. Now in a towering rage and completely frustrated, the Maharajah shouts that everyone except himself has gone crazy.

A septet ensues in which the principals sum up their various reactions ("Ah, how fortune waits in hiding"—"Ah, il destino che sorprese"). The four young people rejoice that they have been united with their true loves at last; the Maharajah laments that all his plans have ended in disaster—with his stupid son choosing a servant girl and Kitty a jungle savage. Scattergood marvels that he, a respectable citizen, has a love child in India, a romantic secret which the mighty Maharajah never will discover. The

Maharanee reflects over her good fortune in being reunited with the charming lover of her Nile adventure. The septet ends in a rousing operatic climax as all point the moral of the tale: Wise men gamble only on the present; only fools gamble on the future.

The Maharajah, fuming that he wants nothing more to do with children or marriage, strides toward his tent. He declares that henceforth he will devote his precious time to his stamp collection. The Maharanee, Sardula and Kodanda follow him inside.

A scene now follows between Kitty and her father. Scattergood again tries to dissuade her from her absurd notion of living in the jungle. Kitty blandly assures him that life will not be as primitive as he imagines: He is to leave Abdul's money with her, then send out a butler and a cook from Chicago. Her father, aghast at the idea, warns her that Abdul probably will kill her when he discovers her scheme. Kitty flippantly observes that a woman has nothing to fear from a man who is a lover, and that it would be nonsense to think of her surrendering completely. Roaring with laughter, Scattergood remarks that sex appeal is the downfall of every superman.

Kitty asks him to send some housekeeping necessities to the cave without unduly disturbing Abdul, then to send more money later to make the place livable. It will all be quite delightful, she says airily—and as for husband Abdul, if he wants to play Samson she'll gladly play Delilah. Kitty sings the name in a soaring coloratura phrase.

During a brief orchestral passage, the Maharajah and his entourage emerge from the tent, which is then dismantled and carried away. His Highness, whose wrath has subsided into a mood of benevolence, bids Kitty an affectionate farewell ("The sun is going and we must go"—"Tramonta il sole e si deve partir"). This marks the beginning of another richly melodic septet in which all, with a certain mocking sentimentality, take leave of each other with the hope that heaven will protect them from their individual follies. They leave Kitty and Abdul with exaggerated gestures of farewell.

During a serene orchestral interlude the scene darkens into twilight. Over the sound of jungle mutterings and twitterings are heard the distant horn calls of the Maharajah's party.

The lovers, lying down on a bed of moss, blend their voices in an impassioned duet, "See how the dying sun"—"Ecco sul verde mar." They sing of the tranquil magic of the jungle and the enveloping friendliness of the forest. Civilization is far away, and in this green enchanted world of their own they ask for nothing more than the beauty and wonder of their love.

Abdul bends over Kitty and passionately embraces her as the theme of the duet fades into silence. Suddenly a mischievous figure sounds softly in the orchestra. With her free arm, Kitty gestures surreptitiously toward the forest. Out of the shadows come servants, who silently carry into the cave a bathtub, a refrigerator and a television set. The curtain falls.

# Luisa Miller

## *by* GIUSEPPE VERDI
### (1813–1901)

### *Libretto by*
#### SALVATORE CAMMARANO

*Based on the drama* KABALE UND LIEBE, *by the German poet-dramatist Johann Christoph Friedrich von Schiller*

#### CHARACTERS

| | |
|---|---|
| Count Walter | Bass |
| Rodolfo, his son (first disguised as Carlo) | Tenor |
| Miller, an old soldier | Baritone |
| Luisa, his daughter | Soprano |
| Federica, Duchess of Ostheim, Count Walter's niece | Contralto |
| Wurm, steward to Count Walter | Bass |
| Laura, a peasant girl | Mezzo-soprano |
| A peasant | Tenor |

Ladies attending the Duchess, pages, servants, archers, men-at-arms, villagers

*Place:* A Tyrolean village
*Time:* Seventeenth century
*First performance:* Teatro San Carlo, Naples, December 8, 1849
*Original language:* Italian

---

*Luisa Miller,* Verdi's fifteenth opera, is a blood-and-thunder melodrama which contains to a satisfying degree the familiar elements of grand opera—emotional upheaval, display of passion, intrigue, star-crossed lovers—all set to broad, sweeping melodies and thunderous choral climaxes.

It has been described as Verdi's first outstanding success since *Ernani,* and as a work that prepared the way for his later triumphs. In this opera the composer shifted his area of plot interest from the larger-than-life world of kings, courtiers, statesmen and epic battles to the *verismo* portrayal of individual human beings in situations involving the play of elemental emotions. Verdi was fortunate in having a libretto based on the soundly constructed drama by Schiller.

Subsequent to its premiere in Naples, where it was acclaimed, it was given in Spain, France, Russia, Hungary, Turkey, South America and England, with performances in Italian, French, German, Hungarian and English. In London (1858), however, it failed. Its first production in America was at the Castle Garden Theater in New York City on July 20, 1854. The Metropolitan Opera Company staged it on December 21, 1929, with Rosa Ponselle in the role of Luisa. Although favorably received, it was given only a limited number of performances. It was absent from the operatic repertoire in this country until its revival during the Metropolitan's 1968–69 season.

The overture, considered one of the best Verdi ever wrote, is dominated by variations on the theme of a dramatic refrain sung by Rodolfo at the conclusion of Act Two.

## ACT ONE
### (*Love*)

[*Scene One*] After a brief introduction the curtain rises on a picturesque Tyrolean village. At one side is the cottage where Luisa and her father live. Opposite is a small church. Visible in the background is the castle of Count Walter. Villagers gathered to celebrate Luisa's birthday greet her in a spirited chorus ("Ti desta, Luisa, regina de' cori") as the queen of their hearts.

Miller, Luisa and her friend Laura appear and thank the peasants for their good wishes. But Luisa, looking around anxiously, frets because a certain young man she has been expecting is nowhere to be seen. Her father tries to reassure her. At the same time he voices certain misgivings about this young man, who calls himself Carlo. He is a complete stranger, not only to Count Walter but to everyone else in the village. Miller hopes his daughter will not be deceived in her love for him.

Luisa answers her father in one of the opera's principal arias, "Lo vidi, e'l primo palpito," the burden of which is that from the first moment she saw Carlo her heart throbbed in rhythm with his. Fate has destined them to be united in eternal love. The aria ends in a brilliant cadenza. As the villagers crowd around to present her with garlands of flowers, Carlo (Rodolfo in disguise) makes his way through the throng and hands her his own bouquet. Luisa exclaims in delight. Miller looks on with concern; the villagers comment on the tender scene.

A long ensemble now ensues, beginning with an ardent duet in which Luisa and Carlo pledge their eternal love ("T'amo d'amor ch'esprimere"). Over the choral accompaniment sung by the villagers, Miller's voice blends in trio form as he expresses his premonition of disaster that may overtake this love affair ("Non so qual voce"). Laura's voice is added to form the quartet which dominates the ensemble. As it approaches its climax the clock in the church tower strikes the hour. With telling dramatic effect, the chorus suddenly is hushed to a whisper as all go into the church singing that the voice of heaven itself seems to be sounding to crown this day of happiness with worship. The ensemble then concludes with a repetition of the opening theme.

All except Miller enter the church. As he himself is about to go in, Wurm, the Count's steward, appears and calls to him. A long colloquy follows. The two men converse in recitative over a foreboding orchestral figure. In a jealous rage, Wurm reminds the old man that it has been a year since he promised Luisa's hand in marriage. But up to now this promise has not been kept.

Miller protests that he made the promise only on condition that Luisa really assured him that she was in love with Wurm. Thereupon the steward upbraids Miller for failing to exercise a father's rightful authority over his child. In a majestic aria, "Sacra la scelta è d'un consorte," Miller replies that a girl's choice of a husband is a sacred privilege that cannot be dictated—it is hers alone. He is no tyrant, Miller sings, but a kind and loving father who would not presume to rule his daughter's heart.

Wurm sneers that this father will pay the penalty for being a foolish, indulgent old man. When Miller demands an explanation, Wurm stuns him with the disclosure that the supposed "Carlo" is none other than Rodolfo, the son of Count Walter. With that he stalks away. Shocked and dismayed, Miller cries that his heart is broken ("Ei m'ha spezzato il cor!").

He continues his lamentation in another powerful aria, "Ah, fu giusto il mio sospetto!" Now his foreboding of disaster is justified: His innocent daughter, this precious gift of heaven, may be betrayed and her honor sullied. In the ringing climax of the aria he prays that a father's love may yet save her from ruin. Overwhelmed by despair, he turns and walks away from the church door.

[*Scene Two*] A room in Count Walter's castle. The Count and Wurm enter through a door at the back. They are followed by several servants, who remain standing at the door. There is a brief conversation in recitative between the two men. Walter fumes in anger when Wurm informs him that Rodolfo has been courting Luisa. Deliberately goading him, Wurm remarks that the boy is headstrong. Walter, abruptly announcing that the Duchess d'Ostheim will arrive shortly, tells Wurm to summon Rodolfo. The steward and the servants leave.

Alone, the Count gives way to the secret fear that is haunting him. He cries that Rodolfo will never know what his happiness has cost his father. Then, in an intensely dramatic aria, "Il mio sangue," he expresses the mingled emotions of anger and guilt that are tormenting him. He would give his life's blood, he storms, to bestow power and position upon his son—but Rodolfo only answers his father's efforts with ingratitude and defiance. For Rodolfo's sake, he himself has committed a crime and now is ridden by guilt. Over a surging chromatic figure in the orchestra, Walter voices his terror of eternal punishment. A ringing cadenza concludes the aria.

Rodolfo enters. Controlling himself with an effort, the Count greets him with a show of affection. He tells Rodolfo that Federica, the Duchess d'Ostheim, his future bride, is on her way to the castle. Rodolfo greets the news with half-concealed expressions of alarm and distress. His father goes on to say that, because Rodolfo and Federica have known each other from childhood, this marriage will be an ideal one. In fact, says the Count, when he made the offer of marriage, the Duchess was overjoyed ("Come l'offerta"). Then in continuing recitative he discloses the sequence of events which have led up to the present situation.

Federica's father had forced her to marry the Duke, who later was slain in battle. But all this time she had cherished a secret love for Rodolfo, and when the King of Lamagne himself asked her to marry him she refused because of that love.[1] When Rodolfo protests that he has no desire for power or position, his father upbraids him for his lack of ambition and peremptorily commands him to obey.

A fanfare announces the arrival of the Duchess and her entourage. The people of the court greet her in a chorus of extravagant praise ("Quale un sorriso"). Moved by her warm wel-

---

[1] Lamagne: presumably a mythical kingdom; geographic location not identifiable.

come, she embraces the Count. Presenting Rodolfo to her, he tells her that his son wishes to speak with her alone. Meanwhile he himself will prepare for the royal hunt. All except Federica and Rodolfo leave at a sign from the Count. Rodolfo starts to speak, addressing her as "Duchess" ("Duchessa"). She interrupts to say that, despite all the enticements of court life, her only wish is to be "Federica" to him.

A long and impassioned duet now ensues ("Dall'aule raggianti di vano splendore"). The splendor and luxury of the court, she sings, never have diminished her yearning for her native land here in the Tyrol. Kneeling before her, Rodolfo (aware of the effect his rejection of her will have) begins by saying that, although they shared the joys of childhood, the later years have changed things. Alarmed at his troubled look, Federica asks him to explain. He confesses that he loves someone else.

As Federica recoils, thunderstruck, Rodolfo entreats her to pardon him for causing her this grief ("Deh! la parola amara"). He declares he would rather die than lead her to the altar when his heart belongs to another. The Duchess turns on him in jealous fury and scorn. Let him take her life instead of his own, she bursts out ("Arma, se vuoi, la mano"), and she still will pardon him with her dying breath. But a jealous heart, she warns, knows neither pardon nor pity. Rodolfo implores her forgiveness. As the two reiterate these emotions, the duet rises to its blazing climax. In the throes of anger and despair, Federica and Rodolfo rush away in opposite directions.

[*Scene Three*] The interior of Miller's house. At one side are two doors, one leading to Miller's room, the other to Luisa's. On the wall next to Miller's door hangs his campaign sword along with a military decoration. Through the window of a passageway at the back can be seen part of the village church.

From the distance comes the music of a rousing hunting chorus ("Sciogliete i levrieri"). The hunters call for the dogs to be unleashed and the horses spurred to follow the quarry. There is a brief interlude as Luisa comes out of her room and goes to the window. Anxiously she wonders why Carlo has not left the hunt and returned to her as he had promised. The chorus continues, then dies away as the hunting party rides on.

Suddenly Miller bursts in and throws himself into a chair. He is distraught, and Luisa asks him what has happened. Her father cries out that his worst suspicions have been confirmed: Her lover has deceived her ("Sei tradita"). As Luisa gasps in disbelief, Miller tells her he has just learned that Carlo actually is Rodolfo, the son of Count Walter. (This phrase is sung over a single note insistently repeated in the orchestra, a striking dramatic effect.) What is more, Miller goes on, Rodolfo is to marry a duchess, who this day arrived at the castle. Luisa distractedly begs her father to say no more.

Pacing in fury about the room, Miller suddenly stops and stares at the military decoration hanging on the wall next to his sword. In a menacing, ascending phrase ("Per questa d'onore assisa") he swears on the badge of honor that he will have revenge. Luisa cries out in terror.

Rodolfo, who had appeared in the doorway just in time to hear Miller's words, now strides into the room. Miller lunges at him, but Luisa throws herself between the two men. In a ringing phrase over dark, sustained chords in the orchestra Rodolfo declares that even though his true identity now is known, his heart has not changed. Then in a dramatic gesture he pushes Luisa to her knees in front of her father and kneels beside her. In a passionate outburst ("Son io tuo sposo") he sings that, as her father and God Almighty are witnesses, he is Luisa's betrothed. Miller, deeply moved, warns him of the Count's wrath when he learns of this. With fierce intensity Rodolfo declares that he knows a dreadful secret ("A me soltanto e al cielo") which, when he reveals it, will make the Count beg for mercy.

Luisa suddenly exclaims that someone is entering the house. Rushing to the door, Rodolfo comes face to face with his father. He demands to know why he has come ("Tu, signor, fra queste soglie!"). This marks the beginning of the fiery ensemble which concludes the act.

The Count thunders that he has come, with a father's authority, to put an end to this squalid intrigue. Rodolfo shouts that he will not tolerate this insult to the woman he loves. This "pure" love, Count Walter sneers, has been bought and paid for. In mounting fury, Rodolfo draws his sword, but then sheathes it and steps back. He will spare the life of the man who gave him his own, he storms—and now the score is even ("La vita mi donasti"). Luisa collapses in the arms of her father, who roars that he will avenge this vile affront to a soldier's honor. Beside himself with rage, Count Walter snarls that this fool will rue his insolence, then shouts for his archers.

His men come rushing in followed by Laura and the villagers. Despite Rodolfo's frantic protests, the Count orders the archers to bind Luisa and her father in chains. As Miller curses him, Luisa kneels before the Count and begs for mercy. Thereupon Miller roughly pulls her to her feet. In furious defiance, he thunders that his daughter will kneel only to God—never to a tyrant ("Fra mortali ancora oppressa").

Rodolfo, torn between love and filial duty, sings that despite his devotion to Luisa, he still must remain loyal to his father. The Count relentlessly reminds him that his word is law ("Tu piegarti, tu"). Turning on Luisa and her father, he warns them of dire punishment to follow. The voices of the four blend in a quartet passage. Luisa's entreaties rise in a soaring obbligato ("Ad immagin tua creata"). With the archers and villagers singing that the Count must be obeyed, the voices crescendo into a typically overpowering Verdian chorus.

At its climax, Rodolfo draws his sword and, planting himself in front of Luisa, defies anyone to touch her ("Da questo acciar svenato"). At that, Count Walter pushes Luisa toward the archers, at the same time daring Rodolfo to strike him. Placing the point of his sword on Luisa's heart, Rodolfo shouts that he will kill her rather than see her fall into the hands of such murderous ruffians. Here Verdi wrote one of the most memorable tenor passages in the opera. Rodolfo's phrase of defiance—"Ah, pria che l'abbiano"—rises at its climax to a high C flat. Glaring at him, the Count sardonically asks why he does not make good his threat. Rodolfo's wild rage abruptly changes to icy calm. In a *sotto voce* phrase rising in half steps with an effect of terrible menace ("Trema! svelato agl'uomini") he whispers to his father that he now will reveal how Walter acquired the title of Count. With that he rushes out of the room.

Walter, staggering back in horror, calls after him. Crying that he will grant Luisa her freedom, he stumbles blindly from the room. Luisa sinks half fainting to her knees. Expressing their consternation in a thunderous phrase, the villagers crowd around her. The archers rush away as the curtain falls.

## ACT TWO
### (*Intrigue*)

[*Scene One*] The interior of Miller's cottage. As the curtain rises, Laura and the villagers crowd in calling for Luisa. She comes out of her room, looks into the anxious faces of the throng and asks what has happened. The villagers explain in an ensuing chorus ("Al villaggio dai campi"), which is another fine example of Verdi's remarkable instinct for dramatic choral effects. They sing that as they came through the mountain pass they saw the archers lead away an old man in chains. Realizing that the man is her father, Luisa expresses her despair in an obbligato phrase over the choral accompaniment. The villagers exhort her to have courage.

She frantically tries to rush away to the castle to intercede for her father, but Laura restrains her. At that moment Wurm appears. Ordering the villagers to leave, he informs Luisa that her father has been imprisoned for threatening Count Walter ("Ei, del Conte vassallo"). Such defiance from a vassal is a serious crime; his life hangs in the balance. As Luisa pleads for him, the treacherous Wurm tells her that there is one way she can save her father's life. The Count, he says, will spare Miller if she will send Rodolfo a letter which he—Wurm—will now dictate. With that he leads Luisa to a table and hands her a pen.

Over an ominous orchestral figure of octave skips, Luisa, hypnotized by fear, writes as Wurm begins with the words "Wurm, io giammai." For an instant she recoils, then forces herself to continue. Wurm dictates that she only pretended to love Rodolfo because of his wealth and royal position—it was selfish ambition alone that drove her on. And now, to escape Rodolfo's avenging anger, she will flee with her real lover.

In sudden fury, Luisa flings down the pen to protest this outrage ("Lo speri invano!"). In an ensuing aria ("Tu puniscimi, o signore"), one of the most dramatic in the opera, she sings that she will endure God's punishment without a murmur if only he will deliver her from the clutches of the monsters who demand that she save her father's life at the price of her honor.

With icy contempt, Wurm remarks that if she does not wish to agree to the terms she is free to go. He turns as if to leave. In desperation, Luisa finishes the letter and hands it to him. Wurm reads it over, then with gloating satisfaction states the final terms of his fiendish bargain. The first: Luisa is to swear on her father's life that she wrote the letter voluntarily ("Sul capo del padre"); the second: She is to go to the castle and confess to the Duchess d'Ostheim that she is in love with Wurm "Un sol cenno ancor t'è prescritto"). This marks the beginning of one of the principal duets in the opera.

Wurm relentlessly presses his advantage. When Luisa, trapped, implies her consent to his diabolical scheme, Wurm, with an evil smile, assures her that her father will be freed. Luisa bitterly denounces him for his sadistic cruelty ("A brani, o perfido"), then demands that her father be released at once so that he at least can comfort her in her own hour of doom.

In cynical mockery Wurm promises her that time will solve all these problems—he still hopes that she willingly will become his bride. On these mingled expressions of fury, anguish and vengeful cruelty, the duet brings the scene to its close.

[*Scene Two*] A room in Walter's castle. Musing alone, the Count reveals that Rodolfo has been driven close to madness by his father's command to marry the Duchess. But there is no turning back now, the Count mutters. His reflections are interrupted by the entrance of Wurm. A long duet follows, in which a crucial turn of the plot is disclosed. In recitative, the two discuss the next step in their machinations. Luisa agreed to all the conditions, Wurm says with malicious relish, and will come secretly to the castle today. They will somehow contrive to place her incriminating letter in Rodolfo's hands. Looking intently at the Count, Wurm asks what caused his change of heart during his argument with Rodolfo over Luisa. A terrible threat from his son, the Count replies.

In mysterious, guilt-ridden tones he goes on to explain ("L'alto retaggio non ho bramato"): For Rodolfo's sake he schemed to gain control of the old Count's estates and wealth—and in so doing committed a monstrous crime. Wurm (well aware of how deeply he himself is implicated) uneasily reminds Walter that he aided his plans by finding out that Rodolfo was determined to marry Luisa—a marriage which would have disinherited him, thus thwarting his father's designs. As the duet continues, the two recall how they ambushed the old Count in the forest and murdered him.

While Walter gives way to guilt and remorse, Wurm boasts that their crime never will come to light. Everyone, he says with a show of bravado, believes their version of the affair: The old Count was slain by brigands. Walter whirls on him with a cry of desperation: "No, not everyone!" ("Non tutti!"). In hushed, fear-stricken phrases, Walter tells him that Rodolfo, walking in the forest, heard the fatal shots. Rushing to the spot, he found the old Count still alive. Before he died, he named his assassins.

Wurm, now beside himself with terror, wails that he is lost. From this point on the duet rises to a frenzied climax. Walter answers that Wurm is not alone in his guilt—the devil himself has chained them together in their doom ("Congiunto non t'ha Satanno a' miei destin?"). Wurm, staring wildly around, shouts that his life no longer is safe in this haunted castle. The duet concludes with a ringing unison phrase.[2]

A moment later Walter announces the Duchess Federica and motions Wurm to leave. Recovering his composure, the Count informs Federica that Rodolfo has overcome his infatuation for Luisa. As proof, he adds, Luisa herself is being brought to the castle to explain the situation. Thereupon Walter opens a secret door and admits Luisa accompanied by Wurm. The latter presents her to the Duchess. In an aside, he whispers a warning to Luisa about the danger facing her father.

Looking at her, Federica muses admiringly on Luisa's comely appearance and her expression of candor and honesty. Luisa secretly laments that the happiness she expected will now be accorded another woman ("A costei sarà concesso"). From this point the scene builds into a long dramatic ensemble.

Federica asks Luisa point-blank whom she loves. In quiet desperation, Luisa answers that her lover is Wurm. He acknowledges her confession with an ironic bow. Federica asks sharply: What of Rodolfo? He came in disguise, Luisa replies—why, she never knew, but there were no words of love between them. The Duchess' face brightens, while Luisa's darkens with jealous rage.

The inquisition continues. Noticing the angry look in Luisa's eyes, Federica intuitively demands to know if she is lying. The two men watch her tensely, wondering if she will break under the strain. When the Duchess commands Luisa to speak, Walter, in a vicious undertone, warns her to speak for the sake of her father. In a stricken voice, Luisa answers that she can only repeat what she has said before: She has always loved Wurm ("Lo stesso da Luisa udrete ognor"). Aside, she wonders if her uncontrollable jealousy is driving her mad ("Come celar le smanie").

Here begins one of the most remarkable ensembles to be found in any of the earlier Verdi operas. It is sung unaccompanied to the very end of the scene in staccato unison phrases alternately loud and soft, vividly reflecting the emotional upheaval of the situation. Luisa laments that she is being devastated by jealousy and despair ("Ahimè, l'infranto core"). The Duchess exults in her conquest over her rival ("Un sogno di letizia"). Walter and Wurm, relishing the success of their evil conspiracy, sing that fortune has smiled on them ("Pinto ha di vivo giubilo"). They vow to

[2] This number has been described as the first of the great Verdian bass-baritone duets, foreshadowing "Solenne in quest'ora," from La Forza del Destino.

keep the hapless Luisa in their power. At the conclusion of the quartet there is a tremendous orchestral fanfare.

[*Scene Three*] The hanging gardens of Count Walter's castle. At the back is the door to Rodolfo's apartment, from which he enters with Luisa's note in his hand. A peasant follows him in. Rodolfo orders the man to explain how he managed to get the note.

Luisa, the peasant says, earnestly begged him to take the note secretly to Wurm—and at all costs to keep the knowledge of it from Rodolfo. He adds slyly that he decided instead to bring the note here because he suspected some intrigue, and considered the possibility of a reward. Rodolfo throws him a purse and dismisses him.

In stunned disbelief, Rodolfo cries out that Luisa cannot be guilty of such perfidy. Yet here is the letter in her own handwriting. His father, then, knew: Underneath that tenderness is a black, deceitful heart . . . her love is a wretched illusion. Rodolfo portrays his disillusionment in one of the opera's finest arias, "Quando le sere al placido." He recalls the moment when he first looked into Luisa's eyes, heard her avowal of love and pressed his lips to hers. But even then she perjured herself and betrayed him. The aria ends in a cry of anguish—"Ah! mi tradia!"

As Rodolfo turns to leave, he is suddenly confronted by Wurm. The two stand face to face for a moment, then Rodolfo hands the other the letter. When Wurm has read it, Rodolfo takes it back. Now, he says in cold fury, the hour of death has come for both of them. He holds out two pistols and curtly invites Wurm to take his choice. As Wurm staggers back in consternation, Rodolfo bursts out that they will die together. He takes aim, but before he can fire, Wurm dodges aside and fires into the air. Rodolfo, in blind fury, lowers his pistol with a scream of "Coward!"

The sound of the shot brings Walter and his men-at-arms rushing into the gardens. Wurm pushes his way through the crowd and vanishes. With a despairing cry, Rodolfo falls to his knees before his father. The Count, in a deliberate pretense of sympathy, tries to calm him. He has repented his severity, he says, and no longer will stand between his son and his chosen love. Rodolfo, although surprised at this change of heart, laments that it is all too late—Luisa has deceived him. Now he asks only for death. Not death, the Count interjects, but revenge.

Uncomprehending, Rodolfo asks what he means. His father thereupon urges him to marry Federica to show his contempt for his betrayer. Desperate and confused, Rodolfo first refuses, then consents. Following up his advantage, Walter goads him on by appealing to his pride. Finally, exhausted by his emotion, Rodolfo resignedly sings that he is ready for either the altar or the tomb and will bow to his fate ("L'ara o l'avello apprestami!").

Touched by his grief, the soldiers and villagers, in an accompanying chorus ("Del genitor propizio"), exhort him to trust in his father's love. The count himself unctuously counsels him to forget the one who so cruelly betrayed him. This ensemble brings the act to a close. As the curtain falls, Walter leads Rodolfo away.

## ACT THREE
### (Poison)

A room in Miller's house. Luisa is writing at a table on which are a lighted lamp, a basket of fruit and a cup of milk. At one side of the room, Laura and a group of peasants who have come to comfort Luisa stand gazing sadly at her. Through an open window at the back can be seen the village church, lighted up.

In a brief chorus ("Come in un giorno") the peasants comment on how, in one short day, sorrow has left its mark on Luisa. Laura entreats her to take some food to restore her strength. Gently refusing, Luisa asks her visitors to respect her grief.

Earthly food, she sings melodramatically, never again will pass her lips ("A questo labbro"); she will soon taste of celestial joys. (A descriptive arpeggio in the orchestral underscores this thought.) Suddenly she sees the lights of the church through the open window and asks what is happening. Laura informs her that there is a special ceremony at the church at which the new Count is being invested with his title as lord of the estates. Turning to the peasants, Laura sings that Luisa would die if she were told that at this very moment preparations are being made for the wedding of a certain royal couple. As the peasants comment softly in chorus, Miller enters. Luisa throws herself into his arms. Laura leads the peasants away.

The remainder of the scene is taken up with a long recitative and duet, another of the principal numbers in the opera, which foreshadows the great baritone and soprano duets in later works such as *Traviata* and *Rigoletto*.

It begins as Miller expresses his concern over Luisa's pallid, sorrowful mien ("Pallida, mesta sei"). He goes on to say that he has heard the entire story from Wurm, and now knows how much his daughter has sacrificed to save her father. Luisa tells him she has indeed renounced her true love—then adds meaningfully to herself: "But only on this earth."

She hands her father the letter she has just written and entreats him to see that it reaches its destination. Alarmed, Miller begins reading in half-spoken recitative: "Orribil tradimento ne disgiunse, o Rodolfo." The letter asks Rodolfo not to believe this monstrous deception. She is bound by an oath to reveal no more. But there is a home—far beyond the reach of lying and deceit— where they can be together forever. He is to meet here there at midnight.

Miller trembles violently. The letter falls from his hands. In a stricken voice he asks: "Where is this home?" ("Quella dimora saria?"). Luisa replies quietly: "La tomba." Miller utters an anguished cry as an ascending chromatic figure erupts in the orchestra. Then Luisa, as though in a trance, sings that the tomb is a rose-strewn bed—a sweet resting place for those whose lives are pure ("La tomba è un letto"). Only for those who are evil is the tomb a place of darkness and horror; for guiltless, loving hearts it is the gateway to eternal peace.

In agonized protest, Miller cries that she dare not take her own life—there is no pardon for suicide ("Pel suicida non v'ha perdono!"). Tormented by grief, Luisa bursts out: "Is not love to blame?" ("È colpa amore!"). Sobbing, Miller throws himself into a chair and launches into a refrain of bitter reproach ("Di rughe il volto, mira"). A father's love for his child, he sings, should be returned to comfort him in his old age. But as for him, his only reward is a harvest of tears—he himself will be the first to enter the tomb prepared for him by an ungrateful child.

Stricken with remorse, Luisa tears up the letter and promises her father to abandon thoughts of suicide. They embrace joyfully as they sing in a climactic phrase ("Ah! in quest'amplesso l'anima oblia") that in their devotion to each other they can forget their sorrow. With sudden urgency Luisa says they must leave this place at once—there is great danger here. She tells her father to get some rest; they will leave at dawn. Miller starts for his room, then turns and embraces Luisa. Together they sing the beautiful concluding theme of the duet—"Andrem, raminghi e poveri." As fugitives, they will wander wherever Fate will lead them, begging for their bread if they must. But father and daughter will never part, and the Lord will bless them.

Miller slowly goes to his room. A moment later Luisa hears the sound of organ music from the church. Kneeling, she sings quietly that this will be her last prayer in her beloved home ("Ah! l'ultima

preghiera"). Tomorrow she will pray among strangers. The serenity of the prayer theme brings to mind Desdemona's prayer in
*Otello*.

As Luisa remains kneeling with bowed head, Rodolfo, enveloped
in a cloak, appears in the doorway. In an undertone he orders
the servant who is with him to inform his father that everything
is ready for the wedding ceremony and that he will await him at
Miller's home. Then, glaring at Luisa, who is still unaware of his
presence, he murmurs ominously that she prays—and it is time to
pray. He takes a vial from his pocket and pours some of its
contents into the cup of milk on the table.

At that moment Luisa sees him and springs to her feet. Holding
her note to Wurm in his outstretched hand, Rodolfo harshly asks
if she wrote it. Gasping for breath, Luisa answers yes. As though
struck, Rodolfo collapses into a chair, clutches his throat and calls
for a drink. Luisa quickly hands him the cup of milk. The liquid
is bitter, Rodolfo exclaims. Suddenly realizing that he drank from
the cup into which he poured the poison, he asks Luisa to taste.
He watches her in fascinated horror as she drinks, then murmurs
dolorously: "Tutto è compiuto"—"Everything is accomplished."
The two stare at each other in terrible, deathlike silence, which
is shattered after a long moment by a crashing chord in the
orchestra.

Rodolfo tells Luisa to go. Another lover, he says, is waiting for
her, another bride is waiting for him at the altar. But they will
wait in vain, he adds somewhat irrationally. With that he leaps to
his feet, begins pacing furiously back and forth, then flings away
his sword. This sword with which he once defended the innocent,
he rages, now is useless. As he chokes with anger, Luisa again
offers him the cup of milk, saying it will restore him. In bitter
mockery he remarks that his betrayer well knows what she is
offering him.

When Luisa recoils at this brutal jibe, Rodolfo exhorts her to
leave him, singing that he cannot comprehend how a creature
so beautiful can have the heart of a demon ("Ah! lungi quel
volto lusinghier"). Losing control, he breaks down weeping. Luisa,
trying vainly to calm him, says that there is more reason for his
tears than for his anger ("Piangi, il tuo dolore"). Rodolfo replies
that these tears are the dews of death. The duet is suddenly
interrupted by the sound of a clock striking.

Taking Luisa's hand, Rodolfo sings that now has come the last
hour between them and eternity ("Donna, per noi terrible").
Warning her not to perjure herself now, he demands to know if

she really loved Wurm. Distractedly she tries to evade answering. Again cautioning her not to lie, Rodolfo storms that before the lamp goes out she will be face to face with the Almighty. Thrusting the empty cup before her, he tells her that they have both drunk the fatal poison. Luisa totters as though about to faint. Rodolfo carries her to a chair.

Recovering, Luisa sings that death has released her from her oath, and she can now reveal the truth. She then tells how, to save her father, she wrote the letter of renunciation as Wurm dictated it ("Avean mio padre"). Now she will die innocent. The dreadful realization of his fatal mistake dawns upon Rodolfo. Half crazed by remorse, he calls down a terrible curse upon himself and his father ("Maledetto il dì ch'io nacqui"). God, he rages, created him in a moment of anger. Luisa implores him to spare her the horror of outraging Almighty God at the moment of death.

At the fiery climax of the duet, Miller rushes in. Rodolfo, drawing his sword, shouts that he will now expiate the crime of being Luisa's assassin. He pauses as he hears Luisa say that she feels the calm of death. Throwing down his sword, Rodolfo rushes to her. He turns to Miller and says that all hope is gone—Luisa has drunk poison. For a moment Miller stands transfixed, then takes Luisa in his arms. In a serene refrain ("Padre ricevi l'estremo") she bids farewell to her father and Rodolfo. Their voices blend with hers in a moving trio as they pour out their grief. Luisa dies in her father's arms.

Count Walter, the villagers and the men-at-arms rush in and crowd around Miller and Rodolfo, who are kneeling beside Luisa's body. Rodolfo looks up and sees Wurm standing in the doorway. Screaming that death will be his punishment, Rodolfo seizes his sword, lunges at Wurm and kills him on the spot. He whirls to face Count Walter and in the next moment falls dead at his feet. His father stares down at his body sobbing: "Figliol" The throng thunders a cry of horror as the curtain falls.

# Lulu

## *by* ALBAN BERG

## (1885–1935)

*Libretto by the composer, based on two tragedies by the German dramatist Frank Wedekind:* ERDGEIST (EARTH SPIRIT and DIE BÜCHSE DER PANDORA (PANDORA'S BOX)

### CHARACTERS

| | |
|---|---|
| Lulu | High soprano |
| Dr. Ludwig Schön, a newspaper publisher | Baritone |
| Alwa, his son, a composer | Tenor |
| Dr. Goll, a medical health officer | Speaking role |
| Walter Schwarz, an artist | Lyric tenor |
| An Animal Trainer ⎫ Rodrigo, the Athlete ⎭ | Basso buffo |
| Schigolch, an old man posing as Lulu's father | Bass-baritone |
| The Prince, an African explorer | Tenor buffo |
| The Schoolboy | Soprano |
| Countess Geschwitz | Dramatic mezzo-soprano |
| Director of the theater | Basso buffo |
| Theater checkroom girl | Alto |
| A servant | Mimed |

*Place:* A town in Germany; Paris, London
*Time:* Circa 1920
*First performance:* Stadttheater, Zürich, June 2, 1937
*Original language:* German

---

Berg began work on *Lulu* in 1929, seven years after the completion of *Wozzeck*. He had finished the first two acts and about one third of the last act at the time of his death in 1935. However, in 1934, the composer had made an orchestral suite which he called the *Lulu Suites* consisting of five symphonic excerpts from the opera. This was first performed in November of 1934.

*Lulu* is a relentlessly realistic study of a woman—an amoral, passionate creature who lived and loved according to the laws of her own demonic nature. Within that world of her own, she experienced ecstasy and despair, triumph and defeat, trust and betrayal. It was her destiny to destroy those she loved—and then at the last to wreak her own destruction as the victim of a monstrous act of violence.

As a disciple of Arnold Schönberg (to whom he dedicated the opera), Berg adapted that composer's astringent twelve-tone idiom to a warmer, more fluid harmonic structure to delineate the complex emotions of the characters in *Lulu*. Although predominantly a twelve-tone score—and certainly not an opera in the conventional sense—*Lulu* has moments of intense lyricism and rich instrumentation evocative of Verdi and Wagner. In his musical pattern, Berg selected certain identifying forms of the various characters: for Lulu, a single twelve-tone series; for Dr. Schön, the sonata; for Alwa, the rondo; for Countess Geschwitz, the pentatonic (five-tone) scale.

In constructing the work for the stage, Berg had to combine Wedekind's *Erdgeist* and *Büchse der Pandora* to conform to the dramatic requirements of an opera. To solve the problem, he devised a film sequence, with musical accompaniment, which was to serve as a bridge between the first half of the opera (based on *Erdgeist*) and the second (based on *Büchse*). This manner of staging, with rear-projection films and slides, is generally followed in performances today.

The incomplete third act is usually presented in the form of an epilogue—almost all in mime to the accompaniment of Berg's symphonic variations. In this version, the act takes place in London, where Lulu is murdered by Jack the Ripper.

The score of the opera is enormously difficult and demands singing and acting talent of the highest order. Since its premiere some three decades ago, *Lulu* is slowly finding its place in the operatic repertoire. In fact, it has been given regularly in Germany by the Hamburg State Opera for the past ten years. This company gave the first performance in New York (in German) at the Metropolitan Opera House, Lincoln Center, on June 6, 1967. *Lulu* also has been performed by the Santa Fe Opera Company and (in English) by Sarah Caldwell's American National Opera Company.

There is no overture. The curtain rises immediately on the Prologue.

## PROLOGUE

The entrance to a circus tent. At one side stands a clown carrying an enormous drum. In front of the entrance is the Animal Trainer (Ringmaster), dressed in top hat, frock coat, white trousers and riding boots; he has a whip in one hand and a revolver in the other. He addresses the audience in a long monologue ("Hereinspaziert in die Menagerie") in which he invites the "proud ladies and gentlemen" to gaze upon the inhabitants of the menagerie. These he sardonically describes in terms of derogatory human attributes: the rapacious tiger, the greedy bear, the exhibitionistic monkey, the venomous reptile.

Then the Trainer calls backstage and orders August, a stagehand, to bring forth his prize specimen, the serpent. The stagehand comes in with Lulu in his arms. She is dressed in the Pierrot costume for the opening act. Here is a creature, the Trainer proclaims in the manner of a sideshow barker, who was born for seduction and murder. When Lulu glares at him for this gratuitous insult, he tries to makes amends. There is really nothing extraordinary about this creature at the moment, the Trainer says, but there may be some surprises later on. At his command, the assistant carries Lulu offstage. As she passes the Trainer, he pats her hips and murmurs that she is his greatest treasure.

Then in stentorian tones he invites the audience to witness a breath-taking spectacle: He will place his head between the jaws of the beast—the name of which they doubtless know.

## ACT ONE

[*Scene One*] The studio of the Artist (Schwarz). Lulu, in her Pierrot costume, holding a shepherd's crook in her hand, is posing on a dais. The Artist stands at his easel in front of her half-finished portrait. Dr. Schön, hat in hand and with his overcoat on, is sitting on an ottoman watching the Artist. From behind a Spanish screen in front of the door of the room comes the voice of Alwa. He asks if he may come in, then appears.

Casually greeting his father and then the Artist, Alwa goes over to the portrait. With great enthusiasm he exclaims that he wants to engage Lulu as his leading lady in his opera. Lulu demurely remarks that she could not dance well enough to play the role. Dr. Schön interrupts to ask Alwa why he came to the studio. To ask him to attend the rehearsal of his opera, Alwa replies. As

Schön rises to leave, Lulu asks Alwa to reserve a box for her at the opening performance.

Alwa and his father pause to inquire why Lulu's husband is not present. Evading the question, Lulu pointedly requests Dr. Schön to convey her greetings to his fiancée. Deliberately ignoring the remark, Schön turns back to the portrait and criticizes the Artist's work. Then he and Alwa leave.

No sooner have they gone than the Artist, with brush and palette still in his hands, rushes to the dais with a passionate cry. Lulu fends him off, warning him that her husband will arrive at any moment. This marks the beginning of a tumultuous duet.

There is a noise outside, and the two listen apprehensively for a moment. Then the Artist goes back to his easel. Suddenly he throws down his brush and palette, exclaiming that he cannot go on. Lulu, exasperated by his behavior, orders him to continue painting, but the Artist, losing control of himself, lunges toward her. She hurls the shepherd's crook in his face and rushes toward the door with the Artist in pursuit. Dodging him, Lulu scurries up a stepladder at the rear of the studio. Ecstatically she cries that from this height she can see all the cities of the world ("Ich sehe über alle Städte"). The Artist, now in a frenzy, tries to pull her down and in so doing knocks over the ladder. In falling, it shatters a piece of sculpture. Staring at the wreckage, the Artist shrieks that he is ruined. Then he again tries to seize the girl.

Evading his grasp, Lulu staggers toward the couch, on which she collapses. The Artist swiftly locks the door of the studio, then kneels beside Lulu and covers her hand with kisses. Eyes closed, she warns him that her husband will soon arrive. Oblivious to the warning, the Artist cries out that he loves her. Lulu, with eyes still closed, murmurs as though in a dream that she once loved a student with 175 scars. But the Artist amorously babbles on, first calling her "Nelly," then "Eva." Reminding him that her name is Lulu, she pushes him away with a gesture of revulsion. As he tries to continue his violent love-making, the voice of Lulu's husband is heard outside. Panic-stricken, Lulu begs the Artist to hide her. When he starts toward the door she holds him back, crying that her husband will kill them both.

In the next moment the husband (Dr. Goll, the medical health officer) batters down the door and lunges into the room. Glaring madly at Lulu and the Artist, he rushes toward them brandishing his cane and screaming a curse. Suddenly he gasps for breath, then falls to the floor dying of a stroke. With a gasp of horror, the Artist kneels and tries to lift the body, calling on Lulu to help him. Shrinking back in fear, Lulu refuses. The Artist hurries out to call a doctor.

Alone, Lulu voices her thoughts in a brief monologue called the *canzonetta* ("auf einmal springt er auf"). Crouching near the door, she wonders if her husband perhaps will suddenly spring to his feet. Softly she calls to him by her nickname for him: "Pussi." She waits, as though expecting him to answer. Then she warily circles the body, singing that her husband's eyes are following her every step. Gingerly touching the body with her foot, she cringes back. In almost childlke awe she says that now he is really dead . . . the dance is over. He has deserted her—and now what is she to do?

The Artist returns saying that the doctor is on his way. Lulu casually observes that her husband is past all medical help and is quite obviously dead. Shocked at her callousness, the Artist upbraids her. Taking her by the hand, he leads her to the couch and begins questioning her to the accompaniment of a rising and falling chromatic theme in the orchestra ("Kannst du die Wahrheit sagen?"). He asks if she knows how to speak the truth . . . if she believes in a Creator . . . if she has ever loved.

As though in a trance, Lulu answers every question with "I don't know." Then suddenly coming to her senses, she asks the Artist what it is that he really wants to know. Completely baffled by her inexplicable behavior, he roughly orders her to change her clothes. With a surprised glance at him, Lulu goes into the other room.

Staring down at the dead man, the Artist addresses him in a brief dramatic refrain ("Ich möchte tauschen mit dir"). He would gladly change places, he sings. He will give her back, he goes on irrationally, along with his own youth as well. This happiness is more than he can bear—it fills him with hellish terror. In a sudden frantic outburst, the Artist begs the dead man to awaken, then swears that he never touched his wife. Becoming calmer, he sings that his only wish was to bring her a bit of happiness.

His monologue is interrupted as Lulu enters from the adjoining room holding up the top of her dress at the back. She asks him to hook it up because her hand is shaking The Artist complies as the curtain slowly falls. The music continues into a long orchestral interlude, part of which is in canon form—the theme is that associated with the Artist's hopeless passion for Lulu. There is no pause in the accompaniment as the curtain rises on the next scene.

[*Scene Two*] An elegantly appointed salon in Lulu's home. She is now married to the Artist. On one wall hangs the portrait of Lulu as Pierrot. She herself is lying on a chaise longue, gazing at her reflection in a hand mirror. She rubs her forehead thoughtfully, then puts the mirror aside with a petulant frown.

The Artist enters, carrying his brush and palette and a packet of letters. Lulu smiles in greeting. Spoken dialogue follows. The Artist hands Lulu a letter which she identifies from the perfumed envelope as from "the Corticelli." She slips the letter into her bosom. The Artist excitedly tells her that his portrait of her as "the Dancer" has been sold for fifty thousand marks. And that, he adds exultantly, makes the third painting he has sold since he and Lulu were married.

He hands Lulu another letter, which she reads aloud. It announces the engagement of Charlotte Marie Adelaide, daughter of Counselor Heinrich Ritter von Zarnikov, to Dr. Ludwig Schön. The Artist remarks rather cynically that the eminent doctor at long last has made up his mind to announce his engagement publicly. After all, what could possibly stand in the way of marriage for a man of his importance? In silence, Lulu folds the letter and puts it aside. When the Artist says that they must send Dr. Schön a congratulatory note, Lulu enigmatically observes that they already have congratulated him. "You may do so again if you wish," she casually tells her husband.

Saying it is time to get to work, the Artist kisses Lulu and tells her she looks particularly attractive this morning. He kneels and impetuously takes her in his arms. The doorbell rings; he curses the interruption. Lulu tells him not to answer the bell, but the Artist reminds her that it may be the art dealer. "And even if it were the Emperor of China," Lulu murmurs languorously. The implication is lost on the Artist, who goes out to answer the door.

During a brief orchestral passage, Lulu abandons herself to her amorous thoughts and lies with eyes closed. The mood passes, and she sits up. The Artist returns and tells her that the visitor is only a beggar, for whom he has no small change. Again saying he must get to work, the Artist goes into the adjoining room.

Straightening her dress and arranging her hair, Lulu goes to the door and admits the beggar—who actually is Schigolch, a bedraggled, asthmatic old man. The music of the long soliloquy which ensues is designated as "chamber music for a woodwind ensemble." It is throughout in a deliberate, dragging tempo, reflecting the labored speech of the old man.

Looking around, Schigolch remarks rather querulously that he expected the Artist to be a "different" sort of a fellow. He then admits that he has come for money—two hundred marks, or perhaps three hundred. . . . Shrugging resignedly, Lulu gives him the money. Schigolch, neglecting to thank her, compliments her on her new home—taking particular note of the luxurious rugs. Rather amused, Lulu remarks that she likes to walk on them barefoot. The old man leers, then suddenly gasps for breath; Lulu offers him a drink. Recovering himself, he notices her portrait and exclaims: "It is really you!"

In a rather aimless way, Schigolch begins plying Lulu with questions: How does she spend her time . . . is she still studying French? When Lulu, in growing impatience, sharply asks why all this matters to him, he obsequiously answers that his only concern is that his "little Lulu" will never suffer privation. He caresses her knee suggestively. Pushing his hand away, she says that not "within the memory of man" has she been called "Lulu" —and it also has been a long time since she danced. Schigolch asks, puzzled: "What, then, are you now?" In a spoken phrase, Lulu replies bitterly: "An animal."

The doorbell rings, and Lulu gets up quickly. Schigolch, aware that he must leave, rises with a painful effort. Helping him to the door, Lulu accompanies him outside. For a moment the stage is empty. An orchestral passage in discordant, rising chromatics underscores the scurrilous character of the old man. This chromaticism is associated with Schigolch throughout the opera.

Lulu returns with Dr. Schön, who is obviously angry and excited. He asks what her father is doing in her house ("Was tut den Ihr Vater?"), then adds spitefully that if he were her husband he would never allow that wretch inside the door. This marks the beginning of a long duet (designated in the score as "sonata") which later builds into one of the most climactic scenes in the opera.

Coolly ignoring Schön's show of temper, Lulu asks why he has come. Thereupon Schön tells her she must stop visiting him. If Walter (the Artist) were not so naïve, Schön goes on, he long ago would have become aware of her deceitfulness. Lulu answers contemptuously that Walter, like all lovers, is blind. He knows her only as a woman who satisfies his desires.

There must be an end to this, Schön bursts out. Lulu's answer is a shrug. Goaded by her indifference, Schön furiously reminds her of what he has done for her: Twice he found her a husband . . . and even found a position for her current spouse. More than that, he has made it possible for her to live in luxury. Whatever she may feel about the situation, Schön goes on, he no longer wants anything to do with it. During this tirade, his voice blends with that of Lulu's as she blandly repeats that, so far as her adoring husband is concerned, she exists solely for his pleasure.

When Lulu asks why he has decided to break off their relationship, Schön tells her he has become engaged—and he wishes to bring his bride into a home that is without shame. She is indeed enchanting, Lulu says mockingly, but there is no reason why they themselves should not continue to meet.

Schön retorts furiously that they will never meet again—except in the presence of her husband. Lulu repeats the word "husband," and instantly her demeanor changes. With quiet intensity she answers Schön in a spoken passage over a sinister theme in the orchestra ("Wenn ich einem Menschen auf dieser Welt gehöre"): If she ever belonged to anyone in this world, it is to him alone. He took her in—a petty thief who tried to steal his watch—gave her food and made a home for her. No one else in the world has ever shown her such love and care.

With desperate insistence, Schön begs Lulu not to stand in the way of his marriage. He implores her to give him his freedom for the sake of his important position in the business world. And what is more, she must no longer be seen going in and out of his house at all hours. Growing angry, Lulu sarcastically assures him that she has no objections to his marriage, but warns him that he cannot discard her at his own convenience. Furthermore, she adds, she is not in the slightest jealous of this "child." Schön retorts that his bride-to-be is not much younger than herself.

The quarrel is interrupted by the entrance of the Artist. Noting the hostile expressions on the faces of the two, he asks what is wrong. Lulu and Schön glower at him in silence. Taking Lulu's arm, the Artist tries to lead her toward the studio, but she impatiently draws away from him. Indicating Schön, she says that he has grown tired of her. With that she hurries into the studio. Schön, in an aside, murmurs that now the matter must be settled once for all.

Puzzled and suspicious, the Artist confronts Schön. The ensuing colloquy is partly sung and partly spoken. Schön begins by reminding the Artist that he married "half a million" ("Du hast eine halbe Million geheiratet"), that he has won recognition as an artist and now has a secure position in the world. Obviously struggling to get to the point, Schön exhorts the bewildered Artist to assume more responsibility as a husband. He must not entrust her to someone else, Schön adds meaningfully.

Beginning to understand Schön's insinuations, the Artist is dumfounded. Schön, insidiously plotting his revenge upon Lulu, unctuously assures the Artist that he has come not to cause a scandal but to avert one. When Walter hotly interrupts that Schön has never understood Lulu, Schön declares that he cannot allow him to go on in his blind innocence. The woman, he says, does have qualities of respectability—she has, in fact, improved enormously since he first knew her.

That was when she was twelve, Schön explains in answer to Walter's startled question. Thereupon he proceeds to detail Lulu's past in a mélange of lies and innuendo. He first saw her as a flower girl in front of a cafe, took her into his home and put her in the care of a woman he engaged to rear her. Walter mutters that Lulu spoke only of an "aunt" who raised her. Deliberately ignoring the remark, Schön goes on to say that it was through him that Lulu met her first husband, Dr. Goll.

Relentlessly continuing, Schön says that Lulu—determined to become his wife after Dr. Goll's death—did her utmost to come between him and his present fiancée, whom he met as a widower. Stunned and incredulous, Walter says brokenly that Lulu told him nothing of all this and swore to him that she had never been in love before. With deliberate cruelty, Schön observes that one cannot apply conventional standards of behavior to a person of "Mignon's" origin.

At the name "Mignon," Walter looks at Schön questioningly. He soon learns that while he himself affectionately called Lulu "Eva," she was "Mignon" to Schön and "Nelly" to Goll. When Schön admits that he never knew her real name, the Artist bitterly remarks that perhaps she alone knows.

Schön's next disclosure—for Walter's benefit—is that Lulu's father, contrary to her story that he died in an insane asylum, actually was in the Artist's own studio this very day. When Walter scoffs at this, Schön points to the two liquor glasses on the table as mute evidence of the "father's" visit. In despair, Walter cries that everything is a lie.

The dialogue continues in duet form with mounting dramatic intensity. Schön, having reduced the Artist to a state of helpless confusion, urges him to take a firm hand with Lulu—she requires "authority." Walter sobs that Lulu swore by her mother's grave that she had never been in love before. Schön sardonically answers that Lulu never knew her mother, much less her mother's grave.

Collapsing on a chair, the Artist cries that there is a terrible pain in his chest. Looking down at him, Schön, with cruel irony, exhorts him to take good care of Lulu—"after all, she is yours"

("Wahr' sie Dir, weil sie Dein ist"). Overwhelmed by shame and despair, Walter screams in anguish. Schön remorselessly urges him to act at once—or lose the woman he loves.

Suddenly calm, Walter gets to his feet and says he will now have a talk with Lulu. Taking his hand in a spurious gesture of encouragement, Schön guides Walter out of the room. Closing the door after him, he murmurs with evil satisfaction that this was a hard bit of work. Then, in sudden alarm, Schön realizes that the Artist did not go into his studio, but into the adjoining room. At that moment agonizing groans come from the other side of the door.

Schön rushes to the door and finds it locked. As he frantically tries to force it open, Lulu bursts out of the studio in a state of hysterical excitement. Schön shouts at her to fetch a hatchet from the kitchen. Lulu, regaining control of herself, says that Walter no doubt will open the door himself—once he has finished weeping. Schön, furious with her, orders her to do as she is told.

The doorbell rings. Exclaiming that he must not be found in the apartment, Schön tiptoes out and closes the door behind him. Lulu glides to the locked door of the adjoining room and crouches there listening. Schön reappears with Alwa, who is excitedly telling him that a revolution has broken out in Paris. Ignoring him, Schön hammers on the locked door and shouts to the Artist to open it. Again he orders Lulu to bring the hatchet. Alwa, completely oblivious to the uproar, babbles that no one in the editorial office knows what to write about the Paris revolution.

Lulu finally returns with the hatchet, with which Schön and Alwa break open the door. The two stagger back in horror. Lulu looks into the room and recoils with a shriek of terror. She runs to Alwa, who has collapsed upon the sofa, and begs him to take her away. He pushes her into the studio as Schön, wiping his brow, goes into the room. A moment later he emerges, shaken by what he has seen. Gesturing toward the room, he cries, in a symbolic phrase: "There lies my betrothal, bleeding to death."[1] Alwa shouts that Schön has brought this curse upon himself, then denounces his father for his wretched treatment of Lulu.

Lulu reappears, dressed in traveling clothes. When Schön asks her what she will tell the police, she coldly answers that he can do the talking. Cursing the Artist, Schön goes to the telephone and reports the details of the suicide: ". . . cut his throat with a razor

---

[1] The key word in the phrase is "betrothal"—*Verlobung*, used here in an esoteric sense to describe Schön's awareness of disaster.

. . . persecution complex. . ." As he talks, there is a brief exchange between Lulu and Alwa about Walter's tragic act.

Completing the telephone call, Schön comes forward, saying that now at last he can retire from the world. The three are startled by the ringing of the doorbell—the police have arrived. As Schön starts toward the door Lulu tells him there is blood on his hands. She sprinkles perfume on her handkerchief and wipes off the blood. When Schön reminds her that the blood is her husband's, she casually remarks that it will leave no trace. Outraged at her cruel indifference, Schön screams: "You monster!" Lulu answers imperturbably: "But you will marry me." Going toward the door, she murmurs affably: "Have patience, children." The curtain falls.

[*Scene Three*] Before the curtain rises there is an orchestral interlude and at its conclusion a jazz band is heard. This ragtime, which forms the basis of the melodrama of the opening part of the scene, continues throughout the ensuing dialogue. In the dressing room of a theater, Lulu is preparing to dance in a pantomime. Alwa, pouring champagne into two glasses, is speaking to Lulu, who is putting on her costume behind a screen.

Alwa says that never before has he seen a theater audience so excited. Lulu asks him if he has seen his father in the theater, then tells him that the Prince will be there to see her perform. His Highness, she explains, wants to marry her and take her to Africa. In a resplendent ballet costume she emerges from behind the screen. Alwa gasps in admiration, but suddenly clutches his hand to his chest as though in pain.

At this point the music of the jazz band stops and the orchestra takes up the accompaniment. Here for the first time is heard the "rondo" theme associated with Alwa. Deliberately tantalizing Alwa, Lulu asks if he remembers the first time she came to his room. Alwa replies in a passionate refrain ("Sie trugen ein dunkelblaues Kleid"). He recalls that she wore a dark blue dress and that she seemed to be an otherworldly being far beyond his reach. He adored her more than his own mother. He remembers that when his mother died he threatened to fight his father in a duel unless he married Lulu immediately.

She tells Alwa that his father had told her of the incident. But now, she goes on (over the music of the jazz band, which resumes at this point), Dr. Schön must be prepared to recognize her as a successful actress—he insisted she go on the stage so that she could be seen by some patron of the arts rich enough to marry her.

When Alwa vehemently protests that no one must take her away from him, Lulu meaningfully answers that she knows—even without looking—that there are those in the audience who are considering that very possibility. She reminds him that, after all, it is in his stage work that she is on display before the public. At the sound of the call bell, she turns to go onstage. In a brilliant coloratura phrase, Lulu sings that the thought of her appearance onstage is like an icy chill that courses through her body. Alwa shakes his head uncomprehendingly as he watches her leave.

Alone, he muses in a recitative passage that this woman is an ideal subject for an opera: Scene One, the health officer—impossible; Scene Two, the Artist—still more impossible; Scene Three —but why go on? His reflections are interrupted by the entrance of the Prince. Introducing himself, His Highness launches into a fatuous discourse about Lulu ("Würden Sie es für möglich halten"). He has been studying her spiritual qualities, he declares, as reflected in her dancing, and has come to the conclusion that she symbolizes the joy of living. As a wife she would make any man supremely happy. In an aside he adds: "As *my* wife."

His monologue is interrupted by the frantic ringing of the call bell. There is an uproar outside and then the door bursts open and Lulu staggers in. She falls into a chair. An attendant explains that she fainted in the middle of her dance. Lulu, who seems to have lost control of herself, gasps that Dr. Schön and his fiancée were in the audience.

A moment later Schön himself strides in and furiously confronts Lulu, accusing her of using the ballet to revenge herself upon him. An agitated sextet ensues, blending the voices of Schön, Lulu, Alwa, the Prince, the attendant and the stage manager. Schön fiercely orders Lulu to return to the stage and finish her dance. Lulu defiantly refuses to dance before his fiancée. The Prince and the stage manager express their consternation. Lulu protests that she is too exhausted to go on, and the attendant implores Schön to allow her a few moments' rest. When Alwa asks the stage manager to continue the performance with the next number until Lulu can recover, Schön storms that she has a contract and must dance in spite of everything. Lulu finally agrees to do so after she has rested. At a sign from Schön, all the others leave.

Whirling on Lulu, Schön again irrationally accuses her of using her role as an instrument of sheer revenge ("Wie kannst Du die Szene gegen mich ausspielen?"). This introduces the long, in-

tensely dramatic scene (designated as a "sonata") which concludes
the act. It is a scene in which Lulu quietly but remorselessly
destroys Schön's will to resist and reduces him to helpless despair.
Her weapons in turn are sarcasm, flattery, cajolery, seductiveness.

She taunts him with hints of a liaison with the Prince, who is
to take her to Africa. With a sneer she advises him to hurry back
to his innocent bride-to-be. When Schön, goaded to the edge of
madness, raises his fist, Lulu insolently dares him to strike her.
The man rushes to the door, screaming that he must escape, then
breaks down sobbing that he does not know where to go. Watching him with venomous satisfaction, Lulu voices her triumph in a
phrase that soars to the topmost range of the voice (the musical
notation is F above high C): "This is a moment of indescribable
joy—the tyrant is weeping!" ("Mir tut dieses Augenblick wohl
. . . der Gewaltmensch weint!").

Completely demoralized, Schön asks Lulu what he is to do.
She thereupon hands him paper and pen and tells him to write
as she dictates. As though hypnotized, Schön obeys. This "letter
scene" is in the form of a canon: As Lulu dictates, Schön repeats
the words as he writes them down. The letter informs Dr. Schön's
fiancée that he is breaking off their engagement because he is
no longer worthy of her. His message is being dictated by the
woman who wholly dominates his life.

Schön, sobbing abjectly, signs his name. Lulu harshly dictates
a postscript warning his fiancée not to try to save him. In utter
despair, Schön cries out that the hour of execution has come.
Lulu, ignoring him, arranges her ballet costume and goes out to
the stage. The curtain falls to the accompaniment of thunderous
chords.

## ACT TWO

[*Scene One*] A luxurious salon in Dr. Schön's home. He and
Lulu are now married. Clad in negligee, she is sitting in an armchair. Nearby, seated on the ottoman, is the Countess Geschwitz,
a handsome woman in mannish attire. Dr. Schön is standing at
left. The opening recitative is dominated by the pentatonic music
identifying the Countess. Making a social call, she says she is
looking forward to seeing Lulu at the ball for women artists.
She makes it clear to Schön that a man would be persona non
grata. Looking admiringly at Lulu's portrait, the Countess inquires
about the artist. Both Lulu and Schön are evasive and embar-

rassed. Sensing their discomfiture, the Countess takes her leave. Lulu accompanies her out of the room.

Left alone, Schön abandons himself to bitter reflection in a brief monologue in arioso style ("Das mein Lebens abend"). Here he is, in the evening of his life, after thirty years of striving, in a house ridden with evil. He is not safe in his own home . . . there may be spies behind the draperies. Drawing his revolver, he stares apprehensively at the windows. Stealthily he pulls the drapes aside but finds no one there. Staggering back, he bursts out that he is going mad. He looks around with an expression of utter revulsion. Hearing Lulu's footsteps outside, he hides his revolver.

Though obviously preoccupied with thoughts of the Countess, Lulu asks Schön if he will take her for a drive. He answers impatiently that he must go to the stock exchange. Deliberately enticing him, Lulu comes close and gazes up at him amorously. In an insinuating phrase ("Ich fürchte Vieles") she sings that the one thing she is not afraid of is his love for her. Unable to resist her, Schön pushes her gently toward the bedroom.

The stage is momentarily empty. Then the Countess Geschwitz enters, cautiously looks around and hides behind the fire screen. A moment later Schigolch comes limping in, gasping for breath and complaining about the "slippery floors" in the house. A bizarre scene follows.

The Athlete (Rodrigo) appears on the balcony at the rear of the room holding the young Schoolboy by the arm. As he drags him down the steps, the boy struggles to free himself from Rodrigo's grasp. The ensemble which now builds up is constructed on the chromaticism characterizing Schigolch.

From the leering comments made by the old man and Rodrigo, it becomes clear that this youngster has fallen into Lulu's clutches and is hopelessly in love with her. In fact, he tells the two that he has written a poem to her. They comment in cynical amusement. Schigolch, staring lecherously at the boy, remarks that his eyes have enslaved Lulu. Turning to Rodrigo, the old man sings: "We are finished!" The two clink glasses and with sardonic formality drink a toast to each other.

Lulu, dressed in a revealing gown set off by a corsage of orchids, makes a dramatic entrance. The Schoolboy gapes openmouthed at her; she leans provocatively over him for a moment, inviting him to smell the orchids. Schigolch and the Athlete ask her if she is expecting the Prince ("Sie erwarten wohl den Prinzen?"). Showing her irritation at the question, Lulu turns and goes up the stairs to the balcony. In a continuation of the ensemble, both Schigolch and Rodrigo admit—to the utter bewilderment of the Schoolboy—that they wanted to marry Lulu. It also now becomes clear that Schigolch is not her father—as he has pretended. In fact, he tells Rodrigo that Lulu never had a father.

She appears just in time to overhear his remark. Smiling, she admits it is true and that she is a "wonder child." The ensuing action verges on farce. When Schigolch and the Athlete express concern about Dr. Schön, Lulu calmly assures them that he is at the stock exchange. As Rodrigo is bragging about how he will toss the Doctor into the air if he shows up, the manservant announces Alwa. Cursing him, Rodrigo scurries behind the draperies; the Schoolboy ducks under the table; Schigolch, taking the key to the balcony room from Lulu, starts crawling slowly up the stairs.

Alwa, in a dinner jacket, immediately begins talking to Lulu about his opera, then notices Schigolch on the stairs. Startled, he asks Lulu who he is. She glibly answers that he is an army comrade of Dr. Schön's who was wounded in the war. Alwa asks if his father is at home and Lulu tells him he is at the stock exchange. The servant, entering with a bottle of champagne and glasses, stares brazenly at Lulu. Alwa notices the look and angrily asks him what is wrong. Lulu tries to make light of the matter. The servant, obviously unable to control his feelings, rushes out.

Lulu hastily brings Alwa's thoughts back to himself with insinuating flattery, saying that what she admires most about him is his strength of character ("Was ich immer am höchsten"). He is the only person in the world, she tells him, who has protected her without robbing her of her self-respect. Alwa, of course, falls victim to her blandishments. With a show of modesty, he admits his intuitions have been correct. During this conversation, Schön appears on the balcony, glares down at his son, then withdraws.

Alwa masks his amorous thoughts behind a façade of high-sounding phrases—none of which, obviously, swerve Lulu from her intention to make him her next victim. With tantalizing candor she assures him that it is because of his regard for her that she can give herself to him without reservation. Alwa is completely swept away.

The dialogue is interrupted by the entrance of the servant, who is still in a state of uncontrollable agitation. Alwa sharply asks him if he is ill; Lulu again intervenes. Schön reappears and looks down balefully at the hapless servant, who walks out unsteadily balancing his tray.

Alwa, losing control of himself, begins making violent love to

Lulu, quite unaware that Schön and the Athlete emerge to watch the scene briefly. Finally Alwa throws himself into Lulu's arms crying: "Mignon, I love you!"[2] Stroking his hair, she speaks in an eerie, haunting half whisper: "I poisoned your mother."

The two are completely oblivious to the sinister pantomime in progress behind them. Rodrigo, looking out from behind the draperies, sees Schön. The latter takes aim at him with his revolver. Rodrigo frantically points to Lulu and Alwa, but Schön holds his aim on him. Before Rodrigo can dodge back behind the draperies, Lulu catches sight of him and then sees Schön on the balcony. She leaps to her feet with a gasp of fright. Pocketing his revolver, Schön comes down the stairs with a newspaper in his hand. He strides over to Alwa, who is still on his knees and staring at Lulu as though in a trance.

Grasping his son by the shoulders, Schön pulls him to his feet and shouts that revolution has broken out in Paris. Alwa shows no sign of having heard what he said. Schön dementedly babbles that no one in the editorial department knows what to write about the situation. With that he drags Alwa out of the room.

The Athlete, panic-stricken, tries to escape up the stairs but Lulu bars his way, warning that Schön will kill him. In desperation, Rodrigo dodges behind the draperies a moment before Schön, revolver in hand, reappears. Confronting Lulu, he furiously denounces her for dragging him into the mire of her own corruption ("Du Kreatur, die mich durch die Strassenkot"). This marks the beginning of a scene designated as a "five-strophic aria."

At the height of his tirade, Lulu interrupts to ask with infuriating insolence what he thinks of her dress. Beside himself with anger, Schön roars at her to get out before she drives him to killing his own son. Suddenly he thrusts the revolver at her and commands her to kill herself. Almost playfully, Lulu points the gun at him and inadvertently fires a shot into the ceiling. At that moment the Athlete darts out from his hiding place, bounds up the stairs and vanishes.

Schön, catching sight of him, demands to know if Lulu has hidden any other men in the house, then begins to search the room. He discovers the Countess Geschwitz behind the fire screen. As she begs Lulu to save her, Schön roughly drags her into the

---

[2] This phrase ("Mignon, ich liebe Dich") marks the midpoint of the "Alwa Rondo," which has been described as the lyrical focus of the entire opera. It is Berg's expression of his personal affection for the extraordinary character he created in Lulu.

other room and slams the door, snarling after her: "Now you will have to stay until the end."

Exhausted by his rage, he flings himself down beside Lulu, thrusts the revolver into her hands and says there are enough bullets left for her to make an end of things. Lulu quietly tells him he can do so himself by divorcing her.

That would indeed be the end ("Das war noch übrig"), Schön retorts with savage irony, and would leave the way clear for his successor to her affections. But how, he asks, can divorce be the end for two people who are fused together as one? Frantic with rage, he tries to wrest the revolver from her.

Now aroused and frightened by his violence, Lulu tears herself away from him and in a ringing refrain known as "Lulu's Song"— the "coloratura Lied"—("Wenn sich die Menschen") she speaks out in her own defense. If men have killed themselves for her, she sings, their rash actions do not demean her. He knows as well as she why they married; if he has sacrificed his old age to her, she has given him her youth in return. In a climactic phrase (again at the topmost range of the voice) she declares that she has always been true to herself—and no one ever has had reason to regard her otherwise.[3]

Schön, screaming in uncontrollable frenzy, forces Lulu to her knees and turns the revolver in her hand toward her. At that moment the Schoolboy, under the table, shouts for help. Schön whirls toward the table and at that instant Lulu fires five shots into his back and keeps pulling the trigger of the empty gun. As Schön slumps down, the Schoolboy scrambles from his hiding place and helps him to a chair. In spite of his agony, Schön gasps: "Another one!"

Lulu bends over him, but he weakly thrusts her away and calls for Alwa. He comes headlong down the stairs from the balcony. When Schön asks for water, Lulu pours a glass of champagne and brings it to him as she wails that it was she who fired the shots. The Schoolboy whimpers that she is innocent. Schön raises the glass to his lips. When Alwa, with the Schoolboy's help, lifts him to his feet to take him to the adjoining room, Schön warns his son not to let Lulu escape—because *he* will be the next one. When they reach the door, and Alwa opens it, the Countess Geschwitz rushes out. Schön collapses and dies on the threshold. Lulu, kneeling down and tenderly stroking his brow, murmurs that now it is over.

She rises and turns to go up the stairs, but Alwa bars her way.

---

[3] Berg called this Lulu's "confession of faith."

The Countess and the Schoolboy stand by helplessly. Now genuinely terrified over the debacle she has brought about, Lulu implores Alwa not to hand her over to the police. She promises to be faithful to him forever, throwing her arms around his knees in a melodramatic gesture of entreaty.

Alwa looks down at her in mingled pity and contempt. There is a clamorous pounding at the door as the police, presumably called by neighbors who heard the sound of gunfire, demand entrance. Pushing Lulu violently away, Alwa goes to open the door. The Schoolboy, in helpless terror, whines that now he will be hounded out of school. The curtain falls. The orchestral accompaniment continues without interruption into a tumultuous interlude which sustains the feverish mood of the preceding scene. The music gradually subsides to a slow, deliberate tempo; it is based on the *Erdgeist* theme and the portrait motive.[4]

[*Scene Two*] The room in Schön's house as in Scene One. The Countess Geschwitz is sitting in a chair, a rug over her knees. Seated near her on the ottoman is the Athlete. Alwa, deep in thought, is pacing back and forth. The three are waiting for Schigolch, who is coming from the prison hospital where Lulu has been confined as a victim of cholera. An epidemic has been raging through the city. Rodrigo—for reasons which will become apparent later—is posing as Alwa's servant.

As the scene opens, the Countess, Rodrigo and Alwa are discussing Lulu. Rodrigo wonders if the cholera has left its mark on her as it has on the Countess. The latter says that the affliction which disfigures ordinary people only makes Lulu more beautiful —and Lulu now is lovelier than she has ever been.

In any case, Rodrigo says, he intends to go on his way to his next theatrical engagement without Lulu. When the Countess expresses shocked surprise that he would permit his fiancée to travel alone, the Athlete explains in a brief refrain ("Erstens fahrt noch der Alte"). To begin with, he sings, the old man (Schigolch) is going with her to protect her. Furthermore, he (Rodrigo) is obliged to wait for his show costumes, which include a pair of rose-colored tights. He fumes that the effect of his acrobatic costumes will be spoiled because he has gained weight

[4] Berg wrote this music to accompany the film sequence which in the opera establishes the connection between Wedekind's two dramas. Additionally, the retrograde pattern of the harmonies reflects the misfortune that now overtakes Lulu. From the peak of social position as the wife of Dr. Schön, she plunges to the status of murderess, spends a year in prison and then is liberated to go eventually to her doom.

while lying in a hospital bed for three months as an accomplice in the Countess' fantastic "conspiracy." The Countess expresses disgust over the Athlete's lack of consideration for Lulu.

Alwa expresses misgivings about the Countess' plan to spirit Lulu out of the hospital, but he warmly commends her for her unselfish efforts in the girl's behalf. In token of his gratitude he offers to reimburse Geschwitz for her personal expenses with a loan of twenty thousand marks. The foregoing is partly in spoken dialogue.

Before she can reply, Schigolch comes in—grumbling as usual. The musical accompaniment is an exact repeat, in slow motion, of that heard when the old man came into the house complaining about the "slippery floors" at the beginning of the act. Schigolch explains he has been busy arranging for passports for the Countess, Lulu and himself, and adds that he knows of an excellent hotel in Paris. The Countess interrupts to tell him that Rodrigo expects him to accompany Lulu alone. Probably because Rodrigo is afraid of becoming infected, Schigolch sneers. Rodrigo somewhat cynically remarks that there will be no harm in having her disinfected before their honeymoon. Alwa proffers the Countess a wallet with ten thousand marks but she refuses to take it. She and Schigolch leave for the hospital.

No sooner have they gone than Rodrigo and Alwa begin quarreling about money. In the ensuing interval of spoken dialogue the events leading up to the present situation in the opera are disclosed. Rodrigo angrily upbraids Alwa for offering the Countess Geschwitz money when he (Rodrigo) is practically penniless, having spent everything in a harebrained scheme to effect Lulu's release from prison following the murder of Schön.

What is more, Rodrigo goes on, he is doing Alwa a favor by acting as his servant, so that no new servants (who might report the "conspirators" to the police) need be engaged. And finally, he is willing to risk his life to make his prospective bride (Lulu) "the greatest woman acrobat of the age."

Alwa retorts that he knows that the Countess has paid Rodrigo every cent she owes him—and is even now paying him a monthly salary. Under the circumstances, says Alwa, he is somewhat suspicious of Rodrigo's professed unselfish love for the murderess. In any case, he no doubt would have ended up a drunken beggar had it not been for the generosity of the Countess.

Infuriated, the Athlete asks Alwa what would have happened to him if he had not sold his father's scurrilous rag of a newspaper for two million marks. The net result of *that* windfall was that

Alwa composed a miserable opera—in which Lulu's legs are to play the "leading role," and which no theater in the world would think of performing.

The two are about to come to blows when the doorbell rings. Rodrigo, greatly excited, cries that now he will see his bride at last, after a year's time. But Alwa warns him to hide. The visitor turns out to be the Schoolboy. He tells the exasperated Alwa that he has just escaped from the house of correction and has come to ask help in "liberating the woman." He goes into some vague explanation about the testimony at Lulu's trial.

He is interrupted when Rodrigo emerges from behind a curtain and gives a deliberately awkward imitation of a servant. But he promptly drops his masquerade when he sees the Schoolboy. Enraged, he threatens him with a beating. Rodrigo realizes, of course, that the boy has been romantically involved with Lulu and he is bent on revenge. He tells the Schoolboy that "the woman" (significantly, he does not call her Lulu) has been dead for three weeks.

When the boy refuses to believe it, Rodrigo thrusts a newspaper in front of him and points to an item which reports that the murderess of Dr. Ludwig Schön is a cholera victim. Rodrigo snatches the paper away before the Schoolboy can finish reading the first sentence. He finally accepts the fact that Lulu is dead when Alwa assures him it is so. The boy grieves for her but adds, with a cynicism far beyond his years, that he will find some other way to go to the devil. Rodrigo, infuriated at the boy's insolence, throws him bodily out of the room.

A moment later Lulu appears on the balcony with Schigolch. She walks haltingly, leaning on the old man's arm as though barely able to support herself. The music which accompanies her entrance is a slow-motion passage corresponding to that of her first appearance in Act Two. Wearing the Countess' black dress, her face ghostly white and skeletonlike, she is a veritable apparition. The Athlete gasps in anger and dismay. He rages that such a creature could never appear in his circus act and that he intends to denounce her to the police as an impostor. Shouting that he will sue for damages enough to support him for the rest of his life, he storms away.

Lulu, Alwa and Schigolch look at each other with expressions of relief. The old man takes his leave, saying he will get the sleeping car tickets and return for Lulu in half an hour. Lulu sits down on the sofa and then her demeanor and her appearance mysteriously undergo a complete transformation. She again becomes the alluring creature of the earlier scenes. In a soaring phrase ("O Freiheit! O Gott im Himmel!") she exults that she is free at last after two long years of imprisonment. Alwa hands her a drink.

Looking around, she asks what happened to her portrait. Alwa goes to the fireplace and turns the portrait around to face her. He explains that the Countess first thought of hanging it in her home, but then feared that the police might find it as incriminating evidence if they searched the premises. Without the slightest show of concern or regret, Lulu murmurs that now her most ardent admirer is in prison in her place.

Then in a long passage in spoken words Lulu tells Alwa the incredible story of how the Countess sacrificed herself to help her escape from prison. First she volunteered as a nurse in a Hamburg hospital during the cholera epidemic. Purloining the contaminated clothing of a dead victim, she brought the garments to the prison. Both she and Lulu were stricken with cholera and taken to the isolation ward of the prison hospital. As they lay side by side in the same room, the Countess applied makeup so that the two resembled each other. On the day Lulu was discharged from the ward as cured, the Countess put on her prison garb while Lulu donned the Countess' clothes. And now, Lulu comments with cruel amusement, the Countess is in prison as the murderess of Dr. Schön.

Alwa, dumfounded, asks why she pretended to be desperately ill when she arrived with Schigolch. Simply to get rid of Rodrigo, Lulu answers. With sensual abandon she stretches out her arms and asks Alwa for a kiss. He takes her in his embrace and responds with fierce ardor. With calculated viciousness, she reminds him that she shot his father. Alwa's answer is to beg her for another kiss.

For a moment he looks into her eyes. With feverish intensity he sings that, but for their innocent look, he would regard her as the cleverest harlot who ever lured a man to his doom. In a high coloratura phrase, Lulu gaily answers that she wishes she were. She asks him to flee across the border with her so that they can see each other as often as they wish ("so oft wir wollen"). The two repeat the words in parallel musical phrases.

Now hopelessly under her spell, Alwa, in the aria entitled "Hymn" ("Durch dieses Kleid"), apostrophizes Lulu's body in voluptuously erotic terms over surging glissandi in the orchestra.

As he buries his face in her lap she murmurs malevolently: "Is this the sofa on which your father bled to death?" In passion and despair Alwa screams: "Silence!" The curtain falls to dark, foreboding chords as at the end of Scene Three in the first act.


## ACT THREE

While this act is frequently presented in the "pantomime" version—as mentioned earlier—Berg adhered closely to the Wedekind dramas in bringing the opera to a close. The vocal parts are complete in what is known as the "short score." While some of the instrumentation exists only in outline, it is apparent that the composer completed the musical framework of the entire act before his death.

In the scoring, he indicated special effects with surrealistic overtones—mainly produced by means of an instrument called the orchestrion, a mechanical orchestra in the form of an organ, invented about 1851.

The act is in two scenes, which are linked by entr'acte music in the form of four elaborately developed variations of the *Lulu Suite*. Each in turn delineates the further steps in Lulu's dissolution—from the time she fled to Paris following her release from prison in Germany to her doom in London.

[*Scene One*] The action takes place mainly in the glittering salons of the demimonde in Paris, where Lulu had arrived with Alwa and Schigolch, and was later joined by the Countess Geschwitz. There she becomes enmeshed with an unsavory group of underworld characters. Chief among these is the scoundrelly Marquis Casti-Piani, who not only blackmails Lulu but contrives the financial ruin of Alwa. Lulu is rescued from exposure and arrest through the efforts of the Countess Geschwitz, and then the four make their way to London.

[*Scene Two*] Lulu, now a common streetwalker, lives in wretched poverty in a slum garret. Sharing her existence there are the Countess, Alwa, Schigolch and Rodrigo, who remain loyal to Lulu despite her degradation. The Countess herself treasures her last possession—the portrait of Lulu painted by her artist-husband, Walter Schwarz.

Soon the final catastrophe strikes. Alwa is killed in a quarrel with one of the men solicited by Lulu. Not long after, Lulu is stabbed by Jack the Ripper, the last man to accompany her to her garret. The murder takes place offstage, with Lulu's dying shriek bringing the action to a horrifying climax.

Confronted by the Countess Geschwitz as he makes his escape, Jack the Ripper strikes her down. The tragedy ends with her dying words: "Lulu, my angel, let me see you once again. I am near you, I will stay near you, to eternity."

# Macbeth

### *by* GIUSEPPE VERDI
### (1813–1901)

### *Libretto by*
#### FRANCESCO MARIA PIAVE

### *Based on Shakespeare's play*

#### CHARACTERS

| | |
|---|---|
| Duncan (Duncano), King of Scotland | Mute |
| Macbeth (Macbetto) ) generals in | ( Baritone |
| Banquo (Banco)      ) King Duncan's army | ( Bass |
| Lady Macbeth | Soprano |
| Macduff, a Scottish nobleman | Tenor |
| Malcolm, son of Duncan | Tenor |
| Fleance, son of Banquo | Mute |
| Gentlewoman to Lady Macbeth | Mezzo-soprano |
| A doctor | Bass |
| Servant to Macbeth | Bass |
| A herald | Bass |
| Hecate, goddess of witchcraft | Mute |

Witches, messengers of the King, Scottish nobles, peasants, assassins, English soldiers, aerial spirits, apparitions

*Place:* Scotland and England
*Time:* About the year 1040
*First performance:* Teatro Pergola, Florence, Italy, March 14, 1847
*Original language:* Italian

———————————

Of *Macbeth,* his tenth opera, Verdi wrote: "Here is this *Macbeth,* which I love above all my other operas." His affection for this work seems to have been rooted in his love for Shakespeare, which dated from his early years. Verdi himself wrote a prose version of the libretto, which he then gave to Piave to turn into verse to conform to conventional libretto requirements. The first performance in Florence was greeted with restrained enthusiasm—

mainly because this opera was in many respects a departure from the conventional form. In *Macbeth*, Verdi was trying his hand at something new: music drama, in which character delineation took precedence over a mere succession of tuneful arias and concerted numbers. But the public soon "caught on"; subsequent performances were wildly acclaimed.

Verdi's abiding fondness for *Macbeth* prompted him to make drastic revisions after it had been in the repertoire almost twenty years. He rewrote most of the third act, revised two important arias, and completely changed the ending of the opera itself. The new version was presented at the Théâtre Lyrique in Paris on April 21, 1865. There it received only fourteen performances. Verdi, keenly disappointed, conceded that it was "a fiasco." Today it is usually performed in its original version, which retains its popular appeal because of its unique power and intensity of expression.

There is a brief but dramatic prelude mingling the fanfare of trumpets with swift chromatic passages. Also heard is a fragmentary refrain later associated with Lady Macbeth's sleepwalking scene in Act Four.

## ACT ONE

[*Scene One*] The curtain rises on a desolate heath, its gloomy expanse visible in flashes of lightning. An eerie theme sounds in the English horns, then a harsh fanfare of brass underscores the wildness of the scene. As lightning flares and thunder crashes, the witches gather. To a staccato accompaniment, the First, Second and Third Witches being their colloquy—"Che faceste? Dite su" ("Where hast thou been, sister?").

One says she has been killing swine. Her companion tells how she came upon a sailor's wife munching chestnuts and asked her for some. The woman told the witch to go to the devil—and for that bit of insolence one sailor's wife will become a widow—her husband will drown at sea. The other witches cackle their approval of this summary punishment as they dance in a circle to the macabre accompaniment.

Suddenly there is a drum roll. The dance becomes wilder as the witches shriek that Macbeth is on his way. In a moment, he and Banquo appear. The two men comment in recitative on the day's fateful events and on the hideous spectacle of the witches ("Giorni non vidi"). Macbeth commands them to speak ("Or via parlate!"). In sonorous, prophetic tones ("Salve, o Macbetto") they hail him as Thane of Glamis and Cawdor, and as King of Scotland. They tell Banquo that he will be the father of future kings. As their voices die away in a sinister whisper, the witches vanish.

A moment later a messenger arrives and tells Macbeth he has been made Thane of Cawdor by the King. (He already had the title of Thane of Glamis.) Macbeth first exults that two prophecies already have been fulfilled, and the third promises him a throne. Yet he wonders why evil thoughts cross his brain. Banquo comments in an aside that even in a moment of triumph the forces of darkness can trap an unwary victim ("Oh, come s'empie costui"). The voices of the two men blend in a brief but fiery duet. They leave, followed by the messenger. The witches return and hail Macbeth and his destiny in another frenzied chorus ("S'allontanarono!").

[*Scene Two*] A hall in Macbeth's castle. After a short introduction of successively rising chromatic phrases (foreshadowing the duet in *Otello*), Lady Macbeth enters. Over a sustained chord, she reads aloud a letter from Macbeth describing the witches prophecy ("Nel dì della vittoria"). She reflects with satisfaction on the ambition which is spurring Macbeth ("Ambizioso spirto tu sei"), then in an ensuing cavatina ("Vieni! t'affretta! Accendere!") she ponders if he will now let scruples stand in his way.

A servant comes in to tell her that King Duncan is coming to the castle this night with Macbeth. Lady Macbeth, realizing that destiny already is at work, repeats with evil gloating: "Duncano sarà qui? Qui la notte?" Then in an aria of savage exultation she calls on the infernal spirits to assist her in plotting murder ("Or tutti sorgete, ministri infernali").

Macbeth enters. With deliberate emphasis, Lady Macbeth greets him as "Cawdor," then exhorts him not to falter in his resolve to kill King Duncan. A strain of martial music announces the arrival of the King and his retinue. Duncan enters with Macduff, Malcolm and Banquo, and all are ceremoniously greeted by Macbeth, his Lady and their court. The assemblage then leaves the hall.

Macbeth returns alone, deep in thought. Calling a servant, he orders him to tell Lady Macbeth to prepare his nightly drink and to ring a bell when it is ready. Suddenly he staggers back with a gasp of terror, then cries out: "Is this a dagger which I see before me?" ("Mi si affaccia un pugnal?"). Here follows the musical version of his famous soliloquy ("A me precorri sul confuso") in which he steels himself to the murder of Duncan and attempts to justify his act to himself.

He tries to convince himself that the dagger is only a figment of his imagination. In fear-stricken tones he implores the "sure and firm-set earth" not to hear his footsteps lest his whereabouts be discovered ("Immobil terra!").

Suddenly a bell rings. Macbeth intones over dark chords in the orchestra: "Non udirlo, Duncano" "Hear it not, Duncan, for it is a knell/ That summons thee to heaven, or to hell"). He leaves on his murderous errand. Lady Macbeth enters to a foreboding phrase in the orchestra. Haunted by the suspicion that the plot may have gone wrong, she starts in momentary fear as she hears the shriek of an owl—the bird of evil omen. Then Macbeth bursts into the room, a bloody knife in his hand. Shaken with guilt and terror, he cries out: "Tutto è finito!"

This marks the beginning of a long duet. Macbeth, panic-stricken, tells of the murder, describing how the courtiers guarding Duncan prayed in their sleep for his protection. To that prayer, Macbeth groans, he could not say "Amen." Lady Macbeth venomously asks for more details. In growing terror, Macbeth goes on—"Allor questa voce m'intesi nel petto" ("Methought I heard a voice cry, 'Sleep no more!/ Macbeth does murder sleep'").

Lady Macbeth derides him for giving way to remorse. She tells him to take the dagger back into the room and smear the blood on the courtiers as evidence of their guilt ("Il pugnal là riportate"). When Macbeth abjectly refuses to go, she snatches the dagger from his hands and stalks toward the King's room. Macbeth stares at his bloody hands and cries out in horror and despair: "Oh questa mano! non potrebbe l'Oceano queste mani a me lavar!" ("Oh, these hands! Not Ocean's waves could wipe this blood clean!").[1] The sound of knocking within increases his terror. Lady Macbeth returns and chides him contemptuously for his cowardice: "My hands are of your colour . . . A little water clears us of this deed."

When the knocking is repeated, Lady Macbeth tells her husband that they must hurry to their chamber so that they will not be found near the scene of the crime. They leave as the music dies into silence.

Macduff comes in with Banquo, saying he had been ordered by

[1] A paraphrase of Shakespeare: "What hands are here? ha! they pluck out mine eyes!/Will all great Neptune's ocean wash this blood/ Clean from my hand?"

the King to wake him early. Banquo then tells of the strange and terrible things that have happened during the night: "Oh qual orrenda notte!"

This marks the beginning of the powerful ensemble which closes the act. Both men go into the King's room, discover the murder, then rouse the household with their cries of horror. All in the castle are aghast at the news, then express their feelings in the closing chorus, "Schiudi, inferno, la bocca ed inghiott" ("Open wide thy portals, Hell!").

## ACT TWO

[*Scene One*] A room in the castle. In a brief recitative passage, Macbeth and Lady Macbeth discuss the situation confronting them. Macbeth is moody and distraught; his wife sharply asks him why he has been avoiding her ("Perchè mi sfuggi"). The deed is done, she says, and now he is King. Moreover, Duncan's son, Malcolm, fled to England and is being accused of the murder of his own father. Now the throne is left vacant—for Macbeth.

But Macbeth recalls that the witches prophesied that Banquo would be the father of kings ("Banco padre di regi"). A short recitative follows in which Macbeth and Lady Macbeth plot Banquo's murder. Macbeth leaves to accomplish this. Alone, Lady Macbeth sings the dramatic aria "La luce langue," in which she reflects on the evil this night will bring. The darkness will hide yet another murder . . . more blood . . . but so be it. In a ferocious outburst, she exults in her power—"O voluttà del soglio!" This phrase is introduced by a powerful ascending passage in the orchestra. Concluding the aria, Lady Macbeth gloats that he who was destined to be King soon will be dead ("Cadrà fra poco esanime chi fu predetto Re").

[*Scene Two*] A park. Macbeth's castle in the distance. In the foreground, a band of assassins talk among themselves in a sinister chorus ("Chi v'impose unirvi a noi?"). It has a strong resemblance to the "Zitti, zitti" chorus in *Rigoletto*. They reveal that they have been ordered by Macbeth to kill Banquo, who will arrive with his son Fleance. In a staccato passage ("Sparve il sol"), they sing that the sun has set, bringing on the darkness that hides bloody deeds. Now Banquo's hour of doom is near. The voices die to a whisper as the assassins slink away to wait in ambush.

Banquo enters with Fleance, warning him that danger lurks in this gloomy spot. He expresses his foreboding in an impressive aria, "Come dal ciel precipita," which is introduced by a dark, tremulous passage in the strings. The two go into the park. A moment later Banquo's cries are heard as an assassin strikes him down. He shouts to Fleance to save himself. Fleance, pursued by a murderer, dashes across the park as a trumpet passage blares out a theme of doom.

[*Scene Three*] A magnificent banquet room in Macbeth's castle. Gathered there are Macbeth, Lady Macbeth, Macduff and the lords and ladies of the court. The assemblage hails Macbeth and his Lady as King and Queen ("Salve, o Re"). Macbeth toasts Lady Macbeth, who responds with the "Brindisi" ("Si colmi il calice"). She is joined by the chorus.

As Macbeth is lifting his glass with the others, one of the assassins appears at a side door. Macbeth leaves the table and goes over to him. The assassin tells him that Banquo's murder was accomplished, but that his son escaped. Macbeth, shaken by the news, returns to the table. Controlling himself with an effort, he announces that Banquo has not kept his promise to attend the banquet ("Banco falla!"). He himself will sit in the absent guest's place.

But as he goes toward the chair, he sees Banquo's ghost sitting in it. Recoiling in terror, he shouts: "Non dirmi ch'io fossi! le ciocche cruenti non scuotermi incontro" ("Thou canst not say I did it: never shake/ Thy gory locks at me!"). He sings the second phrase in a hushed descending chromatic passage.

Lady Macbeth and the guests stare at him in alarm. In an aside, Lady Macbeth sneers: "Are you a man?" Macbeth cries out: "Yes—and a brave one to face what I see before me." Glaring at the apparition, he raves: "Can sepulchers give back the dead?" ("Il sepolcro può render gli uccisi?"). As it slowly fades from sight, Macbeth becomes calm and calls for a toast to the absent Banquo. Lady Macbeth repeats the "Brindisi," with the chorus joining.

Suddenly the ghost reappears. Macbeth, now on the verge of madness, commands it to leave ("Spirto d'abisso!"), then defiantly shouts that he is not afraid. Swirling chromatics in the strings underscore his terror. Lady Macbeth, in an aside, angrily berates him for his panic. In a passage which begins *sotto voce* then rises to a frenzied outburst, Macbeth sings that the ghost cries for blood, and blood it shall have. Today, the witches will tell him what the future will bring ("Sangue a me quell'ombra chiede"). The guests look on in consternation.

This scene introduces the ensemble which builds into the intensely dramatic finale of the act. Macduff and the lords and ladies voice their horror over Macbeth's frenzied outbursts ("Biechi arcani!"). They sing that an accursed power rules over this land, where now only the guilty can remain. Soon it will become a lair of thieves and assassins. Lady Macbeth rages at her husband for his faintheartedness. Macbeth himself rants that the witches will give him the key to the future. These sentiments blend in the mighty climax of the act.

## ACT THREE

A dark cave. In the center a caldron boils. Thunder and lightning.

There is an introductory chorus of incantation sung by the witches ("Tre volte miagola la gatta"). Dancing around the caldron, they sing about the "ingredients" that make up their infernal brew. A ballet follows in which they invoke Hecate, goddess of witchcraft. In pantomime, she tells them that Macbeth is approaching, then instructs them in the manner in which his doom is to be brought about.[2]

Following the ballet (or, in the original version, after the Incantation Scene), Macbeth enters with his soldiers. Ordering them to wait, he enters the cavern and commands the witches to tell him what his fate is to be ("Ch'io sappia il mio destin"). Then follows the Apparition Scene. Over dark, brooding chords in the orchestra, the witches unfold Macbeth's future.

First they ask him if he wishes to hear the prophecies from "the unknown powers" ("Dalle incognite posse") or from themselves. Invoke the powers—if they have the answers, Macbeth commands. Thereupon a helmeted head emerges from the ground. It warns Macbeth to beware of Macduff ("Da Macduffo ti guarda prudente").

Next a bloody child arises. It tells Macbeth that none born of women can harm him ("Nessun nato di donna ti nuoce").

Finally there is the apparition of a crowned child, holding the branch of a tree in his hand. It tells Macbeth that he never will be vanquished until the day he sees the Birnam Wood marching against him ("Fin che il bosco di Birnam vedrai ravviarsi e venir contro te!").[3]

---

[2] The ballet was written for the Paris version of the opera, presented at the Théâtre Lyrique in 1865. Verdi had revised the opera in 1864.

[3] In Shakespeare: ". . . until/ Great Birnam wood to high Dunsinane hill/ Shall come against him."

Macbeth exults over these auguries of his triumph ("Oh! lieto augurio!"), then asks the witches if Banquo's sons ever will seize his throne. They warn him not to ask. Fiercely Macbeth demands an answer, threateningly brandishing his sword. Instantly the caldron sinks into the ground and then Macbeth hears the wailing of bagpipes. As he stares in surprise, a procession of eight kings marches across the stage. The eighth is Banquo, who is carrying a mirror.

In a frenzy, Macbeth draws his sword and rushes at the phantoms, commanding them to disappear ("Fuggi, regal fantasima!"). To the accompaniment of an orchestral fanfare, he counts them as they march by. In terror-stricken tones he asks the witches if these phantoms will live. When the witches answer yes, Macbeth faints. The witches, in a striking phrase sung on a single note, invoke the spirits of the air to revive the King ("Aerei spirti").[4]

The witches then disappear as Macbeth staggers to his feet. Lady Macbeth enters. In the ensuing dialogue Macbeth tells her of his talk with the witches, of the three apparitions and their prophecies, and of the vision of Banquo's sons, who are destined to become the future kings of Scotland. Lady Macbeth curses them. She and Macbeth together vow that Macduff's wife and babies will perish in the flames of the castle of Fife, and that Banquo's son Fleance will be tracked down and killed. The duet comes to a climax in a trenchant passage that begins in tones of suppressed fury and swells to a furious cry for vengeance ("Ora di morte omai").

## ACT FOUR

[*Scene One*] A desolate region on the border between England and Scotland. In the distance the forest of Birnam. A group of Scottish refugees sings a chorus of lamentation over the oppression of their country by the tyrant ("Patria oppressa!").

Macduff, standing at one side, crushed by sorrow and despair, mourns his wife and children, murdered by Macbeth ("O figli miei"). In a moving aria ("Ah, la paterna mano") he grieves because he was not with his loved ones to protect them from their slayer, then vows revenge for this foul deed.

To a flourish of drums and a fanfare of trumpets, Malcolm enters at the head of a company of English soldiers. When he learns from his men that they are in the forest of Birnam, he

---

[4] In the Paris version, a chorus of spirits ("Ondine e silfidi") and a ballet follow.

orders that each soldier is to cut a branch and carry it with him ("Svelga ognuno e porti un ramo"). Malcolm and Macduff, drawing their swords, then take their places at the head of the company. In a rousing chorus ("La patria tradita") they sing that they will free their country from the chains of the oppressor.

[*Scene Two*] A room in Macbeth's castle. It is night. There is a long orchestral interlude which establishes the eerie mood of the Sleepwalking Scene. A doctor and a gentlewoman are in the room. In a brief recitative, they disclose that Lady Macbeth has been walking in her sleep, and they have waited for two nights to watch her. Tonight, says the gentlewoman, she will certainly appear.

As she speaks, Lady Macbeth enters carrying a candle. She sets the candle down, rubs her hands as though washing them, then begins the great aria "Una macchia è qui tuttora . . . via, ti dico, o maledetta!"—"There is still a spot here . . . out, damned spot . . . out, I say!" At the beginning of the aria there is a rising figure in the orchestra which keeps repeating like an accusing voice, while through the shuddering accompaniment comes the moaning of the English horn. In the interpretation of Lady Macbeth's tormenting thoughts, the aria ranges from a low C flat to a high D flat, encompassing more than two octaves.

The doctor and the gentlewoman stand transfixed with horror as Lady Macbeth recalls, one by one, the murders which have stained her hands. All the perfumes of Arabia, she murmurs in her dreadful nightmare, will not wash away the smell of human blood. As she ends the aria on a high pianissimo phrase, "Andiam, Macbetto" (she imagines she hears someone knocking), the doctor and the gentlewoman intone a prayer.

[*Scene Three*] A hall in the castle. Macbeth enters raging against the thanes who have united with England against him ("Perfidi! All' Anglo contro me v'unite!"). Defiantly he recalls the prophecy that "none born of woman" can harm him. Suddenly he is overwhelmed by hopelessness and despair. In the aria, "Pietà, rispetto, amore," he sings that honor, respect and love—the comforts of a man's later years—will be denied him. His only epitaph will be curses.[5]

---

[5] From Shakespeare: "My way of life is fallen into the sear, the yellow leaf;/ And that which should accompany old age,/ As honour, love, obedience, troops of friends,/ I must not look to have; but, in their stead,/ Curses, not loud but deep . . ."

A gentlewoman enters and informs Macbeth that Lady Macbeth is dead. Too numbed by tragedy to grieve, Macbeth cries out in bitter scorn: "La vita! che importa? È il racconto d'un povero idiota! Vento e suono che nulla dinota!"—"What is life? It is a tale/ Told by an idiot, full of sound and fury,/ Signifying nothing!"[6]

Macbeth's soldiers rush in shouting that "Birnam Wood" is approaching. Realizing that the prophecy has come true, he curses the witches for betraying him. Calling for his sword and shield, he exhorts his soldiers to fight. They respond in a brief but stormy chorus, "Dunque all' armi!"

The scene quickly shifts to a plain, where English soldiers, each carrying a branch, are slowly advancing. Malcolm and Macduff appear. Macduff orders the warriors to discard their branches, unsheathe their swords and follow him into battle. All rush off.

After a short orchestral interlude, Macbeth dashes in pursued by Macduff, who cries that at last he has tracked down the murderer of his wife and children. Turning on him, Macbeth dares Macduff to kill him, shouting that no man born of woman can harm him—"nato di donna ucidermi non può." Roaring that he was not born, but "was from his mother's womb untimely ripp'd" ("Nato non sono: strappato fui dal sen materno"), Macduff plunges his sword into Macbeth's body.

As Macbeth falls, a group of women and children rush in, stare in horror at the dying man, then break out into lamentation over this day of bloodshed ("Infausto giorno!"). Raising himself, Macbeth begins his final aria, "Mal per me che m'affidai." In an evil moment, he sings, he put his trust in witches' prophecies—and now they have destroyed him. As his life ebbs away, he gasps that he dies "at war with earth and heaven" ("muoio . . . al cielo . . . al mondo in ira").[7]

There is a triumphant shout offstage, then Malcolm and Macduff enter with their soldiers, who drag in Macbeth's followers as

---

[6] In Shakespeare, this is the conclusion of Macbeth's famous soliloquy on hearing of Lady Macbeth's death. It begins: "She should have died hereafter;/ There would have been a time for such a word./ To-morrow, and to-morrow, and to-morrow,/ Creeps in this petty pace from day to day . . ."

[7] This aria's curious history was once described by Carl Ebert, manager of the Städtische Oper in West Berlin, in an interview with Harold C. Schonberg of the New York *Times*. In staging the opera in 1931, Mr. Ebert said, he was convinced that Verdi, with his infallible sense of theater, would have written a final aria for Macbeth, rather than have him die offstage—as in the Paris version. Mr. Ebert undertook a search and eventually found the missing aria at Sant' Agata, Verdi's home.

prisoners. Other soldiers, thanes and the populace crowd in. Kneeling before Malcolm, Macduff says he slew Macbeth, then hails Malcolm as King ("Salve, O Re!"). All onstage repeat the acclamation, then join in the chorus which brings the opera to its fiery climax. The curtain falls.

# Mourning Becomes Electra

*by* MARVIN DAVID LEVY

( 1932–    )

*Libretto by*
HENRY BUTLER

*Based on the play by Eugene O'Neill*

### CHARACTERS

| | |
|---|---|
| Christine Mannon | Dramatic soprano |
| Lavinia Mannon, her daughter | Soprano (spinto or dramatic) |
| Jed, an old servant of the Mannons | Bass |
| Adam Brant, a sea captain | Dramatic baritone |
| Peter Niles, Lavinia's suitor | Lyric baritone |
| Helen Niles, his sister | Lyric soprano |
| General Ezra Mannon, Christine's husband | Bass-baritone |
| Orin Mannon, his son | High baritone or Tenor |

Servants (sopranos), townspeople (altos), townsmen (tenors), soldiers, sailors, dock workers

*Place:* A small seaport village in New England
*Time:* Spring and summer of 1865–66
*First performance:* Metropolitan Opera House, Lincoln Center, New York City, March 17, 1967
*Original language:* English

---

*Mourning Becomes Electra,* by the young American composer Marvin David Levy (his first full-length opera), is an operatic retelling of the *Oresteia* trilogy by the Greek dramatist Aeschylus. The immediate source of the Levy opera is the trilogy by Eugene O'Neill, who himself retold the legend in terms of the doom-haunted lives of a New England family in 1865.

In the play's transition from antiquity to the nineteenth century, Agamemnon becomes Ezra Mannon; Clytemnestra, Christine; Electra, Lavinia; Orestes, Orin; Aegisthus, Adam Brant. But both in the plays and the opera the baleful theme of the legend remains the same: The plight of human beings caught in the remorseless grip of their own destinies.

The opera's three acts bear the titles of the three O'Neill plays —*Homecoming, The Hunted, The Haunted*. Librettist Butler condensed the six-hour trilogy into three hours, omitting certain secondary characters, paraphrasing the dialogue, but retaining the basic dramatic elements.

Although the music is essentially atonal, some of the passages are handled in almost conventional melodic style. In fact, Mr. Levy uses his own concept of the Wagnerian leitmotiv. Certain orchestral and vocal phrases recur—not to identify a character in the Wagnerian sense, but in association with the thought or emotion which impels the action of the moment. An ultramodern touch in the orchestration is the brief use of electronic tape for synthetic background sounds to heighten dramatic effects.

There is no overture. The curtain rises after a short orchestral introduction in which the dominant theme, briefly stated, is the one associated with Christine in fleeting moments of tenderness.

## ACT ONE
### Homecoming

[*Scene One*] The porch of the Mannon house, with a view between two huge decaying columns on either side. A basket of freshly cut flowers makes a splash of color against the grimness. It is late afternoon in April. Christine, with an air of nervous excitement, stares down the garden path. Over the "frustrated love" theme in the orchestra, she softly calls the name of "Adam."

A moment later Lavinia, returning from the village, rushes up to the porch. She is about to go into the house when Christine stops her. Lavinia breathlessly tells her that her father has returned from the battle front and will be home this evening. Christine seems unconcerned over this news, but then asks anxiously about Orin. He will be home in a day or two, Lavinia tells her; he suffered a head wound in battle but it is not serious.

With rather forced composure Christine informs her daughter that she has invited Captain Adam Brant for the afternoon. There is a gasp of angry surprise from Lavinia. Christine casually adds that she had met Brant by chance while visiting her father in New York, and she thought perhaps his visit here would please

Lavinia. The latter asks maliciously if the flowers are in honor of the Captain, then testily reminds her mother that General Mannon also will be home this evening.

Christine spitefully comments on Lavinia's strange look of adoration when she speaks of her father, then observes that a daughter should look elsewhere for love. With vicious emphasis, Lavinia retorts: "As her mother has done!" Christine chokes back her fury as Jed enters to announce that Captain Brant has arrived. Here the dissonant theme of "frustrated love" again sounds in the orchestra. Christine, going to meet Brant, gestures to Lavinia to follow. Ignoring her, Lavinia asks Jed what he knows about Adam Brant. In a melodic but somber refrain, Jed relates that Brant is the offspring of David Mannon, Lavinia's uncle, and a servant girl named Marie Brantone. The curse that destroyed them both lives on, Jed says, and now their son has come back to the house his parents disgraced. Lavinia furiously protests that this sordid story must be a lie.

Jed leaves as Christine returns with Brant. Lavinia greets him with icy politeness—fighting down her secret passionate feelings toward him. For Christine's benefit, Lavinia says to Brant that for a moment she mistook him for her father. Chagrined, Christine goes into the house.

Ignoring Lavinia's brusqueness, Brant affably remarks that he is glad of the chance to see her again—reminding her of their secret tryst "that evening last month." The colloquy continues in half-spoken, half-sung recitative. Lavinia rudely turns aside Brant's friendly overtures. When at last he tries to embrace her, she repulses him violently, cursing him as the spawn of a servant girl. In a towering rage, Brant seizes her, storming that there is no hiding from the truth: David Mannon committed suicide. When his mother brought David's son back to the Mannon house, begging for help for her child, she was hounded to her grave by Ezra Mannon, "the upright judge," who mouthed sanctimonious prayers all the while. And now, Lavinia interjects over a menacing triplet figure in the orchestra, Adam Brant is taking his shameful revenge here in the house of Mannon.

As they stand glaring at each other, Christine rushes in asking what has happened. Lavinia turns on her in wild fury. They will no longer use her, she rages, to mask their clandestine designs, for now she knows. . . . She followed her mother to her tryst with Adam in New York. There, outside the door, she listened to their love-making. With hysterical intensity Lavinia repeats her mother's words as she pleads for Adam's kisses. Brant, shattered by Lavinia's outburst, goes toward her in an effort to calm her, but Christine restrains him with: "No, Adam, no!"[1]

At Christine's mention of Adam's name there is an abrupt change of mood. With grim candor, Christine declares that she loves Adam Brant. She asks him to leave her alone with Lavinia. Brant complies, and then the two women stand face to face. One of the principal duets in the opera now ensues, in which mother and daughter futilely strive to understand each other. It begins with Lavinia's half-whispered question: "What lie will you ask me to believe?"

Christine speaks despairingly of the wall of hatred between them. That hatred was spawned here in the "tomb of the Mannons," she says, during her life with a husband she could not love. Somewhat moved, Lavinia asks if she always hated Mannon. Over the theme of "dead love" in the orchestra, Christine replies that she loved him once—and tried also to love his daughter. But that daughter was only the pain he inflicted upon her. Lavinia asks: "What of Orin?"

He was born in Mannon's absence, Christine says, when she could forget his cruelty. Her son was hers and hers alone . . . with no one to stand in the way of her love for him. And now this love, Lavinia murmurs desolately, is given to Adam Brant. In a poignant phrase, underscored by a variation of the double minor-third chord, Lavinia sings that she should pity, but she cannot pity what she does not understand. Reiterating these thoughts, the two women bring the duet to a moving climax on a lingering phrase which dies softly away. In this moment Christine and Lavinia seem to have bridged the gulf between them.

With shattering suddenness, the scene again erupts into violence. As Christine turns as if to join Brant, Lavinia warns her that Mannon never will let her go. Christine screams defiantly that he cannot stop her. With equal violence, Lavinia replies that she will help her father thwart her escape. Despite her rage, Christine realizes that Lavinia's real purpose is to eliminate her as a rival for Adam's love. Goaded by this thought, she lunges at her daughter. At that moment Adam rushes in and seizes her by the

---

[1] Here in the orchestration the composer makes use of one of the fundamental harmonic devices in the opera—a chord of two minor thirds set a diminished octave apart. Its powerful dissonance symbolizes the hatred and misunderstanding which alienate the characters from each other. This device is used throughout the opera.

arm. Spent by her fury, Christine concedes her defeat, murmuring that Lavinia has won . . . Adam will be sent away. She sardonically asks Lavinia if she wishes to be present at their last farewell.

Glaring at her, Lavinia says she is not counting on an easy victory. As she turns to go into the house she snarls a warning that she will be watching—she does not want her father to see Adam Brant here.

Brant, taking the half-fainting Christine in his arms, cries out: "I will not leave you!" Here for the first time is heard the "poison" theme, which foreshadows the murder of Ezra Mannon. It occurs again several measures later when Christine sings that "one does foolish things for love." With fierce intensity, underscored by rising chromatic figures in the orchestra, she goes on to say that she prayed that Ezra Mannon would not come back alive from the war—prayed so hard that she actually believed he never would. But she always has known, she adds darkly, that she must one day free herself.

With a furtive look around, she asks Adam, in spoken recitative, if he has the vial she asked him to buy for her. He hands it to her. Suddenly aware of her terrible resolve, Adam cries out in protest. As the "poison" theme blares again and again in the orchestra, Christine dementedly implores him to help her in her evil plotting. Everyone knows, she argues, that Mannon has a failing heart . . . if he dies they will be above suspicion. Seeing his hesitation, she plays her trump card: It must be Ezra's life or her own. Faced with this ultimatum, Brant promises to do whatever she asks.

A rising chromatic passage erupts in the orchestra, marking the beginning of their impassioned love duet. Clasped in each other's arms, they sing that the love which blossomed out of hate will bind them together forever. They will sail away to the Blessed Isles, where the sound of the surf will obliterate this nightmare of cruelty and fear. The duet rises to a ringing climax, then subsides into softly sung lyrical phrases.

Their moment of happiness is interrupted by the sound of a cannon shot and the blare of martial music in the distance. Christine exclaims this means that Ezra has returned, and tells Adam that he must leave at once. After an embrace, Adam hurries down the garden path. Watching him, Christine sings that now they are bound together in Mannon's death . . . Adam can never leave her. She goes into the house as the martial music and the babble of voices grow louder.

Helen and Peter Niles come bounding in from the garden. Calling gaily for Lavinia, they go into the house to look for her. Jed and the other servants come out to greet the townspeople now crowding on the scene. In a brief choral phrase they hail the return of the illustrious General Mannon. The General, resplendent in his uniform, enters and shakes hands with his well-wishers. The ensemble continues as the townsfolk comment that the great man's "foreign wife" does not come out to greet him, but waits for him in the shadows of this strange house. Their voices drop almost to a whisper as they look around apprehensively, then the chorus builds up again into a rousing tribute to General Ezra Mannon.

After the General acknowledges the plaudits, the crowd gradually disperses. Mannon and Jed talk together. Peter and Helen reappear with Lavinia. The young suitor reminds her that she promised to give him an answer when her father returned. But Lavinia, gazing ardently at Mannon, scarcely notices Peter. As she comes toward her father, Jed tactfully ushers Peter and Helen back into the house. Lavinia suddenly throws herself into Mannon's arms. At that moment he sees Christine at the window above the porch. As she moves away, Mannon frees himself from Lavinia's embrace and hurries into the house. A moment later he is heard calling his wife's name. Lavinia, fuming in jealous rage, stands glaring at the house as the scene fades. There is an orchestral interlude which continues without pause into the next scene. Heard prominently is a variation of the "death" motive, later expressed in Orin's phrase: "How death becomes the Mannons." As the curtain rises we hear the theme of "dead love."

[*Scene Two*] Ezra Mannon's bedroom, where the General lies asleep on a big four-poster. It is night; moonlight shines through the windows. As the "poison" theme sounds in the orchestra, Christine rises from the bed, puts on a dressing gown, then looks intently at her sleeping husband. Sinking into a chair, she begins to weep quietly.

Suddenly Ezra awakens and calls her name, marking the beginning of the long duet which culminates in Mannon's murder. Responding to her husband's call, Christine tells him that her sleep was disturbed by Lavinia's pacing up and down the hall outside all night long, like a sentry. Mannon remarks rather plaintively that at least there is someone who loves him. He raises himself, lights a candle and asks Christine if she can bear to look at him. When she turns away with a grimace he entreats her not to leave him ("Do not go, Christine"). The orchestral harmonies here and in the ensuing refrain are based on the minor-third chord, with its dissonance accentuating the misunderstanding which separates husband and wife. Mannon tells Christine that he thought of her constantly on the battlefield and prayed that he would not die before he saw her again. He admits that he has denied her the love she needed, but implores her to let him live out his "numbered days" with her.

Exhausted by his emotion, he sinks back gasping for breath. Feigning concern, Christine asks if his heart is paining him. Her question rouses Mannon to accusing anger and drives him to the verge of delirium. As Christine vainly tries to quiet him he rants that in this house, which is not his own, "they" are waiting for death to set her free. Losing control under his accusations, Christine rages that after the bitter cruelty he has inflicted on her he can never again lay claim to her love. Mannon, in a spasm of fury, lunges at her. Recoiling, Christine begins to taunt him venomously about her infidelity with Adam Brant—"a Mannon, too." Goaded beyond endurance, Mannon screams a curse, then falls back writhing in pain. Gesturing to the night table, he gasps for his medicine.

Christine picks up the bottle, sets it down again. In a swift movement she goes into her room, which adjoins the bedroom, and returns with the bottle of poison Adam brought her. She pours some of the poison into a glass of water, lifts Mannon's head and literally forces him to drink. This action takes place to the accompaniment of the serpentine harmonies of rising and falling chromatics.

In a paroxysm of agony, Mannon pushes Christine violently away from the bed. She stumbles back against the wall, where she stands transfixed as Ezra screams: "Lavinia!" The "poison" theme sounds clamorously in the orchestra. Lavinia bursts into the room, picks up the bottle of poison on the night table and goes to her father. Mannon clutches her wrists to prevent her from giving him any more of the poison, then points to Christine and gasps: "The medicine! Guilty!" Dazed and uncomprehending, Lavinia takes him in her arms. Seconds later his dead body slips from her grasp. Looking down at him, Lavinia wildly implores him not to leave her.

For a moment there is a terrible silence. Then, in ironic contrast to the horror of the scene, the jaunty music of the town band is heard in the distance. Lavinia looks up at her mother, who is staring at the bottle Lavinia still holds in her hands. She looks at her father, then back to Christine. The dreadful truth dawns upon her. Paralyzed with horror, the two women stare at each other. As the dissonant minor-third chords again blare out in the orchestra, Christine collapses fainting. The curtain falls.

## ACT TWO
### *The Hunted*

[*Scene One*] Interior of the Mannon home. The divided set shows the parlor at right; at left is the library-study, where is placed the bier of Ezra Mannon. A brief orchestral introduction begins softly. Christine is in the library receiving the condolences of the townspeople. Meanwhile Orin, in Union Army uniform, with his head bandaged, enters the parlor followed by Lavinia, dressed in deep mourning. Moving restlessly about the room, Orin asks where his mother is. Lavinia, telling him he must wait, watches him apprehensively as he touches Christine's favorite chair and murmurs that he dreamed of her sitting there to welcome him when he returned home. Several townspeople come in, pay their respects, then leave.

In a brief duet, Lavinia and Orin comment on their father's death. Staring at the portraits of the Mannons on the walls, Orin querulously asks why his father should crowd this tomblike house with one more ghost. Lavinia sharply rebukes him. He again asks impatiently for his mother.

With insidious tenderness, reflected in the curving, lyrical line of the music, Lavinia tells Orin that she has need of his strength now . . . he must put his trust in her. Their mother, she goes on, only will weaken his resolve. Orin upbraids her angrily for feuding with Christine. Their colloquy is interrupted by the approach of Christine, Helen and Peter. Orin and his mother rush into each other's arms, and in a brief duet express their happiness over their reunion. Lavinia watches them for a moment in cold anger, then goes into the library and stands at her father's bier. Helen and Peter stand in awkward embarrassment at the entrance to the parlor.

Aware of the situation, Christine becomes the gracious hostess and admonishes Orin to play the gallant to Helen. The tension eases as they exchange greetings and join in a laugh. Christine exclaims that the sound of laughter is strange to this grim old house. She and Orin urge Helen to sing the song they all remember from happier days. To encourage her, Christine begins singing: "Bring my dress of soft silk." Helen then takes up the song about the maiden with flowers in her hair, whose dearest treasure is her lover's golden ring on her finger. As Helen ends the song, Orin impulsively takes her in his arms and begins to waltz. This moment of tenderness is shattered by Lavinia's sudden appearance in the doorway. Glowering at Orin, she calls out that her father is waiting. The others stare at her in stunned surprise. Helen and Peter turn to leave. Christine, controlling herself with an effort, courteously bids them goodbye, and Orin escorts them down the hallway to the door.

Alone for the moment, Christine looks at the frowning portraits of the Mannons and sings defiantly that they cannot destroy her happiness, because her son has come back to her. As though to flout their disapproval, she waltzes about the room. Orin returns and watches her morosely for a moment. She embraces him affectionately, then half-teasingly asks if he is angry with her. In answer, he leads her to a chair, sits at her feet and begins to tell her how much he longed for her during his absence.

This marks the beginning of a lyrical duet. Christine is momentarily disturbed when Orin sings dreamily about finding his mother in the Blessed Isles. She remembers that it was there that Adam Brant had promised to take her after the quarrel with Lavinia. (The two words are sung in a repetition of the rising five-note phrase Adam sang in Act One.) In the continuation of the duet, mother and son reveal their deep affection for each other.

Ironically, the spell of their intimacy is broken by a gesture. When Christine enfolds Orin in her arms, he reaches up and amorously strokes her hair. She shrinks back in a movement of distaste, thinking of Ezra's familiar caress. The discordant minor-third harmonies which dominated her scene with her husband sound in the orchestra.

Nervous and irritated, Christine says that Lavinia, blaming her for Mannon's death, hates her bitterly. When Orin starts to say that Lavinia wrote him, Christine—shrewdly anticipating his next thought—interrupts to say that Captain Brant came only to court Lavinia. She warns Orin never to believe anything Lavinia tells him . . . he must trust only in his mother's love. Orin looks at her ardently, then in sudden fury vows he will kill Brant if he ever comes to the Mannon house again. Christine, aghast at his wild look, exclaims: "So like your father!"

Lavinia appears in the doorway. Orin kisses his mother, then walks submissively out of the room and into the library, where he stands looking down at the bier. Lavinia, ignoring her mother, watches him. In mingled grief and despair, Orin marvels "how death becomes the Mannons." This powerful, brooding phrase constitutes the "death" theme, a dominating leitmotiv of the opera. Orin repeats it in a continuation of the refrain in which he apostrophizes his father. It is his duty, he sings, to pray but not to mourn, because his father taught him that a soldier does not weep.

Blending with Orin's lamentation is the savage undercurrent of conversation between Lavinia and Christine, and thus the scene continues briefly in trio form. Lavinia demands to know why Mannon, on his deathbed, cried: "Guilty!" Again trying to turn aside suspicion, Christine answers that he had forced her to confess her love affair with Brant. Deliberately goading her, Lavinia asks if she also has confessed this to Orin. Christine retaliates by reminding her that Orin has sworn to kill Brant. Realizing she has failed in this skirmish, Lavinia storms out of the room.

She goes into the library, locks the door behind her and confronts Orin. She asks him point-blank if Christine has convinced him that his sister is insane. When Orin answers evasively, Lavinia assures him she is not mad—but what she knows could drive her to madness. Orin implores her to desist. Thereupon Lavinia takes from the bosom of her dress the bottle of poison. As the "poison" theme flares up in the orchestra she cries out that she here and now accuses her mother and her lover of murder.

Orin gasps in horror. Lavinia shouts that the two are guilty beyond doubt because Adam Brant promised Christine that they would be together forever. Here the double minor-third chords and the "poison" theme clash harshly in the orchestra. Orin tries to snatch the bottle out of Lavinia's hand. In the parlor, Christine distractedly calls Adam's name, then begins pounding frantically on the door of the library, begging Orin to let her in.

When Orin starts for the door, Lavinia blocks his path, asking if he will believe his mother's guilt when he sees her in her lover's arms. Then in a swift movement she places the poison bottle on the bier beside the body. Standing so that she hides the view of the bier from the door, she commands Orin to let their mother come in. Christine stumbles into the room, gasping that she is afraid. She cowers before Orin's ferocious glare. At that moment Lavinia moves to one side, exposing the poison. Christine staggers back with a piercing wail of anguish and terror. Lavinia snatches up the bottle, literally drags Orin from the room and slams the door after her.

Christine hurls herself against the door, screaming that the guilt is not Adam's, but hers alone. Frenziedly she prays for punishment . . . she herself will bear God's wrath, but Adam must not die. Sinking to her knees she chants the four words like a litany and continues mouthing them silently as the scene fades. An orchestral interlude bridges to the next scene. Prominent in this interlude is a foreboding four-note motive later associated with Orin's disintegrating mental state.

[*Scene Two*] The foredeck of Adam Brant's clipper ship moored alongside a dock in Boston Harbor. The captain's cabin is at stage level, with the main deck above; the scene is played on these two levels. A gangway connects the main deck with the pier. Harbor sounds, fragments of sea chanties, bells and foghorns are heard over an orchestral accompaniment which is serene and at the same time sinister.

Adam Brant appears, nervously paces the deck and peers apprehensively into the shadows on the dock. His agitation increases to the point where he strikes the gunwale with his fist. Then in a soliloquy ("Too weak to kill the man I hate") he reflects on the change that Christine has wrought in his life. Cursing his weakness and irresolution, he confesses to himself that he will never again follow the sea because this woman's consuming love has destroyed his courage and his pride. As he stares moodily into space, Christine emerges furtively out of the shadows. The "poison" theme rises briefly in the orchestra, symbolizing her haunting guilt. Brant rushes to her side and helps her across the gangway to the deck.

Christine throws herself into Brant's arms, crying: "Hold me, Adam!" This marks the beginning of the duet which later builds into the opera's principal quartet as Lavinia and Orin appear on the scene. Brant leads Christine to his cabin, where he asks her what happened after he left her home. As she begins her story— saying Lavinia heard Mannon accuse her before he died—Lavinia and Orin stealthily approach the cabin skylight on the main deck. There they crouch and listen as Christine goes on with her story. Several times during her recital Orin almost loses control of himself but is restrained by Lavinia.

Unconsciously trying to shift the blame from herself, Christine relates how Lavinia held the bottle of poison in her hand. She suppresses a scream of terror as she recalls the dreadful moment later at the bier. As Brant tries to comfort her she implores him to leave this ship at once. Suddenly realizing what she is asking him to do, she is stricken with remorse. An explosive chromatic figure in the orchestra underscores her reaction. But Brant, in sorrow and resignation, sings that now it is all too late—this ship and the sea have finished with him forever. Christine sobs that she has brought him nothing but misfortune.

To this, Brant replies in musical phrases of simple eloquence that she brings the gift of love. The refrain, with its affirmative theme, introduces the lyrical quartet in which the four principals express their profound emotions of hopeless longing, their hunger for love and their regret over the happiness they have lost forever. Here is one of the few moments of compassion and understanding in the entire opera. The duet rises to a poignant climax on a powerful minor chord.

For a brief interval there is a deep silence. Then Brant quietly assures Christine that somehow they will find a way to be together. He leads her to the deck. Lavinia and Orin withdraw into the shadows and hide. On the pier, Christine and Brant stand for a moment in each other's arms, murmuring: "We will not say goodbye." Then Brant watches as Christine hurries away.

Lavinia and Orin reappear on deck and quickly go down into the cabin, where they look around carefully. At the sound of Brant's returning footsteps Orin slips behind the door and draws a knife from his belt. Lavinia stands waiting. There is a succession of hammering discords in the orchestra. Brant enters, looks at Lavinia in stunned disbelief. Orin leaps forward and plunges his knife into Adam's body. With an expression of utter bewilderment on his face, Adam stretches his arms toward Lavinia, then crashes forward across the table and rolls to the floor. Lavinia looks down at him and shudders violently. Orin, as though in a trance, kneels beside the body. He wonders aloud if it is Adam Brant or he himself who has died on this night.

Lavinia harshly orders him to carry out the rest of their plan: This must be made to seem the work of marauders . . . a killing during a robbery. She sends him into the other room to break the locks on the cabin door to indicate a forced entry. To the accompaniment of clashing dissonances in the brass, Lavinia, overwhelmed by anguish and remorse, falls to her knees beside Brant's body. A variation of the theme of "frustrated love" wells up in the orchestra.

Orin re-enters and looks at her in astonishment. Noticing him, Lavinia rises abruptly and sacrilegiously prays that the soul of Adam Brant may repose in peace. With a look of revulsion, Orin turns and strides out of the cabin. About to follow, Lavinia looks down at Adam's body and snarls: "and burn in hell!" A brass fanfare in the orchestra underscores her imprecation.

As the cabin fades into the gloom, Lavinia and Orin make their way to the pier and vanish. The entire scene fades, with the music continuing in a somber, meditative mood. This changes abruptly into a nervous, agitated figure which builds into a violent climax just before the rise of the curtain on the next scene.

[*Scene Three*] The exterior of the Mannon home, with all the windows shuttered. It is dawn of the day after Adam's murder. Christine, in a frenzy of excitement, paces back and forth. Finally, exhausted by her emotions, she leans against one of the pillars and in a dramatic soliloquy ("Nothing . . . why am I so afraid?") gives way to her tormenting thoughts. The fear that stabs at her heart will not let her sleep, she sings, and she will never sleep until Adam comes to her. She tries to silence the imagined voices of the "Mannon dead," who are haunting her with their demand for vengeance. Defiantly she sings that she will not let them drag her to the grave to lie beside them there.

As she gasps for breath after her outburst, Lavinia and Orin come up the drive. Orin makes a wild lunge toward his mother but Lavinia manages to hold him back. He then tells Christine that they followed her last night and saw her with her lover. Covering her ears, she tries to run into the house. Orin catches her by the wrists, forces her arms apart and hurls the words into her face: "Brant is dead. My knife is in his heart!" The "poison-guilt" motive storms in the orchestra.

With a high-pitched moan of agony, Christine sinks to the ground where she lies shaken by sobs. Orin, suddenly stricken by her grief, kneels beside her and begs her not to weep. Lavinia coldly orders him into the house. Christine's moaning rises and falls softly in long-drawn phrases. About to go inside, Orin pauses. Now that Father is not here to punish, he murmurs eerily, perhaps they can open the shutters and let in the sunlight.

Lavinia looks down at Christine, whose face is an expressionless mask. "The deed had to be done," she says gently but sternly, "and now Father can rest." She tries to help Christine to her feet. At her touch, Christine's reason seems suddenly to give way completely, and she bursts into insane ranting—"Time to sleep! Blot out the stars!" This marks the beginning of her long aria, one of the most dramatic in the opera. God will not leave them alone, she cries. He sits in the dark shadow of death and destroys them with the fatal power of love. Lost in her madness, Christine imagines she sees Adam and stretches her arms toward the vision. She repeats the tender phrase he sang to her aboard his ship—"You bring the gift of love." As she begs for a "morningless and never-waking sleep," her voice rises in frenzied exultation, then sinks to a dying whisper.

Lavinia, who has been watching her mother in growing horror, makes a desperate effort to bring her back to her senses. As Christine stumbles up the steps to the door, Lavinia cries out: "Mother! You can live!" Christine in maniacal fury shrieks: "Live?" She bursts into demoniac laughter. With that she raises her hands in front of her face as though to blot out forever the sight of her daughter's hated face, then turns and staggers into the house.

Lavinia makes an involuntary move toward the door, but turns around and stands motionless. From the orchestra comes the menacing thunder of bass drums, mingled with the skeletal rattle of a xylophone and the snarling riffle of snare drums. Through the clamor comes the sound of a pistol shot. Lavinia recoils with a shuddering scream of "Justice!" From the study comes Orin's cry of horror as he finds Christine's body. He staggers out of the house and falls on his knees beside Lavinia, sobbing that he drove his mother to her death. Drawing him close in a comforting gesture, Lavinia assures her brother that she loves him and will help him forget. Orin gets up, stumbles up the steps and, still weeping bitterly, stands leaning against one of the columns.

There is general confusion as Jed, followed by servants and field workers, rushes in exclaiming that they heard a shot. Lavinia, cold and impassive, orders Jed to go for the doctor. He is to say, she goes on with menacing emphasis, that Christine Mannon killed herself in grief over her husband's death. Jed, with a grim nod of understanding, leaves. The servants and workers stare at Lavinia uncomprehendingly as the curtain falls.

## ACT THREE
### The Haunted

[*Scene One*] The interior of the Mannon house, as in Act Two, Scene One. A summer evening a year after the events of Act Two. The covered furniture and draped portraits give the rooms a look of emptiness and desertion.

After a brief orchestral passage, Jed enters the library and unveils the portrait of Ezra Mannon. In the parlor, a servant turns up the lights as Helen and Peter come in. Jed, in a brief refrain, wonders if the returning Mannons will preside over this house or if its sorrow still will be master. His voice blends with Helen's and Peter's as they sing the waltz theme of the song Helen sang at Christine's request on their previous visit. Peter teases Helen about being a future bride. They laugh gaily and begin waltzing together. When Jed comes in from the study Helen impulsively tries to get him to dance with her. He refuses good-naturedly. After a brief byplay, all leave to prepare for the arrival of Lavinia and Orin.

Heralded by descending chromatic harmonies in the orchestra, Orin appears in the study. Now with beard and mustache, he bears a striking resemblance to his father. He is thin and haggard, with an expression of dejection. Staring at Mannon's portrait, he murmurs: "We are home, Father." Meanwhile, Lavinia enters the parlor. She too has changed—to the extent that she is almost the exact image of her mother. She has an air of unusual vivaciousness and looks around approvingly at the preparations made for her homecoming.

But her demeanor changes when Orin, in answer to her call, comes in from the study. She looks at him apprehensively as he says plaintively that he had hoped Mother would be here. But only *they* are here, he adds, pointing to the portraits. The remarkable colloquy which now ensues discloses in part the events of the past year, and also Lavinia's desperate efforts to exorcise the demons of their guilt.

Lavinia alternately cajoles and bullies her helpless brother. She reminds him that he promised to forget the Mannons when he sailed with her to his "dream islands" to find peace. Instead, she goes on reproachfully, he insisted on returning to face his guilt and thus destroy it forever. Well then, he must now face the truth. As though hypnotized, Orin kneels before her, and she is suddenly the relentless inquisitor.

Step by step, Lavinia forces Orin to repeat after her—as though cross-examining a witness—that their mother murdered their father, that she did this to be free to join her lover, that she died by her own hand, that her death was an act of justice. Finally, he must swear that all of the foregoing is true. The torturing effect of the ordeal is underscored by the discordant arpeggios which sound during the pauses in the inquisition. Cringing before her, Orin forces out his "confession," then breaks down sobbing. Lavinia, having accomplished her purpose, takes him in her arms as a mother comforts her child and sings quietly: "It is all over now."

At the sound of footsteps in the hall outside, Lavinia helps Orin to his feet; he moves to one side of the room. Peter enters carrying a candelabra. He catches sight of Lavinia and gasps in surprise at her changed appearance. At this point Orin steps forward. His manner has changed from childish self-pity to cynical mockery. He remarks to Peter—ignoring his friendly greeting—that Lavinia was very much taken with the romantic charm of the tropical islands they visited. The brown-skinned men fascinated her, he says. Controlling her anger, Lavinia pointedly tells him that Helen is waiting for him. Orin stalks out, sneering that Peter is not likely to be as entertaining a companion as the captain of a clipper ship.

Peter, utterly bewildered, asks Lavinia what he means. She shrugs off the question, realizing that he is too naïve to cope with the situation. When he extravagantly praises her beauty, she expresses her reaction in a melodramatic aria which is a mélange of spurious emotion and deliberate seductiveness. The burden of her aria is that, through loneliness, frustration and despair, she learned at last what Peter himself always knew: that she must give her love unselfishly to him. At the conclusion of the aria she throws herself into Peter's arms and the two stand in a passionate embrace.

Helen and Orin suddenly appear in the doorway. In bitter reproach, Orin asks Lavinia if this means that he must give her up forever. To save the situation, Lavinia, as tactfully as possible, suggests that it is time to leave. Peter leads Orin away for a private talk. Helen, alone with Lavinia, voices her misgivings about Orin in a simple, moving refrain. The truth is, she says, that Orin never will allow his sister to become Peter's wife. He is haunted by fear and speaks of secret crimes. This is beyond her understanding, Helen says sadly, but her only thought is to save him from himself. She adds compassionately that God will forgive them for whatever wrongs they have done. With cruel contempt, Lavinia answers that she does not need God's forgiveness . . . she has forgiven herself. With that she turns on her heel and goes into the alcove. Helen is nonplused by her rudeness.

A moment later Orin slips furtively into the room. He is holding a large envelope, which he hands to Helen with instructions to give it to Peter. Lavinia, overhearing, steps out of the alcove. Orin angrily warns her not to interfere. Brushing him aside, she demands the envelope from Helen, who looks questioningly at Orin. Lavinia, realizing that Orin may, at this moment, slip beyond her power, insinuatingly says that her brother knows that she always will do what is best for him. Orin reacts to this with a sneer. For a moment the three stare at each other in silence.

Suddenly Orin, abjectly admitting defeat, nods to Helen, who hands the envelope to Lavinia. Turning despairingly to Helen, he tells her that the Orin she loved was killed in battle . . . she must forget him. Bursting into tears, she hurries away. Whirling on Lavinia, Orin struggles for the envelope and finally snatches it out of her hands.

In baffled fury, Lavinia demands to know what he has written. The history of the Mannon crimes, Orin replies, in which she has a place of honor as the "strangest criminal of all." Terrified, Lavinia warns him that the law can punish them both for what they had to do. Orin retorts that she alone is guilty of her mother's death. Suddenly calm, he declares that the moment has come for Lavinia to plan his death. He warns her, however, that while he lives he will not let her go.

Beginning to be frightened by his mad demeanor, Lavinia cries that she will not remain in this house where she has spent half her life in darkness . . . she will no longer be denied the joy of love. With a satanic sneer, Orin asks if she means love with the naked island men.

The next few moments of this scene are almost a repetition of the action in Act One, Scene Two, when Christine taunts Mannon into his fatal outburst of rage. With the same deliberate malice, Lavinia tells Orin that she would indeed find love with the naked islanders if she chose. Like his father, Orin loses all control. Shouting he will kill her, he seizes Lavinia by the throat, then hurls her to the floor.

Exhausted by his rage, Orin stares down at his sister with blank eyes. From this moment on, the tide of madness slowly engulfs him. In broken, low-toned phrases he entreats Lavinia to forgive him. The fateful moment has come at last, he murmurs, and now —again—one Mannon must destroy another. Lavinia beseeches him to be silent.

A look of depraved desire comes over Orin's face. Over a sinister figure of writhing chromatics in the orchestra, he sings that Lavinia must belong to him . . . they are bound together by love and guilt. Caressing her hair, he murmurs that now she is neither sister nor mother, but "a strange woman with the same beautiful hair." Suddenly, in a burst of insane passion, he tries to kiss her.

Gasping in horror, Lavinia struggles out of his arms, then screams that he is too vile to live . . . may he die and set her free. The word "die" seems to shock Orin out of his violence. Like a sleepwalker he glides to the door, where he turns and stares vacantly at his sister. Almost childishly he begs her not to cry, but in the next instant, again in the grip of his madness, he adds sardonically: "The damned do not cry." Tossing the envelope on the table, he walks into the study and locks the door.

Lavinia runs to the door, tries futilely to open it and begs Orin to let her in. Oblivious to everything, he goes slowly to the desk and takes a pistol out of the drawer. Lavinia, frantic with despair, comes back into the parlor, sees the envelope and snatches it to her bosom. In the study, Orin sinks to his knees.

In his madness, he imagines he sees his mother. He sings that he is afraid of the shadows in the hall and begs her to hide him in her arms. His voice trails away in a falsetto wail. Raising the pistol to his head, he fires.

Lavinia, screaming his name, lunges toward the door, then stops. Turning back, she puts the envelope in a drawer, which she locks. As the "madness" theme thunders in the orchestra she raises her eyes and glares defiantly into the accusing eyes of the Mannon portraits on the walls. Then, grim and erect, she stalks out of the room.

The orchestral accompaniment surges into a thundering passage of descending chromatics. The harmonies thematically underscore the brooding tragedy of the Mannon family and the finality of their doom. This effect is further intensified by a three-chord figure powerfully stated by the brasses.

[*Scene Two*] Outside the Mannon house, late afternoon three days later. The shutters are thrown back, the windows open. Lavinia enters carrying a basket of flowers. She is in deep mourning and is startlingly changed in appearance, her face a mask of tragedy. Her manner is grim, desperate and defiant.

Jed comes out of the house. Lavinia hands him the flowers, then sits at the top of the steps of the portico in statuesque immobility. Looking at her with concern, Jed urges her to come inside and give up this endless waiting. Orin is at rest, he says, and now she must sleep. Lavinia answers that in this house she never will sleep. She adds that she will marry Peter and leave this abode of death. A moment later Peter appears. Jed leaves and Lavinia rises excitedly. As she waits for him to come up the drive she leans against one of the columns and closes her eyes.

Peter is drawn and tense, his eyes downcast, his fists clenched. When he comes closer to Lavinia he makes a visible effort to shake off his black mood. She greets him without opening her eyes; he sits down on the steps and looks up at her. Then she returns his gaze and is startled by his stricken expression. Gently taking her hand, Peter tries to reassure her. They will soon marry, he says. In a flash of bitterness he adds that he will take her away from this haunted house, this ugly town and its uglier gossip.

Taken aback by his anger, Lavinia probes for the cause of his bitter mood. Peter confesses he is being tormented by the stories he has been hearing about the Mannons: Ezra Mannon's death . . . his wife's suicide . . . and then Orin's. . . . In suppressed rage, Lavinia murmurs that she hopes there is a hell for the good. Peter goes on to mention a letter Helen has told him about—a letter he should see. But most important, he adds, he is to ask Lavinia before God if she will dare marry him. When Lavinia answers with a fervent "Yes," Peter cries that now there is nothing more to fear.

Not God, not the living—only the dead are to be feared, Lavinia replies. The dead will destroy them, she adds darkly, unless he wants her enough to kill for her . . . as she has done for him. Then she feverishly begs him to carry her into the house and make her a bride before the eyes of the Mannons to "shame them into silence." The theme of "frustrated love" reverberates in the orchestra. With terrible abandon, Lavinia cries out: "Love me— Adam!" The sound of the name brings her to her senses. Laughing vacantly, she wonders why she called Peter by that name. Outraged by her shameless ardor and now aware of the truth, Peter answers: It is because she loved Adam Brant, and Orin knew. Lavinia murmurs desolately that the dead always come between them—it is useless to fight back. This is sung to a variation of the "death" theme heard during Lavinia's scene with Orin just before his suicide.

In a final attempt to confirm his suspicions, Peter demands that Lavinia show him the letter Orin wrote. Lavinia replies in spoken words: "Not while I live!" Recoiling as though struck in the face, Peter stares at her in horror and disbelief. Turning away from him, Lavinia quietly tells Peter she can never marry him. Almost tenderly she says that now he knows all he needs to know, and he must never come to the Mannon house again. Plunged into despair, Peter slowly walks away. Lavinia, nearly fainting, turns, sees he is gone, then cries out that it is not true that she loved . . . She stops abruptly, squares her shoulders and turns again toward the house.

Calling Jed, she orders him to take all the flowers out of the house, close the shutters and nail them fast . . . she does not wish to see the sun. Jed stares at her in bewilderment and reminds her that she had planned to go away. With a hollow laugh, Lavinia says there is no place to go—her home always has been here. Brusquely she orders Jed to do as he is told.

Standing alone, Lavinia begins the aria which concludes the

opera, "Welcome me, House of Mannon." It expresses her renunciation of life and her surrender to the evil destiny of the Mannons. She will never leave this house, she sings over the intermingled themes of "love" and "death," nor will anyone else ever enter it again. She will live out her life with the annihilating guilt and wickedness of this house. In a ringing phrase she calls down upon herself the punishment for the crimes of all the Mannons. Her voice trails away in quavering, disconnected phrases, reflecting her withdrawal from reality.

Finally identifying herself completely with the dead Mannons, Lavinia sings: "I know you will bless me with a long and lonely life." She stands staring like a blind person into the sunlight. Jed appears at one of the windows and closes the shutters with a bang. As though on signal, Lavinia turns, walks stiffly into the house and closes the door behind her. A murmurous figure in the orchestra, similar to that heard at the very beginning of the opera, fades into silence as the curtain falls.

# Nabucco
## (*Nebuchadnezzar*)

### *by* GIUSEPPE VERDI
### (1813–1901)

### *Libretto by*
#### TEMISTOCLE SOLERA

*Based on the Book of Jeremiah in the Old Testament*

#### CHARACTERS

| | |
|---|---|
| Nabucco (Nebuchadnezzar) King of Babylon | Baritone |
| Ishmael, nephew of Sedecia, the King of Jerusalem | Tenor |
| Zacharius, Chief Priest of the Hebrews | Bass |
| Fenena, daughter of Nabucco | Mezzo-soprano |
| Abigail, a slave girl, believed to be Nabucco's other daughter | Soprano |
| High Priest of Baal | Bass |
| Abdallo, an old official of Nabucco's court | Tenor |
| Anna, sister of Zacharius | Soprano |

Hebrews, Levites, Assyrians, vestal virgins, soldiers

*Place:* Jerusalem and Babylon
*Time:* Biblical era of the captivity of the Jews
*First performance:* La Scala, Milan, March 9, 1842
*Original language:* Italian

---

*Nabucco,* Verdi's third opera, was his first great success. It not only made him a new operatic hero in Italy but spread his fame throughout Europe. This roughhewn music, with its powerful dramatic thrust, was in an idiom unfamiliar to a public accustomed to the suavities of Donizetti and Bellini, and the opera's premiere generated the wildest excitement. The score has what Italians call *ruvidezza,* translated as "rudeness, coarseness, roughness." Admittedly it has its crudities—but it is a forthright expression of the sufferings of a people. To the Italians, it was a ringing protest against oppression, particularly the famous chorus of the captive

Hebrews "Va, pensiero sull'ali dorate," which practically everyone in Italy soon knew by heart.

Before the curtain rises there is an overture, the *Sinfonia*, which majestically states several choral themes heard in the opera. One is the chorus of the Levites in Act Two, the other the chorus of the captive Hebrews. This overture is considered to be the first since Rossini's *William Tell* to be linked with development of the dramatic action. The fact that it was singled out for critical praise is somewhat ironical. It is recorded that Verdi composed the overture in a cafe as an afterthought at the suggestion of his brother-in-law.

## ACT ONE

In the Temple of Solomon, in Jerusalem. Assembled in the Temple, the Hebrews, Levites and vestal virgins lament the defeat of the city by Nabucco in an ensemble, "Gli arredi festivi." They are panic-stricken over the imminent arrival of the hated King of Babylon and his barbarous hordes. The festive hangings of the Temple, the people sing, must be torn into shreds to symbolize their grief and shame. In a unison refrain, "I candidi veli," the Levites exhort the vestal virgins to pray for deliverance. The vestals call on the Lord of Hosts for help and mercy ("Gran Nume, che voli"), then all the people implore their God to avert the destruction of the Temple.

Suddenly the High Priest Zacharius strides on the scene, half dragging Fenena, daughter of Nabucco. With them is Anna, the High Priest's sister. In a ringing cavatina, "Sperate, o figli," Zacharius bids the Israelites take heart, because the Lord has given a precious hostage into their hands—Fenena, the King's own daughter. He goes on to remind them that Jehovah sent Moses to protect his people in Egypt. And because they put their trust in the Lord, not a single man of Gideon's army perished. The High Priest exhorts the Jews not to be afraid.

At that moment there is a noise offstage and the people cry out in alarm. Ishmael enters with a band of Hebrew soldiers and announces that the dread Assyrian King and his mighty army are closing in on the city. Zacharius, trying to calm the populace, steps forward to say that the Lord will surely prevent the enemy from desecrating Zion. With that he hands Fenena over to Ishmael, saying that she is a symbol of the Lord's assurance. Then in a solo interlude, "Come notte a sol fulgente," he implores the God of

Abraham to give his people victory in the coming battle. The people repeat his supplication, then follow him from the Temple. Only Fenena and Ishmael remain.

Ishmael tries to embrace Fenena but she sternly repulses him, asking how he dare speak of love in this hour of disaster. In recitative, Ishmael tells her that, as a captive, she is even more beautiful to him than when he saw her in the Babylonian court where he served as ambassador for the King of Judah, his uncle. He recalls that Fenena, risking the anger of her jealous sister Abigail, there later freed him from prison. Now, in turn, he will set her free, Ishmael cries.

Fenena warns him that if he does he will betray his own people. Ishmael answers that his love is stronger than loyalty. At that moment Abigail, sword in hand, rushes in at the head of a band of Assyrian soldiers disguised as Hebrews. Ishmael and Fenena shrink back in terror as Abigail shouts that the Temple has been captured. In a stormy refrain, "Prode guerrier," she turns on the lovers with savage scorn. She derides Ishmael for his love for Fenena, then warns the girl that now nothing can save her from a sister's revenge.

Suddenly she glides to Ishmael's side and whispers that she too loves him ("Io t'amava . . . Il regno"); she offers him her kingdom and her heart. If that love is returned, she sings, she can save him and his people. Ishmael disdains her offer, replying that he has no fears for himself but is concerned only for the safety of his people. A brief trio ensues as Fenena joins to sing that her prayers are not for herself but for her persecuted people. Abigail reiterates her avowal while Ishmael continues to rebuff her.

As the trio ends, a panic-stricken throng of Hebrew men and women, Levites and soldiers swarms on the scene crying that the raging Nabucco, brandishing his bloody sword, is advancing on the Temple ("Lo vedete? Fulminado!"). The defenders have been routed and the King, astride his horse, is nearing the Holy of Holies. The people fall back in terror as Abigail and her soldiers hail Nabucco. The shouts of the invaders are heard outside. Zacharius demands to know how the enemy found the secret passage into the city. Ishmael tells him it was the work of Babylonian spies. Abigail sneers that his excuses are in vain—the King approaches. Heralded by a military band, Nabucco arrogantly rides his horse to the very threshold of the Temple. There Zacharius bars his way, warning the King not to desecrate the House of God ("Questa è di Dio stanza"). Nabucco asks impudently: "What God?" Thereupon Zacharius seizes Fenena, holds the point of his dagger against her body and warns the King that if he dares profane the Temple his daughter will die then and there ("Pria che tu profani il templo"[1]).

Momentarily awed by Zacharius' fury, Nabucco dismounts. He threatens, however, that this defiance will bring even greater destruction down upon Zion ("Tremin gl'insani"). This marks the beginning of the ensemble which concludes the act.

Fenena begs her father to show mercy to the conquered people. Ishmael and Zacharius implore God to change the heart of this cruel King and to save his victims from chains. Abigail, in soaring obbligato passages characterized by a rushing semiquaver figure, exults that now she can revenge herself on the woman who stands between her and the man she loves ("L'impeto acqueta del mio furore"). These passages are underscored by the choral accompaniment sung by the people as they beseech God for deliverance.

In a solo passage ("Oventi, il capo a terra") Nabucco taunts the Jews because their God did not dare come to their aid. Goaded to murderous fury, Zacharius raises his dagger to stab Fenena, screaming that if the conqueror thirsts for blood, the first drop to be spilled will be his daughter's ("Iniquo mira!"). Ishmael leaps forward and tears the dagger from Zacharius' hand. Snatching Fenena out of his grasp, Ishmael pushes her into her father's arms, crying that now she has been saved by love.

Nabucco, in savage triumph, orders his soldiers to plunder and destroy, to burn the Temple and to spare no one—the only crime will be to show pity. Abigail sings that if she cannot tear her love for Ishmael out of her heart, at least the destruction of the Jews will slake her thirst for revenge. Zacharius and the Hebrews turn on Ishmael and curse him for his traitorous act in saving Fenena's life. These conflicting sentiments blend as the ensemble thunders to its climax.

## ACT TWO

[*Scene One*] Nabucco's palace in Babylon. Abigail, holding a parchment, comes in excitedly. In a dramatic recitative and aria she traces the course of events. She sings that she has discovered a fateful document ("O fatal scritto") which reveals that she is not Nabucco's daughter but the child of a slave. Now, as the supposed daughter of a king, she is worse than a slave. Nabucco, who has

[1] This phrase is almost identical to that sung by Rigoletto when he commands the courtiers to leave in Act Three of that opera.

gone to wage a war of extermination against Judea, has left Fenena, her hated rival, in charge of the throne. She herself has been scorned and rejected. But these fools, she muses, do not know the heart of Abigail. She will have her revenge—and it will destroy all of them ("Su tutti il mio furore"). These phrases, sung in rising half steps with octave skips, give an extraordinarily menacing effect. Fenena, Nabucco, the kingdom—perhaps even herself—will be brought to ruin before she will allow the secret of her lowly birth to be discovered.

Then, as though exhausted by her fury, she reflects in quiet despair over the time when she too could find joy in her heart—when she could share another's grief. Now who is there to restore to her one single moment of lost tenderness? These emotions are expressed in a flowing cantabile, "Anch'io dischiuso un giorno."

Her reverie is interrupted by the entrance of the High Priest of Baal followed by members of the court. He announces that the accursed Fenena has betrayed her country by ordering the captive Jews to be freed. This rabble must be curbed, he and the others sing in a unison choral passage, and for this reason they are offering the crown to her—Abigail. To clear the way for this palace revolution they already have spread the report that Nabucco has been slain in battle ("Noi gia sparso"). Now the Assyrians are calling on Abigail to save the Empire.

Realizing that her plans for revenge suddenly have come to fruition, Abigail replies in savage exultation that now she will mount the throne on bloodied steps ("Salgo già del trono aurato"). Now the Assyrians will see that the scepter truly belongs to her. What is more, she adds cryptically, they will see the King's own daughter kneeling at the feet of a slave. (This concluding phrase is sung in a striking passage of sixteenth notes descending from high C.) In a choral accompaniment to the aria, the High Priest and the court sing that Baal himself will share Abigail's revenge.[2]

[*Scene Two*] A hall in the palace. At right a door leading to a gallery; at left a door to Nabucco's apartment. It is evening. Lamps illuminate the scene. Zacharius enters, followed by a Levite carrying the Tablets of the Law. In recitative Zacharius explains that he has been chosen by the Lord to bring the message of

---

[2] This scene, with its vigorous declamation and response, has been pointed out as being typical of the new energy with which Verdi was imbuing his operas. Its grim mood foreshadows the vindictive cruelty of the priests in *Aïda*. The difficult aria itself is noteworthy for its two-octave range.

salvation to the unbelievers. In the ensuing aria, "Tu sul labbro dei veggenti," he sings that through his lips the Lord will speak to the Assyrians and the Holy Writ will prevail over false idols. At the conclusion of the aria he and the Levites enter the door to Nabucco's apartment, now occupied by Fenena.

A moment later a group of Levites cautiously enters through the other door. In hushed tones they wonder who has sent them to this dangerous place. The answer comes from Ishmael, who, apparently unnoticed, has followed them into the room. The Levites gasp in surprise at seeing him. It was the High Priest himself who sent them here, Ishmael tells the astonished Levites. They turn on him in furious denunciation ("Maledetto del Signor!"). This is one of the most striking choruses in the opera—a square-cut melody sung in *presto* tempo, with which Verdi achieved an extraordinarily dramatic effect. He uses the same device—written for male voices —in later operas, notably in the "Zitti, zitti" chorus in *Rigoletto*.

When Ishmael begs for mercy, the Levites revile him as an outcast, shouting that he has betrayed his brothers and bears the mark of Cain. Ishmael begs for death rather than this disgrace. His despairing cry, "Oh, la morte, per pietà," blends with the denunciations of the Levites. As they stand glaring at him, Zacharius and the Levite carrying the Tablets of the Law return accompanied by Fenena and Anna. The latter steps forward and asks the Levites to pardon Ishmael because the woman he saved is not an enemy but a Jewess. Fenena has been converted to Judaism. Ishmael and the Levites are stunned. Zacharius corroborates Anna's assertion.

Shouting is heard offstage, and a moment later Abdallo, an elderly official in Nabucco's court, rushes in. He approaches Fenena and tells her that Nabucco has been slain ("Donna regal! deh fuggi!"). He warns her to flee because the populace has chosen Abigail as Queen. At that point the High Priest of Baal and Abigail come storming in at the head of a shouting crowd of Assyrians. Confronting Fenena, Abigail demands the scepter. Fenena retorts that she will die rather than give it up.

Nabucco and his warriors come charging through the crowd. Thrusting himself between the two women, the King snatches the crown from Fenena's head, puts it on his own and defies anyone to remove it ("Dal capo mio la prendi"). A booming figure in the bass underscores his defiance.

A powerful ensemble begins here as Nabucco expresses the terror and confusion of the moment in a *sotto voce* phrase of suppressed fury—"S'appressan gl'istanti." His voice is joined by those of Abigail, Fenena, Ishmael and Zacharius, who repeat this theme. Finally all onstage burst into a tremendous chorus of lamentation.

Nabucco suddenly silences the crowd with a gesture. On the verge of madness, he cries out that he has cast down not only the god of the Babylonians but the God of the Hebrews as well ("S'oda or me, Babilonesi!"). Now there is no God but Nabucco. Here Verdi achieves a telling effect as each of Nabucco's recitative phrases begins a half tone higher than the preceding one.

While Nabucco's warriors hail him, Fenena, Zacharius and the Hebrews cry out in horror at the King's blasphemy. As Nabucco wildly repeats that he is God, Zacharius calls down the curse of Jehovah on him ("Insano! a terra, a terra"). Nabucco orders his soldiers to drag Zacharius to the foot of the King's statue and there put him to death. Fenena steps forward crying that she, as a Jewess, will die with him. In blind fury, Nabucco forces her to her knees and screams: "Giù! prostrati! non so più re, son Dio!" ("Bow down! I am no longer King! I am God!").

As a chromatic descending passage explodes in the orchestra, there is a crash of thunder. A bolt of lightning blasts the crown from Nabucco's head. In a horrified whisper the onlookers comment that heaven has punished the King for his insolence. There is a moment of absolute silence.

Nabucco, now a hopeless lunatic, stares vacantly before him. Then, lost in his madness, he asks, in the ensuing aria: "Che mi toglie il regno scretto?" ("Who has robbed me of my scepter?"). He shrinks back from the horrid phantoms he sees and murmurs that the crimson sky is sprinkling his brow with drops of blood. With a final despairing cry for help, Nabucco falls in a faint. Abigail picks up the crown and sings with malevolent satisfaction that the hosts of Baal have lost none of their greatness ("Ma del popolo di Belo non fia spento lo splendor"). The curtain falls.

## ACT THREE[3]

The sumptuous hanging gardens of Babylon, where Abigail is holding court. Dignitaries and courtiers are in attendance. The High Priest stands at an altar flanked by the golden statue of Baal. There is a crowd of citizens, soldiers and priests. In chorus, "E' l'Assiria una regina," they pay homage to the new Queen, Abigail.

---

[3] In some stage versions this act begins with the chorus of the captive Hebrews, "Va, pensiero, sull'ali dorate," followed by Zacharius' aria fortelling the doom of Babylon—"Oh, chi piange?"

The High Priest hands her a warrant authorizing the extermination of the Jews—first of all the traitorous Fenena. Abigail studies the document, craftily pretending to be puzzled by its demands.

At that moment Nabucco, an apparition in torn robes and unkempt beard, staggers into the room. (The music here depicts him as a weak and doddering old man.) A scene in recitative follows. At first Abigail angrily commands that the old man be taken back to his cell. With sudden kingly authority Nabucco asks who dares speak in his presence. Instantly Abigail's manner softens, and she asks him to follow her. His mind wandering, Nabucco asks: "Where?" Here is the council chamber, he goes on, and here is his throne—and he well knows how to mount it. Lurching up the steps toward the throne, he stops and glares at Abigail, asking who this interloper is. Abigail swiftly rises and dismisses the court.

Here begins the great confrontation scene, which is in the form of a long and brilliant duet beginning with Nabucco's question as he faces Abigail: "Donna, chi sei?" ("Woman, who are you?").[4] When she replies that she is the guardian of the throne he brands her as an imposter. Pitilessly exploiting Nabucco's confused state of mind, Abigail tricks him into signing the death warrants of the captive Jews and Fenena. In a momentary flash of sanity, the King realizes he has now doomed his own daughter. He cries out in anguish: "È sangue mio!" Remorselessly following up her advantage, Abigail says softly: "You have another daughter." But Nabucco, still in possession of his senses, tells her she is nothing but a slave and commands her to kneel before her master. Then he distractedly searches in his robes for the secret document which proves she was born a slave.

Abigail thereupon draws the document from her bosom and tears it to shreds before his eyes. In a dazzling coloratura phrase, "Tale ti rendo, o misero," she sings that thus she gives the King back his lie. Nabucco despairingly cries that his power is gone and that he is only a shadow of a king ("L'ombra son io del re"). In malicious exultation Abigail sings that her hour of glory has come ("Oh, dell'ambita gloria") and that now an empire will kneel at the feet of a slave.

A fanfare of trumpets interrupts the duet. Abigail tells Nabucco that it signals the death of the Hebrews whom he himself con-

---

[4] The forerunner of a great line of Verdian duets—Macbeth and his wife, Rigoletto and Gilda, Violetta and Germont in *La Traviata*, Amelia and Riccardo in *Un Ballo in Maschera*, Leonora and Padre Guardiano in *La Forza del Destino*, Desdemona and Otello, etc.

demned. He shouts for the guards but Abigail tells him that these very guards are holding him prisoner—the prisoner of a slave. Totally helpless in Abigail's power, the King abjectly begs her to have mercy on a father mad with grief ("Deh perdona a un padre che delira!").[5] He will give her the throne, he sings, if she only will give him his daughter's life. In cruel triumph Abigail scorns his plea—"Esci! invan mi chiedi pace!" Now he will see how well a slave can wear the robe of royalty. This brings the duet to a fiery conclusion. In the closing passages, a chromatically descending figure depicts Nabucco's despair and symbolizes his defeat.

The scene now changes to the banks of the Euphrates, where the Hebrews are toiling as slaves in chains. Here they sing the famous chorus "Va, pensiero, sull'ali dorate," in which they voice their anguished longing for their homeland and freedom. They bid their thoughts to fly "on gilded wings" to the banks of their beloved Jordan and to Zion, ruined though it is. This great chorus, which begins in unison, has certain melancholy overtones of ancient psalms.

Listening to their lamentations, Zacharius springs to his feet and berates them for their self-pitying, womanish tears ("Oh, chi piange? di femmine imbelli"). Then in a ringing aria, "Del futuro nel buio discerno," he prophesies the utter destruction of Babylon, where "not one stone will be left upon another" ("Niuna pietra ove sorse l'altera"). In choral accompaniment, the Hebrews sing that this man has inspired them with the holy fire of courage.

## ACT FOUR

The throne room in Nabucco's palace, where he is seen sitting motionless in a deathlike sleep. There is a brief prelude dominated by the theme of the *Marcia Funebre* (as Verdi called it) which will be heard later in the act as Fenena is led to her execution.

Suddenly Nabucco awakes, still in the grip of a terrible dream. Hearing the funeral march, he fancies it a call to arms and shouts for his horse, his sword, his warriors. Outside, a crowd bellows the name of Fenena, then a band blares the funeral march. Rushing to a window, Nabucco sees Fenena, her hands bound, walking between two files of soldiers. Barely able to comprehend what he sees, the King gasps that Fenena is weeping. This exclamation

[5] In this portrayal of paternal love, Verdi set the pattern—so to speak— of similar characterizations in later operas, such as Rigoletto, Boccanegra, Germont and Amonasro.

is underscored by a poignant phrase in the orchestra. Then he hears the shout: "Fenena a morte!"

Suddenly conscious of the impending tragedy, Nabucco runs to the door of the throne room, finds to his horror that it is bolted. He is a prisoner. In terrible despair he falls to his knees and prays to the God of the Hebrews for pardon ("Dio degli Ebrei, perdono!"). He promises to raise an altar to Jehovah, to renounce his paganism, and henceforth to worship only the True and Omnipotent God. At the conclusion of the prayer he leaps to his feet and with a furious effort again tries to wrench open the door.

As he struggles, the door is flung open from the outside and Abdallo, the King's venerable official, bursts in with a group of Babylonian soldiers. Nabucco, believing them to be his captors, roars at them to leave him alone. Abdallo and the soldiers assure him that they have come to rescue him. Crying out that his mind now is clear, the King demands his sword ("Abdallo, il brando mio!"). As Abdallo hands it to him, Nabucco shouts that he will save Fenena. Over a blazing fanfare, Abdallo and the soldiers promise the annihilation of the Babylonian traitors.

Brandishing his sword, Nabucco commands the soldiers to follow him ("o prodi miei, seguitemi!"). Reason has returned, he sings, and he is King of Assyria once more; his enemies will see his crown blaze like the sun. Followed by the soldiers, he strides out.

The next scene takes place in the hanging gardens, as shown previously. Present are Zacharius, Anna, Fenena, courtiers, Hebrews, guards and the populace. The High Priest of Baal stands at the temple portico beside a sacrificial altar. On the other side stand two executioners with axes.

To the strains of the funeral march, Fenena and the condemned Hebrews are led in. Fenena approaches Zacharius and kneels before him. In a brief recitative passage ("Va! la palma del martirio") Zacharius gently bids her accept the martyr's crown and go to her reward in heaven. In a poignant aria, "Oh, dischiuso e'il firmamento," Fenena serenely resigns herself to her fate.

Without warning, from offstage comes a mighty shout of "Viva Nabucco!" Just as the High Priest vainly commands the execution to proceed, the King, Abdallo and the soldiers rush in. Pointing with his sword to the golden statue of Baal, Nabucco orders his soldiers to destroy it at once. Before they can touch it, the statue crashes to the ground in a mass of rubble.

In a triumphant refrain, "Ah, torna Israello, torna alle gioie," Nabucco bids the children of Israel return to their homeland and rebuild the Temple of their God. Then he discloses that Abigail, tormented by her guilt, has taken poison. Turning to Fenena, he asks her to kneel in worship to Jehovah. Thereupon the entire assemblage joins in the great prayer "Immenso Jeova."

At its conclusion, a sudden hush falls over the throng. All watch in consternation as Abigail, half carried by two soldiers, makes her way through the crowd and stands before Nabucco. There she makes her final confession of guilt and her dying entreaty for pity ("Su me . . . morente . . . esanime"). Holding out her arms as if to embrace Fenena and Ishmael, she sings to Nabucco that these two always have loved each other and have always put their trust in the King. But now, she asks brokenly, who will absolve her of guilt? In her death throes, she cries: "Solleva Iddio l'affitto. Te chiamo . . . o Dio . . . non maledire a me!" ("God alone can lift the burden. Oh, God, do not condemn me!").

As a tremendous fanfare resounds in the orchestra, Zacharius proclaims that henceforth the King of Assyria will be the servant of Jehovah ("Servendo a Jeova sarai de' regi il re!"). The curtain falls.

## Les Pêcheurs de Perles

*by* GEORGES BIZET

(1838–75)

*Libretto by*
MICHEL CARRÉ *and* E. CORMON

#### CHARACTERS

| | |
|---|---|
| Zurga, king of the pearl fishers | Baritone |
| Nadir, his friend | Tenor |
| Leila, a Brahmin priestess | Soprano |
| Nourabad, a Brahmin high priest | Bass |

Pearl fishermen, priests, priestesses, natives, slaves, dancers

*Place:* Ceylon
*Time:* Legendary
*First performance:* Théâtre Lyrique, Paris, September 29, 1863
*Original language:* French

---

*Les Pêcheurs de Perles,* composed twelve years before *Carmen,* met with indifferent success and for a long period suffered undeserved neglect. There is a wealth of pleasing melody in the score, with music of impressive impact and power underscoring the dramatic climaxes of the action. Although the opera as a whole may be comparatively unfamiliar, one number is universally known—the beautiful tenor aria sung by Nadir near the end of the first act, "Je crois entendre encore" (often sung in Italian under the title of "Mi par d'udir ancora").

## ACT ONE

An open sandy beach on the island of Ceylon, with huts of the pearl fishermen to the right and left. The sea is visible in the background. Toward the rear, on a rock overlooking the sea, stand the ruins of an ancient Indian temple. Gathered for a day of festivity, the fisherfolk sing a spirited chorus ("Sur la grève en feu"), during which tribal dances are performed by dancing girls. The people call on the dancers to drive away the evil spirits and then go on to sing about their destined task of braving the dangers of the sea in search of pearls.

Zurga, a leader of the fishermen, interrupts the singing and dancing to announce that on this day they must select a chieftain. He himself is elected king by acclamation, the fishermen hailing him and pledging allegiance in a brief but sturdy chorus ("Ce lui que nous voulons pour maître"). As Zurga shakes hands with the men, a newcomer is seen approaching. When he comes nearer Zurga recognizes him as his friend Nadir, a young courier and jungle hunter.

Welcomed by Zurga and the crowd, Nadir describes, in a melodious, swinging refrain, the adventures he has had, telling how he has roamed through savannahs and forests, stalking the tiger, the jaguar, and the panther ("Des savanes et des forêts"). He lives a lonely life in the demon-haunted jungles, he continues, seeing no human being for a year at a time. The men join him in the concluding phrases of his song as he shakes hands and hails them as boon companions. Zurga invites him to stay and live with the fishermen and join them in their pleasures. Nadir promptly decides to do so. The dancing then resumes, and the people repeat the refrain of the opening chorus, after which they leave the scene.

Nadir and Zurga, now alone, begin reminiscing about the past. They speak of an oath of friendship to which they both swore and assure each other that they have never broken it. When Zurga proposes a toast to the fact that they once successfully resisted temptation and have since forgotten their days of folly, Nadir gravely says they will never forget. As long as they live, he avers, they will remember their last voyage together—that night when they put into the harbor of the city of Candy and visited the Brahmin temple there. The priests were calling the faithful to worship, Nadir says softly.

In a sonorous duet ("Au fond du temple"—"Del tempio al limitar")—one of the great tenor-baritone duets in opera—the two men relive the experience that prompted them to take the oath of which they have been speaking. A veiled woman emerged from the exotic gloom of the sacred temple and walked toward them with the grace and dignity of a goddess. The worshipers, murmuring in wonder and awe, prostrated themselves before her. As she passed the two men she raised her veil for an instant, and they saw a face of ravishing beauty. She mysteriously disappeared, Nadir and Zurga following her in vain. Both were consumed by passion for her, and their rivalry made them bitter enemies for a time.

They eventually came to their senses, however, and took an oath never again to allow anything to break their friendship. Each promised the other that he would never try to find the mysterious and beautiful priestess. The duet ends in ringing phrases as they pledge each other friendship to the death ("Amitié sainte, unis nos âmes fraternelles").

As they clasp hands a fisherman appears and tells Zurga that a boat has landed near by. Saying that he has been awaiting it, Zurga tells Nadir that its arrival has to do with an ancient custom that prevails among the pearl fishermen. Each year a beautiful virgin, whose identity is kept secret, is brought to the seashore to pray for the safety of the fishermen when they go on their dangerous quest for pearls ("Une fille inconnue et belle"). Her face hidden by a veil, she stands on the rock near the ruined temple, chanting prayers to drive away evil spirits and calm the sea. No one may look at her or come near her during her vigil.

Heralded by shouts of the crowd, a veiled woman appears, followed by Nourabad, high priest of Brahma, and four other priests. It is Leila, the Brahmin priestess whom Nadir and Zurga saw in the temple at Candy. A crowd of women go before her, scattering flowers in her path and singing a chorus of welcome ("Sois la bienvenue"). Approaching her, Zurga asks in solemn tones if she will keep the oath she has taken ("Seule au milieu de nous"). She must promise to keep her face concealed, to pray day and night at the brink of the sea, and to deny herself friend or lover. Leila swears to the oath in the name of Brahma. If she is faithful, Zurga proclaims, she will be rewarded with the most beautiful pearl that can be found in the sea. But if she betrays her oath and yields to love, he adds menacingly, she will be accursed and Brahma will demand her life as forfeit. The crowd repeats the curse which Zurga utters—"Malheur à toi!"

As Leila recoils at Zurga's warning, Nadir comes forward with an exclamation of dismay over the harshness of the penalty imposed. Leila murmurs that she recognizes his voice. Taking her hand, Zurga notices that she is trembling in fear, whereupon he urges her to renounce her oath while there is yet time. Gazing at Nadir through her veil, Leila firmly answers that she will remain to accomplish her destined task. At the sound of her voice Nadir starts toward her, but checks himself.

In a ringing ensemble Zurga, Nourabad, the priests, and the people declare that Leila has promised to be faithful. Leila responds. All kneel and offer a prayer to Brahma for protection ("Brahma, divin Brahma"). Zurga then leads Leila into the ruined temple, with Nourabad and the priests following, while the fishermen go down to the shore. Zurga returns to Nadir, shakes his hand, and then leaves.

Gazing up at the temple, Nadir wonders if the voice he heard was that of Leila or only an illusion. He reproaches himself for not having confessed to Zurga that he had been false to his oath—that after seeing Leila at the temple he had followed her to her secret retreat. There he had looked upon her and listened to her singing. In the famous aria "Je crois entendre encore" Nadir recalls the fascination of her voice as it drifted to him through the palms. He sees again the vision of loveliness revealed when the night breeze swept aside her flowing veils. The aria ends on a note of longing and tenderness as Nadir abandons himself to his blissful dream. Lost in reflection, he lies down on a mat before one of the huts and gradually falls asleep. The voices of the fishermen drift up from the shore in a soft choral phrase.

Nourabad and the priests now lead Leila out of the temple to the rock overlooking the sea. The priests light a fire in a brazier and then command Leila to sing. She sings a stately invocation to Brahma ("O Dieu Brahma"), which is answered by the voices of the fishermen on the shore. Nadir awakes, exclaiming that he hears the voice that once enchanted him. As he listens, Leila sings an exquisite refrain ("Dans le ciel sans voile"), which artfully conceals a message of love in phrases of prayer to Brahma. Under the starry sky, she sings, her heart and voice go out to the one she adores. The voices of the people are heard again, urging her to continue her enthralling song, and Leila's tones soar above the ensemble in a beautiful obbligato.

Springing to his feet, Nadir steals to the foot of the great rock. Leila lifts her veil for an instant and looks down at him. Crying out her name, Nadir assures her that he will remain near and defend her with his life if need be. Their voices blend in phrases of adoration over the accompaniment of the chorus as the curtain falls.

## ACT TWO

The interior of the ruined temple above the sea. At the rear is a terrace overlooking the rocky cliff at the water's edge. The scene is flooded with moonlight. An unseen chorus softly chants an invocation to night ("L'ombre descend des cieux"). Leila, Nourabad, and the priests are seen on the terrace. The high priest tells Leila that the fishermen have returned to land and that her nightly vigil is over. When she apprehensively asks if she is to be left alone in the temple, Nourabad assures her that she will be safe. On one side of the temple, he says, is the rocky, inaccessible shore, while the only other approach is guarded by the priests, fully armed. He tells her that if she remains faithful she may sleep without thought of fear.

Leila replies that when she was a mere child her courage was tested in the face of death. In a dramatic refrain ("J'étais encore enfant") she relates how one night a fugitive sought refuge in her home from a band of enemies. Moved by his pleas for protection, she concealed him. When his pursuers appeared she refused to answer their questions, even though they threatened her with their daggers. The fugitive was thus able to escape, but before he left her home he showed his gratitude by giving her a golden chain, telling her to keep it in memory of the man whose life she had saved.

Her steadfastness will likewise be rewarded under the Brahmin law, Nourabad promises at the conclusion of her story. But if she fails, he reminds her grimly, torture and death await her. Exhorting her to think on her vows, Nourabad leaves with the priests. The chanting of the chorus is heard again.

Momentarily giving way to fear, Leila recovers her composure as she looks toward the terrace. Her heart tells her, she murmurs, that her lover is near. In a tender refrain ("Comme autrefois dans la nuit sombre") she rejoices that, as in days past, her lover watches over her from his hiding place in the shadows of the jungle so that she may sleep in peace. She voices her happiness in the thought that he is near. As she ends her song the strains of a guzla[1] sound from below the rocks. Then Nadir's voice is heard in a brief serenade ("De mon amie, fleur endormie"), singing of his beloved who is held captive in a palace of azure and gold in the depths of a crystal sea. Soon he appears and Leila rushes into his arms.

The duet that follows is one of the loveliest numbers in the opera ("Par cet étroit sentier qui borde un sombre abîme"). When Leila asks how he made his way over the treacherous rocks along the shore, Nadir replies that the god of love guided his footsteps. Trembling with fear, Leila implores him to flee, for death is certain if he is discovered. She tries to free herself from his embrace, crying that she must not betray her oath.

[1] Or gusla—a single-stringed instrument with a bowl-shaped body and a sounding board of skin or parchment.

Nadir passionately sings of the nights when he listened enchanted as she sang in her secret retreat, and in an answering refrain Leila recalls the bliss of those moments. Though he had sworn never to see her again, Nadir says, he was drawn to her by the fatal power of love. Leila replies that she has waited for him during the long nights of her vigil at the sea, always knowing that he would come to her.

Suddenly she tears herself away, crying that terrible danger threatens and imploring him to remember the penalty she must pay for breaking her oath. But when Nadir answers that neither a sacred oath nor death itself can separate them now, Leila throws herself into his arms, rapturously exclaiming that she would give her life for this one moment of bliss. As they stand in passionate embrace, thunder rumbles in the distance. Gazing up at the sky, the lovers sing that they will defy the storm's wrath and Brahma's anger as well.

Warned by a sense of imminent danger, Leila begs Nadir to leave at once. Promising that he will return the next evening, he embraces her in farewell. At that moment Nourabad appears on the terrace and sees the lovers. Muttering that treason has been committed, the high priest rushes away. He reappears shortly, followed by priests whom he sends in pursuit of Nadir. The sounds of the storm grow louder, and from the shore come the voices of the fisherfolk expressing their fear of impending disaster and praying for protection against the fury of the tempest ("Quelle voix nous appelle?").

As Nourabad strides toward Leila, the priests drag in Nadir. The people, who have rushed up from the shore and have crowded into the temple, exclaim in horror as Nourabad points to Nadir and Leila and thunders that they have violated the sacred oath. A dramatic ensemble develops as the priests surround them with drawn daggers ("Pour eux point de grâce! Non!"). The crowd roars that no mercy must be shown and that the culprits must die. Leila resigns herself to her fate, while Nadir, vowing that he will never ask for mercy, defies the threats of the people.

The uproar is suddenly halted by Zurga, who forces his way through the angry crowd to Leila and Nadir. He reminds the fishermen that they have elected him king and have given him the power to pronounce judgment on his subjects. In an aside, Leila and Nadir murmur their thanks to him. The fishermen draw back, muttering resentfully that if it is Zurga's wish, mercy will be extended to the traitors. Turning to Leila and Nadir, Zurga quietly tells them to go.

Thereupon Nourabad strides forward, declaring angrily that at least they will know by whom they have been betrayed. With that he tears the veil from Leila's face. Staggering back in surprise as he recognizes Leila, Zurga, in terrible fury, shouts for revenge. Frenzied by the thought that Nadir has betrayed his vow of friendship, Zurga rages that neither mercy nor pity will be shown the offenders—both must die. The ensemble continues as the priests and the fishermen renew their denunciations. As the storm breaks in full fury, they kneel and intone a grim invocation to Brahma, swearing that they will exact the ultimate penalty for the sacrilege which has been committed. Nadir is led away by the fishermen and Leila by the priests as the curtain falls.

## ACT THREE

[*Scene One*] The interior of Zurga's tent, which is enclosed by draperies. Pacing up and down, Zurga gives way to remorse and despair over having doomed Leila and Nadir ("L'orage s'est calmé"). His anger, like the storm, has spent its force, he soliloquizes, and now he realizes that he acted out of jealous hatred and a mad desire for revenge. Crying out that the terrible judgment he pronounced must surely be an evil dream, he declares that he is certain that Nadir did not betray him. And yet he has doomed not only his dearest friend but the beautiful Leila, whom he adored. Overwhelmed by his anguish, he sinks exhausted on a couch.

Escorted by two fishermen, Leila appears at the entrance of the tent, saying that she must speak with him alone. Dismissing the fishermen, Zurga tells her to enter. A spirited duet ensues ("Je frémis je chancelle"). Aside, Leila wonders how she can placate this fierce chieftain, while Zurga murmurs that she is more beautiful than ever in the hour of her doom. When he quietly tells her not to be afraid, she kneels at his feet and implores him to spare Nadir's life, insisting that he is innocent. She swears that it was only by chance that he found her. In an undertone Zurga says that perhaps Nadir did not break the pact they made.

Leila begs Zurga to spare Nadir so that she can more easily face her own punishment. He gave her all his love, she says tenderly, and she loved him in return. At those words Zurga cries out that he might have saved Nadir's life because of their friendship, but now he must die. In the effort to save Nadir's life by declaring her love for him, Zurga says sardonically, she has sealed his fate. Losing all control, Zurga confesses to Leila that he too loved her and that now jealousy is goading him to revenge. At one stroke he will destroy the woman who spurned him and the friend who betrayed his trust.

The duet rises to a stormy climax as Leila distractedly entreats him to take revenge on her alone. When he rejects her pleas, Leila warns that he will be haunted by remorse for this deed as long as he lives, while death will forever unite her with Nadir. Zurga rages that they will pay the penalty for their ignoble passion.

At the conclusion of the duet Nourabad and a group of fishermen appear. Shouts are heard in the distance. The hour of doom has come, Nourabad announces, and Leila declares that she is ready. Zurga orders her to go. As she leaves she takes a golden chain from around her neck and hands it to a young fisherman, telling him to take it to her mother as a token of remembrance. When Leila is led away Zurga snatches the chain from the fisherman's hands, examines it carefully, and then rushes out of the tent. The chain he holds is the one he gave Leila long ago for saving his life.

[*Scene Two*] A wild and desolate spot in the jungle, where a huge pyre has been built. Grouped in front of the pyre, the people watch a barbaric dance and then invoke Brahma in a fierce chorus ("Dès que le soleil"). They exult that as soon as the sun rises they will strike the avenging blow. The blood of the guilty ones will flow like wine, inspiring them with holy joy.

To the strains of a funeral march Nourabad appears, followed by Leila and Nadir, who are in chains. The high priest chants that Zurga has delivered the malefactors into the hands of the people, and the crowd repeats his words in savage exultation. Seeing a red glow spreading over the horizon, the people exclaim that dawn is breaking and that the fatal hour is at hand.

They are startled when Zurga rushes in, torch in hand. Shouting that the gods have rained down fire from heaven and that their village is being ravaged by flames, he calls on them to save their children while there is yet time. The people run toward their homes in mad disorder. Nourabad, however, remains behind and, unobserved by Zurga, Leila, and Nadir, conceals himself near the pyre.

Zurga tells Leila and Nadir that he started the fire in the village to distract the attention of the people. Saying that Leila once saved his life and that now he will save hers, he severs the chains of the captives. Nourabad steals away to inform the people of their king's treachery.

Zurga, Leila, and Nadir join in a dramatic trio ("O lumière sainte"). Leila and Nadir give thanks for their deliverance. Gazing at the lovers, Zurga declares that he will gladly face the death to which he has now doomed himself, for he could not bear the anguish of losing Leila to Nadir. In brief solo interludes Leila and Nadir sing rapturously of the happiness that awaits them in some paradise far from this scene of terror. The trio is resumed as Leila and Nadir exult over their release, while Zurga cries out in wonder and despair over their great love.

As shouts of the returning crowd come from the distance, Zurga leads Leila and Nadir to a secret path by which they can escape. In another brief trio passage Leila and Nadir bid farewell to Zurga, who cries that his task has been accomplished ("Plus de crainte, ô douce étreinte").

Nourabad rushes in at the head of the throng, points to Zurga, and denounces him as the arch-traitor who set the village on fire. He has destroyed their homes and threatened their lives, the high priest shouts, and then calls upon the people to pronounce the traitor's sentence. With fierce cries they hurl themselves on Zurga, drag him to the pyre, and force him to ascend. A moment later Zurga, shouting that he has given Leila his life, disappears in the flames ("Adieu, ma Leila, je te donne ma vie!").

Gazing at the pyre, the crowd chants that the will of the gods has been done and that the infamous traitor has met his just doom ("C'est l'arrêt de Dieu"). Then they turn to the flaming jungle behind them and cry in fear-stricken tones that the angry gods are avenging themselves on the people. As they prostrate themselves and rise again with a thunderous cry to Brahma, the curtain falls.

# Pique-Dame
## (*The Queen of Spades*)

*by* PETER ILYITCH TSCHAIKOWSKY
(1840–93)

### Libretto by
M. I. TSCHAIKOWSKY

*Based on a story by Pushkin*

#### CHARACTERS

| | |
|---|---|
| Czekalinsky | Tenor |
| Ssurin | Bass |
| Hermann, a young officer | Tenor |
| Count Tomsky | Baritone |
| Prince Yeletsky | Baritone |
| The Countess | Mezzo-soprano |
| Lisa, her granddaughter, betrothed to Prince Yeletsky | Soprano |
| Pauline, Lisa's companion | Contralto |
| Governess | Mezzo-soprano |
| Mascha, Lisa's maid | Soprano |
| Master of ceremonies | Tenor |
| Chloë ⎫ Persons in the Interlude, | Soprano |
| Daphnis (Pauline) ⎬ *The Sincere Shepherdess* | Contralto |
| Plutus (Tomsky) ⎭ | Baritone |
| Tschaplitsky ⎫ gamblers | Tenor |
| Narumoff ⎭ | Bass |

Servants, governesses, townspeople, guests, gamblers, children, actors

*Place:* St. Petersburg
*Time:* End of the eighteenth century
*First performance:* St. Petersburg, December 19, 1890
*Original language:* Russian

---

Pushkin's strange and dramatic story about the Queen of Spades greatly interested Tschaikowsky, and he composed the opera with much enthusiasm. Written about three years before his death, the score contains few set arias or ensembles. Much of it is in recitative sung over a symphonic accompaniment.

There is a brief prelude which opens with somber chords suggestive of a "fate" motive. This is followed by themes which will be heard in arias sung by Hermann and Lisa, and these are merged into a dramatic climax.

## ACT ONE

[*Scene One*] A public garden in St. Petersburg on a beautiful spring day. There are pleasant walks and playgrounds, and a grove is visible in the background. The park is thronged with children, maids, nurses, and governesses. Several little girls, playing the game of "cat and mouse," begin singing the words of their game ("Gorew, gorew yasno"). This builds into a gay ensemble as maids, nurses, governesses, and small boys sing various refrains. The maids urge the children to dance and sing and to make the most of their carefree childhood. The governesses complain that they must spend their days watching over noisy and disobedient youngsters. A group of boys playing soldiers marches by, singing a brave chorus about facing shot and shell in defense of the fatherland. Many of the small children troop after the boys, and the women leave to follow their charges.

Czekalinsky and Ssurin, two young-men-about-town, stroll in, discussing last night's card game. It lasted all night, as usual, Ssurin says. Czekalinsky mentions their friend Hermann and his strange obsession for cards. He sits at the card table watching every move of the game but never plays. Perhaps he is working out some system to win, Ssurin suggests with a laugh. Czekalinsky dryly observes that there may be another reason why Hermann does not play—he has no money.

While the two are talking they meet Hermann and his companion, Count Tomsky. Hermann, moody and preoccupied, does not notice Czekalinsky and Ssurin as they pass. When Tomsky asks why he is sad he mumbles a vague answer. Tomsky says he cannot understand why Hermann's usual gaiety has given way to melancholy. Now he sits at the gaming tables all night long, never playing, but watching the game with a strangely troubled expression.

Admitting that the cards have a powerful fascination for him, Hermann finally confesses that the real reason for his perturbed state of mind is that he is in love with a beautiful woman he has seen at the gambling house. She is proud and high-born, and he does not dare approach her. He gives voice to his emotions in an impassioned refrain ("Sravenja vsye perebiraya"), in which he compares her to an angel. He is tormented by the thought that her heart may belong to someone else. Only a kiss from her, he sighs, would soothe his anguish.

Tomsky urges him to pluck up courage and tell the lady about his love, but Hermann answers that as an officer in modest circumstances he could never hope to win her. In that case, Tomsky says, with practical logic, he had better find himself another girl. Hermann protests that there can never be another woman in his life but this beautiful creature. As the two continue on their way Tomsky advises Hermann to control his emotions lest they drive him to madness.

When they have gone strollers throng into the park and join in a tuneful chorus ("Nakonetz to Bog poslal nam"). They rejoice that the month of May, with its sunshine and laughter, has come at last, and that the biting winds of early spring have given way to warm and refreshing breezes. At the conclusion of the chorus Hermann and Tomsky reappear, still discussing the lady whom Hermann adores from afar. Tomsky asks if she has ever given him a sign of returning his affections. At times, Hermann replies, it seems as though she looks at him with an expression of mingled love and pity. But it is hopeless, and there is only one course left to him, Hermann adds melodramatically, and that is to die.

At that moment Prince Yeletsky approaches with Czekalinsky and Ssurin, who are congratulating him on his betrothal to Lisa. Tomsky adds his congratulations as he and Hermann greet the Prince. The voices of Hermann and Yeletsky blend briefly. The Prince revels in the beautiful May day which has brought him so much happiness, while Hermann, aside, reflects that what is a blessing for others is misfortune for him.

As Tomsky asks the Prince who his future bride is, Lisa and the Countess appear. Yeletsky proudly indicates Lisa. Hermann staggers back in surprise and dismay as he recognizes her, realizing that the woman he worships is to be the bride of another. Lisa and the Countess, in their turn, are startled at seeing the mysterious stranger whom they have noticed at the gambling house. Tomsky, turning to Hermann with a look of pity, quietly remarks that his problem is solved. Czekalinsky and Ssurin, talking together, remain in the background.

A brief but impressive quintet ensues ("Mnye strashno! on opyat peredo mnoy"). Lisa and the Countess exclaim over the strange coincidence of their meeting with Hermann and wonder if it bodes some misfortune. Hermann declares that the sight of the Countess fills him with a nameless fear and then laments that he has lost forever the woman he loves. Tomsky sympathizes with Hermann's suffering and then notes that Lisa seems strangely agitated upon seeing him. Prince Yeletsky also notices Lisa's apparent confusion and wonders why this sudden change has come over her.

After the quintet Tomsky approaches the Countess, who asks him about Hermann. Continuing the conversation, they walk a little distance away, while Prince Yeletsky sings ardently to Lisa of their future happiness. Glaring after them as they leave arm in arm, Hermann mutters that unseen disaster will soon blast the Prince's happiness like a bolt of lightning. A low rumble of thunder sounds in the distance as Hermann seats himself on a bench and abandons himself to gloomy thoughts.

Tomsky, having taken leave of the Countess, comes forward and is joined by Czekalinsky and Ssurin. They refer to the Countess as a rather frightening old hag, and then Tomsky asks the other two if they have ever heard the story of how the Countess, who was called the Queen of Spades, fell in love with the Jack of Spades. As Czekalinsky and Ssurin entreat him to tell the story, Hermann looks up expectantly and listens with intense interest. In a dramatic monologue ("O, tack poslushayte!") Tomsky relates that the Countess, in her youth, was a reigning beauty of Paris. Because of her all-absorbing passion for cards she was called the Queen of Spades. One of her lovers, the Count Saint-Germain, was skilled in black magic, and he taught her a secret combination of three cards which enabled her always to win. She not only cheated at cards but betrayed her husband by making love to another, to whom she told the card secret. One day when she was playing at Versailles she lost almost all her fortune, having suddenly forgotten the combination which Saint-Germain had taught her.

She looked up from the table to see a mysterious stranger gazing at her. He approached and invited her to walk in the garden with him, saying that there, in the light of the full moon, he would tell her the secret of the three cards. Having taught her the trick, the stranger—who, of course, was the devil in disguise—said that if she went back to the game and doubled her bets she would win all she had lost and a fortune besides. This proved true, and she was even able to recoup her husband's losses. But one night when she was at a game with another admirer to whom she had told the secret, the devil appeared and warned her that if she told the secret of the three cards to a third lover she would die on the spot.

As Tomsky speaks the storm comes nearer, with the thunder rumbling louder and louder. Laughing over the story, Tomsky, Czekalinsky, and Ssurin hurry away, leaving Hermann alone.

Soon crowds of people come running by, all scurrying for shelter from the storm, which is about to break. They sing an agitated chorus, urging all to seek cover ("Kack bistro groza nastupila"). As the storm rages about him Hermann voices his thoughts about Tomsky's story in a dramatic soliloquy ("Poluchish smertelniy oodar ti"). Repeating the devil's warning to the Countess, he suddenly gives way to his anger and jealousy. Shouting to the lightning and thunder to be his witnesses, he swears that he will win Lisa for himself. As he rushes away the curtain falls.

[*Scene Two*] Lisa's room. At one side is a glass-enclosed porch, beyond which a garden is visible. Lisa is seated at the piano. With her are Pauline and a group of girls who have come to celebrate Lisa's engagement. Lisa and Pauline sing a charming pastoral duet ("Oojh vetcher oblakov"), which is applauded by the other young ladies in chorus. Then Pauline sings a solo, a sentimental and melancholy song of unrequited love ("Podrugi miliya").

When Lisa and the others appear deeply moved Pauline makes amends for this mournful interlude by suggesting that they sing a gay folk song they all know—the song of Mashenka. Dancing about and clapping their hands to mark the rhythm, Pauline and the other girls sing a typically Russian song about a girl who scorned a rich suitor and married the lad of her choice ("Nuka svetik Mashenka"). Lisa does not join them but stands looking thoughtfully out at the garden.

The singing and dancing are interrupted by the governess, who comes bustling in and scolds the girls for their undignified conduct. Warning them to behave with decorum befitting young ladies of society, the governess stalks out, the girls meekly following. Pauline remains behind for a moment in an effort to cheer Lisa and then affectionately bids her good night.

Mascha, the maid, comes in, puts out all the lights but one, and is about to close the door to the garden. Lisa tells her to leave it open and then dismisses her. Gazing into the garden, she sings, in a beautiful aria, of the thoughts that are troubling her ("Otkooda yeti slezi"). She wonders why she is haunted by a strange longing that moves her to tears, despite the fact that she has everything her heart desires. She is loved by the Prince, who is handsome, gracious, and charming. And yet when he is near she becomes frightened and bewildered, because another man seems always to be standing at his side. It is the stranger of the gambling house. In passionate phrases she confides the secret of her love to the night, singing that it is as mysterious and inscrutable as the stranger himself.

As she moves away from the door Hermann comes in from the garden. Lisa, seeing him, shrinks back in surprise and alarm. A dramatic colloquy ensues. Hermann implores her to let him speak, if only to say good-by. When she excitedly orders him to leave he draws a pistol from his pocket and threatens to kill himself. At Lisa's restraining gesture he puts the weapon away. In a passionate refrain he confesses his love for her ("Vet yeto moi posledniy smertniy tchass"). By giving her love to another, he cries, she has sealed his doom. He asks only one embrace before they part forever, and then he can go willingly to his death. As he kneels supplicatingly before her she bursts into tears. Hermann asks if her tears mean acceptance or refusal, and when her manner indicates that she has yielded to his plea, he is wild with joy.

Their conversation is interrupted by a knock on the door. The Countess' voice is heard outside. Warning Hermann that it is too late to escape, she tells him to hide behind a curtain. Composing herself, Lisa opens the door to admit the Countess and several of her maids. She demands to know why Lisa is not asleep and asks to whom she was talking. Lisa replies that she was merely reciting a few lines from *Werther*.[1] Fuming that the erratic notions of the younger generation are beyond her comprehension, the Countess orders Lisa to go to bed and then sweeps out of the room.

No sooner has she gone than Hermann emerges from his hiding place, thoughtfully murmuring the words of the devil's prophecy about the cards as related in Tomsky's story. Lisa meanwhile locks the door after the Countess. As she turns to Hermann he renews his entreaties for her love. Lisa sharply orders him to go at once, but when he says that to go is to die, she yields. Rushing into each other's arms, they pledge their love in exultant phrases as the curtain falls.

## ACT TWO

[*Scene One*] The luxurious ballroom in the home of a diplomat. Guests in masquerade costumes and evening dress are dancing.

---

[1] Goethe's famous romantic novel, *Die Leiden des jungen Werthers* (*The Sorrows of Werther*).

A group of choristers seated on one side of the room sings an impressive number hailing the festivities ("Radostno, veselo v djen sey"). After the chorus the master of ceremonies announces that fireworks will be shown in the garden. As all the guests leave to view the display, Tomsky, Czekalinsky, and Ssurin, all masked, come in. They are discussing Hermann's eccentric behavior of late. Ssurin declares that he is trying to solve the riddle of the three cards, but Tomsky insists that Hermann is not gullible enough to be taken in by anything so fantastic. Czekalinsky and Ssurin decide to have a bit of sport at Hermann's expense over the matter of the cards. They go out into the garden with Tomsky.

As servants set up the scenery for the Interlude in the center of the room Lisa and the Prince come in, both unmasked. The Prince anxiously asks Lisa the reason for her sadness, but she replies evasively. Looking at her earnestly, Yeletsky entreats her, in an eloquent refrain, to believe in his love ("Postoyte na odno mgnovenje"). Begging Lisa to confess her fears to him, he declares that he will protect her from every danger. He can no longer bear the torment of her silence, he says, and entreats her to trust in him. At the conclusion of the refrain Lisa and Yeletsky walk slowly toward the garden.

Hermann now enters wearing a costume but no mask. He is reading a note from Lisa telling him to meet her after the performance. Hermann muses that if he could solve the riddle of the cards he could quickly win his fortune and then take Lisa away with him. At that moment Czekalinsky and Ssurin creep up behind Hermann and in whispered tones ask if he is the third lover who will bring about the Countess's death through the three cards. Then they vanish. Hermann leaps to his feet in terror, fearing that he has heard the ghostly voice of fate. The voices of Czekalinsky, Ssurin, and several other masqueraders are heard outside, repeating, "Three cards!" Hermann distractedly rushes away.

The Interlude, a pastoral play entitled *The Sincere Shepherdess*, is now performed for the entertainment of the guests. It has the classic characters of Daphnis, Chloë, Plutus, and a group of shepherds and shepherdesses. They sing a chorus in the Mozartean vein ("Pod tenju goostoju"), after which a saraband is danced. Daphnis (played by Pauline) and Chloë then enter and sing a charming love duet ("Moy milenkiy drujok").

They are interrupted by Plutus (played by Tomsky), who makes an impressive entrance in a golden chariot. With him is the goddess Fortuna. Plutus descends from his chariot with a flourish and promises Chloë a dazzling array of treasures in return for her love ("Ya gori zolotiya"). But Chloë spurns him and proclaims that her heart belongs to Daphnis, trembling and fainthearted though he is. Thereupon Plutus, in a towering rage, gets into his chariot and rides away, leaving Fortuna behind. She blesses Daphnis and Chloë, and the happiness of all is chanted by the chorus ("Prishel konetz muchenjam").

After the play the guests again mingle. Hermann, walking through the crowd, comes face to face with the Countess. As they stare at each other in confusion, Ssurin, masked, walks stealthily behind Hermann and asks him if he is pleased with his bride. Ssurin disappears before Hermann can turn and see him. Frightened and bewildered by this voice apparently out of nowhere, Hermann wonders if he is going mad.

At that moment Lisa, wearing a mask, cautiously approaches, gives Hermann a key to her house, and tells him how to gain access to the Countess' room. He must come at midnight, she says, because the Countess will still be playing cards downstairs. Behind the portrait of the Countess, Lisa goes on, is a secret door which leads to her own room. She tells him to come the next day, but Hermann declares that he must be there this very night. If that is his will, Lisa says submissively, she can do nothing but assent. With that she leaves. Looking after her, Hermann reflects that it is not his will but the will of fate. Exulting over the fact that he will at last learn the secret of the three cards, he hurries away.

There is an excited stir as the master of ceremonies announces that the Czarina Katerina has arrived. Led by the choir, the guests hail her in a brief but stirring chorus ("Slavsya sim Ekaterina"). As the Czarina enters with her retinue the curtain falls.

[*Scene Two*] The bedroom of the Countess. Several small lamps shed a dim light. At one side is a large window, in front of which is an armchair. Near the window is a door leading to the boudoir and another door at the rear. On the other side of the room is a large portrait of the Countess as a beautiful young woman—the Queen of Spades—behind which is the secret door leading to Lisa's room.

Somber chords sound in the orchestra as Hermann appears. For a moment he wavers, wondering if this attempt to learn the Countess' secret is too fantastic to succeed. He starts toward the secret door, deciding to abandon his plan and go to Lisa's room, when he suddenly stops and stares at the portrait as though hypnotized. The clock strikes midnight.

In a dramatic recitative he declares that the portrait has enchanted him and that he cannot leave ("A, vot ona, 'Veneroyu moscovskoy'"). He laments that he did not know the Countess in the days of her youth and beauty. But even now, he muses, her fatal spell is driving him relentlessly along the path of his destiny. Hearing the sound of voices outside, Hermann conceals himself behind the curtains of the bed.

The Countess enters, attended by her maids, who sing a brief chorus urging her to rest after her tiring day ("Blagodetelnitza nasha"). They escort the Countess into her boudoir. Lisa and Mascha come in. Lisa reveals that Hermann is in the house and warns Mascha not to disclose his presence. Declaring that she has made up her mind to be his bride, Lisa says that she will obey him unquestioningly. She goes out through the secret door, while Mascha leaves by the door at the rear.

The Countess, now in her nightdress, reappears with her maids, who sing another chorus of their song. They try to lead her to the bed, but she impatiently pushes them away and seats herself in the chair by the window. She fumes at their inane expressions of solicitude as they flutter around trying to make her comfortable. When she is settled they withdraw to the rear of the room.

In a long recitative the Countess expresses her distaste for the boorish society of the present day and then abandons herself to thoughts of the past ("Ah, postil mne yetot svet"). She meditates about the brilliant levees at the court where Madame Pompadour held sway, and murmurs the names of the dukes with whom she danced. She recalls the songs she sang for the royal audiences. It was at Chantilly, she remembers, that she danced with the King. Suddenly she starts as though awakening from a dream. Looking around, she sees the maids, still waiting to be dismissed. She sends them away and then gradually falls asleep, softly singing a little French song she remembered from her youth ("Je crains de lui parler la nuit").

A moment after the Countess' voice dies away Hermann emerges from his hiding place and stands before her. She wakes with a start and stares at him in terror. Assuring her that he intends no harm, Hermann tells her that he has come to learn the secret of the three cards. As the Countess rises in alarm Hermann kneels before her and in a dramatic refrain endeavors to persuade her to reveal the secret ("Yesli, kogda-nibud znali"). If there is one spark of compassion left in her heart, he cries wildly in a melodramatic appeal to her emotions, if she can recall the happiness that love for child, sweetheart, or husband ever brought into her life, then she must tell him the names of the three cards.

The Countess glares at him with cold contempt. Goaded to fury by her silence, Hermann draws his pistol. Raising her hands as though to fend him off, the Countess falls back dead. Stunned with horror, Hermann stammers that his threat was only a joke and repeats his entreaties. He takes the Countess' hand, then recoils, gasping that she is dead.

Lisa suddenly comes through the secret door. Hermann rushes to her, crying that the secret of the cards is lost forever. For a moment Lisa does not understand. Pointing to the Countess' body, Hermann moans that she is dead. Lisa rushes over and kneels sobbing at the feet of the dead woman. Shaken with remorse, Hermann pleads that he did not seek her death—he only wanted the secret of the three cards. Lisa turns on him in fury and despair, crying out that now she realizes that it was not for her love that he came here but only because of his evil passion for cards. Her trust, she sobs, has been rewarded with betrayal. Hermann tries to explain. In a ringing phrase Lisa brands him a scoundrel and orders him to go. As he staggers from the room Lisa sinks unconscious at the feet of the Countess. The curtain falls.


## ACT THREE

[*Scene One*] Hermann's quarters in the barracks. Moonlight shows through the windows and the moaning of the wind is heard. Hermann is seated at a table, reading a letter by the light of a candle. From the distance comes the music of a funeral march and then the sound of trumpets and drums. Over a somber theme played by the woodwinds, Hermann reads, in a spoken voice, the letter from Lisa in which she writes that she is certain that he did not intentionally kill the Countess. She is remorseful for having blamed him and asks him to meet her at the quay at midnight so that she can ask his forgiveness and end her suffering.

Hermann bitterly reproaches himself for having caused her this sorrow. He wearily rests his head on his arms and falls asleep. A ghostly chorus is heard singing a chorale ("Gospodu molussya ya"). Hermann springs to his feet in terror, exclaiming that he hears the hymn that was sung at the Countess' funeral. He recalls the grim details of the rites—the candles, the incense, the old woman lying like a pale waxen image in her coffin. He cringes in terror as he tries to drive away the vision of the Countess' face, with one eye winking at him.

Suddenly there is a knock on the window, which is flung open by a blast of wind. The candle is blown out. As Hermann rushes in panic toward the door, the ghost of the Countess stands in his path. Softly she murmurs that she cannot rest in her grave. She tells Hermann that he must marry Lisa to save her, and then speaks the names of the three magic cards—three, seven, ace. With that the phantom disappears. As though demented, Hermann dances around the room shouting the combination. Quickly putting on his uniform, he rushes out.

[*Scene Two*] The canal near the Winter Palace. The Neva quay and the Peter-Paul fortress are seen in the background. Lisa, dressed in mourning, is standing under an archway, waiting for Hermann. It is nearly midnight, and Lisa fears that perhaps Hermann will fail to meet her. In a long soliloquy she voices her anxiety and despair ("Oojh polnoch blisitsya"). At first she refuses to admit that Hermann is capable of deceiving her, but finally, overwhelmed by hopelessness, she laments that she has allowed herself to be dazzled by glittering illusions and has been lured to her destruction by a betrayer and a murderer. In the next moment she cries for her lover and reproaches herself for doubting him. Then she sobs that her dream of love is over, that the forbidden desires to which she yielded are destroying her.

As she stands weeping she sees Hermann approaching. Ecstatically crying out that he has justified her faith in him, she rushes into his arms. Their voices blend in a brief but tender duet as they sing that sorrow and despair will be forgotten in the bliss of their future ("O da minovali stradanya"). When Lisa asks where they will go Hermann answers that he must first return to the gambling house and win his fortune. As Lisa looks at him in astonishment he begins to talk wildly about how the Countess came to him today and told him the secret of the three cards. With a distracted laugh he describes how the Countess died of fright when he threatened her with his pistol. Lisa is crushed when she realizes that he was instrumental in causing the Countess' death.

Their voices blend again as Lisa reiterates that the desires to which she yielded have betrayed her into the hands of a demon. Hermann raves that nothing matters now—he knows the secret of the three cards and destiny will have its way. He babbles that he is the fatal third lover who doomed the Countess through the three, the seven, and the ace. Lisa tries to calm him, but it is too late. Completely out of his mind, he no longer recognizes her.

Pushing her roughly aside, he runs away like a madman. Crazed by anguish, Lisa rushes to the quay and hurls herself into the river.

[*Scene Three*] The gambling house. Tomsky, Czekalinsky, Ssurin, Tschaplitsky, Narumoff, and other guests are seated at tables, drinking and playing cards. They sing a lively chorus in praise of wine, youth, and merriment ("Budem pit i veselitsya"). After an interlude at cards the Prince enters and is cordially greeted by Tomsky, who remarks that he has not seen him in his old haunts for many a year. One always returns, the Prince replies in French, and then goes on to say that he has reversed the proverb: Unlucky in love, lucky at cards. When Tomsky looks at him with a puzzled expression the Prince explains that his engagement was broken off. The rest of the story, he says, is too sad to tell.

The conversation is interrupted by the other players, who noisily demand a song from Tomsky. After much coaxing Tomsky sings a lively ditty ("Yeslib miliya dyevitzi"), in which he compares the pretty girls to birds with whom he would like to bill and coo. His listeners gaily repeat his words and then all join in a lusty chorus, the burden of which is that God made the world as round as a coin ("Tack v nenastniye dni sobiraliss oni").

After the chorus the men resume their card games. Suddenly Hermann bursts in and lurches over to a table. Observing him, Prince Yeletsky remarks to Tomsky that his foreboding has come true and asks him to serve as his second if the need should arise. Hermann announces that he will play cards, whereupon Czekalinsky, Ssurin, and some of the others cynically remark that a miracle has come to pass ("Vot tchudessa on stal igrat"). This introduces an ensemble which builds up as Hermann bets on the three and the seven and wins enormous sums. Flushed with his triumphs, Hermann calls for champagne. Glass in hand, he sings that life is like a game of cards—you wager, and then you win or you lose. Only one thing is certain: In the end Death will claim his share of the stakes.

After his song he calls for another game. The Prince challenges him. Hermann stakes all he has won on a single card. The other players urge the contestants to desist from this mad gamble. Ignoring them, Prince Yeletsky looks intently at Hermann and murmurs that at last he will get even with him.

Czekalinsky deals. "Ace wins!" cries Hermann, showing his card. The Prince says quietly, "Your queen has lost." As Hermann looks at him, dumfounded, Yeletsky tells him to look at the card in his hand. Hermann is unable to believe his eyes. Instead of an ace he holds the queen of spades. At that moment the phantom of the Countess materializes in the background, looking as she appeared in the portrait in her room. In a frenzy Hermann screams that she has tricked him by stealing his ace of hearts. Defiantly crying that he still will escape her fatal power, he plunges a knife into his breast.

The other players crowd around him. As they support him he looks up at the Prince and gasps a plea for forgiveness. In the ecstasy of death he envisions Lisa hovering over him like an angel. As he dies an unseen chorus majestically intones a prayer for his soul ("Gospodj! Prosti yemu!"). The curtain falls.

# Porgy and Bess

## *by* GEORGE GERSHWIN
### (1898–1937)

### *Libretto by*
#### DU BOSE HEYWARD
#### *lyrics by* DU BOSE HEYWARD *and* IRA GERSHWIN

*Based on the play* PORGY, *by Du Bose and Dorothy Heyward*

#### CHARACTERS

| | |
|---|---|
| Porgy, a cripple | Bass-baritone |
| Crown, a tough stevedore | Baritone |
| Bess, Crown's girl | Soprano |
| Robbins, an inhabitant of Catfish Row | Tenor |
| Serena, his wife | Soprano |
| Jake, skipper of a fishing boat | Baritone |
| Clara, his wife | Soprano |
| Maria, proprietress of the cookshop | Contralto |
| Sporting Life, a dope peddler | Tenor |
| Mingo | Tenor |
| Peter, the Honey Man | Tenor |
| Lily, the Strawberry Woman, Peter's wife | Mezzo-soprano |
| Frazier, a Negro "lawyer" | Baritone |
| Annie | Mezzo-soprano |
| Jim, a cotton picker | Baritone |
| Undertaker | Baritone |
| Crab Man | Tenor |
| Alan Archdale | |
| Detective | |
| Policemen | Speaking parts |
| Coroner | |
| Scipio | |

Inhabitants of Catfish Row, fishermen, children, stevedores

*Place:* Catfish Row, Charleston, South Carolina, U.S.A.
*Time:* The recent past
*First performance:* Boston, Massachusetts, Sepember 30, 1935
*Original language:* English

Presented by the Theatre Guild, *Porgy and Bess* was given its premiere with such famous Negro singer-actors as Todd Duncan (Porgy), Anne Brown (Bess), Warren Coleman (Crown) and John W. Bubbles (Sporting Life). It opened at the Alvin Theater, New York City, on October 10, 1935.

The first European performance was in Zurich in 1945. In 1952 an all-Negro company headed by Metropolitan Opera soprano Leontyne Price made a triumphant tour of Europe. The company performed to great acclaim in Moscow in 1955–56.

Recognized as the first truly American opera to make a genuine success, the music of *Porgy and Bess* is founded on the jazz rhythms of the 1920s. Gershwin developed an idiom of his own, based on one segment of American life. While critics at first argued whether it was high-class musical comedy or low-class grand opera, the eventual consensus was that it is a folk opera of the highest order. Not all of the musical numbers (some thirty-one are indexed) can be called operatic, but all are solidly constructed on a soundly conceived harmonic basis. In certain instances, Gershwin made effective use of the Wagnerian leitmotiv technique —at least to the extent of identifying analogous situations by means of the same themes in different harmonic patterns.

In this opera the characters sing and speak in "Gullah" dialect, the language of the Negroes living in the coastal areas of South Carolina and Georgia. To assure authenticity, Gershwin spent some months in the area among the people there.

As musician and composer, George Gershwin traveled the road from Tin Pan Alley to the concert hall and the operatic stage. He supplied all or part of the music for some twenty-two Broadway musical comedies—practically all of them outstanding successes. His first successful attempt at a serious work was the famous *Rhapsody in Blue*, in 1924. The *Concerto in F* came a year later, and *An American in Paris* followed in 1928. Then he turned to opera, and *Porgy and Bess* was his last major work. It has been seen and heard by more people than any other American opera.

On July 11, 1937, George Gershwin, thirty-nine years old, died in Hollywood. He was then on the threshold of even greater fame as a potent force in American music.

There is no overture. The curtain rises after a brief orchestral introduction in a brisk jazz tempo, with scoring for xylophone, triangle, chimes and brass.

## ACT ONE

[*Scene One*] Jasbo Brown's room on Catfish Row on a summer night. At the piano, Jasbo is playing a blues number in a slow, hypnotic rhythm. In the dim half light, a half-dozen couples are swaying trancelike to the music as they sing "Da-doo-da, wa-wa, O-wa-de-wa" in softly accented phrases, almost like an incantation.

The lights dim out, then come up on another group on the stage, in the center of which Clara sits with her baby in her arms. Rocking back and forth, she sings the tender lullaby "Summertime." Its languorous tempo reflects the happy-go-lucky mood of Catfish Row at this time of year when "the livin' is easy, an' the cotton is high."

Again the lights fade and then come up on still another group— Mingo and his friends shooting dice. The easy rhythms change to a driving syncopation over the beat of tom-toms. Kneeling in a circle and rolling the dice, Mingo and the other players break into a chorus sung in typical crap game jargon, "Roll dem bones." Around them, Catfish Row stirs into its usual nocturnal activity. Couples stroll back and forth, children scamper about laughing and playing games.

As conversation continues in quasi-recitative among the players, an argument develops. Sporting Life produces his own dice; Jake, rolling them, begins complaining about his bad luck. Thereupon Mingo snatches them up and shows them to Jake, who exclaims that they are the dice that "cleaned out the game last Saturday night." Sporting Life curses Mingo. The three men glower at each other.

At this juncture Serena and Robbins appear. Ignoring his wife's plea not to join the game, Robbins kneels down and begins throwing the dice. Clara comes in with her baby in her arms. Watching the game, she sings a reprise of "Summertime." In a choral accompaniment, the men sing in dice game chatter: "Seven come seven." At the close of the chorus, Jake walks over to Clara and notices that the baby is still wide awake.

Taking the child from her, he sings his own "lullaby," one of the most engaging numbers in the opera, "A woman is a sometime thing." In catchy jazz rhythm, Jake, with good-natured cynicism, warns his offspring that woman will born him, mourn him and tie him to her apron strings until some other woman comes to claim him. She in turn will take his clothes and leave him. At the climax of the refrain, the dice players join in a lusty chorus.

With a self-satisfied air, Jake hands the baby back to Clara bragging that he has put the child to sleep. As he turns back to the game there is a loud wail from the child. The players laugh derisively. Clara leaves, remarking disdainfully that her baby has better sense than to listen to Jake's foolishness.

Just as the players are about to resume, Maria, standing in the doorway of her shop, calls out that Porgy is coming. She orders the boy Scipio to open the iron gate at the end of the street to let him in. Seated in a small cart drawn by a goat, Porgy rides in like a charioteer to the accompaniment of an imposing theme which musically identifies him in the style of a Wagnerian leitmotiv. The crowd greets him noisily; the dice players welcome him as "the ol' crap shark."

From his cart, Porgy responds with a courtly "good evenin'" to the ladies present. Over a chromatic triad figure in the orchestra, he announces that his luck is riding high: He has a pocketful of money which will go to any man who "has the guts to shoot it off me."

Just as the men are about to roll the dice, one of the players calls out that Crown is approaching—and he seems to be in an ugly mood. Porgy asks if Bess is with him, which prompts Jake to taunt him about being "soft" on Crown's girl. Porgy hotly denies this. But when Maria and Serena sneer that Bess is unfit for decent company, Porgy angrily rebukes them in a memorable phrase sung over sustained chords in the orchestra: "Between the Gawd-fearin' women and the Gawd-dammin' men, that gal ain't got a chance."

Then he gives voice to his mingled bitterness and defiance in a moving refrain, "They pass by singin'." Women will have nothing to do with a cripple, he sings. They pass his door, look in, then go on their way. A cripple is fated to travel the lonesome road alone. As he ends the refrain on a melancholy phrase, Crown is heard shouting outside. A moment later he swaggers in with Bess.

First he loudly orders Sporting Life to bring him a drink, and the latter immediately hands him a pint bottle. Crown drinks and hands the bottle to Bess, who follows suit and then passes the bottle to Robbins. Crown roughly snatches it out of his hands. Throwing down his money, Crown announces he is ready to play.

Robbins is the first to throw. Mingo tauntingly remarks that Robbins' wife allows him only fifty cents to gamble with. Bess steps forward and offers to stake him to the game. Porgy takes due note of this, then pointedly offers Robbins some timely advice by way of a reprise of "A woman is a sometime thing." Bess and the dice players join him in a choral interlude.

As the game continues, with the players calling their throws in crap game jargon, the tension increases. Crown, suspicious, ill tempered, and getting drunker, warns that he will stand for no cheating. Losing all his throws, he rubs the dice with a rabbit's foot for luck. Robbins sneers that he is too drunk to read the dice. Not drunk enough, Crown retorts, then asks Sporting Life for a packet of dope. Bess sharply warns the peddler not to give Crown the "happy dust," but she obediently pays the peddler for it when Crown orders her to. Peter steps between the two men with a well-intentioned warning that dice and "happy dust" do not mix. Crown threatens him with his fist, but the others restrain him. As the game is resumed, Sporting Life wins the pot. In a brief choral passage in canon form, some of the group comment that Crown is "cockeyed drunk." He cuts them short with a menacing gesture and a snarl.

Jake calls out that it is Porgy's turn to roll the dice. Eyes half closed, swaying from side to side, Porgy begins to sing "Oh, little stars, roll" like an incantation over sustained chords in the orchestra. He rolls and takes the pot as Crown glares in mounting anger. With a jeering laugh, Porgy rolls again—but this time he loses. Robbins throws next, makes his point and picks up the money.

Grabbing Robbins' wrist, Crown threatens to kill him ("Touch that money an' meet yo' Gawd!"). This marks the beginning of the opera's first big ensemble scene, which culminates in Crown's murder of Robbins. With reckless courage, Robbins defies Crown. The onlookers, all in terror of Crown and realizing what will happen, implore each other to head off the fight—but no one moves. Suddenly the two men lunge at each other. Serena, distractedly begging for help, tries to go to her husband's aid but is held back by Jake and Clara.

As the chorus rises to a frenzied climax, Crown and Robbins crouch face to face in the shafts of light streaming from windows suddenly flung open. Crown brandishes his cotton hook. Then, as an ascending chromatic passage erupts in the orchestra, he seizes Robbins and kills him with one terrible blow of the cotton hook. Robbins' body falls in front of Porgy's door. Crown stands staring at his victim as though hypnotized.

Rushing to his side, Bess urges him to flee before the police arrive. At the word "police," the onlookers, who have been watching the scene in stunned silence, vanish as if by magic. When

Crown asks where she will hide, Bess casually replies that there
will always be a man around to take care of her. He had better
be "temporary," Crown growls menacingly. As he turns to go,
Bess takes money from her stocking and gives it to him.

A moment later, Sporting Life appears. Bess asks him for
"happy dust" to steady her nerves. Giving her the powder, the
peddler insinuatingly suggests that she go to New York with him.
There, he says, they will make a "swell team." When Bess scornfully rebuffs him he slinks away.

During an ensuing orchestral interlude, Bess tries the doors
of the nearby houses, looking for a place to hide from the police.
Some are locked, others are opened and then slammed in her
face. She finally reaches the door of Maria's shop, where Maria
answers her desperate plea for help with an insult. Despairingly,
Bess asks who lives across the street. Porgy, Maria tells her, adding callously that he would be of no help to a woman of her kind—
he is only a crippled beggar.

With a hopeless gesture, Bess walks slowly toward the iron
gate at the end of the street. At the sound of a police whistle
she stops, then turns back toward Porgy's house. She recoils in
horror as she comes upon Serena, still crouched over Robbins'
body. Averting her eyes, Bess hurries into Porgy's house. The
curtain slowly falls as a variation of the theme of Porgy's loneliness ("They pass by singin'") begins in the orchestra and builds
into a surging climax.

[*Scene Two*] Serena's room, the following night. Robbins' body
lies on a bed in the center of the room. Serena is seated at the
foot, with the mourners huddled around her. This entire scene
is given over to one of the most overpowering ensembles in the
opera. A choral adaptation of the typical Negro spiritual, it is
dominated by the descending chromatic figure of its opening
phrase—"He's gone, gone, gone"—in the tempo of a funeral march.

During the chanting, visitors come to pay their respects. The
first of these are Porgy and Bess. Serena glares as Bess, observing
the funeral custom, goes toward the bed with a gift of burial
money. The widow angrily protests that she does not need Crown's
money to bury her husband. Bess quietly replies that it is not
Crown's money, but Porgy's. Somewhat mollified, Serena tells her
to put it in the saucer with the rest of the burial collection.

One of the mourners raises her voice in fervent appeal—"Come
on, sister, come on, brudder, fill up de saucer." This theme is

taken up by the chorus. Peter and Lily enter and add their contributions while the mourners pray for more money to take care of the widow and her fatherless children. As the chorus of entreaty rises to a climax, there is a dramatic interruption.

A commotion is heard outside and in the next moment a detective, a white man, and two policemen burst into the room. A scene in spoken dialogue ensues. Serena leaps to her feet as the other Negroes cower in fear. The detective begins a brutal inquisition, first asking Serena if her husband left any funeral insurance. When Serena answers no, the detective tells her to see to it that Robbins is buried the next day. Whirling on Peter, the detective accuses him of murdering Robbins, and warns him that he will be hanged for it. When Peter denies it, the detective draws his pistol and demands that he name the killer. Peter stammers that Crown is guilty.

Still not satisfied, the detective turns on Porgy. At first the cripple is silent, even when threatened with the pistol. Then he quietly protests that he knows nothing at all about the killing. In baffled fury, the detective orders the policemen to take Peter to jail as a material witness and keep him there until Crown is caught.

Crown is on the loose, Porgy says, and there isn't a rope long enough to hang him. So much the worse for the old man, the detective growls. Turning to Serena, he snarls that unless Robbins is buried the next day, the Board of Health will turn his body over to the medical students. Serena's lamentations mingle with Peter's anguished cries of protest as the policemen drag him away.

Stunned and bewildered, the Negroes huddle together. Porgy, in a recitative passage, reflects on the cruel irony of the situation: Peter, an innocent man, is dragged off to jail; Crown, a killer, goes on his lawless way unpunished. The dolorous chant, "Gone, gone, gone," breaks out again, softly at first, then crescendoing to a wild outburst of grief.

As a heavy, pulsating rhythm begins in the orchestra, Serena suddenly gives way to her sorrow in the poignant aria "My man's gone now." Instead of being comforted by her husband, she wails, Old Man Sorrow will be her only companion as she travels on to the Promised Land. The mourners, swaying to the beat of the music, join in a keening accompaniment. Serena ends the aria on a descending phrase of utter despair.

Meanwhile, the undertaker enters, quietly watches the scene, then takes up the matter of funeral arrangements with Serena. When she tells him there are only fifteen dollars in the burial saucer, he observes, with professional solicitude, that that is hardly enough to bury a grown man. Remembering the detective's warning, Serena begs the undertaker to bury her husband in the graveyard to keep his body out of the hands of the medical students.

Moved by her frantic plea, the undertaker finally agrees to provide "the box and one carriage," even though it means losing money. Emptying the contents of the burial saucer into his pocket, the undertaker leaves.

The mood of the scene now changes abruptly from profound sorrow to a kind of mystical ecstasy. The transformation occurs when Bess leaps to her feet and bursts out in an exuberant phrase: "The train is at the station an' you better get aboard." The words are sung in a gradually increasing rhythm imitating the starting of a train. The mourners, responding to Bess's mood of exaltation, express their feelings in the jubilant chorus "Leavin' today."

This marks the beginning of the spectacular ensemble which concludes the act. With joyous abandon, the mourners sing of the "rollin' drivin' wheels" of the heavenly train that will carry them to the Promised Land to meet their departed brother. The chorus, impelled by the driving syncopation of the orchestral accompaniment, rises to a tremendous climax.

## ACT TWO

[*Scene One*] Before the rise of the curtain, the chimes of St. Michael's Church, adjacent to Catfish Row, mingle with the voices of Jake and his fishing crew singing a wordless fragment of a sailor's ditty. The chimes strike nine. At the curtain the men are seen repairing their nets and swaying to the rhythm of the music. Jake strikes up a chanty about taking his boat out to the banks to fish ("Oh, I'm goin' out to the Blackfish Banks").

Spoken dialogue and recitative follow. Annie calls down from her window to remind the sailors about the picnic and the parade, which is due to start at ten o'clock. Clara anxiously warns Jake to keep a weather eye open for the September storms. Laughing, Jake answers he must go out in spite of hurricanes to make money for his son's college education.

Porgy, at the window of his room, strums his banjo and sings the delightful number "I got plenty o' nuttin'." It is an eloquent expression of his serene contentment with his lot in life—he has his "gal and his song" and needs nothing more. In a brief choral interlude ("Porgy change"), the listening neighbors marvel at the change which has come over Porgy since Bess has come into his life. All are happy about the couple except Serena, who observes bitterly that only a killer like Crown is a match for a woman like Bess.

A succession of episodic but musically integrated scenes, contributing to the development of the plot, now follows. In the first of these, Sporting Life enters Maria's shop. She watches him grimly as he pours a packet of dope into his palm. Just as he is about to inhale the powder, she blows it out of his hand. He turns on her with a curse. Eyeing him coldly, Maria warns him not to peddle "happy dust" in her shop.

Then in one swift movement she seizes him by the throat, forces him down on the table top and picks up a carving knife. With the knife poised at his throat, she pours out her contempt for him in what is virtually an "aria" in spoken words over an ominous, throbbing accompaniment ("I hates your struttin' style"). She vows that if he does not stop peddling dope to the people of Catfish Row she will carve him up and feed his carcass to the buzzards. Neighbors who have crowded in to watch the encounter laugh at his plight. The hapless peddler gasps in terror. Fortunately for him, Lawyer Frazier, a shyster, walks into the shop at that moment. Maria releases her victim and casually greets the lawyer.

Frazier tells her he is looking for a man named Porgy. Called from his house across the street by Maria, he is questioned by the lawyer about Bess. When Porgy declares that she is now his woman, Frazier informs him that Bess must divorce Crown to make the present arrangement "legal." In a remarkable demonstration of extralegal skulduggery, Frazier talks Porgy into buying a "divorce" for one dollar and a half. When the fraudulent document is duly signed and sealed, the shyster triumphantly observes that it has cost only one dollar and a half to change a woman to a lady. With that he struts away. The onlookers, in gleeful derision, chant "Woman to lady."

The merriment suddenly evaporates when Scipio calls out that a white man is approaching. When the stranger enters and announces he is looking for a man named Porgy, the crowd stares at him in suspicious silence. But when he adds that he comes with good news, the neighbors bring Porgy forward to meet him. Introducing himself as Mister Archdale, the visitor tells Porgy that his friend Peter will soon be back home. Peter's family once were in his service, he explains, and he has furnished bond for him. Porgy and all the others call down a blessing on Peter's benefactor.

As he is leaving, he encounters Lawyer Frazier. Knowing his

man, Archdale remarks that he hopes the lawyer is "not selling any more divorces." Thereupon Porgy shows him the spurious document. Archdale sternly warns Frazier to close up his "divorce mill" or go to jail. He adds magnanimously that he will not report the lawyer this time. Cringing, Frazier mumbles his thanks.

To the accompaniment of a menacing trill high in the strings, a huge bird suddenly swoops low over the crowd. Porgy cries that it is a buzzard, a bird of evil omen. The people voice their superstitious terror in a choral phrase, "Drive him off!" In a dramatic aria, "Buzzard, keep on flyin'," Porgy defiantly sings that the buzzard's menace is powerless against two people who can share love and laughter. No longer will the creature's evil shadow darken his door, nor will he be its helpless prey. In the ringing climax of the aria, Porgy sings that for him there will be no more loneliness and despair—because Porgy is "young again." All the neighbors join him in a thunderous closing phrase: "Buzzard, keep on flyin'!"

Porgy limps to his room and the others disperse, leaving only Bess and Sporting Life. Sidling up to her, the peddler again tries to persuade her to go to New York with him. Again Bess angrily rebuffs him. Still persisting, he offers her dope and tries to pour some of the powder into her hand. Snatching away her hand, Bess cries that she is through with dope.

At that moment, Porgy, unseen, opens his door and overhears the two. Still holding the powder toward Bess, Sporting Life taunts that nobody ever is through with "happy dust." Porgy's hand emerges from the doorway and seizes the peddler's wrist in a vicelike grip. Forcing Sporting Life to his knees, Porgy warns him to stay away from Bess, then sends him sprawling from the doorstep. Leering at Bess, Sporting Life remarks that when all her other men have deserted her, he and his "happy dust" still will be close by. He saunters away as Porgy curses him.

Porgy turns to Bess and begins the famous duet "Bess, you is my woman now," the best-known number in the opera. He sings that her love has blotted out the bitter, lonely past, and Bess responds that she will be his forever—"mornin' time an' evenin' time an' summer time an' winter time." The duet ends on a serene chord as they embrace.

The raucous sound of a brass band breaks the mood of the scene. The residents of Catfish Row, all in their best finery, stream out of their houses and begin dancing to the music of the band. In a rousing chorus ("Oh, I can't sit down") they look forward to a day of fun at a picnic on Kittiwah Island.

Porgy and Bess watch the gay procession follow the band on the way to the wharf. Maria, carrying a huge basket, comes by and admonishes Bess to hurry. Bess replies that she does not want to leave Porgy, but at his insistence she reluctantly joins Maria. Gazing fondly after her, Porgy turns back to his room with a joyous reprise of his song—"Got my gal, got my song."

[*Scene Two*] Kittiwah Island. The same day. The scene opens to the beat of African drums, to which the picnickers are dancing with characteristic abandon. More music is supplied by an "orchestra" composed of youngsters playing mouth organs, combs, bones and washboards. One beats out a bass rhythm on an overturned washtub. Caught up in the frenzy of the music, the picknickers burst into a wild, barbaric chorus, "I ain't got no shame." At its conclusion, Sporting Life ambles forward and entertains the crowd with one of the most engaging numbers in the opera, "It ain't necessarily so." A gem of musical wit, it is Sporting Life's saturnine commentary on some of the familiar Bible stories—David and Goliath, Jonah and the whale, Moses in the bulrushes, and Methuselah. The crowd joins Sporting Life in the closing phrases.

But one of the listeners is Serena, who is outraged at this mockery of biblical tales. Stalking through the crowd, she denounces Sporting Life and his listeners in hellfire-and-damnation terms ("Shame on all you sinners"), warning them that the Lord surely will punish them for their godless ways. As they squirm under her accusing gaze, she orders them to pack up their baskets and hurry to the boat which is about to sail back to the mainland. Gathering up their belongings, the picnickers scamper toward the wharf. Last to leave are Serena and Maria, who calls to Bess to hurry.

As the two women disappear, Bess, carrying a picnic basket, appears and hastens after them. A sharp whistle from a nearby thicket stops her in her tracks. Dropping her basket, she gasps: "Crown!" This marks the beginning of the long duet which is one of the most dramatic episodes in the opera. It is sung partly in recitative, partly in lyrical interludes. Crown, who has been hiding on the island since the murder of Robbins, tells Bess he has managed to stay alive by foraging for food. When he avidly tries to embrace her, she protests that she will miss the boat back to the mainland.

Barring her way, he reminds her that he promised to come back for her at cotton-picking time. Now, he says, his friend Johnny can get them aboard the river boat to Savannah. Vainly trying to elude him, Bess tells him that she has been living with Porgy.

Crown greets this with a sneer and again reminds her that any such arrangement was to be strictly "temporary." Menacingly he asks if she would prefer a crippled beggar to a man like Crown.

In tones of desperate entreaty, Bess answers that she cannot bear the thought of Porgy waiting for her in vain when the boat returns to Catfish Row. Again a mocking laugh from Crown. Resorting to feminine guile, Bess pleads that she is getting old . . . for five long years she has been at his beck and call . . . now, a strong man like Crown needs a young girl. . . . As for herself, the only man who needs her is Porgy. But Crown, wild with desire, keeps repeating that Bess is his woman. The two reiterate these assertions in duet form as the scene builds to a climax.

Bess tries to break away as the steamboat whistle sounds. Crown seizes her in a passionate embrace and kisses her to the accompaniment of a strongly accentuated orchestral theme which may be identified as the "kiss" motive. For a moment Bess fiercely resists him, then voluptuously enfolds him in her arms. In savage triumph, Crown sings, over a discordant variation of the "kiss" motive, the concluding phrase of the duet: "Wid you and me it will always be the same." Then, as an ascending chromatic figure flares in the orchestra, Crown violently pushes Bess into a palmetto thicket. She struggles to her feet and slowly backs away from him deeper into the foliage. He follows her like an animal stalking its prey. The curtain falls as the orchestra thunderously repeats—this time in strident open fifths—the closing theme of the duet.

[Scene Three] Catfish Row. Before dawn a week later. The fishermen are getting ready to leave. Jake enters, carrying a lantern and a net, and calls his men together. One of them remarks that he sees signs of a storm, but Jake cautions him not to scare the womenfolk with that kind of talk. Trooping out, the men sing a reprise of the chanty heard at the beginning of the act.

As their singing dies away in the distance, a piercing wail comes from Porgy's room, where Bess is lying ill and delirious. As Maria explains to Serena, Lily and Peter, anxiously listening with her outside, Bess had wandered into the palmetto jungle on her way home from the picnic and was lost for two days. Now, burning with fever and out of her mind, she imagines she is still on Kittiwah Island fighting off Crown's advances, and pleads desperately for help. Phrases of the music of that turbulent scene echo in the orchestra.

After a time, Porgy comes out and tells the others that Bess finally has fallen asleep. They discuss taking Bess to the white man's hospital, but Serena declares that she can heal the sick woman with prayer. Falling to her knees, she begins chanting with religious fervor: "Oh, Doctor Jesus!" The others also kneel and shout their responses as Serena prays that the devil may be driven out of the body of this poor sick woman. She ends the supplication with a confident "Amen." Then with calm finality she says that Doctor Jesus has taken the case; by five o'clock Bess will be well. As the music continues on a serene, *Tristan*-like theme, the others look at her in awe and gratitude.

Meanwhile, in Catfish Row, life goes on. Lily and Peter—once more the Strawberry Woman and the Honey Man—wander off on their rounds. The Crab Man comes by, makes a sale to Maria, and goes on his way chanting.

Porgy, sitting deep in thought on his doorstep, looks up startled as Bess calls his name over the theme of "Bess, you is my woman now." She appears at the door. Dressed in a nightgown, she looks haggard and exhausted. Sitting down beside Porgy, she murmurs, childlike, that it is lonely in the room without him ("I lonesome here all by myself"). This phrase marks the beginning of a long and moving duet, the theme of which is based on Porgy's aria. Porgy tells her how she wandered back to Catfish Row in a raging fever and was put to bed by Maria. Of this, Bess says with a sob, she remembers nothing at all.

Comforting her, Porgy says gently that he knows she has been with Crown, but that does not matter now—he does not want her ever to go away. Bess confesses that she has promised to go with Crown when he comes back for her at cotton-picking time. She shrinks back in fear as a look of dark anger crosses Porgy's face. Grimly but calmly he says that he will never keep a woman against her will.

In a passionate refrain ("I wants to stay here") Bess pours out her love for Porgy and reveals her haunting terror of Crown. She is unworthy of Porgy's love, she cries—but when Crown touches her with his hot hands she cannot resist him. Distractedly she begs Porgy to save her from Crown's evil spell.

Porgy answers in a ringing refrain ("Bess, you don' need to be afraid") that with him by her side she will find happiness—and he himself will take care of Crown. Over a majestic accompaniment, the duet rises to a fiery climax.

As the two go inside, Clara and Maria enter. Clara apprehensively remarks about the ominous look of the sea, which, she says, seems to be waiting for the sound of the hurricane bell. Maria scoffs at the possibility of a hurricane but betrays a certain anxiety.

A restless sextuplet figure stirs in the orchestra like a rising storm wind. This figure gradually builds into a surging chromatic passage depicting the approach of the hurricane. People rush back and forth shouting warnings. From the distance comes the clangor of the hurricane bell. Clara, hysterically calling Jake's name, stumbles into the courtyard and falls in a faint. The orchestral accompaniment, simulating the howl of the storm, rises to a violent climax as the curtain falls.

[*Scene Four*] Serena's room. It is dawn of the following day, with the hurricane raging at its height. Huddled in groups, the terror-stricken Negroes pray for help and protection in the dramatic ensemble which continues throughout the scene. During the first part, a humming chorus takes the place of the orchestral accompaniment. The prayers intermingle in a religious frenzy, with each group making its individual appeal for mercy.

The singing intensifies as the storm wind howls louder. At times the voices sink almost to a whisper as the Negroes chant that the sky will fall, the sun will rise in the west and the moon will set in the sea. They shriek in fear as lightning blazes and thunder crashes, to the accompaniment of rampaging chromatics in the orchestra.

Clara, hugging her baby close, goes to a window and peeps through a crack in the shutter. There is a sudden, startled silence as she calmly begins singing a reprise of "Summertime." When the chanting chorus is resumed, there is a brief colloquy, like an obbligato, between Porgy and Bess. As though thinking aloud, Bess says that no one could live through a storm like this on Kittiwah Island. She looks at Porgy with an expression of profound relief and adds: "I guess you got me for keeps." Divining her meaning, Porgy replies: "Ain' I tell you dat?"

Another blaze of lightning is accompanied by a particularly violent outburst of the storm. In rising terror the Negroes chant: "Oh, dere's somebody knockin' at de do'!" In a momentarily amusing byplay, Mingo and Peter urge each other to open the door to prove no one is there—but neither has the courage. Maria finally goes toward it but stops in her tracks at the sound of loud knocking. Several men fling themselves against the shaking door as those in the room scream in terror. But in spite of their efforts the door is slowly pushed inward.

In the glare of the lightning, the towering figure of Crown looms on the threshold. He sees Bess and strides over to her; the other Negroes shrink back in fear. When he asks Bess why she has no greeting for "her man," she replies coldly that Porgy is her man now. She flares up when Crown answers with a cruelly insulting remark about Porgy. Now violently angry, Crown threatens Bess.

Over the theme of "Bess, you is my woman now," Bess repeats that she is Porgy's woman, which brings a sneering laugh from Crown. Lunging suddenly at her, he throws her to the floor. When Porgy crawls to her defense, Crown sends him sprawling. The protesting cries of the Negroes mingle with the increasing clamor of the storm.

Serena thrusts herself in front of Crown and warns that God will surely strike him dead. With a brazen laugh, Crown answers that he and God fought it out all the way back from Kittiwah—and now he and God are friends. At this point the Negroes again take up their chanting. Momentarily struck by a superstitious fear, Crown roars at them to be quiet. Over the wailing of the chorus he babbles that those in a hurry to meet Judgment Day need only step outside into the hurricane. He blasphemously calls on God to laugh with him at these cringing mortals.

Then in insolent defiance he bursts into an earthy ditty in exuberant jazz tempo: "A red-headed woman make a choo-choo jump its track." As though to counter its vulgarity, the shocked Negroes sing a choralelike chant: "Lord save us, don't listen to that Crown." In an ironic obbligato, Crown reprises the song, its jazz beat jarring against the solemn rhythm of the prayer.

The final notes are cut off abruptly by a scream from Clara, who is standing at the window. Bess, looking out, cries that Jake's boat is floating upside down in the river. Clara, in wild panic, pushes her baby into Bess's arms and rushes out into the storm. Bess calls for a man to go to Clara's aid, but no one stirs. Crown, making the most of the situation, sardonically asks Porgy why he does not answer when a woman calls. Porgy glares at him in helpless fury.

Shouting that he will get Clara and then come back and get Bess, Crown swaggers to the door. As he opens it, the howling wind blows out the lamp. In the darkness the terrified Negroes again sing the prayer which opened the scene: "Oh, Doctor Jesus!" It is sung to the accompaniment of an undulating sextuplet figure over an insistently repeated theme in the bass. The prayer continues to its conclusion after the curtain slowly falls.

## ACT THREE

[*Scene One*] Catfish Row, the next night. Again the Negroes are gathered to mourn one of their number—this time it is Jake, who was lost in the hurricane. In one of the most beautiful numbers in the opera, "Clara, don't you be down-hearted," they offer their comfort to the grief-stricken widow.

As the singing softly continues, the scene changes to Maria's shop where she is seen at her work. Sporting Life appears on the street outside, listens to the singing, then bursts into a harsh, sneering laugh. Maria upbraids him furiously for mocking those who are grieving for their dead. In quasi-recitative, there is a sharp exchange between the two. Why mourn over a man who is dead, Sporting Life remarks insolently, when there are plenty of men left living who like pretty women? Maria, intuitively aware that he is thinking of Bess, reminds him that the woman he himself has in mind already has her man. Two men, Sporting Life observes meaningfully. This remark puzzles Maria, who believes Crown is dead. When a woman has two men, Sporting Life goes on, there is likely to be a "carvin'," with the police picking up the pieces. Maria turns away in disgust; the peddler strolls off toward the iron gate at the end of the street.

A moment later Bess appears at the window of Porgy's room with Clara's baby in her arms. As she sings a reprise of "Summertime," the mourners, each carrying a lantern, come out of Clara's house and go to their own homes. The action which now follows takes place during a long orchestral interlude dominated by an ominous quadruplet figure in the bass.

Crown suddenly appears at the iron gate, drops to his hands and knees and begins crawling stealthily toward Porgy's door. There, above him, the shutter opens slowly. A hand holding a long knife emerges, then plunges the knife into Crown's back. The knife is withdrawn and hurled to the ground. Crown in his agony writhes almost to his feet. Porgy leans from the window, closes his hands around Crown's throat and holds him until he stops struggling. In one violent movement, Porgy hurls his adversary's body to the ground. With a ferocious laugh of triumph, Porgy screams: "Bess, you got a man now, you got Porgy!" The curtain falls to a thunderous phrase in the orchestra.

[*Scene Two*] Catfish Row, the next afternoon. The scene opens with an orchestral interlude marked by a nervously undulating quadruplet figure and a distorted fragment of the "Summertime" theme. The first half of this scene is in spoken dialogue and recitative.

A detective and a coroner come to Catfish Row to question Serena about the murder of Crown. Abetted by Annie and another neighbor woman, Serena pretends to be very sick. Appearing at the window with her head wrapped in a towel, and groaning with every step, she insists she has been in bed for three days, with the other women nursing her. She of course disclaims any knowledge of what happened, admitting only that Crown killed her husband two months ago. The women's solemn denials, sung in trio form with seriocomic effect, drive the detective into a fuming rage. Annie calmly closes the shutter in his face.

Balked and exasperated, the detective snarls that he nevertheless will find a witness for the coroner's inquest. He strides to Porgy's door, viciously kicks it open and bellows an order to come out. To the accompaniment of the syncopated theme heard at the end of the duet sung by Porgy and Bess in Act Two, Scene One, Bess helps Porgy to the doorstep, then stands beside him with the baby in her arms. Sporting Life glides in unobserved and stands listening.

The coroner, with a show of friendliness, begins to question Porgy about Crown. On his guard, the cripple pretends he has difficulty remembering the man. Then he is told he is being called as a witness to identify the body. Recoiling in abject terror, Porgy begs to be spared the ordeal, but the officers threaten him with jail if he refuses to go. They leave to bring policemen to assist in the proceedings.

Sporting Life walks over to Porgy and Bess, standing paralyzed with fright. Steadying herself, Bess advises Porgy to shut his eyes and only pretend to look at the body. Thereupon Sporting Life venomously remarks that when a murderer is forced to look at the body of his victim, the victim's wounds will begin to bleed. And that, he adds maliciously as Porgy screams in terror, is how the cops find the killer.

At that moment the policemen arrive. They seize Porgy and drag him away through the iron gate as he hysterically protests that no one can make him look at Crown's face. Bess cries out in despair while Sporting Life laughs sardonically. With vicious relish he tells her that, far from being merely a witness, Porgy will be locked up in jail—and probably will be hanged for Crown's murder.

Bess, now completely demoralized, is an easy prey for the dope peddler. He inveigles her into taking some of the white powder.

Her senses numbed, she listens as though hypnotized as he describes how he will take her to New York and show her the exciting life of the big city. In the opera's famous blues number, "There's a boat dat's leavin' soon for New York," he urges her to come with him. He promises to buy her a mansion on upper Fifth Avenue, to dress her in the latest Paris styles, and then go "struttin' through Harlem."

Suddenly coming to her senses, Bess turns on Sporting Life in furious denunication and orders him away. Instead of going he holds out a second packet of dope toward her. As the "Summertime" theme sounds in the orchestra, she knocks the powder out of his hand. With a shrug, he murmurs, in a phrase from "It ain't necessarily so," that he will leave the second "shot" where she can find it. Bess stares at it for a moment, then abruptly turns into the room and slams the door. Sporting Life, with an evil smile, lights a cigarette and walks away. As the curtain falls, the orchestra states the theme of his blues number.

[*Scene Three*] Catfish Row, a week later. The scene opens with an orchestral interlude descriptive of another day in Catfish Row. A young man lies asleep in a doorway, a street sweeper appears, then two workmen pass by. More people gradually appear, and a choral refrain develops as they greet each other ("Good mornin', sistuh, good mornin', brudder"). Children dance by to a carefree waltz tune ("Sure to go to Heaven").

At the end of the chorus the clang of the patrol wagon is heard in the distance. Mingo runs toward the iron gate shouting that Porgy has come home. The news of his arrival has a strange effect upon the people: Instead of rushing to greet him, they gather in small groups and look apprehensively toward the gate. When he finally enters, they make an obvious effort to bid him a warm welcome. As the syncopated theme of the duet in Act Two again is heard, Porgy makes his way to one of Maria's tables and sits down.

Delighted at being the center of attraction, Porgy begins telling how he outwitted the police by keeping his eyes shut when he was told to look at Crown's body. He cautions his neighbors not to let Bess know he has returned, because he has a surprise for her. Mingo, Peter and several others surreptitiously try to leave as Porgy happily distributes the presents he has brought to celebrate his return: a mouth organ for Scipio, a feather-trimmed hat for Lily, and finally a red dress for Bess. But now he begins to notice that his friends are leaving. To win their attention, he launches into the story of how he concealed his dice in his mouth, lured the other inmates of the jail into a crap game and won all their money.

When the story seems to fail to impress his listeners, Porgy impatiently calls for Bess, and becomes more and more mystified when there is no answer. He catches sight of Mingo trying to sneak away and upbraids him for his strange behavior. At the same time, he notices that almost all of his neighbors have left.

Suddenly he sees Serena sitting on his doorstep with a baby in her arms. Crawling over to her, he remarks slyly that he has been gone only a week—and here she is with a new baby. Serena, unable to face Porgy, turns to go inside. As she does so, Porgy catches sight of the baby's face and recognizes it as Bess's child—and his own.

Excited and alarmed, he calls Bess's name. When there is no answer, he turns to Maria—the only one left on the scene—and begs her to tell him what has happened. Maria answers evasively that Bess was not worthy of him. Porgy retorts that he is not interested in her opinions. In an ensuing refrain, "Oh, where's my Bess," he piteously begs for some word of her. This introduces a poignant trio sung by Maria, Porgy and Serena.

The women try to convince Porgy that Bess is a faithless creature who fell under the evil influence of Sporting Life, neglected her child and abandoned herself to dope and liquor. Deaf to their entreaties to forget her, Porgy repeats over and over that he cannot live without his Bess and implores the women to tell him where she has gone.

At the conclusion of the trio Lily appears—and it is she who finally tells him what has happened. Bess left Catfish Row, Lily tells Porgy, and Serena has taken her child to raise as her own. Overjoyed to know that Bess is alive, Porgy asks where she has gone. To New York, Lily says, "a thousand miles up north, pas' the custom house."

Suddenly resolved, Porgy calls for his goat and cart. All the neighbors crowd around, wondering what is happening. Ignoring the pleas of Serena and Maria to stay in Catfish Row with his friends, Porgy declares that he is going to "Noo York" because he must be with his Bess. He stretches out his arms, and two men help him into his cart.

In an exultant refrain he sings, "I'm on my way to a Heavenly Lan'l" He is joined by the chorus in a triumphant affirmation of his love and faith. The orchestra majestically sounds the theme of "Bess, you is my woman now" as the curtain falls.

# Prince Igor

*by* ALEKSANDR PORFIREVITCH BORODIN

(1834–87)

*Libevetto by the Composer*

Based on *The Song of the Army of Igor,* a Russian poem dating from the fourteenth century

### CHARACTERS

| | |
|---|---|
| Igor Sviatoslavitch, Prince of Séversk | Baritone |
| Jaroslavna, his wife of his second marriage | Soprano |
| Vladimir Igorevitch, his son by his first marriage | Tenor |
| Prince Galitsky (Vladimir Jaroslavitch), brother of Jaroslavna | Bass |
| Kontchak } Khans of Polovtsy | Bass |
| Gzak | Bass |
| Kontchakovna, daughter of Kontchak | Alto |
| Ovlour, a Polovtsian convert to Christianity | Tenor |
| Skoula } goudok (or gudok) players | Bass |
| Eroshka | Tenor |
| Maid to Jaroslavna | Soprano |
| A young Polovtsian girl | Soprano |

Russian nobility, boyars, old men, Russian soldiers, dancing girls, the populace, Polovtsian khans, companions of Kontchakovna, slaves, prisoners, guards, Polovtsian soldiers

*Place:* Novgorod, in Russia, and the Tartar region in Central Asia

*Time:* 1185

*First performance:* Maryinsky Theater, St. Petersburg, November 4, 1890

*Original language:* Russian

---

This dramatic and colorful opera, so imbued with the spirit of ancient Russia, has a fantastic history. Borodin, a professor of chemistry and an eminent scientist in his own right, was equally renowned as a composer who is credited with writing the first Russian music of national character to be acclaimed outside his own country. He was one of the group known as the "Russian Five," or the "Mighty Five"—the others being Rimsky-Korsakov, Glazounov, Cui and Balakirev.

Although Borodin worked on *Prince Igor* for eighteen years, he left it uncompleted at the time of his death. His friends Nikolai Andreyevitch Rimsky-Korsakov and Alexandre Konstantinovitch Glazounov finished the work from his notes and sketches, and orchestrated the score. In fact, the overture and all of Act Three except the opening march were composed by Glazounov. But the themes at the core of the opera are Borodin's. To infuse it with the true Russian musical expression, he delved into Russian history and folk music. The idea had been suggested to him by Vladimir Vassilievitch Stassov, the Russian nationalist writer and critic.

The score is richly and vigorously melodic and especially overpowering in the great choruses. Outside Russia, the opera usually has been sung in Italian or French. *Prince Igor* is famous for its *Polovtsian Dances,* a standard classical item in ballet and symphonic repertoire.

*Prince Igor* received its first production in the version completed and edited by Rimsky-Korsakov and Glazunov in Moscow on January 30, 1898. The opera was given its American premiere, in Italian, at the Metropolitan Opera House on December 30, 1890, with Frances Alda, Pasquale Amato and Adamo Didur heading the cast. It was presented during three successive seasons thereafter, then was dropped from the repertoire. Since that time it has rarely been presented in the United States as a complete opera, although the *Polovtsian Dances* are often programed. An interesting contemporary sidelight is that some of the themes from the opera were adapted for the score of the Broadway musical *Kismet,* presented in 1953.

*Prince Igor* was successfully revived, in an English translation, by the New York City Opera Company during its 1968 and 1969 seasons.

The long overture states the principal themes of the opera in elaborate symphonic style, with emphasis on the sensuous melodies of the romantic episodes.

## Prologue

A public square in front of the cathedral in the town of Poutivle. Soldiers and nobles of Prince Igor's court are about to start a campaign against the Khan Kontchak, of the Tartar tribe of Polovtsy. As a great throng of townspeople watches, Prince Igor, his wife, the Princess Jaroslavna, and boyars emerge from the cathedral in a solemn procession.

The crowd bursts into a mighty chorus praising the Prince for his exploits. They hail him as "the sun in all his glory" ("Al fulgente Sol, gloria"—"Au soleil brillant gloire"), and their acclamations include his son Vladimir along with his chief ministers. From the Don to the Danube, they sing, Prince Igor will declare the glory of Russia.

The Prince cries out that the hour of decision is at hand, but at that moment the sky suddenly is darkened by an eclipse of the sun. The people, staring at the sky in terror, cry out that this is a portent of disaster ("Esser potra presagio"—"c'est la présage fatal") and implore the Prince not to undertake the campaign.

But as the eclipse passes and the sky brightens again, Igor sings that whether the sign foretells good or evil no one can escape his fate ("Il ciel espri l'oscuro"—"Au ciel s'il passe"). Meanwhile, he will go forth to fight in a just cause. In a ringing phrase he commands his forces to prepare for battle, then leaves to review his troops. The Princess and the boyars follow.

Skoula and Eroshka, two rascally gudok players,[1] now come wandering in. In a brief recitative ("Amico: in andar"—"Amis, allez là bas") they sing that they are not interested in fighting—they would much rather spend their time in feasting and drinking. And so they have decided to stay at home in the service of Prince Galitsky. With that they toss their weapons aside and sneak away.

Following the review of his troops, Prince Igor returns with his wife. A duet ensues as he bids his followers to say farewell to their wives ("Salutsiam le spose"—"Appelez nos dames"). Jaroslavna begs him not to go because there have been omens of misfortune, but Igor replies that he must go for the sake of his honor and the fatherland.

A brief quartet passage follows as Vladimir and Prince Galitsky add their voices to sing that there is no turning back now. Igor asks Galitsky, as the Princess' brother, to watch over her during his absence. The treacherous Galitsky pretends to be grateful for

---

[1] These two comic characters are stock figures in traditional Russian opera. They have their counterparts, for example, in the drunken monks in *Boris Godunof*. The instrument the two play, the gudok, is an old Russian three-stringed viol resembling a cello.

the duty Igor has entrusted to him. Thus, he says, he will repay the Prince for having befriended him when he was banished from his home by his own father. Igor rather impatiently shrugs off Galitsky's fawning expressions of gratitude. Jaroslavna leaves with the other women of the court.

Igor turns to an old priest and asks his blessing. The priest complies, with the chorus of the people again hailing Prince Igor and Vladimir as heroes going into battle for the glory of Russia.

## ACT ONE

[*Scene One*] The court of Prince Galitsky's palace in Poutivle. The populace, led by Skoula and Eroshka, now are singing the praises of Galitsky. They also comment on the latest court gossip: Some gay young blades, with Galitsky's connivance, have carried off several girls for their own pleasures. To the huge amusement of the crowd, Eroshka imitates the voice of a girl begging the Prince to allow her to go home.

Galitsky himself strides in. He declares, in a brief recitative, that he does not share Igor's enthusiasm for the hard life of a soldier—his tastes run to merrymaking and a life of luxury. Then in a long and lusty aria ("Se di Poutivle principe"—"Si l'on me trouvait") he describes what life in court would be like if he ruled in Igor's place. It would be given over to pleasure—endless revelry with the most beautiful women in Russia always at hand. He climaxes the aria with a roaring invitation to drink.

A group interrupts to ask him what would happen to the Princess. She is much too serious-minded, Galitsky answers carelessly. She can go to a convent and pray for his sinful soul if she likes—just so long as she doesn't interfere with his carousing. The throng hails him delightedly.

As the Prince turns to go indoors he is met by a group of young girls who, in an agitated chorus ("Ah! che viltà"—"Ah! mécréants!"), tell the Prince that one of the girls has been abducted by his men. Galitsky casually assures them that she will be safe in his hands. When the girls beg him to have pity on the victim, the Prince angrily orders them to be off. They run away in terror. Skoula and Eroshka, watching, sardonically commend Galitsky for his firm hand with women.

These two court jesters now deliberately set out to incite the populace against Prince Igor and Jaroslavna. In recitative, they sing that the Princess has no authority in the palace now because Igor and all his palace guards are away at war. What is more, she is stingy with her wine and deserves no sympathy whatever. But with Galitsky, the two go on, things are different—he lets the wine flow like water. As if to prove their point, the servants roll out a huge cask of wine. The populace howls in glee.

Thereupon Skoula and Eroshka launch into a mock-serious song in praise of their generous patron, Prince Galitsky, "Chi cercasse un buon signore"—"Qui récherche un bon maître." They urge everyone to rally to the Prince, whose hospitality has no equal. To rouse the guillible populace still more, Skoula and Eroshka remind them how hard they are forced to labor under Igor's stern rule— joyless servitude from dawn till dusk. But under Galitsky's benevolent regime they will be asked to do nothing but sing and dance and play.

The brawling crowd responds, in the roaring chorus which closes the scene ("È ver! Si puo donargli"—"Que n'est-il donc dans Poutivle"), that Galitsky is the man they want as leader. Prince Igor and his army are far away and there is nothing more to fear. In frenzied excitement the people clamor for a meeting of the Parliament to overthrow Prince Igor. Then, shouting "Glory to Prince Galitsky," the crowd storms away.

Skoula and Eroshka, reeling drunk and holding each other up, bellow out a nonsensical phrase about "going home to mama" as they stagger in the wake of the mob.

[*Scene Two*] The palace apartment of the Princess Jaroslavna. She is sitting alone, lost in thought. In recitative ("Da lungo tempo Igor"—"Depuis longtemps Igor") she laments the long absence of Prince Igor and Vladimir. She is haunted by a premonition of disaster. This introduces the aria in which she recalls the happy days before Igor rode away to battle ("Or più non va, mio desiato Igor"—"Le temps n'est plus, où mon Igor"). She hears him calling to her in her dreams, only to awaken to anguish and bitter loneliness. As she ends the aria on a poignant phrase, she buries her face in her hands, abandoning herself to her grief.

Suddenly her old nurse bustles in with the news that a group of girls has come to ask the Princess' help. These are the girls who previously had appealed to Prince Galitsky. In an excited chorus ("Noi veniam ploranti"—"Nous venons, princesse") they entreat the Princess to intercede in behalf of the girl who has been abducted. Her captor, they wail, not only derided their pleas for mercy, but threatened them as well. The girls beg Jaroslavna to punish the betrayer.

When the Princess asks them to name him, the girls are thrown into confusion. They finally summon up enough courage to reply, and do so in a striking chorus, "Principessa, la voce trema"—"O maîtresse, c'est d'une voix." Sung *allegro vivo* in 5/4 tempo, it reflects their hysterical fear as they disclose that the lecherous villain is Prince Galitsky himself. He has wronged them many times before, they declare. Now that he has usurped Prince Igor's power, he shows himself as a cruel tyrant who oppresses the people and spends his time in wild carousing. His followers have plundered the land; not a woman is safe in the town.

Just as they finish their chorus of accusation, Galitsky himself walks in. Screaming in terror, the girls rush away. In recitative, over ominous chords in the orchestra, Jaroslavna asks Galitsky if what the girls have told her is true. A long and heated colloquy follows as the Prince insolently replies that this whole affair is none of her business. What he wants, he adds brusquely, he takes. With a sneer he remarks that in the palace it is customary to greet a guest with wine and good cheer. Obviously, he adds, the Princess' own brother is not as welcome as the stinking rabble who fill her ears with their wretched complaints.

Exasperated by his mockery, Jaroslavna reminds Galitsky that she still is Princess in this palace and warns him that he will answer for his shameless conduct when Igor returns. Galitsky coolly retorts that at the moment he is the ruling Prince at the behest of the people of Poutivle. With infuriating arrogance he advises his sister to keep this fact in mind and not risk his anger.

When the Princess turns on him wrathfully for threatening her, Galitsky changes his tactics. He was only joking, he tells her placatingly ("Ho detto per celiar"—"c'etait pour plaisanter"). He likes to see her angry, he says, because when she is angry she is more beautiful than ever. With deliberate malice he reminds her that she still is young and attractive, that her husband is far away and that living alone is dreary business. Does she not, he inquires, even have a secret lover to comfort her?

Goaded to fury by his insinuations, Jaroslavna storms that she has had enough of his insolence ("Dell'insolenze il colmo"—"Assez d'audace et d'insolence". As rightful Princess she has the power to send him under guard to his father in Galicia, where he will receive the punishment he deserves. Jaroslavna furiously commands Galitsky to release the girl he has abducted, then orders him out of her sight.

With a contemptuous shrug, the Prince promises to free the girl —and then look about for another who will be more agreeable. He leaves to the accompaniment of a descending chromatic passage. Jaroslavna, spent by her anger, murmurs that she has no more strength left to fight.

As she sits brooding, she suddenly is aroused by the entrance of the council of boyars. She welcomes them eagerly, but they bring only news of further misfortune. In a dramatic chorus ("Fa' cuor, Principessa"—"Ecoute, princesse") underscored by a somber, insistent rhythm, they sing that the fearsome Khan Gzak and his Tartar hordes have crossed the Russian frontier and are at the gates of Poutivle. But the worst news of all is that Prince Igor has been badly wounded and has been taken captive along with his brother and Vladimir, Igor's son. Overcome by horror, Jaroslavna falls in a faint. Quickly revived, she asks the boyars what now can be done to save the city from the invaders. In another vigorous refrain ("Maintes fois, lutant sans crainte"), sung mostly in unison, they assure the Princess that they have successfully defended Poutivle before and—with God's help—will do so again.

Deeply moved by their loyalty, Jaroslavna sings that the fighting spirit of the boyars has given her new hope. She bows low to them in a regal gesture of thanks.

Suddenly from outside comes the clangor of the alarm bell, followed by the terrified screams of women. As a powerful sustained chord reverberates in the orchestra, the boyars shout that the tocsin signals that the enemy is upon them ("Campane d'allarme son"—"La cloche d'alarme, hélas!"). This marks the beginning of the closing ensemble of the act.

As the red glow of the burning city begins to show through the windows of the palace, the voices of the boyars blend with those of the women in the streets below as they cry for help. Jaroslavna's voice soars above the chorus in an agonized plea to the Blessed Virgin to save the people from the wrath of an angry God who is punishing them for their sins. The boyars, drawing their swords, vow they will defend the Princess with their lives as the chorus surges to its climax. The curtain falls.

## ACT II

The camp of Khan Kontchak of the Polovtsy. It is evening. In a sinuous, flowing chorus ("O fior languente"—"O fleur fanée") a group of Tartar girls sings about the beauty of the night and how its enchantment will turn their lovers' thoughts to them.

Now follows the *Dance of the Polovtsian Maidens*, the first of the tribal dances which Khan Kontchak has arranged for the entertainment of his royal captives—Prince Igor, his brother and Vladimir.

After the dance, Kontchakovna, daughter of the Khan, sings a beautiful invocation to night ("O notte virginall"—"Oh! descends des cieux bleu"), accompanied by the chorus of girls. It is also an expression of passionate longing for her lover. Her song ends on a phrase in the lower reaches of the contralto register, with the music dying gently away.

The mood of the scene abruptly changes as the Russian prisoners and their guards are seen approaching in the background. They are greeted warmly by Kontchakovna and the girls, who offer them food and wine. The prisoners thank them in a brief chorus ("Que Dieu donne aux belles filles"). They then go on their way and the women also leave the scene. The Polovtsian patrol passes by on its rounds of the camp. As the guards move on, the renegade Ovlour[2] enters to take his post standing guard.

Then to the accompaniment of quiet, sustained chords in the orchestra, Vladimir enters. In recitative ("Fugge fra brividi il Sol" —"Lentement baissa le jour") he muses that, with the sunset, the steppe is enveloped in mysterious shadows. The warm south wind stirs him to thoughts of Kontchakovna. He gives voice to his passionate longing in the ensuing cavatina ("Ah, vien, rispondi al mio sospir"—"Ah, viens, réponds au tendre appel"), one of the finest numbers in the opera. In its lyrical concluding phrase, ending on an octave interval, Vladimir entreats his beloved to come to his arms.

As an agitated theme stirs in the orchestra, Kontchakovna emerges from her tent and rushes to Vladimir's embrace. A rapturous love duet follows ("Si: io t'adoro"—"Quel amour égale"). But at its conclusion, on a long, sustained chord, the romantic mood is suddenly broken as Kontchakovna asks if Prince Igor will give his consent to their marriage. There is no hope of that, Vladimir answers ruefully, so long as he and his father remain captives. Kontchakovna assures him that her own father would have no objections to the union. Suddenly Vladimir warns that Igor is approaching. The lovers hastily separate and leave.

To the accompaniment of a somber phrase in the orchestra, Prince Igor enters. Brooding over his defeat and captivity ("Ohimè!

---

[2] A rather shadowy figure, whose identity is not too clearly established. As a Christianized Polovtsy—and thus a traitor to his Tartar tribe—he seeks to join the Russians. To that end, he puts himself at Igor's service and engineers the Prince's escape from Kontchak's camp.

Nel cor mi graverà"—"Hélas! mon âme est triste"), he is haunted by memories of the past and thinks of the fateful portent of the eclipse. In another of the opera's fine arias ("Ma pur lontano in gran miraggio"—"Et puis je vois dans un mirage"), Igor laments his disgrace. He thinks of his wife, waiting in vain for him. He cries out that if God will give him his freedom he will redeem his own honor and save Russia from the invader—for there still is time. But the aria ends on a note of hopelessness as Igor sings that there is no escape from the torment of his conscience.

As he stares at the dawn which now is beginning to brighten the sky, Ovlour approaches. Saying that the dawn is a symbol of a new life, he tells Igor he will help him escape—at this very moment a horse is saddled and waiting. The Prince scorns the offer. He thanks Ovlour for his loyalty but rejects the idea out of hand. Taken aback by Igor's angry refusal, the renegade leaves.

A moment later Kontchak strides in. A long colloquy follows. The Khan jovially asks Prince Igor why he is so sad ("E sempre il ciel ti guidi"—"Que le ciel te bénisse!"). When Igor replies that it is because he is a captive, Kontchak assures him that—far from being a prisoner—he is an honored guest. The Tartar adds that he respects bravery and courage on the field of battle; he admires Igor for these sterling qualities and would like nothing better than to be his friend and ally. Kontchak impulsively offers the Prince lavish gifts—his fastest horse, his most beautiful slave girls, priceless treasures—anything to make him happy.

Igor gravely thanks the Tartar for his generosity but tells him that he can never be happy while he is a prisoner. Thereupon Kontchak offers the Prince his freedom—if he will promise not to resume the war against the Polovtsy once he returns to his homeland.

To that, Igor promptly replies that he will make no such promise. He will fight Kontchak to the death . . . he will march into the Tartar country and dip water out of the River Don with his helmet. Kontchak, philosophically accepting the situation, commends Prince Igor on his frankness. He remarks, somewhat wistfully, that if they could be allies they would hunt together like two tigers, and their armies would be invincible. With that he invites Igor to enjoy the entertainment he has prepared.

At Kontchak's command, singers and dancers appear and perform the *Polovtsian Dances*. To a stirring choral accompaniment the dances rise to a pitch of wild, barbaric abandon. A sensuous chorus of young girls is followed by a dance of savage men, with its underlying rhythm of four sharply accented descending notes,

then by a movement of young men with bows and arrows symbolizing war games. A voluptuous dance follows to the accompaniment
of an insinuating oriental melody. The scene comes to a blazing
climax with a fanfare of trumpets and crashing of cymbals as all
onstage hail the victorious leader Khan Kontchak.

## ACT III

Before the rise of the curtain the *Polovtsian March* is played.
It begins quietly, then builds into a climax in a fanfare of trumpets.
The scene opens on the Polovtsy camp, where the tribesmen are
awaiting the arrival of the triumphant Khan Gzak and his army.
Soon the soldiers appear, some guarding Russian captives, others
carrying the booty of war. Khan Gzak and his officers ride in on
horseback and are greeted by Khan Kontchak. Prince Igor, Vladimir and the other Russian prisoners stand to one side, watching
the scene intently. All the men in the throng hail Khan Gzak in
a resounding chorus ("I trionfatori cinti"—"Nos guerriers vain-
queurs"). Kontchak follows with a vigorous aria ("La clava ancor
possente"—"Le glaive en main"). He exults in the victory over the
Russians. The warriors break in with shouts of acclaim. Kontchak
announces that a council of war will be held. He sings of the
burning of the villages, of the devastation of the land, where
now only wild beasts howl. Here mothers sorrow over their children
lost in the trackless steppe, where the scream of the eagle calls
the ravening beasts to their grisly banquet. This is sung to rising
and falling chromatic figures in the orchestra. Kontchak hails Gzak
as a hero, boastfully singing that both now rule the world. The
warriors respond with a fierce cry of acclamation.

To a fanfare of trumpets, Kontchak invites all to share the
spoils of war, then orders the most beautiful of the captive women
to be brought to his tent. He declares that a war council will
be held the next day to plan the campaign. The Tartars, in
a savage chorus ("Al gran consiglio"—"Au grand conseil"), hail
the prospect of another foray against the Russians and debate
whether to sack Kiev or Poltava.

Meanwhile, the Russian prisoners observe the scene in rising
anger at the bragging Polovtsy. In an ensuing ensemble, led by
Igor and Vladimir, they rage over the report that Poutivle has been
destroyed and their wives and children taken captive. The Russians
urge Prince Igor to accept Ovlour's help in trying to escape to
Russia, so that he can save the fatherland while there still is time.

To infuriate the prisoners still more, the Tartar guards burst into a chorus of praise of the two victorious khans, comparing them to the splendor of the sun and the moon ("Il vittorioso è pari al sol"—"Kontchâk est semble au soleil!"). As the Russians angrily withdraw to their tents, the guards call for kumiss,[3] then begin drinking and dancing. The scene climaxes in a drunken orgy which leaves most of the guards sprawled asleep on the ground.

As darkness falls, Ovlour cautiously makes his way to Prince Igor's tent and calls to him softly. In quasi-recitative he discloses the plan for escape. The guards are dead drunk, he reports, and now the Prince and Vladimir can safely make their way to the river. At the signal, a whistle, they are to swim across to the other side, where horses are saddled and waiting. The Prince says he is ready to go. Ovlour hurries away.

A moment later Kontchakovna rushes to Vladimir's tent and calls out his name. An impassioned duet ensues ("L'amor tuo si dissolve?"—"L'amour fut éphémere?") as Kontchakovna asks Vladimir if it is true that he is deserting her now. She knows of his plan to escape but desperately implores him not to leave her. She will not even ask to be his bride, she sings, and would be happy to be his slave. Vladimir sorrowfully replies that, despite his love for her, his first duty is to his country. As he sings farewell, his father storms out of his tent.

A stormy trio follows. Igor angrily asks Vladimir if he intends to throw his lot with the Polovtsy and thus betray his country. Kontchakovna continues her entreaties, while Vladimir cries that he lacks the strength to resist her love. Suddenly Igor hears Ovlour's whistle and tries to drag Vladimir away. Kontchakovna holds him in her embrace; Vladimir begs his father to allow him one last kiss of farewell. Igor vainly tries to tear him from Kontchakovna's arms, then dashes away.

Kontchakovna, screaming that she will sound the alarm, strikes furiously on a sheet of iron used as an alarm bell. As the Polovtsy rush in from all sides she tells them that Prince Igor has escaped with the help of the traitorous Ovlour. Roaring in fury, some of the Tartars dash away in pursuit, while others shout that Vladimir must be executed on the spot. Kontchakovna throws herself in front of him, saying she will die with him. The Tartars retreat before her defiance. The pursuers return to report that the River Don is rising so fast that they cannot cross to follow the fugitives.

At that point, Khan Kontchak and the other chieftains stride

---

[3] A drink made from fermented camel's milk.

in. He is surprised to see his daughter and Vladimir. The Tartars, threatening to close in on Vladimir, tell Kontchak about Igor's escape and Ovlour's treachery. Kontchak sternly orders that Vladimir is not to be harmed. Then in calm but impressive phrases he declares that the fugitive Prince is a respected foe and a brave man who has done exactly what the Khan himself would do in the same situation. Then he adds harshly: for the guards, death; Vladimir is to live.

For a moment the other chieftains stare at him in consternation, then burst into a chorus of angry protest ("È pronto ognun ad obbedir"—"A t'obéir chacun est prêt"). They are willing to follow his leadership in battle, they sing, but this prisoner is another matter. Though the old "falcon" has flown home, the young one still is in their grasp—a prime target for an arrow. The chieftains then demand that all the Russians be slain before they too escape. Kontchak imperturbably replies that now they have the young falcon they will keep him "chained"—with a mate.

Turning to Vladimir, Kontchak presents Kontchakovna to him as his bride ("Si tu di mia famiglia"—"Soi donc de ma famille") —now he no longer is an enemy but a dear son-in-law. Then to the chieftains he proclaims: "Tomorrow we march on Russia!" All the Tartars shout their approval as the curtain falls.

## ACT IV

A square in Poutivle adjacent to the city wall. On a terrace, Jaroslavna stands alone. It is dawn. She pours out her anguish and longing in the great aria known as "Jaroslavna's Lament" ("Udirà lo sposo diletto"—"Dans le douleur est mon pauvre coeur"). It is based on the same theme heard in Act II as the captive Prince Igor expressed his longing for his wife. She sings that she longs to fly like a bird to the banks of the Don so that she could bathe her husband's wounds. She invokes the aid of the wind that roars across the steppe, the mighty River Dnieper and the sun itself, pleading for the return of her beloved Prince Igor. The aria concludes with a cry of despair. Jaroslavna remains staring over the ramparts.

A crowd of villagers passes. In a mournful chorus ("Qual fragor selvaggio"—"Est-ce un vent d'orage") they sing that it was not the storm nor the wolves that laid their town in ruins—the destroyer was Khan Gzak. The voices die away in an unaccompanied phrase as the crowd straggles out of sight.

In quasi-recitative, Jaroslavna reflects on the desolate landscape

ravaged by the Polovtsy. Suddenly she catches sight of two horse-
men in the distance. An insistent rhythm in the orchestra, gradually
increasing in intensity, underscores her rising excitement as she
describes the two coming closer: One is dressed like a Polovtsy,
the other has the bearing of a noble Russian. Then at last she
discerns that the riders are Prince Igor and Ovlour. Jaroslavna
greets her husband with a shout of joy and the two rush into
each other's arms. Then follows the rapturous love duet, "È ver,
non à illusion la tua"—"J'ai cru rêver! Mon Dieu, merci," one of
the most beautiful numbers in the opera. Curiously, at the conclusion of the duet, the romantic sentiments give way to a warlike
mood as Igor and Jaroslavna vow death to the khans. Gazing fondly
into each other's eyes, they walk slowly to the entrance of the
citadel.

Just before they enter, Eroshka and Skoula wander in unsteadily,
both half drunk. To the accompaniment of their gudoks, they
launch into an amusing duet ("Or fiammegia il sole"—"Le soleil
rayonne!"). Unaware of the Prince and the Princess, they comment
sardonically on Igor's heroic "exploits."

Now that a new "sun" (Prince Galitsky) is beaming upon the
town, they bellow, there is no need to weep for Prince Igor, who
is far away as a prisoner of Khan Kontchak. Rather, weep for the
brave Russian soldiers whom Igor led to their doom. With Russian
gold, this great Prince built bridges that never were crossed. The
flooded River Kayala carried away one bridge, and with it Igor's
army—and Igor's glory. Now from the Danube to the sea the
Russian people curse the name of Prince Igor.

But as the two are bawling out the end of their song, they
catch sight of Prince Igor and Jaroslavna at the door of the citadel.
Clutching each other in terror, they babble that now they certainly
will be beheaded, executed, drawn and quartered. In drunken
solemnity they ponder the situation—the matter, they agree, requires great cunning. Suddenly they have an inspiration: They
will ring the town alarm bell in the nearby tower, call all the
people together and be the first to announce that the glorious
Prince Igor has returned home.

This they promptly do. The townspeople crowd excitedly into
the square, asking the reason for the alarm. When Skoula and
Eroshka shout that the "Prince" has arrived, the people angrily
denounce them as drunken scoundrels hand in glove with a traitor.
As the crowd is about to close in on them, Skoula points to the
citadel shouting: "There is Igor, son of Sviatoslav, and the Polovtsy
who brought him home!"

The throng rushes toward Igor and Jaroslavna, who now come forward followed by the boyars and the elder statesmen of the Kremlin. The people hail them in the thunderous closing chorus of the opera, "Placa alfin la tetra sorte"—"Le ciel calme enfin nos peine." The curtain falls.

# I Puritani
## (*I Puritani di Scozia—The Puritans of Scotland*)
### *by* VINCENZO BELLINI
### (1801–35)

### *Libretto by*
#### COUNT CARLO PEPOLI

After the play *Têtes Rondes et Cavaliers* (*Roundheads and Cavaliers*), by François Ancelot and Xavier-Boniface Saintine. In its general outline, the plot is based on *Old Mortality*, by Sir Walter Scott.

#### CHARACTERS
*(Italian version of English names as used by Bellini)*

| | |
|---|---|
| Lord Gualtiero Valton (Walter Walton), Puritan Governor General of Plymouth | Bass |
| Sir Giorgio Valton, Puritan, his brother | Bass |
| Elvira Valton, Gualtiero's daughter | Soprano |
| Sir Riccardo Forto (Forth), Puritan, Elvira's suitor | Baritone |
| Sir Bruno Robertson (Benno Robertson), Puritan official | Tenor |
| Enrichetta di Francia (Henrietta of France), Stuart Queen, widow of Charles the First | Soprano |
| Lord Arturo Talbo (Talbot), Stuart Cavalier | Tenor |

Soldiers of Oliver Cromwell, men-at-arms of Lord Arturo, ladies-in-waiting, lords and ladies of the court, heralds, pages, servants, villagers.

*Place:* Plymouth, England
*Time:* The 1650s, during the English wars between Oliver Cromwell and the Stuarts
*First Performance:* Théâtre-Italien, Paris, January 25, 1835
*Original language:* Italian

---

Although burdened by an implausible and rather ridiculous libretto, *I Puritani*, Bellini's tenth and last opera, contains some of his finest music. His ingratiating melodies, with their glittering coloratura embellishments, stamped him as a master of the great *bel canto* operatic writing of the seventeenth century and a peer of Rossini and Donizetti.

At its premiere the opera was a sensational success and subsequently was heard on stages all over the world. The cast was headed by four of the most renowned singers in operatic history: Giulia Grisi (Elvira), Giovanni Battista Rubini (Arturo), Antonio Tamburini (Riccardo) and Luigi Lablache (Giorgio). These four singers later toured together for many years, billed as the *I Puritani Quartet*.

It was as Elvira that Marcella Sembrich made her debut (in her first role on any stage) in Athens on June 7, 1877. She also sang the role in the first performance of *I Puritani* at the Metropolitan, on October 29, 1883. It was not given there again until February 18, 1918—with Giuseppe De Luca as Riccardo—then disappeared from the repertoire after five performances.

The opera next appeared in America on October 3, 1955, when Maria Callas sang Elvira at the Chicago Lyric Theater with Giuseppe Di Stefano, Ettore Bastianini and Nicola Rossi-Lemeni. On May 24, 1960, Joan Sutherland made a sensational success as Elvira in a revival of the opera at the Glyndebourne Festival. The inclusion of *I Puritani* arias in the concert programs of Miss Sutherland and Miss Callas very probably has been responsible for the revival of interest in the virtually lost art of *bel canto* singing.

Inept libretto aside, *I Puritani* is rarely given today simply because it is beyond the capabilities of most singers. It requires coloratura singing not only by the sopranos but by the baritones as well—not to mention a tenor role which soars to two high Ds and three high Fs above high C.

Bellini's career was tragically cut short when he was in his thirty-fourth year and at the height of his creative powers. A few days before the performance of *I Puritani* which was to open the 1835 season at the Théâtre-Italien, the composer—who had remained in Paris since the premiere—was stricken with intestinal fever. He died in the Paris suburb of Puteaux on September 24, 1835.

It is said that during the entire performance everyone in the opera house—performers, instrumentalists and audience—wept with grief. Afterward, the cast and musicians joined in a great requiem mass directed by Rossini and Cherubini at the Church of the Invalides.

There is a brief introduction which opens with a fanfare, then leads into a plaintive, flowing melody expressive of the romantic elements of the opera.

## ACT ONE

The curtain rises on a seventeenth-century castle, bristling with fortifications, in Plymouth, England.[1] Its towers are silhouetted against the early morning sky. Bruno and a company of Cromwell's soldiers are discovered; they stir into activity as a trumpet sounds. In a chorus ("Quanto la tromba squilla") they sing that the trumpet sounds the call to the battle in which they will annihilate the proud Stuarts.

Then, to the sound of organ music from inside the castle, Bruno bids the warriors sing a morning hymn of praise to the Creator. Kneeling, the Puritans join in a moving and dignified anthem: "La luna, il sol, le stelle." It dies away in a phrase of quiet reverence.

The mood of the scene suddenly changes as the villagers crowd in with a gay chorus hailing Elvira on the day of her betrothal ("Garzon, che mira Elvira"). They bring the chorus to a rousing finish, then move from the scene with the soldiers, leaving Bruno standing alone.

A moment later Riccardo enters, and dialogue in recitative follows. Riccardo says despondently that these nuptial choruses are funeral dirges to his ears because he has lost Elvira. Her father, he tells Bruno, had promised him Elvira's hand, but when he arrived at the castle with his troops he learned that she is in love with the hated Stuart Cavalier Arturo Talbo. Her father, Riccardo fumes, can do nothing to change her heart. Bruno advises him to forget his disappointment by devoting his life to the service of his country.

But Riccardo, inconsolable, expresses his despair in a melodramatic aria, "Ah, per sempre io te perdei." He laments that he has lost Elvira forever and that nothing is left him but oblivion. The aria illustrates the vocal agility demanded of male as well as female singers in this opera. As Bruno vainly tries to turn Riccardo's thoughts to patriotism, the disgruntled suitor bids farewell to his dreams of bliss ("Bel sogno beato d'amore e contento").

The scene changes to Elvira's apartment in the castle, where she is seen in conversation with Sir Giorgio, her uncle—whom she

[1] For reasons of his own, the librettist, Pepoli, located Plymouth, which is several hundred miles from the Scottish border, in Scotland.

affectionately calls her "second father." In recitative, Giorgio tells her how happy he is that today she is to be a bride.

Thinking he means she will marry Riccardo, Elvira protests in alarm and dismay that she will never be a bride. In an ensuing aria ("Sai com'arde in petto mio") she declares that if she is dragged to the altar she will die of grief.

Thereupon Giorgio informs her that the Cavalier she really loves is on his way to the castle. Elvira, scarcely able to believe this news, literally weeps for joy. A long duet follows ("Piangi, o figlia, sul mio seno") in which Giorgio explains how he persuaded Elvira's father to allow her to marry the man of her choice. He finally won Lord Valton's consent, Giorgio says, by warning him that if Elvira was forced to marry another, she would die ("se ad altre nozze andrà, misera perià!").

As Elvira fervently embraces her uncle, trumpets are heard outside. Giorgio says that Arturo and his soldiers have arrived. In a brief choral phrase the soldiers announce Arturo Talbo, and the people of the castle respond with a greeting. In a ringing duet ("A quel nome" . . . "A quel suono") Elvira and her uncle express their mutual joy over the fortunate turn of events. In a choral accompaniment the people pay homage to the brave Cavalier.

The next scene takes place in the great hall of the castle. To the accompaniment of a spirited introduction in 6/8 tempo, Lord Arturo enters from one side accompanied by esquires and pages carrying nuptial gifts. From the other side come Elvira, Lord Valton and Sir Giorgio. They are followed by ladies and gentlemen of the court, and peasants carrying garlands of flowers. The company salutes the forthcoming nuptials in a majestic chorus, "Ad Arturo, A Elvira! Onor!"

In an interlude, Arturo steps forward with a gallant tribute to his bride ("A te, o cara, amor talora"). She responds with an avowal of her love. As the ensemble builds to its fiery climax the voices of the lovers soar above in an obbligato of brilliant coloratura phrases.

All then leave the hall, with only the principals remaining. In an aside to Bruno, Lord Valton reminds him of the order he has given: Anyone who leaves the castle without Valton's permission will be put to death. Dialogue in recitative follows. Turning to the lovers, Lord Valton tells them they must go to the altar without him. He then gives Arturo a note admitting him to the nuptial temple and asks Giorgio to accompany the bridal pair at the ceremony.

At that moment Enrichetta enters escorted by Bruno. Valton tells her she has been called before the English Parliament in London. Enrichetta asks him why she must go. Evasively, Valton replies that he must do his duty. Arturo, aside, asks Giorgio if this woman is an adherent of the Stuarts ("E de' Stuardi amica?"). Giorgio explains that she has been Valton's prisoner for many months and is believed to be a spy for the Stuarts.

Exclaiming that this summons means her doom, Arturo gives her a pitying look. Enrichetta gazes at him beseechingly. Valton bids Elvira to prepare for her nuptials, orders Bruno to saddle his horse, then tells Enrichetta that they must leave at once. Before he goes he gives his paternal blessing to Elvira and Arturo. He exits with the others, leaving Enrichetta and Arturo alone.

Turning to Enrichetta, Arturo urges her to put her trust in him and assures her that he will help her in every possible way. When he asks the reason for her fear she replies that her death now is only a matter of time. Arturo shudders. When Enrichetta asks him why, he answers that he trembles not only for her—whoever she may be—but for himself as well. Moreover, he is haunted by the memory of his father, who died for his loyalty to the Stuarts. But no matter who she is, Arturo goes on, he is determined to save her.

It is too late, Enrichetta says, then identifies herself as the daughter of King Henry and the wife of Charles the First of France. Like them, her fate will be the headman's ax ("È tarde, figlia Enrico, a Carlo sposa"). Thunderstruck, Arturo kneels in homage to his Queen.

This colloquy leads into a dramatic duet. Arturo vehemently declares he will help her escape or die in the attempt. Enrichetta begs him not to risk his life for her, but to think of Elvira, who even now is waiting for him at the altar. Arturo implores her not to mention the name of his beloved lest the thought of her swerve him from his purpose ("Non parlar di lei che adoro"). Enrichetta desperately insists that she is resigned to her fate—her life is over, but his is still before him. Arturo cries that he will save his Queen or die with the name of his beloved on his lips. He ends his declaration on a ringing phrase of defiance. At that instant, in startling contrast to the grim mood of the scene, Elvira's voice is heard in a joyous coloratura phrase expressive of her happiness.

A moment later she appears with Giorgio. Crowned with a wreath of roses and wearing a pearl necklace, she carries the wedding veil given her by Arturo. In a lilting refrain ("Son vergine vezzosa") she sings about her bridal finery. Looking on admiringly, Enrichetta, Arturo and Giorgio comment on her child-like joy over being a bride. Their voices blend with hers in a quartet ("Semiro il suo candore") which continues until the end of the scene.

During an interlude, Elvira—like a child playing a game—asks Enrichetta if she may put the wedding veil on her head "in a new fashion" ("il velo in foggia nuova"). Amused, Enrichetta consents. In a continuation of the quartet, Elvira gleefully admires the effect; Giorgio and Arturo asks Enrichetta to indulge Elvira's childish whim; Enrichetta herself comments that the veil will hide the sorrow in her face.

Lord Valton and his retinue interrupt the ensemble briefly to remind Elvira that the hour of the wedding is drawing near. At the conclusion of the quartet, Elvira leaves with her father, after being assured by the other three that Arturo will place the wedding veil on her own head at the proper time. Giorgio follows her, and Enrichetta and Arturo again are left alone.

As Arturo, looking around cautiously, takes from his belt the note given him previously by Lord Valton, Enrichetta, in recitative, observes that the white veil should adorn the head of a bride-to-be—but not her own ("Sulla verginea testa"). She is about to take it off when Arturo restrains her. It is heaven's will, he tells her, that the veil was placed upon her head. It will conceal her face, and thus when they leave the castle it will deceive the sentry into thinking that Arturo is escorting his bride.

Just as Arturo is about to lead her away, Riccardo appears and with drawn sword bars his path. In bitter anger, Riccardo—of course mistaking the veiled Enrichetta for Elvira—accuses Arturo of trying to steal his promised bride ("Ferma, invan rapir pretendi"), then challenges him to fight. This marks the beginning of a tempestuous musical dialogue—another example of the difficult coloratura parts Bellini wrote for male voices in the opera. Arturo draws his sword and accepts the challenge.

As the two adversaries are about to lunge at each other, En-richetta, imploring them not to sacrifice their lives for her sake, interposes herself between them. In so doing she disarranges the veil, revealing her face. Riccardo, recognizing her as the Queen, staggers back in surprise. Arturo sardonically dares him now to make good his challenge to fight ("Tua voce altera"). To Arturo's utter amazement, Riccardo replies that he will do nothing to prevent his leaving with the Queen.

There is a brief passage in quasi-recitative. Arturo, now losing all hope of marrying Elvira, swears he will always love her. Enrichetta wonders if her good fortune is a dream, and if now she can be reunited with her son. Riccardo, glaring at Arturo, gloats that his rival will suffer even more than he himself has suffered—he will lose his beloved and his country as well. In ironic contrast, a chorus behind the scenes hails the wedding day.

Arturo, about to rush away with Enrichetta, suddenly turns to Riccardo and asks if he will swear to say nothing until they are safely outside the castle walls. Riccardo swears to it. The other two then disappear. After a few moments Riccardo goes to an adjoining balcony overlooking the castle ramparts and watches the fugitives vanish into the distance.

Lord Valton, Sir Giorgio, Bruno, Elvira and the ladies of the wedding party now enter. Elvira, looking around anxiously, asks where Arturo is ("Dov'è Arturo?"), and her question is echoed by Valton, Giorgio and the court. This marks the beginning of the tempestuous ensemble which concludes the act.

As all stare at Riccardo in consternation, he breaks the news that Arturo and the royal prisoner have escaped. Pandemonium erupts as the alarm bell of the fortress clangs and cannon are fired off. Over a clamorous orchestral accompaniment, the men and women denounce the Cavalier bridegroom as a vile traitor ("Col vil cavaliero!").

Their outcries are suddenly hushed as Elvira totters forward, staring wildly around. Shocked out of her senses, she sings in disconnected phrases that Arturo's beloved wears a white veil . . . he calls her his bride and her name is Elvira ("La dama Arturo"). Then in anguished tones she asks: "But am I not Elvira?" There is a gasp of horror from the onlookers.

In the grip of her madness, Elvira imagines she sees Arturo. With passionate intensity she implores him to come to the temple where they will be united forever ("Oh, vieni al tempio, fedele Arturo"). She repeats her avowals over a choral accompaniment.

In mounting delirium she upbraids Arturo for his betrayal and wails that the flames of rage are devouring her heart ("Qual febbre vorace m'uccide"). Then, exhausted by her outburst, she stares with unseeing eyes as the Puritans thunder out a malediction against the traitorous fugitives ("Non casa, non spiaggia raccologa i fuggenti!"). May they be denied home and haven, and may they be accursed eternally in life and in death—"eterno sia il penar." On this phrase the ensemble comes to its blazing conclusion.

## ACT TWO

A large room in the castle, with side doors leading to Elvira's apartment and to other rooms. Villagers, Puritans and Bruno are gathered together discussing the misfortune which has befallen Elvira. A brief orchestral introduction states a melancholy theme which is taken up in a chorus of lamentation, "Piangon le ciglia, si spezza il cor." The villagers and Puritans sing that Elvira surely will die of unrequited love . . . she wanders over the castle grounds weeping and crying, "Pity! pity!"

Giorgio enters and all eagerly ask for news of Elvira. Sometimes she is sad, sometimes happy, Giorgio reports, and she seems to hover between reason and insanity. At the urging of his listeners, Giorgio, although protesting he is too grief-stricken to speak, describes Elvira's plight in the aria "Cinta di fiori e col bel crin disciolto." He tells how she wanders aimlessly about, wearing a chaplet of roses, her hair disheveled, repeating: "Where is Elvira?" Or, dressed in her wedding gown, she repeats her vows as though at the altar. At other times she sings sadly of love to the accompaniment of her harp, then in the agony of her grief she cries for death. The aria is sung to accompanying choral phrases as the listeners call down the avenging lightning of heaven upon Elvira's betrayer ("Si, cada il folgore sul traditor").

As the aria ends, Riccardo enters with a document and electrifies the company with the news that Arturo has been condemned to death by the English Parliament. The people express their satisfaction in a choral phrase. Riccardo continues reading the parliamentary decree to the effect that Lord Valton has been declared innocent of any conspiracy and that his honors will be restored to him. But what will honors mean to him, the people ask, when he finds that his beloved daughter is hopelessly insane?

At that, Riccardo asks Giorgio if there is any hope. In a recitative passage ("Medic'arte n'assicura") Giorgio explains that Elvira's physicians have declared that any sudden joy or sorrow might serve to shock the girl out of her madness. In a menacing phrase ("Qual mai merita, Arturo") the Puritans murmur that a dire fate surely awaits the culprit responsible for this debacle.

Riccardo steps forward and in continuing recitative ("In me duce premier, parla Cromvello") proclaims that in the name of Cromwell the Puritans must hunt down the traitor who has stained English ground with blood. And when he is brought to justice, there will be neither pity nor pardon for him. The Puritans and villagers rush away. Riccardo and Giorgio remain.

Suddenly they hear Elvira's voice. In a dolorous, wailing phrase ("O rendetemi la speme") she asks for the boon of hope or the release of death. A moment later she appears, and then follows the opera's famous Mad Scene—a dramatic and musical parallel to that in Donizetti's *Lucia di Lammermoor*.

Hopelessly out of her mind, Elvira recalls how her lover called to her "in his voice so soft and sweet ("Qui la voce sua soave") and swore eternal fidelity. But then he cruelly deserted her, and now she asks only for a ray of hope—or death. The phrase she sang just before she entered is heard here again. Looking at the two men with the vacant stare of the demented, Elvira identifies Giorgio as her father and Riccardo—much to his despair—as Arturo. When she takes his hand and gently asks him to come to the wedding he breaks into sobs. In a tender phrase ("Ah! se piangi ancor tu sai") she tries to comfort him.

Both men, shaken by her grief and confusion, vainly try to bring her to her senses. But, lost in her dream world, she implores Arturo to join her. In a refrain of passionate entreaty ("Vien, diletto, è in ciel la luna") she brings the scene to a close. The voices of Giorgio and Riccardo blend with hers as they express their pity and compassion. As the accompaniment dies into silence, Bruno appears and gently leads Elvira away.

Then, as a rhythmic, martial theme sounds in the orchestra, Giorgio grasps Riccardo's arm as though about to confide an important secret. With intense emphasis he tells him that he must save his rival's life. When Riccardo flatly refuses, Giorgio pointedly reminds him why it was that Arturo and his prisoner managed to escape—referrring, of course, to the fact that Riccardo himself made that escape possible. Bridling at this, Riccardo retorts that it is the English Parliament that has doomed Arturo ("Fu voler del Parlamento"). He himself, he adds, neither hates nor fears him —but die the traitor must.

Giorgio accuses him of acting out of jealousy and guilt ("Un geloso e reo tormento"). He warns Riccardo that if he dooms his rival, not one person but two will die. Then, Giorgio goes on in foreboding tones ("Se tra il bujo un fantasma vedrai"), the ghost of Elvira, accusing him of causing her death ("io son morte per te"), will hound him to his grave. And with her will be the avenging phantom of Arturo.

Partly out of supersitious fear, Riccardo's anger subsides somewhat. The two men, in effect, then strike a bargain: If Arturo is captured unarmed, Riccardo promises to spare his life; if he returns to give battle, Giorgio agrees to fight him to the death. And their own battle cry will be: "Country, victory and honor!" ("Patria, vittoria, onor!").

This climactic phrase brings the long colloquy to one of the opera's most famous numbers—the "Liberty Duet"—"Suoni la tromba" ("Let the trumpets sound"). Its theme brings to mind the chorus "D'immenso giubilo," the opening of Act Three of *Lucia di Lammermoor*.

In an exuberant, martial refrain, Giorgio and Riccardo sing of the glorious privilege of fighting for liberty and dying for one's country. When the trumpet sounds at dawn, they will sally forth to do battle with all perfidious tyrants and destroy their power forever. The two conclude the duet with a thunderous repetition of their battle cry.[2]

## ACT THREE

A garden and a grove of trees outside Elvira's apartment in the castle. Lights in the apartment shine through the windows. There is a long orchestral introduction with a dark, brooding theme welling up in the bass.

As it diminuendos into silence, Arturo rushes in crying that at last he is saved ("Son salvo"). He exults that he has outrun his pursuers. In recitative he expresses his happiness over having returned safely from exile to his beloved country ("Oh patria! Oh amore!"), where he can again embrace his adored bride-to-be.

Unseen by Arturo, Elvira, dressed in white, passes by the window of her apartment. A moment later she is heard singing a plaintive ballad ("A una fonte afflito") about a lonely troubadour sitting beside a fountain and pining for his love. In joyful surprise, Arturo exclaims that he hears his own love song, then eagerly calls Elvira's name. When there is no answer he himself takes up the ballad, hoping this will bring Elvira to his side.

But just as he concludes the aria he is startled by the sound of a drum and a babble of voices from beyond the castle walls. In a brief choral phrase ("Agli spaldi, alle torri andiam") Cromwell's

---

[2] In another version, Giorgio and Riccardo end the duet by repeating the terms of their bargain: If Arturo is defenseless, he will be pardoned; if he returns in arms, he must die.

soldiers call out that they will search for the fugitive near the ramparts.

In desperation Arturo is about to hide inside the castle, but then realizes that this might well put both Elvira and himself at the mercy of his pursuers. Instead, he decides to sing his troubadour song ("Corre a valle, corre a morte"), in the hope that it will awaken in Elvira the memory of their love and thus bring her to him.[3] This verse describes the suffering and loneliness of the exile.

As he ends the serenade, Elvira appears, walking as though in a dream. Still out of her mind, she piteously calls Arturo's name. He rushes forward and kneels at her feet. At that instant Elvira recovers her senses and recognizes him. Holding her in his arms, Arturo cries that now love has reunited them and there is nothing more to fear.

Then, singing that this reunion has banished all his sorrow ("Nel mirarti un solo instante"), Arturo begins the main section of the great duet which is one of the musical pinnacles of the opera. During its course Elvira asks Arturo—to his complete bewilderment—if the prisoner with whom he escaped is now his wife. He in turn asks if she does not realize that the prisoner was none other than the Stuart Queen—who would have died at the hands of the Puritans had he not helped her escape from the castle.

When the truth finally dawns upon Elvira ("Qual lume rapido"), she abandons herself to the rapture of being reunited with her lover. The two then repeat their avowals in the magnificent finale of the duet ("Star seco ognor"[4]).

But as the two stand clasped in each other's arms, the sound of drums again is heard—a sound which shocks Elvira back into temporary insanity. To Arturo's horror, she begins to murmur incoherently about trampling on the wedding veil. Collapsing at Arturo's feet, Elvira frantically entreats him not to desert her again for the woman with whom he fled ("no, colei più non t'avra"). Outside, the soldiers are heard in a triumphant shout of "England and Cromwell" ("Anglia, Cromvello!").

As Arturo distractedly tries to bring Elvira to her senses, Riccardo, Giorgio and Bruno, followed by soldiers and villagers,

[3] In another version this aria begins: "Cerca il sonno a notte scura."
[4] This phrase is sung by Arturo at the beginning of the refrain, which contains an F above high C. Elvira's answering refrain begins with "Caro, non ho parola," after which the two voices join.

burst upon the scene, with the soldiers savagely clamoring for Arturo's death ("Te alla morte condanno!").

Suddenly Elvira tears herself from Arturo's arms and staggers forward as though waking from a nightmare. The violence of the scene has produced still another shock which has restored her reason. Arturo strides to her side and in a simple yet majestic refrain ("Credeasi misera") sings that Elvira suffered because she believed he betrayed her. Now he will defy his enemies and die with her. This marks the beginning of the overpowering ensemble which concludes the opera. In a repetition of the refrain ("Qual mai funerea"), Elvira wonders what dreadful sound awoke her from her madness, and declares that she is ready to die with her lover.

As the ensemble gathers intensity, the Puritans rage that the traitor must die; the people express horror over the lovers' impending doom; Riccardo and Giorgio voice their pity for the hapless pair. Then, after clasping Elvira in a farewell embrace, Arturo suddenly whirls and faces his captors. In a reprise of the theme heard before he furiously denounces them for subjecting Elvira to this inhuman ordeal ("Arrestatevi—scostate!"). As for himself, he rages, let them do their worst. Over the chorus of soldiers shouting for vengeance, Arturo reiterates his denunciation in an obbligato which soars to a high C and beyond to two high Fs.

A blare of trumpets cuts through the uproar. Soldiers rush in and hand a message to Giorgio, who reads it with Riccardo. Together they announce that the Stuarts have been defeated, the captives have been pardoned and freedom once again reigns in England ("l'Anglia terra ha liberta"). Joyfully embracing, Elvira and Arturo join the throng in a final jubilant chorus in praise of love and victory. The curtain falls.

# The Rake's Progress
## (*Der Wüstling—Carriera d'un Libertino*)
### *by* IGOR STRAVINSKY
### (1882–1971)

### *Libretto by*
#### W. H. AUDEN and CHESTER KALLMAN

Suggested by a series of engravings by the eighteenth-century artist William Hogarth (1697–1764), who satirized the social customs of his day

#### CHARACTERS

| | |
|---|---|
| Trulove | Bass |
| Anne, his daughter | Soprano |
| Tom Rakewell | Tenor |
| Nick Shadow | Baritone |
| Mother Goose | Mezzo-soprano |
| Baba the Turk | Mezzo-soprano |
| Sellem, an auctioneer | Tenor |
| Keeper of the Madhouse | Bass |

Whores and Roaring Boys, servants, citizens, madmen

*Place:* England
*Time:* Eighteenth century
*First performance:* Teatro La Fenice, Venice, September 11, 1951
*Original language:* English

---

Igor Stravinsky was seventy years old when he completed *The Rake's Progress*, yet the work is anything but traditional in its harmonic structure or dramatic concept. It is true that the listener hears echoes of Mozart, Bellini, Rossini and other classical composers, but one soon becomes aware of subtle musical ironies.

An aria, for example, begins in conventional form, then imperceptibly changes its character as dissonances transform its harmonic structure. An eighteenth-century arioso is unexpectedly brought into the twentieth century through the medium of the atonal pattern of the accompaniment. At the same time there are emotional passages in which Stravinsky's astringent, complex harmonies give way to simple, unabashed melody. These contrasting musical forms give the opera a stimulating freshness and an element of surprise.

*The Rake* is the composer's fourth opera. In 1914 he wrote *Le Rossignol,* a three-act opera; in 1917 *Renard,* a satirical chamber opera; in 1921 *Mavra,* a Russo-Italian comic opera.

The first American performance of *The Rake* was given at the Metropolitan in English on February 14, 1953. Critical reaction was mixed, and after seven performances it was dropped from the repertoire. In Europe, however, it is a staple operatic item—most of the smaller houses in Europe have produced it since World War II. It was given by the Hamburg State Opera at the Metropolitan Opera House, Lincoln Center, on June 29, 1967, during the German company's visit to America. The production was staged by Gian-Carlo Menotti.

Derived from the engravings of eighteenth-century London life by Hogarth, the plot actually is a version of the Faustian legend. To the motley assemblage of characters depicted by Hogarth, the librettists Auden and Kallman added the Mephistophelean figure of Nick Shadow. He is the devil to whom Tom Rakewell sells his soul—but not with the legendary consequences. The devil fails to collect his fee when Tom, at the last moment, is redeemed by the love of Anne, the girl he rejected and deserted.

There is a brief prelude in waltz tempo, with trumpet passages in the manner of a fanfare.

## ACT ONE

[*Scene One*] The garden of Trulove's house in the country on a spring afternoon. The house is at right; a garden gate at the back. Downstage left is an arbor, where Anne and Tom Rakewell are seated.

In a lilting duet ("The woods are green") Anne and Tom sing of the magic of spring in the month of May, when the world is the special province of lovers. Trulove steals in and watches them unobserved. His voice blends with theirs in a trio as he expresses the hope that lovers' avowals will be more than empty promises ("O may a father's prudent fears"). He reflects that all too often we find out too late what really is in the hearts of others—and in

our own as well. He listens with paternal anxiety as Anne and
Tom, in the conclusion of their duet, pledge eternal fidelity.

Coming forward, Trulove tells Anne she is wanted in the
kitchen, then turns to talk to Tom. A brief scene in recitative
follows. Trulove informs Tom that, through a friend he has found
a bookkeeper's position for him in London. Tom assumes an air
of humble gratitude, but then says that he has other plans and
cannot accept the offer. When Trulove bridles somewhat at this,
Tom hastens to assure him that his daughter certainly will not
marry a poor man. She may marry a poor man, Trulove answers
pompously, so long as he is honest and not lazy. With that parting
shot he goes into the house. Tom looks after him with a sneer.

In an ensuing recitative ("Here I stand"), followed by an aria
("Since it is not by merit"), Tom expresses his cynical philosophy
of life. He has no intention of slaving away in a countinghouse
to pile up wealth for others. For his part, he agrees with the
learned doctors who assert that striving for good works is futile,
because one's achievements are foreordained. That being the case,
Tom reasons, he will put himself into the hands of his Fate.

He continues this line of thought in the aria. He is resolved
to trust to Fortune and live by his wits; the world is large and
his whole life is ahead of him. He ends his aria with a flippant
variation of the old adage: "Wishes, be horses; this beggar shall
ride!" Pacing back and forth, deep in thought, Tom makes a
wish for money.

Instantly, Nick Shadow materializes at the garden gate as an
insinuating glissando sounds in the orchestra. Tom turns with a
gasp of surprise as Nick speaks his name inquiringly. He identifies himself; Nick, with a courtly bow, does the same, adding
that he is the bearer of good news. It has to do with a long-
lost relative of Tom—an uncle. The news is so good, in fact,
that he should call his friends together to share it, Nick goes on.
Tom promptly hurries into the house to summon Anne and her
father. Nick unlatches the gate and strides into the garden.

When the others return, Nick discloses the reason for his visit
in a Bellinian aria of mocking elegance ("Fair lady, gracious
gentlemen"). Tom Rakewell, says Nick, had an uncle whom he
—Nick—served for many years. He left England to seek his fortune
in strange lands. Making money, in fact, was his sole aim in life.
But at the last, when he lay dying, he realized that all his gold
had bought him neither joy nor solace in his old age. He longed
to go back to England, where, he believed, his wealth could

bring happiness to a young man he vaguely remembered as his nephew.

Slyly pausing for effect, Nick announces that the benevolent uncle is dead. He himself has come to inform Tom Rakewell that this long-neglected relative remembered his kin on his deathbed—and Tom is now a rich man.

An exuberant quartet follows in a parody of the conventional operatic ensemble. It begins as Tom exults over the astounding success of his first wish ("I wished but once"). He thanks Nick profusely for his services. Shadow ironically thanks him in turn, and the phrase "be thanked" is taken up by Anne and Trulove to lead into the choralelike climax of the quartet. In a melodramatic refrain ("My Anne, behold") Anne and Tom rejoice in their good fortune.

Nick finally interrupts the happy proceedings by apologetically reminding Tom that the inheritance involves certain legal matters which must be attended to. In short, they must be off to London. That can wait, Tom murmurs, his head in the clouds. But Trulove and Anne urge him to settle the estate at once so that the marriage can be arranged. Tom thereupon agrees to go; Nick tells him a carriage is waiting down the road. Shadow leaves for a talk with Trulove while Anne and Tom bid each other farewell in a graceful *duettino* ("Farewell for now").

When Trulove and Nick reappear, Tom asks Shadow what his customary fee is for such valuable services. Then and there, Nick Shadow binds the unsuspecting Tom to a Mephistophelean contract: They will settle the account one year and a day from the present date for whatever sum Tom considers fair and just. Tom, of course, agrees.

In an ensuing refrain ("Dear Father Trulove") Tom assures his prospective father-in-law that he will send for him and Anne as soon as his affairs are settled. And then all London will be at Anne's feet. Trulove is pleased, but Anne seems suddenly apprehensive and turns away. Tom sings confidently that success comes to him who is clever enough to play the game and win. Anne wonders why she feels certain misgivings at this happy moment. Trulove fears that Tom's sudden good fortune only will encourage him in his sinful ways. These thoughts are voiced in a trio which brings the scene to a close. Anne, Tom and Trulove go toward the garden gate. Nick holds it open for them as they pass through, with Anne and her father singing a final "farewell." Alone, Nick Shadow turns to the audience with the phrase: "The progress of a rake begins."

[*Scene Two*] After a prelude dominated by harsh, agitated dissonances, the curtain rises on Mother Goose's brothel in London. Tom, Nick and Mother Goose are sitting at a table downstage drinking. Prominent backstage is a large cuckoo clock. Milling about are the whores and Roaring Boys, London's eighteenth-century hoodlums. In a two-part chorus ("With air commanding") in descriptively crude harmonies, the Roaring Boys boast of how they roam the streets at night unchallenged, stirring up trouble. The whores respond with a chorus acclaiming their own exploits in Cupid's campaigns. The two groups join in a lusty climax to sing a toast to Venus and Mars.

A scene in recitative follows. Nick asks Tom to explain to Mother Goose that he has been thoroughly schooled to enjoy the life of pleasure which now awaits him—this by way of proof that Nick has fulfilled his duties as Tom's "godfather." In a phrase sung on a single note, as though saying his catechism, Tom replies that he was told that his first duty is to himself, and that he must ignore the precepts of every teacher except Nature. Mother Goose and Nick comment approvingly.

Plying him with wine, the two ask him to define Beauty, Pleasure and Love. In lyrical phrases, Tom recites that Beauty is something which Youth owns, but money can buy. It has one flaw: It dies. Pleasure is the stuff of dreams—it can be anything from a hat to a cat. Then over a sinuous figure in the orchestra, he attempts to define Love. Leaping to his feet, he exclaims that the very word fills him with terror. As Mother Goose refills his wineglass, the cuckoo clock sounds the hour of one. Tom cries out that he must go before it is too late. Thereupon Nick makes a commanding gesture toward the clock, which turns backward and coos the hour of twelve in exact synchronization with the notes of a descending figure in the orchestra. Nick casually assures Tom that there is plenty of time for pleasure—he may repent at leisure.

Tom sits down and wildly gulps another drink. The whores and Roaring Boys break into a raucous chorus about the pleasures of the night ("Soon dawn will glitter"). At its conclusion, Nick rises to announce that a young friend of his, Mister Tom Rakewell, wishes to favor them with a song by way of initiation into their company.

As all applaud, Tom comes forward and sings the cavatina "Love, too frequently betrayed." It is a plaintive song in a minor key, in which Tom laments that he has been unfaithful to Anne.

He implores the Goddess of Love not to desert him in his darkest hour.

In a brief refrain ("How sad a song") the whores murmur pensively that the young man is most charming in his sorrow. They offer him the solace of their kisses. Mother Goose dispels the sentimental mood by declaring that tonight she claims Tom as her prize. As though on signal, the men and women, facing each other, form a lane. Taking Tom's hand, Mother Goose leads him slowly through the lane toward a door at the back. Nick, standing to one side, watches them with malevolent satisfaction.

The whores and Roaring Boys, mingling again, sing a madrigal-like chorus in nonsensical doggerel keyed to the word "Lanterloo." At its conclusion Nick raises his glass in the direction of the door at the back. With sinister meaning, he wishes his "master" sweet dreams . . . and let him dream on, for to awake is to die. The curtain falls.

[*Scene Three*] The garden of Trulove's house (as in Scene One) on an autumn night. There is a full moon. During a brief, serene orchestral introduction, Anne, in traveling clothes, enters from the house. In recitative, she reveals that she has had no word from Tom. She sings that she will go to London to find him because she knows he needs her help. In the following aria, "Quietly, Night, O find him," Anne offers an invocation to the night. In poetic terms she implores the moon to help her find her lover. The aria ends on a descending phrase which reflects her longing and despair.

Suddenly her father calls her from the house. She turns to go inside, then pauses. For a moment she is torn between loyalty to her father and devotion to Tom. Her father is strong, she decides finally, while Tom is weak and needs her help. Sinking to her knees, she sings a brief but moving prayer for guidance, "O God, protect dear Tom."

In the next moment, Anne makes her decision. Rising swiftly, she expresses her resolve in the brilliant cabaletta which concludes the act, "I go to him." Even though Tom has cast her off, she sings, she must keep the faith, because love cannot falter or change. No matter how wretched he may be, she will not desert him now. This remarkable aria in C major begins with Mozartean simplicity. Its center section, with its distorted harmonies, reflects Anne's grief and uncertainty. Then it returns to the C-major mode, embellished with chromatic figures and roulades. Anne brings the aria to an exultant climax on a high C. The curtain falls.

# ACT TWO

[*Scene One*] A room in Tom's house on a London square. The morning sun pours through the window. Street vendors are heard. Tom is having breakfast. At a particularly loud noise, he strides to the window and slams it shut. Staring morosely at the scene outside, he abandons himself to bitter reflection in a long soliloquy in the form of two arias interspersed with recitative. In the first ("Vary the song, O London, change")—sung in the florid style of eighteenth-century opera—he voices his contempt for the spurious harmonies of the city. None of its music, he sings, can fill the void in his heart.

In the ensuing recitative ("Nature, green unnatural Mother"), over a staccato rhythm in the bass, he gives vent to his loathing of the vaunted delights of "civilized" society: the food which chokes him, the wine which is bitter in his mouth . . . the witless card playing . . . the fatuous matrons and their marriageable daughters . . . the strumpets and their more obvious charms. . . . Tom breaks off his reflections with an expression of disgust, then suddenly remembers Anne. Stricken with remorse, he murmurs that he does not dare even think of her.

For a moment he sits plunged in gloom. Then again he bursts into an aria, one of furious scorn ("Up Nature, the hunt is on") for the senselessness and corruption of life in the city. He rails against the frustration of his search for the meaning of his existence. Finally, numbed by despair, he sighs in a spoken phrase: "I wish I were happy."

Instantly, Nick Shadow slips into the room. He glides over to Tom, hands him a circus playbill and asks if he recognizes the person pictured on it. Tom replies that it is Baba the Turk, the bearded lady of the circus. With amused sarcasm, he remarks that fearless heroes of the battlefield have been known to faint dead away at the sight of her. After more banter, Tom suspiciously asks Nick why he has brought up the subject of Baba.

To his utter consternation, Nick suggests that Tom marry her. In quasi-recitative over a rhythmic, skipping figure in the orchestra, Shadow cynically gives his reasons: Human beings, he says, are enslaved by either their desires or their obligations. To be completely free, one must ignore both desire and duty. Marrying Baba the Turk, Nick gravely assures Tom, will symbolize his liberation.

Shadow elaborates on this specious reasoning in an ensuing

aria, "In Youth the panting slave pursues." The conventional man, he sings, wastes his powers in the futile pursuit of women and success. In the end, he has nothing to show for his efforts except old age and regret. To escape that wretched fate, a man must be strong enough to will his own destiny. Only he who cannot be enslaved by passion or swayed by reason is free and beyond the law.

At the conclusion of the aria Nick looks at Tom with a quizzical expression. Tom looks back at him and begins to laugh—quietly at first, then louder and louder. Nick joins in and the two shake hands. With Shadow's help, Tom begins to dress himself for an evening's frolic. During the preparations, the two sing a duet ("My tale shall be told"), in an exuberant 6/8 rhythm, in which they anticipate the delights they will share in their conquest of Baba the Turk. It will be a story that will be told by young and old around the fire for years to come. Finally Tom, resplendent in the finery of an eighteenth-century dandy, and Nick together hail the future success of "Tom Rakewell, Esquire." Like Mephistopheles and the youthful Faust, the two rush off to begin their adventure as the curtain falls.

[Scene Two] A street in front of Tom's house in London on an autumn evening. The entrance is reached by a semicircular flight of stairs. At left a servants' entrance; at right a tree. As a winding figure in thirds sounds in the orchestra, Anne enters. She looks anxiously up at the entrance, then walks slowly up the steps and timidly lifts the knocker. But when a servant appears she scurries down the steps and hides against the wall under the tree until he has passed by.

In the following recitative and arioso ("O heart, be stronger") she sings that she will conquer her terror of this strange city and act with courage inspired by love. In the concluding phrases she declares that love has the power to cheat hell of its prey.

Anne shrinks back startled as a procession of servants appears carrying oddly shaped packages into the servants' entrance. Then a sedan chair is carried in, preceded by servants with torches. A young man steps out and Anne gasps in surprise as she recognizes Tom. When she rushes forward to throw herself into his arms he gently restrains her. A dramatic duet follows. Tormented by guilt, Tom beseeches her to go back to her home and never think of him again. When she replies that she will not leave without him, he implores her to listen to reason ("Listen, listen to me"). London, he sings, is a haunt of evil where it is wise to be afraid. Heedless of his warning, Anne answers that there is nothing to be afraid of because she is protected by his love. Tom bitterly protests that he no longer is worthy of her—the city has corrupted him beyond redemption. The duet ends with his anguished cry: "O Anne!"

The mood of tenderness and sorrow is shattered when Baba the Turk thrusts her head through the curtains of the sedan chair and upbraids Tom for making her wait. Anne is stunned when Tom tells her that this apparition is his wife. A trio follows, beginning with a phrase sung by Anne ("Could it then have been known"), who laments that love which blossomed in spring has died in shame in autumn. Tom voices his hopelessness and despair. Baba speculates venomously on the identity of a possible rival who shows up on her wedding day. The trio comes to an end —with a touch of irony—on the word "forever." For Anne and Tom it is a cry of despair; for Baba it is a petulant objection to being kept waiting.

Anne rushes away. Tom helps Baba alight from the sedan chair. Patting his cheek, she asks him who "that girl" was. Only a milkmaid who wanted money, Tom answers casually. With that he escorts Baba up the steps to the entrance of the house.

From the distance comes the sound of a crowd shouting a welcome to Baba the Turk. By the time she and Tom reach the top of the stairs, the townspeople throng to the scene. Tom goes into the house. Baba, veiled, stands before them in the pose of a star performer. In chorus, they beg her to show herself just once before she retires. With an imperious, theatrical gesture, Baba removes her veil, revealing her flowing black beard. The applause of the crowd mingles with a fanfare as the curtain falls.

[*Scene Three*] Tom's room (same as Scene One). Now it is cluttered with a fantastic jumble of objects—stuffed animals and birds, display cases of stones and fossils, bric-a-brac, glassware and so on. After a brief orchestral introduction, the curtain rises to reveal Baba and Tom at breakfast. Tom, obviously in a bad humor, is scowling. Baba is chattering away, scarcely stopping for breath. She babbles in the form of an amusing aria ("As I was saying") to the accompaniment of a twittering figure in the orchestra. Into Tom's unwilling ears she pours the detailed description of the souvenirs she has collected during her circus travels— musical glasses, Chinese fans, a bottle of water from the River Jordan, snuffboxes, stuffed birds . . . and so on and so on.

Eventually she becomes aware that Tom has not spoken a

single word, and asks him what is wrong. When he snaps at her she affectionately puts her arms around his neck, then tries to coax him into good humor by singing, unaccompanied, a silly little song, "Come, sweet, come." Exasperated, Tom pushes her violently away and roars at her to sit down.

Thereupon Baba, bursting into tears of rage, abandons herself to a wild orgy of destruction. She gives voice to her fury in a spectacular aria which begins with the words "Scorned, abused, neglected, baited." Each word is sung a half tone higher, and at each word Baba seizes an object in her collection and smashes it to bits. Beside herself with jealousy, she accuses Tom of still being in love with her young rival. She screams that, sigh as he may, the "milkmaid" will never be his wife. Baba brings the aria to an end on a rising chromatic phrase sung on the word "never."

Suddenly Tom tears off his wig and pushes it down over Baba's face back to front. Her voice is instantly cut off at the climax of the phrase. For the rest of the scene she sits motionless and silent. Ignoring her, Tom paces sullenly back and forth, his hands in his pockets. Then, flinging himself down on the sofa, he mutters that he cannot find relief in tears—only one remedy is left him: sleep.

He falls asleep as a single sustained note sounds in the orchestra, to be followed by a mysterious skipping figure in the bass. A door silently opens and Nick Shadow peeps in. After a cautious look around he wheels in a large object covered by a dust sheet. He pulls off the sheet to reveal a weird contraption—a kind of cabinet with a hopper on top and a door in the front.

Nick takes a loaf of bread from the table and puts it into the cabinet. Next he throws into the hopper a piece of broken vase he has picked up off the floor. Then he turns a wheel. The broken china falls into the cabinet and the loaf of bread slides out of a chute. After repeating the operation to see that everything is working properly, he puts the loaf of bread back into the cabinet and takes out the piece of broken china, which he keeps in his hand. It is obvious that the machine is the clumsiest kind of a fake. Singing softly to himself, Nick replaces the dust cover, wheels the contraption to Tom's bedside, then stands looking down at him.

In his sleep, Tom murmurs that he wishes "it were true." Waking, he sits bolt upright and stares at Nick in surprise. Then in an agitated refrain he tells Shadow about his strange dream: He had invented a wonderful machine which could change stones into bread. Thus, through his genius, he was able to banish hunger from the world.

With the theatrical gesture of a magician, Nick whips the cover off the machine and asks Tom if it resembles that in his dream. It is the same, Tom gasps, then says excitedly that he needs a stone to make it work. Nick hands him the piece of broken vase; Tom drops it into the hopper, turns the wheel, and out comes the loaf of bread. Incredulous, Tom snatches up the loaf and tastes it. Overwhelmed, he sinks to his knees and murmurs in awe: "A miracle!" In a simple, quiet phrase, almost like a prayer, he wonders if this one good deed will make him worthy of Anne.

This leads into a long duet and a following recitative which conclude the act. Gazing in mystical exaltation at his magic machine, Tom sings that it will open to man the gates of paradise from which he once was driven ("Thanks to this excellent device"). Nick, sidling to the front of the stage, winks broadly at the audience and observes that any sensible person can see that his young master is a fool ("A word to all my friends"). Yet, he adds slyly, there are business opportunities here for the smart investor.

Tom takes up the duet to sing that mankind, freed at last from the thrall of hunger, poverty and pain, will shout hallelujahs in praise of this marvelous contrivance. Nick, in turn, comments cynically that idlers and the scheming poor would be eager to invest in this worthless toy—the bigger the lie the easier the victim.

Carried away by the ideal of saving humanity, Tom sings in melodramatic phrases that man now will attain his highest state of being and assume his rightful place as monarch of the universe. Nick's voice blends with Tom's in the closing measures of the duet as he urges the audience to seize the chance to profit by investing in this machine—a clever fraud which is bound to pay big dividends.

As Tom stands transported by his dream, Shadow, in ensuing recitative, brusquely reminds him that the device is not yet a reality. First it must be mass-produced, then advertised and sold. This, of course, will require capital. Brought suddenly back to earth, Tom ruefully admits that he knows nothing about such things and wonders if, after all, this noble vision is only an illusion like everything else. But Nick quickly assures him that these matters have been taken care of—he already has interested a number of reputable financiers who are impatiently waiting to get the project under way. Tom thanks him effusively, and is all for meeting the investors at once. He and Nick begin wheeling the machine out of the room. At the door, Shadow pauses to ask Tom if he will tell the good news to his wife. Tom replies harshly: "I have no wife. I've buried her." The curtain falls.

## ACT THREE

[*Scene One*] Tom's house. The same as in Act Two, Scene Three, except that everything is covered with dust and cobwebs. Baba, with Tom's wig covering her face, is still sitting motionless at the table. It is an afternoon in spring.

Before the curtain rises a brief choral phrase is heard ("Ruin! Disaster! Shame!") like an ominous chant over a restlessly rising and falling accompaniment. The Crowd of Reputable Citizens then is revealed examining the objects in the room. In chorus ("What curious phenomena") they exclaim over the weird display and indicate that an auction is about to take place. From offstage again comes the chant of "Ruin! Disaster! Shame!"

The people of the crowd, looking at each other with malicious I-told-you-so expressions, now come forward and in a hushed chorus sing directly to the audience. In this chorus they disclose the extent of the catastrophe. Hundreds have been ruined by Tom Rakewell's ill-fated venture in promoting his magic machine: Merchants have gone mad, widows are selling their clothing to buy food, starving children are roaming the streets, even duchesses have been driven to suicide. And Tom Rakewell alone is to blame for the debacle. At the conclusion of the chorus the people turn back to their examination of Baba's collection.

A moment later Anne enters. She looks around, then goes quickly from group to group asking if they have seen Tom Rakewell. All in turn give her vague, confusing answers: He fled to America . . . he died of fever . . . he is a Methodist, a Papist . . . he's converting the Jews . . . he is being hounded by creditors. . . . Anne runs from the room in despair. Looking after her, the crowd mutters that this poor girl probably is another of Tom's victims.

Then Sellem the auctioneer bursts into the room followed by servants who scurry about setting up a dais for him. When it is finally in place Sellem mounts it and launches into his auctioneer's routine ("Ladies, gentlemen, be all welcome"). He bellows that this will be the "ne plus ultra" of auctions. Those fortunate enough to be present are ordained to establish the divine balance in

Nature: Thousands lose so that other thousands may gain. He bows to vociferous applause.

Sellem then turns his attention to the objects on display and calls for bids. This he does in one of the longest arias in the opera ("Who hears me, knows me"), sung to the staccato accompaniment of single-note figures which have the effect of building up the excitement of the scene. Occasionally he is interrupted by shouted bids from the crowd, whereupon he demands higher and higher offers. In two amusing interludes he calls out the bids, then bangs his gavel in true auctioneer fashion.

Finally, with elaborately mysterious movements, he walks over to Baba. In a brief refrain, sung *mezza voce* in a deliberate waltz tempo, he calls attention to the prize offering of the day. He expertly stirs the curiosity of the crowd by speculating on what might lie behind the mask of this figure—a precious jewel . . . an oracle . . . an octopus . . . perhaps even an angel . . . ? The crowd grows wild with excitement and the bidding becomes more frantic. Scarcely able to make himself heard, Sellem begins shouting the final bids, starting with "fifty." By the time he reaches "one hundred" the uproar is at its height. Bellowing "going, going, gone," he snatches the wig from Baba's face. There is a sudden, stunned silence as the crowd gapes in disbelief.

Like an automaton, Baba instantly begins singing the cadenza exactly at the point where, in the preceding scene, she was cut off on the word "never" when Tom covered her face. Then, as though regaining consciousness, she stands up. Snatching up a veil lying on the table, she dusts herself off. Glaring at Sellem and the crowd, she furiously denounces them for stealing her treasures. When the people cower back she orders them out. Her tirade is interrupted by the voices of Tom and Nick outside, calling out like street hawkers: "Old wives for sale!" All in the room listen in bewilderment.

Here begins a long and involved ensemble which brings the scene to a close. Baba reacts angrily to the sound of the men's voices; the people exclaim in surprise. Anne rushes in and goes to the window looking for Tom. She and Baba then confront each other and Baba beckons to the girl to come closer. When Sellem tries to continue with the auction, Baba cuts him short.

Turning to Anne in a complete change of manner, Baba tells her to find Tom again and set him straight ("You love him"). This marks the beginning of a duet which is one of the most melodious in the opera. The lad is scatterbrained, Baba sings, but not entirely bad. She assures Anne that—good or bad—he still loves her.

In mingled happiness and remorse, Anne sings that it is she who has been untrue, because she doubted Tom's love. Sellem and the chorus comment sympathetically. Continuing the duet, Baba warns Anne about Tom's companion, a snake who has poisoned his victim. With that she gently dismisses the girl. When Anne anxiously asks Baba where she herself will go, Baba replies that a lady of talent has nothing to fear.

In a flowing refrain ("I shall go back") Baba explains that she will go back to the stage—her own world of good manners and wealth. She has been away too long, and now this interlude must end. In the continuation of the duet Baba reiterates these thoughts; Anne wonders if she can win back Tom's love at the expense of Baba's happiness. The voices of Sellem and the crowd provide a choral accompaniment. The people marvel at the strange turn of events while Sellem laments the ruinous interruption of his auction.

At the conclusion of the ensemble the voices of Tom and Nick again are heard outside. They sing a simple, rather charming nonsense song, "If boys had wings." As before, everyone in the room stops and listens intently. Then, as all express their various reactions, the concluding ensemble of the scene begins. Anne exclaims happily as she recognizes Tom's voice; Baba exhorts her to go to him: Sellem and the crowd cry that the archthief has reappeared—his crime is grave, and now the law is closing in.

In chorus, Baba, Sellem and the people warn Anne that she must act quickly if she wishes to save the man she loves. Anne's voice rises above the chorus in a coloratura obbligato as she expresses the hope that her love will give her the courage to save Tom. As the ensemble ends, Anne turns to Baba with a fervent "God bless you!" She rushes away. From the distance come the voices of Tom and Nick in the ending of their ditty.

Baba turns to Sellem and imperiously orders him to call her carriage. Startled out of his pompous manner, Sellem jumps to obey—apparently forgetting that the carriage was to be one of the prize items of his auction. Regally motioning the gaping crowd aside, Baba stalks to the carriage. At the door she turns and sternly informs all that the next time they see her, they will pay. She gets in and rides away to a majestic fanfare. Staring after her, the crowd murmurs that it has been a hectic day. The curtain falls.

[*Scene Two*] A gloomy churchyard at night. At front and center is a newly dug grave; behind it a flat raised tomb, with a sexton's spade leaning against it. At right is a yew tree. Before the curtain rises there is a brief, somber orchestral introduction.

Tom and Nick enter hurriedly. Nick carries a small black bag. To the accompaniment of a sinister theme in thirds, Tom looks apprehensively around. Then, over an eerie, throbbing figure in the bass, he voices his premonition of danger ("How dark and dreadful is this place"). He sings that the strange look on Nick's face strikes fear into his heart. With ominous calm, Shadow reminds him that a year and a day have passed. Now, according to their contract, it is time to settle accounts. This is sung with ironic effect to the tune of the ditty Nick and Tom sang during the auction scene.

Terror-stricken, Tom implores Shadow to be patient. Now he is a beggar, he goes on, but as soon as he is rich again he will pay every cent he owes. In a foreboding *mezza voce*, Shadow tells him he does not want his money. He wants his soul. He commands Tom to make certain that he now recognizes the person he was fool enough to hire for this fee.

There, Nick snarls, is his grave—and here are the means for his last exit. He may take his choice. Thereupon Nick takes from his bag a knife, a rope, a vial of poison and a revolver.

In wild despair, Tom begs the hills to hide him from his impending doom, or the sea to cover him. He cries out against the caprice of fate that made an unknown uncle choose him as his heir. Nick gloatingly sings that nothing now can hide his sins and that there will be rejoicing in hell when he arrives. On the stroke of midnight, Shadow declares, Tom must kill himself. Slowly he begins to count as a distant clock strikes. Tom abjectly begs for mercy. But on the stroke of nine, Nick holds up his hand. There is a deep silence.

His manner suddenly unctuous, Nick remarks that although Tom has presumed upon their friendship, Nick Shadow always is the gentleman. He will forgive Tom his breach of faith and will suggest a pleasanter way to decide his fate. They will play a game of cards. The scene continues in a dramatic recitative.

Nick asks Tom if he has a deck of cards. Taking one from his pocket, Tom remarks with grim humor that this is all that is left him in this world—or the next. Nick comments approvingly that a jest always makes the game go well. The rules, he goes on, are as follows: Nick Shadow will cut three cards. If Tom can name them, he is free. If not . . . Nick points to the contents of the black bag.

To the accompaniment of a nervous, darting figure in the orchestra, the game proceeds. Nick cuts the cards, then holds the exposed card away from Tom and toward the audience. Tom trembles with fear. Suddenly he murmurs Anne's name and instantly regains control of himself. He names the card: queen of hearts. Nick casually tosses the card aside. The clock strikes once. As Tom raises his head in a gesture of thanks, Shadow observes to the audience that this sportive gentleman gambles "the peace of hope against the guineas of despair."

Again Nick cuts the cards and again Tom, seized by terror, wonders what power can help him name the right card. Nick tauntingly remarks that, as Lady Luck has been his good friend before, he might well give her a second chance.

At that moment the sexton's spade leaning against the tomb clatters to the ground. Startled and angry at the noise, Tom, with the expletive "The deuce!" kicks the spade away. For an instant he stares at it, then in a flash of understanding he names the card: two of spades. The clock strikes again. Glaring at Tom in baffled fury, Nick sneeringly remarks that he is to be congratulated on his luck. Then in menacing tones he reminds Tom that his last chance has come. Quaking in terror, Tom hides his face in his arms and leans against the tomb.

Nick swiftly picks up one of the discarded cards, holds it up and in a brief refrain addresses the audience. The simpler the trick, he sings, the easier the deception. He explains that he has taught his guileless pupil to believe that things do not repeat themselves. But the next card will contradict this precept. It will be the queen of hearts again—and for Tom Rakewell it will be the queen of hell. He calls to Tom to name the final card.

In a brief duet passage the two sing that this time Fortune has given neither help nor hint. Nick maliciously asks the "love-lucky" Tom if he is afraid. Tom, who has been looking wildly about, suddenly turns his face away from the ground as though he had seen some unspeakable horror. He gasps that he caught sight of the imprint of cloven hoofs. The goats are back, Nick murmurs casually, now that spring's returned. In an anguished phrase, Tom voices the words "return" and "love."

Suddenly from far off comes Anne's voice calling, "Return!" In a following phrase she sings that love can cheat hell itself of its victim. Tom, without realizing what he is doing, sings the word "love" with her, then checks himself. Nick stands as though turned to stone. As a tremendous fanfare bursts out in the orchestra, Tom exultantly welcomes love—which at this moment has returned to save his life—as his queen of hearts. Thus naming the fateful card, he tears the remainder of the deck out of the still motionless Shadow's grasp. The clock strikes twelve. With a joyous cry, Tom falls senseless to the ground.

To the accompaniment of thunderous, hammering chords, Nick Shadow roars that the failure of his scheme has damned him to the torment of ice and flame ("I burn! I freeze! In shame I hear"). Then he commits his final act of revenge: With a sorcerer's gesture, he makes Tom insane. Howling in terror, Nick sinks slowly out of sight into the grave. As the hammering rhythms die away into silence, the scene is plunged into darkness. Then the action continues.

A tender theme imitative of forest murmurs begins in the orchestra. The dawn gradually brightens the churchyard, where the open grave is now covered with a mound of green grass. Tom, hopelessly mad and smiling vacantly, puts grass on his head and begins singing in a childlike voice. In a simple, poignant melody he sings that he is Adonis, beloved of Venus. As the quiet woodland theme is again taken up by the orchestra the curtain slowly falls.

[Scene Three] A large room fronting a row of cells in Bedlam, the famous hospital for the insane in old London. At the back is a raised platform with a straw pallet. Tom is standing before it facing a chorus of madmen, who include a blind man with a broken fiddle, a crippled soldier, a man with a telescope and three witchlike creatures. Throughout the ensuing scene the conventional harmonic patterns are broken by eerie dissonances, reflecting the mental distortions of the insane.

In a brief arioso in mock-heroic style, Tom exhorts his hearers —whom he calls "shades"—to array themselves in festive attire to welcome the goddess Venus, who has promised to visit her Adonis. The inmates respond in a derisive chorus that Venus never will keep her promise to a madman.

Crushed by their taunts, Tom sinks down on the pallet and buries his face in his hands. The others begin to dance before him in a grotesque minuet, meanwhile singing a chorus of despair, "Leave all love and hope behind." As it concludes with a phrase of utter desolation—"In a night that never ends"—a key scrapes in the rusty lock of the door. The inmates scurry to their cells, warning each other of the Keeper's whip. The Keeper enters with Anne. Pointing to Tom, who is still sitting motionless, he assures

Anne that this inmate is harmless. He will answer only to the name of "Adonis," the Keeper says, and advises Anne to indulge his fancy. When he leaves, she softly calls "Adonis." Tom leaps to his feet and joyfully hails her as Venus, his Queen.

In a brief but stately arioso, he sings that he waited for her so long that he almost believed the blasphemous madmen who told him she would never appear. With great dignity he invites her to mount her throne, then leads her gently to the pallet. Kneeling before her, he implores her to hear his "confession."

Here begins the duet ("In a foolish dream") which is one of the opera's finest numbers. It is virtually in the style of a Bach aria, with intertwining harmonies of striking poignancy. It is a lyrical declaration of penitence, forgiveness and mutual love in terms of classical mythology. As it ends on a serene phrase ("Nor now no notion of 'Almost' or 'Too late'") Tom suddenly collapses on the pallet. Anne cradles him in her arms. Still addressing her as "immortal queen," he asks her to sing him to sleep.

His head on her breast, Anne sings the beautiful lullaby "Gently, little boat." Between the two verses, and at its conclusion, the inmates listening in their cells sing that the music has released them from the torment of their madness.

After a brief silence, the Keeper and Trulove enter. Saying that the story is ended at last, Anne's father bids her come home. As sustained chords sweep through the orchestra, Anne gently lowers Tom to the pallet. Looking down at him, she murmurs that though she has kept her vow of faith, he no longer needs her now. She sings goodbye and joins her father. In an ensuing *duettino* ("Every wearied body"), set in measured, Handelian rhythm, they sing that the end of life is inevitable; what God has ordained will come to pass. They slowly leave followed by the Keeper.

A moment later Tom wakes up, leaps to his feet and stares wildly around. Frantically he calls for Venus. In recitative phrases in the style of eighteenth-century opera he bids her join him in "the holy rites of love." The sound of his voice brings the other inmates rushing from their cells. As they crowd around him he shouts dementedly for Achilles, Helen, Eurydice, Orpheus, Persephone. In mingled fury and anguish he demands to know where the others have hidden his beloved Venus. In bewilderment they murmur that no one has been here.

Tom suddenly staggers back, gasping that he feels death approaching. Now in the grip of his fantasies, he implores Orpheus to strike his lyre in a hymn of sorrow . . . let nymphs and shepherds weep for the beautiful Adonis whom Venus loved. This too is sung in the classically ornate style of eighteenth-century opera. With this final expression of despair, Tom falls back dying on the pallet. Like a Greek chorus, the inmates break into lamentation for Adonis ("weep for the dear of Venus"). The curtain falls.

## EPILOGUE

This is sung in front of the curtain by Baba, Tom, Nick, Anne and Trulove. Baba is without her beard and the men are without their wigs. To a lighthearted, bubbling accompaniment they comment in turn on what has happened onstage.

Anne observes that not every rake is lucky enough to have a faithful sweetheart rescue him; Baba declares that all men, good or bad, are mad; Tom warns that young men who dream they are Vergil or Caesar will wake up to find they are only ordinary rakes. Nick finally remarks that it has been rumored that he does not exist—and sometimes he wishes he didn't. Then all join to point the moral of the tale ("So let us sing as one"): For idle hands and hearts, the devil finds work to do. Pointing at the audience, they bow and leave the stage.

# La Rondine
## (*The Swallow*)

*by* GIACOMO PUCCINI

(1858–1924)

*Libretto by*
GIUSEPPE ADAMI

Based on a libretto by A. M. Willner and Heinz Reichert

### CHARACTERS

| | |
|---|---|
| Magda de Civry, a demimondaine, mistress of Rambaldo | Soprano |
| Rambaldo Fernandez, a Parisian banker | Baritone |
| Ruggero Lastouc, a student, son of a friend of Rambaldo's | Tenor |
| Prunier, a poet | Tenor |
| Lisette, Magda's maid | Soprano |
| Bianca ⎫ | Soprano |
| Yvette ⎬ friends of Magda | Soprano |
| Suzy ⎭ | Mezzo-soprano |
| Périchaud ⎫ | Baritone/Bass |
| Gobin ⎬ friends of Rambaldo | Tenor |
| Crébillon ⎭ | Baritone/Bass |
| Georgette ⎫ | Soprano |
| Gabriella ⎬ grisettes | Soprano |
| Lolette ⎭ | Mezzo-soprano |
| Rabonnier, a painter | Bass |
| A student | Tenor |
| Major-domo | Bass |

Students, artists, ladies and gentlemen, grisettes, cocottes, flower girls, dancers, waiters

*Place:* Paris and Côte d'Azur
*Time:* During the Second French Empire (1852–70, under Napoleon III)
*First performance:* Monte Carlo Theater, March 27, 1917
*Original language:* Italian

Puccini's eighth opera, *La Rondine* was composed after such international successes as *Manon Lescaut, La Bohème, Tosca* and *Madama Butterfly*. While it has echoes of these works, this opera is in an entirely different vein—light, lyrical and abounding in ingratiating dance rhythms. It is notable for interesting experiments in harmonization which are more sophisticated than those in *La Bohème* or *Tosca*, by way of comparison.

When Puccini was in Vienna in 1912 he heard a number of light operas and was attracted by the effervescent gaiety of the music. Interested in trying his hand at this style of composition, he began work. The writing, however, was beset by a succession of financial and political complications. First of all, two Viennese theater directors had offered him about 200,000 crowns (at the time the equivalent of $50,000) for an operetta. Puccini, who flatly refused to have anything to do with operettas, turned down the project, but the directors persisted in offering him a contract. Meanwhile, during negotiations, war had broken out between Italy and Austria, and Puccini was censured in some quarters for "dealing with the enemy."

Toward the end of the war, matters eventually came to a mutually satisfactory conclusion. The directors having compromised by accepting a "lyric comedy" instead of an "operetta," Puccini honored his contract and *La Rondine* emerged.

Puccini had first decided to write the opera in the style of genuine *opéra comique*, with spoken dialogue, but dropped the idea in favor of recitative. Incidentally, the tenor role of Prunier (created by Tito Schipa at the Monte Carlo premiere) originally was written for baritone.

Although considered one of the composer's lesser operas, *La Rondine* is a charming work with a sound plot and abundant melody. Puccini himself once said it was his favorite among all his operas. The title refers to the prophecy of the poet Prunier, who tells Magda that, like the swallow, she will one day leave her home but—also like the swallow—she will always return.

One of the outstanding interpreters of the role of Magda was the late Lucrezia Bori. In the Metropolitan Opera's first performance of the opera on March 10, 1928, she sang the role with Beniamino Gigli as Ruggero. Early in 1936 the then impresario Edward Johnson scheduled a series of performances for Miss Bori. Her performance as Magda on a Metropolitan broadcast on Saturday afternoon, March 21, 1936, marked her farewell appearance in opera.

The brief orchestral introduction is dominated by an undulating three-chord figure which continues thematically into the scene. This figure, as a theme, is one of the most important in the score. It might be called the leitmotiv of Magda's renunciation. It is heard prominently in Act Three when Ruggero brings Magda the letter from his mother, and also when Magda tells him she cannot marry him because of her past.

## ACT ONE

A luxurious salon in Magda's home in Paris. At back, right, is a large veranda with windows through which the Tuileries can be seen in the deepening twilight. The portiered entrance to the salon is in the back wall, to the left. A door in the left wall leads to the boudoir. There is a fireplace with a mirror over the mantelpiece; placed about are armchairs, divans and tables. Downstage, a grand piano covered with a rich brocade on which stands a vase of red roses.

Rambaldo is seen at right rear with his friends—Périchaud, Gobin and Crébillon. Prunier, lounging against the piano, is gossiping with Yvette, Bianca and Suzy; Magda is pouring coffee, which Lisette hands around to the guests.

The scene ensues in recitative interspersed with musical dialogue in various ensemble forms. Prunier, cynical but good-humored, informs the three girls that something very serious is happening in Paris: An epidemic of love has broken out ("Una cosa assai grave"). High society has been smitten by overpowering passion.

Lisette, happening by at the moment, scoffs at this as sentimental nonsense. In these days, she remarks, one simply answers any romantic proposal with "yes," and that ends the matter. Feigning annoyance, Prunier insists that Magda dismiss this impertinent minx on the spot. With an indulgent shrug, Magda remarks that in her house outrageous behavior is more or less the rule. Lisette flounces away.

At Magda's invitation, Prunier continues his discourse on the mysterious epidemic which is raging in Paris ("La Malattia diciamo epidemia"). It is caused, he explains gravely, by a dangerous microbe which strikes the heart. In a brief trio ("E un microbo sottile") Yvette, Bianca and Suzy comment in mock alarm. Prunier goes on to say that no one is immune—not even Doretta.

And who, the others promptly ask, is Doretta? When the poet tells them she is the heroine of his latest song, the girls insist that he sing it. He pretends reluctance. Magda thereupon calls for silence, then announces that the illustrious poet Prunier has deigned to favor the company with his latest masterpiece.

Seating himself at the piano, Prunier strikes a romantic pose, then plays an introductory arpeggio. As a hush falls over the company he begins his song, "Chi il bel sogno di Doretta." It is a simple yet graceful ditty about a maiden who dreamed she was being wooed by a king who promised to make her rich and happy. But she spurned him, saying that not all his gold could bring her happiness.

Magda, listening intently, slowly approaches the piano. The poet stops playing, rises and says quietly that he does not know how to end the story of Doretta. Perhaps, he adds to Magda, she can finish it. The simple story intrigues her, Magda answers, then sings a reprise of Prunier's song. One day, so her version goes, a young student kissed Doretta's lips and the madness of love engulfed her. Magda's guests, fascinated, express their admiration in a hushed, spoken phrase.

In a passionate, soaring climax, Magda—now thinking not of "Doretta" but of herself—sings of the golden dream of love that once was hers ("O sogno d'or poter amar così"). Prunier impulsively takes the red roses from the vase on the piano and scatters them at Magda's feet. The men and women crowd around with effusive expressions of approbation.

As a sinuous theme continues in the orchestra, Prunier, Magda and Rambaldo—as though aware of each other's thoughts—comment with veiled irony. Rambaldo remarks rather sardonically that the tide of passion swept him off his feet. Magda, taken aback by his unaccustomed show of feeling, says that it was the poet—not herself—who inspired these emotions.

Prunier disclaims any credit. In each soul, he declares sententiously, there lurks a romantic demon whose power is absolute ("Nel fondo d'ogni anima"). Rambaldo, looking intently at Magda, remarks that he has exorcised his particular demon with holy water. If she wishes to see him, he adds in an ironic jest, here he is. With that Rambaldo takes from his pocket a jewel case with a pearl necklace and hands it to Magda. She takes it with a gasp of surprise, then shows it around.

Rambaldo tells her he had planned to present this gift earlier, but the present occasion seems more appropriate. Annoyed at his insinuating tone, Magda retorts that he has heard her answer to him in the song she sang a moment ago. With a slight bow, Rambaldo turns and walks to the other side of the room. Prunier, watching Magda, murmurs that the "Doretta" of his song was unyielding, but her real-life counterpart probably will surrender to the lure of treasure.

Suddenly, to the accompaniment of a staccato phrase in the orchestra, Lisette enters and hurries over to Rambaldo. In a *vivace* passage reflecting her breathless haste ("quel signore giunse ancora") she tells him that the young man who has called seven times before is here again and now refuses to go away without seeing the master of the house. Turning to Magda, Rambaldo asks if he may be permitted to introduce the son of an old family friend. She curtly reminds him that he is in his own house and can do as he pleases. Rambaldo sends Lisette to bring in the visitor.

As the orchestra takes up a syncopated waltz theme, Prunier rather peevishly again asks Magda why she does not get rid of this saucy maid of hers. Magda good-naturedly defends Lisette as a good girl who brings a ray of sunshine into her mistress' life. At this, her three friends, Bianca, Yvette and Suzy, wryly comment that hers is the kind of life they would gladly lead—especially with so lavish a provider. As for themselves, they complain, the problem is always the same: money.

In a quasi-recitative passage, Magda rebukes the girls for thinking of nothing but money ("Denaro! Nient'altro denaro!"). She is certain, she says, that—like herself—they look back fondly on the days when they were grisettes: They had no money but were rich in happiness with their sweethearts.

Bemused by her recollections, Magda begins to sing about the carefree hours she spent dancing at Chez Bullier—dancing the night away as a voice whispered magic words into her ear. Then, to the accompaniment of one of the opera's ravishing waltz tunes, Magda relates how the voice of love ("Fanciulla, è sbocciato l'amore!") yet warned her that ecstasy must be paid for in anguish. The owner of that voice was an ardent young student. After a night of dancing he ordered two glasses of bock, threw down twenty sous and told the waiter to keep the change. The girls laugh over this example of reckless extravagance, then entreat Magda to tell the rest of her story. The young man, she continues, asked her name ("Il tuo nome vuoi dir?"), but she would not tell him. Instead, they both wrote their names on the table top, then for a long time looked silently into each other's eyes.

Suddenly she became frightened and ran away, but she could not escape the throbbing music and the sound of her lover's voice. In a poignant phrase that dies away on a high note, Magda expresses her longing to relive the joy of that adventure.

As she sits lost in thought, Prunier rejoins the group. Yvette, Bianca and Suzy, disappointed with the commonplace ending of Magda's romance, mockingly discuss it with the poet. They have a most unusual subject for a poem, they tell him ("Poeta, un argomento!"): A pure, modest maiden fled in fright from a ballroom and a beer glass. Her passionate lover's curly hair and bushy side whiskers had quite turned her head—and so she ran home to her old guardian aunt. Giggling over their own joke, the three girls waltz in a circle around Prunier.

Purposely misunderstanding their nonsensical version of Magda's story, the poet remarks that an old aunt with side whiskers could never inspire him to flights of poetic fancy. But the niece undoubtedly could, Magda says with a smile. That would depend, Prunier replies fatuously, entirely on whether she could meet a poet's exalted standards ("Può darsi . . . ma qualora"). To be worthy of him, she must be beautiful, charming, worldly and refined—in short, a combination of Galatea, Berenice, Francesca and Salome.

With pretended seriousness, Magda asks how all these feminine virtues can be discovered. Quite simply, the poet answers: Every woman's character is plainly written in the palm of her hand. The women, of course, beg him to read their palms at once. Prunier declares that this procedure requires the utmost secrecy. On his orders Yvette, Bianca and Suzy set up a screen in one corner of the room. Thus out of view of the other guests, they seat themselves around Prunier; Magda is the first to stretch forth her hand. At this point the focus of the action shifts.

As the waltz theme of Magda's story sounds in the orchestra, Lisette enters, shows Rambaldo the visitor's card, then brings him in. He is Ruggero Lastouc. Although Rambaldo greets him cordially, the young man is ill at ease. Apologizing for his intrusion, he hands Rambaldo a letter of introduction from his father. As the other begins reading, the action shifts back to Prunier. Assuming a prophetic air, he tells Magda that her palm has revealed her destiny.

In a brief refrain over a series of soft chords in the orchestra, Prunier prophesies that Magda, like the swallow, is fated to leave her home for a distant land ("forse, come la rondine"), a land of sunshine and—perhaps—love. Magda asks apprehensively if this prophecy might also mean misfortune. Destiny, Prunier replies gravely, always has two faces: one smiling, the other sad.

As Prunier next reads Bianca's palm (advising her in the future to accept whoever has the most to offer), Rambaldo finishes reading

Ruggero's letter of introduction and learns that he is visiting Paris for the first time. Calling to Prunier, he asks him if he can suggest where Ruggero might best spend his first evening in the city. In bed, Prunier answers flippantly. Walking over to the visitor, he condescendingly informs him that the so-called pleasures of Paris are nothing more than illusion.

Thereupon Lisette, to everyone's consternation, cries that Prunier is wrong—Paris is the most wonderful city in the world. Exasperated by her interruption, Prunier orders her to be silent. Ignoring him, Lisette hands Ruggero a pencil and a piece of paper, then asks the guests to name the most exciting night clubs in Paris for the visitor's benefit.

Over an exuberant accompaniment in polka rhythm, they call out the names: Le Bal Musard . . . Frascati . . . Cadet . . . Pré Catalan; and finally, from Lisette, Chez Bullier. Ruggero, though utterly bewildered, dutifully writes down the names. He shakes hands with Rambaldo, then turns to leave—forgetting to pick up the piece of paper. Lisette, drawing aside the portiere at the doorway for him, urges him to choose Chez Bullier. There, she sings ("Amore è là"), love reigns supreme in a realm of laughter and delight. She follows him out.

Magda, Prunier, Rambaldo and the others, who have been watching the scene from the veranda, burst out laughing. As Magda comes forward—the pearl necklace dangling carelessly from her hand—she remarks that Prunier and the others should have shown more consideration for Ruggero and spared him embarrassment. Rambaldo dryly comments that a night at Bullier's probably will make up for it—to which Bianca adds that Bullier's is famous for its miracles. Magda, repeating the name softly to herself, tosses the necklace on the nearby table.

Rambaldo, Prunier and the guests now leave. The closing action of the scene takes place to the accompaniment of a melodious waltz theme. Magda rings for Lisette, orders her to call her carriage, then countermands the order. Lisette reminds Magda that this is her night off. Told she may leave, the maid turns out all the lights in the room and hurries out.

Sitting in the faint glow of a light on the veranda, Magda softly repeats Prunier's prophecy in the same musical phrases: "Forse come la rondine . . ." ("Like the swallow, I may go to a distant land . . ."). She notices the sheet of paper which Ruggero had left on the table. Magda picks it up, then drops it as though having made a sudden decision. As a sustained chord sounds

faintly in the orchestra, she whispers, "Bullier's," then runs smiling
into her boudoir.

To the accompaniment of a unison figure, which is repeated in
changes of key, Lisette appears. She is carrying a shawl and a
gaudy hat. Tiptoeing to the boudoir door, she listens, then turns
away—only to run into Prunier in top hat and overcoat with a
turned-up collar. He takes her in his arms and kisses her. With
a startled gasp, she tears herself away. The ensuing musical dialogue is remarkable for the fact that its curious blend of tenderness
and irony is underscored by the accompanying theme itself. Prunier tells Lisette that she could not possibly imagine how much
he despises her ("Tu sapessi a quale prezzo di disprezzo").
She is utterly unworthy of him—and yet he loves her.

The two then go on to argue comically about what Lisette is
wearing. Prunier bluntly disapproves of her entire costume, despite
Lisette's protests that she has borrowed her mistress' best frock,
coat and hat. Prunier sends her to change into a costume more
acceptable to him, meanwhile calling in mock despair on the nine
muses to forgive him for consorting with a creature so unworthy
of him.

When he is finally satisfied with Lisette's appearance, the two
start for the door arm in arm and make their exit on a softly
sung but melodramatic phrase: "sono te" ("I am thine!"). No
sooner have they left than Magda emerges from her boudoir. She
is in the simple dress of a grisette. As the tender waltz theme
sounds in the orchestra she fastens a rose in her hair, drapes a
shawl around her shoulders and goes toward the door. In a brief
musical phrase she sings: "Who knows what Doretta dreamed?"
("Che il mistero di Doretta"). At the door she turns, goes back
to the mirror and asks her reflection: "Who would recognize me
now?" She leaves as the curtain falls.


## ACT TWO

The ballroom at Chez Bullier. At left, a curving stairway leading
down from the entrance; at right, steps lead up to a balcony.
In the left wall, two large windows give a view of the street.
In the ballroom, profusely decorated with flowers, is a throng of
students, grisettes, courtesans, men about town and couples out for
a night of fun. Flower girls and waiters move among the tables.

In the brilliant ensemble writing of this act, Puccini mingled
the decadent, sophisticated gaiety of Paris with the nostalgic
sentimentality of prewar Vienna. The resulting *Schwärmerei* is

evoked by the irresistible waltz rhythms that dominate the entire act. There are echoes of *Rosenkavalier,* of Lehár, of Johann Strauss. But the melodies are not borrowed; they are Puccini's own. These waltzes are the composer's accolade to Vienna. He loved the city and paid a generous musical tribute to its irrepressible spirit.

The scene opens with a tumultuous ensemble (reminiscent of the Café Momus scene in *La Bohème*) blending the voices of flower girls, brash young students and other merrymakers. Imperceptibly, the action focuses on a table where Ruggero sits alone. Some of the girls begin eyeing him curiously and remark on his solemn demeanor ("Così solo! È funebre!"). Their inquisitiveness getting the better of them, they crowd around his table and ask him his name. Is it, perhaps, Armando . . . Marcello . . . Ernesto . . . Alberto . . . ? Ruggero, in mingled embarrassment and irritation, only glares at them. Finally giving him up as hopeless, the girls move away with a burst of derisive laughter.

With a sudden change in the mood of the music, Magda appears on the stairway and looks around in timid hesitation. A group of eight students, noticing her, comment that although she is poorly dressed she has the air of a lady of quality. One young man advances up the stairs and offers her his arm. Magda shrinks back in embarrassment. In a brief chorus ("Siam studenti, gaudenti") the youths introduce themselves as pleasure-seeking students endowed with every desirable masculine trait—except money. They offer to serve as her escort for the evening.

Anxious to evade them, Magda says she has an appointment. Looking around in desperation, she suddenly notices Ruggero and smothers an exclamation of surprise. Drawing their own conclusions, the students gallantly lead her to Ruggero's table. In high good spirits they give the lovers their blessing and go on their way laughing.

Magda, in charming confusion, haltingly apologizes to Ruggero for intruding on him in this manner. She only wanted to escape the attentions of the students, she explains, and will leave as soon as they are out of sight. Touched by her distress, Ruggero invites her to sit beside him. From this point on the dialogue continues over shifting rhythms in the orchestra: a sensuous, sustained figure, a staccato rhythm and an ebullient Viennese waltz.

Entreating Magda not to leave, Ruggero tells her that in her shyness and modesty she is like the girls in his native Montauban ("Così timida e sola"). They are not like the girls here. They prefer to dance to old-fashioned tunes, and to set off their beauty they need only a simple ornament—or perhaps a single flower such as she herself is wearing in her hair. Ruggero invites Magda to dance but she demurs, protesting that she cannot dance like the girls in Montauban. Saying he is certain she dances divinely, Ruggero offers his arms and draws her to the dance floor. In an aside, Magda murmurs that this adventure is like the one she had long ago ("L'avventura strana come nei dì lontani").

As the two mingle with the other dancers their voices blend in a brief duet ("Nella dolce carezza"). This introduces the splendid waltz chorus which dominates the act. While the music gradually grows wilder and more abandoned, Magda and Ruggero dance their way to the stairs and go up to the balcony. There they pause to watch the scene below and sing of the enchantment of this moment ("Dolcezza! Ebbrezza"). For a brief interval they go to the garden outside, and from a distance their voices blend with the chorus in a surging climax.

The music subsides as the crowd drifts toward the adjoining garden. Lisette and Prunier enter, with Lisette complaining over the poet's domineering attitude toward her—she cannot sneeze or turn right or left without being criticized. Prunier blandly answers that it is all a part of her education: Perhaps, by some miracle, he may be able to teach her how to behave properly. Still bickering, they dance their way toward the garden.

Magda and Ruggero return and make their way back to their table, where—exhausted but beaming happily—they drop into their chairs. At this point, Magda virtually re-creates the romantic episode of her past. She says she is thirsty. Ruggero orders two glasses of bock from a passing waiter. Thereupon Magda asks if he will grant her a favor: Give the waiter twenty sous and tell him to keep the change. Ruggero, puzzled, smiles at this whimsical request.

As though her thoughts were far away, Magda vaguely explains that the generous tip brings back the memory of an old aunt. Then she repeats the refrain sung by Yvette, Bianca and Suzy in the first act when they told Prunier about the frightened maiden who ran away from "a ballroom and a beer glass" ("Una fuga, una festa"). Noticing Ruggero's bewildered look, she adds softly that all this is only a fairy tale. The waiter brings the beer. Magda proposes a toast "to all your loves" ("A nostri amori"). Frowning, Ruggero sets down his glass without responding. With earnest emphasis he declares he could love one woman only—and to her he would dedicate his whole life. Impressed by his sincerity, Magda gravely echoes his words.

Fearing he has offended her, Ruggero speaks in tender reas-

surance. They are friends, he says, and yet he does not know
her name. Still re-creating the past, she says she would rather
write her name than say it, singing the identical phrase in which
she had told her friends of her adventure. With a small pencil
Ruggero hands her, Magda writes a name: Paulette. Reading
it approvingly, he writes his name beside hers on the table top.
Now, Magda says softly, there will always be something of themselves in this place. Ruggero answers that these names will fade—
but her enchantment will live in his heart forever.

Then, gazing into each other's eyes, they give voice to their
emotions in an impassioned duet, "Perchè mai cercate," one of
the opera's most lyrical moments. The duet ends not on a vocal
phrase but in a long kiss as the love theme surges up in the
orchestra.

Oblivious to everything, Magda and Ruggero remain locked in
each other's arms. A group of night club patrons, coming chattering and laughing down the staircase, notice the two and lapse into
respectful silence. In a pianissimo choral phrase ("Non facciamo
rumore") they comment that such love is not a matter for laughter.
With exaggerated gestures of secrecy they steal away.

Lisette and Prunier, who had come in shortly after the others,
stagger back in surprise as they catch sight of Magda and Ruggero
—who are still in a passionate embrace. At Lisette's startled cry
when she believes she recognized her mistress, the lovers separate
in confusion. Now follows a delightful scene with variations on the
"mistaken identity" theme, a dramatic vignette which is played out
over a flood of Puccinian melody.

To begin with, Prunier and Magda instantly recognize each
other, and, unobserved by Ruggero, Magda puts a warning finger
to her lips. Lisette, who keeps insisting that the woman is her
mistress, is even more astounded when she recognizes Ruggero.
Prunier hastily admonishes her that she has been drinking too much
and has simply been deceived by the woman's remarkable resemblance to Magda. With elaborate courtesy he presents Lisette to
Ruggero, telling him she is eager to know if her previous advice
to come to Chez Bullier has brought him luck. In answer, Ruggero
gallantly turns to Magda.

Unsuspectingly, he now introduces Magda to Prunier and Lisette
as "Paulette," adding the information that Prunier is a very famous
poet. Lisette, sitting down beside Magda, confidentially tells her
she is the very image of her mistress. She must be a charming
woman, Ruggero puts in. Just as she would be, Lisette says with
naïve tactlessness, indicating Magda, if she were wearing the

right clothing. "As you are, for example," Magda remarks, highly amused. Thereupon Lisette explains that all her finery costs her nothing—it is all borrowed from her mistress. To Lisette's annoyance, Prunier roars with laughter.

In an aside, Magda, with a touch of feminine malice, asks Prunier if his companion is his "Salome" or his "Berenice." The poet is stung by this jibe at his conceit. Meanwhile, Ruggero has ordered champagne and proposes a toast to love. The response is sung by all four in a unison phrase.

With glass upraised, Ruggero turns to Magda, and in the beautiful aria "Bevo al tuo fresco sorriso" sings a toast to her beauty and her laughter. In an answering phrase Magda sings that now her dream will last forever ("È il mio sogno che savvera"), and then the four voices blend in a glowing paean to all lovers. They are joined in a choral ensemble by the other patrons, who meanwhile have returned to the ballroom. As the great chorus rises to its climax, the four lovers are deluged with flowers thrown from the balcony and from every part of the ballroom. Several girls step out from the crowd and crown Prunier with a garland.

A moment later, as the throng is gradually dispersing, the romantic mood of the scene is suddenly shattered. The music changes to a rapid, menacing rhythm. Rambaldo appears at the top of the staircase. Prunier, catching sight of him, whispers a warning to Magda. Terrified, she asks the poet to get Ruggero out of sight. Prunier makes a reassuring gesture, then turns to Lisette to warn her of her master's presence. Before she can recover from her fright, the poet orders Ruggero to take her into the garden.

(In contrast to this moment of tension, there is an amusing byplay on the other side of the ballroom. A grisette runs away with an aging roué's top hat. He stumbles after her, forgetting to pay his check. The waiter, in turn, chases after him and triumphantly returns with the money a few moments later, to the vast amusement of the onlookers.)

Prunier, watching Rambaldo approaching down the stairs, urges Magda to leave at once. To his dismay she refuses to move. At a loss as to his next maneuver, the poet, while futilely trying to keep Magda in the background, greets Rambaldo with ostentatious cordiality. Taking his hand, he enthuses over the large emerald the banker is wearing. Rambaldo's answer is an icy stare. With a gesture of hopelessness, Prunier turns on his heel and retreats into the garden.

Face to face with Magda, Rambaldo demands an explanation.

Magda replies in a poignant refrain: "L'amo! Ma voi non lo sapete." He will never know, she sings, how much she has longed for true love—and now she has found it. As for him, everything is over. Moved by Rambaldo's incredulous look, Magda grasps his hand in an impulsive gesture of pity and begs his forgiveness for hurting him. Bowing, Rambaldo coldly says he hopes she will not regret her actions. With that he turns and without looking back stalks from the ballroom.

Magda collapses into a chair and for a long time stares motionlessly into space. In the grim, cold light of dawn, now beginning to show through the windows, the ballroom with its disordered tables, overturned glasses and wilted flowers is a tawdry reminder of the frenzied gaiety of the night. Outside, a wistful, ghostly voice sings that a cool fragrance heralds the dawn that robs the night of its magic and transforms love into an illusion ("Nella trepida luce d'un mattin").

Ruggero reappears carrying Magda's shawl. Calling "Paulette," he gently reminds her that it is dawn and they must go. Magda rises and faces him uncomprehendingly. Only then does he notice with alarm that she is deathly pale. As though waking from a trance, Magda comes toward him with arms outstretched. In mingled passion and despair she apostrophizes her dream of love in a reprise of the theme of Ruggero's aria ("Ti amo! Ma tu non sai"). Their voices blend in an ecstatic unison phrase as the curtain falls.


## ACT THREE

A cottage on the Côte d'Azur, where Magda and Ruggero are in seclusion. In front, a terrace with tables and chairs. Beyond, an open field and farther off an olive grove, with a path leading down to the sea. At the back a wall, covered with ivy and climbing roses, with an opening in the middle. It is afternoon of a beautiful spring day.

As the curtain rises, the lovers are having tea on the terrace. They give expression to their bliss in a long duet in waltz tempo which begins when Magda sings that the murmur of the sea enhances the charm of this spring day ("Anche il mare respira"). At the conclusion of the duet they sit in silence for a few moments and then Ruggero turns to more practical matters—namely, money.

The bills are piling up, he tells Magda ruefully, pulling several from his pockets. Even the landlord, he says, is eying his tenants suspiciously. Ruggero discloses that he wrote his father three days ago for money but has had no reply. Perhaps, he adds with a chuckle, they will have to go begging. Magda utters an exclamation of distaste.

Shrugging off his financial troubles, Ruggero says he has a happy secret to tell—one his beloved probably can guess: He has asked his father for his consent to their marriage. Magda, nonplused, can only stammer that she had not expected such news. This should not surprise her, Ruggero says with disarming simplicity, because he has sworn to love her forever.

Taking her in his arms, he tells her of his own dream of marital happiness in the opera's best-known aria "Dimmi che vuoi seguirmi." He asks her to follow him to his home high on a hill surrounded by the serene beauty of nature. In this idyllic spot their love will come to its fruition. His mother will be there to protect her against all care and sorrow, and soon they may hear the laughter of a child. But perhaps—who knows?—their life in this haven of sun and shadow will be but a prelude to their golden future, their final golden dream. He ends the aria on a tender questioning phrase—"E chi sa?"

Overwhelmed by emotion, Magda sobs in his arms. Kissing her hair with tender reverence, Ruggero releases her and walks slowly from the scene. Alone, Magda is wracked by terror and guilt. In an agitated refrain ("Chi più dirgli?") she asks herself the agonizing question: How can she tell her trusting lover of her past? With a single word she will shatter their happiness forever . . . and yet she dare not live a lie to hold Ruggero's love. Plunged into despair, Magda goes into the cottage.

As an ascending chromatic passage erupts in the orchestra, Lisette and Prunier come hurrying in—wrangling, as usual. Lisette appears to be panic-stricken because she fears they have lost their way and will never find Magda's cottage. Prunier sneers that, as usual, she is overplaying the scene. Lisette wails that he has ruined her life.

A long and hectic argument ensues in duet form as Prunier launches into a diatribe on the general subject of Lisette's disastrous lack of talent as an actress ("Non mi stupisce"). He had been fool enough to hope, he fumes, that he could make her a star—on the assumption that she had wit enough to learn the ditties he composed for her stage debut in Nice. And what happened? The "star" vanished without a trace.

Lisette, covering her ears, moans that she still can hear the hisses that greeted her performance ("il sibilare di quella gente"). All she asks now is silence. Here, in this remote spot, she has it,

Prunier remarks sardonically. As for her stage debut, he adds, he had hoped to make her forget—at least for one evening—that she is nothing more than a servant. Ignoring him, Lisette looks wildly around in comic terror, exclaiming that she hears mysterious hisses. Prunier sarcastically observes that she is obviously a victim of his highest theatrical ambitions.

Then, realizing that the girl is quite beside herself with unreasoning fear, the poet changes his tactics. He assures her that they are now at Magda's cottage and that in this lovers' retreat she is safe from the cruel taunts of the theater audience in Nice. And here, he goes on pompously, he will restore her to the kind of life she is fitted for—far from the world's strife ("fuori del mondo").

At that moment, Magda's valet comes across the terrace with some letters on a tray. Prunier asks him to inform the lady of the house that two friends from Paris have come to visit her. No sooner has the valet left than Lisette turns on Prunier in a furious outburst ("Alla fine m'hai seccato!"). She has had enough of his high and mighty airs and his nagging criticism of her, she rages. Now that he has destroyed all her dreams and illusions, she asks only that he leave her in peace. Roused to genuine anger by her accusations, Prunier retorts scornfully that gratitude never has been one of her virtues. Losing all control, Lisette screams, "I hate you!"

The two recover themselves quickly as Magda appears. Prunier tells her they have come only to ask if she is happy. Her absence, he says, is the talk of all Paris—and when he tells her friends the truth they refuse to believe him. They cannot understand how a sophisticated woman of Paris can resign herself to rural domesticity for the sake of a love affair. Magda sharply protests his insinuations.

Quickly changing the subject, she asks Prunier why he and Lisette actually have come to this place. With obvious relish he explains that the theater patrons of Nice ("Il teatro di Nizza") have decreed that Lisette is not destined to become one of the immortals of the stage. He adds, however, that his real reason for coming is to ask if Lisette may be permitted to resume her position as a maid. Magda assents, and Lisette, with a sigh of relief, says that now at last she is happy. As though to symbolize her return to the status of servant, she takes off her hat.

Then, over a repetition of the musical theme first heard during the dialogue between Prunier and Lisette near the close of Act One, Prunier speaks candidly to Magda. Lisette, he begins, is happy because she has returned to the place and station where she belongs. And this, he tells Magda, is what she herself must do: leave this dream world and go back to her own reality. Magda angrily tries to silence him. The poet tells her he is only doing his duty: He was asked to give her this message by one who understands her and can solve all her problems.

With that he abruptly turns to Lisette and bids her farewell. In an unaccompanied recitative he requests Magda's permission to ask Lisette one more question. She nods. In a stage whisper, he asks Lisette at what time she will be free this evening. At ten o'clock, she answers. Saying he will meet her then, Prunier struts jauntily away.

Turning to Magda, Lisette remarks briskly that the house is obviously in need of tidying up and that she will be glad to serve her mistress as before. She hurries out and returns shortly, dressed in her maid's uniform, and curtsies to Magda.

A moment later, as the "renunciation" theme is heard in the orchestra, Ruggero rushes in and excitedly shows Magda a letter from his mother. Magda turns pale and sways unsteadily, as though about to faint. Alarmed, Ruggero leads her to a chair, then assures her that all is well: His mother has given his bride-to-be her blessing. He hands Magda the letter. Controlling herself with an effort, she begins reading to the accompaniment of a simple yet eloquent theme.

Ruggero's mother writes ("Figliuolo, tu mi dici") that she weeps with happiness when she thinks of the gracious lady whose heart he has won and who will be the mother of his children. If she is modest and virtuous, then she is indeed truly blessed. Here, at the ancestral hearth, everyone impatiently waits to meet her son's chosen bride. Magda stops reading, her voice choked with sobs. Tearfully she reads the letter's closing phrase: "Donale il bacio mio!" ("Give her a kiss from me!").

As Ruggero kisses Magda on the forehead she tears herself away, crying in anguish that she dare not receive his mother's kiss ("No! non posso riceverlo!"). Here again the "renunciation" theme is heard.[1] This marks the beginning of the farewell duet which ends the opera. In despairing tones Magda tells Ruggero that, stained by her past, she is not worthy of entering his home as his bride. She has had other lovers, she confesses, who bought her affections with their ill-gotten wealth.

[1] A few measures later, a new and powerful theme takes over. It is reiterated in an extraordinary succession of changes of key, illustrative of Puccini's experiments with new harmonizations.

But it is he himself, she goes on, who has given her the greatest treasure of all—his steadfast love—and she cannot and will not repay him with lies. Falling on his knees, Ruggero wildly implores her not to leave him and plunge his life into ruin ("Taci! le tue parole"). Magda answers that leaving him is worse than death—but she must go because she loves him too much to betray him.

Fiercely clinging to her, Ruggero reiterates his entreaties; Magda, with desperate insistence, repeats that she will not add to her guilt by ruining his life. Suddenly calm, she takes his face in her hands and looks with passionate intensity into his eyes. Only he, she sings, has known her innermost soul ("L'anima mia che solo tu conosci"), and it will be his forever. And when this pain is only a memory, he will return to his home, she will return to her sorrow.

Gently releasing Ruggero, Magda rises. Lisette comes from the cottage, and her look shows that she understands. She goes to Magda and supports her as she begins to walk away. After a few steps Magda turns and sings her final phrase of farewell, "che sia mio questo dolore" ("let me bear our sorrow alone"). Weeping bitterly, Ruggero collapses as the curtain falls.

# Suor Angelica

*by* GIACOMO PUCCINI

(1858–1924)

*Libretto by*
GIOVACCHINO FORZANO

### CHARACTERS

| | |
|---|---|
| Sister Angelica | Soprano |
| The Princess | Contralto |
| The Abbess | Mezzo-soprano |
| The Monitor | Mezzo-soprano |
| Mistress of the Novices | Contralto |
| Sister Genevieve | Soprano |
| Sister Lucilla | Mute |
| Sister Osmina | Mezzo-soprano |
| Sister Dolcina | Mezzo-soprano |
| The Nursing Sister (Infirmary) | Mezzo-soprano |
| The Tourières | Mezzo-sopranos |
| The Novices | Mezzo-sopranos |
| The Lay Sisters | Soprano, Mezzo-soprano |

Chorus of women, children, men (behind scenes)

*Place:* A nunnery in a mountain region of Italy
*Time:* Latter part of the seventeenth century
*First performance:* Metropolitan Opera House, New York City,
    December 14, 1918
*Original language:* Italian

---

*Suor Angelica* is the second one-act work of the operatic triptych known as *Il Trittico*—the first being *Il Tabarro,* the third *Gianni Schicchi.* It is the story of the beautiful daughter of a Florentine nobleman, who entered a nunnery to expiate the sin of being an unmarried mother. Haunted by her guilt, and crushed by unjust punishment visited upon her by a vengeful relative, Suor Angelica commits suicide.

Ironically, of the three operas, this was Puccini's favorite. But along with *Il Tabarro* it failed to sustain the interest of the public, and both operas lasted only two seasons at the Metropolitan. *Gianni Schicchi*, on the other hand, won enduring popularity. The Italian premiere of the triptych, in Rome on January 11, 1919, with Arturo Toscanini conducting, was an outstanding personal triumph for Puccini. At the world premiere in New York, the role of Suor Angelica was created by Geraldine Farrar.

In the opinion of some commentators, two elements have hindered the success of *Suor Angelica:* For a short work, it is too episodic, with too many loosely connected scenes; also, it employs only women's voices, which makes for a certain monotony.

Yet in its entirety, it is a touching work, full of sweeping Puccinian melody and melancholy tenderness. Throughout, the composer sustains an ethereal mood, combining religious ecstasy with elemental human emotions.

There is no overture. The curtain rises to a bell-like theme in the orchestra which echoes the majestic theme of the great *Te Deum* in the first act of *Tosca.*

An open space in front of a small church, with arcades to the right and left. Toward the back, at one side, a garden may be seen; on the other side, part of a cemetery. In the foreground a shrine with a fountain, and some cypresses. It is a clear evening in spring.

Over the ringing of bells, the voices of the nuns in the chapel are heard singing the *Ave Maria.* Two Lay Sisters, late for chapel, hurry toward the entrance. For a moment they pause to listen to the birds singing in the cypresses, then they go inside.

Sister Angelica, also late, walks quickly to the chapel. But before she enters she kneels down and kisses the threshold—an act of penance for being late. A few moments later her voice is heard alone in a brief phrase as she joins in the *Ave Maria*—"Prega per noi peccatori."

The chorus ends, and the Abbess comes out of the chapel followed by the nuns walking two by two. When she pauses before the shrine the sisters bow low as they pass her. The Abbess blesses them and leaves. The sisters talk together in small groups. They fall silent as the Monitor and the Mistress of the Novices come forward and confront the two who were late. They sternly reprove them for this infraction of the rules ("Sorelle in umiltà). Sister Angelica also was late, says the Monitor, but she made the proper penance. Because they neglected to do so, they not only must kiss the threshold but must say twenty prayers for the poor and needy. The two Lay Sisters express their contrition in a brief invocation to the Savior ("Cristo Signore") and go to their cells.

The Monitor and the Mistress then turn to Sister Lucilla and Sister Osmina and chide them for breaking other rules. For making the nuns laugh in chapel, Lucilla is ordered to work at her spinning wheel in complete silence. Osmina, caught hiding a bunch of roses in her sleeve, is told to go to her cell at once. Denying the accusation, Osmina marches to her cell and defiantly slams the door.

The remaining sisters, innocent of any infractions, are rewarded by being allowed to play and rest awhile. Sister Angelica, having made her amends, is included in this privilege. To the accompaniment of serene arpeggios she busies herself watering the flowers. Meanwhile, Sister Genevieve, in a sprightly melody, calls to the nuns to observe how the rays of the setting sun soon will turn the water of the fountain into gold. Perhaps, she sings, they will again see the miracle which has happened three times before ("Comincian le tre sere").

In answer to a young nun's question about the miracle, the Mistress of the Novices explains: On three evenings of every year ("Per tre sere dell'anno solamente") in the past, the sunset has turned the water to gold. But this has not happened for a year —and during that interval a sister has died. The nuns listen silently, absorbed in their own thoughts, as a requiemlike theme sounds in the orchestra.

Taking up the refrain, Sister Genevieve sings ("O sorelle in pio lavoro") that they must now sprinkle the fountain's golden water on the grave of the departed Sister Bianca Rosa. In mystical, symbolic phrases, Sister Angelica interrupts to express her own thoughts. Mysteriously she sings ("I desideri sono i fiori") that earthly desires bloom and die like flowers—but in death there is life eternal.

The reflective theme of the scene is carried on by Sister Genevieve, who recalls the days when she was a shepherdess. Looking upward, she wonders if it is a sin to long to hold a fleecy lamb in her arms again ("Mio, tu sai che prima"). If it is, she adds, then she asks forgiveness from the Lamb of God. Next to confess is Sister Dolcina, who admits having an insatiable craving for sweetmeats. She is reproached with gentle severity by the other nuns.

At that point Sister Genevieve turns to Sister Angelica and asks if she has any fond desires. The change of mood is reflected in the darkening harmonies in the orchestra. Angelica firmly answers "no" and goes on watering the flowers. In an ensemble phrase the sisters comment that Sister Angelica is lying. She has a desire, they sing ("Noi lo sappiamo"). Her dearest wish is to hear from her relatives—for seven long years she has had no word. She was banished from a home of wealth and nobility, so the Abbess said, and had to take the veil. The nuns look at each other questioningly, asking: "How . . . why . . . ?"

Their conjectures are interrupted by the Nursing Sister, who rushes in to ask help from Sister Angelica. The Nurse cries that Sister Chiara was stung by wasps as she was trimming a rosebush in the garden. The poor girl is now lying in her cell in great pain. Sister Angelica tells the Nurse to make a potion of herbs and flowers dipped in milk. It will be bitter, Angelica warns, but it will ease the pain. As the Nurse thanks her profusely, Angelica murmurs she is glad to be able to help.[1]

Suddenly there is great excitement as two convent attendants (tourières) arrive leading a donkey laden with gifts for the sisters. They crowd around and in a lively ensemble express their delight over the contributions—filberts, almonds, flour, butter, lentils, milk. Then one attendant stirs up more excitement by announcing that a distinguished visitor has arrived at the convent in a splendid carriage.

Angelica, rushing forward, asks in startled tones if the carriage is emblazoned with a coat of arms in ivory . . . if it is upholstered in pale blue silk. The attendant shrugs. In chorus, the nuns remark that Angelica has turned pale and is trembling. When the bell sounds to announce the visitor, they chatter excitedly, wondering who it may be. Angelica meanwhile stands apart; eyes upraised, she implores the Virgin Mother for help, as though haunted by a premonition of misfortune. Watching her, Genevieve silences the nuns with a gesture, then approaches Angelica. In a phrase of lyrical tenderness she expresses the hope that, at long last, Sister Angelica will have a visitor. Deeply moved, Angelica thanks her.

As a kind of fanfare sounds in the orchestra, the Abbess enters to announce the visitor. The nuns gaze compassionately at Angelica, who stands as though in a trance. When the Abbess calls her name, the spell seems to be broken. With a wave of her hands, the Abbess dismisses the other nuns, who go toward the fountain, where the water has turned to gold in the light of the setting sun. There they fill their watering cans and go toward the cemetery. Angelica breathlessly asks the Abbess who the visitor is

---

[1] In the original score this scene is marked for an optional cut.

("Madre, parlate!"). She sings that she has waited for seven long years, and now . . .

The Abbess interrupts to say that the visitor is her aunt, the Princess. Angelica greets the news with a choking cry. Sternly warning Angelica that she must be obedient and submissive, because the Blessed Mother will hear her every word, the Abbess leaves. Angelica walks toward the arcade, then stops a few paces from a door in the side wall.

A moment later, as a foreboding theme sweeps through the bass, the Princess is escorted in by the portress and the Abbess. A tall, forbidding figure with aristocratic bearing, she stares coldly at Sister Angelica. Almost losing control, Angelica rushes toward her, but halts when the Princess stretches forth her hand in an imperious gesture. Angelica feverishly kisses it, then falls to her knees sobbing. The Princess only looks down at her contemptuously. Now follows the climactic scene of the opera, which is in the form of a long, dramatic duet.

It begins as the Princess recalls how Angelica's father, the Prince Gualtiero ("Principe Gualtiero, vostro padre"), and her mother, Princess Clara, when they both died twenty years ago, left their children in the Princess' care. Their inheritance she sings, was left in equal shares—but the will gave her, the Princess, the power to change it in the event of some "indiscretion" on the part of the heirs. With that she hands a document to Angelica and peremptorily orders her to read it, then sign it.

Confused and frightened, Angelica timidly begs for some show of love and pity. In answer, the Princess tells her why she must sign this document—which will cancel forever all claims to her inheritance: Her young sister, Anna Viola, is to be married. In phrases of poignant tenderness, Angelica asks a blessing on her sister. There is a striking change of key here from the grim minor accompaniment to the Princess' words to the major harmonies of Angelica's.

When Angelica asks whom Viola is marrying, the Princess vindictively replies that the bridegroom is a man whose love can overlook the disgrace which Angelica has brought upon her ancient and honorable name ("Chi per amore condono"). Outraged by this insult, Angelica asks how it is possible for her mother's own sister to show such cruelty. In a furious outburst, the Princess denounces Angelica for daring to invoke her mother's name. Then in a sudden change of mood, she launches into a somber, almost mystical refrain ("Di frequente las sera") in which she describes how every evening she kneels in her chapel to commune with the spirit of

Angelica's mother. But when this ecstasy has passed, she goes on as the harmonies darken in the orchestra, only one thought remains: Angelica, and her need for repentance.

Angelica softly answers that she has always prayed to the Blessed Mother for forgiveness ("Tutto offerto alla Vergine") —but one thing she will not promise even her. In anguish and despair she screams: "To forget my son!" She abandons herself to her grief and hopeless longing for her baby in a tortured refrain, "Mio figliol" Then in a frenzy she rages that the Princess must tell her what has happened to her child, or be forever cursed.

The Princess calmly tells Angelica that her son died two years ago. With an agonized cry, Angelica falls to the ground. The ensuing wordless action takes place to the accompaniment of a powerfully dramatic orchestral passage. The Princess rises as though to help Angelica, checks herself and goes over to a sacred image on the wall. There, leaning on her cane, she stands with head bowed as though in prayer. The scene gradually darkens. Angelica, racked by sobs, remains kneeling. The portress enters, places a candle on the table, then pauses as the Princess says a few words to her. She goes out and returns a moment later with the Abbess, who brings an inkwell and a quill.

Angelica stares at her, then realizes what she must do. Dragging herself to the table, she signs the document, buries her face in her hands and turns away. The Princess picks up the document and takes a step toward Angelica, who shrinks back with a gesture of horror. The Princess goes toward the door, turns toward Angelica with a look of gloating and contempt, then disappears. Angelica, wailing in anguish, falls to her knees. The gloom of night envelops the scene; in the background the nuns are seen lighting the votive lanterns on the tombstones.

Angelica now pours out her longing for her dead son in the opera's principal aria, "Senza mamma, o bimbo." As though hypnotized, she cries out for death to release her so that she can be with her son. Sister Genevieve and the other nuns move slowly toward her through the gloom like white ghosts. In a choral accompaniment to Angelica's final rapturous invocation to the Blessed Virgin, they sing that her prayers will be answered. The convent bells chime as they withdraw to their cells. Angelica, walking as though in a dream, slowly follows.

There is a brief, serene orchestral interlude, during which Angelica reappears. She is carrying an earthenware jar, which she places at the foot of a cypress tree after filling it with water from the fountain. She then gathers a small heap of twigs and leaves and sets them afire with a flint. On the flames she places the jar, then stands watching it intently for a moment. Now Sister Angelica's healing potion, she murmurs ("Suor Angelica ha sempre"), will do its work. The flowers on which she has lavished loving care will in return give her the blessed gift of poison . . . the gift of eternal peace.

Facing the cells, she begins the song of farewell, "Addio, buone sorelle." Her son is calling her, she sings, and she now will go to meet him in paradise, where they will be together for all eternity. With a cry of exultation she rushes to the shrine, kisses the cross, then picks up the jar and drinks the poison. She gasps in pain as it takes effect. The jar drops from her hands.

Her expression of serene resignation suddenly changes to one of horror at the realization of her terrible crime of suicide. In agony and remorse she screams that she is damned forever ("Ah! son dannata!"). Wildly she implores the Madonna for a sign of pardon for this deadliest of sins ("O Madonna, salvami!"). It was the love of her son, she wails, that led her to this act of madness.

Through the mists of approaching death, Angelica hears the voices of angels interceding for her ("O gloriosa virginum"). Her voice soars over the swelling chorus as she makes her final entreaty for absolution. A vision appears before her: A dazzling glow envelops the chapel as the doors slowly open. The Blessed Virgin emerges leading a small, fair-haired boy. She gently pushes him toward Angelica as the unseen chorus bursts into a triumphant phrase—"Gloriosa virginum! Salve, Maria!"

The boy takes one step toward Angelica, then another and finally another. The voices of the angelic choir fade into a lingering pianissimo. Angelica, dying, sinks gently to the ground. The curtain falls.

# Il Tabarro
## (*The Cloak*)

### *by* GIACOMO PUCCINI
### (1858–1924)

### *Libretto by*
#### GIUSEPPE ADAMI

*Based on* LA HOUPPELANDE, *a story by Didier Gold*

#### CHARACTERS

| | |
|---|---|
| Michele, owner and captain of a barge | Baritone |
| Luigi, a stevedore | Tenor |
| Tinca, a stevedore | Tenor |
| Talpa, a stevedore | Bass |
| Giorgetta, wife of Michele | Soprano |
| Frugola, wife of Talpa | Mezzo-soprano |

Stevedores, a street singer, milliners, an organ-grinder, two lovers

*Place:* Paris
*Time:* About 1850
*First performance:* Metropolitan Opera House, New York City, December 14, 1918
*Original language:* Italian

---

*Il Tabarro* is the first one-act opera of Puccini's triptych *Il Trittico,* the second and third being *Suor Angelica* and *Gianni Schicchi.* It is a story of passion, violence and revenge in the *verismo* pattern of *Cavalleria Rusticana* and *Pagliacci,* concerned with tragic upheaval in the lives of simple people.

Its setting is the Paris of *La Bohème* (written twenty years earlier), but not the gay, happy-go-lucky world of the artists. *Il Tabarro* has to do with the harsh existence of working people, who can only dream of a better life they never will know.

The opera never achieved the success of *Gianni Schicchi,* and it is revived only occasionally. Yet it has a plot of great dramatic thrust and a sound harmonic structure embellished by glowing melody. Despite its comparative obscurity, it is one of Puccini's most effective works. A recent revival was the performance of the triptych by the New York City Opera Company at the New York State Theater, Lincoln Center, on February 23, 1967.

The entire action takes place on Michele's barge anchored at a wharf on the Seine. A gangplank connects it with the wharf. The barge is neat and brightly painted, with its flat roof surrounded by a low, white fence lined with pots of geraniums. Laundry is drying on a clothesline; a cage of canaries hangs beside the cabin door.

As the scene opens, Michele, pipe in mouth, is sitting at the helm of the barge and staring into the sunset. Giorgetta is busy taking in her wash, watering her plants and cleaning the canary cage. Stevedores are carrying sacks of cement out of the hold and loading them on a dray on the wharf. From the distance comes the long-drawn whistle of a tugboat, mingled with the moan of foghorns.

To the accompaniment of a barcarolelike rhythm in the orchestra, which continues during most of the opening scene, the stevedores sing a kind of sea chanty ("Oh! Issa! oh!"). Its theme is that they must hurry to get the day's work done, because if they are late getting home their sweethearts may wander off with some other lads.

Giorgetta, pausing in her work, asks Michele what he is thinking about as he stares into the sunset and smokes his pipe ("O Michele? Non sei stanco"). He shrugs off the question and asks if the stevedores have finished. In a brief refrain ("Han lavorato tanto") Giorgetta expresses her concern for the hard-working stevedores, then asks Michele if she may serve them a drink as a reward for their day's work. Michele commends her for her thoughtfulness and tells her to bring out a bottle of wine.

Teasing her about thinking of the stevedores instead of her husband, Michele affectionately tries to embrace her. She resists him, and when he asks for a kiss she offers only her cheek. With a sharp look at her, Michele releases her and goes below deck. The chorus of stevedores again is heard briefly.

A moment later Luigi crosses the gangplank to the barge. Obviously fatigued, he grumbles about the never-ending heat ("Si soffoca, padrona"). This marks the beginning of an ensemble which blends the voices of Giorgetta and Luigi, then Tinca and Talpa. With a passionate look at Luigi, Giorgetta remarks that the heat, like everything else, will have an end. She adds that the wine she is about to serve him will help matters. As she goes into the cabin, Tinca and Talpa, each carrying a sack of cement, stagger up out of the hold. Like Luigi, they complain about the heat and their backbreaking work.

Giorgetta reappears with a pitcher of wine and pours out drinks for the three men. Luigi gaily sings that "a good friend" has come to their assistance, and the four drain their glasses. Spying an organ-grinder passing on the wharf, Luigi throws him a coin and asks him to play. The man obliges with a number comically out of tune. Tinca and Talpa roar out the praises of wine; Tinca is rapidly getting drunk.

Looking seductively at Luigi, Giorgetta sings that the only kind of music that interests her is music one can dance to. Tinca drunkenly offers to be her partner and she good-naturedly accepts. Luigi twits the stevedore about his clumsiness, then pushes him aside and takes Giorgetta in his arms. They dance together like lovers.

Suddenly Michele emerges from the hold. Giorgetta and Luigi abruptly stop dancing. Motioning the organ-grinder to leave, Luigi throws him another coin, then follows Tinca and Talpa down into the hold. Michele approaches Giorgetta, who makes an obvious effort to appear casual.

A colloquy follows as she asks him if he plans to sail the next day. ("Dunque, che cosi credi?"). Through the music of the dialogue comes the voice of a street singer who now appears on the wharf. His plaintive cry, "Who will buy my latest songs" ("Chi vuol l'ultima canzonetta"), is in ironic contrast to the nagging conversation between Giorgetta and Michele. She tries to find out why he has decided to leave Luigi and the other stevedores behind. As for Luigi, Michele answers, it would be better for him if he stayed in Paris—and, in any case, his mind is not always on his work.

Listening with growing irritation, Giorgetta turns away momentarily and becomes aware of the sunset. In a brief refrain ("Già descende la sera") she admires its flaming beauty, but then reflects sadly that the end of another day also brings closer the end of summer. Forebodingly, she murmurs that the sun seems drenched in blood.

Her thoughts are interrupted by the approach of Frugola. Giorgetta sarcastically comments that, as usual, she probably is chasing her husband. Michele growls that she has good reason—he drinks too much. The real reason, Giorgetta retorts, is that Frugola is jealous.

From this point on, Puccini blends several musical themes into a remarkable ensemble which focuses the action of a complex scene. As Giorgetta and Michele continue their dialogue, the street singer and an itinerant harpist, on a street across the Seine, entertain a group of milliners who have just come out of their shop. The street singer favors the girls with one of his ballads, "Primavera, non cercare," a bittersweet story about a girl named Mimi whose heart was broken in a love affair. The girls, moved by Mimi's plight, buy copies of the ballad and then go on their way singing its refrain, "anche il cuore di Mimi!"

Meanwhile, Giorgetta and Michele continue their bickering. He patiently tries to discover why she is angry with him: Has he mistreated or neglected her? No, Giorgetta answers—then bursts out that his brooding is driving her to distraction. She cries that she would rather be cursed and beaten—anything but this silence. Again she demands to know why he is acting so strangely. Instead of answering, Michele goes toward the prow of the barge and checks the mooring. With mocking effect, the chorus of the milliners is heard in the distance, repeating the "Mimi" refrain about unrequited love. Giorgetta, listening, murmurs that she is always happy when she is in Paris. Michele nods significantly.

The scene is interrupted by the entrance of Frugola, who comes aboard carrying a bag filled with junk she has collected. A frowzy, unkempt woman of about fifty, she shouts an effusive greeting. Michele responds with a wave of his hand, then retreats below deck. Frugola loudly asks Giorgetta if she has seen Talpa, her husband. In an ensuing refrain ("il mio uomo") she explains that, to relieve his aching muscles, she rubbed him down with rum. He absorbed enough through his pores to make him drunk.

Then she opens her sack and enthusiastically displays its contents—a fantastic jumble of odds and ends. In a refrain introduced by a swaying, harplike figure in the orchestra, she describes her wares ("Se tu sapessi"). She offers Giorgetta a comb—"good as new"—then enumerates the rest of her treasures. There are scraps of silk and lace, silver buckles, golden lockets—all souvenirs of forgotten love affairs or moments of tender passion.

When Giorgetta points to a certain package, Frugola rambles on that it contains fresh beef for her beloved cat, Corporal. With that she launches into extravagant praise of her pet ("Cuore di manzo per Caporale"). He is a very superior cat, she sings, and her only true friend. Human beings may betray her, but Corporal never will. He has a most admirable philosophy of life: Being a king in a cave is better than being a slave in a palace. It is better to be satisfied with two slices of beef than to hunger for love and die of a broken heart.

Frugola's babbling is interrupted as Talpa and Luigi come out of the hold with Michele. A scene in ensemble follows. Michele asks Luigi if he will help load another cargo tomorrow ("O Luigi, domani"). Tinca and the other stevedores emerge from the hold and start to cross the gangplank. When Frugola catches sight of Tinca she begins to upbraid him about his drinking. If she were his wife, she tells him, she would nag him into sobriety. And take all the joy out of life, Tinca retorts. Only in drinking, he goes on, can one forget the bitterness of living.

Luigi, who has been listening intently to the conversation, enlarges on Tinca's point of view in one of the opera's major arias, "Hai ben ragione." Tinca is right, he sings. For the poor there is no other escape from misery. They are doomed to live by the sweat of their brows without hope of reward. The doors to a better life are forever closed against them. It is useless to struggle—the wise man accepts this as a fact of life and bows to his fate. There is only one answer—drinking, Tinca comments sardonically. Giorgetta angrily tells him to be quiet. Taken aback, Tinca slinks away.

In contrast to Luigi's bitter mood, Frugola sings lightheartedly that her dream of happiness is a cottage in the country ("Ho sognato una casetta"). Giorgetta declares that the place of her dreams is Paris—she blossoms like a flower when she breathes the air of the city ("E ben altro il mio sogno"). She laments that Michele will not leave this dismal existence aboard his barge.

Then she recalls the village outside Paris where she and Luigi grew up. It was Belleville, Luigi explains. In an ensuing duet ("Come me, l'ha nel sangue!") he and Giorgetta reminisce about the happy days of their childhood. In the climax of the duet ("Ma chi lascia il sobborgo") they sing that their memories of the gay and exciting life in Belleville are tinged with sorrow, because they know they never can return to the place which is their true home. The duet ends on a soaring unison phrase. Frugola, deeply moved, murmurs that she can understand their longing and sorrow.

Talpa dispels this nostalgic mood by inviting Giorgetta and Luigi to have supper with him and his wife. Luigi declines, explaining that he must have a talk with Michele. Talpa and Frugola leave arm in arm, repeating the plaintive refrain about the cottage of their dreams.

Alone, Giorgetta and Luigi voice their emotions in an impassioned duet ("O Luigi! Bada a te!"). When Giorgetta softly repeats his name, Luigi impulsively tries to take her in his arms. Fighting

for self-control, she warns him that Michele might find them together—and he would kill them both if he found out they were
lovers. But in the next moment they declare that not even the
threat of death can keep them from each other's arms.

They hear Michele approaching and quickly draw apart. Luigi
asks the skipper if he will take him along on the trip to Rouen.
Michele scoffs at the suggestion, telling Luigi that there is no
work to be had in that city. As Luigi shrugs resignedly, Michele
leaves to attend to his barge duties.

No sooner has he gone than Giorgetta, tormented by anxiety
and desire, asks Luigi why he wants to go to Rouen ("Dimmi:
perchè gli hai chiesto"). This marks the beginning of one of the
finest duets in the opera. Luigi replies that he asked to go because he cannot bear to share her with someone else. To a blazing
orchestral accompaniment, they abandon themselves to their emotions and reiterate their avowals.

As they become calmer, Giorgetta tells Luigi to return later
for their rendezvous. She will leave the gangplank in place; he
is to wait until she gives him the signal by lighting a match—
as she has done before. Its flame will be like a star in heaven,
she sings, a blazing symbol of their love. The duet continues with
increasing intensity. At its climax, Luigi cries that if Giorgetta
spurned his love he would kill her in his jealous madness and
fashion her heart into a beautiful jewel. Giorgetta, fearing that
her husband is approaching, frantically signs Luigi to leave. He
goes quickly. There is a suspenseful pause in the music.

Then Michele, carrying a lantern, comes out of the cabin. Looking sharply at his wife he asks why she has not gone to bed
("Perchè non vai a letto?"). Here begins another of the opera's
great duets. First, in quasi-recitative, they talk about Luigi and
Tinca. Giorgetta commends her husband for keeping Luigi on the
crew, but urges him to dismiss Tinca, who drinks too much.
Michele remarks dryly that he drinks only to keep from strangling
his unfaithful wife. Giorgetta testily says she is not interested in
family gossip.

As the music takes on a deeper emotional quality, Michele
comes closer to Giorgetta and asks why she no longer loves him.
To evade answering, she says she is tired and will go to bed—
although she dreads the hot, gloomy cabin. Michele, trying to
soften her mood, tenderly recalls the happier days when they
shared the cabin with their baby. Shaken by the memory, Giorgetta sobs. Michele sings eloquently of the times when he held

her in his arms, when he kissed her and enfolded her warm body in his cloak.

But that golden September is gone, Michele sings in somber phrases. Now their baby is dead and their lives no longer mean anything. He himself has only his old age to offer a young wife. Stricken by his pleading for her love, Giorgetta tries to end the ordeal, but Michele will not let her go. He reminds her of how much they once were in love and abjectly begs her to give him back her heart. He holds out his arms to her.

Giorgetta protests that, neither for herself nor for him, can things be the same again; life has changed them both. Michele stubbornly refuses to believe that this has come to pass. In complete despair, Giorgetta tells him she is going to bed, then hurries into the cabin. Glaring after her, Michele snarls in a savage undertone: "You harlot!" ("Sguldrina!"). The outburst is underscored by somber chords in the bass.

At length he gets up and attends to the red and green navigating lights of his barge. In ironic contrast to his turbulent mood, two lovers passing on the wharf are heard singing that lips are made for kissing and that the precious hours of night must not be wasted ("Bocca di rosa fresca"). As their voices die away, the stillness is broken by the sound of a bugle from a distant military barracks.

Michele turns and stalks slowly toward the cabin, where he stands listening intently. In tones of despair, he murmurs: "Nulla! Silenzio!" There is a menacing drum roll and a trombone passage, dark and foreboding. This introduces the magnificent aria which is the musical climax of the opera. Tortured by suspicion and jealousy, Michele wonders who is the lover for whom Giorgetta, lying sleepless in the cabin, is waiting ("Chi l'ha trasformata?"). Is it Talpa? He is too old. Tinca? She despises that sot. Luigi? No . . . he spoke first of leaving the crew, then asked as a favor to be taken along to Rouen.[1]

The thought of his mysterious rival goads Michele to wild fury. He cries that he will seek out the guilty man . . . beat him . . . crush him . . . scream into his face: "It is you! It is you!" ("Sei tu! Sei tu!"). A terrible destiny has chained their lives together and now they both face the black abyss ("giù insiem nel gorgo

---

[1] In another version of this scene (as given in the Ricordi score, copyright 1918), Michele remains seated, wraps his cloak around him and stares out over the Seine. In the aria he addresses his thoughts to the river, which he compares to endlessly flowing eternity ("Scorri, fiume eterno").

più profondo!"). A rising and falling chromatic figure in the accompaniment heightens the impact of the words. The aria ends on a phrase of overpowering menace: "La pace è nella morte!" ("Only your death will bring me peace").

Exhausted by his rage, Michele sinks down beside the tiller and slowly lights his pipe. Luigi, watching from the shadows of the wharf, mistakes the flare of the match for Giorgetta's signal, runs across the gangplank and leaps aboard. His action is reflected in a hurrying rhythmic figure in the orchestra. Michele waits until the intruder comes closer. Suddenly recognizing Luigi, he springs at him like a wild animal and grasps him by the throat. Luigi screams in terror. Over a clamorous accompaniment, Michele tries to force a confession from his captive, who momentarily struggles free and whips out his knife. Michele twists his arm until the knife clatters to the deck. Now Luigi will go to Rouen as he asked, Michele howls, but as a bloated corpse in the river.

Then in a paroxysm of fury he again seizes Luigi by the throat and shouts that only a confession will free him. Luigi gasps that it is true: He loves her. Relentlessly tightening his grip, Michele forces Luigi to repeat the words. The boy's answer is cut short in the final convulsion of death. As though demented, Michele glares down at the body.

Suddenly Giorgetta, calling his name, rushes from the cabin. Michele quickly lifts Luigi's body in his arms and covers it with his cloak. Wailing that she is frightened, Giorgetta comes closer. With stony calm, Michele murmurs that he was aware that she was not able to go to sleep. Giorgetta, with a deliberate touch of coquetry, asks him to forgive her thoughtless words and rude behavior, then asks if she may sit beside him.

With sinister meaning that even now is lost on Giorgetta, Michele in turn asks: "Where? Under my cloak?" The cloak, Giorgetta answers, reminds her of something he often told her: Every person carries a mysterious cloak, under which he conceals either "a secret joy or a secret sorrow."

Michele leaps to his feet, flings back the cloak, and in a thunderous voice shouts: "And sometimes a crime!" ("Qualche volta un delitto!"). Luigi's body rolls grotesquely at Giorgetta's feet. She staggers back with a scream of horror.

Michele violently seizes her and, forcing her down, thrusts her face against the face of her dead lover. The curtain falls.

# Werther

### by JULES MASSENET
### (1842–1912)

### Libretto by
#### ÉDOUARD BLAU, PAUL MILLIET and GEORGES HARTMANN

Based on the novel *Die Leiden des Jungen Werthers* (*The Sorrows of Young Werther*), by the German poet and novelist Johann Wolfgang von Goethe

#### CHARACTERS

| | |
|---|---:|
| Werther, a young poet | Tenor |
| Charlotte, daughter of the Bailiff | Mezzo-soprano |
| Sophie, her sister | Soprano |
| The Bailiff, a widower | Bass |
| Albert, fiancé of Charlotte, later her husband | Baritone |
| Schmidt ⎱ friends of the Bailiff | ⎰ Tenor |
| Johann ⎰ | ⎱ Bass |
| Brühlmann  a young boy and girl | |
| Kätchen     who appear briefly | Treble voices ⎰ |

Younger children of the Bailiff (Fritz, Max, Hans, Karl, Gretel, Clara), servants, townsfolk

*Place:* Wetzlar, in Prussia
*Time:* About 1780
*First performance:* World premiere (in German), Imperial Opera, Vienna, February 16, 1892; first performance in French, Geneva, Switzerland, December 27, 1892
*Original language:* French

---

*Werther*, the ninth of Massenet's twenty-five operas, was his most popular with the exception of *Manon*. It was a favorite with French audiences, having been performed some thirteen hundred times at the Opéra-Comique in Paris following its premiere in Geneva.

In America, *Werther* was performed for the first time in March 1894. Subsequently, Mary Garden, while with the Chicago Opera

Company, made the role of Charlotte one of her most memorable interpretations.

The Metropolitan presented *Werther* for the first time in April 1894 with a cast headed by Emma Eames and Jean De Reszke. In November 1909 and March 1910 revivals there, the cast was headed by Geraldine Farrar, Edmond Clémont, Alma Gluck and Dinh Gilly.

The San Francisco Opera staged the opera for the first time in November 1935 with the role of Werther sung by Tito Schipa, considered the finest Werther in the opera's later history. The most recent New York performance was given by the New York City Opera Company during its 1947–48 season. Abroad, the work was produced by Sir Michael Redgrave at Glyndebourne in June 1966. *Werther* was scheduled for the Metropolitan Opera's 1970–71 season for the first time in sixty years, with a cast headed by Christa Ludwig and Franco Corelli.

Massenet's craftsmanship, unerring musical instinct and sure sense of the dramatic give the opera a sound theatrical quality. The music ranges from unabashed romanticism to a kind of refined sensuality. There is a wealth of flowing melody combined with a fragile charm peculiarly French. Massenet makes effective use of identifying themes to heighten characterization, and the vocal line is supported by superb orchestration.

There is a brief, lyrical prelude, the themes of which reflect the realistic as well as the romantic elements in Werther's personality. The dominant theme is that heard later when the poet sees Charlotte's house for the first time.

## ACT ONE

At left, the terrace at the entrance of the Bailiff's house; beyond, a courtyard with a fountain. At right, a garden. An afternoon in July. The Bailiff, seated on the terrace, is surrounded by his younger children, whom he is teaching Christmas carols.

Stopping them in the middle of a chorus, the bailiff scolds them for singing too loudly, then asks them to begin again ("Assez! Recommençons"). The children do so, singing as loudly as before and without expression. Annoyed, the Bailiff asks if they would dare sing in such an unmusical manner if their sister Charlotte were there to hear them. This admonition impresses the youngsters, and they repeat the carol ("Jésus vient de naître") to their father's satisfaction. In fact, he is so well pleased that he ends the carol with them.

Schmidt and Johann appear and stand listening in the doorway. The children run to them affectionately. Johann twits the Bailiff for rushing the Christmas season by teaching the children Christmas carols in July. The Bailiff answers rather testily that not everyone's artistic sensibilities are as easily offended as Johann's—and besides, it is not easy to teach children because they do not pay attention.

Their colloquy is interrupted by the entrance of Sophie. The scene continues in quasi-recitative and brief solo passages. Greeting Sophie, Schmidt inquires about Charlotte. Sophie answers that her sister is getting dressed for the family ball which is to be held at Wetzlar this evening. In a brief refrain ("Koffel a mis sa redingcote") Schmidt describes how friends and neighbors are eagerly preparing for this gala event. Koffel is brushing up his frock coat, Steiner is hiring the brewer's horse, Hoffmann and Goulden are renting a coach and a buggy. Even that melancholy young poet, Werther, seems lately to be taking a more cheerful view of life.

The three men discuss Werther briefly. The Bailiff says he likes the young man, but the other two consider him too withdrawn and gloomy. When the Bailiff tells them that the Prince has even offered Werther a diplomatic post, Schmidt and Johann scoff that he is much too provincial for such a sophisticated position.

With that the two take their leave, telling the Bailiff they will meet him later at the Golden Grape—where they intend to collect the drinks he owes them. They add that the waitress has promised them lobster for dinner. The Bailiff jokingly calls them a pair of gluttons, then asks if they will not wait to see Charlotte. They answer that they will see her later at the ball.

Schmidt pauses to ask when Albert will return. He has not mentioned returning in his letters, the Bailiff replies, but he writes that his business is going well. Schmidt comments that Albert is a fine young man who will make an ideal husband for Charlotte. Finally leaving arm in arm, Schmidt and Johann sing a lusty duet in praise of Bacchus ("Vivat Bacchus, semper vivat!").

The Bailiff calls the children together again to rehearse the Christmas carol "note by note." He sends Sophie to bring Charlotte, then goes into the house with the children. Werther appears, accompanied by a young peasant who has shown him the way to the Bailiff's house. Walking slowly to the fountain, the poet sings the first of the opera's arias, a lyrical invocation to the pastoral beauty of this quiet spot ("O nature, plein de grace"). In an introductory recitative ("Je ne sais si je veille") he wonders if he is awake or dreaming, because this place is like paradise itself. In the aria, he hails Nature as the eternal mother, forever young and adorable ("Mere eternellement jeune").

A graceful arpeggio follows the conclusion of the aria, and then the sound of the children singing is heard. Listening, Werther murmurs that the bitterness of life cannot sully their innocence.

As he muses beside the fountain, Charlotte appears. The children, excitedly calling her name, rush out of the house to greet her. The Bailiff follows, and Charlotte asks him if he is pleased with their singing. Reasonably so, he answers, but the children assure Charlotte that Papa is "tres content" with their performance. Gazing at Charlotte in her party finery, the Bailiff effusively praises her beauty. All their friends, he exclaims, will be jealous of her.

Modestly turning aside the compliment, Charlotte remarks that their "jealous" friends are late in arriving—and that will allow her time to give the children their supper. Thereupon she fetches a large loaf of bread and a dish of butter, then distributes the slices to her brothers and sisters.

At the sound of carriage wheels in the distance, the Bailiff tells Charlotte to hurry because the guests are arriving. At that moment he notices Werther approaching and welcomes him with pompous courtesy ("Vous venez visiter"). Introducing Charlotte, he explains she is mother to her brothers and sisters, who were left motherless by the death of his wife. Charlotte, somewhat embarrassed, apologizes to Werther for being remiss in her greeting. The children, she adds primly, refuse to eat their meals unless she herself serves them. Werther acknowledges with a gallant bow.

During a brief orchestral interlude, the guests begin to arrive. With them come Brühlmann and Kätchen, a young couple so wrapped up in each other that they pay no attention to the Bailiff as he greets them. Holding hands, they sigh ecstatically over "the divine Klopstock," whose poetry obviously has inspired them.[1] The Bailiff, with an indulgent laugh, advises the lad to save his rhapsodies until he gets to the ball, in order not to delay the proceedings at present.

A brief byplay follows. Approaching Werther with one of the

[1] This is a reference to Friedrich Gottlieb Klopstock (1724–1803), a German poet. He was notable for his iconoclastic rejection of contemporary classic forms in favor of unrhymed odes expressing intensely religious emotions.

youngest children in her arms, Charlotte tells the child to "kiss her cousin." Taken aback, Werther wonders if he is worthy of the name. Charlotte observes, rather enigmatically, that there are so many cousins that it would be unfortunate if he proved unworthy of the relationship. She then turns to Sophie and asks her to take charge of the children tonight in her stead. Sophie willingly assents, but remarks that the children would much rather be with Charlotte.

Deeply touched by the rapport between the sisters, Werther expresses his admiration in an impassioned refrain, "O spectacle ideal." It is at the same time a declaration of his love for Charlotte.

He and Charlotte then leave with the other guests. Brühlmann and Kätchen, still oblivious to everything, remain at the fountain for a moment, then wander hand in hand after the others. The Bailiff, watching them with a smile, muses that the "divine Klopstock" and young love present a riddle beyond his understanding.

Sophie sends the children into the house. Then, hearing her father reprise a few bars of "Vivat Bacchus," she quietly brings him his hat and cane, mischievously reminding him that he promised to meet Schmidt and Johann at the Golden Grape. The Bailiff—somewhat abashed because Sophie knows he is anxious to join his convivial friends—at first demurs, then struts away, jauntily swinging his cane. Sophie accompanies him to the garden gate and closes it after him.

As she turns back to the house, Albert appears. With an exclamation of surprise, Sophie runs to him and they embrace. Their dialogue continues over a recurring six-note figure in the accompaniment. Albert's first question is about Charlotte. Sophie explains that this is one of the rare occasions when she is away from the house. Why, she asks, has he kept his arrival a secret? He replies that he wanted to surprise Charlotte, and now he wants to know if she thought about him during his six months' absence. Sophie assures him that Charlotte—who, after all, is to be his bride—thought of him constantly, as did everyone else in the house.

And meanwhile, Sophie goes on, she and the others have been busy preparing for the wedding—and she hopes there will be dancing. Albert promises that it will be a gay affair because he wants everyone to share his happiness. But for the present no one is to know that he has returned, he tells Sophie, then urges her to go into the house before they are discovered. With a tender "Goodnight, dear brother-in-law," she goes in and closes the door.

Alone, Albert expresses his happiness over his return in the melodious aria "Quelle prière de reconnaissance." He marvels how these familiar surroundings have taken on a new meaning, and looks forward with passionate longing to his first meeting with Charlotte after his absence.

As he slowly walks away, immersed in his thoughts, the scene gradually darkens and the moonlight glimmers through the trees. Here begins the exquisite music of the "Clair de Lune" scene, one of Massenet's finest creations. The sensuous theme, stated by the strings in elegant contours, is evidence of the composer's gift for orchestral effect. The music inevitably brings to mind Debussy's more impressionistic evocation of night in his own "Clair de Lune."

Charlotte and Werther, returning from the ball, walk arm in arm through the garden gate, then sing the great duet "Il faut nous séparer." Charlotte bids the poet goodnight; he responds with a passionate avowal of his love. She deprecates his extravagant praise of her beauty, saying that he really knows nothing about her.

In answer, Werther exclaims that their souls are linked together ("Mon áme a reconnu"). He declares that her own brothers and sisters will bear witness that she is the loveliest of women. Yes . . . the children know, Charlotte replies ("Vous avez dit vrai"), but that is only because these orphaned little ones see in her the image of their beloved mother. Even now, Charlotte goes on, they add to her own anguish by asking why "those men in black" carried their mother away.

But Werther, almost beside himself with ardor, scarcely hears what Charlotte is saying. In an impassioned refrain ("Rêve! Extase!") he again apostrophizes her beauty and reiterates his avowals. Disturbed by the violence of his emotions, Charlotte tells him he must go. At that moment, the Bailiff is heard calling out that Albert has arrived. Werther, staggering back in stunned surprise, repeats the name questioningly. In stricken tones, Charlotte tells him that Albert is the man she promised her dying mother she would marry.

Looking into Werther's eyes, she declares that when he was near she had forgotten that oath. Though crushed by despair, the poet tells her she must keep her promise—but if she does, he will die. As the "Clair de Lune" theme, in a minor key, sounds softly in the orchestra, Charlotte turns and leaves. Alone, Werther cries out in anguish: "She is betrothed to another!" The curtain falls.

## ACT TWO

Before the curtain rises there is a brief prelude entitled *Les Tilleuls* ("The Lime Trees"), in the rhythm of a country dance. Its principal theme is associated with the convivial personalities of Schmidt and Johann.

The scene is the square before the Golden Grape at Wetzlar on a pleasant Sunday afternoon in September. Across the square is the Protestant church, next to it the parsonage. Schmidt and Johann are seated at a table outside the inn. Enjoying their wine, they sing a variation of their favorite tune, "Vivat Bacchus," in praise of wine, the weather and life in general.

They pause to listen to the sound of the organ in the church. Schmidt suggests they join in singing the service, whereupon they strike up an impromptu hymn of their own ("De bénir le Seigneur"). Sung in an ingenious imitation of the canon form, its burden is that each man should praise the Lord in his own way. At its conclusion, Johann tells his companion that on this day the rector is being honored for his fifty years of married life. Schmidt remarks that this is indeed an admirable achievement—but he himself could never have survived it. At that moment they both catch sight of Charlotte and Albert crossing the square on their way to the church. There, says Johann, are two people who were willing to take the risk of marriage. He and Schmidt gravely drink to the health of these two brave souls and then go inside the tavern.

Meanwhile, Charlotte and Albert sit down on a bench under a lime tree near the entrance of the parsonage. In a melodious duet ("Voici trois mois") they reflect on the happiness they have shared during the three months of their marriage. At the conclusion of the duet, organ music again is heard and the two enter the church.

As they do so, Werther appears on the other side of the square and grimly watches them. A sudden change in the orchestral accompaniment from the simple melody of the organ music to foreboding harmonies reflects his emotional turmoil. He gives expression to his thoughts in the dramatic recitative and aria "Un autre est son époux . . . J'aurais sur mon poitrine"—known as the *Désolation de Werther*.

In the recitative he sings that if God had granted him this angel, he would have devoted his life to her. Now his love for her is blasphemy. But for a caprice of fate, he goes on in the aria, he could be holding this most glorious of God's creations in his arms, to be his own forever. In a climactic phrase of anguish, Werther sings that this dream is shattered. Staggering to the bench under the lime tree, he buries his face in his hands. The clamorous orchestral accompaniment gradually subsides.

As Werther remains motionless on the bench, Schmidt and Johann emerge from the inn leading young Brühlmann, who is beside himself as the result of a lovers' quarrel. The two men try to assure the lad that his Kätchen will come back to him, but Brühlmann is inconsolable. After all, Johann tells him, a seven-year courtship cannot possibly have been in vain. In any case, Schmidt adds gaily, taking the boy by the arm, he can forget his troubles at the rector's anniversary party. With that the men literally drag the distraught youngster away.

Albert, coming out of the church alone, sees Werther. Going to him, he impulsively puts his hand on the poet's shoulder in a comforting gesture. Werther, startled, leaps to his feet as though trying to avoid the other. A dramatic colloquy follows.

Restraining Werther, Albert sings that he understands his sorrow and is grateful to him for his abnegation. In an ensuing refrain ("Mais celle qui devint ma femme") he sings that he is aware that Werther and Charlotte once met, and that the poet dreamed of love. But now that dream has vanished, and he knows what agony this has cost. And to know, Albert adds, grasping Werther's hand, is to forgive.

In an equally moving refrain ("Vous l'avez dit") Werther answers that he has indeed tried to remain loyal. Rather than continue to harbor unworthy desires for what he has lost he will resist temptation and go away forever. When the storm of passion is over and the pain is gone, the consolation of true friendship will sustain him.

The scene is interrupted by Sophie, who comes tripping in to the accompaniment of a sprightly figure in the orchestra. Bubbling with happiness, she shows the two men a bouquet and sings that she has plundered the garden for the choicest flowers ("Voyez le beau bouquet"). Smiling up at Werther, she promises to ask him for the first dance at the anniversary party. Taking note of his crestfallen expression, Sophie exclaims that on this beautiful day everyone should be happy. She elaborates on this theme with joyous abandon in a sparkling aria, "Du gai soleil."

Werther, however, is unmoved by Sophie's gaiety. Albert, in order to be alone with him, tells Sophie to present her bouquet to the anniversary couple. With a significant look at Werther,

Albert observes that while one looks far and wide for happiness, perhaps it is before one's very eyes—with a smile on her face and flowers in her hands. Werther's only reaction is stony silence.

Sophie comes skipping back, reminds Werther that he is to have the first minuet with her, then sings a reprise of her aria. Ending the number on an exuberant phrase, she hurries away followed by Albert.

Werther abandons himself to gloomy reflections to the accompaniment of somber chords in the orchestra. He asks himself if his love for Charlotte has been pure and untainted, then bursts out remorsefully that he has lived a lie: His love has been sullied by impure desire. Tormented by guilt, he cries out that he must go away to escape the consequences of his shameless weakness.

He is about to rush away when he sees Charlotte on the threshold of the church. He stands as though hypnotized as she approaches with downcast eyes, murmuring that prayer has given her new strength. Noticing Werther, she asks if he plans to attend the rector's anniversary party. He replies that it would mean only the torment of seeing her there with another man. Charlotte gazes at him compassionately.

Here begins one of the principal duets of the opera. As the "Clair de Lune" theme sounds in the orchestra, Werther recalls the day they first met ("Ah! qu'il es loin, ce jour") and the rapture they shared in that moment. Charlotte, determined not to weaken, coldly reminds him that she is now the wife of Albert —who loves her. "Who could help loving you?" Werther interjects wildly.

Trying to reason with him, Charlotte asks if there are not other women who could inspire his love ("N'est-il donc pas d'autre femme") . . . why must he love *her?* As well ask a madman the reason for his madness, Werther storms. When Charlotte resolutely tells him he must go, he wildly implores her not to send him away. The scene builds in intensity as Charlotte entreats Werther to have consideration for her own peace of mind. Her plea brings him to his senses.

In quiet resignation he sings that her peace of mind is all he desires—yet he cannot promise to go away forever. No . . . not forever, she tells him fervently, but only for a little while. In fact, she adds, she will expect him back on Christmas Day. With that she leaves to the accompaniment of a descending chromatic theme in the orchestra which underscores Werther's emotional upheaval.

In a melodramatic soliloquy ("Oui! ce qu'elle m'ordonne") Werther resolves to act in accordance with Charlotte's plea for peace of mind. His self-sacrifice may cost him his life, but what does it matter! What is death but the drawing aside of the veil which separates the known from the unknown? Is it a sin to seek relief from suffering?

Werther continues his philosophizing in one of the opera's principal arias, "Lorsque l'enfant revient d'un voyage." When a wandering child returns home unexpectedly, he sings, his father greets him with joy and relief—not rebuke. By the same token, will not God, the Father of mankind, welcome back an erring son and pardon his sins? In the impassioned climax of the aria Werther cries that although he cannot claim to know the Almighty Father, he puts his trust in Him and implores His help in his hour of anguish. He ends the aria in a half-spoken phrase of desperate entreaty.

As Werther turns and walks slowly away, he meets Sophie, who tells him the anniversary procession is ready to start and is waiting for him. Werther brusquely tells her he is leaving. Staring at him in surprise, Sophie asks when he will return. Never, Werther snaps, then strides away. Calling after him, Sophie bursts into tears.

Charlotte, Albert and the other members of the party rush in, find Sophie weeping and excitedly ask what has happened. She sobs that Wether told her he was going away forever, then rushed away like a madman. Charlotte gasps: "Forever!" Albert, suddenly realizing what Werther's action means to her, says in a grim aside: "He loves her!"

As the gay music of the anniversary celebration blares out in ironic contrast to the tragic mood of the scene, the curtain falls.

## ACT THREE

There is a brief prelude—mostly on the theme heard during the Letter Scene which opens the act. The curtain rises to show the home of Charlotte and Albert early on Christmas Eve. Albert is absent. Charlotte is sitting at a table reading a letter from Werther. Here follows another of the opera's famous arias, known as the "Air de lettres" ("Ah, Werther, qui m'aurait dit").

In recitative, Charlotte muses that Werther's absence has served only to bring him closer to her. Throwing the letters on the table, she murmurs that she cannot bring herself to destroy them. In an ensuing refrain ("Je vous écris") sung over a barcarolelike accompaniment in 6/8 tempo, Charlotte reads Werther's latest letter. It quite simply states the fact that he is alone.

Charlotte notes that there is no word of reproof, of love or regret, of blame or rebuke. This intensifies her feeling of guilt: She blames herself for her hardheartedness, for making Werther suffer in loneliness and frustration. This she expresses in an unaccompanied passage. In the letter, Werther adds that as he writes he hears the happy cries of children playing outside his window. They remind him of the tender care Charlotte lavishes on her brothers and sisters. They too will forget him. . . .

They never will forget him, Charlotte exclaims, and will welcome him when he comes back. But the tone of his letter disturbs her. He reminds her that when she set Christmas as the day of his return ("Tu m'as dit: a Noël"), his answer was: "Never!" When that day comes, it will become clear who was right—Charlotte or Werther. But if he does not return ("Mais si je ne dois reparaitre") he asks only that she weep in memory of him. As the somber letter theme sounds in the orchestra, Charlotte finishes reading and sobs quietly.

Sophie runs in—effervescent as always—and chides her sister for keeping to herself while Albert is away. Father, she says, is unhappy about the situation. Noticing Charlotte's tears, Sophie asks if she is ill. Charlotte hastily assures her that she is merely tired but will soon regain her spirits and laugh again.

With childlike enthusiasm, Sophie responds in another characteristically lighthearted air ("Ah! le rire est béni") that laughter is a blessing. It is born of light and is as free as a bird, she sings in coloratura phrases. But suddenly she becomes serious, and the mood of the music changes with her. Leading Charlotte to a chair, Sophie kneels before her.

No longer prattling like a child, she says gravely that she is old enough to know the reason for her sister's tears, as well as for the general air of gloom which has settled over the household. It is all because Werther has gone away. At the sound of his name, Charlotte makes an involuntary movement; she tries to control herself but breaks into tears. The reaction is not lost on Sophie, who apologizes for mentioning Werther's name.

In an ensuing aria, "Va! laissez couler mes larmes"—known as the *Air des Larmes*—Charlotte sings that it is best to let tears flow unchecked. Unshed tears beat like waves upon the heart until at last it breaks. The aria ends on a descending phrase expressive of Charlotte's grief.

Alarmed by her despondent manner, Sophie begs her sister to leave her lonely house and come back to live with her family until Albert returns. Things will be merry at home . . . the children will sing their lovely Christmas carols to brighten the hours. The mention of Christmas brings Charlotte's thoughts back to Werther's letter. In an aside, she repeats the phrase from his letter—"If I should fail to return." Fighting back her tears, she promises Sophie that she will come home. The sisters tenderly embrace.

After Sophie leaves, Charlotte sinks down at the table in utter despair. Then, in a moving prayer ("Seigneur Dieu! J'ai suivi ta loi"), she asks for strength to resist the temptation to surrender to Werther's love. The test is cruel, she cries, and her strength is failing. She implores God's help in her hour of trial. At the conclusion of the aria her voice dies away in a whispered plea.

As she sits hopeless and dejected, Werther suddenly appears in the doorway. Charlotte looks up and cries out his name over a thundering phrase in the orchestra. Werther, pale and haggard, stares at Charlotte as though on the verge of madness. There is a long pause as the two gaze at each other.

Then in broken phrases Werther says that every hour he was away he swore he would never come back to her. On her very threshold he fought against himself, but it was all in vain. Trying to hide her emotions and to calm him, Charlotte says that there was no reason for him to stay away—everyone was eagerly waiting for his return. Werther interrupts to ask if she too was waiting. Pointedly ignoring the question, she hastens to add that even in the house itself nothing has changed. Looking around, Werther murmurs: "Nothing . . . except the hearts."

Yes . . . everything is as he remembers it, he goes on (Charlotte repeats the phrase in a musical echo of his own). Werther notices the harpsichord and recalls how he and Charlotte sang together, then speaks of the books they read to each other. Suddenly he notices two pistols in a box on the table. Making a movement as if to pick them up, he murmurs ominously that these he also remembers. He held them once . . . when he was thinking of the final rest for which he longed.

His gesture is unobserved by Charlotte, who has turned to pick up a book from the harpsichord. She hands him a volume of verses by his favorite poet, Ossian, remarking that he had once asked her to translate them.[2] With a melodramatic sigh, Werther begins reading over a harp accompaniment. This introduces one of the most famous arias in the opera, "Pourquoi me réveiller."

2 Ossian: a bard and epic hero of Gaelic folklore of the third century A.D. His poetry, flowery and romantic, was claimed to have been translated by James MacPherson in The Poems of Ossian (published 1760–62).

Appropriately, it is a lover's lament, in which he asks why the voices of spring should awaken him, when the awakening will bring only sadness and desolation. The aria ends in an impassioned climax. Charlotte, realizing that Werther is describing his own feelings in terms of Ossian's verses, begs him not to go on reading.

Believing she has at last betrayed her true feelings toward him, Werther sings that now she understands ("Ciel! Ai-je compris?"). They must throw off all pretense and submit to the divine decree of love. The scene continues in duet form as Charlotte protests that she must not allow herself to love the poet, while he reiterates his avowals. In momentary surrender, Charlotte yields to his embrace, then tears herself from his arms. Crying that she cannot endure this anguish, she bids Werther goodbye forever and rushes into her room, closing the door behind her.

Imploring her not to leave him, Werther staggers toward the door, then stops and listens. As dark harmonies reverberate in the orchestra and then subside into a long, sustained chord, he murmurs that it is goodbye at last . . . Charlotte has condemned him to death. Walking slowly toward the entrance door of the house, he sings that now Mother Earth may prepare to receive her son ("Prends le deuil, ô nature!"). He must die, carrying his torment with him to the grave. Flinging open the door, he rushes blindly away.

A moment later Albert walks in, his face grim. Told previously that Werther had returned, he is puzzled at finding no one in the room and the door wide open. Frowning darkly, he looks at the door of Charlotte's room and sharply calls her name. The door opens and she appears, gasping in surprise as she sees her husband. When Albert asks her if anything is wrong she manages to answer that she was merely startled at seeing him. With harsh insistence, Albert demands to know who has been in the house. Confused and terrified, Charlotte is speechless.

At that moment a servant enters and hands Albert a letter. He looks at it, recognizes Werther's handwriting, then glares at Charlotte. Slowly and deliberately he reads Werther's message: He is going on a long journey and wishes to borrow Albert's pistols. Charlotte wails that this is an omen of disaster. In cold fury, her husband orders her to give Werther the weapons. As though hypnotized, Charlotte walks to the desk where the pistols are lying in the box. With Albert's eyes fixed on her in a stare of icy hatred, she closes the box and hands it to the servant, who carries it away. Albert crushes Werther's letter in his hand, hurls it from him in violent anger, then strides from the room.

As foreboding bass harmonies reverberate in the orchestra and then flare up into a harsh chromatic figure, Charlotte frantically prays that she may reach Werther in time. The curtain falls.

## ACT FOUR

In the original score there is a long symphonic interlude called —with a certain irony—*La Nuit de Noël*, which recapitulates some of the themes heard in the previous acts. Its general character is dark and foreboding, heavy with Tschaikowskian gloom and the premonition of death. In some productions the interlude is omitted and the act is played as the second part of Act Three.

Werther's study. On the table is a three-branched candlestick, with books and papers scattered about. Through a large window at one side the snow-covered houses of the village are visible. Prominently seen is the house of the Bailiff, which is brightly lighted. In the study a ray of moonlight strikes across the floor and faintly reveals the form of Werther. He has shot himself and lies near death on the floor near the table.

As somber chords reverberate in the orchestra, the door is suddenly flung open and Charlotte enters. Looking around, she excitedly calls Werther's name. Then, going around the table, she comes upon Werther's form. With a cry of horror, she kneels and gently lifts him in her arms. Refusing to believe he is dead ("Non! Non! c'est impossible!"), she distractedly implores him to speak to her. This marks the beginning of the poignant death scene which brings the opera to its tragic climax.

Werther slowly opens his eyes. Recognizing Charlotte, he asks her to forgive him. Charlotte protests that it is she who must be forgiven, because she herself has shed the blood now gushing from his wound. Werther murmurs that because she had kept her love unstained she has spared him remorse in his hour of death. He sinks slowly back into her arms.

Panic-stricken, Charlotte calls for help. Reviving, Werther asks her not to call anyone ("n'appelle personne") . . . it is good to be alone at this moment when Death will allow him to say: "Je t'adore." In a flood of grief and passion, Charlotte bursts out into an avowal of her love: "Et moi, Werther, je t'aime!" At last she confesses that from the day they first met she knew they were destined to love each other.

"And now," she goes on, as the "Clair de Lune" theme softly echoes in the orchestra, "take this last kiss as the seal of our love ("Ah! ton baiser") . . . and in this last kiss let us forget all our anguish." Over shimmering chords in the orchestra, the voices of the lovers die away together on the phrase "Tout oublions."

Suddenly from the Bailiff's house comes the sound of childish voices singing a Christmas carol ("Noël! Jésus vient de naître"). Charlotte recoils at the stinging irony of these sounds of joy in an hour of pain and death. Werther murmurs that these sinless children are singing a hymn of redemption. Now in the grip of delirium, he entreats Charlotte not to weep for him . . . this is not death . . . it is birth into new life. As though to add to Charlotte's torment, she hears Sophie's voice soaring over the children's chorus in an exultant phrase of the carol ("Dieu permet d'etre heureux!").

Looking into Werther's face, Charlotte now realizes that he is at the point of death. As though to keep him from being physically taken away from her, she clasps him frenziedly to her breast, crying: "You shall live!" ("Tu vivre!").

For the last time, Werther opens his eyes. In serene phrases he asks Charlotte to grant him one final request ("La bas, au fond du cimetiere"): He wishes to be buried under the two large linden trees at the back of the cemetery. But if the Church denies Christian burial to one who has taken his own life, then let him be buried in some secret, quiet place. And there, in the twilight, a woman will come and bless his last resting place with her tears.

As the theme of Ossian's poem ("Pourquoi me réveiller") surges through the orchestra, Werther dies in Charlotte's arms. With a cry of agony, she falls sobbing over his body. From outside comes the happy laughter of the children, mingled with the lilting chorus of the Christmas carol. The curtain falls.

# Der Zigeunerbaron
## (*The Gypsy Baron*)
### *by* JOHANN STRAUSS
### (1825–99)

*Libretto by*
IGNAZ SCHNITZER

*Based on the novel* SAFFI, *by the Hungarian novelist Mór Jókai.*

### CHARACTERS

| | |
|---|---|
| Ottokar, a young farm hand | Tenor |
| Lodovico Carnero, emissary of Empress Maria Theresa of Austria, Commissioner of Public Morals | High baritone |
| Sandor Barinkay, a young, impoverished Hungarian nobleman | Tenor |
| Czipra, an old gypsy woman | Mezzo-soprano |
| Saffi, a gypsy girl, supposed daughter of Czipra | Mezzo-soprano |
| Kalman Zsupan, a wealthy pig farmer | Baritone |
| Arsena, daughter of Zsupan | Soprano |
| Mirabella, mother of Ottokar and governess of Arsena | Soprano |
| Count Peter Homonay, Hungarian statesman and hussar | Baritone |
| Pali, a gypsy | Tenor |

Peasants, gypsies, soldiers, nobles of the court, citizens of Vienna.

*Place:* Hungary
*Time:* About 1750, during the reign of Maria Theresa
*First performance:* Theater an der Wien, October 24, 1885
*Original language:* German

---

This gay and tuneful operetta, rich in melody and fiery Hungarian rhythms, is second in popularity only to the composer's *Die Fleder-*

*maus.* Written about ten years after *Fledermaus,* it is another one of some fifteen works Strauss composed for the stage. While in Budapest to conduct one of his operettas, Strauss visited the Hungarian novelist Mór Jókai, who showed him his novel *Saffi.* It was a story of eighteenth-century Hungary—about the time when that province passed from Turkish to Austrian domination. Intrigued by its romantic and patriotic elements, Strauss saw in this subject the opportunity to unite—musically, at least—the ebullient spirits of the Hungarians and the Austrians. The result was a lusty, dashing, Hungarian gypsy piece, topped off with true Viennese *schmaltz.*

Strauss took two years to write *Zigeunerbaron,* making the most effective use of the dance forms which had made him the "Waltz King" of Europe. At the height of his fame as a composer of dance tunes (he wrote more than five hundred of them) he turned to light opera and operetta. With his incomparable talent for melody, he was highly respected as a musician by the great composers of his time—and these included men like Wagner, Richard Strauss and Brahms. His contemporaries said of him that he brought the spirit of the cafe into the opera house.

*Zigeunerbaron* opens with a typically Straussian overture, a collage of the major themes in symphonic style. First, a martial rhythm builds into the czardas theme, followed by the *andantino* of the finale of Act One. Then a wild marching rhythm leads into the gay waltz of the Vienna scene, with the theme of the *Werberlied* (Recruiting Song) following. The overture then returns to the 6/8 tempo of the Boatmen's Chorus at the opening of Act One, and into a brilliant climax.

## ACT ONE

A lonely clearing in the forest. In the background a stone tower rises above the ruins of a castle. In the foreground is a dilapidated, roofless hut; at right a gypsy cabin with a smoking chimney. Near stage front is a peasant house, trim and well kept, with a balcony. This is the home of  Zsupan, the pig farmer, richest landowner in the region.

There is a brief orchestral prelude in a minor key, interspersed with bird calls. Then from behind the scenes comes the Boatmen's Chorus ("Das war kein rechter Schifferknecht"). In a barcarolelike rhythm they sing that anyone who is afraid of the water never will be a good sailor; the true seaman places his trust in his boat and oars. In a poetic turn, the sailors sing that they will sail the sea of life together with their sweethearts.

As the chorus ends, Ottokar appears, carrying a shovel and a pickax. He is vainly searching for buried treasure which, according to legend, had been hidden in the vicinity of the castle by its owner, Baron Barinkay, who had died in exile. Ottokar has been at this task for months and now he complains ("Jeden Tag, Müh und Plag'") that he has been working like a slave to no avail. He curses his bad luck.

Czipra, the old gypsy woman, watches him and cackles in glee at his disappointment. She describes how she has seen Ottokar digging away day after day without finding anything ("Vergebens haben sie gesucht"). Ottokar finally throws down his tools in disgust.

As the barcarole again is heard behind the scene, Czipra comes out of her hut. Spoken dialogue follows as she asks Ottokar what he is looking for—although she knows what it is as well as he does. Ignoring his rudeness when he tells her to mind her own business, she asks why he bothers to look for treasure when there is something more precious for him in a neighbor's house. When he asks what that may be, she answers that it is Arsena, the pretty daughter of Zsupan. With that she goes back into her hut.

Ottokar is dismayed because the gypsy woman knows about his secret love and—what is worse—probably knows he intends to meet Arsena at this very spot tonight. Suddenly hearing voices, he withdraws to one side.

Carnero and Sandor Barinkay enter, followed by officials and a crowd of villagers. In an amusing patter song ("Als flotter Geist doch früh verwaisst") Barinkay describes his exciting adventures as he roamed the world over. He explains that he has been everywhere and has done everything. He traveled with a circus as an animal trainer, and all the animals simply adored him—giraffes, lions, tigers, hyenas, crocodiles and even alligators.

In a rousing waltz refrain, in which he is joined by the chorus ("Ja, das Alles auf Ehr"), Barinkay boasts that he has done all this and more. And when you know what you're about, he sings, everything is easy. In a second stanza he modestly describes how he excelled as juggler, fire-eater, sword swallower, acrobat and magician.[1]

---

[1] This paraphrase of Barinkay's couplet closely follows the translation of the original German. There are different versions—as is true of other patter songs in the operetta.

In ensuing dialogue it is explained that Carnero, as emissary of Empress Maria Theresa of Austria, has been assigned to reinstate Barinkay as lord of his ancestral land. This includes the ruined castle, a swamp under four feet of water and a nearby gypsy village. As Barinkay ruefully contemplates his inheritance, he notices the trim peasant house and asks whose it is. Carnero explains that it is the home of Kalman Zsupan, the "Prince of Pigs." His wealth includes not only thousands of pigs but a very pretty daughter, Arsena. Barinkay pricks up his ears.

Carnero leers amiably. Then, remembering his official position, he pompously declares that feminine beauty is of no interest to him. "Well then," says Barinkay, "let's get on with settling my affairs." They look around for witnesses to sign the necessary documents. First they knock on the door of the hut, bringing out Czipra. In answer to Carnero's questions, she says she lives here with the gypsies, who have gone to market but will return at sundown. Carnero introduces Barinkay to her as her lord and master, the rightful heir to this estate, who has just returned from exile.

Looking at him sharply, Czipra exclaims that her gift of prophecy did not desert her—she knows that this stranger is Barinkay. When Carnero suspiciously asks who told her she replies that she read the cards.

At that moment Saffi comes out of the hut and stares fixedly at Barinkay. She ignores Czipra's order to go inside and, with her eyes on Barinkay, murmurs that he casts a strange spell over her ("Bezaubernd wirkt auf mich sein Blick"). At Czipra's repeated bidding, Saffi re-enters the hut. Barinkay steps forward and asks the gypsy to tell his fortune. In a dramatic refrain ("Bald wird man dich viel umwerben") she prophesies a wonderful future—a treasure is waiting for him. He will find a loving wife who will be told in a dream on her wedding night where this treasure is hidden.

Carnero ironically compliments Czipra on her fortunetelling and asks her to prophesy for him. She mischievously obliges in a continuation of her aria ("Verloren hast du einen Schatz!"). The treasure *he* will soon find will be the sweetheart he lost, who was as scrawny as a sparrow but will come back to him as round as a barrel. And another prize will be restored to him—something that once was no bigger than his hand and now has grown taller than a beanpole. Czipra sings that Carnero will shortly discover these treasures. She chortles gleefully.

Embarrassed, Carnero blusters that this is all nonsense and

orders Czipra to sign the documents. When she protests that writing is much too difficult for her, he tells her to draw a cross. After all, he snaps, this isn't a bargain with the devil. Sign, says Barinkay. "You command, I obey," Czipra replies. Seeing her mark, Carnero gasps that it is a drude's foot (*Drudenfuss*), a sign of witchcraft.[2] The onlookers comment with laughter. Saying that this is the only kind of writing she knows, Czipra shuffles away cackling to herself.

Zsupan, called out of his house, now strides up and asks what is wanted of him. When Carnero tells him that he is to sign a document as witness, the pig farmer replies in a patter song which is another of the comic highlights of the opera ("Ja, das Schreiben und das Lesen"), for which Strauss wrote an earthy, bombastic melody quite in keeping with the character of the pig farmer.

Reading and writing, Zsupan sings, never were his long suit. From childhood on, pigs were his specialty. He knows nothing about poetry; his aesthetic fancies run to pig bristles and bacon. On the subject of fattening pigs, for example, he is the final authority. There isn't a skinny one in his drove of five thousand, which are known far and wide for their tempting sleekness. Strutting about, Zsupan brings his song to a bellowing climax.

An interval of spoken dialogue follows. Carnero informs Zsupan —who, in fact, had taken over the lands of the exiled Baron Barinkay, Sandor's father, and had become enormously wealthy —that the documents he is to sign as second witness will restore Sandor Barinkay to his rightful inheritance. Zsupan, outwardly cordial to Barinkay, fumes over his return but promptly marks the documents with his signature—a splotch of ink. A pig, he explains proudly, is his personal signature.

Barinkay, amused, remarks that he has heard about Zsupan's pretty daughter, Arsena. With such a father, of course she is pretty, says Zsupan. Thereupon Barinkay makes a startling offer: In order to avoid the nuisance of lawsuits over who is now the owner of the ancestral estate, he proposes to settle everything out of court by marrying Arsena.

Zsupan is flabbergasted but recovers quickly. He sends his servant into his house to fetch Arsena and her governess, Mirabella. He is to tell them that a suitor is waiting and that they are to bring a betrothal cake with them. A few moments later Mira-

---

[2] *Drudenfuss*—the pentagram (five-pointed star), an ancient symbol against witches.

bella comes rushing out of the house exclaiming she must have a look at Arsena's suitor.[3]

Suddenly she catches sight of Carnero and, much to his discomfiture, greets him as her long-lost husband. As the crowd stares in amazement, Carnero explains to Barinkay and Zsupan that it was at the Battle of Belgrade in 1718 that he became separated from his wife and child. Thereupon Mirabella drags Ottokar forward and tells him that here is his father. The young man jumps into Carnero's arms with a cry of "Vater!" The three then embrace to general exclamations of surprise from the onlookers. Carried away, Carnero also tries to embrace one of the young peasant girls, whom he calls "niece." Mirabella drags him away.

The scene is interrupted by the appearance of Arsena, veiled and dressed in bridal finery, with a group of peasant girls. A long ensemble begins ("Dem Freier naht die Braut") as the peasants hail the bride-to-be. Arsena sings that another suitor has come along—from whom, however, she will conceal her face for the time being. Barinkay, charmed, tries to approach her but she demurely evades him. Zsupan impatiently tells her to drop her veil. Carnero interrupts to say that as Commissioner of Morals he will enforce the rules of propriety. He and Zsupan inform Barinkay that, according to custom, all parties concerned must first partake of the betrothal cake and wine; then the suitor's turn will come. The cake is brought in as the peasant girls invite all to share it as a symbol of a happy marriage ("Hochzeitskuchen bitte zu versuchen").

In a brief passage in quasi-recitative, Barinkay formally presents himself as Arsena's suitor. She herself is dismayed at being confronted by another swain when she is currently being wooed by Ottokar. Carnero announces that, as the betrothal cake has been eaten, the moment has come for the bride-to-be to drop her veil. The music continues in ensemble form interspersed with solo passages. Dropping her veil, Arsena resignedly sings that if Barinkay takes a fancy to her it means she will have to give up Ottokar.

Gazing at her, Barinkay enthuses over her beauty in a sensuous refrain ("Ach, sie da, ein herrlich Frauenbild"). Zsupan's voice blends with his as the pig farmer sings that Arsena's good looks are an exact copy of his own when he was a smart young lieutenant of twenty. Mirabella acclaims Zsupan as a veritable Apollo.

The voices of Barinkay and Arsena now blend in an obbligato

[3] At this point in the sequence of musical numbers there is a couplet in which Mirabella relates how she was captured by a Turkish pasha at the Battle of Belgrade. This number is generally omitted.

to a choral passage, with the peasants singing Arsena's praises. Barinkay effusively compliments her on her beauty and asks her to marry him. But Arsena, quite unimpressed, sings that while his attentions certainly are flattering, his wife she will never be—and she will say it ten times over. On these various sentiments the ensemble comes to a rousing climax.

In a brief refrain ("Ein Falter schwirrt um's Licht") following the ensemble, Arsena sings that a suitor has been attracted to her like a moth to a flame. Whoever chooses her, she declares in a spoken phrase, must be—at the very least—a baron.

When Barinkay, shocked and infuriated by her snobbery, flares up at this implied insult, she calmly tells him to come back when he has proof of his nobility. With that she flounces off. Zsupan jokingly observes that he can't force his daughter to marry someone she doesn't want. In any case, he adds, she hasn't chosen *him*. He advises Barinkay to go to bed and then see to it, when he wakes up, that he is really a baron. Then Zsupan jovially invites everyone to come to his house and toast the "future" bride. Angry and chagrined, Barinkay watches him leave with the crowd.

As he is brooding disconsolately he suddenly hears Saffi's voice in the opening phrases of her gypsy song, "So elend und so treu ist Keiner auf Erden." This is the *Zigeunerlied* one of the most dramatic numbers in the opera. Its somber, haunting quality is focused in the ancient warning cry of the Hungarian gypsy— "Dschingrah, dschingrah!" No one on earth, Saffi sings as Barinkay listens fascinated, is so wretched and yet so loyal as the gypsy. When he is near, women must guard their children and men their horses.

At midpoint in the refrain, the mood changes with lightning swiftness from lamentation to defiance. When the gypsy appears, the song goes on, flee for your lives because the gypsy comes as an implacable foe. In the second stanza the mood shifts to one of calm reassurance: When the gypsy is your friend you can trust him. Give him your hand . . . he will never fail you. Saffi ends the *Zigeunerlied* with a defiant shout of "Heijah!" In spoken dialogue, Barinkay exclaims that he knows this song because his mother sang it to him long ago. Czipra, who has followed Saffi on the scene, tells him that his mother learned it from the gypsies when she and the Baron, Sandor's father, lived in the castle before their exile. The gypsies, who were allowed to encamp on the estate, made the Baron their Voyevode, or leader. Czipra then identifies Saffi as her daughter.

While they are talking, they suddenly become aware that Ottokar

is cautiously approaching Zsupan's house and is calling to Arsena
("Arsena, es harrt auf dem Balcon"). He and Arsena pledge their
love in a lyrical duet which marks the beginning of the long and
stirring finale of Act One. Barinkay, furious at discovering that
Ottokar is his rival for Arsena's love, swears revenge. Saffi and
Czipra join him but warn him not to let his anger goad him into
violence. Their voices blend in an accompaniment to the romantic
phrases of the lovers' duet. As Ottokar gives Arsena a golden
locket set with his picture, Barinkay, beside himself with rage,
lunges toward the balcony. Saffi and Czipra restrain him. At that
moment the gypsy chorus is heard in the distance. Arsena and
Ottokar bid each other goodnight.

Barinkay, Saffi and Czipra listen in rising excitement as the
voices come closer. During a brief orchestral interlude, the tribe
crowds on the stage and all join in a choral reprise of the *Zigeunerlied*.

As they stand facing Barinkay, who looks at them in bewilderment, Czipra says they have come to swear allegiance to him as
their Voyevode—they are now his loyal subjects and he can trust
them ("Du kannst die Zigeuner getrost vertrauen"). Turning to
the gypsies, she exhorts them to pledge their faith to the new
leader. They respond in a lusty chorus, "Er nimmt uns're Huldi-
gung an." Barinkay acknowledges their homage.

As the cheers die down, Barinkay declares that now he will
settle accounts with neighbor Zsupan. With that he strides over
to Zsupan's house and knocks loudly on the door. Zsupan emerges
followed by Arsena, Carnero, Mirabella and the crowd of villagers who have been celebrating with him. When he asks what
the commotion is all about, Barinkay answers that if he insists
on having a baron for a son-in-law, he now has one. "I," says
Barinkay, "am a baron." The villagers exclaim in surprise.

In a triumphant refrain ("Komm her und schau mir die Leute
an") Barinkay bids Zsupan look upon the people whose Voyevode
—Baron—he has now become. He is the Gypsy Baron. Saffi steps
forward and in an equally exultant refrain ("Hier im diesem
Land") hails the Hungarian who, inspired by the song of a poor
gypsy girl, has returned to serve his fatherland. Her voice blends
with Barinkay's and Czipra's in a brief passage commenting on
the magical power of her song.

There is a moment of silence. Then the villagers burst into
jeering laughter at the idea of a "Voyevode of the Gypsies."
Ignoring the insult, Barinkay asks Arsena if she will marry him.
A "gypsy" baron, she replies contemptuously, won't do. Thereupon

Barinkay turns to Saffi and asks her to be his wife. When she protests that this is a cruel joke, Barinkay cries that her faithful heart has won his love and trust. Carnero steps forward and declares that Saffi cannot go with Barinkay because it is against the law of the land for a Hungarian to marry a gypsy. As Barinkay angrily defies him, the gypsies shout that they will protect their Voyevode. Zsupan roars that he will not allow his daughter to be spurned and made a laughingstock.

The scene builds up to a turbulent pitch as the two groups—Zsupan's villagers and Barinkay's gypsies—face each other and hurl insults. A fight finally breaks out as Carnero orders Barinkay's arrest. After a furious scuffle the voices of the combatants blend in the thrilling chorus which closes the act, with villagers and gypsies alike claiming victory.

## ACT TWO

A gypsy encampment near the tower of the ruined castle, seen at one side. On the other, the gypsies' forge and smithy. Czipra, half reclining, lies in front of the tower. Saffi lies with her head on Czipra's lap. Above them in a ragged opening in the tower, Barinkay lies asleep. Czipra sings softly that she is keeping watch over this lovely child and her master's land ("Mein Aug' bewacht"). This marks the beginning of the Treasure Scene, sung in trio and duet form by Czipra, Saffi and Barinkay.

Slowly awaking, Barinkay wonders if his happiness is real or only a dream. Gazing tenderly down at Saffi, he calls to awaken her. When he fondly calls her "his wife," she somewhat sullenly asks if he still is jesting about marrying her. Barinkay answers in a passionate refrain ("In dieser Nacht, voll herrlicher Pracht") that on this wondrous night he came to know that Saffi is his only love. Her beauty has completely enchanted him and his heart is hers. Overwhelmed by his ardor, Saffi yields to his embrace. They pledge their love in a lyrical continuation of the duet ("O Blick an Blick"), one of the loveliest numbers in the operetta.

At its conclusion Saffi remarks on the strange look on Czipra's face. In explanation the old gypsy says that last night she had a dream ("Ein Greis hat mir im Traum erschienen"). She saw Saffi's father, who told her where the ancestral treasure is hidden. The young suitor has only to lift a certain marble stone in the wall of the tower. Barinkay cries excitedly that the dream is true and that the treasure already is his. Czipra and Saffi urge him to begin the search at once. Barinkay's voice blends with theirs in a staccato trio as he strikes the stones with a hammer in time with the music.

Suddenly he shouts that one stone has a hollow sound. He pulls it away. In a triumphant phrase ("s'ist grandios! Der Schatz!") he sings that he has found the treasure as he brings out a large rough-hewn chest from the hollow behind the stone. Czipra and Saffi gasp in amazement as Barinkay opens the chest to reveal a glittering array of gold and jewels. The three express their joy over their good fortune in a trio ("Ha, seht es winkt, es blinkt, es klingt") which is one of Strauss's finest waltzes.

This treasure, they sing, will buy all the things they have longed for—lackeys, fine clothes, wine, parties, masquerades, horses and palaces. Czipra cautions the lovers not to squander their wealth, so that its pleasures may last. Barinkay and Saffi, though dazzled by their riches, sing that love and trust still are more precious than gold.

It is now daylight and the gypsy camp is stirring to life. Hearing the sound of voices, Barinkay quickly puts the chest back into the hollow and replaces the stone. Pali, one of the gypsies, enters and calls on the tribe to go to work. The gypsies crowd in, the men going to their forges and the women watching. All join in the Anvil Chorus ("Ja, das Eisen wird gefüge"), which brings to mind a similar scene in Verdi's *Il Trovatore*. The theme of the chorus is that the gypsies will forge the iron into weapons with which they will strike their enemies blow for blow ("Schlag auf Schlag").[4]

Carnero now comes in with Mirabella, Arsena, Ottokar and a group of officials. He upbraids Barinkay for "living in sin" with a gypsy girl. When Sandor angrily retorts that she is his wife, Carnero asks who married them. Barinkay and Saffi reply in what is perhaps the most beautiful melody in the score, "Wer uns getraut?" It was the *Dompfaff*, the bullfinch, who married them under the blue cathedral dome of the sky, the lovers sing. And then the nightingale serenaded them, singing that love is a power sent from heaven. Witnesses to the marriage were two storks, those symbols of a happy household, which clapped their bills loudly and wished the couple well.[5]

---

[4] Here, in some versions of the opera, there is a comic byplay in dialogue involving Zsupan and a trio of gypsies—Pali, Ferko and Jozsi—who steal his watch and his moneybags.

[5] In the original score this scene is followed by a *Sittenskommissions* (Morals Commission) couplet, sung in unison by Carnero, Mirabella and Zsupan. It is usually omitted.

As the onlookers warmly applaud the lovers, they are startled by a shout from Ottokar, who meanwhile has been exploring the tower. He cries that he has found gold. When all rush toward the tower, Barinkay steps in their way declaring that this treasure is his own discovery and belongs to him alone. Carnero demands that it be turned over to him as a "war chest." Barinkay contemptuously rejects the idea.

The argument is interrupted by a fanfare offstage. A moment later Count Homonay enters, followed by his bodyguards, hussars and vivandières. Barinkay greets him with appropriate dignity as his noble patron. Homonay announces that he has come to recruit men to fight in the war against Spain. He himself, he adds, is too old to fight—but he still can sing the famous Hungarian recruiting song, the *Werberlied*. He thereupon launches into the song, a call to arms in a thumping martial rhythm ("Her die Hand, es muss ja sein!"). It describes the traditional Magyar recruiting custom: a handshake, a glass of wine—and you're in the army. Then when the recruit exchanges his hat for the shako he is ready to fight for the fatherland. All onstage roar out the chorus, which bristles with martial spirit and defiance . . . victory or death . . . our blood will stain the earth before we surrender. The *Werberlied* ends with a fierce shout of "Strike hard!" ("Schlagt ein!").

Then the mood changes in a flash to one of wild abandon as soldiers and peasants sing and dance the czardas ("Wir Alle wollen lustig sein"). It is a song in praise of the dashing hussar, who, next to fighting, loves wine, women and song.

After the czardas the recruiting begins. Zsupan and Ottokar unsuspectingly drink wine and shake hands, and find themselves in the army. Barinkay not only enlists but offers his treasure to Count Homonay to help pay for the war. As patriotic fervor rises to fever pitch, Count Homonay proclaims that the war will not last long, that victory is assured and that all will meet in Vienna to celebrate the triumph of the Hungarians. The crowd sings of the delights of Vienna in a sparkling Viennese waltz, "So voll Fröhlichkeit."

But during the merriment, Carnero, Mirabella, Arsena and Ottokar stand glumly to one side, eying the gypsies in disapproval. Disgruntled by his failure to get possession of Barinkay's treasure for his own use, Carnero complains to Homonay that, in spite of all the noble palaver, his authority has been flouted by this gypsy rabble ("Noch eben in Gloria"). The others join him in denouncing the gypsies as outlaws and thieves.

Suddenly Czipra, glaring at them, bursts out that she will no longer keep silent in the face of their insults ("Genug, nicht langer schweig ich mehr"). Now they will learn that the gypsy girl whom they scorn as a hussy is far above them in rank and station. This child, Czipra cries, does not belong to her. The others gasp in amazement.

Thereupon she hands Homonay a document. In suspenseful phrases ("Ich hab gewacht") she sings that while she watched over this child she also guarded the document she now entrusts to the Count. It will reveal the whole truth.

Reading it quickly, Homonay points to Saffi and declares that there stands the daughter of a prince. There is general consternation. Her father, Homonay goes on, was the last pasha of Hungary. Everyone present joins in a chorus acclaiming the newly discovered princess, "Ein Fürstenkind, ein Wunder ist gescheh'n!"

But Saffi's happiness is cut short when Barinkay tells her he must leave ("Ach, von Euch muss ich geh'n"). As she stares at him in dismay and unbelief, he says he is leaving only because he loves her. At that moment, as though to underscore the irony of the situation, the throng bursts into the *Werberlied*. The voices of Mirabella, Arsena, Zsupan, Czipra and Ottokar blend with the chorus in contrasting expressions of disappointment over this turn of events.

Barinkay himself, despite Saffi's tearful protests, calls for the recruiting wine. He seals his decision by clasping Homonay's hand. After a momentary struggle with himself he declares that while he would gladly die for love, he first will die for the fatherland. He holds out his hand and Homonay grasps it, shouting: "Forward! On to battle—and then to Vienna!"

Now follows the great closing chorus of the act—a reprise of the *Werberlied*. All urge the hussars to go forward into battle and smite the foe for the glory of the fatherland. The curtain falls.

## ACT III

Before the Kärntnerthor in Vienna. The populace is awaiting the arrival of the victorious Hungarians. Zsupan struts in and is welcomed by Arsena, Mirabella and Carnero. When Arsena asks her father about his exploits, he sums up the course of the war in a hilarious patter song. He begins by describing how the army returned after the campaign on the banks of the Tagus in Spain ("Von des Tajo Strand"), where they "taught the enemy manners." As for himself, he came through the war unscathed—except for a spot of sunburn. Next he launches into a nonsensical story of how he dealt with a Spanish soldier who tried to shoot him with an unloaded gun. Finally he brags about his scandalous flirtation with a pretty Spanish woman. He enchanted her, of course, and when he gallantly kissed her hand he managed to slip a diamond ring from her finger. He is now wearing it as a token of her affection.

There were many such beautiful donnas, Zsupan goes on, but none of them made him forget his duties as a soldier. At intervals during his recital his listeners comment admiringly in chorus.

There is a fanfare of trumpets announcing the return of the troops, led in by Barinkay and Ottokar. They sing the lusty Soldiers' Chorus ("Hurra, die Schlacht mitgemacht"). It expresses the usual operatic sentiments about the soldier bravely facing shot and shell and asking only a kiss from his beloved as his reward when—and if—he returns home.

As for Barinkay, he is awarded for his heroism in battle by being made a true baron. Zsupan hails the accolade, saying that Barinkay now can qualify as his son-in-law and marry Arsena. Then he will claim her now, Barinkay sings in a phrase which begins the closing ensemble of the opera ("Ich halte um deine Tochter an"). He amazes everyone by announcing that he claims Arsena not for himself but for the faithful Ottokar. The two young lovers rush into each other's arms.

Homonay asks Barinkay if he now intends to stay single. Before he can answer, the Count announces that the marriage of a certain Hungarian nobleman and a gypsy girl has been given legal sanction. Barinkay turns to Saffi and in a tender phrase sings that here is the queen of his heart. Gazing into his eyes, Saffi sings the phrase of her gypsy song—"give the gypsy your hand, for he comes as a friend." Barinkay, taking her in his arms, sings jubilantly that everything has turned out for the best—he has won both a victory in battle and a beautiful wife.

Then he swings into a reprise of his patter song in Act One, "Ja, das Alles auf Ehr." The chorus joins him in the lilting refrain: "When you know what you're about, everything is easy." The curtain falls.

# PART II

## THE CONCERT OPERAS

# CONCERT OPERAS

What is a "concert opera"? The term is comparatively new to the operatic lexicon, and does not necessarily define the form in which any particular opera originally was composed. Opera, of course, is meant for the stage—complete with dramatic action, scenery, costumes, lighting effects and so on. Concert opera dispenses with some of these elements, focusing the attention on the music itself.

The usual method of presentation is with singers and orchestra onstage, the singers in formal dress or in costume. There is little or no stage action *per se,* although the singers sometimes heighten the effect of an aria or an ensemble with stylized gestures.

Obviously, almost any opera thus can become a "concert opera." Even Berlioz' titanic *Les Troyens* has been presented with stunning effectiveness by singers in evening gowns and white tie and tails.

Certain operas, however, lend themselves logically to concert opera performances—for today's audiences, at any rate. This is particularly true of works of the early classical period—from Monteverdi to Purcell, Scarlatti, Lully and Handel. The reason for their adaptability is—paradoxically—the same reason they vanished from the operatic repertoire. Their inherent weakness was the libretto. The plots, based on classical subjects, were stilted, with little relation to flesh-and-blood human beings or human emotions. Dramatic characterization was almost entirely absent—it was the music that defined mood and motivation.

In other words, everything depended upon the singer and his vocal interpretation. As a result, opera in the sixteenth, seventeenth and eighteenth centuries nourished the most extraordinary singers in the history of the operatic stage. This was the age of the *castrati* and of the women singers who were the practitioners of true *bel canto*—artists who could sing the florid arias with instrumental precision.

Within the past decade there has been a revival of interest in concert opera presentations of forgotten masterpieces. These have made it possible for opera lovers to enjoy much magnificent music which otherwise would have been lost to posterity. The operas listed in this section comprise a representative repertoire of works revived in recent performances by such organizations as the Handel Society of New York, the American Opera Society, the Little Orchestra Society and the American Chamber Opera Society.

# Anna Bolena

### *by* GAETANO DONIZETTI
### (1797–1848)

### *Libretto by*
#### FELICE ROMANI

#### CHARACTERS

| | |
|---|---|
| Enrico (Henry VIII), King of England | Bass |
| Anna Bolena (Anne Boleyn), his wife | Soprano |
| Giovanna (Jane Seymour), Anna's lady in waiting | Mezzo-soprano |
| Rochefort (Lord Rochford), Anna's brother | Bass |
| Lord Richard Percy, Anna's first love | Tenor |
| Smeton (Smeaton), the Queen's page | Contralto |
| Hervey, the King's officer, Governor of the Tower of London | Tenor |

Lords, courtiers, ladies in waiting, huntsmen, soldiers

*Place:* England—the first act in Windsor, the second in London
*Time:* 1536
*First Performance:* Teatro Carcana, Milan, December 26, 1830
*Original language:* Italian

---

Donizetti's twenty-third opera was long considered by his contemporaries as his masterpiece, and enjoyed that distinction at least until he composed the operas acknowledged as his greatest—*L'Elisir d'Amore, Lucia di Lammermoor* and *Don Pasquale*.

*Anna Bolena* was the first opera Donizetti wrote in his own individual style, rather than in imitation of Rossini, who had strongly influenced his earlier works. It is recorded that he composed the opera—completing the score in one month—at the Lake Como villa of the renowned eighteenth-century *bel canto* soprano Giuditta Pasta, who created the role of Anna. After its sensationally successful premiere it was heard all over Europe. In England the legendary basso Luigi Lablache scored his greatest success in it.

Although it vanished from the operatic repertoire—possibly because of the tragic nature of the plot—*Anna Bolena* has had successful revivals during the past decade or so. A La Scala production in 1957 by Count Luchino Visconti was hailed as one of the finest restorations of recent times. What was probably its first American performance was given that same year in concert form by the American Opera Society. The Society presented it again in November 1966. It was given in English by the Santa Fe Opera Company during its 1959 season, and by the Dallas Civic Opera in 1968.

The opera's plot, a page out of English history, closely follows the course of events during the reign of the notorious Henry VIII. The chief deviations are Anna Bolena's madness and the betrothal of Anna and Richard Percy—events which have no historical basis.

The long and stirring overture states the principal themes of the opera.

## ACT ONE

[*Scene One*] At Windsor Castle, the chief topic of gossip among the courtiers and others of the Queen's court is the marital discord between Enrico and Anna. In an opening chorus ("Nè venne il Re? Silenzio!") the courtiers discuss the rumor that the King has rejected Anna and is infatuated with another woman. Although Anna is acutely aware of the King's wavering affections, she does not know who her rival is.

Giovanna enters. In an aside (the cavatina "Ella di me, solecita"), she wonders apprehensively why the Queen has summoned her. Does she perhaps suspect that her own lady in waiting is her rival for the King's affections?

Anna enters with Smeton and her attendants to await the arrival of the King. She notices the expressions of concern on the faces of those in her entourage and, in recitative ("Si taciturna e mesta"), asks the reason. She confesses that she herself is troubled by an unknown fear. To dispel the gloom she asks the page to entertain the company with a ballad. Smeton obliges with a plaintive love song (romanza: "Dehl non volero constringere"). But when he sings a phrase alluding to "first love," Anna abruptly silences him. There is a stir of alarm in the court. Then, almost to herself, Anna sings about a first love that was hers long ago (cavatina: "Come innocente giovane").

Asking Giovanna to approach, the Queen tells her that there is a lesson to be learned from her sorrow: The power and glory

of the throne can break a proud spirit (aria: "Non v'ha sguardo").
Again Giovanna wonders if the Queen knows her guilty secret.
Saying wearily that there is no point in waiting any longer for
the King, Anna retires with her retinue. Giovanna remains alone.

Torn between her loyalty to Anna and her ambition to be
Queen, Giovanna reflects on the Queen's ominous words (recitative: "Oh! qual parlar fu il suo!"). Suddenly there is a knock on a
secret door to the chamber, and a moment later Enrico cautiously
enters. A long duet ensues ("Vederci alla faccia del sole"). The
King declares that these clandestine meetings must come to an
end: He has decided to proclaim his love for Giovanna to all
the kingdom. When she replies that in order to win her love he
must make her his Queen, Enrico agrees—but adds resentfully
that Anna imposed exactly the same conditions solely to win the
throne. Trying to justify his repudiation of Anna, he declares that
she was guilty of loving another before she married him—and even
after. When he proffers Giovanna his kingdom, she flatly refuses
until he reluctantly promises not to punish Anna for her supposed
infidelity.

[*Scene Two*] Richard Percy, recalled from exile by Enrico,
arrives at Windsor and is warmly greeted by Lord Rochefort.
Percy eagerly asks about Anna. Divining his thoughts, Rochefort
reminds him that she is now the Queen, and if he dared reveal
his true feelings toward her it would doom them both. In the
cavatina "Da quel di che, lei perduta" Percy describes the anguish
he suffered in exile, knowing that he had lost Anna forever. Yet
he clings to the hope that even now she will give him one word
of comfort. As a fanfare announces the King's return from the
hunt, Rochefort again vainly warns Percy not to invite disaster.

Enrico comes in escorted by huntsmen and his palace guards,
with Hervey at their head. Anna appears with her retinue. The
King greets her with mocking cordiality, then notices Percy, who
is standing apart. As Enrico welcomes him back to court, Anna
gasps in surprise, murmuring that she did not know he had been
pardoned.

Percy kneels before Enrico, thanks him for his pardon and
reaches out to kiss his hand. The King brusquely withdraws it,
remarking with sinister emphasis that thanks are due someone else
who interceded for him: the Queen herself. Impetuously, Percy
kneels and kisses Anna's hand. Aware of the King's eyes upon
her, she makes a supreme effort to control herself.

Calling Hervey to him, Enrico, in an aside, tells him to watch

Percy's every move from this moment on. Hervey assures him that he will set the trap for Percy. Enrico's order, in recitative ("Questa di per voi"), leads into the fiery quartet (Enrico, Anna, Percy, Rochefort) and chorus which conclude the scene. Anna laments that her love for Percy can never be requited; Percy, heedless of Rochefort's warning, exults that Anna's very presence has restored his hope and courage; Enrico—for reasons of his own—virtually forces Percy to agree to remain at the castle. As the King leaves with his huntsmen, he remarks that he is now in search of another kind of quarry.

[*Scene Three*] Smeton steals into the Queen's apartment. He takes from inside his shirt a portrait miniature of Anna which he had purloined and which he now plans to return before the theft is discovered. Gazing at it avidly, he pours out his frustrated love in the cavatina "Ah, pare che per incanto."

Hearing footsteps outside, Smeton thrusts the portrait back inside his shirt and hides behind the draperies. Anna, nervous and excited, hurries in followed by Rochefort. At her brother's insistence she consents—against her better judgment—to permit Percy to see her. Assuring her he will stand guard over their tryst, Rochefort leaves and a moment later Percy enters.

A long and dramatic duet follows ("La fronte mia solcata"). Warning him that they are both courting death by daring to meet in this fashion, Anna desperately begs Percy to forswear her love and flee England. Crying that death is better than a life without her, Percy draws his sword and turns the point toward his heart.

At that moment Smeton springs from his hiding place and wrests the weapon aside. Raging, Percy turns on the page with sword poised, whereupon Smeton draws and prepares to lunge. With a shriek of terror, Anna falls fainting. Rochefort rushes in exclaiming that Enrico is approaching.

The King strides in, sees Percy and Smeton at sword's point and bellows for his guards. Glaring at the two adversaries, the King snarls that their guilty looks have trapped them, and the Queen as well. Shouting that he is ready to die to defend the Queen's innocence, Smeton tears open his shirt in a melodramatic gesture of sacrifice. With that the portrait falls to the floor. There is a stunned silence as Enrico picks it up. Here, he says with evil relish, is the final proof. Percy stares at Smeton in baffled fury.

Anna revives and staggers to her feet. Thrusting the portrait close to her face, Enrico cries that here is the accuser. A tumultuous ensemble then ensues ("I quegli sguardi impresso"). The more Anna protests her innocence, the more ferocious the King's accusations become; Percy voices his utter despair over Anna's apparent betrayal of his love; Smeton, Rochefort and Giovanna reproach themselves for inadvertently casting suspicion on the guiltless Queen. At the conclusion of the ensemble, Enrico peremptorily orders Anna and the three men to the Tower.

## ACT TWO

[*Scene One*] An apartment in the Tower of London, where Anna is imprisoned. Before she enters from her chamber, her ladies in waiting ask in a mournful chorus ("O dove mai ne andaromo") why those who once sought the Queen's favors— Giovanna among them—have not come forward to help her now.

When Anna appears they try to console her with assurances of their loyalty. Hervey enters to inform the Queen that her ladies in waiting have been called as witnesses before the Council of Peers. They leave with him. Sinking to her knees, the Queen sings a brief but eloquent prayer ("Dio, che me vedi in core"). She asks to know what shameful thing she has done to merit so cruel a punishment.

Giovanna enters and kneels beside her, and then follows the duet which is one of the great climactic numbers of the opera. Taking note of Giovanna's looks of mingled guilt and dread, the Queen asks if she brings yet more terrible news. Giovanna tells her that the King will see to it that she is found guilty by the servile Council of Peers, and so destroy her. To save her life, she must confess to adultery, which will void her marriage and leave the King free to marry her rival. Horrified, Anna flatly refuses so to debase herself.

Giovanna implores Anna to listen to reason—to take the advice of the woman who is fated to replace her. In wild anger, Anna demands to know if this woman has the effrontery to send the Queen's own lady in waiting to her sovereign with this vile counsel. She calls down a terrible curse on the interloper ("Sul suo capo aggravi un Dio").

Cringing before Anna's fury, Giovanna finally confesses that she herself is the guilty rival. As the Queen stares at her in stunned disbelief, Giovanna goes on to say that it was love, not ambition, that made her surrender to Enrico.

Anna magnanimously forgives Giovanna, saying that the King alone is guilty of this monstrous act of treachery and lust. Shaken by remorse, Giovanna sings that the Queen's forgiveness and pardon are worse punishment than her rage. At the conclusion of the duet, Anna rises and goes to her room, leaving Giovanna sobbing bitterly.

[*Scene Two*] Outside the chamber where the Council of Peers is hearing the evidence against Anna, Hervey and the courtiers discuss Smeton's testimony. Enrico enters and the courtiers withdraw. The King and Hervey sardonically comment on the fact that the hapless Smeton, believing he could save the Queen's life, swore that she committed adultery. Thus he has drawn the net tightly around all the conspirators.

Anna and Percy are brought in and the dramatic confrontation scene follows in trio form. Anna entreats the King to destroy her if he must—but not dishonor her name with a baseless charge of adultery ("A' piedi tuoi mi prosto"). She accuses him of corrupting Smeton and forcing him to lie about her. Percy swears that Anna has never been unfaithful ("Il ver parlati; ascolta"). Enrico's only answer is that Anna and her lover are doomed.

Finally, Percy, goaded beyond endurance by the King's vindictiveness, stuns him with the assertion that Anna is his bride and that the royal marriage has no legality ("Sposi non siam"). In a towering rage, Enrico orders Anna and Percy to be taken immediately before the Council of Peers. There, he shouts, Anna will be forced to confess her illicit love—and that confession will doom them both. The two are led away.

In a brief soliloquy in recitative, Enrico expresses his disbelief in Percy's claim to Anna and concludes they are both lying to save themselves. But if the story is true, he muses, the law will have its way and he still be avenged: Anna's child will bear the stain of illegitimacy.

Giovanna enters. The King greets her ardently and salutes her as his Queen. But she answers that she cannot accept either his love or his throne unless he shows mercy to Anna, whom she herself betrayed. If she could expiate that sin, she goes on, she would spend her life fasting and praying in the darkest corner of the earth. In a dramatic aria, "Per questa fiamma indomita," Giovanna pleads for Anna's life. Enrico storms that now he loathes Anna more than ever because she has caused Giovanna this anguish. Relentlessly he reiterates his decision: Anna must die.

[*Scene Three*] The prison section of the Tower of London, where Percy and Rochefort await execution. Hervey enters and tells them that Enrico has pardoned them. When they learn that

Anna is to die, Percy scornfully rejects the offer of pardon and Rochefort follows suit. In an eloquent aria, "Vivi tu, te ne scongiuro," Percy implores Rochefort to accept the reprieve and find a haven where sorrow and injustice do not exist. Rochefort declares that he will die with his friend. Guards lead both men away.

Anna's ladies in waiting enter and sing a chorus of lamentation ("Chi può vederla"). They gaze at her in grief and pity as she enters, half mad with terror and despair, her clothing in disarray. In her delirium she imagines it is the day of her marriage to the King, and she begs forgiveness of Percy. Lamenting her lost love, she sings a plaintive song, "Al dolce guidami castel natio." She asks to be taken back to the pleasant castle where she spent her youth—there to enjoy again one precious hour of youth.

Percy, Rochefort and Smeton are brought in for a final farewell. Smeton, tormented by remorse, kneels before Anna and cries that he alone is to blame: Because he had hoped to win her love, he accused her of adultery in the belief that the King would repudiate her but spare her life.

Anna, her mind wandering, raises Smeton to his feet and asks wistfully if the strings of his harp are broken. Profoundly moved, the three doomed men pray for the repose of her soul. Suddenly there is a drum roll, the boom of cannon and the ringing of bells. The crowds outside are acclaiming the new Queen. With a prayer of forgiveness on her lips ("Non impreco in quest'ora tremenda"), Anna is led to the scaffold.

# L'Assedio di Corinto
## (*Le Siège de Corinthe—The Siege of Corinth*)
### *by* GIOACCHINO ROSSINI
### (1792–1868)

*Libretto by*
LUIGI BALOCCHI and ALEXANDRE SOUMET

A revised version of *Maometto II,* a two-act libretto by the Duca di Ventignano

#### CHARACTERS

| | |
|---|---|
| Mahomed II (Mahomet), Emperor of the Turks | Bass |
| Cleomene (Cléomène), Governor of Corinth | Tenor |
| Neocle (Néoclès), a young Greek officer | Tenor |
| Omar, Mahomed's adviser | Bass |
| Pamira (Palmyre), Cleomene's daughter | Soprano |
| Ismene, her confidante | Mezzo-soprano |
| Jero (Hiéros), Keeper of the Tombs | Bass |
| Adrasto, a young Greek soldier | Tenor |

Turks, Greek soldiers, serving-women, people of Corinth

*Place:* Corinth, the ancient city in southern Greece
*Time:* 1459
*First performance:* as *Maometto II,* San Carlo, Naples, December 3, 1820; as *Le Siège de Corinthe,* Salle Le Peletier (Opéra), Paris, October 9, 1826
*Original language:* Italian

---

*L'Assedio di Corinto,* the thirtieth of Rossini's thirty-six operas, was the first of his works to be presented in Paris, where it was sung in French. This opera was a reworking of *Maometto II,* which Rossini had composed in 1820 for Naples; for Paris, in 1826, the two acts were expanded to three. In that form, the opera received its first staged performance in Italian in 1828. The plot originally stems from a play by the French dramatist Voltaire, entitled *Mahomet, ou Le Fantisme* (1742). The plot has to do with the final days of Corinth, destroyed in 1459 by the Turks under Mahomed II.

When Rossini went to Paris he took up the study of French prosody in order to rewrite his opera specifically for the French language. He wrote the role of Neocle especially for Adolphe Nourrit (1802–39), who is renowned as the most accomplished singing actor among all the dramatic tenors in the history of opera.

The opera was an immediate success and became permanently established in the early nineteenth-century repertoire. It received its hundredth performance in Paris in 1839, and was presented throughout Italy until about 1870. The first New York performance was in 1883. In the present century it was revived at the Maggio Musicale Fiorentino in 1949, with Renata Tebaldi as Pamira— a role which she also sang in Rome in 1951.

One of the most recent staged revivals abroad was at La Scala in April 1969, under the baton of Thomas Schippers, when Beverly Sills, as Pamira, and Marilyn Horne, as Neocle (the tenor role re-arranged for mezzo), sang with sensational success. In New York, the American Opera Society scheduled the work for performance in November 1969.

Before the rise of the curtain there is a sinfonia in the effervescent Rossinian style, interwoven with several themes heard later in the opera.

## ACT ONE

[*Scene One*] The vestibule of the Palace of the Senate in Corinth. Cleomene, Neocle and Jero are gathered there with the Greek warriors and the populace. In the opening chorus the people comment on Cleomene's grave and anxious demeanor as the city awaits the first attack of Mahomed II and his army. They try to console him by reassuring him of their loyalty ("Signor, un sol tuo cenno").

In an ensuing aria "Del vincitor, superbo di Bisanzio," the Governor voices his despair over the cruel destiny of Corinth and his people at the hands of the ruthless invader. The people commiserate in a brief response ("In cosi reo periglio"). Neocle then steps forward and in a ringing aria, "Guerrieri, a noi s'affida," exhorts the warriors to defend Greece with their lives. Let them remember, he sings, that the choice is victory or slavery. Cleomene, Jero and the warriors join the call to arms, after which the warriors leave.

[*Scene Two*] In a recitative passage beginning "E salva amor la patria," Cleomene informs the populace that the first onslaught of the Turks has been beaten back, and Corinth is saved. Again he urges his people to swear on the altar of the fatherland either to triumph or to die. During the general rejoicing over the news of victory, Neocle reminds Cleomene that he has promised Pamira to him as his bride ("Tua figlia m'e promessa").

[*Scene Three*] Pamira enters. Greeting her affectionately, Cleomene commits her to the protection of Neocle ("T'appressa o figlia"). Neocle exultantly sings that Pamira's love will inspire him to heroic deeds in the coming battles. But Pamira stuns both her father and the young officer by declaring that she has given her heart to one "Alamanzor of Athens." Cleomene angrily reminds her that she has been promised to Neocle, and warns her not to flout paternal authority in this matter. Pamira, however, although torn between obedience to her father and her secret love, refuses to capitulate. The three express their various reactions to the dispute in a long trio, "Destin terribile." They entreat the gods to witness their shame and sorrow over this unfortunate turn of events.

[*Scene Four*] With the invading Turkish army closing in on the walls of Corinth, terror reigns in the city. In a dramatic chorus ("Di morte il suon") the people wail that the air is filled with the sounds of approaching death. Cleomene, in a solo passage, proclaims that he himself will lead the Greek soldiers to victory or death.

Turning to Pamira, he warns that if he is slain in battle the guilt will be hers as a traitor to her country. Brandishing a dagger, he shouts that this will exact payment for her crime. Terrorstricken by his fury, Pamira promises to remain faithful to the Greek cause ("La data fè rammento"). Her refrain builds into a trio with Cleomene and Neocle, then into an ensemble, "La gloria della patria."

[*Scene Five*] An open plaza in Corinth, where the Turkish invaders are confronting the Greek soldiers, who are now standing at bay. In a fiery chorus, "Dal ferro del forte," the Turks threaten the Greeks with annihilation unless the city surrenders.

[*Scene Six*] Mahomed enters with his followers. Flushed with victory, he bids his soldiers make the most of their triumph

("Cessi vittoria di mia voce al suono"). In an ensuing obbligato to the chorus ("Duce di tanti eroi") he boasts of his success and exhorts his men to fight on to greater glory.

[*Scene Seven*] Omar, the Emperor's general, reports that victory is indeed assured, but adds that some of the Greeks are still holding a passage leading to the main fortress. Meanwhile, one of them has been taken captive. Mahomed orders him to be brought before him. Turning to Omar, the Emperor remarks that the present situation recalls his conquest of Athens under the name of "Almanzor." There he came face to face with a beautiful woman ("qual si'offriva donzella"), and now the memory of her beauty banishes all thoughts of revenge as a conqueror.

[*Scene Eight*] Cleomene is brought before Mahomed, and a dramatic confrontation ensues in recitative. Excoriating the Governor as a treacherous rebel ("Capo all'oste ribelle"), the Turk commands him to surrender the city at once. When Cleomene defiantly refuses, Mahomed consigns him to the dungeons.

[*Scene Nine*] Pamira, who meanwhile has entered, sees her father with his captors and bewails the unhappy fate that has overtaken them both ("Oh padre! Ingrata sorte"). She turns supplicatingly to Mahomed, then staggers back in surprise, recognizing him as the suitor she has known as "Almanzor." As she gasps out his name, Cleomene is stupefied by the realization that the man his daughter loves is the archenemy of the Greeks.

Gazing ardently at Pamira, Mahomed begs her to marry him, promising to restore peace to Corinth if she accepts him ("Giorno sarà di pace"). Pamira is about to consent—realizing that thus she can save her people from their doom—when Cleomene again reminds her that she is promised to Neocle. Again Pamira—determined to sacrifice herself—refuses to obey her father. In baffled fury, Cleomene curses her ("Spietata figlia").

The closing ensemble of the act now develops. Mahomed reiterates his fervent pleas and assurances of mercy toward the Greeks; Pamira, in an agony of indecision, laments the cruel dilemma in which she is trapped ("Deh tace a mi fatale"); Cleomene expresses his anguish over her ingratitude and disobedience; the Greek women voice their sympathy for Pamira ("Tristo il giorno"); Mahomed's followers exult over their Emperor's irresistible power.

## ACT TWO[1]

[*Scene One*] A square in Corinth. In a recitative ("Da ferri sciolta") and aria ("Si; m'avvalora il Dio") Cleomene, who had managed to escape his captors, calls down the wrath of the gods on his daughter and Mahomed—who is not only his archfoe but the seducer of his daughter as well. In bitter wrath he vows to fight on to the end for Greece.

[*Scene Two*] The pavilion of Mahomed, where Pamira is awaiting him. Tormented by remorse, she gives way to her emotions in a recitative ("Di ostili tende non è questo") and aria (Dall'asilo dello pace"). Guilt-ridden over her repudiation of Neocle, she sings that her unreasoning love for Mahomed is far more fatal than the assaults of the enemy. She prays to the spirit of her mother for strength to resist Mahomed's blandishments.

[*Scene Three*] The Emperor appears and again importunes Pamira, offering her all the fruits of victory. This marks the beginning of the long duet which comprises the entire scene ("Ti calme alfine"—in the Ricordi score: "Sgombra il timor").

When Pamira still resists, Mahomed adds the promise to show mercy toward her father. Although somewhat moved by the intensity of her protests ("Ciel, qual crudele delirol"), Mahomed continues his entreaties, imploring her to be his Queen. In utter despair, Pamira cries that only death can end her torment.

[*Scene Four*] Overriding all Pamira's objections, Mahomed has gone ahead with preparations for the wedding. Pamira, grief-stricken but resigned, is greeted by the nuptial chorus, "La festa dell'Imene," the burden of which is that she will find happiness in marriage ("Un fortunato Imene"). The nuptial altar is then brought to the center of the scene to the accompaniment of the invocatory chorus, "Divina profeta."

[*Scene Five*] Suddenly Neocle's voice is heard outside, shouting Pamira's name. The throng stares in consternation as Omar enters

[1] In the Italian-language Ricordi score (1891) Act Two begins with a recitative ("Cielo! che divero? destin crudele!") and a brilliant aria ("Dal soggiarmo degli estinti") by Pamira. This is followed by a duet between Pamira and Ismene ("Oh ciel! che fia chi mai s'avanza"), in which they are joined by the chorus of women ("Bella pace scenda almeno"). In the only available English translation of the libretto, these numbers are omitted.

leading Neocle bound in chains. Glaring at him in fury, Mahomed asks him what he wants ("Audace schiavo"). Death or vengeance, Neocle retorts defiantly ("O morte, o vendicarmi"). Then with withering scorn he goes on to say that while the women of Corinth are fighting side by side with their men, Pamira abandons herself to the caresses of the tyrant who would destroy her country. The very flowers in her hair, Neocle storms ("Pugnar tu li vedesti"), are stained with the blood of the Greeks.

Mahomed, momentarily taken aback, turns to Pamira and asks her who this man is. Suddenly and dramatically, she makes the decision that saves Neocle's life. She answers: "He is my brother" ("È mio germano"). A fiery trio ensues ("Si mai gradita"). Neocle, utterly bewildered by Pamira's quixotic action, implores her not to betray her father and her people by marriage with their mortal enemy. Mahomed, declaring that Pamira will be his bride, orders Neocle to be unchained and to witness the nuptials. Pamira cries that she can still hear her father's curse.

Omar and Ismene rush in with the news that the Corinthians have sounded the call to the final battle. (At this point in the staged version, the rear wall of the set opens to show Corinth in the distance, its ramparts crowded with women and soldiers. In a stormy chorus, "L'oltraggio m'è guida," the Greeks hurl defiance at the enemy. Then the voices of the Turks swell the ensemble as they threaten the beleaguered Greeks with fire and death.)

The ensuing action is dominated by a duet between Mahomed and Pamira ("Tu sol puoi, Pamira"), in which the Turk delivers his ultimatum: One word of consent from her will save Corinth; if she remains silent the city will perish. Resolutely Pamira answers that she will perish with it. Neocle applauds her courage in a fervid refrain. Declaring that she will now go back to Corinth and die there with her countrymen, Pamira asks Neocle to go with her.

Beside himself with fury, Mahomed bids them go—and go to die ("Ite a morir, abbene"). Before sunrise, he roars, every Greek will be exterminated and Corinth will vanish from the earth. The Greek chorus of defiance and the chorus of the Turks threatening disaster bring the act to a close.

## ACT THREE

[*Scene One. The Tombs of Corinth*] With the avenging Turks now about to breach the city walls, Neocle and Jero lead the citizens to the refuge of the tombs. Neocle hails this abode of death as their final sanctuary ("Avanziamo, questo è il luogo"), while Jero laments the tragic fate of Greece. Pamira and Ismene, with the other women, offer a prayer ("Signor, che tutto puoi") beseeching the gods to punish those who desecrate their altars.

This is followed by Neocle's incredibly long and difficult aria, "E fia ver, mio Signor." He implores the gods to avert the doom of Greece and to forestall the sacrilege of the Turks. He resolves to rescue Pamira from the lustful embrace of the tyrant—to free her so that she may immolate herself with her people. On this day, he sings with mystical fervor, death will release her from this loathsome earth and her soul will join the soul of her mother.

[*Scene Two*] A room in the Governor's palace. Here Cleomene welcomes back Neocle, who he supposed had been slain by the Turks. Joyously he embraces him as a son who brings him the consolation his own daughter denies him. Pamira still ignores him, Cleomene says, and disdains all family ties. When Neocle tells him she saved his life, the Governor answers that she stained his own with infamy. Even if she now comes repentant, he bursts out, he will plunge a dagger into her heart.

[*Scene Three*] Pamira appears and humbly asks forgiveness of her father. Neocle tries to intercede for her. Cleomene at first flatly rejects her expressions of penitence ("Perfida a che ne vieni"). But when Pamira tells him she has kept faith with Neocle and has spurned Mahomed, Cleomene's wrath melts away. Embracing the two, he gives them his paternal benediction. This leads into an impassioned trio ("Celeste Providenza, il tuo favor"), in which they implore the protection of the gods.

[*Scene Four*] An open square near the tombs, where the people are gathered with Cleomene, Jero, Ismene and the Greek warriors. Jero reports that the Turks are storming the city ("Tutto percorsi il marziale recinto"). Cleomene hails the final hour of death and glory and invokes the blessing of the gods ("A questa morte sacra"). All kneel as Jero performs the ritual of preparation for death: the placing of palm garlands and white veils on the heads of the faithful. Then, in a dramatic aria, "Nube di sangue intrisa," over a choral accompaniment, he foretells the doom of Greece at the hands of her enemies. He bids the people fight on in the spirit of the ancient hero Leonidas, King of Sparta, who died gloriously at Thermopylae. The people respond that the very name inspires them with new courage. The chorus comes to a thunderous conclusion on the phrase "si il sepolcro cangiarsi in altar—andiam!"

[*Scene Five*] As the siege nears its climax, Pamira, Ismene and the other Greek women are gathered in an open square to await the outcome. In recitative ("L'ora fatal s'appressa") Pamira sings that the fatal hour is at hand, then in an ensuing refrain ("Giusto ciel! in tal periglio") she exhorts the women to have the courage to die for Greece. Confusion and terror mount as the clamor of battle comes closer.

[*Scene Six*] Mahomed and his soldiers burst in with savage shouts of triumph. Resolutely facing the attackers, the women defy them to do their worst: If destiny has ordained the doom of the Greeks, then let their conqueror beware his own fate ("Se i Greci tutti, miser! fur spenti, di noi paventi il vincitor").

Mahomed, motioning his followers back, cries that in this moment of victory, revenge will be tempered with mercy. As he strides forward to take Pamira in his arms, she stabs herself, crying that first this dagger will pierce her heart ("Arresta! O questo ferro mi squarcia il sen"). She falls dead at Mahomed's feet. There is a gasp of horror from the crowd. In the background, Corinth is seen in flames, and from the distant ramparts comes the despairing cry of the vanquished defenders: "O patria!"

# Benvenuto Cellini

## *by* HECTOR BERLIOZ

### (1803–69)

### *Libretto by*
#### LÉON DE WAILLY AND AUGUSTE BARBIER

Based on the *Autobiography* of Benvenuto Cellini

#### CHARACTERS

| | |
|---|---|
| Balducci, Papal Treasurer | Bass |
| Teresa, his daughter | Soprano |
| Benvenuto Cellini, a goldsmith | Tenor |
| Ascanio, his apprentice | Mezzo-soprano |
| Francesco ⎰ artisans in Cellini's workshop | ⎱ Tenor |
| Bernardino ⎱ | ⎰ Bass |
| Pope Clement VII | Bass |
| Fieramosca, sculptor to the Pope | Baritone |
| Pompeo, a professional assassin | Baritone |
| Innkeeper | Tenor |

Artists, apprentices, artisans, masquers, carnival actors, monks, townspeople, servants

*Time:* 1532
*Place:* Rome
*First performance:* Grand Opéra, Paris, September 3, 1838 (also given as September 10)
*Original language:* French

NOTE: The role of "Clement VII" was in the Berlioz original. Because of French censorship it was changed to "Cardinal Salviati," the censors having objected to the depiction of a pope on the stage. In most productions, the character is designated as Cardinal Salviati.

---

This opera, the first of three Berlioz wrote, has a strange history. It was a complete failure at its Paris premiere, as well as at its London premiere two weeks afterward. Given fifteen years later in London, with Berlioz conducting, it was a qualified success. By that time the composer had established himself as one of the most gifted orchestral virtuosos of his day, and his ideas were championed by such eminent musicians as Franz Liszt and Robert Schumann.

Liszt, in fact, revived *Benvenuto Cellini* at Weimar in 1855, and Hans von Bülow conducted the opera in Hanover in 1879. Then it vanished from the operatic repertoire. The first American performance was given at Philharmonic Hall, New York, on March 22, 1965, by the Concert Opera Association under the baton of Thomas Scherman.

The stirring overture states some of the opera's most important themes. It begins in a mood reflecting the restless, rebellious spirit of the hero-artist with a theme based on the love duet of Cellini and Teresa in Act Three.

A following section is marked by a pizzicato theme in the basses which foreshadows the aria sung by Pope Clement VII at the beginning of Act Three. The main section of the overture, in sonata form, carries the impetuous "Cellini" theme along with that of the drinking song. The coda reiterates the Clement VII theme. Running through the entire overture is the effervescent gaiety of the Mardi Gras carnival.

## ACT ONE

A room in Balducci's home. Late evening. Balducci is complaining to his daughter, the seventeen-year-old Teresa, that he cannot understand why Pope Clement insists on calling a troublemaker like Cellini to Rome as his official sculptor ("En vérité, c'est bien etrange"). This fellow Cellini is a wild-eyed revolutionary and is obviously up to no good. In any case, a sensible, competent artist, Fieramosca, already is available in Rome. Teresa, who seems completely disinterested, watches her father silently as he leaves the room, shaking his head.

No sooner has he gone, however, than she rushes to the open window and listens to a chorus of masquers in the street. They are singing in anticipation of Mardi Gras, which will begin on the following evening—Shrove Tuesday, 1532.

Suddenly a bouquet of flowers is thrown through the window. Picking it up, Teresa finds a note from Cellini, her lover. She realizes then that the singers were Cellini and his friends and apprentices. In a melodious cavatina, "Entre l'amour et le devoir," she reflects on how she is torn between her love for the sculptor and her filial duty. Then, over a sprightly waltz theme, she sings that she will put off any decisions on the matter until she is older and wiser—like her parents.

At the conclusion of the song, Cellini enters. In the aria "O Teresa, vous que j'aime" he tells her how much he loves her—and at the same time makes it clear that he objects to her being pledged to his rival, the sculptor Fieramosca.

While the two are busy with their love-making, Fieramosca himself comes mincing in on tiptoe, unobserved. He is carrying a huge bouquet of flowers. A trio in tarantella rhythm ensues. While Fieramosca makes simpering avowals of love, Cellini and Teresa—still unaware that he is in the room—ridicule his prowess as a lover and an artist. Unfortunately for the lovers, Fieramosca overhears their plan to run away together to Florence.

As the trio ends, Teresa hears the angry voice of her father outside. At her cry of alarm, Fieramosca darts panic-stricken into Teresa's bedroom. When Balducci comes storming in, flinging open the door, Cellini hides behind it. Scowling at Teresa, Balducci demands to know why she is still up at this late hour. She stammers that there is a strange man in her bedroom. With a bellow of rage Balducci rushes into her room, and while he is gone Teresa helps Cellini escape. Balducci comes back dragging the hapless Fieramosca.

Pandemonium breaks loose as Balducci and Teresa shout for their servants and neighbors to help them rid the premises of this "libertine" who has forced his way into their home. In a tumultuous closing ensemble ("Ah, maître drôle! Ah, libertin!") Fieramosca frantically protests his innocence; Balducci and Teresa denounce him as a lecherous intruder; neighbors and servants, adding their imprecations, comically threaten the cowering young man with dust mops, brooms, meat cleavers and pokers.

## ACT TWO

[*Scene One*] The courtyard of an inn. Cellini, alone, sings the aria "Une heure encore," in which he meditates on whether his first duty is to his art or to his beloved Teresa. His reflections are interrupted by the entrance of a noisy crowd of his apprentices and friends, including two of his fellow artisans, Francesco and Bernardino. Cellini joins them in a lusty drinking song, "Si la terre aux beaux jours se couronne."

A comic byplay follows as the innkeeper comes bustling out.

To the amusement of the crowd, he whines that he will not serve these rascally young artists another drop of wine until they have paid what they owe him ("que voulez-vous? La cave est vide"). Luckily for the indigent debtors, Ascanio suddenly shows up with a bag of gold. In the aria "Cette somme t'est due," he announces that he has come from the papal palace with the advance payment to Master Cellini for the statue of Perseus commissioned by Pope Clement.

The others stare in awe as Cellini—whose mind is on getting away to Florence with Teresa as soon as possible—rather casually takes the purse of gold. Counting the money, he exclaims angrily that Balducci has fobbed him off with a miserable fee quite unworthy of a creative artist.

Then and there, Cellini decides to pay Balducci out for the insult. He tells his friends that tonight at the carnival there will be a pantomime performed by the great Cassandro and his troupe, in which Balducci will be burlesqued by the character of King Midas. Cellini adds that he is certain Balducci and Teresa will be in the audience ("Je sais que Balducci quittera sa demeure"). When the cannon sounds to signal the end of Mardi Gras at dawn on Ash Wednesday, and all the lights are extinguished, says Cellini, he will take advantage of the confusion and abduct Teresa. Disguised in a white monk's habit, he will easily be able to carry out his plan.

But—as before—Fieramosca overhears Cellini's plotting. In desperation he goes for advice to his friend Pompeo, a professional assassin. This worthy obligingly suggests that they double-cross Cellini by disguising themselves in monk's habits and carrying out their own abduction of Teresa. The audacity of the scheme terrifies Fieramosca, but Pompeo confidently assures him that if it comes to swordplay he is more than a match for the likes of Cellini.

Fieramosca, trying to bolster his faltering courage, boasts in a mock-heroic aria ("Que pourrait me résister") that he will win Teresa by vanquishing his hated rival with a single sword thrust. He and Pompeo then leave to prepare for their escapade.

[*Scene Two*] The Piazza Colonna at the height of the carnival. At one side is the stage upon which the pantomime will take place. There is a brief orchestral prelude which echoes the theme of the trio in Act One.

Balducci and Teresa enter and stand near the stage. A moment later Ascanio, in brown monk's garb, and Cellini, in white, enter and converse in undertones about their plot. The simultaneous conversation of the four merges in a quartet. This builds into an ensemble as the citizens, led by Francesco and Bernardino, gather to express their delight at the prospect of seeing the wonderful pantomime called *King Midas or the Donkey's Ears*.

The performance, in *commedia dell'arte* style, begins with an overture in a melodramatic vein. To the accompaniment of descriptive orchestral sound effects, the traditional characters such as Arlequin and Pasquerello go through their antics. They bow in exaggerated humility to King Midas—an obvious caricature of Balducci with the ears of an ass—who bestows a crown upon Pasquerello. Balducci, infuriated, leaps up on the stage and chases the actors off. The crowd roars with laughter.

Then suddenly Cellini and Ascanio enter from one side of the piazza just as Fieramosca and Pompeo come in from the other side. The two rivals are dressed in white monk's habits. They promptly challenge each other and a fight breaks out—Cellini duels with Pompeo, Ascanio with Fieramosca. Ironically, the encounter takes place against a background of moving figures with lanterns—trysting young lovers among the carnival crowd. There is a sudden, ominous silence in the orchestra. Cellini lunges at Pompeo and kills him on the spot. There is a gasp of horror from the crowd, then all throw themselves on Cellini. Tearing himself free, he rushes away just as the cannon shot booms out and all the lights are extinguished.

## ACT THREE

[*Scene One*] Cellini's studio. His goldsmith's furnace is offstage in the rear. It is early the following morning. Teresa rushes in with Ascanio, who is still in his monk's robe. They call out Cellini's name, then hide when Francesco and Bernardino appear. The two artisans urge the foundry workers to their tasks. The latter respond in chorus in a melancholy folk song refrain ("A l'atelier rentrons sans plus attendre"), during which Francesco and Bernardino exit into the foundry.

Ascanio, doing his best to console Teresa—who is now in tears at not finding Cellini—sings a sprightly ballad ("Mais qu'ai-je donc") recalling the goings on at the Mardi Gras carnival. Teresa smiles through her tears as he imitates her own voice as well as those of Cellini, Fieramosca and Balducci.

The two pause to listen to a group of monks outside chanting a prayer to the Virgin Mary. They both sing an obbligato in the form of a hymn, "Sainte Vierge Marie." As their voices die away on a reverent phrase, Cellini bursts in. He is still in his monk's habit.

In an ensuing recitative and air ("Ma dague en main portège par la nuit") he describes how he escaped from the crowd after the fatal duel, then joined a procession of monks to throw his pursuers off his trail. When he tells Ascanio he intends to flee to Florence with Teresa, Ascanio reminds him of his promise to the Pope to finish the statue of Perseus.[1] Cellini snaps that the statue —and the Pope—can go to the devil. He orders Ascanio to inform the apprentices that the foundry will be closed.

Ascanio leaves, but rushes back in with the news that Balducci and Fieramosca at this very moment are outside the door. It bursts open, and the two stride in. Cellini and Ascanio stand shoulder to shoulder to hide Teresa from her father.

A turbulent ensemble now follows. Balducci demands to know where Teresa is, roaring that by this time she no doubt has been dishonored. To preserve what is left of her reputation, she must marry Fieramosca at once. Thereupon Cellini bellows that he will tear his rival limb from limb if he dares touch the girl. All at once there is a dead silence. In the next moment the figure of Pope Clement VII looms in the doorway. The scene continues with a dramatic sextet, "A tous péchés plein indulgence."

The Pope demands to see the statue he has commissioned. When Cellini confesses that it is not yet finished, the Pope sternly declares he will turn the work over to another artist. Infuriated, Cellini shouts that he would not allow "Michelangelo himself" to touch his masterpiece. Seizing a hammer, he lunges toward the mold to smash it to bits, but is restrained by the Pope's guards. In measured, menacing tones ("Je vais entrer à l'atelier") the Pope delivers an ultimatum: Cellini will be pardoned both for his crime of murder and for his insult to His Holiness only if the statue is finished by nightfall. If he fails he will pay with his life. Cellini hastily assures the pontiff that he will require no more than another hour to finish the work. Pope Clement turns and stalks into the foundry, followed by his retinue, leaving Cellini in the hands of four papal guards.

Cellini, thus prevented from escaping, reflects on the course of

[1] One of the most renowned sculptures of medieval Italy and today one of the art treasures of Florence. The bronze statue of the helmeted Perseus, holding aloft the severed head of Medusa as he stands with one foot on her body, is in the Loggia della Signoria.

events in one of the most dramatic arias in the opera, "Sur les monts les plus sauvages." He sings that he would gladly exchange his hectic, stormy life as an artist for the peaceful serenity of a shepherd's existence.

[*Scene Two*] Cellini's foundry, with the furnace in the center. The sculptor is frantically at work, assisted by Francesco and Bernardino. Fieramosca, obviously relishing Cellini's dilemma, warns him that the mold is beginning to congeal because there is not enough metal. Francesco and Bernardino express their dismay.

Inspired by desperation, Cellini shouts to Ascanio and the apprentices to throw into the furnace every bit of metal in the studio—including even some of his completed masterpieces. Cellini works with furious energy. With the casting finally completed, he inscribes on the base of the statue the famous inscription: "Si quiste laeserit, ego tuus ultor ero" ("If anyone harm you, I will be your avenger"). He sings the words on a single note over a sustained chord in the orchestra. Then with his mallet he carefully taps the mold as all in the studio stand transfixed. The mold falls away, and Perseus emerges in all its golden magnificence.

Pope Clement, the apprentices, artisans, friends and townspeople (joined by Fieramosca and Balducci in grudging admiration) hail the crowning achievement of Benvenuto Cellini's genius in a thunderous finale, "Gloire à lui! Les métaux ces fleurs souterraines."

Carmina Burana
*Cantiones Profanae*
(*Secular songs for soloists and chorus*)

by CARL ORFF
( 1895–    )

Based on the *Songs of Benedictbeuern,* a collection of verses written and sung by the goliards, vagabond poets of the twelfth and thirteenth centuries.

---

Although *Carmina Burana* is not an opera, it has become a part of the concert opera repertoire and is usually presented with its dramatic action—inherent in the music—provided by a ballet. The drama of *Carmina Burana*—like that of Berlioz' *Symphonie fantastique*—is admittedly cerebral, yet it belongs to the stage. Written by a man who is considered one of Germany's foremost composers of music for the theater, it is one of the most remarkable choral works of the present day.

Carl Orff went back to the Middle Ages for the inspiration of *Carmina Burana*. He set to music the poetry of the goliards, the picaresque nomads of Europe who sang of pagan joys and the sheer delight of living. Irreverent, witty, earthy and rebellious, the goliards nevertheless were influenced in their songs and verses by the prosody of the ancient Catholic Latin hymns. In much the same way as they satirized church ritual, Orff parodied Gregorian chant in his musical settings. There are echoes of the *Dies Irae* in the opening chorus, for example, and in one or two instances the Gregorian psalm tone is adapted note for note.

The prime source of goliard poetry is a manuscript discovered in 1803 in the monastery of Benedictbeuern in Bavaria about forty miles from Munich, Orff's birthplace. This manuscript provided the material for *Carmina Burana*. It was Orff's first major work and was completed in 1936.

The score consists of musical settings of twenty-five poems (the chorus, "O Fortuna, velut Luna" begins and ends the work); most of the lyrics are in Latin, some in Low German. There is an extraordinary variety of rhythmic patterns—including flamenco, French and Italian dances of the Middle Ages and the simple rhythms of Bavarian folk song.

The work is orchestrated for eight percussion players, with a percussion section of three glockenspiels, xylophone, castanets, wood blocks, small bells, chimes, celesta, two pianos, six tympani, tambourines, two side drums and bass drum.

Following are brief descriptions of the twenty-five musical settings.

## Fortuna Imperatrix Mundi
### Fortune, Empress of the World

1. "O Fortuna, velut Luna." Chorus. Fortune, as evanescent as moonlight, bestows her blessing on man—then as quickly takes it away. A powerful rhythmic thrust characterizes this sardonic chorus of homage to Fate.

2. "Fortune plango vulnera." Chorus. The three verses describe how Fate capriciously strikes down her victims in the very moment of triumph. The song ends with a symbolic warning to a king: Let him beware, for on Fortune's wheel is inscribed the name of Hecuba, goddess of revenge.

## I
### Primo Vere
### In Springtime

3. "Veris leta facies." Small chorus. In unison passages sung in plain-chant style, altos are paired with basses, sopranos with tenors. It is an expression of pagan joy over the return of spring.

4. "Omnia sol temperat." Baritone solo. Also in the Gregorian mode, it is another evocation of spring, when the god of love rules in all hearts.

5. "Ecce gratum." Chorus. Beginning with a solemn four-note Gregorian phrase, it suddenly swings into an impudent staccato rhythm reflecting the abandoned gaiety in anticipation of the return of summer and the season of love.

### Auf dem Anger
### On the Lawn

6. Dance. Orchestral interlude somewhat in the manner of the French and Italian dances of the Middle Ages.

7. "Floret silva." Chorus and small chorus. Sung partly in Latin and partly in Low German, it is a plaintive yet lilting lament of a maiden for her lover who rode away on horseback.

8. "Chramer, gip die varwe mir." Solo sopranos and chorus.

Sung in Low German in the manner of a Bavarian folk song, with hummed choral interludes. A young girl asks a shopkeeper for rouge to paint her cheeks to make her more attractive to the young men.

9. Reie. A round dance—orchestral interlude. This introduces two brief choruses in folk-song style, lyrics in Low German: "Swaz hie gat umbe" and "Chume, chum, geselle min." Both, of course, have to do with the longing of the girls for the boys, and vice versa.

10. "Were diu werlt alle min." Chorus. Sung *allegretto* in unison, this is a delightfully flippant variation of a lover's lament: If all the world belonged to him, he would gladly give it up to hold the Queen of England in his arms.

## II
### In Taberna
### *In the Tavern*

11. "Estunas interius." Baritone solo. One of the principal arias in the score, it is written in the style of true *bel canto* opera. Driven to despair by the aimlessness and frustration of his life, a man abandons himself to thoughts of lust and depravity.

12. "Olim lacus colueram." Tenor solo and chorus. A brief but spectacularly difficult aria, beginning on a high A natural and rising to a D above high C. It is the parodied lament of a beautiful swan, captured and roasted black upon the spit for the feast.

13. "Ego sum abbas." Baritone solo and male chorus. This is sung in unctuous Gregorian style, interrupted by raucous orchestral outbursts, by the drunken Abbot of Cucany, who describes how he meets in the tavern with his cronies for the dice game. Whoever plays against him loses everything—including his garments.

14. "In taberna quando sumus." Male chorus. A roaring chorus, mostly in unison, in which the Abbot's companions drink a toast to everyone from "the sinful brethren" to the Pope, then recite the litany of those who find their joy in wine—which includes everybody "by the hundreds and thousands."

## III
### Cour d'Amours
### *The Court of Love*

15. "Amor volat undique." Soprano solo and boys' chorus. This section is dominated by an undulating figure in thirds. The

*ragazzi* sing of the all-pervading presence of the god of love; the soprano reflects upon the plight of the young girl who has no lover.

16. "Dies, nox et omnia." Baritone solo. A young man complains that he is the most wretched of mortals because the heart of his ladylove is made of ice. A short but difficult aria with an extremely high tessitura—a B natural above the staff in the bass in one of the coloratura passages. In performance, this is usually sung by a tenor.

17. "Stetit puella." Soprano solo. A beguiling melody in flamenco rhythm. The song describes a young girl in a red dress which rustles provocatively as she walks.

18. "Circa mea pectora." Baritone solo and chorus. Another lover's lament, with three verses in waltz tempo sung in Latin while the chorus responds in Low German.

19. "Si puer cum puellula." Sung by three tenors, a baritone and two basses. A striking ensemble on a Gregorian theme (marked *allegro buffo*) sung in unaccompanied triads with solo interpolations. Its theme is a passionate description of two young lovers.

20. "Veni, veni, venias." Double chorus. A lover's exuberant ode to his mistress. The choral response of "Hyrca, hyrce, nazaza trilliviros" has the effect of a demonic incantation.

21. "In trutina." Soprano solo. In a simple melody of Puccinian lyricism, a girl reflects amorously on the temptations of love.

22. "Tempus est iocundum." Soprano and baritone solos with chorus and boys' chorus. One of the most elaborate numbers in the score, it is a pagan hymn to spring, describing how the vernal urge turns the thoughts of youths and maidens to the delights of love.

23. "Dulcissime." Soprano solo. A passionate expression of surrender to the god of love, sung in the form of a brilliant coloratura phrase.

24. "Ave formosissima." Chorus. A hymn to Venus, written in imitation of a majestic Lutheran chorale, in which the goddess is compared to two celebrated heroines of medieval poetry— Blanziflor and Helena, mythological sorceresses.

25. The foregoing leads directly into the finale of *Carmina Burana*, "O Fortuna, velut Luna," a repetition of the opening chorus.

# La Damnation de Faust

*by* HECTOR BERLIOZ

(1803–69)

*Libretto by*
BERLIOZ AND M. GANDONNIÈRE

Based on a translation of Goethe's *Faust* by Gérard de Nerval

### CHARACTERS

| | |
|---|---|
| Marguerite | Mezzo-soprano |
| Faust | Tenor |
| Méphistophélès | Baritone |
| Brander | Bass |

Students, soldiers, peasants, dancers, demons

*Place:* Hungary and Germany
*Time:* Middle Ages
*First performance:* Opéra-Comique, Paris, December 6, 1846
*Original language:* French

---

*La Damnation de Faust* is one of the best examples of concert opera, because Berlioz wrote it to be presented in this form. He himself entitled it an *opéra de concert*. The work began in the form of nine songs with lyrics as translated from Goethe by Nerval. These Berlioz grouped into eight scenes, which he subsequently incorporated into *Faust*.

Berlioz' version of the Faust legend differs somewhat from those of Gounod and Boito. His Faust does not sell his soul to the devil outright; he bargains at first only for the sensual pleasures with which Méphistophélès tempts him. In the end, he offers his soul to save Marguerite, then—a victim of the devil's treachery—rides to hell.

The two original performances in 1846 (December 6 and 20) were failures which cost Berlioz ten thousand francs of his own money. He recouped his losses, however, with successful performances of the first two parts of *Faust* in Russia in 1847.

Although never intended to be presented as an opera, it

subsequently received a number of successful stage productions in
Europe, including England and South America. *Faust* was staged
for the first time as an opera by Raoul Gunsbourg in Monte Carlo
on February 18, 1893. It was first heard in America, in the concert
version, under Leopold Damrosch in New York on February 12,
1880. The operatic version was given by the Metropolitan on
December 7, 1906, with four additional performances during the
1906–7 season. Most performances in recent years have been given
in the original concert form.

## ACT ONE

[*Scene One*] The curtain rises immediately on a pleasant landscape outside Faust's study. Weary after a night of poring over
his books, he muses on the enchantment of the returning spring
("Le vieil hiver a fait place"). Following this aria there is a brief
orchestral interlude with rhythms of a peasant dance and a
martial air.

[*Scene Two*] Faust listens to the singing of the peasants ("Les
bergers quittent leurs troupeau")—the *Ronde de Paysans*. He comments enviously on their carefree gaiety and their lusty enjoyment of life.

[*Scene Three*] Another part of the plain, with a fortress in the
distance.[1] Watching soldiers march out of the fortress, Faust sings
that the specter of war now looms over this pleasant land, with
the sons of the Danube marching into battle ("Mais d'un éclat
guerrir"). The army continues to advance to the strains of the
*Rákóczy March*. At first Faust is inspired to patriotic fervor by
the military pageantry, but then he is haunted by the realization
that victory is won only at the cost of suffering and death.

## ACT TWO

[*Scene Four*] Faust's study in north Germany. A cavernous fireplace dominates the room, and curled up on the hearth is a poodle.
In a despondent mood, Faust laments that the solitude of the
forest has failed to bring him the peace of mind he longs for
("Sans regrets j'ai quitté"). Overwhelmed by despair, he seizes

---

[1] This scene is set in Hungary because Berlioz wanted to introduce a
Hungarian musical theme—which he did in the form of the famous *Rákóczy
March* (*Marche Hongroise*), the dominating music of the scene.

the flask of poison on his table. Just as he raises it to his lips he hears the Easter hymn ("Christ vient de resussiter"). Its majestic strains restore his courage, and he expresses the renewal of his faith in a jubilant obbligato to the chorus ("O souvenirs! O mon âme tremblante"). Overcome by emotion, he falls to his knees and joins in the concluding "hosanna" of the hymn.

[*Scene Five*] The poodle in front of the fireplace vanishes. In its place crouches Méphistophélès. Rising, he takes note of Faust on his knees and sarcastically commends him for his piety ("O pure emotion! Enfant du saint"). A scene in recitative ensues. Eying him suspiciously, Faust asks the devil why he has come ("Qui donc es-tu?"). To show him, the devil replies, that there are other things in life besides the dull study of philosophy—for example, pleasure, power and fortune. In behalf of such pursuits, Méphistophélès adds, he is at his service. Faust accepts the offer on one condition: that he will be granted one moment in time when he can say, "This moment, stay. I am happy" ("Si jamais dis au moment qui passe: Arréte-toi"). The devil assents with an ironic bow, and then the two rush away.

[*Scene Six*] Auerbach's tavern in Leipzig, where Méphistophélès has brought Faust to sample the pleasures of carousing. They listen as students on a spree roar out a drinking song ("À boire encore"). The leader of the crowd, Brander, obliges with a rollicking ditty about a rat ("Certain rat, dans une cuisine")—the *Chanson de Brander*.

It is the story of the rat that grew sleek and plump in the kitchen until the cook slipped poison into his soup. Thereupon he squirmed and moaned as though "in the throes of love"—as the song's cynical refrain goes. Finally, to escape his misery, the rat jumped into the oven, where the kitchen maid saw to it that he was properly roasted. In a sardonic coda the drinkers sing a fugue on the theme of Brander's song, vocalizing on an "Amen."

Méphistophélès steps forward and sneeringly compliments the students on the devotional quality of their choral efforts, then asks leave to respond with a song of his own. This he does with the famous *Song of the Flea* ("Une puce gentile"). The flea was the favorite of a wealthy prince, who one day ordered his tailor to measure the insect for a resplendent court costume. Impressed with his sartorial importance, the flea called in all his brothers and sisters from the provinces and persuaded the prince to confer royal titles upon them. The resident lords and ladies of the court not only were obliged to tolerate the interlopers but were forced to scratch in secret so as not to offend their sovereign. Méphistophélès ends his song with a satirical guffaw, and then he and Faust disappear.

## ACT THREE

[*Scene Seven*] A meadow on the banks of the Elbe, to which Méphistophélès has transported Faust. He is lying on a bed of roses. In a sensual incantation ("Voici des roses") the devil conjures up an idyllic vision for Faust's benefit. Gnomes and sylphs encircle him in a sinuous dance as they invite him to find happiness in dreams ("Dors, heureux Faust"). At the conclusion of the chorus Marguerite emerges from among the roses as Méphistophélès tempts Faust with a vision of her.

## ACT FOUR

[*Scene Eight*] A street near Marguerite's home. Soldiers and students crowd in. The soldiers sing that cities and women are equally difficult to conquer ("Ville entourées")—but both eventually surrender. Then the students strike up a Latin song, "Iam nox stellata velamina pandit" ("Under night's starry vault there is time to drink and love"). The two groups join in an ingenious choral ensemble, after which they leave the scene.

[*Scene Nine*] Méphistophélès comes in with Faust and shows him Marguerite's house. Stealing alone into her room, Faust voices his amorous thoughts in the beautiful aria "Merci doux crépuscule!"

[*Scene Ten*] Suddenly Méphistophélès rushes in and warns that Marguerite is approaching. Trembling with ardor and excitement, Faust hides behind the draperies. As the devil leaves he remarks cynically that he and his sprites will oblige with a nuptial serenade.

[*Scene Eleven*] Marguerite enters. In recitative she wonders why the air has a strange heaviness. She has a premonition of evil, yet is beguiled by thoughts of her lover-to-be . . . will a kind Fate bring him to her? Braiding her hair, she sings the plaintive medieval song about the King of Thule ("Autrefois un roi de Thulé").

The King had received a golden chalice from his Queen as she lay dying, and this he treasured as his most precious possession. As he neared the end of his life he gave away all his lands and wealth, keeping only the chalice. One day he called his barons together for a feast in an ancient castle by the sea. There he drank a final toast from the chalice, then hurled it into the breakers. As it sank out of sight the King grew pale and shuddered in his death throes. Marguerite's voice trails off as she falls asleep.

[*Scene Twelve*] Méphistophélès suddenly materializes. Summoning his demons and will-o'-the-wisps, he commands them to dance in order to charm Marguerite into his power. To a shimmering accompaniment, the *Minuet of the Will-o'-the-Wisps* follows, introducing the dream sequence.

Standing on the steps of a church, the devil draws Marguerite to him with the gestures of a sorcerer. He conjures up a vision of Faust which alternately appears and then vanishes. As the girl raises her arms supplicatingly, the cross on the church lights up. Méphistophélès cowers back and hides his face behind his cloak. Finally Marguerite staggers toward the church and falls fainting on the steps. The demons burst in and circle about her in a frenzied dance. At a magical sign from Méphistophélès the dream fades. Marguerite is seen asleep in her chair. Then the devil sings an insulting "moralizing" serenade ("Chantons à cette belle une chanson morale") about the unfortunate consequences of an innocent maiden's tryst with her lover.[2] The demons chant a suggestive refrain. The devil makes them disappear as Faust approaches.

[*Scene Thirteen*] Marguerite awakens, sees him, and rushes into his arms. Then follows the passionate duet "Ange adoré, dont la céleste image," one of the most beautiful numbers in the score.

[*Scene Fourteen*] As the lovers stand in a blissful embrace, Méphistophélès rushes in exclaiming that the neighbors are converging on the house. With them is Marguerite's mother, whom the village gossips have informed that a stranger has stolen into her home and is making love to her daughter.

Pretending great concern over Marguerite's safety, the devil cries that "this angel" must be saved at all costs ("Il faut sauver

[2] This is a variation on the theme of the serenade sung by Gounod's Méphistophélès, who cynically advises the maiden not to yield to her lover until the wedding ring is safely on her finger.

cet ange"). This marks the beginning of a stormy trio. Faust and Marguerite lament that their dream of love has been shattered. Méphistophélès curses the intruders. The trio blends with the chorus of the townspeople maliciously taunting "Mother Oppenheim." Mingled with their derisive laughter, the ensemble rises to a furious climax.

## ACT FIVE

[*Scene Fifteen*] Marguerite's room. In the romanza "D'amour l'ardente flamme" she abandons herself to thoughts of Faust—his gentle smile, his beautiful eyes, his enchanting voice and the fiery ecstasy of his kisses. In sorrow and longing she waits for his return. From behind the scenes come the voices of the soldiers and students in a reprise of their chorus. With a final despairing cry Marguerite leaves.

[*Scene Sixteen*] Faust alone in a forest. Enchanted by the beauty of the scene, he sings a majestic invocation to Nature, "Nature immense, impénétrable et fière." Méphistophélès appears and watches him unobserved. In a sinister refrain ("Cette ame à moi librement donne") he muses that he still cannot claim Faust's soul because he has not yet said to a moment in time: "Stay. I am happy"—the stipulation of his bargain.

A passage in recitative follows. Making himself known, Méphistophélès informs Faust that Marguerite is in prison, doomed to die for the murder of her mother: She gave her an overdose of the sleeping potion Faust himself had provided so that he and Marguerite could tryst undisturbed.

Faust turns on the devil in fury, accusing him of treachery and ordering him to save the girl. Instantly Méphistophélès hands him a document. Sign it, says the devil, and he will save Marguerite. Scarcely looking at the paper, Faust forthwith signs away his soul. Now sure of his victim, Méphistophélès deliberately suggests that it may already be too late. Shaken by terror, Faust calls on Time to stop ("Temps, arréte-toi")—thus inadvertently sealing his fateful bargain.

In savage exultation, Méphistophélès calls for his horses ("Hola! Vortex, Giaour!"), and then begins the fearsome *Ride to Hell* [*Scenes Seventeen and Eighteen*]. Storm winds howl, hideous monsters roar, huge black birds beat their wings on Faust's head. At the side of the road, terror-stricken peasants pray for mercy.

[*Scene Nineteen*] As the riders near the abyss, the chorus of the damned greets Méphistophélès, chanting in diabolical gibberish ("Irimiru Karabrao! Tradioun Marexil firtrundixe"). When he tells them that Faust has finally signed the pact that damned his soul, the demons hoist the devil on their shoulders with a chorus of fiendish triumph. Then all are engulfed in the flames of hell.

In a brief epilogue, earthly voices are heard recalling the horror of the scene ("Alors l'Enfer se tut")—the shrieking demons, the wail of lost souls in torment.

[*Scene Twenty*] Heaven, where the Blessed Spirits welcome the soul of Marguerite (the *Apotheosis*). In a majestic closing chorus ("Remonte au ciel âme naïve") they sing that this innocent soul has been forgiven the mortal sin committed in error, and that one day Faust himself may be granted divine mercy.

# Dido and Aeneas

*by* HENRY PURCELL

(1659–95)

*Libretto by*
NAHUM TATE

Based on Vergil's *Aeneid*

### CHARACTERS

| | |
|---|---|
| Dido, or Elissa, Queen of Carthage | Soprano |
| Belinda, her lady in waiting | Soprano |
| First Woman | Soprano |
| Second Woman | Mezzo-soprano |
| Sorceress | Mezzo-soprano |
| First Witch | Soprano |
| Second Witch | Soprano |
| Spirit | Soprano |
| Aeneas, a Trojan prince | Tenor or high baritone |
| A sailor | Tenor |

Chorus of courtiers and people, witches, sailors

*Place:* The ancient city of Carthage on the northern coast of Africa
*Time:* Antiquity
*First performance:* London, about 1689
*Original language:* English

---

Henry Purcell is considered the greatest composer of the early classical period in England, a creative artist who brought the music of the Elizabethan age to its finest flowering. He wrote the music for some thirty-five dramatic works, many of them masques, which were spectacles staged for the entertainment of royalty. Outstanding among his stage works, besides *Dido and Aeneas,* are *King Arthur, The Witch of Endor, The Fairy Queen* (based on Shakespeare's *A Midsummer Night's Dream*) and *Dioclesian.*

Much of the history of *Dido and Aeneas* has vanished with the past. It has been established that Purcell composed it for a school for girls in London, where it was first performed about 1689. But —unaccountably—there is no record of its performance for the next two hundred years. The opera was staged in 1895 by students at the Royal Academy of Music for the bicentenary of the composer's death.

In recent times it has been revived with increasing frequency in concert and stage performances, sometimes with ballet to give more movement to the essentially static nature of the plot. It was presented in a modified concert version by the American Chamber Opera Society in New York in 1954 under the baton of Arnold U. Gamson and has since had other performances in various parts of the United States.

The plot of the opera is based on episodes in the *Aeneid* of Vergil. Dido, the reputed founder of the ancient city of Carthage, gives refuge to Aeneas after his flight from Troy during the Trojan War. They fall in love—only to become the victims of a conspiracy brewed by a malevolent sorceress and her witches. An evil sprite in the employ of the sorceress falsely informs Aeneas that the god Jove has commanded him to sail at once to Italy. Aeneas reluctantly obeys and leaves Carthage, whereupon Dido stabs herself on a funeral pyre.

The stately overture, dominated by a theme in rising and falling triads, sets the somber mood of the legend.

## ACT ONE

[*Scene One*] Dido's palace at Carthage. The Queen and Belinda enter with their entourage. In a spirited chorus Belinda and the court exhort Dido to shake off her sorrow for the moment ("Shake the cloud from off your brow"). Belinda reminds her that Fortune still smiles on her and that her empire is growing.

But Dido, inconsolable, answers that she is tormented by a secret grief and that peace of mind is utterly strange to her ("I am prest with torment"). Belinda guesses her secret: She is yearning for Aeneas, who is expected at the palace. They are fated to become lovers, and their love has a two-fold destiny: to save Carthage and to restore ruined Troy.

In a recitative passage ("Where could so much virtue spring?") Dido muses over Aeneas' manly virtues and heroic conquests—he is gentle in peace, yet fierce in war. Belinda and the other women of the court assure the Queen that she has nothing to fear from this great hero.

Aeneas appears and declares his love for Dido. For her, he proclaims, he will defy Destiny itself. He begs her to accept his avowals—if not for his sake, for the sake of the future of Carthage. Belinda surreptitiously urges Aeneas to be ardent in his wooing, for Dido's eyes betray her love even though her lips deny it ("Pursue thy conquest, Love"). The scene ends as the chorus hails the triumph of love and beauty. This is followed by a brief ballet called the *Dance of Victory*.

[Scene Two] The cave of the witches. Introduced by a foreboding theme in the orchestra, the sorceress summons her witches and commands them to put Carthage to the torch. They respond in wild chorus ("Harm's our delight"). The sorceress exults that before sunset they will destroy the hated Queen of Carthage and her royal lover as well.

When the witches ask how this is to be accomplished, the sorceress explains that Aeneas is destined to go to Italy. At the moment, she goes on, he and Dido are idling their time away in hunting. When they return, the sorceress' own mischievous sprite, disguised as the messenger Mercury, will inform Aeneas that Jove has commanded him to set sail this very night.

The witches express their glee in a spiteful, snarling chorus (sung to "ho-ho-ho"), then sing that they will first conjure up a storm to force the lovers to break off the hunt and hasten back to court. Deep in the recesses of their cave, the witches promise, they will prepare hideous charms to work against the lovers. They symbolize their evil machinations in an ensuing *Dance of the Furies*. This closes the act.

## ACT TWO

A clearing in the forest at Diana's spring. Dido, Aeneas and Belinda enter with their train to rest from the hunt. Dido is silent and downcast. In a lyrical refrain repeated by the chorus ("Thanks to these lonesome vales") Belinda sings about the beauty of this secluded spot. In an ensuing aria Dido sings that Diana often comes to bathe in this spring—here, where the unfortunate Actaeon met his fate.[1]

Aeneas, exulting over the spoils of the chase, triumphantly holds aloft a boar's head impaled on his spear. Dido, however, can think

---

[1] Actaeon, the hunter of Greek mythology who surprised the goddess bathing. She changed him into a stag and he was torn to pieces by his own hounds.

only of the approaching storm, which is vividly depicted by rising and falling chromatic phrases in the orchestra. As the storm breaks, Belinda and the chorus urge everyone to flee back to the palace because there is no shelter in the open woods. Just as they are about to rush away, the false Mercury appears in Aeneas' path. He tells him Jove is angry over his amorous dalliance and has commanded him to set sail immediately for Italy. Dido meanwhile goes with the others.

Saying he will obey at once, Aeneas laments that he must leave Dido just when she has surrendered to him ("But ah! What language can I try"). Crying that he would rather die, he rails against the gods for separating him from his beloved.

## ACT THREE

Aboard Aeneas' ship which is about to weigh anchor, the sailors sing a lusty chorus ("Come away, fellow sailors"). Unobserved by them, the sorceress and the witches come forward and balefully sing that their plot thus far has succeeded: Dido is about to be torn from her lover. They burst into savage laughter. In a solo interlude the sorceress gloats that their next duty will be to destroy Aeneas and his ships. Tonight Elissa (Dido) will perish and tomorrow Carthage will be in flames. The witches and sailors join in a dance of wild abandon.

Dido and Belinda approach Aeneas' ship. Crushed by despair, the Queen sings that the gods themselves have conspired against her (Recitative: "Your counsel all is urged in vain"). Aeneas appears. He tells Dido that he cannot explain why the gods have decreed that he must leave her. The Queen turns on him in bitter sarcasm, commending him for his "crocodile tears," and for blaming the gods for his own desertion of her. Contemptuously she tells him to go back to his "promis'd empire" and to leave her alone.

Stung by her disdain, Aeneas cries that he will defy Jove himself for her love ("In spite of Jove's commands"). This builds into a dramatic duet as Dido pours out her scorn and Aeneas vows he will not leave her. Quailing before her wrath, Aeneas resignedly leaves.

Alone, Dido gives way to her despair in the famous aria "When I am laid in earth." At its conclusion she stabs herself and dies. The opera ends with an eloquent chorus of lamentation: "With drooping wings, ye Cupids come."

# Giovanna D'Arco

## *by* GIUSEPPE VERDI

### (1813–1901)

*Libretto by*
TEMISTOCLE SOLERA

Adapted from *The Maid of Orleans,* a play by Schiller

#### CHARACTERS

| | |
|---|---|
| Carlo (Charles VII), King of France | Tenor |
| Giovanna (Joan) | Soprano |
| Giacomo (Jacques), her father | Baritone |
| Delil, an officer of the King | Tenor |
| Talbot, commander of the English army | Bass |

Officials of King Carlo's court, French and English soldiers, grandees, heralds, pages, halberdiers, deputies, magistrates, guards, angels, demons

*Place:* France
*Time:* Circa 1429
*First performance:* La Scala, Milan, February 15, 1845
*Original language:* Italian

---

At the time Verdi began the composition of *Giovanna D'Arco,* he had already achieved operatic fame with *Nabucco, Ernani* and *I Due Foscari.* Asked to write an opera for La Scala, he turned to a version of the Joan of Arc story fashioned by the librettist Solera from the drama by Johann Christoph Friedrich von Schiller.

For operatic purposes, Solera virtually ignored the historical background of the story. Joan, for example, is betrayed to the English by her own father—not by a treacherous countryman, as history records. Moreover, in Solera's libretto, she dies on the battlefield instead of at the stake. But Verdi, as could be expected, compensated for many of the plot's inadequacies through the power of his music, which brings the otherwise static characters to life. Some of the music concededly is routine, some of it simple to the point of naïveté. Yet there are passages of true Verdian eloquence.

*Giovanna* was only moderately successful, and there were comparatively few performances following the premiere. A bizarre revival was staged at Palermo in 1847, when it was provided with an entirely new libretto to satisfy the police censors. Joan was changed to a compatriot of Sappho, and the opera retitled *Orietta of Lesbos*. After that, however, the original rarely showed up on the operatic stage.

Oddly enough, contemporary revivals have met with remarkable success, prompting critics to ask why this early evidence of Verdi's genius has been so undeservedly neglected. *Giovanna* received its American premiere by the American Opera Society in New York on March 1, 1966; in May of that year it was performed in London at the Royal Academy of Music.

There is a long opening sinfonia, reminiscent of the harmonic style of Beethoven, which establishes the tragic mood of the opera. This is followed by a lyrical *andante pastorale* scored for flute, oboe and clarinet.

## PROLOGUE

At the court of King Carlo in Domremy, people of the court and a throng of citizens express their mingled rage and despair over France's evil fate at the hands of the invading English ("Qual v'ha speme?"). Carlo enters. In recitative ("Amici, v'appressate") he announces his abdication and releases all his subjects from further allegiance to him. In the ensuing cavatina ("Sotto una quercia") he relates how the Maid appeared to him in a vision and requested him to lay down his helmet and sword in a certain spot in the nearby forest. By this act of abnegation, she explained, he will save France from divine punishment.

Carlo describes the spot in the forest as it appeared in his vision and asks his listeners if anyone has seen it. They earnestly entreat him not to go there ("Per poco uditeci, fermate!"). Brushing aside their warning, the King goes into the forest and finds the designated spot. A descriptive orchestral interlude accompanies the scene change to the secluded retreat where Giovanna comes to pray for guidance in her destined role as the savior of France.

Meanwhile Giacomo, deeply distressed by his daughter's mysterious behavior, has concealed himself in a cave nearby to find out for himself if Giovanna secretly communes with angels or demons. In a dramatic recitative ("Gelo! terrore m'invade") he expresses his forebodings. Suddenly Carlo enters, and Giacomo watches him as he lays down his helmet and sword.

Giovanna appears. Unaware that she is being observed by her father and the King, she sinks to her knees, and in the beautiful cavatina "Oh, ben s'addice questo" she prays for strength to face her ordeal. She promises to forswear all earthly love if the divine spirits will answer her prayer. The chorus of angels and demons is heard in reply ("Tu sei bella")—the angels exhorting her to be steadfast, the devils tempting her with profane pleasures.

Carlo approaches and Giovanna greets him joyously. Snatching up his helmet and sword, she promises him victory, and in the ensuing cabaletta ("Ah! son guerriera!") she hails the sacred cause of France.

Then follows an interlude in the form of an unaccompanied trio in which the three principals voice their respective reactions (beginning with Giovanna's phrase: "A te, pietosa Vergine"). The cabaletta then continues, after which Giovanna leaves with Carlo. Giacomo laments that his worst fears have been realized.

## ACT ONE

[*Scene One*] The camp of Talbot's army, which has been defeated by the French troops led by King Carlo and Giovanna. In a sorrowful chorus the English bemoan the disaster on the battlefield ("Ai lari! alla patria!"). They express their superstitious horror over the supernatural powers that enabled the Maid to lead the French to victory. The vanquished troops curse their foe ("Perduto Orleano").

The camp is suddenly thrown into an uproar as Giacomo staggers in, glaring wildly about him. Driven to the verge of madness by the shame of Giovanna's liaison with King Carlo, Giacomo begs Talbot, through an interpreter, to be allowed to fight with the English ("Questa rea che vi percuote"). In a ringing aria, "Franco son io, ma in core," he sings that, French though he is, he will help defeat the monarch who has dishonored his daughter. He promises to turn Giovanna over to the English.

Talbot acknowledges the offer ("Vien! di guerra in forte"). Giacomo pours out his rage and grief over Giovanna's apparent perfidy in the aria "So che per via." The soldiers commend him for his courage and self-sacrifice ("Nobile vecchio affretatti"), then hail the opportunity to avenge their defeat ("Vien la vendetta").

[*Scene Two*] The court at Rheims. Giovanna, alone, muses in recitative over the mysterious destiny that has brought her to this fateful moment ("Qui! dove più s'apre"). Then, in one of the opera's most moving arias, "O fastidica foresta," she voices her intense longing for home and family. The tender love of those dear to her, she sings, is stronger even than the divine will which commands her to be the savior of France.

She is about to leave when Carlo enters. When she tells him of her decision to return to her home and leave France to her own destiny, he entreats her to stay ("Dunque, o cruda, e gloria e trono"). This marks the beginning of a long, impassioned duet. Carlo sings that she must not leave him, because she has brought him not only victory but love as well. Now her divine mission is to crown him in the cathedral and thus restore him to the throne of France.

Giovanna, powerless to resist him, finally confesses her love, even though she realizes she is courting her own doom. The unseen chorus of evil spirits rises in gloating triumph ("Vittoria! plaudiamo a Satàna").

## ACT TWO

Outside the Cathedral of Rheims during Carlo's coronation. The throng pays homage to the King in the *Triumphal March* ("Da cielo a noi chi viene"). At the doors of the cathedral, Giacomo waits to confront Giovanna when she emerges with Carlo after the ceremony. In the dramatic romanza "Speme al vecchio era una figlia," he prays that his daughter still may expiate her sins through the ordeal of divine punishment. The doors swing open and Giovanna comes out followed by King Carlo. The throng bursts into a majestic chorus of acclaim, "Te, Dio, lodiam." Carlo pays homage to Giovanna for her heroic defense of France ("Non fuggir donzella"), declaring she is worthy to be revered with St. Denis as the savior of her country.

Thereupon Giacomo rushes forward and launches into furious denunciation ("M'odi, o re"). He accuses both the King and Giovanna of blasphemy, then charges that his daughter holds secret rendezvous with Satan, who has endowed her with infernal powers. He demands that she confess her guilt then and there, but Giovanna remains silent. There is a crash of thunder; Giacomo cries that thus heaven bears witness to the truth of his charges.

A fiery trio follows ("No! forme d'angelo"): Carlo defends Giovanna, who protests her innocence; Giacomo, in a final desperate entreaty, grasps his daughter's hand and begs her, in the name of God, to admit her guilt ("Dimmi, in nome del Dio"). The vast throng, suddenly seized by mass hysteria, bursts out in condemnation of Giovanna ("Sil la colpa è manifesta"). Her guilt has been proved, they shout, cursing her as a witch ("Fuggi, o donna maledetta"). They demand that she be handed over to the English to be burned at the stake.

## ACT THREE

[*Scene One*] The English camp, where Giovanna lies chained during the attack by the French. In an eloquent prayer ("Oh, qual mi scuote") she asks for deliverance from the enemy, then admits having broken her vows of chastity by yielding to the temptation of carnal love.

As she prays, Giacomo approaches and listens spellbound. Overwhelmed by her repentance and convinced at last of her ultimate innocence, he rushes forward and impetuously strikes off her chains. Giovanna fervently embraces him, and then father and daughter express their happiness over their reconciliation in a lyrical duet, "Amai, ma un solo instante," one of the climactic moments of the opera. In its outline it foreshadows the famous Violetta-Germont duet in *La Traviata*.

Inspired with new courage, Giovanna asks her father for his sword ("La tua spadal") and rushes out to lead the French again to victory. Giacomo, following, urges her on with a battle cry: "Ecco! Ella vola!"

[*Scene Two*][1] Giovanna, mortally wounded in the battle, is borne back to the fortress—now recaptured—to die. With her fading strength, she holds aloft the banner of the French emblazoned with the fleur-de-lis. Gazing down at the Maid, King Carlo pours out his grief in one of the opera's finest arias, "Quale più fido amico." In mystic ecstasy, Giovanna sings that she sees the vision of the Virgin bending over her with words of divine consolation and forgiveness ("S'apre il cielo . . . Discende la Pia"). Her voice blends with Carlo's and Giacomo's in a final elegiac trio, and at its conclusion Giovanna falls back lifeless.

All on the scene fall to their knees and in wonder and sorrow

---

[1] Because of the unavailability of an authorized English translation of the libretto, the closing scene of the opera is presented here in an abridged description.

pay homage to the Maid who brought victory and salvation to France ("Oh, prodigio! d'insolito raggio"). Blending with this closing ensemble is the chorus of the mystical voices which inspired Giovanna—the celestial and infernal spirits—now joining in a paean of redemption.

# Giulio Cesare

*by* GEORGE FRIDERIC HANDEL

(1685–1759)

*Libretto by*
NICCOLÒ FRANCESCO HAYM

CHARACTERS

### Romans

| | |
|---|---|
| Giulio Cesare (Caius Julius Caesar) | Bass-baritone |
| Curio, a Roman tribune | Bass |
| Cornelia, wife of Pompey | Contralto |
| Sesto (Sextus Pompey), her son | Tenor |

### Egyptians

| | |
|---|---|
| Cleopatra, Queen of Egypt | Soprano |
| Tolemeo (Ptolemy), her brother, King of Egypt | Bass |
| Achillas, Egyptian general commanding Ptolemy's forces | Bass-baritone |
| Nirenus, confidant of Cleopatra | Bass |

Romans, Egyptians, soldiers, slaves, ladies in waiting

*Place:* Egypt, after the Battle of Pharsalus
*Time:* 48 B.C.
*First performance:* King's Theater, London, February 20, 1724
*Original language:* Italian

---

This opera was written during the period when Handel was at the height of his fame in London as an operatic composer and conductor. It was one of twenty operas he wrote during his association with the Royal Academy of Music.

Of all those works, it perhaps comes closest to being "grand opera" in, say, the Verdian sense. Full of vivid action, *Giulio Cesare* abounds in musical utterances that have trenchant emotional thrust. It offers a fusion of the lyric with the dramatic. In the main, the action centers around Cleopatra's manipulation of the destinies of Caesar and Ptolemy, and how she thus changed the course of Egypt's history.[1]

Premiered with a cast including the famous castrato Senesino (Francesco Bernardi), the soprano Francesca Cuzzoni and the basso Giuseppe Boschi, the opera was a resounding success. After the peak of its popularity had passed, it was revived in 1730 and again in 1787. But with the passing of the vogue for baroque opera in the latter half of the eighteenth century, *Giulio Cesare* disappeared from the stage.

In America, a staged revival of the opera by the New York City Opera Company in 1966 and 1968, with Beverly Sills and Norman Treigle in the leading roles, was outstandingly successful. Subsequent productions have proved popular with the American public.

The brief overture begins with a *maestoso* theme leading into an *allegro* expressive of the turbulent course of events which make up the plot of the opera.

## ACT ONE

[*Scene One*] A broad plain along the Nile, near a bridge. In a brief martial chorus the Egyptians hail the advancing Roman troops. Caesar strides forward and addresses the throng as the conquering hero ("Presti omai l'Egizia terra"). In an ensuing recitative he utters the historic phrase: "I came, I saw, I conquered." He then tells how he defeated Pompey, who too late had sought the aid of King Ptolemy.

During his discourse, Cornelia and Sextus approach and kneel in abject humility before Caesar. Cornelia makes an eloquent plea for mercy, entreating Caesar to sheathe his sword and bring peace to the land. Caesar tells her he comes in the spirit of forgiveness and asks her to bring Pompey to him as a friend.

At this point Achillas enters attended by slaves, one of whom carries a large covered vessel. He removes the cover, revealing the severed head of Pompey. Caesar and the throng gasp in horror; Cornelia falls fainting into Sextus' arms. Achillas imperturbably explains that this trophy is presented by Ptolemy as "proof of his allegiance."

[1] At Pharsalus, in the Grecian province of Thessaly, Caesar routed the army of Pompey during the Roman civil war. Pompey fled to Egypt, where he was beheaded by Ptolemy.

Caesar bursts out in furious denunciation of Ptolemy for this foul deed ("Empio, dirò, tu sei") against a vanquished foe. He commands Achillas to inform Ptolemy that he will seek him in his palace before nightfall, then angrily orders the general out of his sight. Caesar himself leaves hurriedly, followed by the throng.

Cornelia gives voice to her bitter grief in the aria "Priva son d'ogni conforto," after which she leaves with her ladies in waiting. Sextus, in horror and fury, calls on the avenging Eumenides to strike down the murderer of his father ("Svegliatevi nel core, furie d'un alma offera").

[*Scene Two*] A gallery in the palace of Ptolemy. Cleopatra enters with Nirenus, whom she orders to take her to Caesar. She remarks that her beauty will gain more from the conqueror than the bloody trophy presented to him by Ptolemy. A moment later her brother enters and angrily accuses her of trying to usurp the throne. When she answers that she claims only what is rightfully hers, Ptolemy caustically advises her to concern herself with needle and thread instead of crown and scepter. Contemptuously branding him a "boudoir hero," Cleopatra sweeps out of the room.

Achillas comes in and describes Caesar's horror and anger when he saw the head of Pompey. The treacherous general goes on to say that when Caesar comes to the palace tonight, that will be the moment to slay him. Or better still, Achillas adds craftily, he himself will do the deed—if Ptolemy will promise him Pompey's widow as his bride. But Ptolemy, while gloating over the prospect of doing away with Caesar, hedges on the promise to his general, whom he curtly dismisses. Alone, he gives voice to his murderous intentions in the ringing aria "L'empio, sleate, indegno."

[*Scene Three*] At a monument to Pompey in Caesar's camp. It is in the form of an urn flanked by weapons and trophies. Standing before the urn, Caesar reflects on Pompey's fate—yesterday a conqueror who held the world in the palm of his hand, today . . . dust and ashes ("Alma del gran Pompeo").

As he stands there brooding, Cleopatra enters, dressed in a simple gown. Kneeling before Caesar, she identifies herself as "Lydia," one of Cleopatra's serving maids. She begs him to protect her from the lecherous advances of Ptolemy. Caesar assures her that when he sees Ptolemy this very evening, he will intercede in her behalf. With a fervent phrase of thanks, Cleopatra leaves. In a lyrical arietta, "Non è si vago e bello," Caesar muses on "Lydia's" beauty and charm. He too leaves.

A moment later Cleopatra returns with Nirenus, who compliments her on capturing the mighty conqueror's heart on their first meeting. In answer, Cleopatra remarks that now she dares Ptolemy, with all his ruthless power, to take the throne. As for herself, the goddess of love will lead her there. She orders Nirenus to bring Caesar to her chambers after he has seen Ptolemy. There, she murmurs voluptuously, she will proffer the hero a love feast that will make him her slave forever.

Seeing Cornelia approaching, Cleopatra and Nirenus hide. The widow, dressed in deep mourning, goes to Pompey's monument and kneels before it. Still crushed by grief, she sings the moving aria "Nel tuo seno," lamenting that she has lost her greatest treasure. Looking up, she sees a dagger among the trophies displayed. She seizes it, crying that it is destined for Ptolemy's heart. At that moment Sextus steps from behind the monument. He snatches the dagger from his mother, declaring that it is a son's duty to avenge his father's murder. But to whom, he wonders, can they turn for help?

Thereupon Cleopatra and Nirenus emerge from their hiding place. Again identifying herself as "Lydia," Cleopatra tells Cornelia that not only will she herself help, but she will summon certain persons who know how to bring the guilty one to justice. In a brief arietta ("Cara speme questo core") Sextus enthuses over the possibility of accomplishing his revenge. He and Cornelia leave.

In wild exultation, Cleopatra relishes the thought of bringing Ptolemy to book for his crimes, and abandons herself to her emotions in the brilliant aria "Tu la mi stella sei." She thanks the gods for aiding her plans. Midway in the aria her mood suddenly changes to tenderness as she thinks of Caesar ("Qual sia di questo core") . . . she sought a throne and found a loving heart. Cleopatra ends the aria on a passionate phrase.

An intermezzo follows during a change of scene. It is from the Concerto Grosso in G minor.

[Scene Four] The palace of Ptolemy, where a reception in honor of Caesar is in progress. Ptolemy, Achillas and various Egyptian dignitaries are watching the dancing girls. In a lusty refrain ("Belle dee di questo core") Ptolemy urges the guests to enjoy the entertainment.

Caesar and his retinue enter. There is an ironic exchange in recitative between Caesar and Ptolemy, bristling with veiled insults. The two monarchs, with their adherents, sit on either side of the hall. Caesar, watching the Egyptians narrowly, comments about Ptolemy in a remarkable aria, "Va tacito e nassoto." He describes him to his courtiers as a relentless hunter, with weapons at the ready, on the trail of his prey. He will not pause until he has destroyed his victim.

After the aria there is an orchestral interlude during which an ominous byplay takes place. As Caesar and his retinue slowly withdraw, a group of Egyptians stealthily follow. When Caesar turns to look back, they stop in their tracks, then advance on him again as he goes on. The effect is of a hunter stalking a human quarry.

Cornelia and Sextus arrive. In bitter irony, Cornelia commends Ptolemy for his magnanimity toward Pompey. Sextus, cursing Ptolemy, lunges at him with a sword. Instantly the boy and his mother are surrounded by Egyptian guards. Ptolemy orders Sextus imprisoned. He tells Cornelia she will be consigned to his harem, where she will be taught proper respect for the emperor.

Achillas, sidling up to Cornelia, slyly asks her to be his bride, promising her freedom if she consents. Cornelia rebuffs him with furious contempt. When Sextus, overhearing, shouts that his mother would die rather than consort with an Egyptian, Achillas orders him to the dungeon. Clasping her son in her arms, Cornelia desperately pleads for mercy. They bid each other farewell in a poignant duet, "Son nata a lagrimar."

## ACT TWO

[*Scene One*] The palace of Cleopatra. It is a starry night. Nirenus escorts Caesar to Cleopatra's chambers, where he gazes in astonishment at the luxurious furnishings. Cleopatra enters, regally dressed. Approaching Caesar, she gives expression to her amorous feelings in the beguiling aria "V'adoro, pupille," sung over muted strings. Caesar listens in hypnotic fascination.

But the romantic spell is broken when Nirenus bursts in exclaiming that soldiers are at the doors shouting that Caesar must die. He begs Caesar to make his escape. At this point Cleopatra discloses her real identity and cries that weapons cannot harm the Queen of Egypt. Caesar is thunderstruck. Assuring him that she will thwart his enemies, Cleopatra rushes away. A moment later she reappears, declaring that even her power as Queen cannot stem the fury of the invaders. But when she entreats Caesar to flee, he draws his sword and shouts that Caesar knows no fear. In the great aria "Al lampo dell'armi" he voices his defiance. As he rushes out, cries of "death to Caesar" are heard. Sinking to her knees, Cleopatra implores the gods for his protection in the stately aria "Se pietà di me non seati."

[*Scene Two*] In Ptolemy's harem, Cornelia expresses her hopelessness and shame in the arietta "Deh piange—te, oh mesti lumi." Nirenus rushes in with the unwelcome news that Ptolemy is on his way to the harem to speak with her. Even more disturbing is the news that Sextus, with the help of Nirenus, bribed his jailers to free him and is coming to kill Ptolemy.

With deceptive gentleness, Ptolemy attempts to persuade Cornelia to submit to his desires. She turns on him with furious scorn. Enraged, he warns that her refusal only serves to inflame him further ("Si spietata, il tuo rigore"), and that he is determined to have his way with her. At the conclusion of the aria he forces Cornelia to her knees.

At that moment Sextus rushes in with drawn sword and springs toward Ptolemy. But before he can strike, Achillas and his soldiers burst in. One of the soldiers wrenches the sword out of Sextus' hands. At the same time, Achillas thrusts another sword toward Ptolemy and warns him to prepare for battle. He tells him that Caesar, cornered by the Egyptian soldiers, leaped from the palace balcony into the sea and was drowned. Cleopatra, at the head of the Roman troops, is on her way to the palace to avenge Caesar's death.

Then Achillas asks Ptolemy if he will now make good his promise to give him Cornelia as his bride. Ptolemy harshly tells him to get out of his sight, and turns away. Watching him go, Achillas swears revenge. Tossing Sextus the sword wrested from him earlier, the general leaves. When Sextus laments that he has failed in his attempt at revenge and is not worthy to be called his father's son, Cornelia bids him not to lose courage and exhorts him to fight on. Regaining his confidence, Sextus declares he will never rest until the murder is avenged ("L'angue offenso mai riposa").

## ACT THREE

[*Scene One*] The curtain rises to the sound of battle music. The scene is Ptolemy's encampment on the seacoast near Alexandria. In his headquarters, Ptolemy stands gazing at Cleopatra, who is being guarded like a captive by soldiers. With savage satisfaction, Ptolemy boasts that he still is King and conqueror, despite the fact that Achillas betrayed him with the false story of Caesar's death. When Cleopatra defiantly answers that it was not he, but blind Fate, that caused her defeat, Ptolemy orders her to be put in irons. He leaves.

Dejected and alone, Cleopatra gives way to her despair in the aria "Piangerò, la sorte mia," one of the opera's finest numbers. At a sign from her guards, she walks slowly away.

[Scene Two] A spot on the shore near the encampment, where Caesar, staggering from exhaustion, is seen approaching from the water's edge. In recitative, he recalls how he was rescued from the sea . . . once more he has escaped death. But now, he muses, where shall he begin again . . . where are his legions . . . where are his weapons? He continues his reflection in the aria "Aure, deh, per pietà," imploring the sea to restore him to strength, to good fortune and to his beloved.

As he stands facing the sea, Sextus comes in leading Achillas, who is mortally wounded. A dramatic scene in recitative ensues. With his life ebbing away, the general makes his dying confession. First he asks Sextus to go to Cornelia. He is to tell her that it was he—Achillas—who plotted the murder of Pompey. It was because he loved her and wanted her as his bride that he also joined the plot against Caesar. As reward, Ptolemy had promised him Cornelia, but the King treacherously broke his word. In revenge, Achillas says, he betrayed Ptolemy by inciting his own soldiers against him.

Drawing a signet ring from his finger, Achillas tells Sextus to take it to a nearby cavern, where a hundred armed soldiers are concealed. When he shows them the ring they will obey him without question, and will accompany him through a secret underground passage into the city. There they will find Cornelia as a prisoner of Ptolemy. They are to rescue Cornelia and then slay the King. Thus, Achillas gasps, his revenge will be complete and he will die in peace. With that the general falls back dead.

Caesar, who had approached unobserved just as Achillas handed Sextus the ring, now strides forward. Identifying himself, he asks Sextus for the ring. Sextus staggers back in surprise. Caesar tells him that he himself will lead the hidden soldiers to the rescue of Cornelia and of Cleopatra as well. In a ringing aria, "Quel torrente, che cade dal monte," he sings that vengeance, like a mighty torrent, will sweep his enemy to destruction.

[*Scene Three*] Ptolemy's tent on the battlefield, where Cleopatra is held prisoner with her ladies in waiting. She sorrowfully tells them that their days of serving her are over, because she has been condemned to death by this monstrous tyrant—her own brother, who has usurped her crown.

Suddenly, shouting and the clash of weapons are heard outside. In the next moment the entrance curtain of the tent is ripped away and Caesar strides in. Cleopatra stares at him in terror and unbelief, convinced she is seeing a ghost. When he assures her he is not a phantom, but has come to set her free, she rushes to him with a joyous, passionate cry. Caesar tells her that the final, decisive battle is at hand . . . Mars has commanded and he obeys. He will fight for Egypt and for the world itself, inspired by the fire she has kindled within him.

They clasp each other in an impassioned embrace. Cleopatra hails her hero in a dazzling aria, "Da tempeste il legno." Her ladies in waiting adorn her with the royal mantle symbolizing her rightful claim to the throne as Queen of Egypt.

[*Scene Four*] The banks of the Nile, as in Act One. Roman and Egyptian soldiers are arrayed on either side of the scene, with the tribune Curio at the head of the Roman troops. To a blazing martial fanfare, Caesar rides up in his chariot as Egyptian dignitaries escort Cleopatra from her tent. Caesar steps from his chariot to greet her. In recitative, Curio acclaims Caesar as Egypt's liberator. The latter thanks him for his loyal service and assures him that the fame of his troops has spread throughout the world.

Cornelia and Sextus come forward and kneel to receive a cordial greeting from Caesar. Sextus announces that he has slain the tyrant Ptolemy and that now his father is avenged. Caesar says that Pompey was indeed fortunate in having so noble a son. Turning to Cleopatra, he places a golden crown on her head and hails her as Queen of Egypt.

A ballet—the "War Dance," in which youths are vanquished by temple virgins in a simulated battle—is performed before the assemblage. Then Caesar leads Cleopatra forward and the two apostrophize their happiness in a lyrical duet, "Caro! Bella! Più amabile beltà." At its conclusion the throng hails the couple in a mighty chorus of triumph, "Ritorni omai nel nostro core."

# Idomeneo, Re di Creta
## (*Idomeneus, King of Crete*)

*by* WOLFGANG AMADEUS MOZART
(1756–91)

*Libretto by*
ABBÉ GIAMBATTISTA VARESCO

*Based on a French opera by André Campra and A. Danchet*

### CHARACTERS

| | |
|---|---|
| Idomeneo, King of Crete | Tenor |
| Idamante, his son (originally soprano role) | Tenor |
| Ilia, daughter of Priam, King of Troy | Soprano |
| Electra, daughter of Agamemnon, King of Argos | Soprano |
| Arbace, counselor to Idomeneo | Tenor |
| High Priest | Tenor |
| Voice of Neptune | Bass |

Retinues of Idomeneo and Idamante, Cretans, warriors from Crete and Argos, Trojan prisoners, priests of Neptune, dancers

*Place:* The island of Crete
*Time:* Shortly before the end of the Trojan War, circa 1200 B.C.
*First performance:* Munich, January 29, 1781
*Original language:* Italian

---

Mozart composed *Idomeneo* in 1780 when he was commissioned to write an *opera seria* for the Munich Carnival of 1781. At the time, he was cathedral organist in Salzburg, and a libretto was furnished him by the Abbé Varesco, chaplain to the Archbishop of Salzburg. The opera is the fifth of Mozart's eleven full-length works for the stage. With its theme of classic tragedy, it is the only one which may correctly be called "grand opera"—as contrasted to the other stage pieces, which fall into the category of *opera buffa*, in which the serious elements of the plot are balanced by situations of comic relief. *Idomeneo* is *opera seria*, a form in which Mozart was intensely interested.

The plot is the story of Idomeneo's return from the Trojan War after years of absence. While the characters involved are from Greek mythology, they are not presented in the frame of historical perspective. As these figures of classic tragedy move through the opera they emerge as a tapestry of human emotions with a quality transcending time.

Although *Idomeneo* has music of grandeur and nobility, it never became a part of operatic repertoire. Written toward the end of the vogue for *opera seria*, it was an anachronism. It has been said that this work—like *La Clemenza di Tito*, Mozart's other *opera seria*—was a museum piece the moment it was put on the stage. Following its Munich premiere it was given only once more during Mozart's lifetime.

A notable revival in this century was under the direction of Richard Strauss, who revised the libretto and rescored the opera for the Munich Festival of 1930. Subsequently it was performed at Glyndebourne in 1951, and in America at Tanglewood, Massachusetts, in 1949 (Goldovsky Opera Company); the New York premiere was given by the Little Orchestra Society in 1951, and the Academy Opera Theater presented it in Brooklyn in 1966.

The overture, with its opening unison passage in D major, establishes the intensely serious mood of the opera. A gradual change to a minor key foreshadows tragedy. In the concluding section a brief characteristic theme emerges in the form of a descending figure for woodwinds, and this is heard several times during the opera. The overture leads directly into Ilia's recitative, which begins without a chord.

## ACT ONE

Ilia's apartment in the palace of Idomeneo. In a long recitative ("Quando avran fine omai") she bewails the misfortune which has followed her since the destruction of Troy, where her father, Priam, was slain. She recalls how she was carried away as a captive by the Cretans, then how she was rescued from drowning by Idamante during a storm on the voyage to Crete.

Now she is torn between her love for Idamante and sorrow for her family, lost in the holocaust of Troy. Her grief is even more bitter because she believes that Idamante does not return her love. She is convinced that he is enamored of Electra, who came to the palace as an exile from Argos following the murder of Clytemnestra. Ilia gives voice to her conflicting emotions in the ensuing aria, "Padre, germani, addio," marked by its violent outburst on the word "Grecia" (Greece), on which she lays the blame for her woes.

At the conclusion of the aria Idamante appears with his retinue. He tells Ilia that his father's ships have weathered a terrible storm and are nearing the Cretan coast. Even now, Arbace, Idomeneo's counselor, is searching the shore for him and his men. In gratitude to the gods, Idamante goes on, he will free the Trojan prisoners. Then only one "prisoner" will be left—he himself, who has been captured by Ilia's charms. He elaborates on this thought in the aria "Non ho colpa."

The Trojan prisoners are brought in and they hail their release in a resounding chorus, "Godiam la pace." Electra enters and furiously upbraids Idamante for showing clemency to the enemies of Greece. Her tirade is interrupted by Arbace, who rushes in with the news that another storm has overtaken Idomeneo's fleet and that he has been drowned. Shaken by the news, Idamante calls on his retinue to follow him to the seacoast in search of survivors.

Electra, remaining behind, broods in jealous rage over Idamante's infatuation with Ilia. In the aria "Tutto nel cor vi sento" she calls on the Furies to assist her plans for revenge.

The action now shifts to the storm-wracked seacoast where the wreckage of Idomeneo's ships lies scattered on the sands. The fear-stricken people kneel and pray to the gods to have mercy on those in the grip of the storm ("Pietà! Ajuto o giusto Numi!"). After the prayer they leave the scene, while from the distance come the cries of the sailors, also praying for help.

As their voices die away, Idomeneo appears with a group of his followers, whom he sends on to find help. Left alone, he bitterly reproaches himself for the sinister bargain he made with the sea god Neptune to save his life: He promised to offer up as a sacrifice to Neptune the first mortal he would meet. In the aria "Vedrommi intorno" he reveals his torment at the thought of shedding the blood of an innocent victim. To his horror he sees a figure coming toward him. It is the first mortal he has seen—the unwitting sacrifice. The King curses the gods for their vindictive cruelty toward mankind.

Idamante approaches and generously offers the shipwrecked stranger his assistance. They do not, of course, recognize each other as father and son, yet each senses something vaguely familiar about the other. After several searching questions, they suddenly realize who they are. Idamante joyfully tries to embrace his father, but the horrified King—realizing that his own son will be the victim of his vow to Neptune—warns him not to come near. Stunned by the rebuff, Idamante expresses his bewilderment and anguish in the aria "Il padre adorato ritrovo." The two go their separate ways in utter dejection as the scene ends.

The Cretan warriors and sailors who survived the shipwreck now appear to the accompaniment of a spirited march and are met by the Cretan women, who dance with joy. All join in an exuberant chorus of thanks to Neptune and the sea gods who serve him ("Nettuno s'onori"). This long choral movement is known as a *ciacconna,* the Italian equivalent of the *chaconne,* a device favored by French composers to bring an act to an exciting climax.

## ACT TWO

Idomeneo's palace. The act begins with a long dialogue between the King and Arbace. Idomeneo relates that Neptune, jealous of his success in the Trojan War, threatened to destroy him and his fleet, then forced him to agree to sacrifice a mortal to save himself. That mortal, the King says, is his own son.

When he begs Arbace to help him out of this dilemma, the counselor suggests sending Idamante to accompany Electra back to Greece—thus putting him beyond the consequences of his father's ill-fated bargain. Idomeneo profusely thanks Arbace for his advice. Seeing Ilia approaching, the counselor leaves.[1]

In recitative, Ilia and Idomeneo confide in each other. When she expresses her gratitude for the kindness shown her by Idamante, the King answers that his son is carrying out his father's own wishes. In the beautiful aria "Se il padre perdu" Ilia sings that even as a captive she is fortunate: She has acquired a second father and a second homeland.

When she leaves, the King, reflecting on her words, realizes that Ilia has become reconciled to captivity simply because she is in love with Idamante. Thus the tragedy of his vow is threefold: Ilia's happiness as well as his own will be destroyed by Idamante's death. In the great aria "Fuor del mar" Idomeneo laments that

---

[1] At this point in the original there is an aria for Arbace ("Se il tuo duol"), which is usually omitted. Its theme is that it will be to Idamante's advantage to remove him from the scene. Mozart wrote the entire scene to provide a recitative and aria for the tenor Panzacchi, who created the role of Arbace.

Neptune spared his life only to confront him with a more merciless destiny.[2]

Electra approaches. Having learned from Arbace that Idamante is to accompany her back to Greece, she fervently thanks Idomeneo for his magnanimous decision. When he leaves to make final arrangements she expresses her joy at being united with Idamante in the aria "Idol mio, se ritroso altro amante." She also relishes the thought that she has taken him away from Ilia.

The aria leads directly into a brief march which introduces the barcarole "Placido è il mar," sung by the sailors and people as they are about to embark. Electra is joined by Idamante, Idomeneo and their retinues as they prepare to board ship. In the farewell trio which follows ("Pria di partir, o Dio!") Idamante and Electra thank the King for his benevolence. Idomeneo exhorts his son to fulfill his destiny. In an aside, Idamante expresses his secret grief over parting from Ilia.

Just as the ship is about to sail, a howling storm bursts over the sea. The people voice their terror in an agitated chorus ("Qual nuovo terrore!"). Imploring Neptune to have mercy, they demand to know who among them has incurred the sea god's wrath with evil-doing.

Idomeneo steps forward. In a recitative passage he cries that it is he who has sinned, and he calls on Neptune to punish him alone. He entreats the god not to claim an innocent victim. At that moment an immense sea monster rears up from the waters of the harbor. In the turbulent chorus which concludes the act ("Corriamo, fuggiamo quel mostro") the panic-stricken people urge all to flee for their lives.

## ACT THREE

The garden of Idomeneo's palace. Ilia soliloquizes about her longing for Idamante in the tender aria "Zefferetti lusinghieri," exhorting the breezes to carry her message of love to him. A moment later he enters and dialogue in recitative follows. Idamante tells Ilia that he is hopelessly in love with her, while at the same time he is almost mad with despair over his father's strange behavior toward him. Now, he goes on, he must go forth to slay the monster Neptune has loosed upon the Cretans—and he hopes the encounter will result in his own death.

[2] This aria was written as a special favor to Anton Raaff, who, at the age of sixty-five, created the title role.

Entreating him not to give up hope, Ilia cries that she loves him, and that if he dies she herself will die of grief. This leads to the ecstatic duet "S'io non moro a quisti accente," in which the two pledge their undying love.

As they embrace at the conclusion of the duet, they are discovered by Idomeneo and Electra. In the ensuing recitative, Idamante again implores his father to explain why he continues to treat his own son like an enemy. The King, unable to bring himself to disclose the real reason, advises Idamante, for his own sake, to flee the country. When Idamante asks him at least to show compassion toward Ilia, an innocent captive, Electra is consumed by jealous fury. She is driven to distraction when Ilia—unaware of the irony—turns to her for comfort and advice.

In resignation and despair, Idamante finally says he will obey his father and leave. Sorrowfully he bids Ilia to remain and live in peace. As for himself, he will go wandering alone ("Andrò ramingo e solo"). This phrase introduces the magnificent quartet which the musicologist and critic Edward J. Dent called the most beautiful ensemble ever composed for the stage.

Ilia sings that she is determined to die with her lover; Electra seethes with hate and revenge; Idomeneo cries for death to release him from his disastrous vow. The quartet's overriding theme is expressed in the ensemble phrase "soffrir più non si puo" ("to suffer more is not possible"). It ends in a mood of profound tragedy as Idamante repeats the opening measures: "Andrò ramingo e solo."

Suddenly Arbace rushes in shouting that an angry crowd, led by the High Priest of Neptune, is outside demanding to speak to the King. Suspecting the reason for the uproar, Idomeneo nods understandingly to Arbace, then goes out followed by Electra and Ilia.

Staring after them, Arbace is assailed by ominous thoughts about the future of Crete, which he describes in a recitative ("Sventurata Sidon") and an aria ("Se cola ne' fati è scritto"). He fears that the present misfortunes presage the doom of the kingdom. If Crete is guilty, then let her pay the penalty. He begs the avenging gods to spare the King and his son, offering himself as a sacrifice in their stead.[3]

The scene now shifts to a large square in front of the royal palace. Idomeneo, attended by Arbace and his retinue, is seated on his throne. Confronting him are the High Priest and the clamoring throng.

[3] This scene, which Mozart also wrote for Panzacchi, is usually omitted.

In majestic anger the High Priest tells the King that the savage monster is destroying the city—the streets are running with blood, thousands of his subjects have been swallowed alive by the hideous creature. And yet, the Priest thunders, the King is deaf to their piteous cries for help. In behalf of the people, he calls on Idomeneo to name the person who is to be sacrificed to appease Neptune's wrath. The Priest's excoriation is underscored by a powerful descending figure in the accompaniment.

Thereupon Idomeneo cries out that the sacrificial victim is his own son, Idamante. Pandemonium reigns as the High Priest and the crowd express their horror in a thunderous chorus, "O voto tremendo! spetaccolo orrendo!"

During a brief but stately march the scene changes to the Temple of Neptune. Before it stands a gigantic statue of the sea god. On the scene are Idomeneo, with his court, and the High Priest and the people. The temple priests enter in a procession for the ritual of sacrifice. Idomeneo begins the ceremony with a solemn prayer to Neptune ("Accogli o re del mar") in which the priests join. The people hail the King in a brief choral phrase ("Stupenda vittoria").

The ceremony is interrupted by the blare of trumpets mingled with shouts of triumph. Arbace rushes in and tells Idomeneo that Idamante has slain the sea monster and that the people are saved. But Idomeneo is aghast at the news, realizing that Neptune, who sent the monster to ravage the city, now will exact an even more terrible revenge.

Escorted by the royal guard, Idamante enters, dressed in a white sacrificial robe with a wreath on his head. A dramatic colloquy in recitative now ensues. Idamante declares he is willing to be sacrificed in fulfillment of his father's vow, which finally was revealed to him. Over the King's anguished protest that he cannot slay his innocent son, Idamante says the will of Jove must be obeyed. Then he commits Ilia to his father's care, saying that her love will replace that of the son he has lost. In an ensuing aria, "No, la morte io non pavento," he sings that he will welcome death, knowing that his beloved will live in peace.

Just as Idomeneo steels himself to proceed with the sacrifice, Ilia rushes in. Throwing herself at his feet, she begs him to offer her as the sacrificial victim. She cries that Idamante is innocent —his life must be spared because on him depends the future of Crete. She herself, she goes on, is a Phrygian, a natural enemy of Crete, and therefore deserving of death. As Idomeneo and Idamante vainly try to dissuade her, Electra looks on in jealous rage. Ilia, deaf to all pleas, turns toward the sacrificial altar, but Idamante restrains her.

At this juncture there is a crash of thunder and the giant statue of Neptune begins to sway. To the reverberating accompaniment of trombone chords, a sonorous oracular voice, apparently emanating from the statue, begins to pronounce judgment ("Ho vinto amore").

The oracle proclaims that through the triumph of love King Idomeneo has been pardoned for his sacrilege. But as a king, he cannot be forgiven for repudiating his vow. Therefore he must abdicate in favor of Idamante, who will ascend the throne with Ilia as his bride.

As the voice of the oracle falls silent, Ilia and Idamante rush into each other's arms, and there are expressions of joy and relief from everyone. In sharp contrast, Electra now comes forward and gives vent to her jealous fury in the opera's most spectacular aria, "D'Oreste, d'Ajace ho in seno i tormenti." She sings that rather than see Idamante in the arms of her rival she will follow her brother Orestes down into hell and there share with him the torments of the damned. She begs the Furies to tear out her heart. Bringing the aria to a fiery climax, Electra rushes away.

To the accompaniment of a sweeping phrase in the violins, Idomeneo ascends the throne for the last time. In an eloquent recitative he makes his final declaration: His fateful vow has been rescinded, Neptune has been appeased and now there will be peace forever in Crete. Then he formally presents Idamante and Ilia to their subjects.

In an ensuing aria, "Torna la pace al core," Idomeneo sings that he has been rejuvenated by the spirit of youth, like an ancient tree that bursts into leaf in spring. The people pay tribute to their new monarch and his bride in a mighty chorus ("Scenda Amor, scenda Imeneo"), a hymn of praise to the gods of love and marriage.

# L'Incoronazione di Poppea
## (*The Coronation of Poppea*)
### *by* CLAUDIO MONTEVERDI
### (1567–1643)

### *Libretto by*
#### GIOVANNI FRANCESCO BUSENELLO

Based on Book XIV of the *Annals* of Publius Cornelius Tacitus, a Roman historian

### CHARACTERS

| | |
|---|---|
| Poppea, a courtesan | Soprano |
| Nerone (Nero) | Tenor |
| Arnalta, Poppea's old nurse | Contralto |
| Drusilla, lady in waiting to Ottavia | Soprano |
| Ottone (Otho), Poppea's former lover (in Tacitus, her husband) | Bass |
| Seneca, elder statesman and Stoic philosopher | Bass |
| Ottavia (Octavia), the Empress | Soprano |
| Valetto, a page in Ottavia's service | Tenor |
| Damigella, a maidservant in Ottavia's service | Soprano |
| Liberto, captain of the guard | Baritone |
| Lucano (Lucan), a Roman poet, friend of Nerone's | Tenor |
| Littore (Lictor), a minor Roman official | Bass |
| Primo Soldato | Tenor |
| Secondo Soldato | Tenor |
| Pallade (Pallas Athena), goddess of wisdom | Soprano |
| Amor, god of love | Soprano |

Senators, consults, tribunes, soldiers, disciples of Seneca, servants, people of Rome

*Place:* Rome
*Time:* Circa A.D. 55
*First performance:* Theater of SS. Giovanni ed Paolo, Venice, in the autumn of 1642
*Original language:* Italian

As the work of a musician who invented a basic system of harmony and who was called the founding father of opera, *L'Incoronazione di Poppea* represents the cornerstone of opera as an art form. Monteverdi adapted the madrigal form to operatic creation by making the music as important as the words, thus giving the voice a greater range of expression. He had laid the foundations with *L'Orfeo* (1608), which required an unheard-of orchestra of thirty-six musicians in support of the vocal line.

His contribution to the development of this genre reached its culmination in *Poppea*—the first opera to use a historical subject for its plot. It was Monteverdi's last work, written when he was seventy-five years old. Of his seven operas, only *Poppea* and *L'Orfeo* have survived. His other works, however—hundreds of madrigals, motets, masses and choral pieces—are treasures of the world's musical heritage.

As to the plot of *Poppea*, it is concededly one of the most amoral and immoral in the history of opera. Vice triumphs over virtue, evil over good, cruelty over compassion. Nero and Poppea are the incarnation of corruption, and in their lust and selfish ambition they destroy all who cross their paths. Yet these hapless mortals work out their destinies in music of extraordinary eloquence and majestic power.

A masterpiece of Italian drama in the seventeenth century, *Poppea* established a tradition. It was played in the principal opera houses of Italy and was chosen to inaugurate the first public opera house opened in Naples in 1651. With a revival of interest in Monteverdi's music in the late nineteenth and early twentieth centuries, the opera was produced in Paris during that era.

Occasionally appearing in modern repertoire, *Poppea* was performed in an abridged version at Glyndebourne in 1962. In America there have been performances in Dallas and workshop presentations at universities. The Chicago Lyric Opera produced the work in November 1966. It was presented in its original form (a prologue and three acts) at Caramoor, Katonah, New York, in June 1968 by the New York City Opera under the baton of Julius Rudel.

The opera opens with an imposing sinfonia with its theme sounded forth in majestic chords, reflecting the panoply of the imperial Roman court.

# ACT ONE

[*Scene One*] Poppea's house outside Rome. It is early morning. Two guards lie asleep before the door. Ottone, returning from the wars, enters and in the aria "E pure io torno" expresses his joy over the prospect of seeing his beloved Poppea again. He sings that he is drawn to her as though by some magnetic force. But his ardor turns to despair when he suddenly catches sight of the two soldiers. Recognizing them as Nerone's bodyguards, he realizes that the Emperor has displaced him as Poppea's lover. Crying to the gods to witness his anguish, he rushes away.

His lamentations awaken the guards, who bawl out the customary challenge—which of course does not bring an answer. In an ensuing duet ("Sia maledetto Amor") the two launch into a comical tirade about their military duties. They fervently curse everyone who is in love—particularly Nerone and Poppea for keeping them up all night on guard duty. They curse the vileness of Rome and wind up with a double curse on the army.

The two deplore Nerone's shameful humiliation of his Empress. What is worse, they go on, Rome is being threatened on all sides by enemies—but the Emperor only laughs and goes on making love. Finally, however, they agree that under the circumstances it is wisest to see nothing they are not supposed to see. Their voices sink to a whisper as they warn that the Emperor is approaching.

Nerone enters with Poppea and a long, impassioned duet follows. Poppea seductively implores the Emperor not to leave ("Signor deh, non partire"). Nerone, surfeited for the moment, says he must go, warning her that their rendezvous must be kept secret until he can free himself from the Empress. But when in the next moment he tells Poppea that he will return to be with her forever, she bids him go with her blessing. The duet ends on amorous phrases of avowal.

[*Scene Two*] Inside Poppea's house. Savoring her triumph, Poppea sings that her hopes are high because the god of love himself will lead her to the throne ("Speranza, tu mi vai"). Arnalta comes in and tries to warn her that Ottavia knows of her liaison with Nerone and may exact a terrible revenge. Poppea blithely answers that the god of love and the goddess Fortune both are on her side. Arnalta sardonically observes that she must be mad indeed to put her trust in a blind boy and a capricious old woman.

[*Scene Three*] Ottavia's apartment in the palace. Tormented by jealousy and shame, the Empress abandons herself to bitter reflection in the recitative and aria "Disprezzata regina." Queen of an empire, she is the object of scorn and ridicule as the wronged wife. She laments the unhappy lot of her sex: fated to be enslaved by marriage, destined to suffer the pain of childbearing only to bring into the world tyrants, brutes and murderers.

In her anguish and frustration, Ottavia curses the gods for allowing Nerone to go unpunished—then suddenly expresses horror at her own blasphemy. In a phrase of hopeless resignation, she asks leave to bury her misery in silence.

Drusilla, noting her mistress' distress, naïvely tries to console her with some practical advice: Now that Nerone has been taken from her by Poppea, the Empress is free to choose someone worthier of her. This alone, Drusilla says, will assuage her grief. Ottavia answers that she will bear her burden of sorrow as befits the dignity of an empress.

Seneca comes in with Valetto and in sententious phrases ("O gloriosa del mondo Imperatrice") gives Ottavia the benefit of his counsel. Urging her not to quail before misfortune, he declaims that adversity makes one immune to the blows of fate. The Empress acidly observes that his eloquence is no balm for a wounded heart.

Valetto, exasperated by Seneca's pomposity, turns on him with a flood of stinging rebuke ("Madama, con tua pace"). Asking Ottavia's leave, he warns the philosopher that if he persists in offering the Empress oratory instead of assistance he himself will make a bonfire of his precious books and singe his beard into the bargain. The threat makes no impression on Seneca. Ottavia leaves, followed by the page.

As the philosopher stands deep in thought, Pallas Athena appears before him. In a foreboding refrain ("Seneca, io miro in cielo") she foretells his doom: The planets are in evil conjunction, and before another day dawns he will hear the warning of his fate. Seneca replies that he is not afraid to die—after the turbulent ordeal of life he will welcome the peace of death. The vision of the goddess fades.

Nerone strides in and informs Seneca that he has decided to dethrone the Empress, then marry Poppea and make her his Queen. A dramatic colloquy ensues. Seneca implores the Emperor not to defy the laws of Rome and bring the wrath of the Senate and the people down upon his head. Nerone contemptuously retorts that he cares nothing about public opinion.

The philosopher's persistent talk of "reason" and "conscience" gradually drives Nerone to hysterical fury. In a final effort to bring him to his senses, Seneca reminds him that he is Emperor of Rome and that it is unworthy of him to be swayed by the charms of a woman. Thereupon Nerone furiously denounces him as a presumptuous old meddler and rushes away. Looking after him, Seneca murmurs that he knows only too well what the consequence of the Emperor's mood will be: When lust for power supplants reason, disaster is sure to follow.

[*Scene Four*] Inside Poppea's house. She and Nerone are in each other's arms. With tantalizing guile, Poppea asks if her modest charms are pleasing to him ("Come dolci, Signor"). This marks the beginning of a voluptuous duet. Completely under her spell, he promises to share the Empire with her and bestow upon her the title of "Illustrious Empress." He cries that the royal diadem, all Rome, even Italy itself are mere baubles unworthy to be offered so glorious a queen.

Now confident of her mastery over Nerone, Poppea removes the last obstacle in her path. His trusted counselor Seneca, she says, has let it be known that he is the real power behind the throne— it is he who wields the scepter. In sudden fury Nerone shouts for the Lictor and orders him to go at once to Seneca with this message: He is to die this evening. Then turning back to Poppea he sings that today she will see what love and Nerone together can accomplish ("Ciò che puo far Amore").

[*Scene Five*] Poppea's house. Ottone abjectly entreats Poppea not to desert him. She tells him flatly that she is rejecting his love in favor of a kingdom, then leaves him with a gesture of disdain. Ottone loudly bewails his misfortune. At this point Drusilla enters and takes due note of his self-pitying lamentations. In the ensuing duet ("Già l'oblio seppelli gli andati") she offers him the consolation of her love. He gratefully accepts and swears eternal fidelity. But when she leaves he murmurs that while Drusilla's name is on his lips, Poppea's is in his heart.[1]

[*Scene Six*] This scene is an interlude in the form of an amusing duet between Valetto and Damigella. The love-smitten page describes his emotions in rather simple-minded terms ("Sento un certo non so che"). Damigella twits him about his childish prattle ("Astutello garzonello"), observing that if he really fell in love he probably would lose his mind completely.

[1] End of Act One in the original.

[*Scene Seven*] Seneca's garden. In a recitative passage, the philosopher muses on the blessing of solitude ("Solitudine amata"), which releases the soul from the thrall of earthly corruption. His meditation is interrupted by the Lictor, who asks his pardon for bringing evil tidings. Seneca replies that he knows what the message is: He will obey the Emperor's command, and by this evening he will be dead.

A moment later his friends and disciples throng into the garden, and he announces that his final hour has come ("Amici, è giunta l'hora"). In a stirring chromatic chorus ("Non morir, Seneca") the people beg him not to die. Though moved by their entreaties, he asks them to leave, then orders his servants to prepare his bath. There, he sings in farewell, his innocent blood will flow like a river ("come sangue innocente io vo").[2]

## ACT TWO

[*Scene One*] Nerone's apartments in the palace. Celebrating the death of Seneca, Nerone and his friend, the decadent poet Lucano, stage a drunken orgy. In a duet ("Cantiam amorese canzoni") they hail Poppea as a woman whose talent for love-making is equaled only by her lust for power.

[*Scene Two*] Ottavia's apartment in the palace. A dialogue in recitative takes place in which the Empress orders Ottone to kill Poppea. When he recoils in horror, she warns him not to disobey. He is to disguise himself as a woman to conceal his identity. Ottone cries that he cannot murder in cold blood, whereupon the Empress threatens to accuse him before Nerone of improper conduct toward her. As he well knows, she adds, that will mean unspeakable torture. Terror-stricken, Ottone agrees to carry out her plan.

[*Scene Three*] In an exultant refrain ("Felice cor mio") Drusilla expresses her joy at having won Ottone as her lover. But at the climax of her song he rushes in, almost beside himself with fear and anxiety, and tells her of Ottavia's murderous command. Still bemused by thoughts of romance and oblivious to Ottone's distress, she gaily repeats the phrases of her love song. When he begs her to be silent and listen, she assures him that he can count on her aid

---

[2] According to history, Seneca committed suicide by cutting his wrists in his bath.

without fail. As for the disguise—she not only will give him her garments but will dress him with her own hands.

[*Scene Four*] Poppea's bedroom (or the palace garden). Elated at the news of Seneca's death, Poppea sings a jubilant hymn to the god of love ("Amor, ricorro a te") as her mentor in her campaign for the throne. When Arnalta enters she happily assures the nurse that she will share her good fortune. Noticing that Poppea is overwrought, Arnalta urges her to rest. She sings her to sleep with a hypnotic lullaby which, with its undulations from major to minor, is one the most striking numbers in the opera.

A moment after she leaves, Amor appears. He observes that it is well that Poppea, with eyes closed in sleep, cannot see her murderer approaching. In the ensuing aria, "O sciocchi frali mortali," he muses that slumbering mortals thus think themselves safe from all harm. Fortunately for them, Amor keeps a sleepless vigil. And now he, that same little god, will save this sleeping mortal from the evil fate designed for her.

To the accompaniment of a menacing arpeggio, Ottone, dressed in Drusilla's clothes, creeps toward Poppea's bed. In quasi-recitative he sings that she will never awaken to discover that her murderer is the lover she rejected. Just as he raises his dagger, Amor springs forward and furiously denounces him as a vile assassin. As a god, he cries, he will not waste his arrows on so ignoble a mortal, but will leave him to the hangman's noose. Ottone rushes away.

Poppea awakens and catches sight of the fleeing figure in woman's clothes. Her cries of "Drusilla" bring Arnalta to her side. The nurse shouts for the servants, ordering them to pursue and kill the would-be murderess. They dash away as the music rises to a surging climax. At this point there is another seriocomic touch characteristic of the opera. Amor struts forward and boastfully asserts that it was he alone who saved Poppea because he has willed her to be Empress.

[*Scene Five*] A street in Rome.[3] Drusilla, unaware of what has happened, gloats over the fact that her rival for Ottone's love soon will be eliminated. Suddenly she is surrounded by a shouting throng led by Arnalta and the Lictor. The nurse screams that there is the assassin, who has tried to escape detection by changing her clothes. When Drusilla asks what crime she has committed,

---

[3] Act Three in the original.

Arnalta accuses her of trying to murder Poppea. Drusilla only then realizes with horror that Ottone's fateful disguise has implicated her in the conspiracy.

At that moment Nerone enters and Arnalta repeats her accusations. When Drusilla protests her innocence, the Emperor orders her to be tortured until she confesses and names her accomplices. Impelled by her love for Ottone, she suddenly decides to shoulder the blame and blurts out that she alone plotted the murder. As Nerone savagely orders his soldiers to torture her to the utmost, Ottone rushes in. Over Drusilla's frantic protestations he shouts that he is guilty and begs the Emperor to put him to death.[4]

Nerone, however, consigns him to exile in the desert, with forfeiture of all his titles and his fortune. Turning to Drusilla, he proclaims that he will reward her valorous determination to share her lover's guilt by granting her pardon. Drusilla replies that she asks nothing more than to live and die in exile with Ottone. She thanks Fortune that the Emperor has recognized the power of love in a woman's heart. Angry and exasperated, Nerone orders the lovers out of his sight.

Then he stuns the throng with the proclamation that he has banished Ottavia from the throne and has condemned her to perpetual exile. She is to be taken to the nearest seacoast, put aboard a flimsy boat and left to the mercy of the wind and waves.

Poppea enters as he speaks the final words of his decree. With gloating satisfaction she commends his decision as wise and just. Taking her in his arms, Nerone declares that today he will make her his Empress and invest her with crown and royal purple. Poppea responds with a passionate declaration of love ("Idolo del cor mio"), which marks the beginning of a fervid, sensuous duet.

[*Scene Six*] Ottavia, bereft of her throne and doomed to perpetual exile, bids a poignant farewell to Rome, fatherland and friends in one of the opera's greatest arias, "Addio Roma, addio patria, addio amici." Bold dissonances in the accompaniment underscore the intensity of her grief.

[*Scene Seven*] This scene is another example of the interludes of comic relief which heighten the contrasting impact of the opera's underlying tragedy. In the aria "Io, che son la nutrice"

---

[4] In the original, Ottone confesses that Ottavia commanded him to murder Poppea. Nerone seizes upon this as an excuse to punish the Empress with banishment.

Arnalta gloats over the caprice of fortune which has made her the confidante of the Empress of Rome. Now all those who once scorned her as a humble nurse will bow and scrape and murmur, "Your Ladyship." Born a servant, she will die a lady. She reflects, however, that if she were to be reincarnated she would prefer the reverse: After all, those who live a life of ease leave it regretfully; those who live in misery and hardship welcome the release of death.

[*Scene Eight*] The climactic Coronation Scene is introduced by a stately fanfare, and then the populace hails Nerone and his new Empress in a resounding chorus, "Con il consensu universal." At its conclusion the crowd disperses, leaving Emperor and Empress alone on a darkening stage. In a transport of triumph and sensual ardor, their voices merge in a final duet—the great passacaglia which crowns the opera—"Pur ti miro, pur ti stringo."

# Maria Stuarda
*by* GAETANO DONIZETTI
(1797–1848)


*Libretto by*
GIUSEPPE BARDARI


Based on the play *Maria Stuart*, by Johann Christoph Friedrich von Schiller

### CHARACTERS

| | |
|---|---|
| Elisabetta (Elizabeth), Queen of England | Soprano |
| Maria Stuarda (Mary Stuart), Queen of Scots | Mezzo-soprano |
| Anna (Anne Kennedy) | Soprano |
| Robert, Earl of Leicester, favorite of Queen Elizabeth | Tenor |
| Talbot, lay priest of the Church of England | Baritone |
| Lord Cecil, adviser to Queen Elizabeth | Bass-baritone |

Courtiers, people of the court, soldiers, guards

*Place:* England—Westminster Palace and Fotheringay Castle
*Time:* 1587
*First performance:* La Scala, Milan, December 30, 1835
*Original language:* Italian

---

*Maria Stuarda,* Donizetti's thirty-third opera, has a bizarre history. The first rehearsals for the premiere originally scheduled for October 1834 at the Teatro San Carlo, Naples, were thrown into an uproar when the two *prime donne* playing the leading roles suddenly flew at each other in a no-holds-barred battle. Later at the dress rehearsal before an invited audience, Queen Maria Christina of the Two Sicilies was so horrified by the scene of Maria Stuarda's condemnation that she fainted. Further performances promptly were forbidden by the censors.

To salvage his opera, Donizetti adapted the music to another libretto, entitled *Buondelmonte,* with the locale of the plot in twelfth-century Florence. In that form it was premiered on October 18, 1834—with the same two warring sopranos. It was a failure.

At the 1835 premiere of the opera in its original form, the renowned soprano Maria Malibran created the title role. Although ill and in poor voice, she insisted on singing, with the result that the opera was unfavorably received. To make matters worse, there was more badgering by the censors, who objected to Maria Stuarda calling Elisabetta a "bastard."

Withdrawn after seven performances, the opera was given elsewhere in Italy. Thirty years later, in 1865, it reappeared at the Teatro San Carlo. The next recorded revival was at Bergamo (Donizetti's birthplace) in 1958. The first American performance (1964) was given in concert form by the Little Orchestra Society in New York under the direction of Thomas Scherman. Another concert presentation was given on December 6, 1967, at Carnegie Hall by the American Opera Society under the baton of Allen Sven Oxenburg.

In the context of history, *Maria Stuarda* is a sequel to *Anna Bolena.* It involves the lethal feud between Elizabeth, the daughter of Henry VIII by Anne Boleyn, and Mary Stuart, ex-Queen of France and Queen of Scotland. The situation at the opening of the opera is that Mary has been imprisoned at Fotheringay Castle by her jealous older cousin on charges of treason. Mary defies Elizabeth at the cost of her life.

## ACT ONE

Westminster Palace, where courtiers and people of the court are awaiting the arrival of Elisabetta. After a brief orchestral prelude on a plaintive theme, they express their mood of excited anticipation in the chorus "Qui s'attenda." The Queen appears, and an ensemble ensues during which she discloses her thoughts on the possibility of linking the thrones of England and France by marrying the King of France.

But in the recitative and cavatina which follow, Elisabetta hints that she is in love with someone else. She then discusses the fate of Maria Stuarda with Talbot and Lord Cecil. The lay priest entreats her to show mercy to her rival, while the crafty Lord Cecil, by innuendo, portrays Mary as a dangerous conspirator who must be eliminated.

When they have left, Leicester enters. Elisabetta informs him that he is to be her ambassador to France. She is obviously annoyed when he accepts the post with casual courtesy, but she betrays by look and gesture that her secret love is Leicester himself.

A scene now follows between Talbot and Leicester. The priest gives Leicester a letter from Maria in which she begs the Earl to use his influence to arrange a meeting between her and Elisabetta. Leicester, burning with love for Maria, vows he will risk life itself to save her; Talbot warns him that any such rash action would bring Elisabetta's jealous wrath down upon his head. The thoughts of the two men are expressed in the recitative "Questa imago, questo foglio" and the cavatina "Si fida tanto."

In an audience with the Queen, Leicester shows her the letter from Maria. Elisabetta regards it as conclusive proof that the Queen of Scots is determined not only to usurp her throne but her secret lover as well. At the same time—seeing her chance to humiliate Maria further—Elisabetta agrees to their meeting. Leicester's impassioned pleas in behalf of her rival infuriate the Queen, but she controls herself. The dialogue begins with Leicester's refrain, "Era d'amor l'immagine," which is followed by the duet "Sul crin la rivale la man mi stendea." This number closes the act.

## ACT TWO

In the park at Fotheringay, Maria and her companion Anna are enjoying a moment of freedom from confinement in the castle. As they revel in the beauty of the woods, Maria recalls the smiling landscape of her native France in the cavatina "Oh nube, che lieve per l'aria."

A chorus in the distance is heard announcing the arrival of Elisabetta with her hunting party. It has a certain foreboding quality which heightens Maria's dread of the meeting with her hated rival. Leicester appears and tells her that the Queen arranged the hunting party simply as an excuse to come to Fotheringay to see her. In the ensuing duet, "Da tutti abbandonata," Leicester counsels Maria to be respectful to Elisabetta. He adds, however, that he will have his own revenge if she refuses to show mercy. Overwhelmed by Maria's comeliness and bravery, Leicester impulsively asks her to marry him. Though profoundly moved, she gently evades a direct answer. The Earl leaves to meet Elisabetta.

The Queen arrives with Cecil and her entourage. Maria, escorted by Talbot, greets her with formal respect, and then follows the great sextet, "E sempre la stessa superba," sung by Elisabetta, Maria, Anna, Leicester, Cecil and Talbot.

At its conclusion there follows the famous *Dialogue of the Two Queens*. Forcing herself into an attitude of submissiveness, Maria kneels before Elisabetta and asks forgiveness. But the Queen harshly accuses her of having violated her marriage vows and further charges her with complicity in the murder of her second husband, Henry Darnley.

Goaded to fury, Maria denounces Elisabetta as a despicable creature driven by lust and ambition and calls her the bastard of Anna Bolena ("figlia impura di Bolena"). The epithet, of course, seals Maria's doom.

## ACT THREE

[*Scene One*] Westminster Palace as in Act One. Elisabetta is seated at a table facing Cecil, with Maria's death warrant before her. A dramatic duet ensues, beginning with the Queen's brilliant, florid arietta, "Quella vita a me funesta." Here she makes her decision to sign the death warrant—and also determines to revenge herself on Leicester by ordering him to witness Maria's execution.

Leicester enters, and the scene continues in a powerful trio, "Deh! per pietà suspendi." While the Earl begs Elisabetta to spare Maria's life, Cecil remorselessly demands her death. Enraged by Leicester's show of compassion for her rival, the Queen storms: "Go, worthless one—prepare the tomb for your beloved" ("Vanno indegno, prepara la tomba"). This scene marks the dramatic and musical climax of the role of Elisabetta.

[*Scene Two*] Maria's apartment in Fotheringay Castle. In the aria "Che vuoi?" she expresses her longing for Leicester. Cecil enters with Talbot and hands her the death warrant. When he asks if she wishes a minister of the Church of England to accompany her to the scaffold, Maria contemptuously dismisses him, declaring she will be true to her Catholic faith.

Alone with Maria, Talbot discloses that he is secretly a Catholic priest and can give her absolution. The poignant *Duet of Confession* follows ("Delle mi colpe lo squallido fantasma"). Half mad with fear of approaching doom, Maria imagines she sees the ghost of her murdered husband. She tells Talbot that Darnley died because Elisabetta was jealous of his love for her. As the duet continues, Maria touchingly thanks Talbot for his words of spiritual comfort ("Quando di luce rosea"). She listens with bowed head as he intones the words of absolution ("Lascia contenta al carcere").

Cecil reappears to inform her that Elisabetta will grant her a final request. Resigned and serene, Maria asks that her faithful Anna be permitted to accompany her to the scaffold.

[*Scene Three*] An anteroom off the execution chamber. Here, in a turbulent chorus ("Vedeste? vedemmo"), a crowd of Stuart supporters rages helplessly over the impending execution of their Queen. Anna enters and asks them to lower their voices lest they disturb the queen in her final moments.

Suddenly Maria appears. She is dressed in royal black and is wearing her crown. With resolute calm she tells the courtiers that she is happy to return to God's embrace. As they gaze at her in awed silence, Leicester bursts in and forces his way to her side. In a transport of religious ecstasy, Maria now sings the eloquent *Hymn of Death* ("Deh! Tu di un'umile preghiera").

During this scene two cannon shots have sounded to herald the approaching execution. The third shot booms out, signaling the moment of doom. Taking Leicester's arm, Maria sings her farewell in a refrain inspired by love and courage ("Ah, se un giorno da queste ritorte"). Then, with Anna and Leicester on either side, she walks with firm steps to the scaffold.

# Rodelinda

### *by* GEORGE FRIDERIC HANDEL
(1685–1759)

*Libretto by*
NICCOLÒ FRANCESCO HAYM

CHARACTERS

| | |
|---|---|
| Rodelinda, Queen of the Lombards | Soprano |
| Bertaric, King of the Lombards, her husband | Baritone |
| Grimwald, tyrant of the Lombards | Tenor |
| Hadwig, Bertaric's sister | Contralto |
| Garibald, Duke of Turin, Grimwald's henchman | Bass-baritone |
| Hunolf, a soldier, Bertaric's henchman | Bass |
| Flavius, young son of Rodelinda and Bertaric | Mute |

Men and women of the court, townspeople, nobles, guards

*Place:* Milan
*Time:* Sixth century A.D.
*First performance:* London, February 13, 1725
*Original language:* Italian

---

*Rodelinda* is a dramatic story of treachery, lust for power and the eventual triumph of good over evil in a royal court of the early Christian era. In contrast to most of Handel's opera-oratorios, this work is in a prevailingly minor key, which heightens the tragic aspects of the plot and gives impact to the play of elemental emotions. The musical design of the opera is based on the *da capo* aria, in which recitatives are followed by long, florid arias embellished with roulades, chromatic scales and arpeggios. Handel—as did other composers of the period—wrote these arias for the legendary *castrati,* those extraordinary singers who could encompass seemingly endless coloratura passages in a single long breath.

One of the leading singers in the first performance of *Rodelinda* was the great contralto *castrato* Senesino (Francesco Bernardi), for whom Handel wrote some of his finest arias. Senesino, as Handel's *primo uomo,* sang in Handel operas for more than ten years. Handel authorities agree that *Rodelinda* contains some of the composer's best music. It was given in concert form by the Handel Society of New York at Carnegie Hall on November 23, 1966.

## ACT ONE

Queen Rodelinda mourns her husband, King Bertaric, believing he is dead. Grimwald, the King's archenemy, had succeeded in banishing him, then had falsely reported his death. Plotting to usurp the throne, Grimwald also seeks to marry Rodelinda. Meanwhile, he spurns Hadwig, Bertaric's sister, whom he had first courted.

The unfortunate Hadwig turns for consolation to Garibald, who is treacherously conniving against Grimwald. At first Garibald—in his turn—spurns Hadwig, but then deludes her into thinking he is in love with her. With her help he plans to get the throne away from Grimwald.

Bertaric, returning in secret from exile at the risk of his life, makes his way back to the castle, where his Queen is a virtual prisoner. With him is Hunolf. When Bertaric impetuously resolves to enter the castle, Hunolf restrains him, warning him against risking his own life—as well as Rodelinda's—by so rash an action. Kneeling at the tomb of his ancestors, Bertaric voices his despair and longing in the recitative and aria "Pompe vane di morte . . . Dove sei amato bene."

Alone in the castle, Rodelinda broods over her fate. In the aria "Ombre piante, unre funesta," she sings that in the funeral shadows of the cypresses on the castle grounds she sees an omen of impending disaster.

Grimwald enters. Rodelinda turns on him in fury, denouncing him as a murderer and warning that he will die for his crimes ("Morrai, si l'empio tua testa"). But her anger only serves to inflame his desire, and he expresses his passion and lust in the aria "Se per te giunge a godere."

Realizing resistance is useless, Rodelinda finally consents to marry Grimwald but demands Garibald's death as the price of her surrender. She then manages to evade Grimwald long enough to meet secretly with Bertaric, who has gained entrance to the castle with the connivance of servants. Rodelinda confesses she consented to marry Grimwald only to save her husband's life. Bertaric, horrified, refuses to believe her story and denounces her seeming infidelity in the aria "Si l'infia consorte."

## ACT TWO

[*Scene One*] Bertaric, still in a rage over Rodelinda's betrayal, meets with Hadwig and Hunolf to discuss how they may thwart the conspiracy of Grimwald and Garibald. Although somewhat mollified by assurances that the Queen is faithful to him, Bertaric gives way to his doubt and frustration in the aria "Con ranco mormoriso."

[*Scene Two*] An intermezzo sustains the mood of rising tension and impending conflict. The curtain rises on the hall of the castle where Rodelinda and Grimwald are gathered with their retinues. Confronting Grimwald, Rodelinda makes an eloquent plea for mercy ("Spietati, io vi giurai"). Grimwald, ignoring her protestations, sings that he is bound to her by chains of love ("Prigionera ho l'alma in penna").

In subsequent action, Bertaric and Rodelinda again meet in her apartment, where Bertaric, finally convinced of his wife's fidelity, takes her in his arms. She pledges her devotion in the aria "Ritorna, oh caro e dolce mio tesoro." At this moment they are discovered by Grimwald. Beside himself with rage, he accuses Rodelinda of betraying him with her "paramour" ("Tuo drudo è mio tesoro")—for some reason, he does not believe Bertaric is the King and Rodelinda's husband. He consigns Bertaric to a dungeon. Husband and wife bid each other farewell in one of the opera's finest duets, "Io t'abaccio."

## ACT THREE

There is a prelude and fugue before the rise of the curtain.[1]

[*Scene One*] Grimwald, tormented by the realization of his guilt, voices his terror and remorse in the aria "Tra sospetti, affetti, timori" ("In suspicion, contrition, in terror!").

[*Scene Two*] Bertaric, brooding in his cell, wonders bitterly if, after all, he has been abandoned by those he trusted ("Chi di voi più infedele?"—"Which of you did worse deceive me?").

As he ends the aria he is startled by a sudden noise. A sword is thrust through a crack in the wall and clatters at his feet.

[1] From Handel's G minor Concerto Grosso.

He picks it up just as a figure moves toward him in the darkness. Bertaric lunges at the intruder, only to find that he has wounded Hunolf, to whom Hadwig had given a key to a secret door in the dungeon and who had come to help Bertaric escape. Despite his wound, Hunolf leads Bertaric out of the dungeon, pausing first to tear off the king's cloak—stained with his blood—which he flings to the ground.

A moment later Rodelinda and Hadwig rush in, find the bloody cloak and of course believe Bertaric has been murdered. Rodelinda gives way to her anguish in the aria "Ahi perchè, giusto ciel."

[*Scene Three*] The final scene takes place in a meadow outside the dungeon walls. Grimwald, now half crazed by guilt and fear, staggers in exhausted from trying to escape his imaginary pursuers. In a stormy aria, "Fatto inferno è il mio petto," he cries that the torments of hell are raging in his soul. Then, as though bereft of his reason, he stares vacantly at a group of children passing by and sings a pastoral refrain about the children who tend the meadows ("Pastorello d'un povero armento"). At its conclusion he lies back and falls asleep.

Garibald sneaks in and craftily draws Grimwald's sword from its sheath. Just as he is about to plunge it into Grimwald's heart, the latter wakes up. As Garibald staggers back, Bertaric and Hunolf burst in. Tearing the sword out of Garibald's hands, Bertaric springs at the would-be assassin, who flees in terror. Bertaric follows and kills him offstage. He returns and tells Grimwald, who is stunned at having been saved by the man whom he plotted to rob of his wife and his throne.

Rodelinda comes in with Hunolf, Hadwig and Flavius, followed by people of the court. United at last with her husband, Rodelinda greets him in a fervent aria ("Mio caro bene"). There is general rejoicing as Grimwald restores the crown to Bertaric. Then all join in the great choral finale, "Dopo la notte oscura."

# Semele

## *by* GEORGE FRIDERIC HANDEL
### (1685–1759)

### *Libretto by*
### WILLIAM CONGREVE

Congreve's original work *Semele* was arranged for Handel's use—probably by Newburgh Hamilton, one of the composer's oratorio librettists

### CHARACTERS

| | |
|---|---|
| Jupiter (Jove) | Tenor |
| Juno | Alto |
| Cadmus, King of Thebes | Bass |
| Semele, his daughter | Soprano |
| Athamas, a prince of Boeotia, in love with Semele | Alto |
| Ino, Semele's sister | Alto |
| Somnus, god of sleep | Bass |
| Iris, a messenger from Olympus | Soprano |
| Apollo | Tenor |

Priests, soothsayers, Loves, Graces, Zephyrs, nymphs, swains, attendants

*Place:* Greece
*Time:* Antiquity
*First performance:* Covent Garden, February 10, 1744
*Original language:* English

---

While musical dictionaries list *Semele* as a "stage piece" rather than an opera, it has also been referred to as the "first great full-length English opera." Handel here achieved a blend of oratorio and opera, introducing certain elements (dramatic action, *da capo* arias, recitatives) which move the work out of the realm of pure oratorio.

The English dramatist Congreve (1670–1729) in his libretto took his plot from the Greek legends as related by Ovid and Euripides. In his setting, Handel gave the mythical characters human attributes—susceptibility to the mundane emotions of pride, jealousy, remorse, fear and anger—and thus the opera emerges as a human drama of unique expressiveness. Semele, a beautiful mortal, is loved by Jupiter, and she herself aspires to godhood. Her ambition for immortality destroys her—with Juno's wifely jealousy as the instrument of her destruction.

The work is characterized by a sustained flow of Handelian melody, with majestic choruses and scenes linked by vigorous recitatives. Two of the principal arias—Semele's "O sleep, why dost thou leave me?" and Jupiter's "Where'er you walk"—are familiar in the concert repertoire.

Despite its musical distinction, *Semele* failed completely in London. Withdrawn after three performances and given only once more later in 1744, it was never revived during Handel's lifetime. For some reason, Handel had aroused the ire of the opera faction. They not only damned *Semele* as "profane," but resented what they called an oratorio being staged as an opera. Opposition went beyond a war of words: Hired hoodlums waylaid, beat up and robbed patrons who came to see the performances.

In the intervening years, *Semele* has rarely been given. In a contemporary revival, it was presented in June 1969 at Caramoor, Katonah, New York, by the New York City Opera Company under the direction of Julius Rudel.

The three sections of the long overture can be related to basic elements of the opera's action: the *maestoso* to the solemnity of the sacrificial scene; the fugue to the consequences of Juno's avenging wrath; the gavotte to the pastoral charm of scenes in Act Two.

## ACT ONE

[*Scene One*] The temple of Juno. Flanking the altar is a golden statue of the goddess. Priests are seen performing a sacrificial rite, during which flames leap up from the altar and the statue bows. A priest proclaims that Juno has accepted the sacrifice; the assemblage responds with a chorus of rejoicing: "Lucky omens bless our rites."

In a recitative passage, King Cadmus and Athamas both try to persuade Semele to accept Athamas as her bridegroom. The King urges her to "hear and obey," while Athamas entreats her to give heed to "a lover's prayer."

But Semele, thinking only of her lover, Jove, is unmoved by

their pleas, and in recitative ("What refuge now is left me?") she frets over her dilemma: on one hand, her father's wrath if she disobeys; on the other, Jove's anger if she yields to mortal love. She begs the god to help her ("O Jove, in pity teach me which to choose"). This larghetto refrain leads into a long aria, in baroque style, expressive of tender longing ("The morning lark to mine accords his note").

Athamas, assuming her avowals are meant for him, thinks of his approaching nuptials with joyous anticipation ("Hymen, haste! Thy torch prepare!"). His amorous sighing, in turn, is overheard by Semele's sister, Ino, who is hopelessly in love with him. Furious over his lack of attention to her, she bursts out: "I can no longer hide my passion!" The three others are startled by her outcry, and King Cadmus asks: "Why dost thou untimely grieve?" This marks the beginning of a beautiful quartet in which Ino turns aside the efforts of the others to console her.

At the conclusion of the number, thunder rumbles ominously and the flames on the altar are extinguished. In mingled terror and anger, the priests demand that the nuptial ceremonies (for Semele and Athamas) cease forthwith ("Cease your vows, 'tis impious to proceed"), warning of Jove's avenging wrath. Cadmus sings that while Jove thunders, Juno approves; Athamas implores her aid in winning Semele. In an aside, Semele herself swears to Jove that she loves him alone. There is a crash of thunder and the altar sinks out of sight.

[*Scene Two*] In a long duet ("Hopeless lover, turn thy eyes") Ino commiserates with Athamas over his unrequited love for Semele. She invites him to find consolation in her own arms, but his casual reaction to the suggestion goads her to jealous fury ("Insensible! Ingrate!"). In the concluding sections of the duet ("You've undone me!") they express their mutual confusion and frustration.

[*Scene Three*] Cadmus rushes in and tells Athamas to prepare himself for disastrous news about Semele. In a feverish recitative ("Wing'd with our fears and pious haste") he relates that she has been abducted by Jove, who swooped down in the guise of an enormous eagle with flashing eyes and golden beak. While Athamas breaks into lamentation, Ino secretly gloats over the elimination of her rival. The priests and soothsayers now enter and Cadmus commands them to explain the reason for Semele's abduction.

To his surprise, they burst into a congratulatory chorus ("Hail

Cadmus! Jove salutes the Theban King!"). They compliment him on the fact that the mighty Jove himself has favored him by taking his daughter to the celestial regions to be his companion.

The voice of Semele is heard in an insinuating gavotte refrain ("Endless pleasure, endless love"), as though in mockery of her father's distress over her fate. She sings of her bliss in the arms of the god—whose thunder and lightning now have been tamed by her caresses. The chorus takes up this theme in a kind of parodied madrigal style.

## ACT TWO

[*Scene One*] The act is introduced by a sinfonia. Juno asks Iris, the messenger from Olympus, where Jove has taken Semele. Iris answers that the rendezvous is a palace on the heights of Cithaeron, beyond the reach of mortal eyes. In an ensuing refrain ("There from mortal eyes retiring") she sings that Semele, attended by Loves and Graces, abandons herself to the delights of love.

Juno vents her fury in a stormy recitative ("Awake, Saturnia!"), one of the most dramatic in all Handel's operas. She orders the goddess to destroy Semele—let the Furies tear her to pieces. Iris warns her of the terrible monsters that guard Jove's hideaway ("Hear, mighty queen"): thousand-eyed dragons with forked tongues and brazen wings.

In a frenzied *da capo* aria ("Hence, Iris, away!") Juno commands the messenger to go with her at once to the Maeotian Lake, the abode of Somnus, god of sleep. There she will force the god to exercise his magic to seal the eyes of the dragons guarding Semele's love nest.

[*Scene Two*] An apartment in Semele's palace. Loves and Graces hover around her bed. She awakens and sings the famous aria "O sleep, why dost thou leave me?" While voicing her passionate longing for her lover, she is haunted by the thought that the joys of love are illusory and fleeting.

[*Scene Three*] Jove appears. Semele greets him amorously. He responds in a long *da capo* aria ("Lay your doubts and fears aside"), counseling her to think only of the pleasures of love, now that he has returned. In an ensuing recitative he somewhat gratuitously assures her that "I and Love are one." Semele answers with a voluptuous avowal ("With fond desiring, with bliss expiring"), in which she coquettishly observes that she too can claim that "I and Love are one." Loves and Zephyrs approvingly comment in chorus ("How engaging, how endearing").

Semele lapses into a pensive mood and Jove asks what is troubling her. Wistfully she replies that she is, after all, only a mortal, with all the misgivings and fears that beset a mortal woman. The god immediately suspects her of harboring a dangerous ambition to become immortal, and in the aria "I must with speed amuse her" he resolves to divert her from these thoughts of godhood. Again the Loves and Zephyrs voice their approval of amorous dalliance ("Now Love that everlasting boy invites").

By way of providing Semele with further distractions, Jove tells her he will bring Ino to keep her company for a while. He will then transport the sisters to Arcadia, which he describes in one of the loveliest of all Handel arias, "Where'er you walk."

[*Scene Four*] Semele and Ino embrace. Ino describes how she made the journey under the protection of Jove himself. Then in a lyrical aria, "But hark! The heavenly sphere turns round," she revels in the serene beauty of Arcadia. Semele's voice blends with hers in a pastoral duet ("Prepare then, ye immortal choir"). Loves and Zephyrs respond in a great fugal chorus ("Bless the glad earth with heavenly lays").

## ACT THREE

[*Scene One*] The cave of Somnus. The mood of the scene is established in a remarkable overture with a hypnotic swaying figure in the bass. Roused from sleep by Juno and Iris, the god sings a trancelike invocation to slumber ("Leave me, loathsome light"). His voice dies away to a murmur as sleep overpowers him.

When Iris chides Somnus for his lethargy, Juno remarks that she knows what will keep him awake. Thereupon she offers him the nymph Pasithea for his pleasure. The god's response is instantaneous and enthusiastic. In a delightful buffo aria, "More sweet is that name," he savors the joys of a romantic interlude with the nymph.

Pasithea will be his, Juno promises, if he does her bidding. He is to send his minister, Morpheus, to tantalize Jove with a dream of a woman like Semele—only more beautiful. The purpose is to inflame the god's passion to the point where, when he awakens, he will grant Semele anything she asks. Then Somnus himself is to cast a spell on Ino, so that Juno may take her shape and appear thus before Semele. In an ensuing duet ("Obey my will, thy rod resign") Juno and Somnus agree on the terms of their bargain.

[*Scene Two*] Disguised as Ino, Juno enters Semele's apartment carrying a mirror, which she hands to Semele. Pretending to be dazzled by Semele's beauty, Juno asks if she has become immortal. Unsuspecting, Semele answers that she still is a mortal and is not aware of any change in herself. Juno plies her with spurious compliments. Overwhelmed by the adulation of her supposed sister, Semele, gazing into the mirror, invokes her image in the brilliant aria of self-praise "Myself I shall adore."

Juno then offers Semele practical advice on how to obtain from Jove the immortality she longs for: When he approaches her bed, she is to refuse his caresses until he agrees to discard his mortal disguise and appear in his true form as a god. Inflamed by desire, Jove will grant her wish, and thus she will become a goddess.

Completely carried away, Semele expresses her gratitude in the siciliana aria "Then let my thanks be paid." She promises that when she achieves immortality she will endow her sister with charms like her own. Juno, warning that Jove is approaching, starts to leave; Semele assures her she will follow her advice. In a sardonic aside, the goddess dismisses her as a conceited fool.

[*Scene Three*] Jove rushes in with an impetuous greeting, "Come to my arms, my lovely fair," the opening phrase of his aria. He is astonished when Semele gently but firmly fends off his advances, then launches into a petulant harangue about his insistent demands on her ("I ever am granting"). To placate her, Jove promises, in a vigorous recitative passage ("Speak your desire"), to give her anything she asks. As he swears by all the gods on Olympus, there is a menacing rumble of thunder.

Then, to his utter dismay, Semele demands that he stop masquerading as a mortal and appear before her as the god he really is. Realizing that she is pronouncing her own doom, he warns her not to insist on his granting her wish ("Ah, take heed on what you press"). Semele reiterates her demand in the opera's most spectacular coloratura aria, "No, I'll take no less." At its conclusion she rushes away.

[*Scene Four*] Remorseful and dejected, Jove ponders the fate ordained for Semele ("she must a victim fall"). He resolves to use only his "softest lightning" and "mildest thunderbolts" to mete out her doom . . . but die she must. Juno reappears briefly to gloat over her victory.

[*Scene Five*] Abandoned and resigned to her fate, Semele sings her farewell in the poignant aria "Too late I now repent." It ends in a spoken, unaccompanied phrase of despair: "I can no more." She cringes in terror as she sees Jove descending in a cloud. Semele vanishes as a thunderbolt obliterates the palace.

[*Scene Six*] Cadmus, Athamas, Ino and the priests comment on Semele's doom in a dramatic choral arioso, "Oh, terror and astonishment." In an interlude, Ino recalls, as though in a trance, her strange journey to Arcadia. The god Hermes, she sings, foretold Semele's doom and her own betrothal to Athamas. Cadmus thereupon gives the pair his paternal blessing, and Athamas voices his happiness in the aria "Despair no more shall wound me."

[*Scene Seven*] A bright cloud descends on Mount Cithaeron, and from it emerges Apollo as the god of prophecy. He proclaims that from Semele's ashes a phoenix shall rise in the form of a god mightier than love—in short, Bacchus, the offspring of Semele and Jove. The chorus hails the new deity in a majestic prelude and fugue, "Happy shall we be."

# La Straniera
## (*The Stranger*)

*by* VINCENZO BELLINI

(1801–35)

### *Libretto by*
#### FELICE ROMANI

Based on the Gothic novel *L'Étranger*, by Viscount Charles Victor d'Arlincourt

#### CHARACTERS

| | |
|---|---|
| Alaide (La Straniera) | Soprano |
| Lord Montolino | Bass |
| Isoletta, his daughter, bethrothed to Count Arturo | Mezzo-soprano |
| Arturo, Count of Ravenstel | Tenor |
| Baron Valdeburgo | Baritone |
| The Prior of the Knights Hospitalers | Bass |
| Osburgo, friend of Arturo's | Tenor |

Ladies and gentlemen of the court, huntsmen, peasants, servants

*Place:* The Castle of Montolino in Brittany
*Time:* Circa 1300
*First performance:* La Scala, Milan, February 14, 1829
*Original language:* Italian

---

The famous love affair between Bellini and Giuditta Turina-Cantu, a beautiful, cultured society girl of Milan—twenty-five years old and unhappily married to a millionaire—was said to have been the inspiration for *La Straniera*. He began work on it during the summer of 1828, when he had already made a name for himself with *Bianca e Fernando* and *Il Pirata,* and was the idol of the operatic world. Most of the score was composed while he was living at Giuditta's villa on Lake Como. The pastoral surroundings there, in fact, influenced Bellini's setting for several scenes in the opera.

*La Straniera,* the fourth of Bellini's ten operas, was an unqualified success. Bellini himself reported that the audience howled with enthusiasm. His main source of satisfaction, however, was that the opera established him as a composer in his own right, rather than an imitator of Rossini, for whom he had high respect as a musician.

The plot has all the melodramatic elements of the typical Gothic tale: doomed lovers, renunciation, suicide, frustrated passion—all overlaid with the brooding mystery of sorcery and witchcraft. These elements Bellini fused into the sensuous melodies that are at the core of *bel canto* art.

The opera's overture opens with a thunderous unison chord in the brass, then goes on to state several themes of leading arias and ensembles. Noteworthy is a section in the lively rhythm of a folk dance much like the Scottish reel.

## ACT ONE

[*Scene One*] On the shores of the lake outside the Castle of Montolino. A chorus of peasants and people of Montolino's court hails the approaching wedding of Isoletta and Count Arturo ("Voga, il vento tace"). At its conclusion, Isoletta and Valdeburgo appear. The bride-to-be confides to Valdeburgo that she is in deep distress over Arturo's inexplicable change of heart ("Col cor trafitto"). Apparently, she says, he has fallen hopelessly in love with another woman—a sinister, wild creature known as "La Straniera," who lives alone in a hut on the shore of the lake.

In the aria "Io la vidi" she relates that only yesterday she caught sight of this witch and heard her wail in an unearthly voice: "Abandon all hope, ye who long to recapture the joys of love" ("Ogni speme è a te rapito che riponi nell'amor"). This leads into a duet in which Valdeburgo expresses his grief over Isoletta's plight and tries to console her.

From the distance comes the excited chorus of the people of the castle as they pursue La Straniera to her hut and curse her as a sorceress. As Isoletta and Valdeburgo leave, Montolino and Osburgo appear. When Montolino reveals his apprehension over Arturo's behavior ("Osburgo? Io non divido"), the latter tries to reassure him with the promise to do his best to bring the errant suitor to reason ("Tu pur col vogo").

[*Scene Two*] The interior of La Straniera's hut in the forest. Arturo enters and looks around, musing that a magic spell hovers over this place ("È sgombro il loco")—a spell he is powerless to resist. He stares wonderingly at a portrait of La Straniera, bejeweled and dressed in the robes of a queen. Hearing footsteps, he withdraws to a dark corner of the room.

Alaide enters. In the romanza "Sventurato il cor che fida" she philosophizes on the sorrows of unrequited love. Her reflections are interrupted when Arturo steps out of the shadows and impetuously declares that he has come only to serve her ("In tuo soccorso"). This marks the beginning of a duet. Alaide upbraids him for daring to come to her hut; Arturo replies that an irresistible force draws him to her. Although she confesses that she is mysteriously attracted to him, she implores him to leave. His love, she warns, will destroy them both.

[*Scene Three*] A clearing in the forest. Osburgo and his party sing a hunting chorus, "Campo ai veltri." With them are Arturo and Valdeburgo, whom the hunters had met in the forest. Flatly rejecting Osburgo's suggestion to go back to the castle for the prenuptial festivities, Arturo begs Valdeburgo to go with him to meet Alaide. He promises never to see her again if the Baron disapproves of her ("Tu di me in traccia"). This introduces a long duet in which the two argue the matter. Valdeburgo finally agrees to go.

[*Scene Four*] Alaide's hut. When Valdeburgo sees La Straniera, he greets her like a long-lost friend. Embracing her, he is about to call her by her real name when she stops him ("Cielo! Taci! Qual gioia!"). Arturo is beside himself with joy over Valdeburgo's apparent approval of Alaide. But his hopes are dashed when Valdeburgo tells him, over ominous chords in the orchestra, that he must forswear Alaide: She cannot return his love because another destiny is in store for her. Arturo gives vent to his surprise and rage in the refrain "Un dubbio atroce." Drawing his sword, he is about to lunge at Valdeburgo when Alaide interposes herself with a cry of "Ah, non partir!"

This action sets off the dramatic trio which is one of the opera's most memorable numbers. Its main theme brings to mind the theme of the tenor aria "Ecco ridente" in Rossini's *Il Barbiere di Siviglia*. Valdeburgo tries to convince Arturo that he is not his rival; Arturo forces Alaide to agree to see him at least once more ("Ecco gl'indegni insieme"). Warning Arturo again that their love is accursed, she begs the two men to leave her in peace.

[*Scene Five*] The shore of the lake near the castle. Arturo, tormented by jealousy, is certain that Valdeburgo is his rival, and when he meets the Baron by chance in the forest he challenges him to a duel. Valdeburgo, wounded, staggers and falls into the lake just as Alaide rushes in. Turning on her in fury, Arturo storms that he has just slain her real lover. Horrified, Alaide cries that Valdeburgo is her brother, not her lover. With a despairing shout, Arturo flings down his bloodstained sword and plunges into the lake to save Valdeburgo. Arturo's outcry brings people from the castle rushing to the scene, where they find Alaide crouching alone beside the bloody sword. In a wild chorus, "Un uom nell'- onda," they brand her a witch and accuse her of murdering the Baron. She is dragged away as their prisoner.

## ACT TWO

[*Scene One*] The great hall of the Castle of Montolino, where the trial of La Straniera is taking place. The Prior, as judge, reflects on the evidence in the refrain "Udimmo. Il tuo racconto." Before Alaide is brought in, Osburgo, as first witness, gives damaging testimony against her ("E dubitar ne puoi?").

When the accused—her face veiled—appears and the Prior asks her name, she replies: "La Straniera. A me tal nome." The Prior, recognizing her voice, smothers an exclamation of surprise. Dialogue in recitative follows. When the Prior has heard her testimony he asks if there is anyone she can call as defense witness. There is no one, Alaide answers.

At that moment Arturo bursts in, shouting that Alaide is innocent and that he alone is guilty ("Morte cadrà sul mio"). At the height of the ensuing uproar, Valdeburgo strides in. There is a stunned silence in the court, and then he declares that both Alaide and Arturo are innocent. He makes his plea for mercy in a ringing aria, "Si, li scioliete, o Giudici." The onlookers express their consternation in a stirring chorus.

Ordered by the court to reveal her identity, Alaide answers that she will lift her veil only to the Prior. When she does so, he staggers back in surprise, then says with deep respect: "Go, you are free. And forgive us our sins." Alaide leaves, escorted by Valdeburgo; Arturo, baffled and dejected, walks away alone. The Prior, turning on Osburgo, angrily censures him for giving false testimony against Alaide ("Tu che osasti mentir").

[*Scene Two*] A spot near Alaide's hut. Arturo has come to ask her forgiveness and to beg for her love. He is intercepted, however, by Valdeburgo, who entreats him to abandon his attempts to win Alaide. He adds the warning that Arturo will see her "only over the body of her brother" ("È osar puoi tanto"). This leads into a fiery duet, one of the most impressive numbers of the opera.

Arturo finally promises to renounce Alaide and marry Isoletta, but he makes one final request. He asks that Alaide be allowed to attend the wedding so that he may see her once more. Valdeburgo assents, then exhorts him to be mindful of Isoletta's deep love for him and to be faithful to her.

[*Scene Three*] The church on the day of the wedding. Isoletta, still haunted by thoughts of Arturo's ominous behavior is gloomy and despondent. She gives way to her fears in the aria "Ah! se non m'ami più." In a folowing chorus ("Si, vincesti, e sulta alfine") her serving-women try to reassure her. A wedding hymn is then sung ("È dolce la vergine").

The wedding party arrives, with Arturo in a state bordering on frenzy. Valdeburgo, trying to calm him, assures him that Alaide has consented to be present ("Coraggio: ella ti vede"), but Arturo scarcely seems to hear. When Isoletta approaches, he glares wildly at her and behaves so irrationally that she threatens to halt the ceremony then and there. The church is thrown into an uproar. Alaide meanwhile surreptitiously comes closer to the altar. There the four principals voice their mutual confusion and despair in the great quartet "Che far vuoi tu?" At its climax, Isoletta cries that she will release Arturo from his marriage vows. Thereupon Alaide rushes forward and implores her to take courage and go on to the altar. Then she turns and, half fainting, makes her way toward the door of the church. Almost at the door, Alaide pauses and prays for mercy for all those caught up in this disaster ("Cielo pietoso").

Arturo, at the altar, suddenly turns away from Isoletta and dashes toward the door. Brandishing his sword, he orders Alaide to follow him. At her cry of terror, Valdeburgo and the Prior rush to her side. The Prior stuns the throng by proclaiming that La Straniera is in reality Queen Agnes of Brittany; it has just been learned that her rival for the throne has died and the plot against her life has collapsed. She will now resume her rightful place as Brittany's Queen. Arturo, staring at her in disbelief, dementedly cries that now the truth is known ("Ancor ti trovo"), then plunges his sword into his body. Isoletta kneels sobbing at his side.

The wedding guests comment in chorus on the tragic scene ("Pari all'amor degli angioli"). In solo passages ("Or sei pago"), Alaide laments the ironic destiny that has recalled her to the throne at the sacrifice of her own happiness. A powerful choral expression of grief and compassion ("Al ciel, lo spirto l'abbandona") brings the opera to a close.

# Les Troyens
## (*La Prise de Troie, Les Troyens à Carthage*)
### *by* HECTOR BERLIOZ

## *Libretto by the composer*

Largely based on the first, second and fourth books of the *Aeneid*, by Vergil (Publius Vergilius Maro), 70–19 B.C., Roman poet

### CHARACTERS

| | |
|---|---|
| Cassandra, a Trojan prophetess, daughter of King Priam and Queen Hecuba | Mezzo-soprano |
| Dido, a Tyrian princess, founder and Queen of Carthage | Mezzo-soprano |
| Anna, her sister | Contralto |
| Aeneas, Trojan hero, son of Anchises and Venus | Tenor |
| Ascanius, son of Aeneas | Mezzo-soprano |
| Coroebus, lover of Cassandra | Baritone |
| Panthus, a Trojan priest | Bass |
| Iopas, a Tyrian poet | Tenor |
| Narbal, Dido's minister of state | Bass |
| Hylas, a sailor | Tenor |
| Hector (as a vision) | Bass |

Populace, warriors, sentinels, shades, nymphs, satyrs

*Place:* Troy and Carthage
*Time:* Antiquity
*First performance:* (Les Troyens à Carthage) Théâtre Lyrique, Paris, November 4, 1863
*Original language:* French

---

*Les Troyens,* Berlioz' third stage work, is his acknowledged operatic masterpiece. This titanic score—in its original form comprising almost five hours of music—is one of the most grandiose creations in the history of opera. Sir Donald Tovey called it a "gigantic and convincing masterpiece of music drama," and Romain Rolland regarded it as the *Paradise Lost* of music.

Yet in some respects the opera was a failure. To begin with, the original proved too long for one evening. Berlioz himself wrote to a colleague: "My score is far too long." In any case, he was persuaded to divide the work into two parts: The first two acts of the original five became *La Prise de Troie;* the remaining three became *Les Troyens à Carthage.* It was the latter section which was produced for the first time in Paris.

Misfortune beset the premiere. The singers were underrehearsed and did not understand their roles; the stage mechanism was woefully inadequate for so complicated a production. Finally, the public could not understand the composer's unconventional musical treatment of his subject matter. *Les Troyens* ran for twenty-two performances, then vanished from the stage.

The opera emerged from oblivion some sixteen years later, when it was presented in concert form. The first complete version was given under the baton of Felix Mottl in Karlsruhe on December 6 and 7, 1890. A year later *La Prise de Troie* was performed at Nice and at the Paris Opéra; *Les Troyens à Carthage* was revived by the Opéra-Comique in 1892. But two decades elapsed before Paris finally heard the original opera—in a version somewhat condensed for a single evening performance in 1921.

A subsequent production of the entire work—again with minor cuts—was given by an amateur company in Glasgow in 1935. After another hiatus of some twenty years, interest in the opera revived to such a degree that some critics wondered why this masterpiece had been so long neglected. From about 1957 to the present there have been notable revivals—both staged and in concert form—in Paris, London, Glasgow and America (American Opera Society and the San Francisco Opera).

Berlioz, like Wagner, wrote his own libretto. The Trojan legend as a subject for a grand opera had been suggested to him by the Princess Carolyne von Sayne-Wittgenstein, the companion of Franz Liszt. The idea had a special appeal for Berlioz—the Vergilian epic had been a favorite of his since childhood. He focused the plot of his opera on the story of the fall of Troy and the tragic romance of Dido and Aeneas.

"In form," writes Jacques Barzun in his *Berlioz and His Century,* "both poem and score carried forward . . . the Berlioz principle: choosing musical situations and linking them by the shortest path of recitative. Between larger sections there are no links. The hearer must make the mental jumps with the composer. Yet such is the dramatic force of the music that one need not memorize a libretto. That Troy fell to the Greeks and that Aeneas abandoned Dido is really all the information one requires."

(NOTE: In the following description of the plot, acts and scenes are designated in conformity with the original score.)

## La Prise de Troie
### The Capture of Troy
### ACT ONE

[*Scene One*] The action begins on a day in the tenth year of the Trojan War when the Trojans discover that the besieging Greek army has vanished. Gathered at the site of the enemy's deserted camp, the people—deluded into thinking that the Greeks have broken off the siege—sing the exuberant opening chorus, "Ah! quel bonheur de respirer l'air pur." They rejoice that they are again able to breathe the air of freedom after ten years of war.

They exclaim ("Que de débris!") over the weapons that litter the battlefield—swords, helmets, shields—then recoil in momentary terror as they come upon a grim object. It is the tomb of Achilles, raised by the Greeks in memory of the slain hero. But soon their attention is diverted by another Greek memento, the Wooden Horse ("Ce cheval colossal"). As the people rush pell-mell to view it more closely, Cassandra appears.

[*Scene Two*] Staring after them, she voices her tormenting forebodings in the aria "Mais quel dessin fatal." She sings that she saw the ghost of the slain Trojan hero Hector—itself a portent of catastrophe. And now the Trojans, with King Priam himself leading their drunken celebration over a supposed victory, do not realize they are doomed.

This unhappy King ("Malheureux roi!"), Cassandra intones in a continuation of the aria, will vanish into eternal night—and with him the entire race of Trojans. In anguish she cries that when she tells of the horror she foresees, no one will believe her.

[*Scene Three*] At this point Coroebus comes in and excitedly asks her to join him in the victory celebration. Shocked at his careless gaiety, Cassandra replies that the hour of doom is near. Coroebus implores her to forget her groundless fears and to come with him ("Reviens à toi"). This marks the beginning of a long duet. In vain she prophesies that soon the streets of Troy will run red with blood, that the temple virgins will be dragged naked into the streets and raped. In vain she begs Coroebus to flee before he himself is killed by the Greeks.

But her lover refuses to leave her. In hopeless despair, Cassandra finally relents. She asks for a final kiss to seal their doomed betrothal ("Et mon chaste baiser"), then faints in Coroebus' arms.

[*Scene Four*] An open space before the walls of Troy, where the victory celebration is to continue and where an altar to Pallas Athena has been set up. A triumphal procession enters, led by King Priam and Queen Hecuba. With them are their son Helenus and daughter Polyxena, Aeneas at the head of his soldiers, and his son Ascanius, who leads in a group of children. Also in the procession are Coroebus, Panthus, the priests of Jupiter and Neptune, Trojan dignitaries, magistrates and soldiers. All join in a mighty chorus of thanks to the Trojan gods for Troy's deliverance from the Greeks ("Dieux de la ville eternelle").

Next, a mock combat of young warriors is staged for the entertainment of the King and Queen. At its conclusion the mood of the scene changes abruptly. Andromache, the widow of Hector, enters leading her young son Astyanax. Clad in white robes of mourning, she takes him to the altar as the people express their pity in a solemn choral phrase ("Andromaque et son fils! O destin!"). Astyanax places flowers on the altar while his mother kneels and prays. Then she escorts him to the throne and presents him to Priam and Hecuba, who give the boy their blessing.

Meanwhile, the brooding figure of Cassandra looms in the background. To herself she murmurs the sinister prophecy that Andromache is doomed to even greater disaster than that which will befall Troy. The widow and her son leave the scene as the people again comment sympathetically.

[*Scene Five*] Suddenly Aeneas makes his way through the crowd and tells Priam that he has received word of a frightful disaster that has overtaken Laocoön, the High Priest of Neptune, and his two sons ("Du peuple et des soldats, o roi"). When a group of Trojans urged that the Wooden Horse be taken into the city as a trophy, Laocoön warned that it had been left there by the treacherous Greeks for some evil purpose—and not, as some Trojans believed, as an offering to Pallas Athena.

With that the priest plunged a lance into the horse's flank. A hollow groan reverberated. Then, without warning, two enormous serpents reared up from the sea, coiled themselves around

Laocoön and his two sons and devoured them before the eyes of the horror-stricken Trojans.

The victory celebration erupts into panic, with the people crying that Laocoön's fate was a sign that the gods were angry over his sacrilegious act. The tragedy is commented on in a thunderous ensemble, "Chatiment effroyable," one of the most spectacular numbers in the opera.

Aeneas orders the Horse to be brought into Troy at once. All shout approval. The strains of the *Trojan March* are heard as the crowd rushes away. Cassandra, standing to one side, again sounds her warning—and again no one listens. She wails that she cannot bear the sight of her people singing and dancing on the brink of the abyss ("Non, je ne verrais pas la fête déplorable!"). Crying that fire and death lurk in the entrails of the Horse, Cassandra screams one final, desperate plea: "Arrêtez! Arrêtez!" The crowd surges by unheeding. As she watches the gigantic image being drawn through the gates, she moans in despair: "Le destin tient sa proie! Et Cassandre va mourir sous les débris de Troie!" ("Fate has her prey. And Cassandra will die in the ruins of Troy!").

## ACT TWO

[*Scene One*] Aeneas, asleep in the palace, is visited by the ghost of Hector, which warns him to flee before it is too late ("Ah! fuit fils de Vénus!"). Troy is in ruins . . . King Priam is beyond help. Now the fate of the Trojan race is in Aeneas' hands. He is destined to lead his people to Italy, there to found a new empire which will rule the world.

[*Scene Two*] As the vision fades, Panthus, wounded and carrying images of the gods of Troy, bursts in with the news that the Greeks, springing from the Wooden Horse, massacred the Trojan soldiers, slew Priam and sacked Troy ("La ville ensanglantée"). Coroebus and armed warriors rush in and rally with Aeneas to make a last-ditch stand to save the city. In a defiant chorus ("Le désespoir dirigera nos coups") they call on Mars and the Furies to lead them into battle.

[*Scene Three*] The Temple of Vesta. A group of Trojan women, including Polyxena, are invoking the protection of the goddess Cybele ("Puissant Cybele").

[*Scene Four*] Cassandra appears. In a vigorous aria ("Tous ne périront pas") she proclaims that not all the Trojans will die. Aeneas and his band of warriors survived the final battle, rescued some of the citizens and managed to secure some of King Priam's treasury. The Trojans are now retreating to the safety of Mount Ida.

In stricken tones Cassandra goes on to say that Coroebus was slain, and now she herself has no wish to live. She exhorts the women to kill themselves to escape the ravaging Greeks. When some of the more timid shrink back in terror, Cassandra furiously denounces them as cowards. The others, in a powerful chorus ("Complices de sa gloire"), swear they will never let the Greeks defile them and will die with Cassandra. With cries of "Italy! Italy!" they leap from the parapet of the temple or stab themselves.

As the soldiers swarm in, Cassandra plunges a dagger into her breast, withdraws it and hands it to Polyxena. Stretching her arms toward Mount Ida, Cassandra gasps "Italy!" and falls dead.

### Les Troyens à Carthage
#### The Trojans at Carthage
#### ACT THREE

According to legend, Dido, a princess of Tyre, founded Carthage in north Africa, where she had taken refuge following the murder of her husband, Sychaeus, by her brother Pygmalion. At the time this section of the opera opens, the building of Carthage had been in progress for seven years.

[*Scenes One and Two*] The garden of Queen Dido's palace. The Queen is seated on her throne, with her sister Anna on one side and Narbal, her minister of state, on the other. The Carthaginians hail their Queen in a majestic chorus, "Gloire à Didon."

In a stately aria ("Nous avons au finir sept ans à peine") Dido thanks her people for their efforts during the past seven years in building Carthage into a proud and flourishing city. In the second part of the aria ("Chers Tyriens") she exhorts them to even greater efforts to prove themselves a new race of heroes.

Dido adds, however, that at this very moment Carthage is threatened by Iarbas, the savage chieftain of the Numidians, who are marching on the city. What is worse, Dido says, this insolent barbarian is demanding her hand in marriage. Her outraged subjects swear to defend her against this interloper. Dido thanks them for their allegiance.

[*Scene Three*] Then follows a procession honoring the builders, artisans and laborers who brought Carthage into being. Led by Narbal, they pass in review before the Queen to the accompaniment of a stirring march.

[*Scene Four*] Dido and Anna are left alone and a long duet ensues, beginning with Dido's refrain "Les chants joyeux." She muses that the loyalty of her subjects has restored her happiness and has dispelled a strange fear that has been haunting her.

When Anna asks why she, the adored Queen of a beautiful realm ("Reine, d'un jeune empire"), should be afraid, Dido replies that she has been troubled by a mysterious longing. Knowingly, Anna observes that her sister is longing for love. Dido protests that she will always remain faithful to the memory of her husband ("Non, la veuve fidèle"), and points to Sychaeus' wedding ring on her finger. Anna gently reminds her that Queen Dido is still young and beautiful—and Carthage needs a king.

The duet continues in a surging flood of melody. Dido confesses that her sister's words stir a dangerous joy in her heart ("Sa voix fait naitre dans mon coeur"), while Anna comments that Dido cannot resist the thoughts of love that now stir her ("Ma voix fait naitre dans son sein"). The duet ends as Dido impulsively calls out her husband's name, and Anna asks her forgiveness for having tempted her with thoughts of love.

[*Scene Five*] A moment later Iopas hurries in with the news that a strange fleet, seeking refuge from the storm, has anchored in the harbor. The mariners are asking an audience with the Queen. Dido tells Iopas to bid them welcome. In an ensuing aria ("Errante sur les mers") she recalls how she herself once fled from her native land to wander at the mercy of the elements without hope or haven. Remembering this, she could not now refuse help to those in a similar plight.

[*Scene Six*] Aeneas (disguised as an ordinary seaman), Ascanius, Panthus and other Trojan leaders enter to the strains of the *Trojan March*. Ascanius, acting as spokesman, identifies himself and his companions as Trojans—homeless wanderers after the fall of their city. In proof, he presents Dido with symbolic gifts: the scepter of Ilione, a daughter of Priam's. Queen Hecuba's crown; and the gold-embroidered veil of Helen of Troy.

Panthus then steps forward and explains that their leader, Aeneas, is destined by the gods to sail on until he reaches Italy, where he is to found a new home for the Trojans.

[*Scene Seven*] The conversation is interrupted by Narbal, who rushes in crying that Iarbas is marching on Carthage, plundering and killing as he approaches. Thereupon Aeneas throws off his disguise. He is clad in armor, except for his helmet and buckler. Assuring Dido that he will defend her against the invader, he rallies the Carthaginians around him.

They respond in a resounding chorus ("C'est le fils de Vénus") as a soldier brings Aeneas his helmet, buckler and javelin. Confiding Ascanius to Dido's care, he leads the Carthaginians into battle with the Numidians.

[*Scene Eight*] A symphonic interlude, *Royal Hunt and Storm*, now follows, with ballet, pantomime and chorus. It is a pastoral scene deep in the forest, with nymphs bathing in a pool. They hide as hunting horns are heard in the distance. A storm comes up, and hunters ride by to find shelter. Soon Dido, dressed as Diana the huntress, and Aeneas, still clad in half-armor, appear and find refuge in a grotto.

As the storm rages to its climax, a bolt of lightning splinters a huge tree and sets it afire. Sprites, nymphs and satyrs dance orgiastically around the flames. Wildly they cry "Italy! Italy!"— reminding Aeneas of his destiny. The storm gradually subsides and the woodland creatures vanish. Serene calm pervades the scene once more.

## ACT FOUR

[*Scene One*] The garden of Dido's palace on the shore of the Mediterranean, where the Carthaginians are celebrating Aeneas' victory over Iarbas. Standing apart from the throng, Anna and Narbal are seen in conversation. In quasi-recitative they express concern over Dido. Captivated by Aeneas, she spends her time in feasting and hunting—to the neglect of her duties as Queen.

[*Scenes Two and Three*] Dido and Aeneas enter with Panthus and Ascanius. A victory ballet is presented. The action which follows is staged in a deliberate tableau for purposes of the plot. Dido sits on a couch, her left profile to the audience, and rests her left arm on the shoulder of Ascanius, who kneels beside her in a pose symbolic of Cupid. Aeneas sits at Dido's feet, and the others group themselves at the back of the couch.

[*Scene Four*] Dido asks Iopas to entertain her with a song. Taking up his harp, the poet obliges with a hymn to Ceres, goddess of the harvest ("O blonde Cérès"). But the Queen, bored and restless, stops him, saying apologetically that the music does not soothe her.

Turning to Aeneas, Dido asks him to continue his story of the fall of Troy ("Enée, daignez achever")—and particularly about the fate of Andromache. She listens intently as Aeneas recounts how Andromache had been taken into slavery by Pyrrhus, the son of Achilles, who had slain Hector ("Hélas! en esclavage réduite par Pyrrhus"). Pyrrhus fell in love with her, and his wooing erased the memory of her husband. Andromache married her captor and became the Queen of Epirus.

[*Scene Five*] Enthralled by the story, Dido sings that the example of the widowed Andromache, yielding thus to a new love, freed her from any feelings of remorse ("Tout conspire à vaincre mes remords"). Gazing passionately into her eyes, Aeneas repeats her phrase.

[*Scene Six*] This marks the beginning of the famous quintet, one of the most beautiful ensembles in the opera, blending the voices of Anna, Iopas, Narbal, Dido and Aeneas. During the ensemble, Ascanius gently slips Dido's wedding ring from her finger. She takes it from him, but absent-mindedly leaves it lying on the couch when she rises at the conclusion of the ensemble.

All onstage turn to contemplate the beauty of the deepening twilight, expressing their emotions in a septet, another of the opera's outstanding ensembles ("Tout n'est que paix et charme"). At its close, all except Dido and Aeneas withdraw, and then follows a love duet of surpassing beauty ("Nuit d'ivresse et extase infinie").

It is a lyrical paraphrase of the dialogue between Jessica and Lorenzo in *The Merchant of Venice*.[1] In an undulating 6/8 tempo, the lovers sing of other lovers like themselves on an enchanted, moonlit night: Venus and Anchises, Troilus and Cressida, Diana and Endymion.

Then Dido—with a kind of mischievous irony—sings that "in such a night" the son of Venus was cold to Dido's caresses. In the same vein, Aeneas answers that Queen Dido was gently pardoned for her unjust accusations.

The lovers melt into the shadows and conclude the duet offstage. A moment later the god Mercury materializes in the moon-

[1] In Shakespeare, Act Five, Scene One: "The moon shines bright; in such a night as this,/ When the sweet wind did gently kiss the trees . . ."

light. Striding up to a broken column on which Aeneas had hung his helmet and buckler, Mercury strikes the buckler three times with his caduceus—each time intoning "Italy!" Then he vanishes.

## ACT FIVE

[*Scene One*] The beach at Carthage, where the sailors of the Trojan fleet have pitched their tents. Their ships are lying at anchor near by. Aboard one of them, Hylas, a young sailor, sings a plaintive song about his longing for home ("Vallon sonore").

[*Scene Two*] Panthus and Trojan officers enter and give orders for embarkation. The priest tells the officers that Aeneas, fearing the wrath of the gods over his dallying in Carthage, will do their bidding: He will desert Dido and resume his destined quest for Italy. In an ensuing chorus ("Chaque jour voit grandir la colère des dieux") the Trojans sing that they know only too well that the gods are angry. Shrieks and groans rend the night . . . the ghosts of dead Trojans come to haunt them, all the while repeating "To Italy!" The men go aboard the ships.

[*Scene Three*] Now follows an interlude of comedy relief involving two sentinels who are marching back and forth at their post on the beach. In salty dialogue they tick off their list of complaints: Here they are in Carthage—a snug harbor where the food is good, the wine plentiful and the wenches buxom, gay and willing. And what happens? They must leave all this and start on another dangerous voyage in a harebrained search for some place called Italy. But then, they conclude resignedly, orders are orders, and soldiers must obey.

[*Scene Four*] The mood of the action changes abruptly. Aeneas enters and walks slowly toward the beach. Staring at his ships, he gives way to his gloomy thoughts in the soliloquy "Inutile regrets! Je dois quitter Carthage!" He recalls how Dido looked at him in stunned disbelief when he told her he must leave. In vain he reminded her that not only his own destiny but that of the Trojan race is in his hands. But the look in Dido's eyes, he goes on, shattered his resolve to leave her.

In the great ensuing aria, "Ah! quand viendra l'instant," he sings that he cannot endure the agony of the final farewell. Yet he is determined to see her once again—to clasp her hands, to bathe her feet with his tears. The aria's concluding phrase, rising to a high B flat, is a cry of utter despair.

[*Scene Five*] Suddenly Aeneas staggers back, hearing a voice call his name. Then the ghosts of Priam, Coroebus, Cassandra and Hector materialize before him. Pointing accusing fingers, they warn him to leave Carthage at once ("Il faut vaincre et fonder"). Aeneas promises to go, but cries out in furious protest that the gods themselves will be to blame for the anguish he is causing Dido as the result of their divine commands.

[*Scene Six*] As the visions fade, an *agitato* variation of the *Trojan March* is heard. Aeneas gives orders to his fleet to sail at dawn. Then, turning toward the palace, he sings an impassioned farewell to Dido ("A toi mon âme").

[*Scene Seven*] Just as he concludes the refrain, Dido herself appears. A feverish colloquy ensues, beginning with the Queen's desperate entreaty. She sings ("Errante sur tes pas") that she has pursued him through night and storm to learn if his resolve to leave her is really true. Aeneas can only answer that he must obey the gods. Dido screams a curse at him and rushes away. Gazing after her in despair, Aeneas cries: "Italy!"

[*Scene Eight*] Dido's apartment in her palace. With her are Anna and Narbal. Distractedly the Queen asks them to help her persuade Aeneas not to leave her—at least to delay his departure for several days.

[*Scene Nine*] But at that moment Iopas dashes in to tell the Queen that the Trojan fleet has set sail. Beside herself with fury, Dido orders the Carthaginians to pursue Aeneas and burn his ships to the waterline ("Armez-vous, Tyriens! Carthaginois, courez!"). Then, realizing the futility of her rage, she subsides into the calm of despair. In measured, brooding phrases she recalls how she offered this treacherous adventurer a throne ("Et viola donc la foi"). Bitterly she censures herself for not having exterminated this despicable race of Trojans . . . in revenge she should have forced Aeneas to feast on the flesh of his own son.

Then, in a paroxysm of fury, underscored by a harsh fanfare in the brass, Dido summons the priests of Pluto to officiate in a demoniac ritual of vengeance ("Du prêtre de Pluton"). She orders them to build a pyre and place upon it Aeneas' gifts to her—every memory of him must disappear in the avenging flames of hell. At her maniacal shout of "Sortez," the priests rush away to obey her.

[*Scene Ten*] Alone, Dido gives way to her madness, striking her breast and tearing her hair. Suddenly she stops, exhausted by her fury. In a grief-stricken plea she cries: "Venus, give me back your son" ("Vénus, rends-moi ton fils").

Now follows the lyrical conclusion of the monologue ("Adieu, fière cité"), marked by descending phrases of sorrow and hopelessness. Dido bids farewell to her sister Anna, to the city she founded and to her loyal subjects. Recalling Aeneas' passionate caresses, she repeats a fragment of the love duet! "Aux nuits d'ivresse." The great aria ends on a cadence that dies away into silence: "ma carrière est finie" ("my life is finished!").

[*Scene Eleven*] A terrace overlooking the sea. In the center is the funeral pyre surmounted by a couch and a bust of Aeneas, along with his toga, helmet and sword. The priests of Pluto and the Carthaginians are assembled. In a savage chorus they invoke the divinities of hell ("Dieux de l'oubli! Dieux du Ténare! Hecate . . . Erebus . . . Chaos!").

[*Scene Twelve*] The crowd makes way for Anna and Narbal, who enter followed by Dido. She is veiled, with a chaplet encircling her brow. While the priests sing an invocation to Pluto, Anna and Narbal call down the curse of the gods on the Trojans. Dido mounts the pyre.

Throwing herself on the couch, she snatches up Aeneas' sword. But before she stabs herself she is transfixed by a vision of a conqueror who will rise from the soil of Africa to avenge her. "Hannibal," she cries, then plunges the sword into her breast. Yet even in dying she is tormented by another vision—that of imperial Rome. Gasping "Rome . . . eternal," the Queen dies in Anna's arms.

There is a great outcry from the people. In the turbulent chorus which closes the opera, the Carthaginians swear to eradicate the accursed race of Aeneas ("Haine eternelle à la race d'Enèe"). But over their clamor for revenge come the sounds of the *Trojan March*, symbolic of Rome's future triumph over Carthage. The curtain falls.

# PART III

---

## BRIEF BIOGRAPHIES
## OF FAMOUS SINGERS

Presented here is a roster of opera singers of the past and present whose names are familiar in varying degrees to the opera-going public. Some of these names—those of singers of the Golden Age of opera, for example—are household words. Those of contemporary singers, whose careers have begun auspiciously on the world's opera stages within, say, the past five years, may become equally well known. This is the fervent hope of the authors in selecting what must be considered a representative list of singers of today. Obviously, the list is not complete—and never will be, because new singers on the threshold of promising careers are constantly preparing for their operatic debuts. What is presented here will, hopefully, give some indication of the number of artists whose talent and dedication have contributed so much to the cause of opera as an enduring art form.

ADAM, Theo, baritone: native of Germany. One of the rising young Wagnerian baritones, he has sung Wotan in the *Ring* cycle at Bayreuth and Covent Garden. He made his Metropolitan debut as Hans Sachs in *Die Meistersinger* on February 7, 1969, and also appeared as Wotan in *Das Rheingold* and *Die Walküre*. First major role was King Henry in *Lohengrin* at Bayreuth in 1954. Other roles include Baron Ochs (*Der Rosenkavalier*), Figaro (*Le Nozze di Figaro*), Don Alfonso (*Così Fan Tutte*). Also heard frequently in Europe in concert, lieder recitals and oratorio.

AGAI, Karola, soprano: born in Budapest. Made her operatic debut in 1955 as the Queen of the Night in *Die Zauberflöte*. On February 5, 1969, she appeared at the Metropolitan as a last-minute replacement for Anna Moffo in the title role of *Lucia di Lammermoor*. She made her official debut in the same role February 14, 1969. Other roles include Konstanze (*The Abduction from the Seraglio*), Susanna (*Figaro*), Gilda, Violetta, Olympia-Giulietta-Antonia (*Les Contes d'Hoffmann*), Marguerite (*Faust*), Zerbinetta (*Ariadne auf Naxos*), Adina (*L'Elisir d'Amore*), Rosalinde (*Die Fledermaus*).

ALBANESE, Licia, soprano: born in Bari, Italy. Won Italian national competition in 1935. American debut at Metropolitan Opera in 1940, in *Madama Butterfly*. She claims forty-eight stage roles, 190 times as Butterfly, 130 times as Mimi, 118 times as Violetta in *La Traviata*. Operatic debut was in Parma, Italy, as Cio-cio-san in *Butterfly* in 1933. She has also sung in all the major opera houses in the world. Famous for her roles in Puccini and Verdi operas. On twenty-fifth anniversary of her debut at the Met, she hired Carnegie Hall, an orchestra and conductor, and sang fourteen Puccini arias.

ALBANI, Emma, soprano (1852–1930): born in Chambly, near Montreal. Real name Marie Louise Cecilia Emma Lajeunesse. Made her debut in Milan in 1870 in Bellini's *La Sonnambula*. Counted among the great singers of her time, she was heard most frequently at Covent Garden, where she sang roles ranging from Mimi to Isolde and rivaled Adelina Patti in popularity. Her only appearances at the Metropolitan were in 1892 with the Abbey-Schoeffel-Grau Opera Company. She sang Desdemona in Verdi's *Otello,* and Senta in an Italian version of Wagner's *Der Fliegende Holländer* on March 31, 1892.

ALDA, Frances, soprano (1883–1952): real name Davis, born in Christchurch, New Zealand. Made her debut as Manon at the Paris Opéra-Comique in 1905, and as Gilda at the Metropolitan on December 7, 1908. In 1909 she married Giulio Gatti-Casazza, general manager of the Metropolitan. They were divorced in 1928, and she retired from opera the following year. Miss Alda continued to be active in concert and was a pioneer in radio. She published a book of witty reminiscences about her career and fellow artists: *Men, Women, and Tenors.*

ALEXANDER, John, tenor: born in Meridian, Mississippi. Studied in Cincinnati. After singing with the New York City Opera, he made his Metropolitan debut on December 19, 1961 as Ferrando in *Così Fan Tutte.* He sings the leading tenor roles in *Manon Lescaut, Faust, La Sonnambula, Luisa Miller, Madama Butterfly, Les Contes d'Hoffmann, Die Zauberflöte, La Traviata, Rigoletto, Lucia di Lammermoor, The Last Savage* and *Vanessa.*

ALTHOUSE, Paul, tenor (1889–1954): born in Reading, Pennsylvania. He had two careers at the Metropolitan, where he made his debut as Dimitri in *Boris Godunof* on March 19, 1913. After seven seasons in Italian and French roles, he became a leading singer in European opera houses and with the Chicago Opera. He returned to the Metropolitan as a heldentenor in 1934. On March 16 he became the first American to sing Tristan there. He taught many famous pupils, including Richard Tucker and Eleanor Steber.

ALVA, Luigi, tenor: born in Lima, Peru. A leading lyric tenor in Italy and at Covent Garden, he made his Metropolitan debut as Fenton in *Falstaff* on March 6, 1964. His other roles there include Almaviva in *Il Barbiere di Siviglia,* Don Ottavio in *Don Giovanni,* Elvino in *La Sonnambula* and Ernesto in *Don Pasquale.*

ALVARY, Lorenzo, basso: born in Budapest, Hungary. He has been supplying outstanding characterizations at the Metropolitan since 1942, when he made his debut as Zuniga in *Carmen.* Has sung a total of forty-seven roles, performs in eight languages and studied in Milan and Berlin prior to his stage debut as Ramfis, in Budapest. Enjoys both serious and comic roles. Sings Samuele in *Un Ballo in Maschera.* Favorite roles are Ochs in *Der Rosenkavalier* and Alfonso in *Così.*

AMARA, Lucine, soprano: born in Hartford, Connecticut, but raised in San Francisco. Made her Metropolitan debut in *Don Carlos* in 1950. Sang Nedda in *Pagliacci* December 14, 1951, also Frasquita in *Carmen*. One of her best roles is Liu in *Turandot*. Also sings Ellen Orford in *Peter Grimes*, Mimi, Eva, Ariadne, Donna Elvira and Aïda. She was also Wellgunde in *Das Rheingold* and the Priestess in *Aïda*.

AMATO, Pasquale, baritone (1878–1942): born in Naples, where he made his debut in 1900. He made his Metropolitan debut in *La Traviata* with Sembrich and Caruso on November 20, 1908. He remained in the company as one of its most popular stars until 1920, then also sang with the Chicago Opera. In later years he sang with the Hippodrome Opera and taught at Louisiana State College. His recordings with Caruso sold in the millions.

AMPARAN, Belen, mezzo-soprano: born in Texas of Mexican parentage. Studied at the Conservatory of Mexico City and made her operatic debut there in 1951. She first appeared at the Metropolitan on November 29, 1956, as Giulietta in *Les Contes d'Hoffmann*. Outstanding in mezzo-soprano roles such as Marina in *Boris Godunof*, Preziosilla in *La Forza del Destino*, Dalila in *Samson et Dalila*. Also an authoritative interpreter of modern music.

ANDERSON, Marian, contralto: born in Philadelphia. The distinctive dark quality of her voice was recognized as early as 1925, when she was selected from three hundred contestants for an appearance with the New York Philharmonic. She spent the next ten years studying and singing in Europe, then made her debut in Town Hall, New York, December 30, 1935. She was a well-known concert artist but made her operatic debut as Ulrica in *Un Ballo in Maschera* at the Metropolitan on January 7, 1955, when she was fifty-two years old. Received an Honorary Doctor of Music degree at Ithaca College in 1968.

ANTHONY, Charles, tenor: native of New Orleans, his family name is Caruso. He came to the Metropolitan via the Metropolitan Auditions, which he won in 1952. Made his debut as the Simpleton in *Boris Godunof*. Is familiar in the roles of Vogelgesang in *Die Meistersinger*, Normanno in *Lucia di Lammermoor*, Pong in *Turandot*, Don Ottavio in *Don Giovanni*, Count Almaviva in *Il Barbiere di Siviglia*, Ernesto in *Don Pasquale*. He is also ranked as one of the leading comprimarios at the Metropolitan.

ANTOINE, Josephine, coloratura soprano: born in Boulder, Colorado. Studied at Juilliard School of Music, New York City, and later was a pupil of Marcella Sembrich. Won the Atwater Kent prize in 1929, made her Metropolitan debut as Philine in *Mignon* on January 4, 1936. She sang there until 1942 and subsequently became teacher of singing at the Eastman School in Rochester, New York.

ARAGALL, Giacomo, tenor: born in Barcelona. Had his first singing lesson at the age of twenty. In June 1963 he won first prize in the Verdi Competition in Busseto and made his operatic debut in that composer's *Jérusalem* (originally *I Lombardi alla Prima Crociata*) at the Teatro La Fenice, Venice. He has sung regularly in other leading opera houses in Italy and throughout Europe. He made his debut at the Metropolitan in *Rigoletto* on September 19, 1968.

ARMSTRONG, Karan, soprano: born in Havre, Montana. Won the 1965 Metropolitan Opera National Council Auditions and was subsequently given a Metropolitan contract. She has appeared in a number of operas, including *Die Frau ohne Schatten* and *Hänsel und Gretel*.

ARROYO, Martina, soprano: native of New York City. Won the Metropolitan Auditions in 1958 and made her debut on March 14, 1959, as the offstage Celestial Voice in *Don Carlos*. In February 1965, on two days' notice, she sang Aïda as a replacement for an ailing Birgit Nilsson. Well known for other roles such as Butterfly, Elsa in *Lohengrin*, Leonora in *Il Trovatore*, Amelia in *Un Ballo in Maschera* and Donna Anna in *Don Giovanni*. Her Aïda has also been heard at Covent Garden and the San Carlo in Naples. She was scheduled to sing the role of Elvira in *Ernani* at the opening of the Metropolitan's 1970–71 season.

AUSTRAL, Florence, soprano (1894–1968): born in Melbourne, Australia, real name Wilson. She was best known as a Wagnerian soprano and appeared often as Brünnhilde at Covent Garden, where she made her debut in that role in 1922. Her recordings were some of the first to carry excerpts from the Wagner operas to the far corners of the earth.

BACCALONI, Salvatore, basso buffo (1900–69): born in Rome, received his early musical training in the Sistine Choir there. Made his debut in Rome as Dr. Bartolo in *Il Barbiere di Siviglia,* and went on to build a career as one of the greatest comedians of the operatic stage. His portrayals of Don Pasquale, Gianni Schicchi, Leporello and Dr. Dulcamara were comic masterpieces. He sang at the Metropolitan for twenty-two years after his debut as Dr. Bartolo in *Le Nozze di Figaro* on December 7, 1940. He later acted in films.

BACQUIER, Gabriel, basso: French-born, studied at the Paris Conservatory. He created the title role in Gian-Carlo Menotti's *The Last Savage* (Abdul) in the premiere at the Opéra-Comique, Paris, in 1963. Specializes in such roles as Iago, Don Giovanni, Scarpia and Escamillo. His Metropolitan debut was as the High Priest in *Samson et Dalila* on October 17, 1964.

BADA, Angelo, tenor (1876–1941): born in Novara, Italy. Sang at La Scala, Milan, where he acquired a repertoire of character roles. He made his debut at the Metropolitan in 1908 as the Messenger in *Aïda*, and for thirty years thereafter he appeared in a vast number of character and secondary roles.

BAKOCEVIC, Radmila, soprano: born in Guca, Yugoslavia. Her operatic debut was as Mimi in *La Bohème* at the State Opera in Belgrade. She has appeared in the leading opera houses of Europe and South America. On April 5, 1968, she made her Metropolitan debut as Madama Butterfly. Her roles also include Violetta, Desdemona, Elizabeth (*Don Carlos*), Leonora (*La Forza del Destino*), Maria (*Simon Boccanegra*), Butterfly, Manon Lescaut, Norma, Marguerite (*Faust*), Nicaela, and Susanna (*Le Nozze di Figaro*).

BALDWIN, Marcia, mezzo-soprano: born in Moline, Illinois. She sang with the opera companies of Santa Fe, San Francisco, Cincinnati and Boston, then made her New York recital debut in 1959. Later she appeared on national television in the NBC Opera production of *Boris Godunof* with Giorgio Tozzi. Miss Baldwin made her Metropolitan debut as Javotte in *Manon* on Ocober 25, 1963. She was prominently cast in the Metropolitan's "Opera in the Park" series during the summer of 1968.

BAMPTON, Rose, soprano: born in Cleveland. Studied at the Curtis Institute, Philadelphia. Began her career as a mezzo-soprano, making her Metropolitan debut as Laura in *La Gioconda* on November 28, 1932. She later became a soprano and made history by singing both Aïda and Amneris in the same week. Her other Metropolitan roles included Donna Anna, Leonora (*Il Trovatore*), Alceste, Sieglinde, Elsa (*Lohengrin*), Kundry and Elisabeth (*Tannhäuser*). She married the conductor Wilfrid Pelletier.

BARBIERI, Fedora, mezzo-soprano: born in Trieste, where she began her musical training. She made her operatic debut as Fidalma in *Il Matrimonio Segreto* at the Teatro Communale in Florence in November 1940, and has since appeared in all the world's major opera houses. She made her debut at the Metropolitan as Princess Eboli in *Don Carlos* on November 6, 1950. Her other roles include Amneris, Santuzza, Laura (*La Gioconda*), Adalgisa (*Norma*), Carmen and Dame Quickly (*Falstaff*).

BARDINI, Gaetano, tenor: born in Riparbella, Italy. In 1956 he won the Medaglia d'Oro in the competition in Rome and thereafter appeared in the major opera houses of Europe. His roles include Rodolpho (*La Bohème*), Radames, Andrea Chénier, Cavaradossi and Osaka in *Iris*. For his Metropolitan debut, Bardini replaced Franco Corelli as Dick Johnson in *La Fanciulla del West* in Acts Two and Three on January 17, 1966. Bardini sang the same role (again as a replacement—this time for an indisposed Robert Nagy) in the acoustical test performance of *Fanciulla* on the afternoon of April 11, 1966—the first performance given on the stage of the new opera house at Lincoln Center.

BARIONI, Daniele, tenor: born in Copparo, Italy. Studied in Milan and made his debut there as Turiddu at the Teatro Nuovo in 1954. He subsequently sang in Florence, Mexico City, Cairo and Johannesburg. He made an auspicious Metropolitan debut as Cavaradossi on February 20, 1956.

BARRIENTOS, Maria, coloratura soprano (1884–1946): born in Barcelona, Spain. She was one of the reigning coloraturas at the Metropolitan from 1916 to 1920. Her debut was as Lucia di Lammermoor, on January 31, 1916. She later starred at the Met in revivals of *Le Coq d'Or*, *Lakmé* and *I Puritani*.

BASTIANINI, Ettore, baritone (1922–67): born in Siena, Italy. Made his debut in the bass role of Colline (*La Bohème*) at Ravenna, Italy, in 1945. He created the role of Prince Andrei in the first stage performance of Prokofiev's *War and Peace* in 1953. Made his Metropolitan debut as Germont on December 5, 1953, with outstanding success. One of his greatest roles was that of Gérard in *Andrea Chénier*. He sang his last performance as Rodrigo in *Don Carlos* at the Metropolitan on December 11, 1965. Stricken with cancer of the vocal cords, Bastianini died in Sirmione, Italy, after a career of more than twenty years, with a repertoire of forty-three roles.

BATTISTINI, Mattia, baritone (1857–1928): born in Rome. Many critics claimed that he had the most beautiful voice of any baritone in history. He sang about eighty roles in the principal opera houses of Europe and in the last years of the nineteenth century appeared at Covent Garden, where his Don Giovanni and Rigoletto were ecstatically cheered. After one trip to South America, he swore never to cross an ocean again, and so he never appeared at the Metropolitan or in any opera house in North America.

BAUERMEISTER, Mathilde, soprano (1849–1926): born in Hamburg, Germany. Probably the most famous operatic *seconda* in history (at least until the time of Thelma Votipka), she was sponsored at her debut at Covent Garden in 1865 by the great soprano Therese Tietjens, and at her farewell there in 1905 by Dame Nellie Melba. She alternated between Covent Garden and the Metropolitan, making sixteen crossings to America in all. She sang all the nurses, maids, duennas and ladies in waiting and sometimes went on in emergencies for the star.

BAUM, Kurt, dramatic tenor: native of Prague, Czechoslovakia. Developed his career in the opera houses of Europe. Made his Metropolitan debut as the Singer in *Der Rosenkavalier* on November 27, 1941. Noted for his powerful voice and ringing top tones. Was a member of the Metropolitan for many years as a leading dramatic tenor. Best known as Manrico in *Il Trovatore*.

BENZELL, Mimi, coloratura soprano: born in Bridgeport, Connecticut. Made her Metropolitan debut in the difficult role of the Queen of the Night in Mozart's *Die Zauberflöte* on January 5, 1945. Successful in other coloratura roles such as Philine (*Mignon*), Susanna (*Le Nozze di Figaro*) and Gilda. Her voice was noted for the brilliance of the upper range. In the years before her death in December 1970, Miss Benzell had established a successful career in radio as a commentator on a variety of subjects of interest to women.

BERGANZA, Teresa, Lyric mezzo-soprano: born in Madrid, where she was first heard in public as a recitalist. She made her operatic debut in America (after appearing in the leading opera houses of Europe) in Dallas in the role of Isabella in Rossini's *L'Italiana in Algeri*. Miss Berganza joined the Metropolitan in 1967. Her voice is distinctive as a type of "mezzo coloratura." She is the youngest artist ever to be honored by the Spanish government as "Dame of the Most Noble Order of Isabella La Católica."

BERGER, Erna, coloratura soprano: born in Dresden, Germany. Became one of the leading artists of the Dresden State Opera and later sang in opera houses throughout Europe and in England. Made her debut at the Metropolitan on November 21, 1949, in the season's opening performance, as Sophie in *Der Rosenkavalier*. She won high praise for her musicianship and dramatic talent. Two of her best roles were Gilda and the Queen of the Night. She now teaches in Hamburg.

BERGLUND, Joel, bass-baritone: native of Sweden. Was well known as a Wagnerian singer. Made debut at the Metropolitan as Hans Sachs on January 9, 1946; was also impressive as Wotan. Following his career at the Metropolitan he returned to Sweden and became the impresario of the Stockholm Opera.

BERGONZI, Carlo, dramatic tenor: native of Polesine Parmense, Italy. Currently one of the leading dramatic tenors of the Metropolitan, he has been with the company since his debut as Radames on November 13, 1956. Outstanding in such roles as Andrea Chénier, Canio, Rodolpho, Don Carlos, Edgardo, Pinkerton, Manrico and Ernani which he was scheduled to sing at the opening-night performance of the Metropolitan's 1970–71 season.

BERRY, Walter, baritone: born in Vienna. He is internationally renowned as an interpreter of operatic roles and also as a concert artist. He is famous as the Dyer in *Die Frau ohne Schatten*, and sang this role at his Metropolitan debut on October 2, 1966. He also excels in the roles of Wotan, Baron Ochs, Telramund, Leporello and Wozzeck.

BIBLE, Frances, mezzo-soprano: born in Sackets Harbor, New York. Studied at the Juilliard School of Music and has had an outstanding career as one of the leading singers of the New York City Opera Company. She sings a wide variety of roles, including Cenerentola, Lucretia (*Rape of Lucretia*), Dorabella (*Così Fan Tutte*), and Elizabeth Proctor (*The Crucible*), Augusta Tabor (*The Ballad of Baby Doe*) and Octavian.

BISPHAM, David, dramatic baritone (1857–1921): born in Philadelphia. Counted among the leading singers of the later Golden Age. Began his career as a choir singer and a specialist in oratorio; his repertoire included one hundred oratorio parts. From 1891 he appeared at Covent Garden and at the Metropolitan and was heard in fifty operatic roles. He made his Metropolitan debut as Alberich (*Siegfried*) on December 30, 1896. In this performance with a cast headed by Jean De Reszke, Dame Nellie Melba made her disastrous attempt to sing Brünnhilde. Bispham toured with Lillian Nordica in concert. In 1909 he retired from the operatic stage to sing in concert and to teach.

BJONER, Ingrid, dramatic soprano: native of Norway. She made her debut in Oslo in 1957 as Donna Anna. Subsequently she sang leading roles at the Vienna Staatsoper, the Berlin Städtische Oper, the Hamburg Opera and Bayreuth. Miss Bjoner made her American debut as Elsa in *Lohengrin* in San Francisco in 1960, and her Metropolitan debut in the same role on October 28, 1961.

BJÖRLING, Jussi, dramatic tenor (1911–60): native of Sweden. Studied at the Royal Opera School in Stockholm and made his debut at the Stockholm Opera in 1930 as Don Ottavio in *Don Giovanni*. International success followed rapidly. He was acclaimed in all the great tenor roles. At the height of his career he was recognized as one of the finest singers in contemporary operatic history; his voice was characterized by Caruso's widow as the closest to her husband's in quality. He made his Metropolitan debut as Rodolpho (*La Bohème*) on November 24, 1938. His final appearance was as Turiddu on December 22, 1959. He died suddenly in Stockholm on September 9, 1960.

BOHNEN, Michael, basso (1887–1965): born in Cologne, Germany. Studied at the Cologne Conservatory, made his operatic debut in *Der Freischütz* in Düsseldorf. He then sang in Berlin, Bayreuth, London, Vienna, Barcelona and Stockholm. He made his Metropolitan debut as Francesco in Max von Schillings' *Mona Lisa* on March 1, 1923. He left the Metropolitan at the end of the 1931–32 season. A gifted singing actor, Bohnen was particularly effective in the roles of Gurnemanz, Hagen and Wotan, and his portrayal of Caspar in *Der Freischütz* was considered a classic.

BOKY, Colette, soprano: native of Montreal. In 1962 the Academy of Music of the Province of Quebec awarded her the "Prize of Europe for Singing." She has sung with the Vienna Volksoper, the Bremen Opera, the Munich Opera, at the Odeon Theater in Paris, the Geneva Opera and the Salzburg Festival. In 1964 she sang the role of Mistress Ford in the filmed version of *The Merry Wives of Windsor*. With the Canadian Opera Company at Expo 67, she sang the four soprano roles in *Les Contes d'Hoffmann*. She joined the Metropolitan in 1967.

BONCI, Alessandro, lyric tenor (1870–1940): born in Cesena, Italy. Started singing as a boy soprano in a choir at the age of seven. Made his operatic debut in *Falstaff*. From 1900 he sang at Covent Garden and at the Manhattan Opera House. A lyric tenor, he sang a high D with ease. He was an Italian contemporary of Caruso's. Bonci made his Metropolitan debut as the Duke in *Rigoletto* on November 22, 1907.

BONELLI, Richard, baritone: born in Port Byron, New York. Made his operatic debut as Valentin in *Faust* in 1915, then sang with the San Carlo Opera Company in America, La Scala in Milan, and in German opera houses. From 1925 to 1931 he was a member of the Chicago Civic Opera Company. He made his Metropolitan debut as Germont in *La Traviata* on December 1, 1932. He sang leading roles with the company until 1945.

BORG, Kim, baritone: native of Finland. Made his debut at the Royal Opera of Copenhagen as Colline in *La Bohème*. Frequently appears in European festivals, and is best known for his interpretations of King Marke, Count Almaviva in *Le Nozze di Figaro*, Amfortas and Golaud. On January 30, 1960, he made his Metropolitan debut as King Marke.

BORGIOLI, Dino, tenor (1891–1960): born in Florence, Italy. A fine *tenore di grazia*, he was also successful as an impresario, managing an opera company in London, where he was a noted teacher in the last years of his life. He sang Cavaradossi in *Tosca* in the performance that opened the War Memorial Opera House in San Francisco on October 15, 1932. He sang regularly with the Chicago Opera and for one season at the Metropolitan. His debut there was as Rodolfo in *La Bohème* on December 31, 1934.

BORI, Lucrezia, lyric soprano (1880–1960): born in Valencia, Spain, a descendant of Italy's Borgia family. She was famous for her roles of Mimi, Cio-cio-san, Violetta, Mélisande and Manon. She made her debut as Micaela at the Teatro Costanzi, Rome, in 1908. Her first New York appearance was in *Manon Lescaut* on the opening night (November 11) of the 1912–13 season at the Metropolitan. She retired in 1936 at the age of forty-eight, then devoted herself to fund-raising activities in behalf of the Metropolitan.

BORKH, Inge, soprano: born in Mannheim, Germany. Studied at the Reinhardt School, the Vienna Academy, and also in Italy; made her operatic debut in Switzerland. She has sung in the principal opera houses of Italy, Germany, England and Portugal. In 1953 she made her American debut as Elektra with the San Francisco Opera Company, then followed with her Metropolitan debut as Salome on January 24, 1958. In 1955 she had created leading roles in Respighi's *Fiamma* at La Scala and Werner Egk's *Irish Legend* at the Salzburg Festival. At the Cincinnati May Festival she sang the title role in the American premiere of Benjamin Britten's *Gloriana* on May 8, 1956.

BOTTCHER, Ron, baritone: born in Sandpoint, Idaho. Has sung leading roles with the New York City Opera, the American Opera Society and the Santa Fe Opera. He made his debut with the Santa Fe Opera in 1961 and toured Europe with that company. He appeared with the Metropolitan National Opera Company before coming to the Metropolitan in 1967. His roles include Sharpless in *Madama Butterfly* and Morales in *Carmen*.

BOUCHER, Gene, baritone: native of Missouri. He began his career with the St. Louis Municipal Opera Company. Studied in France on a Fulbright Fellowship, then in 1958 won the American Opera Auditions. He made his Metropolitan debut as the Master of Ceremonies in *Pique-Dame* on September 28, 1965.

BOWER, Beverly, soprano: native of Olean, New York. Began her career as a coloratura, subsequently shifted to more dramatic roles under the tutelage of Helen Jepson. She has sung Tosca at the Vienna Staatsoper and Minnie in *La Fanciulla del West* at the Central City (Colorado) Opera Festival. She has made extensive appearances with the New York City Opera, the Santa Fe Opera and the Vancouver Opera, in addition to singing scores of concerts. She was the first soprano to sing a leading role in the New Metropolitan at Lincoln Center, singing the role of Minnie in an acoustical test performance on April 11, 1966.

BRANDT, Marianne, mezzo-soprano (1842–1921): born in Vienna; real name Marie Bischof. A pupil of Pauline Viardot-García, she was a star of the Berlin Hofoper and in 1882 at Bayreuth was one of the three singers who alternated as Kundry in the original production of *Parsifal*. She sang at the Metropolitan from 1886 to 1890 and was the first to sing Fidelio and Amneris there. She also sang Magdalene in *Die Meistersinger* and Brangäne in *Tristan und Isolde* at the American premieres of these operas.

BRANZELL, Karin, mezzo-soprano: born in Stockholm. In 1919 she joined the Berlin Staatsoper. As one of Gatti-Casazza's discoveries, she made her Metropolitan debut as Fricka in *Die Walküre* on February

6, 1924. She sang there for twenty-two consecutive seasons, and was known for her ability to sing roles in the German, French and Italian repertoire with equal facility.

BRASLAU, Sophie, soprano (1892–1935): born in New York City. Made her debut at the Metropolitan on November 25, 1913, as Feodor in *Boris Godunof,* and was a member of the company for seven years. She sang extensively in concerts with leading orchestras touring Scandinavia, the Netherlands and England.

BRILL, Phyllis, soprano: born in Long Beach, California. Graduate of the University of California, where she was technical assistant to Carl Ebert (stage director). Her roles include Ariadne, Pamina, Marie (*The Bartered Bride*), Lady Billow (*Albert Herring*), Turandot and Donna Anna. She has concertized in the Far East, the Middle East and Europe.

BROOKS, Patricia, soprano: born in New York City. One of the leading singers of the New York City Opera Company, she began her career there as Mistress Marianne in *Der Rosenkavalier* in 1960. A versatile artist, her other roles include Sophie in *Der Rosenkavalier,* Abigail in *The Crucible,* Violetta, Manon, Nedda and Gilda. She also appeared as an actress in off-Broadway productions of *The Iceman Cometh* and *The Grass Harp.* She is the wife of Theodore Mann, New York theatrical producer and director.

BROUWENSTIJN, Gré, soprano: born in Den Helder, Holland. The reigning star of the Amsterdam Opera, she has sung with the San Francisco Opera and became a popular guest artist at Covent Garden, where she first sang as Amelia in *Un Ballo in Maschera* in 1953. She also has sung regularly in Stuttgart, Vienna and Rome. At Covent Garden she has been acclaimed as Aïda, Fidelio, Leonora (*Il Trovatore*), Elizabeth (*Don Carlos*) and Desdemona. In 1959 she sang the title role in *Jenufa* with the Chicago Lyric Opera.

BROWNLEE, John, baritone (1901–69): born in Australia. He was discovered by Dame Nellie Melba and went to England. He sang at Melba's Covent Garden farewell on June 8, 1926. Made his Metropolitan debut as Rigoletto on February 17, 1937, and remained with the company until 1954. He subsequently became director of the Manhattan School of Music.

BRUSON, Renato, baritone: born in Padua, Italy. Made his operatic debut at Spoleto as Count di Luna (*Il Trovatore*) in 1961. On Saturday,

February 1, 1969 (matinee), he made his Metropolitan debut as Lord Enrico Ashton (*Lucia di Lammermoor*). Other roles include Macbeth, Rigoletto, Simon Boccanegra, Germont (*La Traviata*), Rodrigo (*Don Carlos*), Valentin (*Faust*).

BUZEA, Ion, tenor: born in Cluj, Romania. Made his operatic debut with the Cluj Opera in 1959, and subsequently became a member of the Vienna Staatsoper, the Vienna Volksoper and the Zurich Opera. He was first heard in America in April 1969 in the role of Pedro in D'Albert's *Tiefland* with the American Opera Society at Carnegie Hall. On January 6, 1970, he made his Metropolitan debut with outstanding success in the role of Rodolpho in *La Bohème*.

BUMBRY, Grace, mezzo-soprano: native of St. Louis. A protégée of Lotte Lehmann's, she joined the Metropolitan on October 7, 1965, in the role of Princess Eboli in *Don Carlos*, and her debut won high critical praise. She has appeared successfully in festivals at Bayreuth (where her "black Venus" in *Tannhäuser* attracted much attention) and Salzburg. Also outstanding in the role of Amneris, which she sang at La Scala and Covent Garden. She was acclaimed for her Carmen in the Metropolitan's new 1967 production.

CABALLÉ, Montserrat, soprano: native of Barcelona. In Europe, sang at La Scala, Gran Teatro in Barcelona, Basel Opera (three years), Berlin Staatsoper (two years): also at Glyndebourne and at Teatro Colon, Buenos Aires. Made her Metropolitan debut as Marguerite in *Faust* on December 22, 1965. First appearance in America was as substitute for Marilyn Horne in an American Opera Society concert performance of Donizetti's *Lucrezia Borgia* on April 20, 1965. She has mastered forty-six roles in Italian, German, French and Spanish. Roles range from Marguerite in *Faust* and Desdemona to Elizabeth in Donizetti's *Roberto Devereux*, Bellini's *La Straniera*, Mimi, Madeleine in *Andrea Chénier* and *Pamina*. Also sings roles in contemporary operas such as Prokofiev's *Flaming Angel*, Hindemith's *Cardillac* and Berg's *Lulu*. She once learned Leonora in *Il Trovatore* in German in less than two weeks. Miss Caballé is the wife of Bernabé Marti, tenor of the New York City Opera.

CALLAS, Maria, soprano: born in New York City; real name Anna Maria Cecilia Sophia Kalogeropoulos. She studied in Athens with Elvira de Hidalgo and first sang in opera there. Her international career began at the Arena in Verona, Italy, as La Gioconda on August 3, 1947. She is famous for the roles of Norma, Medea, Tosca, Lucia,

Lady Macbeth and Violetta. She sang Norma in Chicago and Dallas and for her Metropolitan debut, on the opening night of the season, on October 29, 1956, before an audience that paid $75,510 to be present. She is credited with the revival of interest in florid operatics, as exemplified by Donizetti and Bellini, and for the rediscovery of the dramatic elements of *bel canto* singing. Absent from the stage since 1964, she announced that she would return in 1970 in a Paris production of Menotti's *The Consul*. She has also made a non-operatic film of *Medea*.

CALVÉ, Emma, soprano (1858–1942): born in Aveyron, France; real name Rose Emma Calvet de Roquer. From a convent at Millau, France, she went out to begin her musical education at the age of fifteen. For a time she studied with Mustafà, one of the last of the great *castrati*, who taught her the mastery of the "fourth voice," a kind of disembodied tone. She sang for a number of years with indifferent success in Belgium, France and Italy, but was encouraged to continue her career by Victor Maurel, the renowned French bass-baritone. Another great influence in her life was Eleanora Duse. Massenet created for her the title roles in *La Navarraise* and *Sapho*. In 1892 she sang the first Santuzza in London, and made her Metropolitan debut in that role on November 29, 1893. She sang at the Metropolitan for thirteen consecutive years. Although she scored in such traditional roles as Lucia, Pamina, Amina, Ophelia (*Hamlet*), Marguerite and Juliet, her overwhelming success was as Carmen. She was considered the greatest Carmen of her time.

CAMPANINI, Italo, dramatic tenor (1846–96): born in Parma, Italy, where he was working as a blacksmith when his potentialities as a singer were discovered. Established as an artist, he toured Europe and the United States with Christine Nilsson and Adelina Patti. He sang in the first American performance of *Aïda* at the Academy of Music in New York City on November 26, 1873. He also sang Faust at the performance that inaugurated the Metropolitan Opera House on October 22, 1883.

CAMPORA, Giuseppe, tenor: born in Cortona, Italy. Made his operatic debut as Rodolpho in Bari, Italy, and later sang at the Rome Opera, La Scala and the San Carlo in Naples. He made his Metropolitan debut as Rodolpho, with Dorothy Kirsten as Mimi, on January 20, 1955.

CANIGLIA, Maria, soprano: born in Naples. Educated at the Royal Conservatory there and graduated in 1929. Made her operatic debut in *Elektra* in Turin in 1930, then sang for three seasons at La Scala.

Her Metropolitan debut was in the role of Desdemona on November 21, 1938, the opening performance of the season. Though she sang with the company for only one season, she was known to all opera lovers as one of the most popular stars in Italy.

CARELLI, Gabor, tenor: born in Budapest, Hungary. Auditioned for Gigli, who was much impressed and took Carelli on tour, then in 1938 arranged for his debut in Florence as Rodolpho in *La Bohème*. Carelli came to the United States and toured with the American Civic Opera for a year, singing 160 performances of *Il Barbiere di Siviglia*. At the Metropolitan, he made his debut as Don Curzio in *Le Nozze di Figaro* on November 17, 1951. He specializes in character roles.

CARLYLE, Joan, soprano: born in London. She began in small roles at Covent Garden but soon rose to stardom there, becoming one of the most popular English singers of the 1960s. Her roles at Covent Garden include the important soprano heroines in contemporary operas by Britten, Tippett and Poulenc, as well as Desdemona, Nedda, Micaela, Mimi, Countess Almaviva, Sophie and Arabella. She also has sung at La Scala.

CARSON, Clarice, soprano: born in Montreal. Received her musical training at the Toronto Conservatory of Music. In 1962 she made her operatic debut as the Mother in *Amahl and the Night Visitors*, and subsequently won scholarships at Les Amis de l'Art and the Quebec Music Festival. Roles include Tosca, Marguerite (*Faust*), Cio-cio-san, Manon, Mimi, Violetta, the Countess (*Le Nozze di Figaro*).

CARUSO, Enrico, dramatic tenor (1873–1921): born in Naples. Began his musical life as a contralto in the boy choir of the Church of San Severino. At twenty-one he made his operatic debut in a forgotten opera called *L'Amico Francesco* at the Teatro Nuovo in Naples. A year later, in 1895, he made his debut in standard opera as Turiddu, which later became one of his great roles. At twenty-five Caruso vaulted into world fame by creating the tenor lead in the world premiere of Giordano's *Fedora* at the Teatro Lirico in Milan. He made his debut at the Metropolitan as the Duke in *Rigoletto* on November 23, 1903. In eighteen seasons there he sang 607 times in thirty-seven different operas. His total repertoire included fifty roles. The last role he sang at the Metropolitan was that of Eleazar in *La Juive* on December 24, 1920. Stricken with pleurisy, he underwent a painful operation, then returned to Naples for a period of convalescence. Though seemingly on the road to recovery, his condition suddenly worsened and he died on August 2, 1921. Acknowledged as the most famous singer in operatic history, Caruso's voice has been preserved on more than 250 records. Offstage, he was a clever cartoonist, and published a book of his drawings.

CASE, Anna, soprano: born in Clinton, New Jersey. Sang with the Metropolitan from 1909 to 1916, appearing in the American premieres of *Boris Godunof* (1912) and *Der Rosenkavalier* (1913). She subsequently was successful as a concert singer and recitalist. She was the wife of Clarence H. Mackay, chairman of the board of the New York Philharmonic Symphony Society.

CASEI, Nedda, mezzo-soprano: native of Baltimore; born Casey. She studied at the Juilliard School of Music, won a scholarship and continued her studies in Milan. Following a series of engagements in Europe, she had a private audition with Leopold Stokowski, who chose her for the role of Jocasta in the 1959 Empire State Festival's *Oedipus Rex*. She made her formal operatic debut as Maddalena in *Rigoletto* in Brussels in 1960 and sang the same role in her Metropolitan debut on October 14, 1965. Her repertoire includes forty roles.

CASSEL, Walter, baritone: born in Council Bluffs, Iowa. He studied in New York, began his stage career at the Radio City Music Hall, then joined the New York City Opera Company. He made his Metropolitan debut as De Brétigny in *Manon* on December 12, 1942, subsequent to winning the Metropolitan Auditions. Two of his most impressive interpretations are Telramund and Scarpia. An accomplished actor as well as singer, he is ranked as one of the foremost American baritones. He created the role of Horace Tabor in Douglas Moore's *The Ballad of Baby Doe* at Central City, Colorado, in 1956 and with the New York City Opera in 1958.

CASSILLY, Richard, dramatic tenor: born in Washington, D.C. Began his professional career on Broadway, where he stepped from the chorus to take over the tenor lead in Gian-Carlo Menotti's *The Saint of Bleecker Street*. For the next eleven years he appeared as leading tenor of the New York City Opera. After several guest appearances with the Hamburg Staatsoper, he became a permanent member of the company in 1966. One of his major roles is Laca in Leos Janáček's *Jenufa*, in which he appeared when the Staatsoper visited New York in 1967. He also has sung Otello at Covent Garden.

CASTAGNA, Bruna, mezzo-soprano: born in Milan. First appeared in popular-priced opera in New York at the old Hippodrome, then made her debut as Amneris at the Metropolitan on March 2, 1936. During the decade of her career at the Metropolitan, she was considered one of the leading mezzos of the company's Italian wing. She sang with distinction the roles of Dame Quickly (*Falstaff*), Laura (*La Gioconda*), Ulrica (*Un Ballo in Maschera*), Adalgisa (*Norma*) and Carmen.

CASTEL, Nico, tenor: born in Lisbon, Portugal. Began musical education in Venezuela, studied in Germany and Italy, was graduated from Temple University, Philadelphia. Following New York Town Hall debut in 1958 as winner of the Winifred Cecil "Joy of Singing" contest, he was engaged by the Santa Fe Opera. Was a member of the New York City Opera Company for ten seasons, has sung more than a hundred roles. Made his Metropolitan debut as Don Basilio in *Le Nozze di Figaro* on March 30, 1970.

CAVALIERI, Lina, soprano (1874–1944): born in Rome. Made her debut as Nedda in *Pagliacci* in Lisbon in 1900. Appeared in the first performances at the Metropolitan of Giordano's *Fedora* (1906), Puccini's *Manon Lescaut* (1907) and Cilèa's *Adriana Lecouvreur* (1907)—all with Caruso. A strikingly beautiful woman, she was known as much for her romantic escapades as for her voice.

CEHANOVSKY, George, baritone: born in in St. Petersburg, he made his operatic debut there as Valentin in *Faust*. He joined the Metropolitan for the 1926–27 season (his debut was as the Mandarin in *Turandot* on November 16) and sang with the company every season until he ended his brilliant career as a character actor in 1966. He established the record for longest continuous service by a featured singer at the Metropolitan. By actual count, he sang eighty character roles there between 1926 and 1953. The total number for his entire career probably is close to a hundred. His farewell appearance was at the gala concert that closed the old opera house on April 16, 1966. Mr. Cehanovsky married the famous soprano Elisabeth Rethberg.

CERNEI, Elena, mezzo-soprano: native of Bucharest, Romania. Graduated from the Bucharest Conservatory in 1955. She joined the Bucharest Opera and Ballet Theater in 1962 and appeared with that organization and the Bucharest Philharmonic more than 350 times. Her first appearance at the Metropolitan was as Dalila on March 17, 1965. Her roles include Carmen, Azucena, Amneris, Octavian, Kneaghina (*Russalka*), the Countess (*Pique-Dame*) and Adalgisa.

CHALIAPIN, Feodor, basso (1873–1938): born in Kazan, he was the first Russian singer to establish an international reputation. Singing the standard roles of Méphistophélès, Don Quixote, Leporello and Don Basilio, he first appeared outside Russia in Milan in 1901 and in Monte Carlo in 1904. He made his Metropolitan debut as Mefistofele in Boito's opera on November 20, 1907. He first appeared in his greatest role, Boris Godunof, in Paris in 1908, when Diaghilev brought the Moussorgsky opera to that city. His interpretation of the role was unprecedented and has never been surpassed. He sang Boris at the Metropolitan, Covent Garden and many other opera houses, making his last appearance in the role in Paris in 1938, the year of his death. He wrote several books and was celebrated as a caricaturist and for his brilliant impersonations.

CHAMLEE, Mario, tenor (1892–1967): born in Los Angeles; real name Archer Chalmondeley. Studied violin during his early years and did not consider singing until he was twenty. He came to the attention of the basso Antonio Scotti, who engaged him for his own company and introduced him to Gatti-Casazza. He made his Metropolitan debut as Cavaradossi on November 22, 1920, and sang with the company from then until 1926, and from 1935 to 1939. Following his retirement from the operatic stage, he opened a vocal studio in Hollywood with his wife, Metropolitan soprano Ruth Miller.

CHOOKASIAN, Lili, contralto: born in Chicago. Launched her operatic career as the result of an audition with Rosa Ponselle, with whom she studied. In 1960 Miss Chookasian made her debut as Azucena with the Baltimore Civic Opera; she also sang Amneris with that company. She was first heard in New York in 1961 when she sang the solo part in Prokofiev's *Alexander Nevsky* with the New York Philharmonic. On March 9, 1962, she made an impressive debut at the Metropolitan as La Cieca in *La Gioconda*. Prior to her operatic career, Miss Chookasian was a member of the voice faculty at Northwestern University.

CHRISTOFF, Boris, basso: native of Bulgaria. Was to make his Metropolitan debut in 1950 in the role of King Philip II in *Don Carlos*, but immigration laws prohibited his coming to the United States. Later, on two separate occasions, negotiations were opened for his appearance as King Philip, but his stipulations as to rehearsal schedules reportedly could not be met by the Metropolitan. Mr. Christoff sings extensively in Europe; one of his greatest roles is Boris Godunof. He has sung with the Chicago Lyric Opera and made one New York appearance with the American Opera Society in a concert performance of Rossini's *Moses*.

CHRISTOPHER, Russell, baritone: born in Grand Rapids, Michigan. Received his music degrees at the University of Michigan, then joined the New York City Opera Company. He has been on the Metropolitan roster since 1963 and has sung more than four hundred performances.

CIGNA, Gina, dramatic soprano: of French-Italian ancestry; real name Genoffeva Sens. Studied piano and voice at the Paris Conservatory, and in 1930 became a member of La Scala. In Milan she created the title role in Respighi's *La Fiamma*. She made her Metropolitan debut on February 6, 1936, as Aïda. During her single season with the company, she also sang Norma, La Gioconda, Donna Elvira and Leonora in *Il Trovatore*. Her career continued in Italy, where she was very popular.

CIONI, Renato, tenor: born on the island of Elba. A pupil of the great baritone Titta Ruffo, he made his opera debut at Spoleto in 1959. Since then he has become particularly successful in the Donizetti-Bellini repertoire and has sung opposite Callas, Tebaldi, Price, Sutherland and Suliotis. In America he has sung often with the San Francisco and Chicago Lyric Opera companies and during the 1968 Lincoln Center Festival appeared with the Rome Opera Company at the Metropolitan in Verdi's *I Due Foscari*. He made his Metropolitan debut as Pollione in *Norma* on the last night of the 1969–70 season, April 18.

CLAUSSEN, Julia, contralto (1879–1941): born in Stockholm. Made her operatic debut at the Royal Stockholm Opera in 1903. From 1912 to 1917 she was a member of the Chicago Civic Opera Company. She made her Metropolitan debut as Dalila to Caruso's Samson on November 23, 1917. She remained with the company for a number of years, mainly in Wagnerian roles.

CLEMENTS, Joy, lyric soprano: born in Dayton, Ohio. Studied at Philadelphia's Academy of Vocal Arts, then joined the New York City Opera, where she was a leading soprano for a number of seasons. She made her Metropolitan debut as the Countess Ceprano in *Rigoletto* on October 23, 1963.

COCHRAN, William, tenor: born in Philadelphia. Studied there at the Curtis Institute. On March 29, 1968, he was a semifinalist (with mezzo-soprano Judith Forst) in the Regional Auditions of the Metropolitan Opera National Council and a winner of the Liederkranz Society

Auditions. Impressed by his voice, Rudolf Bing gave him a Metropolitan contract. One of his first roles was that of Vogelgesang in *Die Meister-singer*.

COLLIER, Marie, dramatic soprano: native of Ballarat, Australia, of Italian-English parents. Began her career with National Theater in Melbourne. In July 1965 she replaced Maria Callas as Tosca at Covent Garden, where she had been the leading soprano for almost a decade. She has appeared in most of the world's leading opera houses. She created the title role of Shostakovich's *Katerina Ismailova* (the revised version of *Lady Macbeth of Mzensk*) in its Western premiere, and also sang the role in the American premiere of the opera with the San Francisco Opera Company in 1964. There also she sang in the American premiere of Janáček's *The Makropoulos Case*. She made a spectacular debut at the Metropolitan as Christine Mannon in David Levy's *Mourning Becomes Electra* on March 17, 1967.

COLZANI, Anselmo, baritone: native of Italy. Made his Metropolitan debut in the title role of *Simon Boccanegra* with Renata Tebaldi on March 7, 1960. He appears frequently in other standard baritone roles, including Falstaff, Amonasro, Nabucco, Barnaba, Rigoletto, Scarpia, Jack Rance and Macbeth.

CONLEY, Eugene, tenor: born in Lynn, Massachusetts. Made his operatic debut in 1941 as the Duke in *Rigoletto* with the Salmaggi Opera Company in New York. In 1942 he toured with Fortune Gallo's San Carlo Company; in 1947 he sang leading roles with the Paris Opéra-Comique. He later appeared in Florence, Turin and Stockholm, and sang *I Puritani* in Milan. For several seasons he was a leading tenor with the New York City Opera. He made his Metropolitan debut as Faust on January 23, 1950, and was Tom Rakewell in the American premiere of Stravinsky's *The Rake's Progress* on February 14, 1953.

CONNER, Nadine, soprano: born in Compton, California. She made her name in radio before making her Metropolitan debut as Pamina in *Die Zauberflöte* on December 22, 1941. She sang her last performance there as Marguerite in *Faust* on March 12, 1960. Though her voice was light, she was an appealing figure onstage and enjoyed popularity in such roles as Pamina, Lauretta (*Gianni Schicchi*), Zerlina (*Don Giovanni*) and Gretel (*Hänsel und Gretel*).

CORELLI, Franco, dramatic tenor: born in Ancona, Italy. Was twenty-three before he considered singing as a career. It began when a friend entered his name in an amateur contest as a joke. He won this contest, and later also won the biggest competition in Italy at Spoleto with his rendition of "Celeste Aïda." In 1953 he was starring at the Rome Opera; the following year he appeared opposite Maria Callas at La Scala. He made his Metropolitan debut as Manrico in *Il Trovatore* on January 27, 1961. Corelli says he has never had a voice lesson. Although he has figured in several temperamental outbursts onstage, he is a serious, disciplined artist and is considered one of the world's leading tenors.

CORENA, Fernando, basso: born in Geneva of Turkish-Italian descent. Called the finest *buffo* singing actor since Salvatore Baccaloni, he made his Metropolitan debut as Leporello in *Don Giovanni* on February 6, 1954. His wide repertoire includes Dr. Bartolo in *Il Barbiere di Siviglia* and *Le Nozze di Figaro*, Don Pasquale, Dr. Dulcamara in *L'Elisir d'Amore*, Lescaut in *Manon*, the Sacristan in *Tosca*, Geronte in *Manon Lescaut*, Fra Melitone in *La Forza del destino*, Gianni Schicchi, Varlaam in *Boris Godunof* and Falstaff.

COSSA, Dominic, baritone: born in Jessup, Pennsylvania. A member of the New York City Opera Company with a repertoire of more than twenty-five roles, which include Figaro, Valentin (*Faust*), Germont (*La Traviata*) and Rigoletto. He has won major awards of the Metropolitan National Council Auditions, Liederkranz Society of New York, Artists Advisory Council and American Opera Auditions. He made his Metropolitan debut as Silvio in *Pagliacci* on January 30, 1970.

COSSOTTO, Fiorenza, mezzo-soprano: born near Vercelli, in the province of Piedmont in northern Italy. Began studying singing at the age of fifteen and received her diploma at the Turin Conservatory. In 1956 she won first place in the competition for study as apprentice singer at La Scala. She was taken into the company and in the first five years there she sang some twenty-four secondary roles. In January 1962 she sang her first leading role at La Scala. On short notice, she replaced Giulietta Simionato, who had become ill, in the role of Leonora in Donizetti's *La Favorita*, playing opposite her husband, basso Ivo Vinco, who was singing Baldassare. Subsequently, the husband-and-wife team appeared as Princess Eboli and King Philip, Rosina and Basilio, Amneris and Ramfis and Azucena and Ferrando. Miss Cossotto made her Metropolitan debut as Amneris on February 6, 1968. Though primarily a mezzo, her voice encompasses the soprano ranges.

COSTA, Mary, soprano: native of Knoxville, Tennessee. She made an impressive debut at the Metropolitan as Violetta on January 6, 1964. A striking blonde, she also scored in other romantic roles such as Manon, Vanessa, Marguerite (*Faust*) and Alice Ford (*Falstaff*).

CRAIN, Jon, tenor: native of St. Louis. Studied at the Juilliard School of Music and with Paul Althouse, Paul Breisach and Enrico Rosati. Toured with the Charles L. Wagner Opera Company and as tenor lead in the Metropolitan's touring company of *Die Fledermaus*. He then joined the New York City Opera Company and was a leading tenor there for more than five years. At the Metropolitan, he appeared as Matteo in Strauss's *Arabella* on January 7, 1957, and later that season as Narraboth in *Salome*.

CRESPIN, Régine, soprano: born in Marseilles of French and Italian parentage. After training at the Paris Conservatory, she rose to fame at the Paris Opéra, the Bayreuth Festival, the Glyndebourne Festival and Covent Garden. With the San Francisco Opera, she sang Dido in the first American stage performance of Berlioz's *Les Troyens*. Her Metropolitan debut was as the Marschallin in *Der Rosenkavalier* on November 19, 1962. Her other roles there include Tosca, Amelia in *Un Ballo in Maschera*, both Sieglinde and Brünnhilde in *Die Walküre*, Senta in *Der Fliegende Holländer* and Kundry in *Parsifal*.

CROOKS, Richard, lyric tenor: born in Trenton, New Jersey. Started his career as a choir singer and later developed into an outstanding concert artist, touring the United States, Great Britain, Scandinavia and Central Europe. First major operatic appearance was as Cavardossi with the Hamburg Opera in 1927. At his Metropolitan debut on February 25, 1933, as Des Grieux in *Manon*, he scored one of the greatest personal triumphs ever won by a singer at the Metropolitan. He remained in the company for ten seasons.

CRUZ-ROMO, Gilda, soprano: native of Mexico. Won a scholarship to the National Conservatory of Music in Mexico in 1960. Made her operatic debut in 1962 with the International Opera Company in Mexico, appeared in the United States with the Dallas Civic Opera in 1966–68. Made her debut with the New York City Opera Company on October 5, 1959, as Margherita and Elena in *Mefistofele*. In 1970 she was the sole winner of a Metropolitan Opera contract in the annual Metropolitan Opera Auditions, also the winner of the $2500 Madame Lilliana Teruzzi Award. She was chosen by the Metropolitan Opera National Council to represent the U.S.A. in the second international *Madama Butterfly* contest held in May–June 1970 in Tokyo, Osaka, and Nagasaki.

CURTIN, Phyllis, soprano: native of Clarksburg, West Virginia. Rose to prominence at the New York City Opera, where she made her debut as Salome. On November 4, 1961, she made her Metropolitan debut as Fiordiligi in *Così Fan Tutte*. She also has sung at La Scala and at the Vienna Staatsoper, as well as with many major symphony orchestras. Her other Metropolitan roles include Eva in *Die Meistersinger* and Rosalinde in *Die Fledermaus*.

CURTIS-VERNA, Mary, soprano: born in Salem, Massachusetts. As Mary Curtis, she sang leading roles with the New York City Opera Company. She then went to Italy for study, and there married the vocal coach Ettore Verna. She made her Metropolitan debut as Leonora in *Il Trovatore* on February 13, 1957, and appeared there in the roles of Donna Anna, Tosca, Maria (*Simon Boccanegra*), Santuzza, Madeleine (*Andrea Chénier*), Aïda, Turandot, Adriana Lecouvreur, Gutrune, Elizabeth (*Don Carlos*) and Alice Ford.

CVEJIC, Biserka, mezzo-soprano: born in Jesenice, Yugoslavia. Made her Metropolitan debut as Amneris on April 14, 1962, and subsequently appeared as Princess de Bouillon (*Adriana Lecouvreur*), Princess Eboli and Azucena. She is a regular member of the Vienna Staatsoper.

DALIS, Irene, mezzo-soprano: native of San Jose, California. Went to Europe in 1952 on a Fulbright grant. On March 16, 1957, she made her Metropolitan debut as Princess Eboli in *Don Carlos*. Her other roles include Brangäne, Dalila, Lady Macbeth, Kundry, Fricka and Amneris.

DALLA RIZZA, Gilda, soprano: born in Verona, Italy. She made her professional debut as Charlotte in Massenet's *Werther*. She was the first Magda in Puccini's *La Rondine* (Monte Carlo, March 27, 1917); Liù, in *Turandot*, was written for her. After a forty-year career she retired to her home in Bassano del Grappa, near Venice.

D'ALVAREZ, Marguerite, mezzo-soprano (1886–1953): born in Liverpool, England. A handsome singing actress, she was one of the stars of Oscar Hammerstein's Manhattan Opera House, where she made her debut as Fidès in *Le Prophète* on August 30, 1909. She later sang with the Chicago Opera until 1922. Her best role was Dalila.

DANCO, Suzanne, soprano: born in Brussels, Belgium. In 1936 she won the International Bel Canto Prize at Venice. Though she sang in opera at Covent Garden and in continental opera houses, she was best known as a major concert artist and in America made a particularly strong impression in the music of Berlioz. She recorded a number of Mozart roles, in which she was specially distinctive.

D'ANGELO, Gianna, soprano: born Jane Angelovitch in Hartford, Connecticut. Made her Metropolitan debut as Gilda on April 15, 1962; appeared later as Lucia, Zerbinetta in *Ariadne auf Naxos*, the Queen of the Night, Norina in *Don Pasquale* and Rosina in *Il Barbiere di Siviglia*.

D'ANGELO, Louis, baritone (1888–1958): born in Naples, Italy. Was first heard in America as a member of the Henry Savage Opera Company in its production of *La Fanciulla del West*. A versatile singing actor, he specialized in comedy characterizations and sang more than three hundred roles. He was first heard at the Metropolitan in the cast of Meyerbeer's *Le Prophète* on February 7, 1918. He remained in the company until 1936, singing a great variety of character roles, sometimes more than one in the same opera.

DARCY, Emory, tenor: born in Chicago. First appeared at the Metropolitan on December 6, 1941, as the Messenger in *Samson et Dalila*. On December 12, 1941, he sang two roles in *Tristan und Isolde*—the offstage sailor's voice and the onstage Melot. Developing his voice as a heldentenor, he later made a good impression as Parsifal during the 1943–44 season, and subsequently sang Siegfried.

DAVY, Gloria, soprano: born in Brooklyn, New York. She studied at the High School of Music and Art and the Juilliard School in New York. She made her operatic debut in Nice as Aïda and again sang the role at her Metropolitan debut on February 12, 1958. During her one Metropolitan season she also appeared as Nedda and Pamina. She then returned to Europe, where she has since sung with the Berlin Deutsche Oper and other prominent companies.

DE HIDALGO, Elvira, coloratura soprano: Spanish by birth, French by marriage and Milanese by adoption. At the age of fifteen she made her operatic debut as Rosina in *Il Barbiere di Siviglia* at the Teatro San Carlo in Naples. At seventeen she made her debut (billed as a "child star") in Paris in the same role, in a cast with Feodor Chaliapin and Titta Ruffo. Immediately engaged for the Metropolitan, she made her debut there, again as Rosina, on March 7, 1910. She did not appear there again until the 1924–25 season, when she sang Rosina and Gilda. During World War II she taught at the Athens Conservatory, where her best pupil was a fourteen-year-old girl named Maria Callas, whose future career she guided.

DE LOS ANGELES, Victoria, soprano: native of Barcelona. Studied in Spain, then made her operatic debut as Countess Almaviva in *Le Nozze di Figaro* in Madrid. Sang at the Paris Opéra, Covent Garden and La Scala. Made her Metropolitan debut as Marguerite in *Faust* on March 17, 1951. Outstanding in roles such as Cio-cio-san, Mimi, Eva (*Die Meistersinger*), Manon, Micaela, Violetta and Mélisande. Her final performances at the Metropolitan were as Mimi and as Lady Harriet in *Martha* in April 1961.

DE LUCA, Giuseppe, baritone (1876–1950): born in Rome. Was an accomplished boy soprano and sang at St. Peter's. He made his debut at the age of twenty-one as Valentin in *Faust* in Piacenza, Italy. Later, at the Teatro Lirico in Milan, he sang in the world premiere of *Adriana Lecouvreur* under the baton of Arturo Toscanini, with Caruso in the cast. He joined La Scala in 1904 and sang in the world premiere of *Madama Butterfly*. On November 25, 1915, he made his Metropolitan debut as Figaro in *Il Barbiere di Siviglia,* and was a leading member of the company for the next twenty years. He sang some one hundred French and Italian roles in more than eight hundred performances, making as many as fifty appearances in a single season. His favorite role was Rigoletto. He was regarded as one of the leading exponents of the art of *bel canto.*

DE PAOLIS, Alessio, tenor (1893–1964); born in Rome. Began his singing career at the age of seven and studied opera at the St. Cecelia Academy. Embarked on his career, he sang a variety of roles in all the leading opera houses of Europe. He made his Metropolitan debut as Guillot in *Manon* on December 8, 1938. A specialist in character roles, he sang more than fifty different parts in Metropolitan productions. He estimated that he had filled two hundred character parts during his career. He was considered by the professionals as the last of the great singing actors of the operatic stage. Mr. De Paolis was killed in an automobile accident near New York City on March 10, 1964.

DE PAUL, Judith, soprano: born in Albany, New York. Studied in Opera Theater Department of the Manhattan School of Music, where she sang in world premieres of Flagello's *Judgment of St. Francis* and Ginastera's *Cantata for Soprano and Orchestra.* Then studied with tenor Kurt Baum, with whom she sang joint concerts in Europe. Also appeared in opera houses in Italy, Austria and Germany. Roles include Tosca, Amelia (*Un Ballo in Maschera*), Aïda, Desdemona, Leonora (*Il Trovatore*), Donna Anna. At the Metropolitan, she appeared in the role of Marianne in *Der Rosenkavalier* during the 1969–70 season.

DE RESZKE, Édouard, baritone (1855–1917): born in Warsaw, Poland, of a noble family named Mieczislaw. A pupil of his brother, Jean, the famous tenor, he made his operatic debut as the King in *Aïda* in Paris on April 22, 1876. Sang throughout Europe and in London, then came to America with Jean. The brothers made their Metropolitan debut in *Roméo et Juliette* on December 14, 1891—Édouard as Friar Laurence and Jean as Roméo. Édouard was an accomplished actor as well as a superb singer, with a repertoire that included all the leading baritone roles. In 1906 he retired to his estate in Poland.

DE RESZKE, Jean, tenor (1850–1925): born in Warsaw. Studied with leading Italian teachers, then made his operatic debut in 1874 in Venice as a baritone, singing the role of Alfonso in *La Favorita*, under the name of "De Reschi." After further study he made his debut in 1879 in Madrid as a tenor in *Robert le Diable*. In 1885, at the Grand Opéra in Paris, he created the title role in Massenet's *Le Cid*. Following his debut at the Metropolitan as Roméo (see above), he and his brother were the mainstays of the company between 1891 and 1903—the great years of the Golden Age. One of his most unforgettable roles was Tristan. In 1902 he retired from the stage and taught singing in Paris. He died in Nice.

DE RESZKE, Josephine, soprano (1855–91): born in Warsaw. She had a successful career in her own right at the Paris Opéra and also sang Aïda at Covent Garden. She sang with her brother Jean when he essayed his first tenor role in Madrid in 1879. The only time she appeared with both of her brothers in the same cast was in Massenet's *Hérodiade* at the Paris Opéra in 1884. She then married and retired.

DEL MONACO, Mario, dramatic tenor: born in Florence. Attended the conservatory in Pesaro where he studied painting and sculpture as well as music. At the age of twenty he was invited by the famous conductor Tullio Serafin to enter a competition in Rome which would enable him to join the school of the Rome Opera. He won first place against eighty competitors. In 1941 he made his operatic debut in Milan as Pinkerton in *Madama Butterfly* and was later engaged by La Scala. His first appearance in the United States was with the San

Francisco Opera in 1950. On November 27 of that year he was guest artist at the Metropolitan as Des Grieux in *Manon Lescaut*. He made his official debut there at the opening of the 1951–52 season (November 13, 1951) as Radames. Then followed a succession of operatic triumphs all over the world. His greatest role is Otello. Del Monaco and his wife together design most of the costumes he wears onstage.

DELCAMPO, Ina, soprano: native of Austria. Studied at the Musik Akademie in Vienna and made her debut in 1957 in Basel, Switzerland, as Elisabeth in *Tannhäuser*. Subsequently sang in opera houses in Europe, England and America. Repertoire includes Amelia (*Un Ballo in Maschera*), Aïda, Lady Macbeth, Tosca, Norma and Senta. She made her Metropolitan debut as Chrysothemis in *Elektra* on March 7, 1968.

DELLA CASA, Lisa, soprano: native of Burgdorf, Switzerland. Made her Metropolitan debut as Countess Almaviva in *Le Nozze di Figaro* on November 20, 1953. Other roles include Eva (*Die Meistersinger*), Cio-cio-san, the Marschallin, Arabella and Pamina. Particularly celebrated in Mozart roles, she also has appeared regularly at Covent Garden and the Vienna Staatsoper.

DESTINN, Emmy, dramatic soprano (1878–1930): born in Prague; real name Kittl. She took her stage name from that of her teacher, Mme. Loewe-Destinn. She made her operatic debut in Berlin in 1898 and was engaged by the Berlin Opera. About 1901 she sang at Bayreuth in the first performance there of *Der Fliegende Holländer*. She was chosen by Strauss for the Berlin premieres of his *Feuersnot* and *Salome* (1901, 1906). On November 16, 1908, she made her debut at the Metropolitan under Toscanini's direction in *Aïda* with Caruso. During the 1910–11 season there, she created the role of Minnie in *La Fanciulla del West*. With a voice of great power and purity, she had a repertoire of more than eighty roles. She also had outstanding gifts as a poet and novelist.

DEUTEKOM, Christine, soprano: born in Amsterdam. Following appearances in Germany, Austria and Spain, she made her debut at the Metropolitan as the Queen of the Night in *Die Zauberflöte* during the 1967–68 season. Her other Mozart roles include Donna Anna and Konstanze (*The Abduction from the Seraglio*). She also sings Marcellina in *Fidelio*.

DI STEFANO, Giuseppe, lyric tenor: born in Catania, Sicily. Made his debut at the Metropolitan as the Duke in *Rigoletto* on February 25, 1947. Other outstanding roles were Fenton (*Falstaff*), Des Grieux and Faust. At the height of his career his voice had an ingratiating, lyric quality that placed him in the first rank of operatic tenors. Though his Metropolitan career was brief, he became one of the great stars in Italian opera houses and at the Vienna Staatsoper.

DÍAZ, Justino, baritone: born in San Juan, Puerto Rico. After coming to the United States, he studied with tenor Frederick Jagel at the New England Conservatory of Music for three years. Continuing his studies at the Metropolitan Opera Studio, he won the National Council's Regional Auditions, then made his Metropolitan debut as Monterone in *Rigoletto* on October 23, 1963. He was chosen to sing Antony in Samuel Barber's *Antony and Cleopatra*, which opened the new Metropolitan at Lincoln Center, New York, on September 16, 1966.

DIDUR, Adamo, basso (1874–1946): born in Sanok, Galicia. Made his operatic debut in Rio de Janeiro in 1894. Sang at La Scala from 1899 to 1903, and subsequently in opera houses in Russia, Spain and England. He made his New York debut as Alvise in *La Gioconda* on November 4, 1907, in a cast that included Lillian Nordica, at the Manhattan Opera House. In 1908 he was signed by the Metropolitan and appeared as Méphistophélès with that company on November 14 in a performance of *Faust* at the Brooklyn Academy of Music. He sang the Metropolitan's first Boris Godunof on March 19, 1912. He was one of the Metropolitan's outstanding bassos.

DIGIUSEPPE, Enrico, tenor: born in Philadelphia. Studied with Richard Bonelli at Curtis Institute and Hans Heinz at Juilliard. In 1959 won American Opera Auditions, which led to European debut in Milan. From 1960 he appeared with some fifteen American opera companies; subsequently became a leading lyric tenor with the New York City Opera Company. Made a successful Metropolitan debut as Pinkerton in *Madama Butterfly* in January 2, 1970.

DIPPEL, Andreas, tenor (1866–1932): born in Cassel, Germany. From 1887 to 1898 he appeared in German opera houses, with interim visits to America. He first appeared at the Metropolitan in a minor opera called *Asrael*, by Franchetti, on the opening night of the 1890–91 season. From 1908 to 1910 he was associated with Gatti-Casazza in the management of the Metropolitan. From 1910 to 1913 he directed opera in Chicago and Philadelphia, then formed his own Wagnerian company.

In later years he taught singing on the Pacific coast. His extensive repertoire included some 150 operas in German, French and Italian, and about sixty oratorios. He died in Hollywood, California.

DOBBS, Mattiwilda, soprano: born in Atlanta, Georgia. Sang with success at Covent Garden and La Scala. Made her Metropolitan debut as Gilda in *Rigoletto* on November 9, 1956. Has also won critical acclaim for her performance in the role of Lucia and as Zerbinetta in *Ariadne auf Naxos*.

DOMINGO, Placido, tenor: born in Madrid, reared in Mexico. Made his operatic debut in Monterrey as Alfredo (*La Traviata*); sang Arturo in *Lucia di Lammermoor* with Joan Sutherland in Dallas in 1961; sang the same role with Lily Pons in Fort Worth in 1962. With the National Opera in Tel Aviv he sang 280 performances of eleven roles. From 1965 he sang in European opera houses. He appeared in the title role of Alberto Ginastera's *Don Rodrigo* in its North American premiere, given by the New York City Opera Company at the opening of the New York State Theater on February 22, 1966. He is rated as an accomplished actor as well as a superb singer. He made his Metropolitan debut as Maurizio in *Adriana Lecouvreur* on October 2, 1968. He sang his first Calaf in *Turandot* with sensational success at the Metropolitan on February 21, 1970.

DÖNCH, Karl, bass-baritone: born in Hagen, Germany. Made his Metropolitan debut as Beckmesser on January 22, 1959. A specialist in character roles, he is particularly effective as the Doctor in *Wozzeck* and the Witch in *Hänsel and Gretel*.

DOOLEY, William, baritone: native of Modesto, California. Made his Metropolitan debut in the title role of *Eugene Onegin* on February 15, 1964. Prior to joining the Metropolitan, he sang extensively in opera houses in Germany, where he had made his debut in Heidelberg as Rodrigo in *Don Carlos*. In 1968 he added Scarpia to his repertoire.

DRISCOLL, Loren, tenor: born in Scotts Bluff, Nebraska. He is a graduate of Syracuse University. He has sung with the Boston Opera, the New York City Opera, the Opera Society of Washington, D.C. and the Santa Fe Opera, and is presently a permanent member of the Berlin Deutsche Oper. In 1957 he sang the role of Tom Rakewell in *The Rake's Progress* under Igor Stravinsky's direction, and in 1962 sang in that composer's *Persephone* at the Berlin Festival. He is well schooled in all of the Mozart operatic repertoire. Driscoll has sung in the world premiere of Roger Sessions' *Montezuma*; in the 1965 premiere of Hans Werner Henze's *The Young Lord*, written especially for him; also in Henze's *The Bassarids*, premiered at the Salzburg Festival in 1966; and in Henze's *Boulevard Solitude*, a modernized version of *Manon Lescaut*, presented by the Santa Fe Opera on August 2, 1967.

DUNN, Mignon, mezzo-soprano: native of Memphis, Tennessee. Made her debut at the Metropolitan as the Nurse in *Boris Godunof* on October 29, 1958. Outstanding in the roles of Carmen, Amneris, Azucena, Fricka and Brangäne. Has also sung with the New York City Opera.

DUX, Claire, soprano (1885–1967): born in Witkowicz, Poland. Though her career was relatively brief, she was much admired for her charm and lovely voice. Her American career was confined to appearances with the Chicago Opera from 1921 to 1924, when she retired upon her marriage to a member of the wealthy Swift family. Her best roles were Nedda in *Pagliacci* and Eva in *Die Meistersinger*.

DVORÁKOVÁ, Ludmila, dramatic soprano: born in Kolin, Czechoslovakia. Wife of the conductor Rudolf Vasata. She made her Metropolitan debut as Leonore in *Fidelio* on January 12, 1966. She is well known in the roles of Isolde, Ortrud and Tosca, and has sung the three Brünnhildes in the *Ring* cycle at Covent Garden.

EAMES, Emma, soprano (1865–1952): born of American parents in Shanghai. Studied voice in Paris and was engaged by the Opéra-Comique in 1888. On March 13, 1889, she made her debut at the Grand Opéra as Juliette in *Roméo et Juliette*—a role hitherto sacred there to Adelina Patti. In the same role, at the age of twenty-six, she made her debut at the Metropolitan on December 14, 1891, with a cast that included Jean and Édouard De Reszke. She sang until 1909, when she retired from the operatic stage. One of her best roles was Sieglinde. Later she toured in concert with her husband, Emilio Edoardo de Gogorza, the Spanish-American baritone. Noted for her delicate beauty and refinement of style, she sometimes was considered "cold" but won the praise of Puccini himself in the role of Tosca.

EASTON, Florence, soprano (1884–1955): born in Middlesbrough, England. Made her first public appearance at the age of eight—as a pianist—and her operatic debut as Cio-cio-san in 1903 with the Moody-Manners Opera Company in London. In 1904–5 she toured the United States with the Savage Opera Company and later sang with the Berlin Opera (1907–13), at Covent Garden (1910) and with the Hamburg

Opera (1913–15). She made her Metropolitan debut as Santuzza on December 7, 1917. Her repertoire extended from Mozart, Weber, Wagner and Puccini to Montemezzi and Deems Taylor; she sang roles in four languages. She was a gifted lieder singer as well as an opera star.

EDELMANN, Otto, bass-baritone: native of Germany. He made his Metropolitan debut as Hans Sachs on November 11, 1954. He is best known for the roles of Sachs, Baron Ochs and the Wotan of *Die Walküre*.

ELGAR, Anne, soprano: born in Wichita, Kansas. Professional name the reverse of real name, Ragle. Studied in New York with Peter J. Wilhousky, Rose Bampton, and George Schick, Metropolitan conductor. At seventeen she won the Metropolitan Opera Guild Scholarship Award, and for two successive seasons was recipient of the Martha Baird Rockefeller Foundation Scholarship. Made her operatic debut at eighteen with the Philadelphia Grand Opera Company; on March 20, 1964, she made her debut with the New York City Opera Company. Repertoire includes more than seventeen major roles, among them Micaela (*Carmen*), Blanche (*Les Dialogues des Carmélites*), Sophie (*Werther* and *Der Rosenkavalier*), Gilda (*Rigoletto*), Pamina, Blonde (*Die Entführung aus dem Serail*), the title role in *The Ballad of Baby Doe* and Zerlina (*Don Giovanni*).

ELIAS, Rosalind, mezzo-soprano: born in Lowell, Massachusetts. Studied at the New England Conservatory of Music in Boston. She is known for her proficiency in the so-called "trouser roles," including Cherubino and Octavian. At the Metropolitan, she made her debut as Grimgerde in *Die Walküre* on February 23, 1954, and has also appeared as Dorabella (*Così Fan Tutte*), Zerlina (*Don Giovanni*), Carmen, Meg (*Falstaff*) and Laura (*La Gioconda*). She created roles in two operas by Samuel Barber—Erika in *Vanessa* and Charmian in *Antony and Cleopatra*.

ELMO, Cloe, mezzo-soprano (1910–65):born in Lecce, Italy. She was the leading mezzo-soprano at La Scala from 1936 to 1943 and sang at the Metropolitan for two seasons, first as Azucena in *Il Trovatore* on November 19, 1947. Equally effective in comedy and drama, she was a celebrated Dame Quickly in *Falstaff*, which she sang at the Metropolitan and in the Toscanini broadcast and recording. In the later years of her life she taught at the conservatory in Ankara, Turkey.

ERNSTER, Dezsö, basso: native of Hungary. His first appearance at the Metropolitan was as Osmin in *The Abduction from the Seraglio* on November 29, 1946. He had previously visited New York as a member of the Salzburg Opera Guild in 1938–39. In the interim, he had spent several years as a prisoner in a Nazi labor camp, an ordeal which robbed his voice of some of its sonorous quality. He was, however, an impressive Wagnerian singer, and one of his best roles was Hagen in *Die Götterdämmerung*.

EVANS, Geraint, bass-baritone: native of Cilfynyyd, Wales. After establishing his reputation at Covent Garden and with the San Francisco Opera, he made his Metropolitan debut as Falstaff on March 25, 1964. It is one of his best roles. He also is famous for his original interpretation of the role of Leporello. He has appeared with distinction as Pizarro (*Fidelio*), Figaro, Wozzeck and Captain Balstrode (*Peter Grimes*).

FARRAR, Geraldine, soprano (1882–1967): born in Melrose, Massachusetts. With Mary Garden, she was the last of the great singers of the Golden Age. She began her vocal studies at the age of twelve in Boston and sang in public there at the age of thirteen. She then studied with Lilli Lehmann, and in 1901 made her debut at the Berlin Royal Opera. She made her Metropolitan debut on November 26, 1906, the opening performance of the season, as Juliette, launching a brilliant career that continued until her farewell as Zaza on April 22, 1922. She and Caruso comprised one of the most popular singing teams in Metropolitan history. On December 28, 1910, Miss Farrar created the role of the Goose Girl in Humperdinck's *Königskinder*. She also toured with her own company in a version of *Carmen*, one of her great roles at the Metropolitan. In 1935 she was heard as intermission commentator for the Metropolitan Opera Saturday afternoon broadcasts. Miss Farrar, who was the wife of Lou Tellegen, the famous star of the silent screen, made several successful silent motion pictures. After she retired from the stage at the age of forty, she devoted much of her time to fundraising activities for the Metropolitan. Her greatest role was probably Madama Butterfly, which she introduced to New York in 1907. Others were Manon, Louise, Tosca, Marguerite and Mimi. She died at her home in Ridgefield, Connecticut, on March 11, 1967.

FARRELL, Eileen, dramatic soprano: born in Willimantic, Connecticut. Over a period of some twenty years before she appeared in opera, she built an impressive career as a concert singer, was frequently heard on radio, made many records—both "pop" and classical with equal success —and raised a family. Her voice developed to majestic size, and she was acclaimed at her Metropolitan debut in the title role of Gluck's *Alceste* on December 6, 1960. Subsequently she won critical praise as La Gioconda and as Leonora in *La Forza del Destino*. On September 29, 1962, she sang in the first American performance (concert) of Parts I and III of Manuel de Falla's *Atlantida*. At the 1962–63 season's opening performance of *Andrea Chénier*, Miss Farrell sang Madeleine; she appeared in that role and as Santuzza during 1964 and 1965. Her greatest role is Cherubini's Medea, which she sang with the American Opera Society and the San Francisco Opera.

FENN, Jean, soprano: born in Riverside, Illinois. Began her operatic career with the New York City Opera Company during the 1952–53 season. She made her debut at the Metropolitan on November 21, 1953, as Musetta in *La Bohème*, and has been a member of the company since that time. Two of her best roles are Marguerite in *Faust* and Eva in *Die Meistersinger*.

FISCHER, Emil, baritone (1838–1914): born in Brunswick, Germany. The first great Wagnerian baritone to be heard in America, he sang in many American premieres of the Wagner operas at the Metropolitan, where he made his debut in 1885, retiring in 1898. He was Hans Sachs in the first American performance of *Die Meistersinger* on January 4, 1886, and his performance of the role was the model for decades to come.

FISCHER-DIESKAU, Dietrich, bass-baritone: born in Berlin. A protean singer, he is unrivaled as a concert artist and also has performed and recorded many operatic roles in Europe, having made his stage debut as Rodrigo in *Don Carlos* in Berlin. He was Don Giovanni in the performance that inaugurated the new Deutsche Oper in Berlin on September 24, 1961. He has sung Wagner roles at Bayreuth and has a repertoire that extends from Mozart roles to those in modern operas by Alban Berg, Hindemith and Hans Werner Henze. His only American operatic appearance was in a concert version of Busoni's *Doktor Faust* in New York in 1964.

FISHER, Suzanne, American soprano. Metropolitan Opera debut as Cio-cio-san on December 26, 1936. She was an interesting singer with a light coloratura voice. Later she sang Marguerite, Micaela and Manon. Also sang Sophie in *Der Rosenkavalier*, in 1937–38 season.

FISHER, Sylvia, soprano: born in Melbourne, Austrialia. One of the most popular stars at Covent Garden since 1949, she has sung many of the great roles there, including Countess Almaviva, Fidelio, Elsa, Sieglinde, the Marschallin, Senta and Isolde.

FLAGELLO, Ezio, basso: born in New York. Made his Metropolitan debut as Leporella on November 13, 1957. Since then he has become one of the company's outstanding bassos in roles such as Pogner in *Die Meistersinger*, Timur in *Turandot*, Wurm in *Luisa Miller*, King Philip in *Don Carlos*, the Maharajah in Menotti's *The Last Savage* and Sir John Falstaff.

FLAGSTAD, Kirsten, dramatic soprano (1895–1962): born in Hamar, Norway. Her father was a conductor and her mother, a singer, was her only teacher. She made her debut at eighteen as Nuri in D'Albert's *Tiefland* at the Olso Opera. Her reputation was confined to Scandinavia for twenty years and she was considering retirement when in 1933 she was engaged to sing secondary roles at the Bayreuth Festival. The following season she sang Sieglinde there and was engaged for the Metropolitan as a replacement for Frieda Leider. Her debut as Sieglinde on February 2, 1935, was one of the great sensations of Metropolitan history. Three days later she appeared as Isolde and added five more Wagner heroines to her Metropolitan repertoire that season. Her performances, usually opposite Lauritz Melchior, were the chief box-office attraction at the Metropolitan until her return to Nazi-occupied Norway in 1942. Because of the controversy surrounding her husband, the Swedish industrialist Henry Johansen, she did not return to the Metropolitan until January 22, 1951, when she reappeared as Isolde. She made her final appearances there the following season in a memorable revival of Gluck's *Alceste*. Her only other non-Wagner role at the Metropolitan was Fidelio. In 1952 she made her last stage appearances at London's Mermaid Theater in Purcell's *Dido and Aeneas*. During the course of her notable career, she also gave many concert tours and appeared triumphantly with the San Francisco Opera and at Covent Garden, La Scala and the Paris Opéra. The extraordinary beauty of her voice is still evident in the last recording she made, as Fricka in *Das Rheingold*, when she was in her sixties.

FLEISCHER, Editha, soprano: native of Germany. She first appeared with the Metropolitan company at the Manhattan Opera House as Woglinde (*Die Götterdämmerung*) during the 1922–23 season. On November 6, 1926, she made her official debut as the First Lady in *Die Zauberflöte*, and was a leading soubrette at the Metropolitan for ten seasons thereafter. Although she also sang leading dramatic roles, she is best remembered as Aennchen in *Der Freischütz*, Adina in *L'Elisir d'Amore,* Marcellina in *Fidelio* and Hänsel in *Hänsel und Gretel.* She sang Hänsel in the Metropolitan's first broadcast, on the afternoon of December 25, 1931.

FLETA, Miguel, tenor (1893–1938): born in Albalete, Spain. Classed as one of the great tenors, his voice was a combination of true lyric quality and dramatic virility. He was the first Calaf in *Turandot.* Widely acclaimed in Europe, Fleta made his Metropolitan debut as Cavaradossi in *Tosca* on November 8, 1923.

FORRESTER, Maureen, contralto: native of Montreal. She made her operatic debut at the age of thirty-six with the New York City Opera Company as Cornelia in Handel's *Giulio Cesare.* She has had a phenomenally successful career as a concert artist. In 1966 she was chairman of the voice department at Philadelphia's Academy of Music. Miss Forrester is the wife of Canadian violinist Eugene Kash, and the couple have five children.

FORST, Judith, mezzo-soprano: native of Vancouver. On March 29, 1968, she sang in the semifinals of the Regional Auditions of the Metropolitan Opera National Council and so impressed impresario Rudolf Bing that he gave her a contract immediately. Previously Miss Forst had sung with the Vancouver, Seattle and Santa Fe Opera companies. She made her Metropolitan debut as the Page in *Rigoletto* on September 19, 1968. Prominent among her first Metropolitan roles was Siebel in *Faust.*

FRANKE, Paul, tenor: born in Boston, where he studied at the New England Conservatory of Music. He made his Metropolitan debut on December 1, 1948, in the small role of a Youth in Montemezzi's *L'Amore dei Tre Re* and has been an active member of the company since that time. One of his outstanding roles is David in *Die Meistersinger.* Also in his repertoire of sixty-six roles are Rodrigo in *Otello,* the Simpleton in *Boris Godunof* and the Captain in *Wozzeck.* He is an accomplished actor.

FREDRICKS, Richard, baritone: native of Los Angeles. Member of the New York City Opera Company. Has sung with the companies of San Francisco, New Orleans, Fort Worth, Honolulu, Houston, Philadelphia, and Miami. On March 25, 1965, he created the role of Jason in the world premiere of Jack Beeson's *Lizzie Borden* with the New York City Opera Company. In February 1969 he sang the role of the Secretary in the English-language premiere of Hans Werner Henze's *The Young Lord* (*Der Junge Lord*) with the San Diego Opera Company, later directed the production and repeated the role with the Houston Grand Opera Company.

FREMSTAD, Olive, dramatic soprano (1872–1951): born in Stockholm. At the age of nine she performed in public as a pianist. Brought to America at the age of twelve, she later was soloist at St. Patrick's Cathedral. In 1893–94 she was a pupil of Lilli Lehmann, then subsequently sang at Bayreuth, Vienna, Munich and Covent Garden. She made her Metropolitan debut on November 23, 1903, as Sieglinde in *Die Walküre*, and became known as one of the Wagnerian "immortals." Her Isolde was acknowledged as one of the finest of her generation.

FRENI, Mirella, soprano: native of Modena, Italy. After her Metropolitan debut as Mimi on September 29, 1965, she was hailed by critics as the finest Mimi since Bori, Sayão and Albanese. Another one of her outstanding roles is Liù in *Turandot*. She is the wife of Leone Magieras, a conductor and a teacher at the Bologna Conservatory.

FRICK, Gottlob, basso: native of Germany. Made his Metropolitan debut on December 27, 1961, as Fafner in *Das Rheingold*. An experienced Wagnerian singer, he is noted for his characterizations of Hunding and Hagen.

GADSKI, Johanna, dramatic soprano (1871–1932): born in Anclam, Prussia, and educated in Stettin. She made her debut at the Metropolitan on January 6, 1900, as Senta in *Der Fliegende Holländer*, and from then until 1917 she was one of the leading Wagnerian singers of the company. Noted for her Isolde and Brünnhilde, she also toured extensively in concert and was a specialist in the songs of Robert Schumann.

GALLI-CURCI, Amelita, coloratura soprano (1882–1963): born in Milan. She studied piano at the Milan Conservatory, then turned to singing, in which she was largely self-taught. Her first appearance in opera was as Gilda in Rome in 1910. She was first heard in America with the Chicago Opera Company at the Lexington Theater in New York City on January 28, 1917, in the title role of Meyerbeer's *Dinorah*. After the famous "Shadow Song," she was recalled twenty-four times, and she responded to almost sixty curtain calls at the end of the opera. She made her Metropolitan debut as Violetta in *La Traviata* on November 14, 1921. She was then forty years old and suffering from the effects of a goiter, but her voice was acknowledged to be one of the most beautiful ever heard. She was spectacularly successful in all the great coloratura roles. Her farewell appearance was as Rosina in *Il Barbiere di Siviglia* on January 24, 1931. Galli-Curci was the wife of the pianist-composer Homer Samuels.

GARCIA, Manuel del Popolo Vincente, tenor (1775–1832): born in Seville, Spain. He first appeared in Paris in 1808, establishing himself as an opera singer. The role of Almaviva in *Il Barbiere di Siviglia* was written for him by Rossini. Later he took up a career as composer and conductor. Garcia composed seventy-one Spanish, nineteen Italian and seven French operas. In 1825 he introduced Italian opera to New York with his own company.

GARCIA, Manuel Patricio Rodriguez, basso (1805–1906): the son of the above, he was born in Madrid. He became one of the greatest singing teachers of the nineteenth century; one of his pupils was Jenny Lind. Scientifically interested in the mechanics of vocal production, he wrote a text on the subject—*Traité complet de l'art du chant*—and also invented the laryngoscope.

GARDEN, Mary, soprano (1874–1967): born in Aberdeen, Scotland. She was brought to America during early childhood and began to study voice at the age of six. Later she returned to Paris and continued her studies there. Her first appearance on any stage was at the Opéra-Comique on April 13, 1900, in the title role of Charpentier's *Louise*. In the second act she replaced another singer, who had become ill. In 1902 she was chosen by Debussy to create the role of Mélisande in his *Pelléas et Mélisande*. She made her first appearance in America in Oscar Hammerstein's Manhattan Opera House as Thaïs in 1907. She joined the Chicago Civic Opera in 1910 and served as the company's general director (or "directa," as she called it) during 1921 and 1922. Although she never sang at the Metropolitan as a member of the company, she appeared there with the visiting Chicago Opera Company. She specialized in French roles and was one of the most brilliant singing actresses in the history of opera.

GARRISON, Mabel, soprano (1886–1963): born in Baltimore. One of the more successful American singers at the Metropolitan, she made her debut there as Frasquita in *Carmen* on November 27, 1914. She was in the company until 1920 and appeared as the Queen of the Night, Gretel, Rosina and the Page in *Les Huguenots*. She later was teacher of singing at Smith College, Northampton, Massachusetts.

GEDDA, Nicolai, lyric-dramatic tenor: native of Stockholm, the son of a Swedish mother and a Russian father who was an orthodox cantor. Made his Metropolitan debut on November 1, 1957, as Faust. An artist of extraordinary versatility, he is multilingual and equally at home in Russian, English, Italian, German, French and Spanish as well as Swedish. The range of his repertoire extends from the Orfeo in Gluck's opera (a role usually sung by a contralto) to Alfredo in *La Traviata*.

GENCER, Leyla, soprano: Born in Istanbul, Turkey. One of the great stars in European houses since World War II. Made her debut in Ankara as Santuzza (*Cavalleria Rusticana*), later sang in world premieres of operas by Poulence and Pizzetti. In the United States she has appeared with the San Francisco Opera and the Philadelphia Opera. Her repertoire of 60 roles ranges from Norma and the heroines of the early Verdi operas to Renata in Prokofiev's *Flaming Angel*, which she sang at the 1959 Spoleto Festival.

GHIAUROV, Nicolai, basso: native of Sofia, Bulgaria. First heard in America at the Chicago Lyric Opera, where he sang to high critical acclaim. At the Metropolitan, he made his debut as Méphistophélès on November 8, 1965. He has been favorably compared with Pinza and Chaliapin—but prefers to be known as "the first Ghiaurov." He began his musical career with the study of piano, violin and clarinet, later turned to singing and made his operatic debut in Sofia.

GHIUSELEV, Nicola, basso: born in Pavlikeni, Bulgaria. Graduated from the Academy of Fine Arts in Sofia. After three years of private study he was engaged by the National Opera of Sofia, where he is still a member. In 1963 he won the second International Competition for Opera Singers in Sofia. He made his Metropolitan debut on December 29, 1966, as Ramfis in *Aïda*. His roles include King Philip in *Don Carlos*, Boris and (in that opera) Pimen, Méphistophélès, Galitsky in *Prince Igor* and the Commendatore in *Don Giovanni*.

GIAIOTTI, BONALDO, basso: a native of Ziraco in the Italian province of Udine. Made his Metropolitan Opera debut as the High Priest in the opening-night performance of *Nabucco* in 1960. Made his debut at the Teatro Nuovo in Milan in 1958, as Colline in *La Bohème*, and later sang Count Des Grieux in *Manon*. More recently he has sung in numerous other Italian opera theaters. First appearance in America occurred at the Cincinnati Summer Opera in 1959, where he sang Don Basilio in *Il Barbiere di Siviglia* as part of an exchange program involving young singers of this country and Italy. He sang Count Rodolfo in

*La Sonnambula*, with Joan Sutherland, in 1969 at the Met. His repertoire ranges from Mozart and Verdi to Wagner and Puccini.

GIANNINI, Dusolina, soprano: born in Philadelphia, she was a pupil of Marcella Sembrich. After her debut in concert in 1923, she went to Europe and made successful operatic appearances in Hamburg, Berlin, Paris, Budapest and at Covent Garden. She made her Metropolitan debut as Aïda on February 12, 1936. During the 1944–45 season she appeared as Tosca with the New York City Opera Company. She recorded the first complete *Aïda* with the La Scala company and sang the leading role in the premiere of *The Scarlet Letter*—an opera written by her brother Vittorio—in Hamburg in 1938.

GIGLI, Beniamino, lyric-dramatic tenor (1890–1957): born in Recanati, Italy. First studied in Rome, then made his operatic debut as Enzo Grimaldo in *La Gioconda* in Rovigo, Italy, in 1914. Made his debut at the Metropolitan as Faust in Boito's *Mefistofele* on November 26, 1920. The following March 7 he sang the title role in the Metropolitan's first *Andrea Chénier*, replacing Caruso, who was recovering from an illness. After Caruso's death later that year (August 2, 1921) Gigli took over his roles. He sang at the Metropolitan until 1934, appearing in twenty-seven different roles. These included Ruggero in Puccini's *La Rondine* at its American premiere in March 1928. He had created the role in the world premiere in Monte Carlo in 1917. During his career he appeared in several German and English films. He returned to the Metropolitan for one season in 1939 and made a farewell American concert tour in 1955. A master of true *bel canto*, Gigli was one of the great tenors of his time.

GLOSSOP, Peter, baritone: born in Sheffield, Yorkshire, England. In 1953 he sang with the Sadler's Wells Company, then made his La Scala debut as Rigoletto in 1966. He opened the 1966 season of the Dallas Civic Opera as Rigoletto, and appeared in the same role in 1967 with the San Francisco Opera. Subsequently, he sang Rigoletto and Iago with the Metropolitan at Newport, Rhode Island. In the fall of 1967 Mr. Glossop toured with the newly formed American National Opera Company, singing the role of Falstaff. On March 6, 1968, he appeared in a revival of Catalani's *La Wally* in New York with the American Opera Society. He again appeared with the San Francisco Opera during its 1968 fall season. Mr. Glossop sings virtually every baritone role Verdi wrote. He is the husband of Joyce Blackham, a leading mezzo-soprano of Sadler's Wells, who sang Carmen in 1967 with the New York City Opera.

GLUCK, Alma, soprano (1866–1938): born in Bucharest; (real name Reba Fierson). She was brought to New York during her childhood. She made her first operatic appearance in New York in the role of Sophie in Massenet's *Werther* with Hammerstein's Manhattan Opera Company on November 16, 1909. On December 23 she sang the role of the Happy Shade in Gluck's *Orfeo ed Euridice,* with Louise Homer as Orfeo, at the Metropolitan. She sang there until 1912. Her voice was noted for its limpid clarity. She was the wife of the violinist Efrem Zimbalist, whom she married in 1914. Her daughter by an earlier marriage is the well-known writer Marcia Davenport.

GOBBI, Tito, baritone: born in Bassano del Grappa, Italy. A singing actor with a powerful stage presence, he sang all the great baritone roles in Italian opera houses and appeared in many Italian films before finally making his Metropolitan debut as Scarpia on January 13, 1956. He also has been a great favorite at Covent Garden and with the opera companies of Chicago and San Francisco. His interpretations of Macbeth, Nabucco, Rigoletto, Iago, Figaro, Simon Boccanegra and Scarpia are outstanding.

GODFREY, Batyah, contralto: born in Portland, Maine. In 1968 she became the first winner of a Lucrezia Bori Scholarship, awarded under a grant from the Bori Foundation to the Metropolitan. She made her Metropolitan debut on February 17, 1969, as "A Voice from Above" in *Die Frau ohne Schatten.* Other roles include Dalila, Ulrica (*Un Ballo in Maschera*), Orfeo (*Orfeo ed Euridice*) and Dame Quickly (*Falstaff*).

GOEKE, Leo, tenor: born in Kirksville, Missouri. Made his first professional appearance with the St. Louis Municipal Opera, where he sang a number of standard tenor roles. His Metropolitan debut was as Gastone in *La Traviata* on February 7, 1970. Later appeared as Count Lerma in *Don Carlos* and in other comprimario roles.

GOODLOE, Robert, basso: born in St. Petersburg, Florida. After winning the Metropolitan Regional Auditions in 1964, he appeared as the Second Knight in a Metropolitan performance of *Parsifal* on March 10, 1965—the first *Parsifal* since the 1960–61 season. Goodloe has sung some twenty comprimario roles at the Metropolitan.

GORIN, Igor, bass-baritone: born in Gradek Jagiell, Russia. Already well known as a concert artist and a singer on radio, he appeared with the New York City Opera during its 1963–64 season as Germont in

*La Traviata*. He made his Metropolitan debut in this role on February 10, 1964.

GORITZ, Otto, baritone (1872–1929): born in Berlin. He made his debut in German opera in 1895 and gained a reputation as a Wagnerian singer. His debut as Klingsor in *Parsifal* at the Metropolitan on December 24, 1903, marked the beginning of a career that continued until 1917, when World War I curtailed the German repertoire.

GORR, Rita, mezzo-soprano: born in Ghent, Belgium. Made her Metropolitan debut as Amneris on October 16, 1962. Roles also include Azucena, Princess Eboli and Dalila. She also has sung at Covent Garden and the Paris Opéra.

GRAMM, Donald, bass-baritone: born in Milwaukee. First sang with the New York City Opera during the season of 1952–53. He made his debut at the Metropolitan on January 10, 1964, as Truffaldino in Strauss's *Ariadne auf Naxos*. He also was seen as Don Alfonso in *Cosi Fan Tutte* and Count Waldner in *Arabella*.

GRECO, Norina, soprano: born in Italy, she has lived in the United States since childhood. She began her stage career as a dancer, then began studying voice at the age of sixteen. She toured three years with the San Carlo Opera Company. Her debut at the Metropolitan took place on December 12, 1940, as Leonora in *Il Trovatore*, replacing Stella Roman, whose arrival from abroad had been delayed. Roles also include Aïda, Santuzza and Tosca.

GREER, Frances, soprano: born in Piggott, Arkansas. At Louisiana State University she studied voice with the baritone Pasquale Amato. Following graduation she toured Europe with the St. Louis Symphony. On her return to the United States she won the Philadelphia Youth Concert Award, and thereafter sang leading roles with the Philadelphia Opera Company. In 1942 she won the Metropolitan Opera Auditions of the Air, then joined the company. She made her debut as Musetta (*La Bohème*) on November 30, 1942.

GRISI, Giulia, soprano (1811–69): born in Milan in a family of musicians and dancers. An aunt and a sister were leading singers of their day, and a sister, Carlotta, was one of the great dancers of the eighteenth century. Giulia made a great success in her debut in Rossini's *Zelmira* in Bologna at the age of seventeen. She sang the first Adalgisa to Giuditta Pasta's Norma in Milan in 1831, and appeared in the premiere casts of *I Puritani* and *I Capuletti ed i Montecchi*. She had a meteoric career, and excelled in the roles of Lucrezia Borgia, Rosina, Norina, Susanna and Pamina. In 1844 she married the leading tenor of the day —a Piedmontese aristocrat known professionally by the name of Mario. They have been described as the handsomest couple in operatic history.

GRIST, Reri, soprano: native of New York City and a graduate of the High School of Music and Art and of Queens College of the City University. She won a Marian Anderson Scholarship and a Blanche Thebom Award. She made her operatic debut with the Santa Fe Opera, and has sung with the San Francisco Opera, the Chicago Opera and the Washington (D.C.) Opera Society. In Europe she has appeared at the Cologne Opera, the Zurich Opera, La Scala, the Vienna State Opera, Glyndebourne and Covent Garden. She made her Metropolitan debut as Rosina in *Il Barbiere di Siviglia* on February 25, 1966. Among her other roles are Sophie in *Der Rosenkavalier* and Zerbinetta in *Ariadne auf Naxos*.

GUEDEN, Hilde, soprano: born in Vienna. Sang at the Vienna State Opera and at the Salzburg Festival. Made her Metropolitan debut as Gilda on November 15, 1951, to great acclaim. She is successful in a wide variety of soprano roles. She was Anne Trulove in the American premiere of Stravinsky's *The Rake's Progress* at the Metropolitan on February 14, 1953.

GUERRERA, Frank, bass-baritone: native of Philadelphia, of Sicilian parentage. Studied at Curtis Institute and made his Metropolitan debut at Escamillo on December 14, 1948 (subsequent to winning the Metropolitan Opera Auditions of the Air). Has appeared regularly in the familiar bass-baritone roles. One of his best-known characterizations is Ping in *Turandot*.

HACKETT, Charles, tenor (1889–1942): born in Worcester, Massachusetts. Made his operatic debut in *Mignon* in Genoa in 1916, and thereafter sang in Milan, London, Rome, Paris, Madrid and Rio de Janeiro. He made his Metropolitan debut as Count Almaviva in *Il Barbiere di Siviglia* on January 31, 1919, sang at the Met for three years, then returned to La Scala. Subsequently he sang with the Chicago Civic Opera and, after 1935, rejoined the Metropolitan for a time. A competent and well-trained artist, he was one of the mainstays of the company's tenor wing.

HARRELL, Mack, baritone (1909–60): born in Celeste, Texas. He studied at the Juilliard School in New York and later taught there. A noted concert artist, he also sang intermittently at the Metropolitan and with the New York City Opera. At the Metropolitan, he made his debut as Biterolf in *Tannhäuser* on December 16, 1940, and was Nick Shadow in the American premiere of Stravinsky's *The Rake's Progress* on February 14, 1953. His last performance there was as Amfortas in *Parsifal* on March 20, 1958.

HARROLD, Orville, tenor (1878–1933): born in Muncie, Indiana. While singing in vaudeville, he was discovered by Oscar Hammerstein. He made his operatic debut at the Manhattan Opera House in 1910 and the next year sang with Hammerstein's company in London. At the Metropolitan, he made his debut on November 22, 1919, as Léopold in Halévy's *La Juive* in a cast headed by Caruso, Ponselle and Léon Rothier. A versatile artist, he appeared in a wide variety of roles.

HARSHAW, Margaret, dramatic soprano: born in Philadelphia, Pennsylvania. A Metropolitan Auditions winner in 1942, she first sang, as a mezzo-soprano, at Covent Garden. She made her Metropolitan debut as the Second Norn in *Die Götterdämmerung* on November 25, 1942. Endowed with a voice of true dramatic quality, a talented actress as well, she sang a wide variety of roles, including Dame Quickly (*Falstaff*), Genevieve (*Pelléas*), Azucena, Amneris, Brünnhilde, Kundry and Erda.

HARVUOT, Clifford, baritone: born in Norwood, Ohio. His first role at the Metropolitan was Kouzka in *Khovanchina,* given on February 16, 1950. One of his outstanding roles is Schaunard (*La Bohème*), and he has capably sung such parts as Rangoni (*Boris Godunof*), Biterolf (*Tannhäuser*), Jokanaan (*Salome*), Yamadori (*Madama Butterfly* ) and Frank (*Die Fledermaus*).

HAUK, Minnie, soprano (1852–1929): born in New York. She first studied in Europe and sang there with great success. For a time she was court singer in Prussia. She became famous as Carmen, which she sang at the opera's American premiere at the New York Academy of Music on October 23, 1878. After 1881 she made three world tours. She appeared for the first time as a member of the Metropolitan on February 20, 1891, as Carmen—which she sang in German. Although not counted among the great voices of her day, Minnie Hauk was a favorite with New York opera audiences for years.

HAWKINS, Osie, baritone: born in Phenix City, Alabama. He made his Metropolitan Opera debut on January 22, 1942, as Donner in *Das Rheingold* and has been with the Metropolitan since that time. After a career there as a singer he became stage manager. His official position as of 1970 was executive stage manager.

HAYWARD, Thomas, tenor: born in Kansas City, Missouri. His mother was a concert singer and his father a violinist. Hayward first sang on radio, then appeared with the Kansas City Civic Opera Company. There he was heard by the movie star Jeanette MacDonald, who urged him to go to New York to study. He became a pupil of Frank La Forge. In 1944 he competed in the Metropolitan Auditions of the Air but failed to reach the finals. Later that year he joined the New York City Opera Company and sang leading roles. In 1945 he again entered the Metropolitan Auditions; this time he won and was given a Metropolitan contract. He made his debut on December 4, 1945, as Tybalt in *Roméo et Juliette*. The high points of his career came when he replaced Jussi Björling as Faust after the first act on December 17, 1953, and sang the same role in place of Richard Tucker on January 8, 1954.

HEMPEL, Frieda, soprano (1885–1955): born in Leipzig. Began her musical career with the study of the piano, then turned to voice. Made her operatic debut in Stettin and in 1906 sang at Bayreuth. Her debut at the Metropolitan was as Marguerite de Valois in *Les Huguenots* on December 27, 1912. She sang a variety of German and Italian roles and was the Marschallin in *Der Rosenkavalier* at its American premiere on December 9, 1913. She remained with the Metropolitan until 1919, then sang in concert for many years afterward.

HERBERT, Ralph, baritone: born in Vienna of a musical family. Made his Metropolitan debut as Count Waldner in *Arabella* on February 10, 1955, when the opera had its first hearing in New York. Other roles included Lescaut (*Manon*), Beckmesser, Alberich (*Der Ring des Nibelungen*) and the Doctor (*Wozzeck*). He also is well known as a stage director, and served in that capacity with the New York City Opera.

HINES, Jerome, basso: native of Hollywood, California; real name Heinz. Made his Metropolitan debut as the Police Officer in *Boris Godunof* on November 21, 1946, and has since been recognized as a leading basso of the company. One of his most famous roles is Méphistophélès. He is also a composer. His principal work is the opera *I Am the Way*, based on the life of Christ. It was first given in 1956 and was subsequently performed more than fifty times in various parts of the country. It was presented at the Metropolitan on April 7, 1968.

HOMER, Louise, mezzo-soprano (1871–1947): born in Pittsburgh. She studied in Paris and made her debut at Vichy in 1898. She made her Metropolitan debut as Amneris on December 22, 1900, and sang there from that time until 1919, succeeding to Mme. Schumann-Heink's roles. She created the title role of *Mona,* the "Ten Thousand Dollar Prize Opera" written by the American composer Horatio Parker and performed at the Metropolitan on March 14, 1912. A fine artist with a magnificent voice, Mme. Homer was one of the great singers of the Golden Age. She was the wife of the American composer Sidney Homer and the aunt of the contemporary composer Samuel Barber.

HOPF, Hans, tenor: native of Germany. He made his Metropolitan debut as Walther in *Die Meistersinger* on March 15, 1952, and appeared thereafter mainly in other Wagnerian roles.

HORNE, Marilyn, mezzo-soprano: born in Bradford, Pennsylvania. Among contemporary singers, Miss Horne has been instrumental in the revival of interest in florid *bel canto* singing, which she performs with outstanding artistry. In her concerts she has gone back beyond Rossini to such long-neglected masters as Giovanni Battista Lampugnani (1706–81) and Johann Simon Mayr (1763–1845). Like Maria Callas, Joan Sutherland, Montserrat Caballé and Teresa Berganza, Miss Horne has mastered the severe technical and stylistic requirements of this type of music. In 1968 she added the role of Carmen to her operatic repertoire. She is the wife of Henry Lewis, conductor of the New Jersey Symphony Orchestra. After opera appearances at Covent Garden and with several American companies, she made her Metropolitan debut on March 3, 1970, as Adalgisa.

HOTTER, Hans, bass-baritone: born in Offenbach, near Frankfurt, Germany. He made his Metropolitan debut on November 9, 1950, as Vanderdecken in *Der Fliegende Holländer,* and was recognized as a gifted singing actor. Other impressive roles are Wotan, Hunding, Kurvenal, Orest (*Elektra*) and Jokanaan. He typified the wide-ranging activities of contemporary singers when he sang an opera performance in Colorado between two appearances at Bayreuth within a space of ten days. He recently staged the Wagner *Ring* cycle at Covent Garden.

HUEHN, Julius, bass-baritone: born of German parentage in Revere, Massachusetts. He made his debut at the Metropolitan as the Herald in *Lohengrin* on December 21, 1935, then sang many performances of Wotan, Amfortas, Telramund and Wolfram. He sang sixty-five performances of Kurvenal in the first seven years after his debut. His career was interrupted by military service, which is said to have adversely affected his voice. He retired from opera in 1946, and in 1952 joined the faculty of the Eastman School of Music in Rochester, N.Y. Mr. Huehn died in June 1971.

HUPP, Rosalind, mezzo-soprano: native of Ohio. Studied at the New England Conservatory of Music and appeared in productions of the Boris Goldovsky and Sarah Caldwell opera companies in Boston. Toured with a *Sound of Music* company (role of Abbess); later engaged by Santa Fe Opera and other community opera companies. Made her Metropolitan debut in 1967 in *Die Walküre*.

HURLEY, Laurel, soprano: native of Allentown, Pennsylvania. First developed her operatic repertoire as a member of the Charles L. Wagner Opera Company and at the Central City (Colorado) Opera Festival. After 1952 she was one of the leading sopranos of the New York City Opera. She made her Metropolitan debut as Oscar in *Un Ballo in Maschera* on February 26, 1955. A talented singer, she is effective in a wide variety of roles.

ILOSFALVY, Robert, tenor: born in Budapest. His fame spread beyond the iron curtain while he was a member of the Budapest Opera from 1953 to 1965. He signed a five-year contract with the Cologne Opera in 1966. His American debut with the San Francisco Opera in 1964 opposite Joan Sutherland in *La Traviata* confirmed his reputation as an extraordinary singer. In 1968 he was hailed at Covent Garden for his performances in *La Traviata* and *Manon Lescaut*.

IVOGÜN, Maria, coloratura soprano: born in Budapest; real name Inge von Günther. Known as one of the finest vocal technicians in the coloratura category, she became a star in Munich and Berlin and then settled in Chicago. She appeared with the Chicago Opera frequently during the 1920s. Her recording of Zerbinetta's aria from *Ariadne auf Naxos* is a collector's treasure.

JAGEL, Frederick, tenor: born in Brooklyn. Began his musical career as a choirboy and during his twenties sang in Broadway productions. He then studied in Milan and launched his career in Italy under the name of Frederico Jaghelli. He sang almost two hundred performances in Italy, Holland and Spain. He made his Metropolitan debut as Radames on November 7, 1927. On a number of occasions, Jagel sang as a last-minute replacement for other indisposed tenors, and he became known as the Metropolitan's "minuteman." He remained at the Metropolitan until 1950 and subsequently taught at the New England Conservatory.

JANSSEN, Herbert, baritone (1895–1965): born in Cologne, Germany. Had a solid reputation as a Wagnerian singer when he joined the Metropolitan, where he made his debut as Wolfram (*Tannhäuser*) on January 28, 1940. His voice, though rather light, was noted for its beautiful quality. He was also a prominent lieder singer.

JANOWITZ, Gundula, soprano: born in Berlin. She studied at the Conservatory in Graz, Austria. Wieland Wagner heard her at Bayreuth and engaged her for the role of the First Flower Maiden in *Parsifal*. Later her career was furthered by Herbert von Karajan. In 1962 came Karajan's new production of *Fidelio*, in which she sang Marcellina. She also appeared in Karajan's Vienna production of *Die Frau ohne Schatten*. In 1964 she sang Ilia in *Idomeneo* at the Glyndebourne Festival. She made her North American debut in September 1967 at Expo 67 as Donna Anna with the Vienna State Opera. Her Metropolitan debut followed two months later as Sieglinde in Karajan's production of *Die Walküre*.

JEPSON, Helen, lyric soprano: born in Titusville, Pennsylvania. Reared in Akron, Ohio, where at the age of fifteen she made her debut with a local opera troupe as Nedda in *Pagliacci*. Later she won five scholarships at the Curtis Institute in Philadelphia, where she studied with the Metropolitan soprano Queena Mario. She made her Metropolitan debut as Helen in John Laurence Seymour's *In the Pasha's Garden* on January 24, 1935.

JERITZA, Maria, dramatic soprano: born in Moravia. Began her stage career as a singer in operettas and later scored in comic operas in Munich and Vienna. Her first operatic success was as Elisabeth in *Tannhäuser* in Vienna in 1910. Thereafter she became a member of the Vienna State Opera and was acclaimed for her acting as well as for her singing. She was the favorite soprano of Richard Strauss and Giacomo Puccini, and was the latter's first choice as Tosca. She made operatic history by singing "Vissi d'arte" while lying on her stomach—setting up a tradition that still persists among the world's Toscas. She created the title role in Strauss's *Ariadne auf Naxos* in Stuttgart in 1912. At the Metropolitan, she made her debut as Marietta in Erich Korngold's *Die Tote Stadt* on November 19, 1921. Jeritza sang most of the leading soprano roles. In 1967, in New York, she received the

Golden Ring of the City of Vienna, presented each year to the person who has done the most for the Austrian capital's artistic life. A dazzling blonde, Jeritza was one of the most flamboyant and glamorous opera stars of her time. Her last performance was in a single return appearance at the Metropolitan as Rosalinde in *Die Fledermaus* in 1952.

JESSNER, Irene, soprano: born in Vienna, the daughter of a physician. She received her musical education at the Vienna Conservatory. Her first engagement was with a provincial opera company in Czechoslovakia, and later she sang extensively in Germany and Austria. She made her Metropolitan debut as Hänsel on December 24, 1936. She remained with the company until 1944. Her best role was the Marschallin in *Der Rosenkavalier*. She later became professor of singing at the Toronto Conservatory.

JOBIN, Andre, tenor: son of Raoul Jobin, former Metropolitan tenor. Trained as an actor with Jean Louis Barrault's repertoire company. Made his debut with the New York City Opera Company in the role of Pelléas on March 18, 1970.

JOBIN, Raoul, tenor: a French-Canadian, Jobin developed his career as a member of the Paris Opéra. After being heard in the Metropolitan Auditions of the Air, he made his debut as Des Grieux in *Manon* on February 19, 1941. He performed effectively as Don José, Valentin (*Faust*), Cavardossi and Hoffmann, and was commended for the appealing warmth of his voice.

JONES, Gwyneth, soprano: born in Pontnewyndd, Wales. Studied as a mezzo-soprano at the Royal College of Music in London. Appeared with the Zurich Opera in the roles of Orfeo and Magdalene (*Die Meistersinger*). Although accepted by Covent Garden as a mezzo, she was persuaded to change to soprano, and sang Amelia in *Un Ballo in Maschera* during the 1963–64 season. The following season she replaced Régine Crespin in *Fidelio* without a stage rehearsal, and also replaced an indisposed Leontyne Price in *Il Trovatore*. She appeared at the Bayreuth Centennial Festival in the summer of 1968 as Eva in *Die Meistersinger,* and at Covent Garden as Elizabeth in *Don Carlos,* one of her outstanding roles. Other roles include Senta, Sieglinde, Lady Macbeth and Octavian. In her American debut as Lady Macbeth with the Dallas Civic Opera on November 23, 1967, she was described as a singer with an enormous voice and a magnetic personality.

JOURNET, Marcel, baritone (1870–1933): born in Grasse, France. He made his operatic debut in Brussels, sang often on the Continent and at Covent Garden. He was first heard at the Metropolitan as Colline in *La Bohème,* in the opera's first performance there on December 18, 1901, with a cast headed by Nellie Melba. He also sang with the Chicago Opera Company. Journet was one of the most accomplished actor-singers of the French school, noted for his elegance of style, polished diction and subtlety of gesture. He left the Metropolitan in 1908 and then sang with the Chicago Opera.

JURINAC, Sena, soprano: born in Bosnia, Yugoslavia. Sang with the Vienna State Opera in 1944–45, and also with other European companies. She was invited to sing at the Metropolitan in the premiere of Samuel Barber's *Vanessa* during the 1957–58 season, but decided not to come to America. She was first heard in America in May 1968 in a New York Philharmonic concert conducted by Leonard Bernstein. She sang Strauss's *Four Last Songs* and in the solo quartet of Beethoven's *Ninth Symphony.* Sings a wide variety of roles: Cherubino, the Composer (*Ariadne auf Naxos*), Leonore (*Fidelio*), Dorabella and Fiordiligi (*Così Fan Tutte*), Donna Elvira and Donna Anna (*Don Giovanni*).

KABAIVANSKA, Raina, soprano: born in Burgass, Bulgaria. Made her Metropolitan debut as Nedda in *Pagliacci* on October 27, 1963. Has appeared as Mimi, Elizabeth (*Don Carlos*), Desdemona, Alice Ford and Leonora (*La Forza del Destino*).

KALIL, Margaret, soprano: born in Monroe, Louisiana. Graduate of Columbia University Teachers College and the Juilliard School of Music, where she had a scholarship. Made her operatic debut as Donna Anna in 1958 with the Chautauqua Opera Company, and her Metropolitan debut as the Celestial Voice in *Don Carlos* on October 7, 1965. Roles include Leonora (*Il Trovatore, La Forza del Destino*), Amelia, the Countess (*Le Nozze di Figaro*), Fiordiligi and Ariadne.

KAPPEL, Gertrude, dramatic soprano: born in Halle, Germany. Appeared extensively in Wagnerian roles in Hanover, Vienna, Munich, London, Madrid and Amsterdam. She made her Metropolitan debut on January 16, 1927, as Isolde—her best role. She sang all the Brünnhildes, also Leonore in *Fidelio,* Kundry, Ortrud, the Marschallin and Elektra. On December 3, 1932, she sang the title role of Elektra in the first performance of Richard Strauss's opera at the Metropolitan. Miss Kappel, whose married name was Mrs. Simon Vukas, died on April 3, 1971, at her villa near Munich. She was 86 years old.

KARLSRUD, Edmond, basso: born in Scobey, Montana. Received his musical training in New York City, then appeared extensively as a concert artist. He made his Metropolitan debut as Hans Foltz in *Die Meistersinger* on January 22, 1969, subsequently appeared in comprimario roles such as Billy Jackrabbit (*La Fanciulla del West*), the Friar (*Don Carlos*), the Duke of Verona (*Roméo et Juliette*) and the Jailer in *Tosca;* has also appeared as the King in *Aïda.*

KELEMEN, Zóltan, bass-baritone: born in Budapest. Made his professional debut in Augsburg, Germany, in 1959, as Kezal in *The Bartered Bride*. Subsequently he appeared as Don Alfonso (*Così Fan Tutte*) and Osmin (*The Abduction from the Seraglio*). In 1962 he started at Bayreuth as a comprimario, singing the Fourth Noble in *Lohengrin* and one of the mastersingers (1963) until promoted to Alberich (*Der Ring des Nibelugen*) in 1964. He was recommended to Herbert von Karajan. He later sang the role of Alberich in at least eight different *Ring* productions. In this role, he made his Metropolitan debut in *Das Rheingold* on November 22, 1968. Other roles include Baron Ochs, Leporello, Falstaff (Verdi's opera and Nicolai's *The Merry Wives of Windsor*), Klingsor (*Parsifal*), the Grand Inquisitor (*Don Carlos*), Gianni Schicchi, Dr. Bartolo (*Le Nozze di Figaro*).

KELLEY, Norman, tenor: born in Bangor, Maine. A graduate of the Rochester Conservatory of Music. With the New York City Opera Company he appeared with outstanding success in such contemporary operas as *The Devil and Daniel Webster, The Crucible* and *The Consul.* He made his Metropolitan debut as Mimi in *Das Rheingold* on January 18, 1957, and later scored as Prince Shuisky in *Boris Godunof,* and in *Wozzeck.* Kelley has won critical acclaim as a talented singing actor.

KELLOGG, Clara Louise, soprano (1842–1916): born in Sumter, South Carolina. One of the leading American women singers of the nineteenth century to make an international reputation. Trained in New York by her mother, she made her operatic debut at the Academy of Music in 1861. She sang in London in 1867. In 1874–75 she organized her own troupe for giving opera in English and sang with the company 125 times. She retired from the stage in 1887. In 1913 she wrote *Memoirs of an American Prima Donna,* an authoritative commentary on famous singers of her day. Miss Kellogg was the wife of the theatrical manager Karl Strakosch. She died in New Hartford, Connecticut.

KELLY, Michael, tenor (1762–1826): born in Dublin. He had an extraordinary career as a singer, composer and writer. He first appeared in public in Dublin in 1779, then in Italy. There he sang extensively and then appeared with the Court Opera in Vienna. There he became a friend of Mozart's and created the roles of Don Basilio and Don Curzio in the first performance of *Le Nozze di Figaro* on May 1, 1786. He returned to London and became actor-manager of the King's Theater. Besides singing on the stage and in oratorios and concerts, he supplied music for more than sixty plays and wrote many songs. He also wrote *Reminiscences,* an account of his own musical life and of the important singers of his day.

KIEPURA, Jan, tenor (1906–66): born in Sosnowiec, Poland, of a wealthy family. While still in his twenties he sang with the Vienna State Opera with sensational success, and subsequently sang in almost every opera house in Europe. In 1930 he appeared with the Chicago Opera Company. He made his Metropolitan debut as Rodolpho in *La Bohème* on February 10, 1938. He and his wife, the soprano Marta Eggerth, became famous as the stars of many *Merry Widow* performances. Kiepura also sang in a number of motion pictures in London and in Hollywood.

KILLEBREW, Gwendolyn, mezzo-soprano: born in Philadelphia, where she began her musical studies. She made her first solo appearance at Philadelphia's Robin Hood Dell. Later, at Temple University, she was soloist in Pablo Casal's *El Pessebro,* with the composer conducting the Philadelphia Orchestra and the Temple University Choir. Miss Killebrew has been a scholarship student at the Juilliard School of Music and also has sung with the Metropolitan Opera Studio. In 1967 she won the gold medal at the international singing contest of Belgium, and also received the Metropolitan Opera National Council's Virginia M. Stoughton Award. On November 21, 1967, she made her Metropolitan debut as Waltraute in *Die Walküre.*

KING, James, tenor: born in Dodge City, Kansas. He rose to prominence in Europe, following his study with baritone Martial Singher, during which his voice changed from baritone to tenor. In Florence and Milan he sang Cavaradossi, then made his debut at the Berlin Opera as the Singer in *Der Rosenkavalier.* Then he sang in Frankfurt, Munich, at the Salzburg Festival and at the Vienna Staatsoper. He made his Metropolitan debut as Florestan in *Fidelio* on January 8, 1965. In 1966 he scored in the role of the Emperor in the first Metropolitan production of *Die Frau ohne Schatten.* His other roles include Siegmund in *Die Walküre* and Don José in *Carmen.*

KIPNIS, Alexander, bass-baritone: born in Zhitomir, in the Russian Ukraine, where he began his musical career as a boy coloratura soprano. He entered the Conservatory of Music in Warsaw (then under the direction of the Russian Imperial Opera) and graduated with highest honors as a conductor. Actually began his adult singing career as a German prisoner in World War I. Studying music in Berlin, he was interred as an enemy alien. In a prison camp, a colonel heard him sing, ordered him to report to the local opera house. For five years he lived a double life: a prisoner by day, an opera star by night. After the war he starred in all the major opera houses of Europe. He was first heard in America on February 12, 1923, as Pogner in *Die Meistersinger*, performed by a German opera company with which Kipnis later toured the country. He made his Metropolitan debut on January 5, 1939, as Gurnemanz in *Parsifal* to great critical acclaim. He was famous as Boris Godunof, his favorite role.

KIRCHOFF, Walther, tenor: born in Berlin. He studied voice with Lilli Lehmann and was the leading tenor with the Berlin Opera from 1906 to 1920. His debut performance as Loge in *Das Rheingold* at the Metropolitan on January 28, 1927, was greeted with thunderous applause, and his was called one of the finest impersonations of the role seen in New York up to that time. He left the company in 1931.

KIRSTEN, Dorothy, soprano: born in Montclair, New Jersey. Studied in Italy and made her operatic debut there. She made her American debut as Pousette in *Manon* with the Chicago Opera Company, then sang with the San Carlo Opera Company, the New York City Opera, and with the San Francisco, New Orleans and Havana opera companies. She made her Metropolitan debut on December 1, 1945, as Mimi. In December 1965, on the twentieth anniversary of her debut, she sang Minnie in *La Fanciulla del West*. Miss Kirsten also appeared in motion pictures with Mario Lanza and Bing Crosby. A talented singing actress, she has been acclaimed for her vivid stage personality.

KNIPLOVÁ, Nadezda, soprano: born in the province of Moravia in Czechoslovakia. A star of the Prague National Theater since 1964, she has since risen to international fame, singing Brünnhilde in Salzburg, Rome, Vienna and San Francisco. Her New York debut was with the Hamburg Opera at the Metropolitan during the 1967 Lincoln Center Festival, when she sang Kostelnitchka in Janáček's *Jenufa*. The following year she was heard at Carnegie Hall with the Little Orchestra

Society in a concert performance of the same composer's *The Makropoulos Case.*

KÓNYA, Sándor, tenor: born in Sarkad, Hungary. Acquired German citizenship and studied in Detmold at the Academy of Music, then in Milan. He made his debut in Bielefeld, Germany, sang at the Berlin Städtische Opera in 1954 and then in Stuttgart, Hamburg and Vienna. He attracted international attention with his first Lohengrin at Bayreuth in 1958. He made his La Scala debut as Radames in May 1960 and in September of that year he first appeared on the American stage as Dick Johnson in *La Fanciulla del West.* He made his Metropolitan debut as Lohengrin on October 28, 1961—one of his best roles—and he is equally effective as Calaf in *Turandot.*

KRAFT, Jean, mezzo-soprano: from Menasha, Wisconsin. Joined the Metropolitan after eight years as a leading singer with the New York City Opera, where she scored in a leading role in the New York premiere of Gian-Carlo Menotti's *Help! Help! the Globolinks!* on December 22, 1969. She made her Metropolitan debut as Flora Bervoix (*La Traviata*) in the broadcast performance on Saturday, March 21, 1970.

KRALL, Heidi, mezzo-soprano: born in Toledo, Ohio, of Swiss parents. She received her early musical training at the Cleveland Institute of Music. She made her operatic debut as Giorgetta in *Il Tabarro* at the Berkshire Music Festival, Tanglewood, Massachusetts. Appearances then followed with the Chatauqua Opera Association, the Montreal Symphony and in a London production of Menotti's *The Consul.* At the Metropolitan, she made her debut as Frasquita in *Carmen* on December 12, 1953. Later she sang Musetta and Marguerite (*Faust*) and appeared in a variety of roles.

KRAUS, Alfredo, tenor: born in Las Palmas, Canary Islands. Studied voice in Barcelona, Valencia and Milan. Made his operatic debut in Cairo as the Duke in *Rigoletto.* From then on he sang in opera houses all over the world, among them the Chicago Lyric Theater. His Metropolitan debut was as the Duke on February 16, 1966. His repertoire ranges from Rinuccio in *Gianni Schicchi* to Arturo in *I Puritani* and the title role in *Werther.*

KRAUSE, Tom, baritone: born in Helsinki, Finland. He made his debut in 1959 with West Berlin's Deutsche Oper as Escamillo, and three years later joined the Hamburg Opera Company, of which he is still a member. He then sang at Bayreuth, the Vienna Opera and La Scala, and was with the Hamburg troupe on its visit to Lincoln Center, New York City, in 1967. He was first heard in America as soloist in the American premiere of Benjamin Britten's *War Requiem*. The title of Kammersänger was conferred on him in Hamburg in 1967. He made his Metropolitan debut as Count Almaviva in *Le Nozze di Figaro* on October 11, 1967. In Hamburg in 1968 he created the title role in Humphrey Searle's *Hamlet*.

KUCHTA, Gladys, dramatic soprano: born in Chicopee, Massachusetts. She studied in New York at the Columbia Opera Workshop, the David Mannes School and the Juilliard School of Music. In 1951 she studied in Milan on a Fulbright grant. That year she made her debut in Florence, singing Elvira to Birgit Nilsson's Donna Anna. Since that time much of her career has been in Germany, where she is a member of the Berlin Städtische Oper. She has sung Brünnhilde (*Die Walküre*) at the Bayreuth Festival. On March 4, 1961, she made her Metropolitan debut as Chrysothemis in *Elektra*. She also sings that title role and has performed it more than sixty-five times. Other roles include Isolde, Sieglinde, Gutrune, Elsa, the Dyer's Wife (*Die Frau ohne Schatten*), Aïda, Turandot, Fidelio and Senta.

KULLMANN, Charles, tenor: born in New Haven, Connecticut, of German parents. First appeared as soloist with the Yale Glee Club, then studied at Juilliard on a scholarship. After three years he was granted a fellowship at the American Conservatory at Fontainebleau, France. On his return to the United States he joined the faculty of Smith College. Later he made his debut with the American Opera Company as Pinkerton, then sang in Berlin, Vienna, Salzburg and at Covent Garden. He made his Metropolitan debut as Faust on December 19, 1935. In fifteen seasons with the company, Kullmann sang some thirty leading roles. In 1954 he returned to the Metropolitan in the character role of Prince Shuisky in *Boris Godunof*, later added Herod (*Salome*) and Tannhäuser to his repertoire. He retired in 1960.

KUNZ, Erich, baritone: born in Vienna. A star of the Vienna Staatsoper since 1941, he also is a master of the Viennese style in operetta and folk song. In opera, his specialty is Mozart roles, though he also is a famous Beckmesser in *Die Meistersinger*, a role that he sang during his one season at the Metropolitan, where he made his debut as Leporello on November 26, 1952.

LABLACHE, Luigi, basso with tenor range (1794–1858): born in Naples of a French father and an Irish mother. From all accounts, one of the most phenomenal singers in history. A giant of a man, he could sing bass and tenor parts with equal facility. In Naples he attended the Conservatorio della Pietà de Turchini and began his career as a buffo. Later he sang in Vienna, Paris and London with enormous success. As a boy in 1809 he sang the alto solos in Mozart's *Requiem* at a memorial service for Haydn, and in 1827 he was one of the torchbearers at the funeral of Beethoven. He sang the bass solos of the Mozart *Requiem* at that service, and the *Lachrymosa* at the funeral of Bellini in 1835. He created the role of Riccardo in *I Puritani*. The soprano Jenny Lind said of him: "Lablache is a genius! And what a voice! And the most perfect actor you could ever see!"

LABÓ, Flaviano, tenor: native of Piacenza, Italy. Made his Metropolitan debut as Alvaro in *La Forza del Destino* on November 29, 1957. In the following season, he was dismissed from the company for failing to perform a role for which he had contracted. He was reinstated, however, some five seasons later. In the interim, he sang at the New York City Opera in leading roles, which included Calaf in *Turandot*. Labó performs with distinction in dramatic tenor roles.

LAMBRINOS, Theodore, baritone: born in Brooklyn. Early in his musical career he was a soloist with the Don Cossack choir. He made his operatic debut in a Hunter College (New York) Workshop production of Rossini's *Il Turco in Italia*. As finalist in the Metropolitan Opera Council's Regional Auditions, he won the Gladys Axman Taylor Award of two thousand dollars. He was one of the four artists of the Metropolitan National Company to join the regular company. Lambrinos made his Metropolitan debut on February 15, 1968, as the Herald in *Lohengrin*.

LAMMERS, Gerda, soprano: born in suburban Berlin. She was well known as a concert and lieder singer before she made her operatic debut as Marie in *Wozzeck* at Cassel in 1955. In that year she sang one of the Walküren at Bayreuth. In 1957 she made a highly successful appearance at Covent Garden as Elektra. She then sang extensively in England and on the Continent. At the Metropolitan, she made her debut as Elektra (her favorite role) on March 16, 1962.

LANDI, Bruno, tenor (1900–68): born in Milan. Made his Metropolitan debut January 12, 1938, as the Duke in *Rigoletto,* and sang with the company for seven seasons. Later made his home Buenos Aires, where he taught singing.

LANG, Edith, soprano: born in Chicago. One of the few American singers to be honored with the title Kammersängerin, she has sung in many European opera houses but is a permanent member of the Hamburg Opera, with which she sang at the Metropolitan during the 1967 Lincoln Center Festival. Her regular roles in Hamburg include Aïda, Tosca, Santuzza and Fidelio. With the San Francisco Opera, she sang the Empress in the American premiere of Strauss's *Die Frau ohne Schatten* on September 17, 1959.

LANGDON, Michael, basso: born in England. He was one of the leading basses at Covent Garden for more than fifteen years. At the Metropolitan he appeared in a single performance as Baron Ochs on November 2, 1964. He was heard again in the United States on May 23, 1968, singing Hunding in a concert version Act I of *Die Walküre* with Eileen Farrell and the New York Philharmonic.

LAUBENTHAL, Rudolf, tenor: born in Düsseldorf. Sang Wagnerian roles at the Berlin Opera and at Covent Garden prior to coming to America. Made his Metropolitan debut as Walther in *Die Meistersinger* on November 9, 1923, and appeared there in Wagner operas for the next decade.

LAURI-VOLPI, Giacomo, tenor: born in Lanuvio, Italy. Made his debut at the Costanzi Theater, Rome, in 1920 as Des Grieux (*Manon*) and subsequently sang in all the leading theaters of Europe. He made his debut at the Metropolitan as the Duke in *Rigoletto* on January 26, 1923. Lauri-Volpi was endowed with a ringing voice of striking dramatic power; his brilliant top tones recalled those of one of the most famous tenors of the early nineteenth century, Francesco Tamagno.

LAWRENCE, Marjorie, dramatic soprano: born near Melbourne, Australia, in a small village called Deans Marsh. She made her debut as Elisabeth in *Tannhäuser* in Monte Carlo in 1932. Shortly afterward she joined the Paris Opéra and was the leading soprano there for three years. She made her Metropolitan debut as Brünnhilde (*Die Walküre*) on December 18, 1935. She made operatic history during a performance of *Die Götterdämmerung* during the Immolation Scene when she leaped astride her horse Grane and rode him toward the funeral pyre. An accomplished actress and a singer with a dynamic personality, Miss Lawrence sang not only all the Wagnerian roles, but also Salome, Aïda, Thaïs, Alceste and Rachel in *La Juive*. In 1942 she was stricken with polio. Exhibiting incredible strength and will power, she continued singing. Progress in her recovery was marked by her appearance as guest at a "welcome home" concert on December 27, 1942, at the Metropolitan, where she sang the Venusberg duet (*Tannhäuser*) with Lauritz Melchior. Though still immobilized, but with her vocal powers undiminished, she sang the role of Venus in a *Tannhäuser* performance on January 22, 1943. Miss Lawrence subsequently became a teacher at Southern Illinois University.

LAZZARI, Virgilio, basso (1890–1965): born in Assisi, Italy. He sang extensively in Europe and was first heard in America on February 13, 1918, as Rodolfo in Catalani's *Loreley* in a performance given by the Chicago Opera Company at the Lexington Theater in New York. He appeared at the Metropolitan for the first time on January 3, 1935, as Leporello, and was commended for his polished characterization of the role. He also was famous for his role of King Archibaldo in Montemezzi's *L'Amore dei Tre Re*, which he sang first in 1917, then for the last time at the Metropolitan in 1949.

LEAR, Evelyn, soprano: born in New York City. Her grandfather was a renowned cantor and her mother, Nina Kwartin, a famous singer. In 1953 Miss Lear studied at the Opera Workshop of the Juilliard School of Music, where she met her future husband, baritone Thomas Stewart. She continued her vocal studies in Europe and sang at Berlin's Deutsche Oper. Then, with her portrayal of the title role of Alban Berg's *Lulu*, she achieved international fame, and she has sung this role in the leading opera houses of the world. In 1961 she created the title role of Klebe's *Alkmene*. She made her Metropolitan debut as Lavinia Mannon in the world premiere of Marvin David Levy's *Mourning Becomes Electra* on March 17, 1967. An unusually talented singing actress, she also has appeared at the Metropolitan as Octavian in *Der Rosenkavalier*, Marie in *Wozzeck*, and the Composer in *Ariadne auf Naxos*.

LEHMANN, Lilli, soprano (1848–1929): born in in Würzburg, Bavaria. She was a pupil of her mother, a singer and harpist. She began her career as a coloratura soprano and sang extensively in German opera houses. In 1875 she studied with Richard Wagner and sang small roles in the first production of the complete *Ring* cycle at Bayreuth. She made her Metropolitan debut on November 25, 1885, singing Carmen in German. She was the first Metropolitan Norma and sang Isolde and the three Brünnhildes at the American premieres of four Wagner operas. She had a repertoire of 170 roles in 119 operas and was a phenomenal vocalist as well as a celebrated eccentric and formidable personality. She left the Metropolitan in 1899, having contributed much to the Golden Age of singing. She later helped found the Salzburg Festival, wrote several books and taught many pupils, including Geraldine Farrar and Olive Fremstad.

LEHMANN, Lotte, soprano: born in Perleberg, Germany. After singing with the Hamburg Opera, she became one of the most loved stars of the Vienna Staatsoper. After singing with the Chicago Opera, she made her Metropolitan debut as Sieglinde in *Die Walküre* on January 11, 1934. Her roles there included Eva, Elsa, Elisabeth and Tosca, as well as her most famous role, the Marschallin in *Der Rosenkavalier*, which she first sang at Covent Garden. She had previously sung the roles of Sophie and Octavian in the same opera. Another of her great roles was Fidelio, which she sang at the Salzburg Festival with Toscanini conducting. Her Metropolitan farewell was as the Marschallin in 1945. One of the great lieder singers of the century, she continued to give concerts until 1951. She later wrote several books, conducted classes in Santa Barbara, California, and helped stage *Der Rosenkavalier* at the Metropolitan in 1962. Her eightieth birthday in 1966 was widely celebrated.

LEIDER, Frida, soprano: born in Berlin. One of the great stars at Bayreuth, in German opera houses and at Covent Garden, she appeared at the Metropolitan for only two seasons after her debut as Isolde on January 16, 1933. Many consider her the finest Isolde of modern times.

LEMNITZ, Tiana, soprano: an Alsatian, she was born when her native city of Metz was under German domination. Her father was a military bandmaster. She received her musical education at Hoch's Conservatory in Frankfurt, then made her operatic debut as Eva in *Die Meistersinger* at Aachen. In the 1930s she declined the invitation of manager Edward Johnson to come to the Metropolitan. She spent much of her subsequent career in East Germany. Noted for her musicianship and the beautiful quality of her voice, she is known is this country mostly through her many records.

LEWIS, Brenda, soprano: born in Sunbury, Pennsylvania. First sang with the Philadelphia Opera Company, then with the New York City Opera Company during the 1945–46 season. In 1949 she appeared in the Broadway production of the late Marc Blitzstein's *Regina*. She made her Metropolitan debut as Musetta on February 26, 1952. Other roles there included Elvira (*Don Giovanni*), Venus (*Tannhäuser*), Rosalinde (*Die Fledermaus*), Vanessa, Salome and Carmen.

LEWIS, Richard, tenor: born in Manchester, England, of a family of musicians. One of the leading tenors at Covent Garden, he is internationally known for outstanding performances in contemporary operas. He was acclaimed for his performace of Aaron in the American premiere of Arnold Schönberg's *Moses and Aaron*, given by the Sarah Caldwell Opera Troupe in Boston in December 1966. He has since appeared in a number of opera and concert performances in this country.

LIND, Jenny, coloratura soprano (1820–87): born in Stockholm. Famous in operatic history as the "Swedish Nightingale." At the age of nine, her voice attracted attention and she was admitted as an actress-pupil to the opera school of the Royal Theater in Stockholm. At thirteen, she appeared as actress or singer in twenty-two performances; at the age of fourteen, in twenty-six; at the age of fifteen, she appeared in eighteen performances and sang her first role in grand opera. When she was sixteen she was made a regular member of the company, and in that year she appeared ninety-two times. By the time she was twenty-one she was an established star of the Stockholm Opera, where she sang Euryanthe, Pamina, Donna Anna, Lucia, Norma, Julia in Spontini's *La Vestale* and Alice in *Robert le Diable*. Then she went to Paris to study with Manuel Garcia. After that—from 1844 to 1849—she toured the Continent and the British Isles with sensational success. In 1850–51 she toured America and Cuba under the management of the flamboyant showman Phineas T. Barnum. She had by that time given up opera and had confined herself to concert appearances. But her legendary appeal gradually waned and she left America in May 1852. Her last appearance in opera was in 1849 but she continued to sing in oratorios and concerts until 1870. In mid-career she married her accompanist, Otto Goldschmidt.

LINDHOLM, Berit, soprano: native of Sweden. Made her debut at the Stockholm Royal Opera in 1963. Was successful in lyric-dramatic roles such as the Countess in *Le Nozze di Figaro* and Tosca, and also as Brünnhilde at the Bayreuth Festival. She made her concert debut in America in an all-Wagner program with Leopold Stokowski and the American Symphony Orchestra at Carnegie Hall on December 7, 1969.

LIPPERT, Marion, soprano: native of Germany. Studied voice in Munich and Milan. Prior to coming to America she sang for more than a decade in operas in the Italian and German repertoire. She has sung in the opera houses of Nürnberg, Hanover, Braunschweig, Berlin, Munich, Florence, Venice, Naples, Barcelona, Lisbon and Vienna. She made her Metropolitan debut as Turandot on October 3, 1968.

LIPTON, Martha, mezzo-soprano: born in New York. During the early part of her career she was frequently heard on radio, then first appeared in operatic roles with the New Opera Company in New York. She made her Metropolitan debut as Siebel (*Faust*) on November 27, 1944, the season's opening performance. Other Metropolitan roles included Mother Goose in *The Rake's Progress*, Fricka, Brangäne, Amneris and Geneviève (*Pelléas et Mélisande*). During the 1961–62 season she sang with the New York City Opera. Miss Lipton's voice was commended for its rich, velvety quality.

LIST, Emanuel, basso (1890–1967): born in Vienna. The leading Wagnerian basso of his time, he appeared frequently at the Berlin Opera, the Vienna Staatsoper and Covent Garden. His Metropolitan debut was as the Landgraf in *Tannhäuser* on December 27, 1933. He sang with the company until 1950. Though he sang all the Wagner bass parts, he was most famous for his Baron Ochs in *Der Rosenkavalier*.

LJUNGBERG, Göta, dramatic soprano (1893–1955): born in Sundsvall, Sweden. Began her musical career in Stockholm, sang later at Covent Garden, then made her debut as Sieglinde at the Metropolitan on January 20, 1932. Other Wagnerian roles there included Elsa, Brünnhilde and Isolde. She also sang Salome and Elektra. A handsome woman with a commanding stage presence, she was impressive in her characterizations.

LONDON, George, bass-baritone: born in Montreal; real name Burnstein. Studied at Los Angeles City College and made his operatic debut there as Antonio (the gardener) in *Le Nozze di Figaro*. London had a notable career abroad, where he was widely acclaimed for his role of Boris, which he sang with the Bolshoi Opera. He sings the role both in Russian and in English. In 1950 he auditioned in Bayreuth for Wieland Wagner, who asked him to sing the Wotans in the 1951 Bayreuth Festival. London, however, refused because he felt he was not yet ready for the roles. Instead, he agreed to sing Amfortas in *Parsifal* at the opening Festival performance. Later he sang the title role in *Der Fliegende Holländer* and the three Wotans under Wieland Wagner's direction. He made his debut at the Metropolitan as Amonasro on November 13, 1951, and continued with the company as one of its leading male singers. There he created the role of Abdul in the American premiere of Menotti's *The Last Savage* on January 24, 1964. In recent years he taught opera at the University of Cincinnati, and in 1968 was president of the American Guild of Musical Artists. He also was named as opera program maker for the new John F. Kennedy Center for the Performing Arts in Washington, D.C., scheduled for opening in 1970.

LORENGAR, Pilar, soprano: born in Zaragoza, Spain. Studied in Madrid, where she made her operatic debut in 1951. In 1955 she made her New York debut in recital, and in that year she appeared for the first time at Covent Garden as Violetta in *La Traviata*. Appearances followed at the Berlin Opera, the Glyndebourne Festival, and in Buenos Aires. She made her operatic debut in America with the San Francisco Opera in the role of Desdemona. At the Metropolitan, she made her debut as a replacement for Elisabeth Schwarzkopf in the role of Donna Elvira on February 11, 1966. Her other roles there are Madama Butterfly, Marguerite, Eva in *Die Meistersinger*, and Pamina in *Die Zauberflöte*.

LORENZ, Max, tenor: born in Düsseldorf. Sang with the Dresden Opera, and after 1934 with the Berlin Opera and at the Bayreuth Festivals. He made his Metropolitan debut as Walther in *Die Meistersinger*, on November 12, 1931, and sang Wagnerian roles with the company for two decades, after which he sang with the Vienna Staatsoper until his retirement in 1965.

LOVE, Shirley, mezzo-soprano: born in Detroit. Made her operatic debut at Wayne State University as Madame Flora in Menotti's *The Medium*. She later joined the Metropolitan Opera Studio and sang the role of the Second Esquire in *Parsifal* in a Metropolitan performance on March 10, 1966. Since then, she has sung character roles such as Martha in *Faust*.

LUDGIN, Chester, baritone: born in New York City. A leading singing actor of the New York City Opera Company, where he has sung all the leading bass-baritone roles. He created the role of John Proctor in Robert Ward's *The Crucible* in the American premiere at the New York City Center on October 26, 1961. He received all his operatic training and experience in the United States and has an active repertoire of seventy-five leading roles.

LUDWIG, Christa, mezzo-soprano: born in Berlin. Her father was the late Anton Ludwig, tenor with the Vienna Volksoper. Her mother, a former opera singer and a leading voice teacher in Vienna, was Christa's only teacher. In September 1946, following a number of concert appearances, Christa was taken on at the Städtische Bühne in Frankfurt as a trainee for small mezzo parts. Her first appearance there was as Prince Orlofsky in *Die Fledermaus* during the 1946–47 season. She sang in numerous operettas and operas in Frankfurt, at the Landestheater in Darmstadt and at the Landestheater in Hanover. Her Vienna Staatsoper debut as Cherubino (at the invitation of Dr. Karl Böhm) in May 1955 launched her on an international career. In 1957 she married the bass-baritone Walter Berry and they appeared as a team in opera and in lieder recitals. She appeared at the Metropolitan for the first time as Brangäne on January 21, 1959, then made her official debut as Cherubino in *Le Nozze di Figaro* on December 10, 1959. She and her husband appeared in the first New York performance of *Die Frau ohne Schatten* at the Metropolitan on October 2, 1966, in which she sang the role of Barak's Wife.

MacNEIL, Cornell, baritone: born in Minneapolis. First sang leading roles with the New York City Opera. Made his Metropolitan debut as Rigoletto on March 21, 1959, and has continued singing leading roles there including Macbeth, Simon Boccanegra, Nabucco, Scarpia and Barnaba in *La Gioconda*.

MACURDY, John, basso: born in Detroit. In 1959 he joined the New York City Opera Company, where he sang all the leading roles for his voice. Also appeared with the Santa Fe Opera, the New Orleans Opera Association, the Houston Grand Opera Association, the San Francisco Opera and under the direction of Boris Goldovsky at the Berkshire Music Center, Tanglewood, Massachusetts. He made his Metropolitan debut as Samuele (Count Warting) in *Un Ballo in Maschera* on December 8, 1962. He created the role of Ezra Mannon in Marvin David Levy's *Mourning Becomes Electra* in 1967.

MADEIRA, Jean, mezzo-soprano: born in Centralia, Illinois; maiden name, Browning. A protégée of Karin Branzell's, she developed a successful career in Europe and for a time was one of the mainstays of the Vienna Staatsoper and the National Theater in Munich. On December 2, 1948, she made her Metropolitan debut as the First Norn in *Die Götterdämmerung*, and subsequently gave vivid portrayals of La Cieca (*La Gioconda*), Ulrica (*Un Ballo in Maschera*), Carmen, Azucena, Herodias (*Salome*) and Clytemnestra (*Elektra*). In 1968 Miss Madeira was presented with a silver clock in recognition of her twenty years of artistic service to the Metropolitan Opera Company.

MAISON, René, tenor (1895–1962): born in Belgium. Studied in Antwerp, Brussels and Paris. Sang with the Monte Carlo Opera from 1922 to 1925, then in Paris with the Opéra and the Opéra-Comique. In America, he appeared for several seasons with the Chicago Opera Company. He made his Metropolitan debut as Walther in *Die Meistersinger* on February 3, 1936.

MALAS, Spiro, basso: born in Baltimore, Maryland. Made professional debut with the Baltimore Opera as Marco in *Gianni Schicchi*, in a production supervised by Rosa Ponselle. After winning 1960–61 American Opera Auditions, he made debut as Colline in *La Bohème* at Teatro Nuovo, Milan. One of five finalists in 1961–62 Metropolitan Opera Auditions. That season he sang Vaarlam in NBC-TV *Boris Godunof*, and in New York City Opera's Gilbert and Sullivan productions. Made grand opera debut with the New York City Opera in 1962–63 season as Bartolo in *Le Nozze di Figaro*. Toured with Sutherland-Williamson Opera Company in Australia, 1965–66, appeared with Sutherland in command performance of *La Fille du Régiment* for Queen Elizabeth at Covent Garden, 1966–67. Sang the role of Tutor in Alberto Ginastera's *Don Rodrigo* in American premiere of the opera on February 22, 1966; sang in American Opera Society's premiere of Haydn's *Orfeo ed Euridice* in February 1968. On March 18, 1970, he appeared in the televised premiere of Jack Beeson's *My Heart's in the Highlands*.

MALIBRAN, Maria, contralto with soprano range (1808–36): born in Paris. One of the legendary singers of the early nineteenth century—along with Giuditta Pasta and her own sister, Pauline Viardot. They were the daughters of Manuel Garcia, and Maria began studying with her father when she was fifteen years old. A year later, in 1824, she appeared in public for the first time in Paris at a musical club founded by her father. On June 7, 1825, she made her operatic debut in London as Rosina. Three weeks later she sang the role of Felicia in the London premiere of Giacomo Meyerbeer's *Il Crociato in Egitto* with sensational success. The next season the Garcia family made its historic visit to New York to bring Italian opera to the public. During their nine-month season, Maria, then eighteen, sang leading roles in six Rossini operas— *Il Barbiere di Siviglia, Otello, La Donna del Lago, La Cenerentola, Semiramide, Il Turco in Italia*—and in *Don Giovanni*. In 1827 she returned to Paris, leaving her husband, François-Eugène Malibran, after a short-lived marriage. From then on—in Paris, London and Italy—she achieved her greatest operatic triumphs. In March 1836 she married the celebrated Belgian violinist Charles Auguste de Bériot. In April tragedy struck: She fell from a horse in London, but despite serious injuries persisted in singing at a choral festival in Manchester. It was said that the strain of performance, coupled with the effects of the injuries, hastened her death, at the age of twenty-eight, on September 23, 1836.

MANGELSDORF, Simone, soprano: born in Leipzig, Germany, of a musical family. Studied voice at the Musikhochschule in Frankfurt and made her operatic debut in Monteverdi's *L'Orfeo* with the Frankfurt Opera. The performance was conducted by the composer Paul Hindemith, who invited her to sing his song cycle *Das Marienleben* in Brussels, Antwerp and Zurich. Miss Mangelsdorf is first soprano with the Städtische Bühne in Cologne and guest artist at opera in Düsseldorf, Nürnberg and Hanover. In 1965 she sang at Bayreuth for the first time, and in 1967 at the Salzburg Festival. For the 1968 Easter Festival there, Herbert von Karajan engaged her to sing Freia in *Das Rheingold*, the role in which she made her Metropolitan debut on November 22, 1968.

MANSKI, Dorothee, soprano (1895–1967): born in New York City. She made her debut as the Witch in *Hänsel und Gretel* on November 5, 1927. A versatile singer, she was one of the leading Wagnerian sopranos during her years at the Metropolitan. She left the company in 1941 to join the faculty of Indiana University. Miss Manski died in Bloomington, Indiana, on February 24, 1967. Her daughter, Inge Manski, also sang at the Metropolitan.

MARAGLIANO, Luisa, soprano: born in Genoa, Italy. Since her opera debut in Verona in 1959, she has become one of the leading sopranos at La Scala and other Italian opera houses, as well as at the Colón in Buenos Aires. She made her American debut as Violetta in Philadelphia in 1961. In 1965 she won Parma's Verdi d'Oro Prize, previously awarded only to Mario del Monaco and Renata Tebaldi. She appeared at the Metropolitan in June 1968 with the Rome Opera Company as Lucrezia Contarini in Verdi's *I Due Foscari*.

MARDONES, José, baritone (1869–1932): born in Fontecha, Spain. First heard with the Boston National Opera Company, he made his Metropolitan debut as the High Priest (*Aïda*) on November 12, 1917, with impressive effect. He remained with the company through the 1925–26 season.

MAREK, Dan, tenor: native of Oklahoma. After studying in California, he became a member of the New York City Opera Company. He made his Metropolitan debut as Arturo in *Lucia di Lammermoor* on September

30, 1965, and continued singing with the company in comprimario roles.

MARIO, Queena, soprano (1896–1951): born Marion Tillotson in Akron, Ohio. A pupil of Marcella Sembrich's, she herself was the teacher of Rose Bampton and Helen Jepson. While touring with the Antonio Scotti Opera Company, she came to the attention of Gatti-Casazza, who invited her to audition. At the Metropolitan, she made her debut as Juliette (*Roméo et Juliette*) on February 10, 1923, and appeared effectively in numerous secondary roles; she had a repertoire of forty-five operas in four languages.

MARSH, Calvin, baritone: born in Morrisville, Pennsylvania. Made his Metropolitan debut as Nachtigall in *Die Meistersinger* on November 11, 1954. He continued with the company in secondary roles until 1963, when he was graduated to featured roles. Recently has sung with the New York City Opera Company.

MARTINELLI, Giovanni, dramatic tenor (1885–1969): born in Montagnana, in the Italian province of Padova, one of fourteen children of a cabinet maker. He made his first operatic appearance in 1910 in Milan in the title role of Verdi's *Ernani* to great applause. In 1911 he came to the attention of Puccini, who selected him to sing Dick Johnson in *La Fanciulla del West* when that opera was produced in Rome. The following year, at Covent Garden, he created the role of Gennaro in Wolf-Ferrari's *The Jewels of the Madonna,* then returned there in 1914 to create the role of Paolo in Riccardo Zandonai's *Francesca da Rimini.* He also sang this role in the American premiere of the opera at the Metropolitan in 1916. Martinelli made a sensational American debut on November 20, 1913, at the Metropolitan as Rodolpho in *La Bohème.* From that time on—particularly following the death of Caruso—he was reigning star of the Metropolitan's tenor wing. He took over the role of Eleazar in Halévy's *La Juive,* made famous by Caruso, and also was enormously effective as Otello. During his career he sang Radames in nearly four hundred performances of *Aïda.* At the age of fifty-six he was named artistic director of the Chicago Opera Company, and in 1948 he sang Tristan, in German, to Flagstad's Isolde with that company. In his prime, Martinelli was acclaimed for the clarion quality of his voice, which had both brilliance and beauty. He died in New York on February 2, 1969.

MARTINI, Nino, tenor: born in Verona, Italy. Made his operatic debut in Italy in *I Puritani* at the age of twenty-one. In the United States, he made his debut in 1931 as the Duke in *Rigoletto* with the Philadelphia Opera Company. Subsequently, he achieved considerable fame as a radio artist, which worked to his advantage when he made his debut at the Metropolitan as the Duke on December 28, 1933. He made a favorable impression in such roles as Edgardo (*Lucia di Lammermoor*), Rinuccio (*Gianni Schicchi*), Rodolpho and Alfredo.

MASCHERINI, Enzo, baritone: born in Italy. Sang with the New York City Opera Company prior to coming to the Metropolitan, where he made his debut as Lescaut in *Manon Lescaut* on December 26, 1949.

MASON, Edith, soprano: born in St. Louis, Missouri. Her debut at the Metropolitan as Sophie in *Der Rosenkavalier* on November 20, 1915, was well received. She left the company two years later, then returned for the 1935–36 season. A mainstay of the Chicago Opera, she was particularly noted as Madama Butterfly.

MATERNA, Amalia, dramatic soprano (1845–1918): born in Styria. She was the first Brünnhilde and the first Kundry in the premiere performances of the Wagnerian operas at Bayreuth. She toured America in 1884 and 1894, and after 1900 taught in Vienna.

MATHIS, Edith, soprano: born in Lucerne, Switzerland. Well known in America through recordings, she is a member of the Hamburg Opera, with which she sang at the Metropolitan in Hindemith's *Mathis der Maler* during the 1967 Lincoln Center Festival. She also has sung leading roles at Covent Garden and Glyndebourne and in Cologne, Berlin and Salzburg. Made her Metropolitan debut as Pamina on January 19, 1970.

MATZENAUER, Margarete, contralto (1881–1963): born in Hungary, the daughter of musicians. Her father was an orchestra conductor, her mother an opera singer. Made her operatic debut in Strasbourg, Germany, and sang there from 1901 to 1904. Thereafter she sang with the Munich Opera and also became well known in Europe as a recitalist. She made an impressive debut at the Metropolitan as Amneris on November 13, 1911, and was one of the leading contraltos of the company from then until 1930. Matzenauer was not only a top-ranking Wagnerian singer, but outstanding in such roles as La Cieca (*La Gioconda*), Octavian and Santuzza. She sang her first Kundry on New Year's Day, 1912, when she replaced Olive Fremstad at one hour's notice and performed without a single rehearsal.

MAUREL, Victor, baritone (1848–1923): born in Marseilles, France. One of the great singing actors of his time, he created three of the famous baritone roles in Milan: Tonio in *Pagliacci* (1892), Iago (1887) and Falstaff (1893). He sang Falstaff at the North American premiere at Metropolitan on February 4, 1895. His debut with the company had been as Iago on December 3, 1894. He remained with the company until 1899 and sang other roles such as Don Giovanni, Rigoletto, Valentin and Escamillo. He was one of the "seven stars" in the famous cast of *Les Huguenots* during these years, the others being Lillian Nordica or Lilli Lehmann, the two De Reszkes, Nellie Melba, Sofia Scalchi or Eugenia Mantelli and Pol Plançon.

MAYNOR, Dorothy, soprano: born in Norfolk, Virginia. An outstanding American singer of 1940s, Miss Maynor (the wife of the Reverend Dr. Shelby Rooks) was primarily a concert artist and sang with practically every major symphony orchestra in the United States. When Serge Koussevitzky heard her audition at Tanglewood for the Berkshire Festival, he exclaimed: "A miracle! A native Flagstad!" In 1963 she founded the Harlem School of the Arts as a cultural center for underprivileged Negro children. It subsequently expanded to include children and adults of all nationalities.

MAYR, Richard, basso (1877–1935): born in Vienna. Studied at the Vienna Conservatory and made his debut as Hagen in *Die Götterdämmerung* at Bayreuth in 1902. Until 1935 he was a member of the Vienna Opera, where he sang a wide range of roles. He was especially known for his buffo characterizations, such as Baron Ochs—the role for which he was famous. He made his Metropolitan debut as Pogner in *Die Meistersinger* on November 2, 1927.

McCORMACK, John, lyric tenor (1884–1945): born in Athlone, Ireland. For the first decade of his career he was an opera singer. It began in 1903, when he won the singing contest at the Feis Ceoil, the annual Dublin music festival, over twelve other tenors. As a result, he was enabled to go to Italy for a year's study. Later he heard Caruso, who served as an inspiration for further study. McCormack then made an outstandingly successful operatic debut as Turiddu at Covent Garden on October 15, 1907. He went on to score in all the great lyric roles. On November 10, 1909, he made his American debut as Alfredo in *La Traviata*, with Luisa Tetrazzini as Violetta, with the Hammerstein company at the Manhattan Opera House. For the next three years he sang with the Philadelphia Opera Company and the Chicago Opera Company, and toured Australia with the Melba Opera Company. On

February 23, 1911, he appeared with Mary Garden in the premiere performance of Victor Herbert's *Natoma* at the Metropolitan Opera House, Philadelphia. His next appearance with the Metropolitan was as Rodolpho (*La Bohème*) on November 14, 1917. McCormack eventually decided that his true métier was the concert field, in which he was without peer. A superb musician, with phrasing, diction and intonation always perfect, he was a master at Irish ballads and simple songs as well as the music of classical composers. McCormack is acknowledged as one of the finest singers of any time.

McCRACKEN, James, dramatic tenor: born in Gary, Indiana. After he made his Metropolitan debut in the small role of Parpignol (*La Bohème*) on November 21, 1953, he sang with the company as a comprimario for the next four seasons. He then went to Europe for further study and graduated into the leading dramatic tenor roles. He was particularly acclaimed for his Otello, the role in which he made a sensational success upon his return to the Metropolitan in 1963. He and his wife, mezzo-soprano Sandra Warfield, make their home in Switzerland and are members of the Zurich Opera.

MEADER, George, tenor: born in Minneapolis, Minnesota. Although he made an inconspicuous debut at the Metropolitan as Victor in Erich W. Korngold's *Die Tote Stadt* on November 19, 1921 (when Jeritza made her American debut in the leading role), he gained a reputation as an accomplished singing actor. He was considered one of the best Davids (*Die Meistersinger*) in Metropolitan annals. Another of his outstanding roles was Wenzel in *The Bartered Bride*.

MEISLE, Kathryn, contralto: born in Philadelphia. Studied at the Philadelphia Conservatory and made her professional debut as soloist with the Minneapolis Symphony in 1921. Was well known as a concert singer before entering opera. She made her operatic debut as Erda with the Chicago Opera in 1923. At the Metropolitan, she made her debut as Amneris on February 28, 1935.

MELBA, Nellie, coloratura soprano (1861–1931): born in Melbourne, Australia; her real name was Helen Porter Mitchell. She took up her singing career while in her twenties—after she had married, borne a son and left her husband. At twenty-seven she went to Paris, where she began studying with Mathilde Marchesi and saw her first opera. After nine months of study she made her debut as Gilda in Brussels, at the Théatre de la Monnaie. At the age of thirty she was a star in both London and Paris. At Covent Garden, she made her debut as Lucia on

May 24, 1888; the following year she sang in Paris. Melba made her Metropolitan debut—also as Lucia—on December 4, 1893. From then on she was the reigning queen of the operatic stage, and sang all the standard coloratura roles with spectacular success. There was one exception: the role of Brünnhilde in *Siegfried,* which she sang on December 30, 1896, with Jean De Reszke in the title role. With the role completely unsuited to her voice, her performance was a disaster. But the capital of Melba's personal musical kingdom was London, where there even were "Melba nights" at the opera. Her final official public appearance was at Covent Garden on June 8, 1926, when she sang scenes from her favorite operas, with the royal family in the audience. She made a farewell speech, then broke down and wept. With a voice of limpid purity, dazzling in its agility, range and intonation, Nellie Melba was ranked as one of the greatest coloratura sopranos of all time.

MELCHIOR, Lauritz, heldentenor: born in Copenhagen. He was one of a long line of illustrious singers who began their careers as baritones—including Donzelli (1790–1873), Zenatello (1876–1949) and Jean De Reszke. He first studied at the Copenhagen Conservatory. After eight years as a baritone, he made his tenor debut as Tannhäuser with the Royal Copenhagen Opera Company. His success won an invitation from Siegfried and Cosima Wagner to study Wagnerian roles at Bayreuth. From then on he became internationally famous for his Wagnerian roles. His debut at the Metropolitan on February 17, 1926, also was in the role of Tannhäuser, and he was then established as the company's leading Wagnerian tenor. During the 1938 through 1940 seasons he averaged a performance every four and a half days. It is a matter of record that he sang the key Wagnerian roles more times than any other tenor in history: 170 Siegmunds, 114 Tannhäusers, 125 young Siegfrieds, 101 Lohengrins, 223 Tristans, 100 *Götterdämmerung* Siegfrieds, 75 Parsifals. He was a tireless performer—he sang fifty-six concerts in fifty-six cities in fifty-six days. Retired and living in California, Melchior in 1965 created a foundation for the musical training of a heldentenor. Also gathering material for his memoirs, he observed that he is the last person alive to have sung under the direction of Cosima Wagner at Bayreuth.

MELIS, Carmen, soprano (1885–1967): born in Cagliari, Sardinia. A pupil of Jean De Reszke, she sang at La Scala under Toscanini's direction and was coached for *La Fanciulla del West,* which she sang in Rome, by Puccini himself. She made one of the first recordings of *Tosca* and during her career sang at Covent Garden, the Manhattan

Opera House (in 1909–10) and with the Boston and Chicago operas. Later in life, she taught at the Pesaro Conservatory, where two of her pupils were Renata Tebaldi and Rita Orlandi.

MELTON, James, tenor (1904–61): born in Moultrie, Georgia. Began his musical education at Vanderbilt University, Nashville, Tennessee, where he studied with Gaetano de Luca, the leading teacher of the Ward Belmont Conservatory. In 1927 he came to New York and sang at the famous Roxy Theater in stage shows which included scenes from operas. He had a successful career in radio, made several film musicals and toured with George Gershwin in 1934. Following appearances with the Cincinnati Zoo Opera and the Chicago Opera, he made his debut at the Metropolitan on December 7, 1942, as Tamino in *Die Zauberflöte*.

MERCER, Ruby, soprano: born in Athens, Ohio. She made her Metropolitan debut as Marguerite (*Faust*) on May 3, 1938, but appeared with the company only infrequently thereafter. She starred in two Broadway musicals, then in 1958 moved to Toronto. There she served as commentator on the Canadian Broadcasting Company's "Opera Time," and also as editor of the magazine *Opera Canada*. She later conducted the "Mr. and Mrs. Opera" program over station WNYC in New York.

MEREDITH, Morley, baritone: native of Winnipeg, Canada. Winning a "Singing Stars of Tomorrow" award enabled him to continue his studies, and he then launched what became a successful concert career. He sang leading roles with the New York City Opera during the 1954–55 season. At his Metropolitan debut on January 3, 1962, he sang the four baritone roles in *Les Contes d'Hoffmann*. He is recognized as a talented singing actor.

MERRILL, Robert, baritone: born in New York City; real name Moishe Miller. One of the leading baritones of the Metropolitan, where he has sung continuously since he made his debut as Germont in *La Traviata* on December 15, 1945. During that time he appeared on six Metropolitan opening nights. He came to the opera via the Metropolitan Auditions, after having become well known as a radio singer and concert artist. In the latter field he is a top-ranking attraction. Endowed with a naturally beautiful voice, Merrill is a favorite in the standard baritone roles. He celebrated his twenty-fifth anniversary at the Metropolitan by singing his debut role of Germont in a performance on October 31, 1970, with Joan Sutherland as Violetta. At the end of the third act, seven other Violettas came up on the stage to applaud him. All told, he has sung the role with 16 famous sopranos.

MEYER, Kerstin, mezzo-soprano: native of Sweden. First began studying voice in 1948 at the Royal Academy in Stockholm and made her debut as Azucena at the Royal Opera there in 1952. Awarded the Christine Nilsson Scholarship, she was able to study at the Mozarteum in Salzburg and in Italy. She returned to the Royal Opera to become the company's leading mezzo. Subsequently sang at the Vienna Staatsoper, the Hamburg Opera, and at Barcelona's Teatro Liceo, where she sang Brangäne to Birgit Nilsson's Isolde. She made her Metropolitan debut as Carmen on October 29, 1960, and appeared thereafter in a number of leading mezzo roles.

MICHALSKI, Raymond, basso: born in Bayonne, New Jersey. He was a piano prodigy and at the age of four played a concert with the New Jersey Symphony. As a young man he studied at the David Mannes School in New York City. His operatic debut was with the Philadelphia Grand Opera Company in 1959, in the role of Nourabad in *Les Pêcheurs de Perles*. Engaged for opera performances in New Orleans and Houston, Michalski learned four roles in eighteen days: Mathieu in *Andrea Chénier*, Nilakantha in *Lakmé*, Friar Laurence in *Roméo et Juliette* and the Grand Inquisitor in *Don Carlos*. On December 29, 1965, he made his Metropolitan debut as the King in *Aïda*.

MILANOV, Zinka, dramatic soprano: born in Zagreb, Yugoslavia; real name Kunc. In Zagreb she studied at the Royal Conservatory of Music. There one of her teachers was the famous Wagnerian soprano Milka Ternina. Later she sang in Prague, Vienna and Salzburg under the baton of Arturo Toscanini. At Salzburg in 1937 she was heard by Edward Johnson, then manager of the Metropolitan, who immediately took an option on her services. He stipulated that she must learn the leading roles in at least three Italian operas—in Italian, a language which she had never sung. Milanov learned the roles and made her debut as Leonora in *Il Trovatore* on December 17, 1937, with great success. For many years after that she was queen of the Italian repertoire at the Metropolitan. When she sang Madeleine in *Andrea Chénier* on her twenty-fifth anniversary with the company in 1962, she was hailed as "the greatest dramatic soprano since Rosa Ponselle." She appeared in 453 Metropolitan performances and retired at the close of the old opera house in 1966.

MILLER, Mildred, mezzo-soprano: born in Cleveland, Ohio; real name Müller. After studying at the New England Conservatory in Boston, she went to Germany for further study, then sang with the Stuttgart Opera and the Munich Opera. Her debut at the Metropolitan as

Cherubino on November 17, 1951, attracted special attention because she was considered ideally suited in appearance and voice for the role. She subsequently scored in such roles as Feodor in *Boris Godunof*, Dorabella in *Così Fan Tutte*, Nicklausse in *Les Contes d'Hoffmann*, Siebel in *Faust* and Magdalene in *Die Meistersinger*.

MILNES, Sherrill, baritone: born in Downers Grove, Illinois. He began his vocal studies at Drake University, Des Moines, Iowa, continued at Northwestern University in Chicago and made his first professional appearance there in concert. He then studied in Europe and made his operatic debut in Milan in the title role of *Il Barbiere di Siviglia*. In 1964 he joined the New York City Opera. He made an excellent impression in his debut as Valentin (*Faust*) at the Metropolitan on December 22, 1965. He was similarly effective as Miller in *Luisa Miller*. He also gave a vivid portrayal of Adam Brant in the Metropolitan's premiere of Marvin David Levy's *Mourning Becomes Electra* in 1967. He has continued with the company in leading baritone roles. He sang the role of Don Carlo in *Ernani* at the opening of the Metropolitan's 1970–71 season.

MITTELMANN, Norman, bass-baritone: born in Winnipeg, Canada, of German parentage. He is a graduate of Curtis Institute and an alumnus of Lotte Lehmann's Master Classes in Santa Barbara, California. He made his operatic debut in Toronto in 1959 as Marcello in *La Bohème*. Later that year he won the Fisher Award in the Metropolitan Auditions, then went to Germany. There he appeared in performances in Essen, Düsseldorf, Stuttgart, Berlin and Vienna. He made his Metropolitan debut as the Herald in *Lohengrin* on October 28, 1961. His other roles include Wolfram (*Tannhäuser*), Renato (*Un Ballo in Maschera*) and Kurvenal.

MÖDL, Marta, dramatic soprano: born in Germany. She began as a mezzo and late in her career reverted to mezzo roles after many years as a dramatic soprano. A star in German opera houses and at many Bayreuth Festivals, she was chosen to sing Fidelio in the performance that reopened the damaged Vienna Staatsoper after World War II. She sang Wagnerian roles at the Metropolitan for three seasons, making her debut as Brünnhilde (*Siegfried*) on January 30, 1957, to Wolfgang Windgassen's Siegfried.

MOFFO, Anna, lyric soprano: born in Wayne, Pennsylvania. She began her meteoric career by winning an award given by the Philadelphia Orchestra for singing "Un bel di," the only aria she knew at the time.

Thanks to a Fulbright scholarship, she was able to go to Italy for study. After her successful debut with the Rome Opera she achieved international fame with her performance as Cio-cio-san in a television production of *Madama Butterfly*. This led to a bid from La Scala, and subsequent appearances with the Vienna Staatsoper, Covent Garden, the Teatro Colón in Buenos Aires, the Chicago Lyric Opera and the San Francisco Opera. She made her Metropolitan debut as Violetta in 1959. Miss Moffo is the wife of Mario Lanfranchi, who directed her television Butterfly.

MOLESE, Michele, tenor: born in New York City. Trained in Milan, he made his debut there at the Teatro Nuovo in 1957. After seven years' experience in provincial Italian opera houses, he came into prominence at the 1963 Spoleto Festival. He then created the role of Kodanda in Menotti's *The Last Savage* at the Paris Opéra-Comique and, in the fall of 1963, joined the New York City Opera. A leading tenor of that company, he sings twenty Italian and twelve French roles and has been acclaimed as Turiddu, Cavaradossi, Rodolpho, Faust, Des Grieux and Tamino.

MOORE, Grace, soprano (1901–47): born in Jellico, Tennessee. While studying voice in Washington, D.C., she managed to arrange a concert appearance with Giovanni Martinelli, at which she sang "Ritorna vincitor" with considerable success. Then she borrowed $300, came to New York and sang in several Broadway musicals. Later she continued her vocal studies in Paris, where she sang at the Opéra-Comique. When she took her first curtain call as the heroine of *Louise,* composer Gustave Charpentier came forward from the audience and conducted the rest of the performance. Under his direction, she made a screen version of the opera. She made her Metropolitan debut as Mimi on February 7, 1928. In 1930 she went to Hollywood, where she made several very successful films, including *One Night of Love* with Tullio Carminati and *New Moon* with Lawrence Tibbett. Miss Moore's career was tragically cut short when she was killed in a plane crash in 1947.

MORELL, Barry, tenor: born in New York City. First sang with the New York City Opera Company at City Center, where he made his debut as Pinkerton in 1955. He made his Metropolitan debut in the same role on November 4, 1958, and has since sung more than seventeen roles with the company. He also has appeared at Covent Garden and in opera in Santiago, Chile.

MORGANA, Nina, soprano: born in Buffalo, New York, of Italian parentage. On the advice of Enrico Caruso, she went to Milan for vocal study. After three years' training she made her operatic debut as Amina in *La Sonnambula* in the city of Alessandria. There the manager of La Scala heard her and engaged her to sing the role in Milan. Returning to the United States, she made her Metropolitan debut as Gilda on November 27, 1920. She then divided her time between opera and concert—Caruso invited her to appear as co-artist on several of his concert tours. Miss Morgana was with the Metropolitan for eleven seasons. She married the well-known concert manager Bruno Zirato.

MOSCONA, Nicola, basso: native of Athens, Greece. Received his early musical training as a choir singer in Athens. He made his operatic debut there as Sparafucile. At the Metropolitan, he made his debut as Ramfis on December 13, 1937, and sang there until 1959. His repertoire includes some thirty-five leading basso roles.

MOSER, Edda, soprano: born in Berlin. She studied at the Berlin Conservatory. Early in her career she sang in concerts in Berlin, then had great success in London singing the works of the contemporary composer Hans Werner Henze. In 1966 she became a member of the Berlin Opera. Herbert von Karajan heard her in 1967 and engaged her for the 1968 Salzburg Easter Festival, to which she was to return in 1969. Miss Moser made her Metropolitan debut as Wellgunde in *Das Rheingold* on February 22, 1969, in the Saturday broadcast performance.

MÜLLER, Maria, soprano (1898–1958): born in Prague. She made her operatic debut as Elsa (*Lohengrin*) in 1920 in the Austrian city of Linz. Sang there, in Prague and in Munich, then came to the United States. She made her Metropolitan debut as Sieglinde in *Die Walküre* on January 21, 1925. She remained with the company for ten years, singing a variety of roles in operas by Mozart, Weber, Verdi and Wagner.

MUNSEL, Patrice, coloratura soprano: born in Spokane, Washington; name originally Munsil. She won the Metropolitan Auditions of the Air at sixteen and made her debut at seventeen as Philine in *Mignon* on December 4, 1943, thus establishing herself as the youngest featured singer in the company's history. She remained with the company until 1957, singing roles such as La Périchole, Adele in *Die Fledermaus*, Zerlina in *Don Giovanni* and Despina in *Così Fan Tutte*. She later starred in a film based on the life of Nellie Melba and appeared in operettas and Broadway musicals.

MUZIO, Claudia, soprano (1892–1936): born in Pavia, Italy. Daughter of Carlo Muzio, a stage manager of Covent Garden and of the Metropolitan during the regime of Maurice Grau. She began her musical training with piano and harp lessons, later turned to vocal studies. In 1912 she made her operatic debut at Arezzo, Italy, in *Manon Lescaut.* Her success led to engagements at other Italian opera houses. In 1913 she sang her first Sieglinde at Turin, and later made her Covent Garden debut as Desdemona. Her Metropolitan debut took place December 4, 1916, when she sang Tosca with Caruso and Scotti. In the season of 1922–23 she left the Metropolitan to join the Chicago Civic Opera Company, where for the next ten years she sang leading Italian roles. She sang a wide variety of roles: the Marschallin, Norma, Isolde, Santuzza, Violetta, Mimi. Her last appearance at the Metropolitan was in 1934.

NAGY, Robert, tenor: born in Lorain, Ohio. He won his Metropolitan Opera contract in 1957 through the National Council Regional Auditions, and made his debut as Gastone in *La Traviata* on November 2, 1957. A well-routined and versatile performer, he was prominent in comprimario roles before undertaking tenor leads in such operas as *Pique-Dame* and *Der Fliegende Holländer.* He has also sung with the New York City Opera Company, where his roles include Faust (*Mefistofele*).

NEBLETT, Carol, soprano: born in Modesto, California. Appeared professionally as a pianist and violinist, then turned to singing. Studied at the Paris Conservatory, then was a member of Lotte Lehmann's classes at the University of California in Los Angeles. Sang in America, Europe and the Middle East. During her debut season with the New York City Opera Company in 1969 she sang the roles of Musetta (*La Bohème*), Margherita and Elena (*Mefistofele*) and Jaroslavna (*Prince Igor*).

NELLI, Herva, dramatic soprano: native of Pittsburgh. She made her Metropolitan debut as Leonora in *La Forza del Destino* on February 17, 1854. She had previously achieved considerable fame as a performer in the Toscanini broadcasts of operas and the recordings emanating from them.

NEWAY, Patricia, soprano: born in Brooklyn, New York. One of the leading sopranos of the New York City Opera Company. Made her debut as Leah in *The Dybbuk* during the 1951–52 season at the City Center. An accomplished musician and a talented actress, she is outstanding in both contemporary and classic operatic roles. Her great success was as Magda in Menotti's *The Consul*.

NIEMANN, Albert, tenor (1831–1917): born near Magdeburg, Germany. A famous singing actor of the Berlin Hofoper, he was Wagner's favorite tenor and was the first Siegmund in *Die Walküre*. He sang at the Metropolitan from 1886 to 1888 and was the first American Tristan, making a profound impression in the role at the age of fifty-seven.

NILSSON, Birgit, dramatic soprano: born in Karup, Sweden; real name Svenson. Made her operatic debut as Agathe in *Der Freischütz* during the 1946–47 season at the Royal Opera House in Stockholm. During the next few years with that company she was heard as Donna Anna, the Marschallin, Sieglinde, Venus and Senta. Her first major engagement outside Sweden was at the Glyndebourne Festival in 1951, when she sang Electra in Mozart's *Idomeneo*. She expanded her repertoire to include Leonore (*Fidelio*), Elsa, Isolde, Salome and the Brünnhildes of the *Ring*. She has sung more than a hundred *Walküre* Brünnhildes. At the Munich Festival in 1955, Miss Nilsson made her debut as Brünnhilde in the complete *Ring* cycle. American audiences heard her for the first time in 1956 when she sang an all-Wagner program at the Hollywood Bowl; she later appeared with the San Francisco and Chicago operas. She made her Metropolitan debut as Isolde on December 18, 1959. Since that time she has been the reigning dramatic soprano of the company. In addition to her Wagnerian triumphs, she is acclaimed for her Verdi and Puccini roles. One of her greatest is Turandot. She also sings Elektra. An international star in every respect, she appears regularly at Bayreuth, Covent Garden and La Scala.

NILSSON, Christine, soprano (1843–1921): born near Wexio, Sweden. She began her career in Stockholm, then went to Paris, where she made her debut at the Théâtre Lyrique in 1864 and sang there for the next three years. From 1868 to 1870 she sang at the Paris Opera, where she created the role of Marguerite in *Faust*. From 1870 to 1874 she toured America, and on October 22, 1883, she made her Metropolitan debut as Marguerite in the performance of *Faust* that inaugurated the Metropolitan Opera House. During her Paris career she was presented with a gold wreath which later was on display at the Museum of Musical History in Stockholm until it was presented to Birgit Nilsson at the ceremonies marking the closing of the old Metropolitan Opera House in 1966. One of the leading operatic sopranos of her day, Christine Nilsson had a range of two and a half octaves.

NISKA, Maralin, soprano: born in San Pedro, California. Studied with Lotte Lehmann and Walter Ducloux, made her professional debut as Manon (*Massenet*) in Los Anglees in 1959. In the fall of 1965, with the Metropolitan Opera National Company, she sang the title role in Carlisle Floyd's *Susannah* in the opening performance of the company's tour in Indianapolis. During the ensuing two-year tour she sang Madama Butterfly, Micaela and Frasquita (*Carmen*), Violetta (*La Traviata*), the Countess (*Le Nozze di Figaro*) and Musetta (*La Bohème*). She joined the New York City Opera in 1967. On July 2, 1968, she sang Madama Butterfly in the performance which opened the new Santa Fe Opera House, rebuilt after the fire of July 1967.

NORDICA, Lillian, dramatic soprano (1857–1914): born Lillian Norton in Farmington, Maine. She began her vocal studies at the age of fourteen in Boston and sang her first professional engagement there with Patrick S. Gilmore's concert band. At twenty-one she toured with the band in the United States and Europe. Later she studied acting, languages and repertoire in Paris and Milan, and made her debut in the latter city as Donna Elvira in 1879. At various times between 1881 and 1887 she sang at the Paris Opéra and at Covent Garden. Her Metropolitan debut occurred on December 18, 1891, when she replaced the ailing Emma Albani as Valentin in *Les Huguenots* in a cast that included Jean and Édouard De Reszke. When Jean De Reszke sang his first Tristan on November 27, 1895, Nordica sang her first Isolde. The year before, she had created the role of Elsa at Bayreuth. Meanwhile, she toured extensively in concerts, and in 1910–11 sang with the Boston Opera Company. During a tour to Australia in 1913 with a concert company, the ship foundered on a reef and the passengers were forced to remain on deck. Nordica, already ill, contracted pneumonia. She finally arrived at Batavia, Java, four months later and died there on May 10, 1914. A brilliant artist and a woman of incredible stamina, Nordica enjoyed more glamorous triumphs than any other American singer of her time. Her repertoire ranged from Gilda and Marguerite through Leonora (*Il Trovatore*) to Aïda, Elsa, Isolde, the three Brünnhildes and Kundry. She once sang Violetta twenty-four hours after a *Walküre* Brünnhilde. In the space of a week, she sang the Brünnhildes in *Die Walküre* and *Die Götterdämmerung* and Marguerite when she was forty-six years old. At fifty-three she learned Isolde in French for a single performance in Paris. Contemporaries said her breathing and tone production were nearly perfect. Added to these qualities were a sure dramatic instinct and a natural feeling for the stage. Toward the end of her career she suffered excruciatingly from rheumatism, but sang in spite of the pain to thunderous applause.

NORDMO-LOEVBERG, Aase, soprano: native of Norway. First heard in New York in concert with the Philadelphia Orchestra in 1958. Made her Metropolitan debut as Elsa on February 11, 1959. She later sang Fidelio, Sieglinde and Eva (*Die Meistersinger*).

NORENA, Eidé, soprano: born in Oslo, Norway. Made her operatic debut in Scandinavia, then sang with success at La Scala, Covent Garden and the Paris Opéra. She was a member of the Chicago Opera Company in 1926–27. At the Metropolitan, she made her debut as Mimi on February 9, 1933. A skilled artist, she appeared frequently with the company during four seasons.

NOVOTNA, Jarmila, soprano: born in Prague. She studied singing there and in Milan, and studied acting with Max Reinhardt. At seventeen, when she was a protégée of Emmy Destinn's, she made her operatic debut as Violetta at the Prague National Opera House. One of her other early successes was as Marie in *The Bartered Bride*, and she sang this role in a film version. In Europe she starred in Offenbach operettas and created Franz Lehár's *Giuditta*. Miss Novotna made her Italian debut at the Arena in Verona as Gilda, with Giacomo Lauri-Volpi as the Duke. On January 5, 1940, she made her Metropolitan debut as Mimi, remaining with the company until 1956. A famous beauty, she starred in the film *The Search*.

OBER, Margaret, contralto: born in Berlin. Sang at Stettin and the Berlin Opera. Her Metropolitan debut was as Ortrud in *Lohengrin* on November 21, 1913, and she sang leading mezzo and contralto roles with the company until 1917. She was Octavian in *Der Rosenkavalier* at the American premiere on Dec. 9, 1913.

OLIVERO, Magda, soprano: born in Saluzzo, Italy. Made her professional debut in Italy in the early thirties as Lauretta in *Gianni Schicchi*. In 1967 she made her United States debut with the Dallas Civic Opera as Cherubini's Medea, and appeared with that company in the title role of Giordano's *Fedora* on November 26, 1969. Was known to be Francesco Cilèa's favorite for the title role of his *Adriana Lecouvreur*.

ORLANDI, Rita, soprano: born in Bologna, Italy. Began her vocal studies there and studied with Carmen Melis. In June 1961 she won first place in the Concorso Internationale per Voci Verdiane in Milan, resulting in her debut in *Suor Angelica* at the Teatro Nuovo. Two years later she sang the title role in the first Milanese performance in 118 years of Verdi's *Giovanna D'Arco*. She has sung the Verdi operatic repertoire throughout Europe. In October 1966 she made her American debut in Rossini's *Mosè in Egitto* with the American Opera Society at Carnegie Hall. Her Metropolitan debut was as Maria in *Simon Boccanegra* on October 17, 1968.

OLSZEWSKA, Maria, contralto (1892–1969): born in Augsburg, Germany. She made her operatic debut in Crefeld (Germany), then sang with the Hamburg Opera, Vienna Opera, Berlin Opera, at the Munich Festivals and at Covent Garden. She made her American debut with the Chicago Opera during the 1930–31 season. She made her debut at the Metropolitan as Brangäne—with Frida Leider making her debut as Isolde—on January 16, 1933. Olszewska was one of the ranking singers of the Metropolitan's contralto wing for the next four years.

OLVIS, William, tenor: born in Hollywood. He first achieved prominence as an Atwater Kent winner in 1949, and in the following year he made his operatic debut as Hans in *The Bartered Bride*. In 1955 he won a Fulbright Fellowship for study in Rome, where he sang with the Rome Opera. He made his Metropolitan debut as the Second Priest in *Die Zauberflöte* on November 18, 1958. Since then he has appeared in both leading and comprimario roles.

ONEGIN, Sigrid, mezzo-soprano (1891–1943): born in Stockholm. Began her musical career as a concert singer in 1912, then turned to opera, making her debut in Stuttgart. She was first heard in America as soloist with the Philadelphia Orchestra in 1922. That same year, on November 22, she made her Metropolitan debut as Amneris, and subsequently toured extensively in concert and opera. A woman of commanding presence, her voice had a quality of nobility combined with an element of tragic intensity.

ORDASSY, Carlotta, soprano: born in Hungary. She was awarded a prize in the International Music Competition in Geneva in 1947. After coming to America, she won the Metropolitan Auditions of the Air. She made her Metropolitan debut as Gerhilde in *Die Walküre* on January 22, 1957.

PANERAI, Rolando, baritone: born in Campi Bisenzio, near Florence, Italy. After his opera debut in *Don Pasquale* in Spoleto in 1946, he became a regular performer at La Scala. He made his American debut as Figaro in *Il Barbiere di Siviglia* with the San Francisco Opera in 1958 and became well known through many recordings. At the 1968 Lincoln Center Festival, he appeared at the Metropolitan with the Rome Opera Company as Figaro in *Le Nozze di Figaro*.

PARADA, Claudia, soprano: born in Santiago de Chile. Trained as a violinist in the conservatory there before studying voice. She made her operatic debut in that city as the Countess in *Le Nozze di Figaro* in 1950, then went to Italy for further study. In 1954 she made her Italian debut as Nedda at the Teatro Nuovo in Milan. Her debut at the Metropolitan was as Amelia in *Un Ballo in Maschera* on February 27, 1962.

PARLY, Ticho, tenor: born in Copenhagen. A former travel agent, he began his singing career as a young man by studying voice at Indiana University with former Metropolitan soprano Dorothee Manski. At first a baritone, he developed his tenor range and built up a repertoire of dramatic tenor roles, including Radames, the Siegfrieds, Lohengrin, Tannhäuser and Florestan. He has appeared in the major opera houses in Europe, in Buenos Aires and in San Francisco.

PASKALIS, Kostas, baritone: born in Athens. Studied at the Athens Conservatory. He joined the Athens Opera as a member of the chorus, then was chosen to sing the title role in *Rigoletto*. He remained there for seven years, singing the standard roles of Verdi, Puccini and Mozart. In 1958 he made his debut with the Vienna Staatsoper as Renato in *Un Ballo in Maschera* under the baton of Dmitri Mitropoulos. He made a successful debut at the Metropolitan in the role of Don Carlo in *La Forza del Destino* on February 17, 1965. His specialty is Italian opera.

PASTA, Giuditta, mezzo-soprano (1798–1865): born Giuditta Negri in Saronno, near Milan. Ranked with Maria Malibran and Pauline Viardot as one of the great singers of the nineteenth century. Entered the conservatory in Milan at fifteen, made an unsuccessful debut three years later and not long after retired from the stage for further vocal study. She reappeared in Venice in 1819. In Paris in 1822, she triumphed in such great *bel canto* roles as Norma, Amina (*La Sonnambula*) and Médée (Cherubini), and for the next decade was a reigning soprano. Her voice encompassed the contralto as well as the soprano range. Pasta continued singing long past her prime and was last heard in London about 1850.

PATTI, Adelina, coloratura soprano (1843–1919): born in Madrid. She made her first public appearance at the age of seven, concertized for years, made her operatic debut at sixteen, then established a career as one of the most phenomenal *prime donne* in musical history. The daughter of parents who were singers, she was brought up in New York. It was there that she made her debut—under the stage name of "the Little Florinda"—as Lucia on November 24, 1859. She made her Covent Garden debut in 1861 and her Paris debut, at the Théâtre Italien, in 1862. Patti lived totally for her art; offstage, her activities—study, eating, sleeping, exercising—were regulated according to an unvarying routine to assure maximum vocal health. Onstage, her sole concern was with the aria or the song. She was an indifferent actress, and habitually came to the footlights for her aria, regardless of the business onstage around her. She could dazzle an audience with her coloratura runs—up to F above high C—then move her listeners to tears with her rendition of a simple ballad. While her greatest roles were Adina (*L'Elisir d'Amore*), Amina (*La Sonnambula*), Norina (*Don Pasquale*), Linda (*Linda di Chamounix*), Lucia and Zerlina, she also sang Violetta, Carmen, Martha and even Aïda. Although she did not sing Wagnerian roles, she sang Elisabeth's Prayer from *Tannhäuser* with the usual sensational results. Patti's "farewell tours" were numerous and legendary, and spanned several continents. She retired officially from the stage in 1906, but her last public appearance was in 1914, when she was seventy-one years old. She had reigned undisputedly as a prima donna for forty-five years. In her final years she lived in her castle—complete with private theater—at Craig-y-Nos, Wales.

PAULY, Rose, dramatic soprano: native of Vienna, where she studied at the Royal Academy. At seventeen she made her debut in *Aïda* with the Hamburg Opera. From Hamburg she went to the Cologne Opera, where she was discovered by Otto Klemperer, who recognized her potentialities as a singer of contemporary opera. In 1927 he brought her to the newly founded Berlin Kroll Opera, where she starred in practically every premiere. With a phenomenal repertoire of sixty-seven roles, she starred in opera houses all over Europe. She was first heard in this country in a concert version of *Elektra* with the New York Philharmonic Symphony on March 18, 1937. She made her Metropolitan debut in this role on January 7, 1938.

PAVAROTTI, Luciano, tenor: born in Modena, Italy. After making his name at La Scala, he came into international prominence at Covent Garden, where one of his successes was opposite Joan Sutherland in *La Fille du Régiment*. In 1967 he made his American debut with the San Francisco Opera and on November 16, 1968, bowed at the Metropolitan as Rodolpho in *La Bohème*.

PEARS, Peter, tenor: born in Farnham, England. A major concert artist, he has sung such operatic roles as Tamino in *Die Zauberflöte* and David in *Die Meistersinger* at Covent Garden. He is best known for his association with Benjamin Britten, with whom he founded the successful Aldeburgh Festival. He created the title role in Britten's *Peter Grimes* at Sadler's Wells in 1945 and since then has had an important role in every new Britten opera.

PECHNER, Gerhard, basso-buffo (1903–69): born in Berlin. Studied singing there at the State Academy. At twenty-one he made his debut at the Berlin Municipal Opera. There he sang basso-buffo and character parts under the batons of Richard Strauss, Bruno Walter and Fritz Busch. He made his Metropolitan debut as the Attorney in *Der Rosenkavalier* on November 27, 1941. An excellent singing actor, Mr. Pechner was famous for his role of Beckmesser, and was also outstanding as Alberich (*Das Rheingold*) and Melitone (*La Forza del Destino*). He sang more than thirty roles at the Metropolitan from 1941 to 1966. An accomplished musician, he played piano by ear at the age of six, then later studied piano and cello. At many of his concerts, he provided his own accompaniments. He was a well-known vocal teacher and operatic coach, and manager of the Liederkranz Society operatic auditions.

PEERCE, Jan, tenor: born in New York; real name Jacob Pearlman. He began his musical career at the age of nine with the study of the violin (a four-dollar instrument bought for him by his mother), then during his teens toured summer camps with his own small jazz combo. He next came to the attention of Samuel (Roxy) Rothafel, who engaged him to sing at the Radio City Music Hall, where he was soloist for six years. This led to a successful career in radio. In 1937 he made his operatic debut as the Duke in *Rigoletto*—with his close friend, Robert Weede, in the title role—with the Columbia Opera Company in Baltimore. At the Metropolitan, he made his debut as Alfredo (*La Traviata*) on November 29, 1941. In addition to his operatic work, he is an outstanding concert singer.

PERTILE, Aureliano, tenor (1885–1952): native of Italy. One of the foremost artists in the era of such singers as Caruso, Scotti, De Luca, Amato, Ruffo and Martinelli. He made his debut at the Metropolitan as Cavaradossi on December 1, 1921, in a cast with Jeritza and Scotti. His career was mainly at La Scala.

PETERS, Roberta, coloratura soprano: born in New York City; real name Rebecca Peterman. She made her Metropolitan debut in her early twenties as Zerlina in *Don Giovanni* on November 17, 1950, when she was engaged on short notice to replace an indisposed singer. This marked the beginning of a brilliant career in opera and on the concert stage. Endowed with a charming personality and a fresh young voice of remarkable flexibility, she scored in a wide variety of roles ranging from Susanna in *Le Nozze di Figaro* to Zerbinetta in *Ariadne auf Naxos*. She was given an honorary degree of Doctor of Music at Ithaca College in 1968.

PETINA, Irra, mezzo-soprano: born in Leningrad, where she received her first musical training. When the Russian Revolution broke out, she fled to China and joined a traveling Russian opera company. Hoping to go to Europe for further study, she came back by way of the United States. While in this country she sang an audition which won her a scholarship at the Curtis Institute. This in turn led to engagements with the Philadelphia Grand Opera Company. Coming to New York she was first heard at the Metropolitan in Howard Hanson's *Merry Mount* during the 1933–34 season. She left the Metropolitan to sing on Broadway, where she was highly successful as leading lady in *Song of Norway* and *Magdalena*. She returned to the Metropolitan during the 1947–48 season. Hers was one of the distinctive Carmens of the 1930s.

PILOU, Jeannette, soprano: born in Alexandria, Egypt, of Greek parents. Made her operatic debut as Violetta (*La Traviata*) in Milan in 1959, then sang extensively in European opera houses. Her Metropolitan debut was as Juliette during the 1967–68 season. In the broadcast performance of *La Traviata* on Saturday, March 21, 1970, she was the replacement for Montserrat Caballé in the role of Violetta.

PINZA, Ezio, basso (1892–1957): born in Rome. He grew up in Ravenna. Prior to taking up singing as a career he was an engineering student and a professional cyclist. At the urging of friends who had heard him sing informally, he took up vocal studies at the Conservatory of Bologna. As he was preparing for his operatic debut, World War I broke out. Pinza joined the Italian artillery and served four years in the Alps—where, as he remarked, he "kept his voice on ice." At twenty-seven he made his operatic debut as the aged King Marke in a performance of *Tristan und Isolde* at the Royal Opera House in Rome. Engagements followed in Turin and La Scala. There Gatti-Casazza heard him and engaged him for the Metropolitan, where he made his debut as the Pontifex Maximus in Spontini's *La Vestale* on November 1, 1926. For the next quarter of a century he was the reigning basso of the Metropolitan, where he triumphed in more than thirty roles. He succeeded Chaliapin in the role of Boris; his interpretations of Méphistophélès and Don Giovanni were the standards. In a historic performance of *Boris Godunof* on March 4, 1929, he and Chaliapin both appeared—with Pinza as Pimen. In 1949 he added to his theatrical laurels by starring on Broadway as the romantic lead in *South Pacific,* one of the greatest musical successes in the history of the New York theater.

PLANÇON, Pol, basso (1854–1914): born in Fumay, Ardennes, France. Made his debut at Lyons in 1887, sang at the Paris Opéra from 1883 to 1893, then at Covent Garden until 1904. Meanwhile, he came to America and made his debut at the Metropolitan as Jupiter in Gounod's *Philémon et Baucis* on November 29, 1893. Plançon was acknowledged as one of the finest singers of the French school, a polished singing actor with an elegant style.

PLISHKA, Paul, basso: born in Old Forge, Pennsylvania. Following his audition for the Metropolitan National Council Regional Auditions in 1963, he was given a contract with the Metropolitan National Company. When it disbanded he was one of three singers taken into the parent company and was assigned to cover sixty-seven roles. He made his debut as the Monk in *La Gioconda* on September 18, 1967. Among his other roles are the Sacristan (*Tosca*), Varlaam (*Boris Godunof*), Zuniga (*Carmen*), Pietro (*Simon Boccanegra*), Dr. Bartolo (*Le Nozze di Figaro*), Quinault (*Adriana Lecouvreur*).

PONS, Lily, coloratura soprano: born in Cannes, France, of French-Italian parentage. She studied piano and voice at the Paris Conservatory, then made her operatic debut in *Louise* at Mulhouse in 1928. She then became a protégée of Maria Gay's, the Spanish mezzo-soprano, who had sung at the Metropolitan during the season of 1908–9. She brought Miss Pons to the attention of Gatti-Casazza, who invited her to audition for the Metropolitan. On January 3, 1931, she made her debut as Lucia with sensational success, in a cast that included Gigli, Pinza and De Luca. One memorable feature of her performance was that in the Mad Scene she sang the much-discussed high F sharp which Donizetti himself had written into a revised version of the scene some hundred years before. Petite and charming, for the next two decades she was one of the leading coloratura sopranos of the company. Also during her operatic career, she starred in radio and motion pictures. In 1936 she appeared with great success in a film called *I Dream Too Much*. Some of the older classic coloratura operas—such as *La Sonnambula, Lakmé* and *Linda di Chamounix*—were revived by the Metropolitan especially for Miss Pons.

PONSELLE, Carmela, mezzo-soprano: born in Meriden, Connecticut, the sister of Rosa; original name Ponzillo. First appeared with her sister as a singing team in vaudeville and motion-picture houses. Branched out into opera and made her Metropolitan debut as Amneris on December 5, 1932. On December 21, 1932, she sang a fine performance as Laura in *La Gioconda,* with Rosa in the title role.

PONSELLE, Rosa, dramatic soprano: born in Meriden, Connecticut, of Italian parentage. She began her spectacular career as a choir singer, then, at the age of thirteen, sang fifteen-dollar-a-week engagements in vaudeville and movie houses with her sister Carmela. She later came to the attention of Caruso, under whose sponsorship she made a highly successful debut at the Metropolitan on November 15, 1918, at the age of twenty-one, singing Leonora to Caruso's Don Alvaro in *La Forza del Destino*. She was the company's foremost dramatic soprano until her retirement in 1936. Her performance of Norma was considered the finest achievement of her operatic career. In the years of her retirement, Miss Ponselle has been teaching and coaching at her estate, Villa Pace, at Stevenson, Maryland. She also has been director of the Baltimore Civic Opera. Her dark-hued, opulent voice—which the late critic Olin Downes described as "the most beautiful voice of her generation"—combined with her regal appearance, made Rosa Ponselle an unforgettable operatic personality.

POPP, Lucia, soprano: born in Bratislava, Czechoslovakia. At eighteen she entered Bratislava Academy for vocal studies. She then went to Vienna, where she auditioned for the Staatsoper and won a contract. Although a permanent member of the Vienna company, she has sung throughout Europe and at Covent Garden. While still in her twenties, she won international acclaim for the Queen of the Night role in the recording of *Die Zauberflöte* under the baton of Otto Klemperer. She made her Metropolitan debut as the Queen of the Night on February 19, 1967.

POSPINOV, Ruza, mezzo-soprano: born in Varazdin, Yugoslavia. In 1963 she became a member of the Croatian National Theater, and made her operatic debut with the Yugoslavian company at the Holland Festival. She was first heard at the Metropolitan as Maddalena (*Rigoletto*) on February 16, 1966. Her repertoire also includes Ulrica (*Un Ballo in Maschera*) and Azucena.

POWERS, Marie, dramatic soprano: born in Ohio. One of the leading actress-singers of the New York City Opera Company, and a gifted performer in contemporary operatic roles. She is famous for her exceptionally vivid characterization of Madame Flora in Menotti's *The Medium*.

PRACHT, Mary Ellen, soprano: born in Shadyside, Ohio. Has sung eight seasons with the Metropolitan Opera, where she has been heard as Marcellina in *Fidelio*, Micaela in *Carmen*, the First Lady in *Die Zauberflöte*, the Guardian of the Threshold in *Die Frau ohne Schatten* and the First Niece in *Peter Grimes*. Also sang in *Elektra* in 1966, as well as in *La Périchole*.

PRANDELLI, Giacinto, tenor: born in Lumezzane, near Brescia, Italy. Began his career at the age of six in the church choir of his native village, then later took up his vocal studies in Rome. He made his operatic debut in *La Bohème* at the Donizetti Theater in Bergamo. His later success in Genoa in *La Traviata*, with the coloratura Toti Dal Monte, led to engagements at La Scala, the Florentine May Festival, Cairo, Lisbon, Paris and London. He made his Metropolitan debut as Alfredo on November 24, 1951, and remained with the company until 1955.

PREVEDI, Bruno, tenor: born in Mantua, Italy. Made his debut as Canio at the Teatro Nuovo in Milan, later appeared in all the leading opera houses in Italy, as well as in Vienna, Barcelona and Budapest. He made his American debut with the Philadelphia Opera Company in 1963 as Alvaro in *La Forza del Destino*. He made his Metropolitan debut as Cavaradossi on March 6, 1965.

PREY, Hermann, baritone: native of Berlin, Germany. His career began when he won a singing contest sponsored by the United States Army in occupied Germany. He subsequently became one of the finest of lieder singers and a prominent performer in German opera houses. He made his Metropolitan debut as Wolfram in *Tannhäuser* on December 17,

1960, returning in 1964 as the Count in *Le Nozze di Figaro* and again in 1967 as Papageno in *Die Zauberflöte*.

PRICE, Leontyne, dramatic soprano: born in Laurel, Mississippi. After studying at the Juilliard School of Music, she made her stage debut in Virgil Thomson's *Four Saints in Three Acts* on Broadway in 1952. Sang in *Porgy and Bess* in 1952–54, and also appeared in NBC-TV productions of *Tosca* and other operas. In 1959 and 1960 she sang at the Vienna Staatsoper and at La Scala. On January 27, 1961, she made a memorable debut at the Metropolitan as Leonora in *Il Trovatore*, with Franco Corelli making his debut as Manrico. Miss Price was chosen by composer Samuel Barber to create the role of Cleopatra in his *Antony and Cleopatra*, which opened the new Metropolitan Opera House at Lincoln Center, New York, on September 16, 1966. A specialist in Verdi operas, her repertoire also includes Mozart and Puccini roles.

RAIMONDI, Gianni, tenor: born in Bologna, Italy, where he made his operatic debut in 1947 as the Duke in *Rigoletto*. He made an impressive debut at the Metropolitan on September 29, 1965, as Rodolpho to the Mimi of Mirella Freni, with whom he had often sung the opera in Italy. A well-routined professional, he has a repertoire of some sixty operatic roles.

RAIMONDI, Ruggero, bass-baritone: native of Bologna, Italy. Sang in the Spoleto Music Festival competition in 1964 and later that year made his operatic debut in *I Vespri Siciliani* with the Rome Opera. He made his Metropolitan debut in *La Bohème* on October 29, 1965, and has a repertoire of thirty-seven roles. He is not related to tenor Gianni Raimondi. Was scheduled to sing the role of Silva in *Ernani* at the opening performance of the Metropolitan's 1970–71 season.

RAISA, Rosa, dramatic soprano (1893–1963): born in Bialystok, Poland. Studied at the Naples Conservatory and made her operatic debut in Parma in 1913. In America, she made her debut as a member of the Chicago Opera Company in *Jewels of the Madonna* on January 24, 1918, and continued as leading soprano of the company for many seasons. At La Scala, on April 25, 1926, she created the role of Princess Turandot. She had appeared at the Metropolitan during the 1919–20 season (with the Chicago company) as Norma, when a critic described her voice as "one of the most beautiful ever heard."

RANKIN, Nell, mezzo-soprano: born in Montgomery, Alabama. After study in the United States and abroad, she made her operatic debut with the Zurich Staatsoper as Ortrud. After singing extensively in Europe, she made her Metropolitan debut as Amneris on November 22, 1951. In the following years she appeared many times as an outstanding performer in such roles as Marina (*Boris Godunof*), Carmen, Madelon (*Andrea Chénier*) and Ulrica (*Un Ballo in Maschera*).

RASKIN, Judith, soprano: born in New York. First sang with the New York City Opera at City Center, where she made an auspicious debut as Despina in *Così Fan Tutte* in 1959. She made her Metropolitan debut as Susanna (*Le Nozze di Figaro*) on February 23, 1962. One of her most effective roles is that of Nannetta in *Falstaff*. She also is noted for her lieder recitals.

RAYMONDI, Lillian, soprano: born in United States. She made her Metropolitan debut as Papagena on November 27, 1942. This role was her specialty. A petite and charming singing actress, she was particularly effective in soubrette parts.

REARDON, John, baritone: born in New York City. Began his vocal studies at Rollins College, Florida, then in 1952 became a pupil of Martial Singher at Aspen, Colorado. Two years later he joined the New York City Opera Company and sang leading roles there for the next twelve years. During that time he appeared in more than fifteen new contemporary works, including Liebermann's *School for Wives*, Moore's *Wings of the Dove*, Floyd's *Wuthering Heights* and Hoiby's *Natalia Petrovna*. He made his Metropolitan debut as Tomsky in *Pique-Dame* on September 28, 1965. Reardon also scored as Orin Mannon in the Metropolitan's premiere of Marvin David Levy's *Mourning Becomes Electra* in 1967.

REBMANN, Liselotte, soprano: born in Stuttgart, Germany. Began her musical studies at the Academy of Music in Stuttgart. After an apprentice period with the Stuttgart Opera she went to Wiesbaden, where she sang some twenty roles during a four-year engagement. A permanent member of the Wurtemberg Staatsoper in Stuttgart, Miss Rebmann appears regularly at other German opera houses. At the 1968 Easter Festival in Salzburg she sang in the new Karajan production of *Das Rheingold* in the role of Woglinde, in which role she made her Metropolitan debut on February 22, 1969, in the Saturday broadcast performance.

REITAN, Roald, baritone: an American of Scandinavian descent. He made his debut as the Gypsy in the *Il Trovatore* which opened the

Metropolitan's 1959–60 season on October 26. He subsequently sang Schaunard (*La Bohème*) and Masetto (*Don Giovanni*) and appeared in comprimario roles such as the Surgeon (*La Forza*), Count Homonay (*Zigeunerbaron*), Wagner (*Faust*) and the jailer Frank (*Die Fledermaus*).

RENAUD, Maurice, bass-baritone (1862–1933): born in Bordeaux. Studied at the Paris Conservatory, then sang at the Opéra-Comique and and in other European opera houses. In America he sang with the Hammerstein company at the Manhattan Opera House, and with the Chicago Opera. His repertoire included roles in fifty operas, and as a singing actor he was excellent in both serious and comic parts. Renaud, like Victor Maurel, was one of the leading exponents of the French school, whose members were noted for the suavity, elegance and stylishness of their characterizations.

RESNIK, Regina, mezzo-soprano: born in New York City. She made her debut while still very young as a dramatic soprano in 1942 as Lady Macbeth with the New Opera Company in New York. She subsequently won the Metropolitan Auditions of the Air and made her debut with the company on December 6, 1944, as a last-minute replacement for Zinka Milanov in *Il Trovatore*, performing without a stage rehearsal. She later appeared in a wide variety of soprano roles from Aïda to Ellen Orford (*Peter Grimes*). In 1956 she shifted to mezzo roles with great success, becoming one of the most popular of Carmens in European opera houses, though she did not sing the role at the Metropolitan until 1968. She became a regular performer at Covent Garden and the Vienna Staatsoper, as well as the Metropolitan. Her other outstanding roles include the Countess in *Pique-Dame*, Dame Quickly in *Falstaff* and Clytemnestra in *Elektra*. Celebrated her twenty-fifth anniversary as a leading singer at the Metropolitan with a performance as Carmen on June 19, 1970.

RETHBERG, Elisabeth, dramatic soprano: born in Schwarzenberg, Germany. Studied piano and voice at the Dresden Conservatory, then auditioned for Fritz Reiner, who was conducting at the Dresden Opera. She made her operatic debut with the company in 1915 and sang there until 1922. Later that year she made her debut at the Metropolitan as Aïda on November 22, then continued with the company as one of the leading singers of German and Italian roles. She also concertized extensively. At Dresden in 1928, she created the title role in Strauss's *Die Ägyptische Helena*. Miss Rethberg was affectionately known to her public as the "Saxon Nightingale." Upon her retirement she married the baritone George Cehanovsky.

REYNOLDS, Anna, mezzo-soprano: native of Great Britain. Studied at the Royal Academy of Music in London as a pianist. Only later, when her studies took her to Rome, did she take up the study of voice. She progressed so rapidly that she soon was singing leading roles in Italian opera houses. Engagements followed for major festivals on the Continent and in Great Britain and Scandinavia. At her debut in the Metropolitan Saturday broacast of *Das Rheingold* on February 22, 1969, Miss Reynolds not only sang the role of Flosshilde, for which she had been scheduled, but also replaced Josephine Veasey, who was ill, as Fricka.

RHODES, Jane, soprano: native of Paris, born into a family of musicians and theater people. She began her musical education at an early age and continued her vocal training while a student at the Sorbonne. Her first prominent role was Marguerite in *Damnation de Faust* at Nancy in 1953 when she was in her early twenties. She sang the same role in her first appearance at the Paris Opéra in 1957. She made her Metropolitan debut as Carmen on November 15, 1960. Her repertoire also includes Salome, Tosca, Senta and leading roles in contemporary works by Dallapiccola, Jolivet and Conrad Beck.

RIDDERBUSCH, Karl, basso: native of Germany. Studied at the Folkwang-Hochschule in Essen, and in 1961 was engaged to sing in Münster, Germany. In 1963 he sang in Essen, and in 1965 with the Deutsche Oper-am-Rhein in Düsseldorf. He made his Bayreuth debut in 1967 as King Henry in *Lohengrin,* also sang Fasolt (*Das Rheingold*) and Titurel (*Parsifal*) there. Later the same year he made his Metropolitan debut as Hunding in *Die Walküre.*

ROBERTO, Francesca, soprano: born in Greenwich, Connecticut. Made her operatic debut in Rome in 1959 in *Madama Butterfly.* Toured with the NBC Opera and the New England Opera Company. She made her professional debut in New York in Menotti's *The Saint of Bleecker Street.* In 1961 she was a finalist in the Metropolitan Opera National Council Auditions. On January 5, 1966, she made her Metropolitan debut as Madama Butterfly. She was the first member of the Metropolitan Opera National Company to be signed by the parent company.

ROBESON, Paul, basso: born in Princeton, New Jersey. A graduate of Rutgers University and Columbia University. He appeared with great success in Broadway productions of *All God's Chillun Got Wings* and *Show Boat,* and was noted as a recitalist. A talented singing actor with a superb voice, he was famous for his characterization of the title role of *The Emperor Jones,* Louis Gruenberg's operatic version of Eugene O'Neill's play. He lived for a number of years in the USSR.

ROBINSON, Gail, soprano: born in Meridian, Mississippi. Sang in the Metropolitan Opera National Council Regional Auditions and went on to win the Fisher Foundation Award at the National Finals in New York. This led to a contract with the Metropolitan Opera Studio and a subsequent debut with the Metropolitan. Repertoire includes the title role in *Lucia di Lammermoor,* Fiordiligi (*Così Fan Tutte*), Rosina (*Il Barbiere di Siviglia*) and Norina (*Don Pasquale*).

ROGGERO, Margaret, soprano: born in New York City. Studied at the David Mannes School of Music and at the Juilliard School in New York. Among her early professional engagements was a role in the Broadway production of Menotti's *The Consul.* On March 20, 1951, she made a striking success of her Metropolitan debut as Suzuki, in the performance in which Victoria de Los Angeles sang Cio-cio-san for the first time. Miss Roggero appeared in the Suzuki role many times thereafter, and scored consistently in many other secondary roles.

ROMAN, Stella, dramatic soprano: born in Chij, Romania, the daughter of a mother who was a gifted amateur pianist. After musical studies in Bucharest, Vienna and Milan, she made her operatic debut as Madeleine in *Andrea Chénier* at the Teatro del Corso in Bologna. In 1940 she sang the role of the Empress in *Die Frau ohne Schatten* at La Scala in the presence of Richard Strauss. Later (1948) she went to his villa in Pontresina, Switzerland, where Strauss coached her in the role of the Marschallin. Meanwhile, she had sung extensively in Europe, Cairo and South America. Her first appearance in America was as Amelia in *Un Ballo in Maschera* with the San Francisco Opera Company. She made an auspicious Metropolitan debut as Aïda on January 1, 1942, and remained with the company until 1950.

ROSSI-LEMENI, Nicola, bass: born in Istanbul, Turkey, of Italian and Russian parentage. His Russian mother helped him to become a notable Boris Godunof and his Italian father to master the art of *bel canto.* He made his operatic debut in 1946 and subsequently became a star in all the major Italian theaters. After his American debut as Boris with the San Francisco Opera in 1951, he sang for one season at the Metropolitan. His debut was as Méphistophélès on the opening night of the 1953–54 season. He later sang Don Giovanni and Boris (in English). His wife is the soprano Virginia Zeani.

ROTHENBERGER, Anneliese, lyric soprano: born in Mannheim, Germany. She first sang at Salzburg in 1954, and then at all the leading European opera houses. Since 1956 she has been a member of the Vienna Staatsoper. She made her Metropolitan debut as Zdenka in *Arabella* on November 18, 1961.

ROTHIER, Léon, basso (1874–1951): born in Reims, France. Studied at the Paris Conservatory and sang at the Paris Opéra, the Opéra-Comique, and at Marseilles and Lyon. He came to America in 1910. On March 29, 1911, he appeared at the Metropolitan in the American premiere of Paul Dukas' *Ariane et Barbe-Bleue,* playing Bluebeard opposite Geraldine Farrar. He remained with the company until 1940. A polished actor-singer, he was an outstanding exponent of the French school, with a repertoire of 120 roles. He gave a New York recital in 1950 at the age of sixty-five.

ROUNSEVILLE, Robert, tenor: born in Attleboro, Massachusetts. A civic fund raised by the people of Attleboro enabled him to study at Tanglewood, where he was heard by a New York City Opera scout in scenes from *Pelléas et Mélisande.* Subsequently he sang Pelléas to Maggie Teyte's Mélisande with the New York City Opera. In 1951 he was chosen by Igor Stravinsky for the role of Tom Rakewell in *The Rake's Progress* at the Venice Festival. He sang in several Broadway productions—notably *Candide, Carousel* and *Show Boat*—and starred in the British film version of *Les Contes d'Hoffmann* with Moira Shearer and Robert Helpmann. As of 1970 he was playing the role of the Padre in the long-run Broadway musical *Man of La Mancha.*

ROSWÄNGE, Helge, tenor: native of Copenhagen, Denmark. Began his musical training in Copenhagen. For more than forty years he was a leading tenor of Central European opera houses, specializing in Italian roles. At the height of his career he had simultaneous contracts with six state operas: Berlin, Vienna, Munich, Dresden, Hamburg and Stuttgart.

RUFFO, Titta, baritone (1877–1953): born in Pisa, Italy, of a poor family, a circumstance which made early musical training difficult. He studied briefly at the Rome Conservatory. His first stage appearance, as the Herald in *Lohengrin,* was such a success that many engagements followed. He made sensational appearances in Italy, South America and Vienna. In America, he was first heard with the Philadelphia-Chicago Opera Company in Philadelphia on November 4 and in New York on November 19, 1912. He made operatic history with the Chicago company for a number of seasons, then on January 19, 1922, he made his Metropolitan debut as Figaro in *Il Barbiere di Siviglia.* He sang with the company until the 1928–29 season. Ruffo's favorites among his many roles were Rigoletto and Hamlet in Ambroise Thomas' now forgotten opera of that name. In the latter role, it was said, he had no rival. He was famous for the tremendous power and incredible range of his voice —from D flat at the bottom to a sustained B flat at the top. Ruffo retired in 1929 and died in Florence in 1953.

RYSANEK, Leonie, soprano: born in Vienna. Received her early training there and sang at the Staatsoper. In 1951 she was coached in the role of Senta by Wieland Wagner in preparation for performances of *Der Fliegende Holländer* at the Bayreuth Festival. She has appeared regularly at Bayreuth since, as Senta and as Sieglinde, Elisabeth and Elsa. She made her debut at the Metropolitan in an impressive performance as Lady Macbeth on February 5, 1959. A gifted musician and a thoroughgoing professional, she sings a wide variety of dramatic soprano roles, and is particularly noted for her portrayal of the Empress in *Die Frau ohne Schatten,* which she sang at the Metropolitan premiere on October 2, 1966. She also sings the Marschallin, Fidelio, Tosca, Desdemona and Abigail in *Nabucco.*

SAMMARCO, Mario, baritone (1873–1930): born in Palermo, Sicily. He was one of those legendary singers who somehow was prevented from singing with the Metropolitan, though he did sing for Hammerstein at the Manhattan Opera House with Melba in 1907 and the next year was Figaro to the Rosina of Tetrazzini. He did, however, appear with the Chicago Opera at the Metropolitan in Wolf-Ferrari's *Jewels of the Madonna* in 1912.

SARFATY, Regina, dramatic soprano: born in New York. Trained at the Juilliard School. Well known to the concert stage prior to her appearance in contemporary opera with the New York City Opera Company, she became prominent in European opera houses, where she is a notable Carmen. During the summers she sings with the Santa Fe Opera.

SAUNDERS, Arlene, soprano: born in Cleveland, Ohio. Began her musical career as a mezzo, then ultimately moved into the soprano repertoire. Her operatic debut was as Dorabella in *Così Fan Tutte* with the Grass Roots Opera Company in Raleigh, North Carolina. Following that, she won the American Opera Auditions, which enabled her to continue study in Cincinnati and then in Italy. She made her New York debut as Giorgetta in *Il Tabarro,* one of the three one-act operas of Puccini's *Il Trittico,* given in its entirety by the New York City Opera for its season's opener on October 5, 1961. She also opened the 1962 season, on October 4, with *Louise.* In 1963 she toured with the Metropolitan, then later that year joined the Hamburg Opera Company. When the company came to New York for the Lincoln Center Festival in 1967, Miss Saunders sang leading roles in three of its seven operas. Now a resident of Hamburg, Miss Saunders was honored by the Hamburg Senate with the title of Kammersängerin.

SAYÃO, Bidú, soprano: born in Rio de Janeiro; real name Balduina De Oliveira Sayão. Began her musical training with piano lessons, then took up the study of voice. Later, in Nice, she became the pupil of Jean De Reszke, studying French diction, style and concert repertoire. Her operatic debut in 1928 as Rosina (*Il Barbiere di Siviglia*) at the Teatro Reale in Rome was so successful that she won an engagement at the Paris Opéra. This was followed by several seasons at the Opéra-Comique. She made her Metropolitan debut as Manon on February 13, 1937, and for thirteen seasons was a great favorite there in roles such as Violetta, Mimi, Mélisande, Susanna, Zerlina, Norina (*Don Pasquale*) and Adina (*L'Elisir d'Amore*). She was celebrated for her refinement of style and as a subtle actress.

SCALCHI, Sofia, mezzo-soprano (1850–1922): born in Turin, Italy. One of the best mezzos of the Golden Age, she sang many roles at Covent Garden, where she was Amneris in the English premiere of *Aïda* in 1876. She was Siebel in *Faust* in the inaugural performance at the Metropolitan on October 22, 1883, and got the best notices the next day. She then sang at the Academy of Music and returned to the Metropolitan for the 1891–92 season.

SCHAULER, Eileen, soprano: born in Millburn, New Jersey. A leading soprano of the New York City Opera. Made her debut in the title role of Dmitri Shostakovich's *Katerina Ismailova* (originally *Lady Macbeth of Mzensk*), given by the company during its spring season of 1965.

SCHIPA, Tito, lyric tenor (1889–1966): born in Lecce, Italy. Studied in Milan, then sang in all the leading opera houses of Italy and in South America. In 1919 he joined the Chicago Civic Opera Company, where he made his debut in *La Sonnambula* on February 5, 1920. He continued there for a number of years as the company's leading lyric tenor. On November 23, 1932, he made his Metropolitan debut as Nemorino in *L'Elisir d'Amore,* and succeeded to some of the roles Gigli had made famous. A true lyric tenor, he was acclaimed for the taste, elegance and refinement of his singing, and was considered one of the most accomplished Mozart singers of his time.

SCHMORR, Robert, tenor: born in New York City. He made his operatic debut with the Washington, D.C., Opera Society as Don Basilio in *Le Nozze di Figaro*, later sang with the Chicago Lyric Theatre and the San Francisco Opera. At the Metropolitan, he made his debut as Goro in *Madama Butterfly* on October 13, 1965. A specialist in character parts, his repertoire includes more than seventy roles.

SCHNORR VON CAROLSFELD, Ludwig, dramatic tenor (1836–1865): born in Munich. While singing with the Dresden Opera, he was heard as *Lohengrin* by Richard Wagner, who chose him to create the role of Tristan. This he did in the premiere performance in Munich on June 10, 1865, with his wife, Malvina Garrigues, creating the role of Isolde. On the following July 15, while rehearsing *Don Giovanni*, Schnorr was stricken with rheumatic fever and on July 21 he died of a stroke. He was twenty-nine years old.

SCHÖFFLER, Paul, basso: born in Dresden. Studied at the Dresden Conservatory, later appeared extensively in leading roles in Europe and at Covent Garden. He won critical praise for his Metropolitan debut role of Jokanaan in *Salome* on January 26, 1950. He was active with the company for the next decade and was particularly celebrated as Hans Sachs.

SCHORR, Friedrich, bass-baritone (1888–1953): born in Nagyvarad, Romania. Was preparing for a career in law when he turned to music on the advice of Adolph Robinson, an American teaching voice in Vienna. Through him, Schorr secured an audition with the Graz Opera, and at the age of twenty-two he made his debut as Wotan in *Die Walküre*. In 1923 Schorr came to New York with the German Grand Opera Company, a debt-ridden aggregation without funds for adequate costumes. The company managed, however, to give a successful debut performance of *Die Meistersinger* in Baltimore—with most of the cast in street clothes. Schorr's performance as Hans Sachs won him a long-term contract with the Metropolitan. He made his debut as Wolfram in *Tannhäuser* on February 14, 1924, and forthwith established himself as the leading Wagnerian of the company. Schorr, like Lauritz Melchior, probably sang his Wagnerian roles more times than any other singer in the history of the composer's operas. Wotan alone he sang more than 250 times in thirty-five cities on three continents. During his stay in New York, he conducted master classes in operatic coaching and established successful summer opera camps. His last appearance at the Metropolitan was as the Wanderer in *Siegfried* on March 2, 1943.

SCHREIER, Peter, tenor: born in Meissen, Germany, to musical parents. At the age of eight he was enrolled in the Kreuzchor, a famous boy choir of Dresden. His first stage appearance following his training at the Dresden Conservatory, was as one of the Three Genii in *Die Zauberflöte* at the Berlin Opera in 1944. He made his official operatic debut as the First Prisoner in *Fidelio* at the Dresden Opera in 1960. Since 1963 he has been under contract to the Deutsche Staatsoper in East Berlin and has been active in Vienna. A Mozart specialist, he made his Metropolitan debut as Tamino on December 25, 1967.

SCHUMANN, Elisabeth, lyric soprano (1891–1952): born in Merseburg, Germany. Sang with the Hamburg Opera and the Vienna Staatsoper. At her Metropolitan debut as Sophie in *Der Rosenkavalier* on November 20, 1914, she was admired for the beautiful lyric quality of her voice. In 1921 she made a concert tour of the United States with Richard Strauss. She returned to Germany, where she became a concert favorite until her death in 1952.

SCHUMANN-HEINK, Ernestine, contralto (1861–1936): born in Prague. A pupil of her mother, she attracted attention at the age of eleven by her singing. Her first public appearance reportedly was as a soloist in Beethoven's *Ninth Symphony* at Graz. She made her operatic debut at the Royal Opera, Dresden, in *Il Trovatore* in 1878, then sang regularly at the Hamburg Opera and at Bayreuth. In 1898 she began a ten-year contract with the Berlin Opera, with leave during the winters to sing at the Metropolitan. There she made an auspicious debut as Ortrud in *Lohengrin* on January 9, 1899. She left the Metropolitan in 1903 and was never again associated with any opera company as a member. However, she created the role of Clytemnestra in *Elektra* in Dresden in 1909. In America, Schumann-Heink became a legendary figure, triumphing in one concert tour after another. She had become a naturalized American citizen in 1905, and during World War I she sang tirelessly at military camps, for Liberty Bond drives and for disabled soldiers. Married three times, with seven children and a stepson, she had sons serving as soldiers on both sides. Schumann-Heink was acknowledged as one of the finest contraltos of her day, a superb Wagnerian interpreter and a brilliant concert artist.

SCHÜTZENDORF, Gustav, bass-baritone (1883–1937): born in Cologne. Studied there at the conservatory. Made his operatic debut in Düsseldorf as Count di Luna in *Il Trovatore*. Made his Metropolitan debut as Faninal (*Der Rosenkavalier*) on November 17, 1922. An accomplished singing actor, one of his most memorable characterizations was Beckmesser in *Die Meistersinger*. Schützendorf was one of five brothers, all of whom were opera singers.

SCHWARZKOPF, Elisabeth, lyric soprano: born in Germany. An artist known for her flawless musicianship and her skill as an actress. She made her Metropolitan debut as the Marschallin (her most famous role) on October 13, 1964. A versatile performer in operatic roles, she is one of the leading exponents of German lieder. Though she was heard at the Metropolitan only as Donna Elvira in *Don Giovanni* and the Marschallin, she sang many roles at Covent Garden and in Italian and German opera houses. She created the role of Anne Trulove in Stravinsky's *The Rake's Progress* in Venice on September 11, 1951.

SCIUTTI, Graziella, soprano: born in Turin. Made her concert debut in Venice in 1950, and later established herself as the leading artist of La Piccola Scala, Milan. She made her operatic debut at the Aix-en-Provence Festival in 1951. In 1954 Miss Sciutti made the first of many appearances in England at the Glyndebourne Festival, and subsequently sang throughout Europe. In America she has sung with the San Francisco Opera and the Dallas Civic Opera.

SCOTT, Norman, bass-baritone (1921–68): born Norman Schultz in New York City. After making his operatic debut in 1946, he sang leading roles with the New England Opera Company in Boston, the Chautauqua (New York) Opera, and with companies in Pittsburgh, New Orleans and Havana. He sang with the New York City Opera Company from 1948 to 1951; in that year (November 15) he made his Metropolitan debut as Monterone in *Rigoletto*. With more than fifty roles in his repertoire, he appeared many times with the company. In 1956 he sang with the Vienna State Opera.

SCOTTI, Antonio, bass-baritone (1866–1936): born in Naples. Made his debut in Malta in Flotow's *Martha* in 1889. He made his Metropolitan debut as Don Giovanni on December 27, 1899, then continued there for many years as the leading baritone of the company's Italian wing. For a time, he toured the United States with his own opera company. Scotti was one of the finest singing actors of his time. One of his greatest roles was Scarpia, which he sang at the American premiere of *Tosca* in 1901. He also sang Sharpless in the New York premiere of *Madama Butterfly* in 1907, and Jack Rance in *La Fanciulla del West* in the Metropolitan world premiere in 1910. His appearances and recordings with Caruso and Farrar made operatic history. On January 1, 1924, the Metropolitan staged a gala *Tosca* to honor Scotti's twenty-fifth consecutive season with the company. He sang Scarpia, with Jeritza as Tosca and Miguel Fleta as Cavaradossi. After thirty-three seasons at the Metropolitan, Scotti made his farewell in his favorite role, that of Chim-Fen in Leoni's *L'Oracolo,* on January 20, 1933.

SCOTTO, Renata, soprano: born in Savona, Italy. Made her debut as Violetta in *La Traviata* at the Teatro Nuovo, Milan, in 1954. Later that same year she made her La Scala debut in Catalani's *La Wally*. She turned down La Scala's offer of secondary parts because she wished to concentrate on leading roles. These she sang for a time in small provincial opera houses. In 1957 she replaced Maria Callas in *La Sonnambula* at the Edinburgh Festival, then returned to La Scala as a star. She made her Metropolitan debut as Cio-cio-san on October 13, 1965. Her repertoire includes fifty roles, both in coloratura and dramatic soprano categories, and she is one of the leading contemporary exponents of *bel canto* singing. Miss Scotto is the wife of Lorenzo Anselmi, a former violinist of the La Scala orchestra who is now her manager.

SCOVOTTI, Jeanette, soprano: born in the United States. Made her Metropolitan debut as Adele in *Die Fledermaus* on November 15, 1962, and appeared thereafter in such roles as Xenia (*Boris Godunof*), Pousette (*Manon*), Nannetta (*Falstaff*) and Olympia (*Les Contes d'Hoffmann*). Effective in soubrette parts, she also has scored as Gilda in *Rigoletto*.

SEEFRIED, Irmgard, soprano: born in Köngetried, Bavaria. A celebrated Mozart singer, she established her career in Europe and sang there in all the leading opera houses. Also an outstanding lieder singer, she often appeared in concerts with her husband, the noted violinist Wolfgang Schneiderhan. She made her Metropolitan debut as Susanna (*Le Nozze di Figaro*) on November 20, 1953, but was not heard at the Metropolitan again.

SEMBRICH, Marcella, coloratura soprano (1858–1935): born in Wisniewszyk, Galicia (Poland); full name Marcella Praxede Marcelline

Kochanska; sang under her mother's maiden name. Studied in Vienna and Milan, then made her professional debut in Athens in 1877. Thereafter she went to Berlin to study German opera and sang for two years with the Dresden Opera. After appearances in London she came to America and toured in concert. She made her Metropolitan debut as Lucia on October 24, 1883. During her first season with the company she sang leading coloratura roles with sensational success—including Zerlina in *Don Giovanni* on October 28, 1883, the first performance of a Mozart score at the Metropolitan. She did not reappear at the Metropolitan until 1898. In 1900 she manged her own opera company in Germany, then returned to the Metropolitan, where she remained a favorite with audiences until she retired from opera in 1909. She taught at the Juilliard School of Music in New York and at the Curtis Institute in Philadelphia. In addition to her operatic accomplishments, Sembrich was one of the first singers to specialize in German lieder. She was recognized as one of the most accomplished musicians in the entire history of singing.

SERENI, Mario, baritone: born in Perugia, Italy. Made his operatic debut in Palermo in *Tannhäuser* in 1955. Appeared at the Teatro Colón, Buenos Aires, in 1956, at La Scala in 1963 and at the Vienna Staatsoper in 1965. In 1957 he made his Metropolitan debut as Gerard in *Andrea Chénier* (November 9). Endowed with a resonant, virile voice, Sereni is outstanding in the standard baritone roles.

SERGI, Arturo, tenor: born in New York City. Made his Metropolitan debut as Dimitri in *Boris Godunof* on March 23, 1963. Also appeared as Otello, Lohengrin, Edgardo (*Lucia di Lammermoor*), Ernani, Walther (*Die Meistersinger*) and Turiddu.

SGARRO, Louis, baritone: born in New York City. After study in New York he made his operatic debut with the Boston Opera Company in the role of the King in *Aida*. Also sang with the San Carlo and the Charles Wagner companies. Later he performed at La Scala and in Trieste. He made his Metropolitan debut as the Major-domo in *Andrea Chénier* on November 16, 1954, and subsequently appeared in numerous comprimario roles, notably in character roles.

SHIRLEY, George, tenor: born in Detroit. First attracted attention at the Glyndebourne Festival, where he successfully sang Tamino in *Die Zauberflöte*. He has appeared in this role many times at the Metropolitan. While abroad, he sang with the Scottish National Opera Company. He made an unscheduled appearance at the Metropolitan as

Ferrando in *Così Fan Tutte*—replacing an indisposed tenor in that difficult role. Previously, he had appeared at the Metropolitan for the first time in the role of Malcolm in *Macbeth*. On November 13, 1961, he made his official debut as Pinkerton in *Madama Butterfly*.

SHUARD, Amy, soprano: born in London. A pupil of the famous soprano Eva Turner, she has been one of her most successful successors in the role of Turandot. A star at Covent Garden, she sings there as Brünnhilde in the annual *Ring* cycle. With the San Francisco Opera, she has sung Brünnhilde, Turandot and Elektra. She also has sung Kundry at Bayreuth.

SIEPI, Cesare, basso: born in Milan. Began his musical career at the age of twelve, singing with what he calls a "white voice." Shortly after he turned thirteen he could sing a low E flat. He increased his musical knowledge by singing with a madrigal group. At eighteen he won a singing contest, the prize being an operatic debut as Sparafucile in an opera house in Schio, near Venice. When he was twenty the Nazis occupied Milan. Just before Siepi was to be drafted into the German army he escaped to Switzerland, where he was held in a detention camp. He and his Milanese friend, the tenor Giuseppe di Stefano, made the rounds of the camps giving concerts. In 1945 the basso sang in a benefit concert to rebuild La Scala and appeared in its opening season the next year. He made his Metropolitan debut as King Philip II (*Don Carlos*) on November 2, 1950, in the opening performance of the season. In 1954 he made a film of *Don Giovanni* in Salzburg with Wilhelm Furtwängler conducting. Resuming his career in America, he sang the lead in a short-run Broadway musical (seventy-six performances) called *Bravo Giovanni*. A six-foot-plus giant with a voice of true basso quality, Siepi is a hard-working, serious artist and an excellent musician. Called the best Don Giovanni on the contemporary operatic stage, he is equally adept in such buffo roles as Don Basilio. In 1970 Mr. Siepi received the highest awared conferred by his native country. He was named a *Commendatore*.

SILJA, Anja, soprano: born in Berlin. Trained in childhood by her grandfather, a part-time singing teacher. At the age of ten, it is said, she knew all the *Ring* and *Tristan* roles by heart. At fifteen she was engaged at Braunschweig, where she made her debut as the Celestial Voice in *Don Carlos*. During the same season she sang Rosina, Micaela and Zerbinetta. In 1956 she added Leonora (*Il Trovatore*) and the Queen of the Night to her repertoire and subsequently, it is reported, Santuzza, the three soprano roles in *Les Contes d'Hoffmann*, Liù and

Turandot, Fiordiligi, Konstanze, Leonore (*Fidelio*) and Salome. In 1960 she sang Senta at Bayreuth and became a protégée of the late Wieland Wagner. She made her American debut in the fall of 1968 as Senta with the Chicago Lyric Opera Company.

SILLS, Beverly, soprano: born Belle Silverman in Brooklyn. As a child, she recalls, she played Galli-Curci records incessantly and memorized twenty-two arias before she was five years old. At eighteen she had a repertoire of fifty operas, thirty of which she could perform. In 1950 she sang fifty-four Violettas in sixty-three nights, and in 1966 sang sixteen Carmens in sixteen days in Cleveland's Music Carnival. Miss Sills began singing in radio at the age of three; at seven she was a regular on Major Bowes' Capital Family Hour. She made her operatic debut with the San Francisco Opera in 1953, and with the New York City Opera in 1955 as Rosalinde in *Die Fledermaus*. With more than thirty-five years of professional singing behind her, Miss Sills has a repertoire of between eighty-five and ninety operas and is equally effective in dramatic, lyric and coloratura roles. A leading soprano of the New York City Opera since her debut there, she played Baby Doe in the premiere of Douglas Moore's *The Ballad of Baby Doe* on April 3, 1958. The only opera she refuses to sing—on the basis of histrionic objections—is *Madama Butterfly*. Her most successful roles have been Cleopatra in *Giulio Cesare*, the Queen in *Le Coq d'Or*, Lucia, Manon and Marguerite. She made her debut at La Scala in 1969.

SIMIONATO, Giulietta, mezzo-soprano: born in Forlì, Italy. At seventeen she won the Bel Canto Grand Prize of the City of Florence against 385 other contenders. This eventually resulted in an offer from La Scala, where she made her operatic debut in 1936 in the small role of Beppe in Mascagni's *L'Amico Fritz*. Dissatisfied with comprimario roles, she left the company to join a touring group, with which she won recognition in leading roles. In 1947 she made her "second debut" at La Scala in *Mignon* with Cesare Siepi and Giuseppe di Stefano. In the United States, she sang with the Chicago Opera in 1954, with the San Francisco Opera in 1955, then made her Metropolitan debut as Azucena in *Il Trovatore* on October 26, 1959, the season's opening performance. With a voice suited to dramatic mezzo roles, Miss Simionato was famous for her ability to sing roulades and rapid coloratura-like passages. Her repertoire included fifty-four roles. She retired in 1966 after a notable career during which she was acclaimed in all the great opera houses from Buenos Aires to Tokyo.

SIMONEAU, Leopold, lyric tenor: born in Canada. Made an auspicious Metropolitan debut as Don Ottavio in *Don Giovanni* on October 18, 1963. Noted for a voice of appealing lyric quality, he has appeared frequently in operatic roles and on the concert stage.

SINGHER, Martial, baritone: native of France. A graduate of the Paris Conservatory, he sang leading roles at the Paris Opéra, where he made his debut as one of the *Ring* Wotans. At the Metropolitan, he made his debut on December 10, 1943, as Dapertutto in *Les Contes d'Hoffmann*. He appeared there in a wide variety of roles until 1958, and then became a noted teacher.

SLEZAK, Leo, tenor (1875–1946): born Leo Schönberg in Moravia. Began his musical studies in Brünn (Czechoslovakian city of Brno), then studied with Jean De Reszke. Made his debut as Lohengrin with the Brünn Opera in 1896, also sang in Berlin and Breslau, and after 1900 was a regular member of the Vienna Opera. In 1909 he sang Otello with sensational success at Covent Garden and repeated this triumph in his Metropolitan debut on November 17 of that same year. He sang with the company for the next four years. Slezak, a six-foot giant with a voice of extraordinary power and brilliance, was not only a great heldentenor but was renowned as a singer of German lieder and other art songs. Onstage, his reputation for practical joking was legendary, the most famous story being about the swan boat in *Lohengrin*. When the boat was pulled offstage without him, he is said to have turned to a super and asked: "When does the next swan leave?" His son, Walter Slezak, is the well-known actor.

SLEZAK, Walter, singing actor: the son of Leo Slezak. He was reared in Vienna and began his musical education at the university there. In Europe, he sang extensively in operetta, and in America he established a career as an actor in musicals and in dramatic productions. He also appeared in a number of films. Slezak appeared at the Metropolitan on November 25, 1959, in a performance of *Der Zigeunerbaron,* speaking the role of Zsupan.

SÖDERSTRÖM, Elisabeth, soprano: born in Stockholm, where she began her musical career. Singing a variety of roles, she became particularly well known for her performances in Mozart and Strauss operas—in *Der Rosenkavalier* she has sung the roles of Octavian, Sophie and the Marschallin. In Salzburg in 1955 she was acclaimed for her role of Ighino, the fifteen-year-old son of the composer Palestrina, in Hans Pfitzner's opera *Palestrina*. Miss Söderström made her Metropolitan debut as Susanna (*Le Nozze di Figaro*) on November 30, 1959, and was commended for her authoritative Mozart style. She remained for four seasons.

SOUZAY, Gérard, baritone: born in Angers, France. Celebrated concert singer and recording artist, an authoritative exponent of art songs by composers such as Schubert, Poulenc, Debussy and Fauré. At the same time, he has scored operatically in such roles as Don Giovanni, Count Almaviva, Golaud (*Pelléas et Mélisande*) and Méphistophélès in Berlioz's *La Damnation de Faust*. In the fall of 1960, Souzay made his New York debut in the title role of *Orfeo* with the New York Opera Company. He made his Metropolitan debut as Count Almaviva on January 21, 1965.

STABILE, Mariano, baritone (1888–1968): born in Palermo, Sicily. One of the leading baritones in Italian opera houses, he sang frequently in London and South America but never appeared in New York. His sole appearances in North America were with the Chicago Opera during the 1924–25 season. Though he sang many roles, he was famous for one in particular, that of Falstaff. He sang it first at La Scala under Toscanini in 1921 and was still singing it in his seventies. Altogether, he gave more than 1200 performances in the part.

STEBER, Eleanor, soprano: born in Wheeling, West Virginia. In 1940 she won the Metropolitan Opera Auditions, and on December 7 of that year made her Metropolitan debut as Sophie in *Der Rosenkavalier*. Her first operatic role actually had been that of Senta in *Der Fliegende Holländer* at the Boston Opera House. As soloist in the premiere radio-TV simulcast of "The Voice of Firestone" in April 1948, Miss Steber became the first prima donna to sing on commercial television in America. During the Metropolitan 1951–52 season, she appeared twenty-five times in seven different roles. On February 9, 1952, she sang in two operas—as Desdemona in *Otello* in the afternoon and Fiordiligi in *Così Fan Tutte* in the evening. She made her continental concert debut with the Vienna Philharmonic at the opening of the Vienna International Festival in June 1953, and her operatic debut as Elsa in *Lohengrin* at the opening of the Bayreuth Festival in July of that year. Miss Steber has appeared with all the major symphony orchestras of the United States. Her operatic repertoire includes some twenty-five leading roles. Her Metropolitan career lasted until 1963.

STELLA, Antonietta, soprano: born in Perugia, Italy. Made an effective debut as Aïda at the Metropolitan on November 13, 1956; sang leading dramatic soprano roles with the company for the next four years and then returned to Italy, where she has appeared in all the major opera houses.

STEVENS, Risë, mezzo-soprano: born Risë Steenberg in the Bronx, New York. Began her musical career at the age of ten on a radio program called "The Children's Hour." While still in her teens, gained stage experience by singing leading roles with the New York Opera-Comique, an amateur company based in Brooklyn. At that time she was a pupil of the late Anna Eugénie Schön-René. She then continued her studies in Europe. She made her professional debut in Prague in 1936 as Mignon and sang with the company for two years. She also sang guest performances at the Staatsoper in Vienna, meanwhile studying and developing the characterization of Octavian in *Der Rosenkavalier,* her most famous role. She made her Metropolitan debut in a broadcast matinee performance of *Mignon* on November 17, 1938. She followed this with her first Metropolitan performance of Octavian on December 19, to high critical acclaim. Another of her most memorable roles was Carmen, the role in which she closed her Metropolitan career in April 1962. She also sang Cherubino, Orfeo and Dalila. In 1964 she became co-manager (with Michael Manuel) of the newly formed Metropolitan Opera National Company. During her career, Miss Stevens appeared successfully in several films, notably *The Chocolate Soldier,* with the late Nelson Eddy.

STEWART, Thomas, baritone: born in San Saba, Texas. After graduating from Baylor University—where he had majored in electronics—he decided on a singing career and went to Juilliard in New York. In 1957 he went to Berlin on a Fulbright grant and there joined the Deutsche Oper. Wieland Wagner heard him and offered him the choice of several Wagnerian roles at Bayreuth. After singing Gunther and Donner (*Die Götterdämmerung* and *Das Rheingold*) he made his official debut as Amfortas. Wolfram (*Tannhäuser*) and the Dutchman followed, then Wotan under Herbert von Karajan in the recorded *Die Walküre.* Although his roles include Golaud, Don Giovanni, Count Almavia, Amonasro and Iago, Stewart describes himself as a confirmed Wagnerite. He made his Metropolitan debut—ten days ahead of time—as Ford in *Falstaff* on March 9, 1966, replacing an indisposed singer. His official debut was as Wolfram on March 19. Stewart is the husband of soprano Evelyn Lear.

STICH-RANDALL, Teresa, soprano: born in West Hartford, Connecticut. Began her musical education as a scholarship student at the

Hartford School of Music. Made her operatic debut as Gilda with the Chicago Lyric Opera Company in 1955, and her Metropolitan debut as Fiordiligi on October 24, 1961. She has become well known as a Mozart specialist; in recent years she has sung extensively in Europe.

STIGNANI, Ebe, mezzo-soprano: native of Italy. One of the few great singers of her time who never sang at the Metropolitan, she was a star in Italian opera houses and at Covent Garden and did appear in America with the Chicago and San Francisco operas. During the 1940s and 1950s she was considered unrivaled in Italy as Adalgisa, Amneris, Azucena and Dame Quickly.

STOJANOVIC, Milka, soprano: native of Yugoslavia. A coaching pupil of Zinka Milanov, she first appeared at the Metropolitan during the 1967–68 season, when she was commended for the attractive quality of her voice and was considered a promising newcomer. In fact, on February 2, 1968, she replaced an indisposed Birgit Nilsson as Aïda to critical acclaim.

STOLZE, Gerhard, tenor: born in Dessau, Germany. Studied dramatics and voice in Dresden, and became a member of the Dresden Opera in 1949. In 1953 he joined the Berlin Staatsoper, and in 1958 the Vienna Staatsoper. His repertoire includes more than a hundred roles, and he sang at Bayreuth fourteen consecutive seasons. He has been awarded the honorary title of Kammersänger. Mr. Stolze made his Metropolitan debut as Loge in *Das Rheingold* on November 22, 1968.

STOSKA, Polyna, soprano: born in Worcester, Massachusetts. After study there and in New York, she appeared successfully in a Broadway production of Kurt Weill's *Street Scene*. She studied for several years in Germany, then returned to join the New York City Opera Company, where one of her most effective roles was the Composer in Strauss's *Ariadne auf Naxos*. She made her Metropolitan debut on November 11, 1947, in a preseason performance of *Don Giovanni*, staged to raise funds for a new production of the *Ring*. In her role of Donna Elvira (to Ezio Pinza's Don), Miss Stoska was commended for the stylishness and professional quality of her singing and acting. She also scored later in the Wagnerian roles of Freia and Gutrune. Miss Stoska sang with the company through the 1949–50 season.

STRACCIARI, Riccardo, baritone (1875–1955): born in Bologna, Italy. After his operatic debut in Bologna in 1900, he became an outstanding baritone and later a famous teacher. His Figaro in *Il Barbiere di Siviglia* was considered unrivaled in his time. He sang with the Chicago Opera, with Antonio Scotti's touring company and at the Metropolitan in 1906–8 and 1917–19.

STRATAS, Teresa, lyric soprano: born in Toronto. There she studied at the Royal Conservatory, then later with soprano Irene Jessner. At the age of twenty-one she won the National Council Regional Auditions and made her Metropolitan debut in *Manon* on October 29, 1959. She continued singing with the company, and was particularly successful in the role of Cio-cio-san, which she sang for the first time at the Metropolitan on March 25, 1968. Her other outstanding roles there include Gretel, Lisa (*Pique-Dame*) and Mimi.

STÜCKGOLD, Grete, soprano: born in London. A leading Wagnerian singer of her day, she also was noted for her Marschallin in *Der Rosenkavalier*. She made her debut in Nürnberg, later sang with the Berlin Städtische Oper with great success. She made her Metropolitan debut as Eva in *Die Meistersinger* on November 2, 1927, and was with the company during five seasons. Equally effective in concert, she was a specialist in lieder singing.

SUKIS, Lillian, soprano: native of Lithuania. Lived in Germany during World War II, then in 1949 went to Canada, where she took up her musical education at McMaster University, Hamilton, Ontario. Later she attended the Artist Diploma Course at the University of Toronto, where she studied with soprano Irene Jessner. In 1965 she sang Lady Billows in the Canadian premiere of Benjamin Britten's *Albert Herring*. She made her Metropolitan debut on March 10, 1966, as a Flower Maiden in *Parsifal*.

SULIOTIS, Elena, soprano: born in Athens of a Greek father and a Russian mother. Moved to Buenos Aires at the age of five, began singing there when she was sixteen. She then went to Milan for study, made her operatic debut in *Cavalleria Rusticana* in Naples in August 1962 and subsequently sang in Catania, Mantua and Trieste. In that city she sang her first *Un Ballo in Maschera* in February 1965. In the fall of 1965 she made a successful American debut as Helen of Troy in Boito's *Mefistofele* with the Chicago Lyric Opera. She made her New York debut on November 15, 1966, in the title role of *Anna Bolena*, in a concert version. Following her debut in Italy, offers came so rapidly that she was learning a new role a month for ten months.

She enjoyed a great success at La Scala as Abigail in *Nabucco* and returned to New York for a concert performance of Norma in 1967. The soprano subsequently changed the spelling of her name to Souliotis.

SULLIVAN, Brian, tenor (1915–69): born in Oakland, California. Began his musical studies at the University of Southern California, made his operatic debut as Count Almaviva in *Il Barbiere di Siviglia* in Long Beach. Acquired further professional experience in motion pictures, operettas, concerts, Broadway musicals. Sang with the Central City (Colorado) Opera Association and at the Berkshire Music Festivals. Sullivan made his Metropolitan debut in the title role of *Peter Grimes* on February 23, 1948, and sang leading roles with the company for more than a decade. In his later years he had developed into a promising heldentenor and had won favorable comment for his singing of the roles of Parsifal and also for Siegfried in *Die Götterdämmerung*.

SUPERVIA, Conchita, mezzo-soprano (1895–1936): born in Barcelona, Spain. Reviving the art of the mezzo coloratura, she was acclaimed at La Scala and Covent Garden and in Paris in the operas of Rossini. Her very Spanish Carmen was both applauded and disliked at Covent Garden; but her records of the principal arias are still cherished by collectors. She died in childbirth while at the height of her career.

SUTHERLAND, Joan, coloratura soprano: native of Australia. Began her vocal studies in Sydney, where in 1947 she appeared in Purcell's *Dido and Aeneas*. As winner of a musical competition, she was able to go to London and enter the Royal College of Music in 1951. During the following years she sang standard leading soprano roles with moderate success. But her first performance as Lucia on February 17, 1959, at Covent Garden—where Donizetti's opera had not been heard for more than thirty years—brought her international fame as a contemporary exponent of the art of *bel canto*. Her first New York appearance was in a concert performance of Bellini's *Beatrice di Tenda* in February 1961. On November 26 of that year she made her sensational debut at the Metropolitan as Lucia. She has since had a succession of triumphs internationally as a singer of the classical *bel canto* operas, which exploit her dazzling technical skill to its fullest extent. Along with Maria Callas, she is credited with the revival of interest in florid coloratura singing, which was the hallmark of opera in the seventeenth and eighteenth centuries. Miss Sutherland is the wife of conductor Richard Bonynge, who also is her pianist and coach.

SVANHOLM, Set, Wagnerian tenor (1904–64): born in Vasteras, Sweden. Began his musical studies in Stockholm, made his operatic debut as Silvio in *Pagliacci* at the Stockholm Royal Opera. Shortly thereafter he gave up music as a career, but later decided to return to opera. In 1936 he made a second debut in Stockholm as Radames. At the Metropolitan, he made a successful debut as Siegfried on November 15, 1946, and continued with the company for the next decade as one of the leading Wagnerian tenors. In 1956 he left the Metropolitan and returned to Stockholm to become head of the Royal Opera.

SVED, Alexander, baritone: born in Budapest, the son of a prosperous industrialist. Sent to study the violin at the Academy of Music, he instead took vocal lessons there in secret. His parents learned of his operatic ambitions when it became necessary to obtain their signature on his first contract with the Budapest Royal Opera. There he made his debut as the Count di Luna in *Il Trovatore*. He then went to Italy to study repertoire with Titta Ruffo, Sammarco and Stracciari. In three seasons he became a leading member of the Vienna Staatsoper, the Rome Royal Opera, La Scala, Covent Garden, and the Teatro Colón of Buenos Aires. He made his Metropolitan debut on December 2, 1940, the season's opening performance, as Renato in *Un Ballo in Maschera*. Sved's repertoire included some thirty roles in Italian, French and German and he also was known internationally as a lieder singer.

SWARTHOUT, Gladys, contralto (1904–69): born in Deepwater, Missouri. Began her musical studies at the Bush Conservatory in Chicago. Made her professional debut as soloist with the Minneapolis Symphony. Sang as a member of the Chicago Civic and Ravinia Opera companies from 1924 to 1929, and after that sang extensively in concert and on radio. She made her Metropolitan debut as La Cieca in *La Gioconda* on November 15, 1929. Miss Swarthout, a handsome woman with a vibrant voice of true contralto quality, was outstanding as a singing actress. She was well known for her fiery portrayal of Carmen, and for her starring roles in five motion pictures.

TAGLIABUE, Carlo, baritone: native of Italy. At twenty-two he made his operatic debut as Amonasro in Lodi, Italy. As his career progressed he sang in most of the important opera houses in Italy, Spain, Portugal, Brazil and Argentina. Again in the role of Amonasro, he made his Metropolitan debut in the season's opening performance on December 2, 1937. His repertoire included more than fifty roles in Italian, French and German.

TAGLIAVINI, Ferruccio, lyric tenor: born in Reggio Emilia, near Bologna, Italy. He lived in this remote village until he was twelve. Without formal schooling, he was tutored with the children of the *padrone*, the wealthy landowner for whom his father worked as overseer. Some years later he replaced the lead in a school operetta and thereafter became known locally as *piccolo Caruso*. Uninterested in singing as a career, he began to study engineering, but finally was persuaded by his father to enter the conservatory at Parma. In 1938 he entered a national singing contest and won over all competitors with his singing of "O Paradiso" from Meyerbeer's *L'Africaine*. First rejecting a scholarship to study in Florence, he finally began to study seriously and made a successful debut as Rodolpho in *La Bohème* on October 28, 1939. From then on he rose to international fame. He made his Metropolitan debut as Rodolpho on January 10, 1947, to one of the wildest receptions heard there since the days of Caruso. He later sang there with his wife, soprano Pia Tassinari, but left the company after four seasons.

TAGLIAVINI, Franco, tenor: born in Reggio Emilia, Italy. Made his operatic debut in *Pagliacci* at the Teatro Nuova, Milan. In 1964 he made his American debut with the San Francisco Opera, then sang with opera companies in Dallas and Los Angeles. In the role of Pollione in *Norma*, he made his Covent Garden debut opposite Joan Sutherland in 1967, and made his Metropolitan debut in the same role with her on March 27, 1970. He is not related to Ferruccio Tagliavini.

TAJO, Italo, basso: born in Pinerolo, near Turin, Italy. He was the son of an engineer whose projects often took him outside Italy. The basso was the only one of five children to be born in Italy, and for that reason was named Italo. After study in Turin, he made his debut, at the age of twenty, as Fafner in *Das Rheingold* at the Teatro Regio in 1935. Later, the conductor Fritz Busch took him to Glyndebourne to study and sing Mozart operas. In America, Tajo made his debut with the Chicago Opera in 1946, then also sang with the San Francisco Opera. He made his Metropolitan debut as Don Basilio in *Il Barbiere di Siviglia* on December 28, 1948. He later married soprano Florence Quartararo and began a new career in musical comedy.

TALLEY, Marion, coloratura soprano: born in Kansas City, Missouri. Sang there in a church choir and gave concerts. Her unusual vocal promise led local residents to raise a fund to send her to New York and Italy for further study. At eighteen she made a highly publicized debut at the Metropolitan as Gilda on February 1, 1926. A delegation from Kansas City attended, and Miss Talley's father, a telegrapher, tapped out the story of his daughter's debut over an Associated Press wire installed backstage. She reportedly earned $350,000 on a two-year barnstorming tour following her debut. She left the Metropolitan in 1930, and her last operatic appearance was in Cleveland on May 4 of that year.

TALVELA, Martti, basso: born in Karelia, Finland. Won a nation-wide Finnish singing contest in 1960, which led to his first professional engagement with the state opera in Helsinki. From there he went to the Royal Opera in Stockholm, where he was heard by the late Wieland Wagner, who arranged for his debut in 1962 at the Bayreuth Festi-val. Later that year he made his first appearance at the Deutsche Oper in Berlin. Appearances followed in Milan, Rome and Vienna. In 1967 he made his debut at the Salzburg Festival with Herbert von Karajan. Mr. Talvela was first heard in America in February 1967 in a per-formance of the Verdi *Requiem* with the Cleveland Orchestra conducted by George Szell. He made an auspicious debut at the Metropolitan on October 7, 1968, as the Grand Inquisitor in *Don Carlos*. Six foot seven in height, Mr. Talvela is the tallest singer on the contemporary operatic stage.

TAMAGNO, Francesco, dramatic tenor (1851–1903): born in Turin, Italy. Made his debut in Parma and later was acclaimed at La Scala. At thirty-five he already was a celebrity in Italy and South America in most of the great dramatic tenor roles. His forte was the delivery of brilliant—almost piercing—high tones, up to a high D flat. A conductor of the time recalled that Tamagno once added five high Cs to a climactic passage in the last act of *William Tell*. In 1887 he created the title role of Verdi's *Otello* at La Scala. After the premiere he sang the opera's famous "Esultate" aria from the balcony of the Albergo Milano to the crowds paying homage to the composer. He made his Metropolitan debut in this role on March 24, 1890.

TARRÉS, Enriqueta, soprano: born in Spain. Trained at the Barcelona Conservatory. She was heard at the Metropolitan during the Lincoln Center Festival of 1967 with the Hamburg Opera in Hindemith's *Mathis der Maler*. The year before, she sang with the San Francisco Opera and has won acclaim at Glyndebourne and the Aix-en-Provence Festival. At Covent Garden she has been heard as Desdemona.

TAUBER, Richard, lyric tenor (1892–1948): born in Linz, Austria. Studied at the Hoch Conservatory in Frankfurt and in 1913 made his debut as Tamino in Chemnitz. From 1914 to 1924 he was a member of the Dresden Opera, then later sang throughout Europe. Although he achieved wide popularity as a singer of operettas—notably Lehár's

—he was recognized as an accomplished Mozart stylist. He made his debut in London in Lehár's *Land of Smiles* (which virtually became his trademark), but scored operatically in such roles as Florestan, Belmonte and Don Ottavio. In the United States he was first heard in 1931 in a series of concerts, which he sang to packed houses. A monocled concert artist with a flashy, exuberant manner, he was at the same time a serious musician and a fine lieder singer. His last appearance was on September 27, 1947, in London in *Don Giovanni*.

TEBALDI, Renata, dramatic soprano: born in Pesaro, Italy, of a musical family. Stricken by polio, she could not walk until she was six years old. She began her musical studies as a pianist, but at seventeen entered the Arrigo Boito Conservatory in Parma for a course in singing. There the famous prewar soprano Carmen Melis heard Miss Tebaldi sing and became her teacher and mentor. She made her operatic debut as Helen of Troy in Boito's *Mefistofele;* about two years later she won critical acclaim in Trieste for her Desdemona. Auditioned by Arturo Toscanini, she sang in the concert celebrating the postwar reopening of La Scala on May 11, 1946. In 1950 Miss Tebaldi made her formal La Scala debut, under the tutelage of Toscanini, as Aïda opposite Mario Del Monaco. This was followed by her Covent Garden debut as Desdemona, and later that year she made her American debut in San Francisco as Aïda. She made her Metropolitan debut as Desdemona (with Del Monaco the Otello) on January 31, 1955, with sensational success. A statuesque woman with an extraordinarily beautiful voice, produced seemingly without effort, Miss Tebaldi is one of the foremost contemporary sopranos. Her favorite role is Adriana Lecouvreur.

TELVA, Marion, contralto (1897–1965): born in St. Louis. Began her career as a concert singer, then came to New York for further study. She made her Metropolitan debut as Dame Quickly in *Falstaff* on January 2, 1925, and performed capably with the company through the season of 1930–31. On November 6, 1928, she sang the role of Muschel in the American premiere of Strauss's *Die Ägyptische Helena*. She also created the role of Mrs. Deane in the premiere of Deems Taylor's *Peter Ibbetson* on February 7, 1931. Her most famous role was Adalgisa in *Norma*.

TERNINA, Milka, dramatic soprano (1863–1940): born in Croatia. Made her operatic debut in Leipzig, then sang in Graz and Bremen. In Munich in 1890 she was named "court singer," and later sang at Bayreuth. She made her Metropolitan debut as Elisabeth in *Tannhäuser* on January 27, 1900. Between that time and her retirement in 1904 she sang other leading Wagnerian roles with the company. She returned to Zagreb to teach, and one of her outstanding pupils was Zinka Milanov. Ternina was one of the leading sopranos of the Golden Age and was the first to sing the role of Tosca in London and New York.

TETRAZZINI, Luisa, coloratura soprano (1871–1940): born in Florence. Made her debut as Inez in *L'Africaine* in 1895 at the Teatro Pagliano in Florence. Thereafter she sang in all the leading European opera houses and toured widely in Russia and South America. When she was thirty-seven she made her American debut with Oscar Hammerstein's Manhattan Opera Company. Hailed as the "new Melba," she sang with the company from 1908 until 1910, then in 1911 made her Metropolitan debut as Lucia on December 27. During the 1913–14 season she appeared with the Chicago Opera Company. She continued to sing with sensational success in opera and concert for the next twenty years. One of the great coloraturas of her time, Tetrazzini's voice had a limpid quality and astonishing agility in its topmost range.

TEYTE, Maggie, soprano: born in Wolverhampton, England. Studied with Jean De Reszke and made her operatic debut as Zerlina in Monte Carlo in 1907. Her subsequent career was associated mainly with the role of Mélisande. After Mary Garden had created the role in Debussy's opera at the Opéra-Comique in 1902, and had then left the company, Miss Teyte was named for the part by Marguerite Carré, wife of the opera director. Miss Teyte was introduced to Debussy, who coached her in the role every day for nine months. In 1908 she made a sensational debut as Mélisande and the next season sang the role sixteen times. She sang it again at Covent Garden in 1910, then once more in 1930. In March 1948 Miss Teyte, at the age of sixty, realized her ambition to appear in *Pelléas et Mélisande* in the United States. She sang the role with the New York City Opera. In her first appearance in this country in 1912, Miss Teyte had sung the title role of Massenet's *Cendrillon*, with Mary Garden as Prince Charming, in the American premiere of the opera in Philadelphia. A gifted artist, Miss Teyte was a leading exponent of French opera and art songs, in which she was noted for her impeccable diction, style and musicianship.

THEBOM, Blanche, mezzo-soprano: born in Monessen, Pennsylvania. Gained her early professional experience in concert and radio. Made her operatic debut as Fricka in *Die Walküre* on December 14, 1944, and thereafter appeared with distinction in leading mezzo roles. On February 14, 1953, she sang the role of Baba the Turk in the first Metropolitan performance of Stravinsky's *The Rake's Progress*. Miss

Thebom retired from the Metropolitan in 1968 to become the director of the Civic Opera in Atlanta, Georgia.

THOMAS, Jess, tenor: born in Hot Springs, South Dakota. While studying for a doctorate in psychology at Stanford University, he sang the role of Fenton in a university production of *Falstaff* and was encouraged to take up an operatic career. At the age of twenty-five he began studying opera, then won the San Francisco Opera Audition, which resulted in several secondary roles with the company. He then went to Germany in search of better opportunities and was engaged by the Karlsruhe Opera. There he sang thirty-eight roles in thirty-eight months. While still under contract at Karlsruhe, he sang thirty guest performances with the Stuttgart Opera. In 1961 he made a successful debut at Bayreuth as Parsifal. He made his Metropolitan debut on December 11, 1962, as Walther in *Die Meistersinger*.

THOMAS, John Charles, baritone (1891–1960): born in Meyersdale, Pennsylvania. While a medical student in Baltimore he was unexpectedly offered a scholarship which enabled him to study singing at the Peabody Conservatory there. He then went abroad for further study and made his first operatic appearance at the Théâtre de la Monnaie in Brussels in the role of King Herod in Massenet's *Hérodiade*. He won an ovation for his rendition of the famous aria "Vision fugitive." Returning to the United States, he sang with the Philadelphia Opera Company for three years, then later with the Chicago Civic Opera. He made his Metropolitan debut on February 2, 1934, as Germont in *La Traviata*, with Rosa Ponselle and Tito Schipa. For many seasons one of the most distinguished members of the company, Thomas was noted for the refinement of his style and his musicianship. He was much in demand as a concert artist.

THOMPSON, Hugh, baritone: born in Tacoma, Washington. The son of Oscar Thompson, distinguished music critic of the New York *Sun* during the era of the thirties and forties, he first took up newspaper work, later turned to singing. After studying at the Juilliard School of Music, he sang extensively with opera companies all over the United States. He made his Metropolitan debut as Schaunard in *La Bohème* on December 1, 1944, a performance reviewed by his father as a "very successful debut." Mr. Thompson also served for a time as stage director at the Metropolitan. In October 1968 he was named co-stage director and artistic assistant of the Opera Guild of Greater Miami.

THORBORG, Kerstin, mezzo-soprano: born in Hedemora, Sweden. Her father was a newspaperman and her mother a talented amateur pianist. She began her vocal studies during childhood. While still a young girl she applied for admission to the opera school of the Stockholm Royal Opera. Of the 1200 applicants, Kerstin Thorborg was one of the three accepted for admission. Several seasons later she made her operatic debut as Amneris. She sang with the Stockholm Royal Opera for four years, thereafter in Prague, Berlin, Buenos Aires and at Covent Garden. She made her Metropolitan debut on December 21, 1936 (the season's opening performance), as Fricka in *Die Walküre*, with Kirsten Flagstad (whom she had not met since they sang Amneris and Aïda in Stockholm almost a decade previously) as Brünnhilde. At the Metropolitan, the two artists sang together in many Wagnerian performances. Thorborg also was a memorable Orfeo at the Metropolitan and a striking Octavian in *Der Rosenkavalier*. She retired from the company in 1949.

TIBBETT, Lawrence, baritone (1896–1960): born in Bakersfield, California, the son of the county sheriff. When Tibbett was six years old, his father was killed in a gun battle with a gang of bandits. While a student in Los Angeles, he enrolled in drama courses which eventually led to professional engagements with Tyrone Power's Shakespearean Repertory Company and with the Civic Repertory Company. Meanwhile he studied voice and later joined a light opera company which gave performances up and down the Pacific coast. After he made a successful operatic debut as Amonasro in a Hollywood Bowl performance of *Aïda*, he decided to embark on a musical career and came to New York for further study. Six months after his arrival he auditioned for the Metropolitan and was accepted. He made his Metropolitan debut on November 24, 1923, in the secondary role of Lavitsky in *Boris Godunof*, and continued singing comprimario roles. It was two years later that Tibbett suddenly became a star overnight. Shortly before the scheduled revival of *Falstaff*—which had been absent from the Metropolitan repertoire for fifteen years—on January 2, 1925, the baritone who was to sing the role of Ford was taken ill, and Tibbett was assigned to replace him. In the second act, after he had sung the famous monologue "E sogno," he was accorded one of the greatest ovations ever heard at the Metropolitan. Tibbett was immediately established as a leading member of the company. He created the title roles in Taylor's *Peter Ibbetson* and Gruenberg's *The Emperor Jones*. When *Simon Boccanegra* was given its first New York performance in January 1932, Tibbett sang the title role. He sang with the company for more than twenty-five years. During that time he also was heard frequently on radio and was the first opera star to appear in singing pictures. He made six films in Hollywood. As an outstanding singing actor, Tibbett was awarded a gold medal by the American Academy of Arts and Letters for "good diction on the stage."

TIETJENS [TITIENS], Therese Johanna Alexandra, soprano (1831–77): distinguished German singer of Hungarian descent. From 1849 she appeared in Hamburg, in other German cities and in Vienna with impressive success in the standard grand opera roles. In 1858 she settled in London, where she became a favorite in comic as well as grand opera roles. She also was outstanding as an oratorio singer.

TOKATYAN, Armand, tenor (1898–1967): born in Alexandria, Egypt. There he began his career in light opera. He made his operatic debut in *Manon Lescaut* at the Dal Verme Theater in Milan, then sang in continental opera houses and in London. In the United States, he appeared with the Philadelphia, Chicago Civic, Los Angeles and San Francisco opera companies. He made his debut at the Metropolitan as Turiddu on February 3, 1923. When Puccini's *La Rondine* was given for the first time at the Metropolitan on March 10, 1928, Tokatyan sang the role of Prunier. He remained with the company for ten seasons.

TOUREL, Jennie, mezzo-soprano: born in Montreal. Began her musical career with the study of piano in Montreal and in Berlin. While in Germany, she was advised to study voice. Subsequently she joined the Opéra-Comique in Paris and sang with the company for four years. She made her Metropolitan debut in the title role of *Mignon* on May 15, 1937, during the company's second "spring season." As a member of the New Opera Company (launched in 1941) she sang the role of Lisa in *Pique-Dame*. Returning to the Metropolitan for the 1943–45 seasons, she appeared as Carmen and as Adalgisa (*Norma*). In the spring of 1964 she was the soloist in Leonard Bernstein's *Kaddish* Symphony performed by the New York Philharmonic under Mr. Bernstein's direction. Miss Tourel, also a distinguished concert artist, began teaching in New York in 1957, privately and at the Juilliard School of Music. In addition, she teaches and performs every summer at the Aspen (Colorado) Music Festival.

TOZZI, Giorgio, basso: born in Chicago. Studied at De Pauw University. Operatic debut in *The Rape of Lucretia*. Early experience at Teatro Nuovo, Milan, La Scala, Municipal Opera in Nice, Munich Opera, Cairo Royal Opera, Stuttgart Municipal Opera. His Metropolitan debut as Alvise in *La Gioconda* was March 9, 1955. Also sings Ramfis,

Sparafucile, Figaro in *Le Nozze di Figaro*, Sarastro in *Die Zauberflöte*, Banquo in *Macbeth*, Arkel in *Pelléas et Mélisande*, Colline in *La Bohème*, the Old Doctor in *Vanessa* and Fiesco in *Simon Boccanegra*. He has also appeared with notable success at the San Francisco Opera and the Salzburg Festival.

TRAUBEL, Helen, dramatic soprano: born in St. Louis. There she began her vocal studies with the teacher who taught her mother, a concert singer. At twenty-two, after seven years of study, Miss Traubel made her professional debut as guest soloist with the St. Louis Symphony under Rudolph Ganz. She toured with the orchestra for two seasons, later sang with the Philadelphia, Minneapolis and New York Philharmonic symphony orchestras. Chosen by Walter Damrosch to sing the role of Mary Rutledge in his *Man Without a Country*, Miss Traubel made her first appearance at the Metropolitan in the opera's premiere on May 12, 1937 (spring season). She sang her first Sieglinde in Chicago (with Kirsten Flagstad as Brünnhilde), then made her memorable debut in that role at the Metropolitan on December 28, 1939, with Flagstad, Melchior and Schorr. She reached the zenith of her operatic career in the role of Isolde—she was reputedly the first American who had received all her musical training in this country to appear in the role at the Metropolitan. She virtually inherited this and other Wagnerian roles from Kirsten Flagstad and did them full justice with a magnificent voice and fine stage presence. Miss Traubel left the Metropolitan at the end of the 1953–54 season and thereafter sang almost exclusively on radio and television and in night clubs. Her memoirs were published (1959) under the title *St. Louis Woman*.

TREBELLI, Zelia, mezzo-soprano (1838–92): born in Paris; real name Guillebert. Her career began in Madrid in 1859 and ended in London in 1889. Her performances in an enormous repertoire at Covent Garden, often in combination with Adelina Patti, are legendary. She made her Metropolitan debut on the third night of its existence, October 26, 1883, as Azucena in *Il Trovatore*. During her only season there, she sang the first Carmen to be heard in the new house.

TREIGLE, Norman, bass-baritone: native of New Orleans. Sang soprano in a church choir at the age of eight, but during his later school years his voice developed into bass. While at Loyola University he had his own program on the school station—"The Voice in the Night"—singing and reciting poetry. He also was active in the New Orleans Little Theatre movement and played many straight dramatic roles. Then he won the New Orleans Opera Auditions of the Air, which led to his debut as Lodovico in *Otello*. In 1953 he joined the New York City Opera Company as leading baritone, and in 1956 created the role of Reverend Olin Blitch in Carlisle Floyd's *Susannah*, in the opera's premiere. He has sung with the company since that time. Treigle has an operatic repertoire of more than fifty roles, as well as a large concert and oratorio repertoire. He has been acclaimed in the title role of Handel's *Giulio Cesare*, which he has sung with Beverly Sills, and as Méphistophélès and Rigoletto.

TROYANOS, Tatiana, mezzo-soprano: born in New York. A rising star in European opera houses, she is a permanent member of the Hamburg Opera and appeared with them at the Metropolitan during the 1967 Lincoln Center Festival as Baba the Turk in Stravinsky's *The Rake's Progress*. She was trained at the Juilliard School and made her debut with the New York City Opera on April 25, 1963, as Hippolyta in Britten's *Midsummer Night's Dream*.

TUCCI, Gabriella, soprano: born in Rome. Made her operatic debut in Spoleto's Teatro Nuovo with Gigli in *La Forza del Destino*. Has sung in all the major opera houses of Italy, as well as in other European cities. Her American debut was with the San Francisco Opera in 1959 in the role of Madeleine in *Andrea Chénier*. She made her Metropolitan debut as Cio-cio-san on October 29, 1960, and has sung sixteen different leading roles there.

TUCKER, Richard, dramatic tenor: born Reuben Tickel in Brooklyn, the son of parents who emigrated from Romania with four other children. At the age of three he was recognized as a musical prodigy for his ability to sing on perfect pitch any melody he heard. His early training began as an alto soloist in a synagogue choir in New York City. At seventeen he began three years of cantorial training, after which he filled engagements as cantor. With the Metropolitan as his objective, he began studying with tenor Paul Althouse, and worked with him from 1939 until Althouse died in 1954. In 1942 Tucker placed third in the Metropolitan Auditions and—with the assistance of the (then) general manager Edward Johnson—gained more experience via a series of radio shows on WGN in Chicago. Two years later he made his operatic debut in *La Traviata* and *Rigoletto* with the Salmaggi company in New York. On January 25, 1945, he made his Metropolitan debut as Enzo in *La Gioconda* to sixteen curtain calls. Since that time he has sung more than 400 performances of at least 28 roles at the Metropolitan and more than 150 on tour. Still an ordained cantor, Tucker—honoring a promise he made to his parents—returns twice a year to the ministry for the Jewish holy days each fall and the traditional Passover Seder service each spring. Tucker closely links his career to that of Caruso, to whom he bears a certain physical resemblance. On April 11, 1970, he celebrated his twenty-fifth year as a leading tenor of the Metropolitan at a gala performance at the opera house, appearing in scenes from *La Traviata, La Gioconda* and *Aïda* with Metropolitan casts headed by Joan Sutherland, Renata Tebaldi and Leontyne Price.

TURNER, Claramae, contralto: born in Dinuba, California; lived in Eureka, California, and in Seattle. First sang in the San Francisco Opera chorus, later progressed to comprimario roles. After five years with the company she joined the Savoy Opera Company and sang leading Gilbert and Sullivan roles. In 1945, in New York, she received a Metropolitan Opera contract and also an offer from Gian-Carlo Menotti to create the role of Madame Flora in *The Medium*. She sang the role in the premiere of the opera at the Brander Matthews Theater, Columbia University on May 8, 1946. Later she was chosen by Arturo Toscanini to sing Ulrica in *Un Ballo in Maschera*, and by Bruno Walter to sing in a Mahler concert. With the New York City Opera she scored a success in singing all three contralto roles in Puccini's *Il Trittico* in one evening—said to be the first time in America that the three roles in the one-act operas had thus been sung by one singer. Miss Turner made her Metropolitan debut as Martha in *Faust* on November 16, 1946. She has a repertoire of more than seventy-five roles.

TURNER, Eva, soprano: born in Oldham, Lancashire, England. She made her name in England with the Carl Rosa Opera Company and then became a star at La Scala, where she sang under Toscanini's direction from 1916 to 1924. She returned in triumph to Covent Garden in 1928 in her most famous role, Turandot, for which she set the model. She later became a noted teacher.

UHDE, Hermann, baritone (1914–66): native of Germany. Reared in a home where both English and German were spoken, and thus was effective in roles in both languages. In his Metropolitan debut on November 18, 1955, as Telramund, he was commended for his projection of the Wagnerian style. He also appeared in non-Wagnerian roles with distinction and was particularly successful as Wozzeck.

ULFUNG, Ragnar, tenor: born in Oslo, Norway. After appearing in small theaters in Oslo and Bergen and in an operetta company in Göteborg, Sweden, he studied in Italy for four years. In 1958 he joined the Stockholm Opera at the invitation of Set Svanholm. In 1965 he became a regular member of the Hamburgische Staatsoper. When the company came to New York for the Lincoln Center Festival in 1967, Ulfung appeared in the role of Steve Buryja in Janáček's *Jenufa*. He won critical acclaim for a spectacular acting-singing performance—which included doing cartwheels during the course of a difficult singing role. In his work, Ulfung stresses acting as much as singing. His repertoire extends from Cavaradossi to the part of the Deaf Mute in Blomdahl's space opera *Aniara*.

UPPMAN, Theodor, baritone: born in Palo Alto, California. After study on the Coast and in New York City, he appeared with the New York City Opera Company, singing the role of Pelléas to Maggie Teyte's Mélisande on March 25, 1948. He made his Metropolitan Opera debut in this role on November 27, 1953, and since then has frequently appeared with both the Metropolitan and the New York City Opera in the standard baritone roles. He is particularly well known as Papageno and Masetto and created the title role in Benjamin Britten's *Billy Budd* at Covent Garden in 1951.

VALDENGO, Giuseppe, baritone: born in Italy. First heard as a member of the New York City Opera Company in 1947. Made an auspicious Metropolitan debut on December 19 of that year as Tonio in *Pagliacci*. A seasoned professional, he sang the standard baritone roles with the company for five seasons.

VALENTINO, Francesco, baritone: born Francis Valentine Dinhaupt in the Bronx, New York. Began singing in church choirs at the age of fifteen and was advised to continue study for a singing career. He studied for three years at the Lamont School of Music in Denver. The choir he sang with there made it possible for him to go to Milan for further study. He remained there for twelve years, following his operatic debut in Parma. Later he sang in Europe and at the Glyndebourne Festival. Returning to the United States, Valentino made his Metropolitan debut on December 9, 1940, as Lord Enrico Ashton in *Lucia di Lammermoor,* and was commended for a performance stylishly sung and acted.

VÄLKKI, Anita, soprano: native of Finland. Well known in European opera houses as the Wagner heroines and as Turandot, she made her Metropolitan debut as the *Walküre* Brünnhilde on January 23, 1962. Since then, she has been heard there as Senta, Kundry, Venus and Turandot.

VALLETTI, Cesare, tenor: born in Rome. Made his operatic debut as Alfredo (*La Traviata*) in Bari, Italy. At the Metropolitan he made a successful debut as Don Ottavio on December 10, 1953, when he was commended for having provided the best Mozart singing heard at the Metropolitan for years. After appearing in many lyric tenor roles, Valletti resigned from the company in 1960. A gifted actor and an impeccable musician, he is an outstanding concert artist.

VAN DYCK, Ernest, tenor (1861–1923): born in Antwerp, Belgium. First a law student, then a journalist in Paris, he began studying voice in Paris. He made his operatic debut there in 1887 as Lohengrin, later sang throughout Europe and in London. He made his Metropolitan debut as Tannhäuser, with Lillian Nordica, on November 29, 1898. He sang with the company until 1902, then taught at conservatories in Antwerp and Brussels. An actor and singer of great skill, he was considered one of the best Wagnerian singers of his time.

VAN GORDON, Cyrena, contralto (1896–1967): born in Camden, Ohio. Received all her musical training in America, mostly at the Cincinnati College of Music. Made her debut in 1915 as Amneris with the Chicago Opera Company, and was a leading contralto of the company for many seasons. At the Metropolitan, she appeared as Amneris in a single performance there on January 18, 1934.

VAN KIRK, Mary, contralto: born in Akron, Ohio. Winner of the 1940–41 Metropolitan Auditions of the Air, following vocal study at Oberlin College. After numerous appearances in concert and oratorio, she made her Metropolitan debut as a Walküre on December 6, 1941.

VAN ROOY, Anton, baritone (1870–1932): born in Rotterdam. Studied in Frankfurt, then sang extensively in concert and oratorio. He sang at Bayreuth and the Berlin Opera and in London. He participated in the first complete *Ring* cycle in Metropolitan history, singing Wotan in *Das Rheingold* on January 12, 1899. Van Rooy was considered one of the greatest Wotans in the history of Wagnerian opera.

VANNI, Helen, soprano: born in Davenport, Iowa. Made her Metropolitan debut as the Page in *Rigoletto* on November 9, 1956, and thereafter established herself—mostly in comprimario roles—as an accomplished performer.

VARNAY, Astrid, soprano: born in Stockholm, the daughter of the late Alexander Varnay, director of the Stockholm Royal Opera, and Maria

Yavor Varnay, coloratura soprano. In 1923 the family came to New York, where Mr. Varnay died. Astrid first studied voice with her mother, then studied music at the New Jersey Musical College. Her progress was such that, within little more than two years, she sang for Kirsten Flagstad, whose verdict was: "an exceptional voice." Miss Varnay's debut at the Metropolitan was made under extraordinary circumstances. On Saturday afternoon, December 6, 1941, just before the scheduled performance of *Die Walküre*, Lottie Lehmann, who was to sing Sieglinde, was taken ill. The twenty-three-year-old Astrid Varnay—who had never sung in opera in her life—substituted with sensational success. Six days later, on December 12, she again substituted in another *Walküre*—this time as Brünnhilde in place of Helen Traubel, who had been taken ill. Miss Varnay's performance was acclaimed as one of the best since Mme. Flagstad had left the company. On February 20, 1942, Miss Varnay created the role of Telea in the Metropolitan premiere of Menotti's *The Island God*. She has a repertoire of some twenty-five operatic roles. Since leaving the Metropolitan in 1956, she has sung in most of the important European opera houses. For many years she was a regular at Bayreuth, where she sang the Brünnhildes, Isolde and Kundry.

VEASEY, Josephine, mezzo-soprano: born in London. In her early teens she took voice lessons, then turned to the study of piano. After appearances in concerts and oratorios in London she then auditioned for the Covent Garden chorus, and at the age of eighteen was the youngest singer ever to appear there. Two seasons later she toured the British Isles with a company called Opera for All. After a four-year interim, during which she was married, she made her formal debut as Cherubino at Covent Garden. Then she began the study of Wagnerian roles—Waltraute in *Die Götterdämmerung* and Fricka in *Das Rheingold;* Wagnerian debuts in Salzburg, Milan and Covent Garden followed. Miss Veasey made her Metropolitan debut as Fricka (*Das Rheingold*) on November 22, 1968.

VELIS, Andrea, tenor: born in New Kensington, Pennsylvania. Began his vocal studies in Pittsburgh at the age of sixteen. Army service in the Far East led to further study under the GI Bill, then to a Fulbright scholarship at the St. Cecilia Conservatory in Rome. After five years of study in Italy, he returned to Pittsburgh, where he concentrated on comprimario roles. Singing with various opera companies in the United States, Velis established a career as a singer-actor, specializing in character roles. Finally he sang at the Cincinnati Zoo Opera under Fausto Cleva, who brought him to the Metropolitan. He made his debut there on October 23, 1961, the season's opening performance, as Joe in *La Fanciulla del West*. With a repertoire of some forty roles, Velis is recognized as one of the Metropolitan's most versatile character actors.

VERRETT, Shirley, mezzo-soprano: born in New Orleans. Began her musical studies in New York and has been active in the concert field. She made her Metropolitan debut as Carmen on September 21, 1968. She also has sung at Covent Garden and in Italy and the Soviet Union.

VIARDOT, Pauline, mezzo-soprano (1821–1910): born in Paris, daughter of Manuel Garcia (the elder) and younger sister of Maria Malibran. Her first operatic appearances were in Paris in 1839 in the Rossinian roles of Desdemona (*Otello*), Rosina (*Il Barbiere di Siviglia*) and La Cenerentola. An accomplished musician, she was an excellent pianist and a composer, and in addition a talented painter and linguist. Viardot was a member of the Paris literary and artistic circles which included George Sand, Chopin, Berlioz, Rossini and Gounod, and her romantic association with the Russian novelist Ivan Turgenev lasted for forty years. One of her greatest operatic roles was Fidès in *Le Prophète*, which Giacomo Meyerbeer wrote with her in mind. In later years she became a famous teacher. One of her pupils was the late Anna Eugénie Schön-René, for many years a member of the Juilliard School of Music in New York, and herself the teacher of Risë Stevens, Charles Kullman, Paul Robeson and the late Mack Harrell.

VICHEGONOV, Lubomir, basso: born in Bulgaria. Made his Metropolitan debut as Sparafucile on December 4, 1948. A singer with sound professional training, he appeared in a number of leading and comprimario roles. For a time, he left the stage to become a concert manager under the name of Luben Vichey, but later resumed his singing career.

VICKERS, Jon, dramatic tenor: born in Prince Albert, Canada. Won critical acclaim with performances at Covent Garden. Made his Metropolitan debut as Canio on January 17, 1960, but made his best impression later as Florestan in *Fidelio*, which he sang on January 28. One of his best roles is Peter Grimes. Vickers, a singer with a brilliant voice and a commanding stage presence, is outstanding as Siegmund in *Die Walküre*. He has sung Parsifal at Bayreuth. He also sings Don José, Otello and Samson.

VINAY, Ramon, dramatic tenor: born in Chile of French-Italian parentage. Established as a businessman in Mexico City while still in his early twenties, Vinay took up vocal studies (as a baritone) because of his interest in opera. He sang his first role—that of Count di Luna in *Il Trovatore*—as a replacement for the baritone in a traveling opera company. Later he went to New York, where he studied with the former Metropolitan stage director Wilhelm von Wymetal and shifted his voice into the tenor range. Coached by him and by tenor René Maison, Vinay sang Otello in Mexico City in 1944. In 1951 he sang Tristan with outstanding success at the Bayreuth Festival under the direction of Wieland Wagner. He made his Metropolitan debut as Don José on February 22, 1946. He last sang at the Metropolitan as a tenor in 1962 but returned in 1966 in the bass-baritone role of Dr. Bartolo in *Il Barbiere di Siviglia*.

VISHNEVSKAYA, Galina, soprano: born in Leningrad. Began her musical studies at the age of sixteen and made her professional debut several years later at the Leningrad Operetta Theater. In 1952 she won a competition for admission to the Bolshoi Opera Theater in Moscow, and soon afterward made her debut there as Tatiana in *Eugen Onegin*. Sang in Russia, Europe and England, then came to the United States. She made her Metropolitan debut as Aïda on November 6, 1961, and won plaudits for her command of the role. She is married to the famous Soviet cellist Mstislav Rostropovich.

VON STADE, Frederica, mezzo-soprano: from Somerville, New Jersey. Graduate of the Mannes College of Music in New York City. Won the Frank Chapman Award in the 1969 National Council Auditions. Made her Metropolitan debut in 1970 as the Third Genie in *Die Zauberflöte*, appeared also as Wowkle in *La Fanciulla del West*.

VOTIPKA, Thelma, soprano: born in Cleveland of Czechoslovakian parents. Began her musical studies at the Oberlin (Ohio) Conservatory of Music. Continuing her vocal instruction in New York, she sang with the German Grand Opera Company in 1929 and 1931, then later with the Chicago Civic, the American and the Philadelphia opera companies. Miss Votipka made her Metropolitan debut as Flora in *La Traviata* on December 16, 1935. With a repertoire of some forty roles, she was one of the Metropolitan's most versatile comprimario singers, and appeared with the company regularly for twenty-seven years. Her last performance was as Marianne in *Der Rosenkavalier* in November 1962. At the famous Gala which closed the old Metropolitan on April 16, 1966, she was invited to sing in the *Carmen* quintet. To her operatic colleagues, Miss Votipka was affectionately known as "Tippy."

WALKER, Edyth, contralto (1870–1950): born in Hopewell, New Jersey. Studied at the Dresden Conservatory, later engaged at the Vienna Staatsoper and sang there for four years as the leading contralto. Made her Metropolitan debut as Amneris on November 30, 1903—with Caruso, Gadski, Scotti and Plançon—and sang with the company until 1906. She then continued her operatic career in Europe. After 1933 Mme. Walker taught at the American Conservatory in Fontainebleau. She was one of the distinguished singers of opera's Golden Age.

WALKER, William, baritone: a native of Fort Worth, Texas. Studied at Texas Christian University. Metropolitan Opera debut as Imperial Commissioner in *Madama Butterfly*, October 16, 1962. Also sings Marcello in *La Bohème*, Valentin, Mercutio, Peter in *Hänsel und Gretel*, Brétigny in *Manon*, Papageno, Kothner in *Die Meistersinger*, Paolo in *Simon Boccanegra*, Yeletsky in *Pique-Dame*. He climbed to leading roles with the Metropolitan Opera.

WALTERS, Jess, baritone: born in the United States. One of the leading baritones of the New Opera Company, which was organized in 1941 and gave performances at the Forty-fourth Street Theater in New York City. He appeared with that company in the title role of Verdi's *Macbeth* and has since been active in concert and opera in the United States and abroad, particularly at Covent Garden.

WARD, David, bass-baritone: born in Dumbarton, Scotland. One of Britain's most distinguished singers, he began in the chorus of the Sadler's Wells Opera and in 1953 graduated to leading roles. In 1958 he joined the Covent Garden Opera, where he sang his first important Wagnerian role—Vanderdecken in *Der Fliegende Holländer*. This led to an engagement at the Bayreuth Festival. Subsequently he sang a notable Wotan in the annual *Ring* cycle at Covent Garden. His Metropolitan debut was as Sarastro in *Die Zauberflöte* on January 3, 1964.

WARFIELD, Sandra, mezzo-soprano: born in Kansas City, Missouri. After studies there and in New York City, she sang with the Chautauqua (New York) Opera Association, the New York Chamber Opera Society and the NBC Television Opera Theater. She made her Metropolitan debut on November 20, 1953, in *Le Nozze di Figaro*, following opera and concert appearances in Europe with her husband, tenor James

McCracken. While abroad, they became leading singers at the Zurich Opera, where they were starred in a revival of Meyerbeer's *Le Prophète*. In 1968 they appeared together as Samson and Dalila during the Metropolitan's summer park season.

WARREN, Leonard, baritone (1911–60); born in the Bronx, New York, of Russian parents; real name Varenoff. Began his musical career as a member of the Radio City Music Hall chorus, won the Metropolitan Auditions of the Air in March 1938. A gift from a patron of the Metropolitan enabled him to spend six months in Italy for study and coaching. He made his Metropolitan debut as Paolo in *Simon Boccanegra* on January 13, 1939, and thereafter became the outstanding contemporary interpreter of Verdi baritone roles. By 1960 he had sung a total of 636 performances of 22 roles at the Metropolitan. His extraordinary voice had a range well over two octaves—from a low G to a high C. On March 4, 1960, Warren was singing the role of Don Carlo in *La Forza del Destino* at the Metropolitan. Stricken by a massive cerebral hemorrhage, he collapsed and died on the stage.

WATSON, Claire, soprano: born in New York City. A pupil of Elisabeth Schumann, she made her operatic debut as Desdemona in Graz, Austria. She made her New York debut on January 19, 1969, in a concert version of *Ariadne auf Naxos* with the Boston Symphony at Carnegie Hall, New York City. Miss Watson is the wife of tenor David Thaw and the great-great-granddaughter of Oliver Shaw, American composer. She appears regularly in Stuttgart, Munich and Vienna, as well as in Italian opera houses and at Covent Garden; also has sung with the San Francisco Opera and the Chicago Lyric Opera. Her roles include Countess Almaviva, Pamina, Elizabeth de Válois, Eva, Gutrune, Sieglinde, Ariadne and the Marschallin.

WEATHERS, Felicia, soprano: born in St. Louis. She sang in the finals of the National Council Auditions in 1957, then won a scholarship which enabled her to study with Charles Kullman and the late Dorothee Manski. Subsequently she won the Metropolitan's Titcomb Award. Study in Europe followed. There Miss Weathers won the Laureate Prize at the International Competition for Young Singers in Sofia, Bulgaria, in 1961. This led to engagements with the Kiel Opera and the Vienna Staatsoper. Her repertoire includes a wide variety of roles in classic and contemporary opera. She made her Metropolitan debut as Lisa in *Pique-Dame* on October 21, 1965, and reappeared in the role later in the season. On June 28, 1967, she sang the role of Teena in Gunther Schuller's *The Visitation* in the American premiere of the opera given by the Hamburg State Opera at the Lincoln Center Festival. Since then, she has become a leading singer in many European opera houses and has been acclaimed for her Madama Butterfly and Salome.

WEEDE, Robert, baritone: born Robert Wiedefeld in Baltimore, Maryland. In 1927 he won the National Federation of Music Clubs contest, then studied at the Eastman School of Music (Rochester, New York) and sang with the Eastman Theater Company. Went to Italy for further study, returning in 1933 to become the leading baritone of the Radio City Music Hall. Made his Metropolitan debut as Tonio in *Pagliacci* in the spring season of 1937. His first appearance with the regular company was on February 27, 1942, when he won an ovation for his singing of Rigoletto. After his retirement from opera, Mr. Weede appeared in the successful Broadway musicals *Most Happy Fella* and *Milk and Honey*. Later he taught voice on the west coast. He returned to the stage as costar in *Cry for Us All* in the spring of 1970.

WELITSCH, Ljuba, dramatic soprano: native of Bulgaria. Studied at the University of Sofia and also in Vienna. She sang at opera houses in Graz, Hamburg and Berlin, and in 1943 was made a permanent member of the Bavarian State Opera in Munich. In that year also she sang Salome in Vienna under the direction of Richard Strauss. She made operatic history with her interpretation of the role—particularly in that she herself danced the Dance of the Seven Veils, an interlude usually assigned to a professional ballet dancer. Her Metropolitan debut in this role on February 4, 1949, brought shouts and cheers from the audience, and her Salome thenceforth became legendary.

WELTING, Patricia, soprano: born in Memphis, Tennessee, graduated from the state university there. She joined the Metropolitan in 1967 and has been heard as Papagena, Adele (*Die Fledermaus*) and Oscar (*Un Ballo in Maschera*).

WERRENRATH, Reinald, baritone (1883–1953): born in Brooklyn, New York. A graduate of New York University. Made his concert debut in New York in 1907 and thereafter established an outstanding career as a concert and oratorio singer. He made his Metropolitan debut as Silvio in *Pagliacci* on February 19, 1919, and was commended for his style and musicianship. He remained at the Metropolitan for three years, then returned to the concert field and to radio.

WETTERGREN, Gertrud, contralto: born in Eslov, Sweden, the daughter of parents who were professional singers. She and her parents frequently appeared together in recitals. Miss Wettergren's musical education was provided by Crown Princess Margaretha of Sweden. After preliminary schooling she attended the Music Academy of Stockholm, then the Royal School of Bratt. She made her operatic debut at the Royal Stockholm Opera as Cherubino, then progressed to leading roles such as Carmen, for which she was famous. Her Metropolitan debut was as Amneris on December 20, 1935. She remained for two seasons appearing also as Dalila and Carmen.

WHITEHILL, Clarence, basso (1871–1932): born in Marengo, Iowa. Made his operatic debut in Brussels in *Roméo et Juliette* in 1899, later sang at the Paris Opéra-Comique and at Bayreuth. Following his Metropolitan debut as Amfortas on November 25, 1909, Whitehill sang leading basso roles with the company for more than twenty years. He was one of the outstanding singers of the Golden Age.

WIEMANN, Ernest, basso: native of Germany. Made his Metropolitan debut as the King in *Lohengrin* on November 17, 1961. A specialist in deep basso roles, he sang effectively in such parts as Sarastro, Hagen, the Landgraf (*Tannhäuser*) and Daland.

WILDERMAN, William, basso: born in Stuttgart, Germany. Developed his operatic career as a member of the New York City Opera Company, appearing effectively in such widely different roles as Horace in Marc Blitzstein's *Regina* and as Falstaff. He first appeared at the Metropolitan in the role of the First Nazarene in *Salome* on January 24, 1958, and thereafter appeared frequently both in leading and comprimario roles.

WILLIAMS, Camilla, soprano: a native of Virginia. A graduate of Virginia State College, Petersburg, she was a teacher before taking up a musical career. After study in the United States and abroad, she was acclaimed for her debut as Cio-cio-san with the Vienna Staatsoper, and won similar plaudits for her American debut in the same role with the New York City Opera. Subsequently, under the auspices of the State Department and ANTA, Miss Williams made a five-and-a-half-month tour of the Far East. Following that, at the invitation of the State Department, she made an unprecedented tour of fourteen North and Central African countries.

WILLIAMS, Nancy, mezzo-soprano: born in Pittsburgh. After study at the New England Conservatory in Boston, she toured with the Goldovsky Opera Company and later appeared with many civic opera groups. She became a member of the Metropolitan company in 1966.

She sang the role of Flora in the *La Traviata* which opened the 1967–68 season.

WILSON, Dolores, soprano: born in Philadelphia of English-Italian parents. Sang frequently on television and radio, then studied in Europe, where she sang extensively. She made her debut as Rosina in *Il Barbiere di Siviglia* in Brescia. Her Metropolitan debut role was that of Lucia on February 8, 1954—a role in which she later replaced Maria Callas on December 11, 1956. Miss Wilson again sang Lucia on March 9, 1959, despite a neck injury. Under the strain of performing, she collapsed in her dressing room after the Mad Scene. This was her last appearance with the company.

WINDGASSEN, Wolfgang, tenor: native of Germany. One of the foremost Wagnerian singers in Europe. When his demands for a high fee were finally met (reportedly $12,000, plus transportation, for not more than eight appearances) he made his Metropolitan debut as Siegmund on January 22, 1957. He sang the title role in *Siegfried* and also the *Götterdämmerung* Siegfried later that season and subsequently returned to Europe. It was reported that illness prevented his return to New York for Parsifal, which, along with Tristan, is one of his most celebrated roles.

WITHERSPOON, Herbert, basso (1873–1935): born in Buffalo, New York. Graduate of Yale University. Studied voice in New York and Paris. Made his concert debut in New York in 1902 with great success, then appeared with the Boston Symphony and other orchestras throughout the United States. His Metropolitan debut was made at one of the company's Sunday night concerts as Pogner in the final scene from *Die Meistersinger* on November 22, 1908. He sang leading roles with the company until 1916. In later years he taught voice, became president of the Chicago Musical College (1925–29) and served as artistic director of the Chicago Civic Opera Company (1931) and director of the Cincinnati Conservatory (1932–33). In 1935 he was appointed general manager of the Metropolitan to succeed Gatti-Casazza. Not long after the appointment, Witherspoon was fatally stricken with a heart attack in his office.

WUNDERLICH, Fritz, lyric tenor (1931–66): born in Kusel, Germany. After establishing a reputation as one of Germany's best specialists in art songs, he made his operatic debut in Salzburg in 1959. Singing extensively in Europe, he was regarded as one of the most gifted artists of his generation. In 1964 he made a successful concert tour of the United States. Wunderlich was scheduled to make his Metropolitan debut as Don Ottavio on October 8, 1966. On September 17 he died in a Heidelberg hospital as the result of injuries suffered in a fall. His voice still may be heard in a number of superb recordings.

YEEND, Francis, soprano: born in Vancouver, Washington. One of the leading singers of the New York City Opera Company. Made her Metropolitan debut as Chrysothemis in *Elektra* on February 13, 1961. She reappeared in that role and later also sang Gutrune in *Die Götterdämmerung*. Outstanding as an actress-singer.

ZEANI, Virginia, soprano: born in Romania. A pupil of the noted tenor Aureliano Pertile in Milan, she became one of the most popular sopranos in Italy. She has sung with the opera companies of Houston, Philadelphia, New Orleans and Montreal, and in 1967 made her Metropolitan debut as Violetta at the Metropolitan. She reappeared there the following year with the Rome Opera Company as Desdemona in Rossini's *Otello*. Other roles include the Verdi Desdemona, the two Manons (Puccini's and Massenet's), Marguerite in *Faust* and Margherita in *Mefistofele*. Her husband is the basso Nicola Rossi-Lemeni.

ZYLIS-GARA, Teresa, soprano: born in Wilno, Poland. Studied piano and voice at the conservatory in Lodz. With German opera companies in Oberhausen and Dortmund she sang Pamina, Madama Butterfly, Violetta, Fiordiligi, Santuzza, Octavian and the Composer in *Ariadne auf Naxos*. At the Deutsche Oper-am-Rhein in Düsseldorf she was acclaimed in the title roles of *L'Incoronazione di Poppea* (1966) and *Anna Bolena* (1967). First appearance in the United States was with the San Francisco Opera in November 1968 as Donna Elvira in *Don Giovanni*. In this role she made her American radio debut in the Metropolitan broadcast on January 4, 1969.

# PART IV

---

## OPERA TODAY:

## A BRIEF SURVEY

Contemporary opera has turned completely away from the classic form that has occupied the stage for more than three hundred years.

Born in the esoteric works of Peri and Monteverdi, opera had moved through the Golden Age of *bel canto* in the seventeenth century, the *opera seria* epoch of Scarlatti and Handel, the operatic rebellion of Gluck and the lush romantic period of Bellini, Rossini and Donizetti. Quickened by the nationalistic spirit of the mid-nineteenth century, it was infused with new life in the hands of Verdi, Wagner and Strauss. And all the while, it moved steadily and irrevocably toward realism.

The focus on dramatic verities first manifested itself in the works of the great operatic melodists—Puccini, Leoncavallo, Mascagni, Giordano, Charpentier—who persisted in writing opera in terms of down-to-earth human experience. And thus *verismo* was born.

In the hands of twentieth-century composers, *verismo* took on a sharper edge, reflecting a more uncompromising view of things, with the music more and more subservient to the drama. This trend was polarized in the atonal operas of Alban Berg—*Wozzeck* and *Lulu*—works which marked the emergence of opera into a new phase.

Subsequently, composers such as Stravinsky, Schönberg, Orff, Milhaud and Poulenc—and to a lesser degree Britten and Menotti, whose works are tempered by lyricism—carried *verismo* to the threshold of the avant-garde. Melody and lyricism now have been relegated to the background in favor of the dramatic values of the libretto. In opera today, *the play's the thing*.

This dictum has altered the technique of operatic expression itself. To begin with, the chief medium of communication is no longer the singer, but the orchestra. With the exception of isolated passages of lyricism, the singer is confined to expressing himself in recitative. *Parlando* has replaced the aria; choral commentary, somewhat in the manner of the classic Greek chorus, takes the place of the great massed ensembles of grand opera.

Nothing must stand in the way of getting the text across to the audience, because it is on this, rather than on the music, that the modern composer depends to promulgate his ideas. To that end, the singer declaims. The orchestral accompaniment is in most cases sparse, angular, atonal and explosive, with extremes of dynamics.

The absence of the sensuous play of human emotions, melodically expressed in the manner of traditional opera, has resulted in a certain degree of operatic asceticism. The appeal of Hans Werner Henze's *Der Junge Lord*, Gunther Schuller's *The Visitation*, Alberto Ginastera's *Bomarzo* or Marvin David Levy's *Mourning Becomes Electra*, for example, is to the intellect rather than to the heart. Dealing with human problems in terms of the present, and reflecting the universal feelings of fear, guilt and uncertainty that beset modern man, these operas have powerful dramatic thrust, with the music relegated to secondary support.

In general, the critical reaction to contemporary operas such as those mentioned is that though they are expertly constructed in their own idiom, and have been performed with great histrionic skill, they lack the essential musical quality which would strike a responsive chord in the hearts of the opera-going public. And that public—even in these sophisticated times—has a weakness for melody and song.

Critics of modern opera say that composers make the music wholly subservient to the text, then submerge the text in a flood of orchestral sound. In the process, opera is "taken away from the singer." Technically, in fact, some of the extremely difficult writing of twelve-tone works restricts the singer to abitrary pitches unrelated to the structural character of song. The effect is to put him into an emotional strait jacket and deny him the opportunity for melodic expression.

To meet the demands of modern opera, singers must be retrained. Traditional vocal techniques adequate for standard opera and *bel canto* singing cannot, in the strict technical sense, be applied to modern works. The writing is extremely complex, with wide skips to the limits of vocal range, problems involving atonality, and the absence of any guiding melodic pattern. Moreover, there are further complexities of rhythm and prosody which most singers are unprepared to handle.

In its break with tradition and its bold experimentation, contemporary opera is part of the musical revolution which erupted in the nineteen sixties. As Aaron Copland expressed it in part:

> The art . . . is in the process of being dismantled, broken down into its component parts, and put together in new ways. . . .

A brand new factor has now to be taken into account—the injection of science and scientific calculation into our musical thinking. A tone is no longer merely a tone, to be accepted as a fact of nature. It can be taken apart like a mechanism and measured in frequencies, in decibels, in duration, and in kinds of attack. It can be reassembled by electronic means, recorded on magnetic tape . . . to produce every possible sound combination, from shattering noise to the most delicate tonal mixtures. . . .

The latest development is computer music. If fed the necessary information, the computer can write its own music *and* perform it. . . . Then we have music without instruments, without performers, and even without composers.[1]

Paradoxically—the musical revolution notwithstanding—opera today is more popular than ever. To this, even dull statistics bear eloquent witness. In 1953 in the United States, there were 386 groups producing opera; in 1956, 600; in 1959, 727. During that six-year period the total number of opera performances climbed from 2704 in 1953 to 3953 in 1959.

In 1966–67 there were 3662 performances of standard operas and 1825 performances of contemporary works. During that period there were performances of about 164 works in the standard repertoire and 171 contemporary operas. At present writing, approximately 272 companies throughout the United States produce modern operas.

In the closing years of the nineteen sixties there were five regularly functioning opera companies in the United States—the Metropolitan, the New York City Opera Company, the San Francisco Opera, the Chicago Lyric Opera and Sarah Caldwell's opera company in Boston. On the international scene, London, Berlin and Paris each supported two first-line professional companies presenting old and new operas. Like the United States, Italy and Germany each had five principal opera establishments; it was claimed that East and West Germany supported about 124 opera houses operating most of the year around.

Of the American companies, only the New York City Opera consistently presented American opera as part of its regular repertoire. Chief among such presentations were *The Ballad of Baby*

[1] *The Contemporary Scene,* by Aaron Copland, *Saturday Review,* June 25, 1966, p. 49.

*Doe, The Crucible, Susannah, The Medium* and *Amahl and the Night Visitors.* An interesting addition to the repertoire was Gian-Carlo Menotti's new one-act opera for children, *Help! Help! the Globolinks!,* given during the 1969–70 season on a double bill with *Amahl.* The New York City Opera also pioneered with such productions as Ginastera's *Don Rodrigo* and *Bomarzo.*

In the main, the other companies confined themselves to standard repertoire, although there were certain ventures into the realm of operatic atonality. In 1966 the San Francisco Opera Company presented the first American performance of Leoš Janáček's *The Makropoulos Case,* premiered in Czechoslovakia almost a half century ago. The company also performed Alban Berg's *Lulu.* Also in 1966, Sarah Caldwell's opera company in Boston staged the first American performance of Arnold Schönberg's thirty-five-year-old atonal opera *Moses and Aaron.* Although the work was described as a spoken drama with musical background, its presentation was hailed as an important operatic event.

At the Metropolitan, the leading contemporary works were Igor Stravinsky's *The Rake's Progress,* Samuel Barber's *Vanessa* and Menotti's *The Last Savage. The Rake's Progress,* premiered in 1953, was given seven times in two seasons. *Vanessa,* premiered during the 1957–58 season, remained in the repertoire for three seasons. *The Last Savage,* presented in the 1963–64 season, achieved some measure of critical acclaim and was given sixteen Metropolitan performances in two seasons.

The company ventured no further into atonal territory than the boundaries indicated by Barber's *Antony and Cleopatra,* which opened the new house at Lincoln Center in 1966, and Marvin David Levy's *Mourning Becomes Electra,* premiered in 1967. Both were spectacular productions, but they failed to register musically with Metropolitan audiences; neither opera was retained in the repertoire.

Avant-garde opera, however, did reach the Metropolitan stage. During the Lincoln Center Festival in 1967, the Hamburg State Opera gave the American premiere of Gunther Schuller's *The Visitation.* Based on the dramatic concepts of Franz Kafka's famous novel *The Trial* (*Der Prozess*), the plot has to do with racism in the United States. It is written in the modern idiom, with the vocal elements largely in the form of *Sprechstimme,* and it contains a number of jazz sections.

Although modern opera has yet to make a place for itself in the repertoire of the established professional companies, it is receiving a sympathetic hearing across the nation in opera workshops and experimental organizations. These have enjoyed an astonishing growth in the past several years. Many are at the amateur level, but some mount professional productions with world-renowned artists singing the leading roles.

Prominent in the latter category are such organizations as the Dallas Civic Opera, memorable for its revival of Cherubini's *Médée* (Medea) with Maria Callas; the Fort Worth Opera Association, with a four-opera season; the Houston Grand Opera Association, with a three-opera season plus an opera workshop; Boris Goldovsky's New England Opera Theater, outstanding for opera in English and new ideas in staging; the Center Opera Company, Minneapolis, which has presented works by Britten (*Albert Herring*), Orff (*Die Kluge*), Kurka (*The Good Soldier Schweik*) and Milhaud (*Sorrows of Orpheus*).

Also noteworthy is the Santa Fe Opera Company, which in 1968 gave the American premiere of *The Bassarids* by Henze, one of the foremost contemporary German composers. This company also produced in 1967 Henze's *Boulevard Solitude,* his version of the classic *Manon Lescaut,* in which Manon is portrayed as a young woman of the "mod" world and her lover (Armand in this version) as a drug addict. The first performance of the composer's comic opera *Der Junge Lord,* in which the central character is a trained ape, was given in 1966 by the San Diego Opera Company.

These companies may be classified as civic opera organizations, a comparatively new type of community cultural enterprise which has proliferated during the past decade. The list at the end of this article will give some idea of their number and the extent of their activities in behalf of opera.

While "live" opera thus may be seen—thanks to these groups— virtually from one end of the country to the other, the recording industry has made this art form more popular than ever. Today a vast number of works—classic and modern—are available complete in superbly engineered recordings, and the list is growing every day. This means that the public is becoming familiar with opera aria by aria; the clarity and the balance between singers and orchestra give the listener a chance to hear the words and thus learn what the opera is about.

At present writing, the role of television in promulgating opera has not been developed to its greatest potential. Those close to this medium are frank to say that opera, in competition with the mass appeal of news, comedy and "soap opera" offered on the home screen, can command only a minority audience. This is reflected in the ratings, with the consequent lack of interest on the part of the sponsor.

Yet television has not ignored opera entirely. Examples of its significant contributions are: A complete performance of *Aïda* filmed at the Baths of Caracalla in Rome; a telecast of a backstage visit with Gian-Carlo Menotti at the Spoleto Festival in Italy, with portions of his production of *Pelléas et Mélisande;* some 100,000 feet of film—now in the Metropolitan archives—of the 1966 premiere of Barber's *Antony and Cleopatra;* the first video color tape of a performance on the stage of the Metropolitan, *Il Barbiere di Siviglia,* photographed and recorded in November 1968 by Nippon Hoso Kyekai, a Japanese broadcasting corporation. Filmed during the final dress rehearsal on November 4 and at the Metropolitan performance on November 7, the video tape of *Il Barbiere* marked opera's entry into the field of electronics and was hailed as the beginning of a new era for this art form.

A further step in the progress of television opera was marked by the telecast of Leoš Janáček's last opera, *The House of the Dead,* on December 3, 1969, as part of the National Educational Television Festival. The production was in charge of Peter Herman Adler, formerly director of the NBC Opera and subsequently musical and artistic director of NET. Janáček's opera (completed in 1928 and premiered in 1930, two years after the composer's death) was presented in an English translation by Marie Winn, with score and libretto edited by Mr. Adler specifically to meet the demands of television.

Later in the season, NET telecast a performance of Jack Beeson's *My Heart's in the Highlands.*

At present writing, operas scheduled for television presentation include: *Peter Grimes,* a coproduction of the British Broadcasting Corporation and National Educational Television, New York broadcast June 3, 1970; *The Abduction from the Seraglio,* NET Opera, scheduled for late fall 1970; *Pique-Dame,* NET Opera, scheduled for spring 1971.

While it is recognized that the potentialities of opera on television are almost limitless, its development involves many complex problems and demands specialized knowledge.

Mr. Adler wrote in part not long ago:

> The production of serious musical television shows is an infinitely complicated process, which cannot be carried through successfully on a haphazard basis. . . . It requires long-range planning, extensive rehearsal time, and, even

more important, a production team whose members under-stand each other as well as they understand the medium in which they work.

On the one hand, few television technicians have the musical experience to find the right balance between ear and eye—a particularly delicate judgment in a medium full of visual temptations. On the other hand, singers whose schooling is aimed at the cavernous areas of halls such as the Met . . . need fundamental retraining if they are to project before the "cruel" eye and ear of the TV camera.

And this means that achievement can only come from slow, quiet growth, together with a budget designed to foster such growth rather than to lure big names and sup-port huge advance publicity.[2]

This then, at a glance, is opera today—an art that is still burgeoning in popularity after having brought the enchantment of song to countless millions the world over for more than three hundred years, an art whose practitioners are now breaking the mold of tradition and striking out in bold experimentation, musi-cally and dramatically, to give it new meaning in the world of tomorrow.

[2] *Music: The Silent Stepchild,* by Peter Herman Adler, *Saturday Review,* April 26, 1969, p. 24.

# PART V

---

## AN OPERA GLOSSARY

A CAPPELLA: choral music sung without accompaniment of any kind.

APPOGGIATURA: an embellishment (*q.v.*), usually in the form of a note just above the principal note.

ARIA: a formalized vocal solo in an opera.

ARIA DA CAPO: typical of nineteenth-century opera. Its form is a first section, a contrasting second section, then a repetition of the first section.

ARIA PARLANTE: sung in loose rhythm closely paralleling rhythm of speech. Not to be confused with *Sprechstimme*, which is musical imitation of tones and rhythms of speech.

ARIOSO: a vocal solo between a recitative passage (*q.v.*) and an aria. It is not as declamatory as recitative nor as elaborate as an aria.

ATONALITY: music which has tone but is intended to sound free of any tonal center.

BALLAD OPERA: a musical play based on ballads or folk songs. An example is *The Beggar's Opera,* by John Gay (1728).

BALLET: a divertissement danced by a special corps of dancers between or during the acts of an opera. Example: "Dance of the Hours" in *La Gioconda.*

BARCAROLE: a boat song characterized by a pulsing sextuple rhythm. One of the most famous in opera is in *Les Contes d'Hoffmann.*

BARITONE: the adult male vocal range between bass and tenor.

BAROQUE: a period in musical history; also, a highly ornamental musical style. Baroque was infused into opera in the late seventeenth and early eighteenth centuries.

BASS, BASSO: the lowest range of the adult male voice.

BASSO CANTANTE: a lyric bass, particularly in the lower range.

BEAT: the *pulse* of the music. Not to be confused with tempo (frequency of beats), measure (grouping of beats) or rhythm (*q.v.*).

BEL CANTO: a smooth, beautiful style of singing, characterized by elegance of tone and delivery, developed by the Italians during the seventeenth and eighteenth centuries.

BOCCA CHIUSA: singing with mouth closed.

BRAVURA: great brilliancy and accuracy in execution.

BRINDISI: a drinking song.

BUFFO, BUFFA: denoting an operatic characterization which is humorous or comically grotesque. A *buffo* is an operatic clown.

CABALETTA: a short song set off by a triplet figure in the accompaniment; also, the second or third part of an aria.

CADENCE: final moment of a melody or phrase of music.

CADENZA: a florid passage in a song or aria—usually near or at the end —sung as a vocal embellishment.

CANTABILE: singing in easy, flowing style.

CASTRATO: an adult male singer whose boy's voice has been retained as the result of castration. During the seventeenth and eighteenth centuries some of the most famous singers in opera were the *castrati*.

CAVATINA: A solo shorter and less elaborate than an aria.

CHAMBER OPERA: intended for a small audience, or to be given in a small theater. Frequently without chorus and with a small cast.

CHEST VOICE, CHEST REGISTER: the vocal tone produced from the chest cavity, a distinguishing feature of big dramatic voices. It is in contrast to the head tone, which is lighter and more lyric. The concept of separate registers, however, has been questioned.

CHORAL OPERA: in which the chorus is predominant, as in most of the operas of Gluck, or in *Boris Godunof*. It has elements of the classic style of Greek drama.

CHORUSMASTER: the man who trains and rehearses an opera chorus.

CLAQUE: a small group of people sometimes hired by opera singers to lead the applause for them.

COLORATURA: florid vocal embellishments, chromatic runs, cadenzas and so on. Also, a soprano with a light, agile voice.

COUNTERTENOR: a male voice with an exceptionally high range.

DIATONIC: within the natural scale without altered notes; non-chromatic. Function is represented by the "white notes" of the piano.

DIVA: a female opera star. *Diva* is the Italian word for "goddess."

DIVISI: divided musical line. Passage in which individuals or choristers who have been singing in unison divide to sing different notes.

DODECAPHONISM: the theory of the twelve-tone scale—twelve equally spaced tones of the tempered system having equal harmonic value. The thematic structure is established as a series of twelve tones, with each tone used once. This is the harmonic system of Alban Berg's *Lulu*.

DRAMMA PER MUSICA: a more specific definition than *opera* for a drama in musical terms.

DYNAMICS: the contrasting action of loud and soft. As applied to opera, the rising and falling of emotional tension as the drama unfolds.

EMBELLISHMENTS: tones added to an essential melody for decorative effect, display or elaboration.

ENSEMBLE: a particular combination of three, four, five or more voices. Also, a chorus.

FALSETTO: a vocal tone minus resonance, produced with a high larynx position.

FINALE: the last scene of an act or of a whole opera. Earlier operas usually ended with a display aria for the star; after about 1750 composers began writing finales for ensemble or chorus.

FIORITURE: flowery embellishments.

FOLK OPERA: made up of folk songs or traditional material. The Spanish zarzuela is a good example.

GRAND OPERA: a term introduced in France circa 1820 to define an elaborate singing show without spoken dialogue, usually on a serious subject.

HABANERA: probably of African origin, this dance in duple rhythm was introduced in Spain from Havana, Cuba. Operatically, the most familiar is the *Habanera* in *Carmen*.

IMPRESARIO: the manager or director of an opera company.

INTERMEZZO: music played between the acts—a kind of bridge between the end of one act and the beginning of another. One of the best known is the *Intermezzo* from *Cavalleria Rusticana*.

KAMMERSÄNGER, KAMMERSÄNGERIN: in Germany and Austria, an honorary title conferred on virtuoso singers—both in concert and in opera.

LEGATO: a marking in music indicating notes that are to be given their full value, creating a smooth-flowing, continuous effect.

LEITMOTIV: a motif recurring throughout an entire opera, associated with a given character, situation or emotion. It was first developed and brought to its highest degree of effectiveness by Richard Wagner.

LIBRETTO: the printed text of an opera, usually available in booklet form.

LIRICO SPINTO: a voice combining the qualities of the lyric and the dramatic; usually applied to the male voice.

MEZZA VOCE: half voice.

MEZZO-SOPRANO: a voice in the range between soprano and contralto.

MISE-EN-SCÈNE: the manner in which a scene is staged (sets, costumes, lighting and so on).

OPERA BUFFA: low-comedy opera.

OPÉRA COMIQUE: opera (not necessarily comic) in which the dialogue bridging the plot situations is spoken instead of sung.

OPERA SERIA: serious or tragic opera.

OPERETTA: a light, amusing musical play, usually with a farcical plot, spoken dialogue and songs instead of arias.

OVERTURE: the technical term for an orchestral introduction or prelude of an opera, which in many cases states certain themes associated with different characters or sometimes plot motivations.

PRIMA DONNA: another name for *diva*.

PROLOGUE: a short or a long scene sung before the main section of an opera to explain the background of the drama. Because it is *sung*, it is different from a prelude or an overture.

PROMPTER'S BOX: a hooded installation at the center of an opera stage at the footlights, where the prompter, unseen by the audience, gives musical cues to the singers.

RECITATIVE: a passage in which the words are sung, but not to strict rhythm nor in the form of a flowing melody. The only accompaniment is an occasional chord played on a harpsichord or by the orchestra.

REFRAIN: a stanza which recurs in a ballad or a song. It may be a solo passage without the extent or elaboration of an aria.

RHYTHM: in a broad sense, "a steady flowing." It is the regular recurrence of grouped strong and weak beats, or heavily and lightly accented tones, in alteration; an arrangement of successive tones, usually in measures.

RITORNELLO: a term applied to instrumental interludes between scenes in baroque opera.

ROMANZA: a term describing an aria predominantly lyric in character.

RUBATO: literally, "robbed." In a rubato passage, the extra time given to one beat is made up by hurrying the other notes within the measure in order to maintain the tempo of the piece. It is used mainly for emphasis.

SCENA: an episode in an opera which integrates the music and the drama, making each equally important. It may be the extension of one of the principal arias of an opera.

SINGSPIEL: the German word for "song-play," spoken dialogue interspersed with songs or arias. It is closely allied to ballad opera and *opéra comique*.

SOPRANO: the highest range of the female voice—or boy's voice before mutation (voice change) occurs. Also designated as treble.

SOTTO VOCE: a kind of whispered singing.

TENOR: the highest range of the adult male voice.

TESSITURA: the prevailing range—not necessarily extremely high or low notes—of a song or aria.

TREMOLO: an uncontrolled wavy or oscillating tone with an unsteady pitch, mainly due to faulty breathing.

TRILL: prolonged singing of a note and the one above or below it in rapid succession. A difficult vocal feat which only the best singers can accomplish.

VERISMO: stark realism in opera, as first exemplified by Puccini, Leoncavallo and Mascagni. A prime characteristic of contemporary opera.

VIBRATO: a pulsating effect on a steady pitch—as distinct from tremolo—imparting a heightened emotional level.

# APPENDIX

# OPERA BIBLIOGRAPHY

*Annals of Opera, 1579–1940,* compiled from original sources by Alfred Loewenberg, with an introduction by Edward J. Dent. Vol. 1: Text. Societas Bibliographica, Genève 8 Rue Verdaine, 1955.

*Berlioz and His Century,* by Jacques Barzun. Cleveland and New York, Meridian Books, World Publishing Company, 1956.

*Bringing Opera to Life,* by Boris Goldovsky. New York, Appleton-Century-Crofts, Division of Meredith Corporation, 1968.

*Callas, Portrait of a Prima Donna,* by George Jellinek. New York, Ziff-Davis Publishing Company, 1960.

*The Collector's Verdi and Puccini,* by Max de Schauensee. Philadelphia and New York, J. B. Lippincott Company, 1962.

*The Concise Oxford Dictionary of Opera,* by Harold Rosenthal and John Warrack. New York, Toronto, Oxford University Press, 1964.

*The Critic at the Opera,* by Dennis Arundel. London, Ernest Benn, Ltd., 1957.

*Crowell's Handbook of World Opera,* compiled by Frank Ledlie Moore, introduction by Darius Milhaud. New York, Thomas Y. Crowell Company, 1961.

*The Decca Book of Opera.* Biographies by Harold Rosenthal, with a foreword by Erich Kleiber. London, Werner-Laurie, 1956.

*Donizetti and the World of Opera in Italy, Paris and Vienna in the First Half of the Nineteenth Century,* by Herbert Weinstock. New York, Pantheon Books, 1963.

*Encyclopedia of the Opera,* by David Ewen. New York, A. A. Wyn, 1955.

*The Essence of Opera,* by Ulrich Weisstein. London, Collier-Macmillan; New York, the Free Press of Glencoe, 1964.

*Five Operas and Richard Strauss,* by Lotte Lehmann. New York, Macmillan, 1964.

*Flagstad, a Personal Memoir,* by Edwin McArthur. New York, Alfred A. Knopf, 1965.

*George Frideric Handel,* by Paul Henry Lang. New York, W. W. Norton, 1966.

*The Great Singers, from the Dawn of Opera to Our Own Time,* by Henry Pleasants. New York, Simon and Schuster, 1966.

*Handel,* by Herbert Weinstock. New York, Alfred A. Knopf, 1946.

*Handel's Oratorios and Masques,* by Winton Dean. London, Oxford University Press, 1959.

*Introduction to Opera,* by Mary Ellis Peltz. New York, Barnes & Noble, 1962.

*Jenny Lind,* by Joan Bailman. London, James Barrie, Ltd., 1956.

*Joan Sutherland,* by Russell Braddon. London, Collins, 1962.

*John McCormack,* by Raymond Foxall. London, Robert Hale, Ltd., 1963.

*Journey Towards Music, a Memoir,* by Victor Gollancz. New York, E. P. Dutton & Company, Inc., 1965.

*Kobbé's Complete Opera Book,* edited and revised by the Earl of Harewood. London & New York, Putnam, 1963.

*Men, Women and Tenors,* by Frances Alda. Boston, Houghton Mifflin, 1937.

*The Metropolitan Opera, 1883–1966, a Candid History,* by Irving Kolodin. New York, Alfred A. Knopf, 1966.

*My Lord, What a Morning,* by Marian Anderson. New York, Viking Press, Inc., 1956.

*Once More, from the Beginning,* by Robert Merrill, with Sanford Dody. New York, Macmillan, 1965.

*100 Great Operas and Their Stories,* by Henry W. Simon; a new and revised edition of *Festival of Opera.* A Dolphin Reference Book. Garden City, New York, Doubleday, 1957, 1960.

*The Opera Companion,* by George Martin. New York, Dodd, Mead, 1961.

*The Opera Guide,* by Arthur Jacobs and Stanley Sadie. London, Hamish Hamilton, 1964.

*The Opera Reader,* compiled and edited by Louis Biancolli. New York, McGraw-Hill, 1953.

*Opera as Theatre,* by George Marek. New York, Harper & Row, 1962.

*The Price of Genius, a Life of Pauline Viardot,* by April Fitzlyon. London, John Calder, Ltd., 1964.

*Producing Opera for America,* by Herbert Graf. Zurich, New York, Atlantis Books, 1961.

*Red Plush and Black Velvet, the Story of Melba and Her Times,* by Joseph Wechsberg. Boston and Toronto, Little, Brown & Company, 1961.

*Renata Tebaldi, the Woman and the Diva,* by Viktor Ilich Serov. New York, Appleton-Century-Crofts, 1961.

*Subway to the Met: Risë Stevens' story* (1st. ed.), by Kyle Crichton. Garden City, New York, Doubleday, 1959.

*Two Centuries of Opera at Covent Garden,* by Harold D. Rosenthal. London, Putnam, 1958.

*Verdi, His Music, His Life and Times,* by George Martin. New York, Dodd, Mead, 1963.

*What Time's the Next Swan,* By Walter Slezak, as told to Smith-Corona Model 88E (1st. ed.). Garden City, New York, Doubleday, 1962.

*World of Opera,* by Wallace Brockway and Herbert Weinstock. New York, Simon & Schuster, 1941.

*World Treasury of Grand Opera,* by George Marek. New York, Harper & Row, 1962.

# CONTEMPORARY OPERA AT A GLANCE

A brief selection of works which typically reflect the trend of opera at the mid-point of the twentieth century and beyond.

*Albert Herring*, by Benjamin Britten. Composed in 1947, the farcical plot is a free adaptation of Maupassant's story *Le Rosier de Madame Husson*. Herring, crowned King of the May, in recognition of his chaste and upright life, goes on a spree and enjoys the worldly pleasures he has missed. World premiere: Glyndebourne, June 20, 1947. American premiere: Berkshire Music Center Opera School, Tanglewood, Massachusetts, Summer 1949.

*Altgeld*, by Will Gay Bottje. Plot concerns three anarchists in the Haymarket bombings in Chicago (1886). Has electronic music and filmed stills. Premiere: March 7, 1969, by Opera Workshop of Southern Illinois University, Carbondale, Illinois.

*Amahl and the Night Visitors*, by Gian-Carlo Menotti. First opera expressly commissioned for television; a lyrical adaptation of the Christmas legend of the three kings. World premiere: NBC Television Opera Theater, New York, Christmas Eve, 1951.

*Antony and Cleopatra*, by Samuel Barber. Based on Shakespeare's tragedy. World premiere: September 16, 1966, opening of new Metropolitan Opera House, Lincoln Center, New York City.

*Ballad of Baby Doe*, by Douglas Moore. Based on the story of the tragic love affair of "Baby Doe," wife of a silver miner, and Horace Tabor, silver-mining tycoon of Leadville, Colorado, during the 1890s. First produced at the Central City Opera House, Central City, Colorado, in July 1956. New York premiere: April 3, 1958, by the New York City Opera Company.

*The Bassarids*, by Hans Werner Henze. Adaptation of *The Bacchae*, by Euripides. World premiere: Salzburg Festival, Summer 1966. American premiere: Santa Fe Opera Company, August 7, 1968.

*Billy Budd*, by Benjamin Britten. Composed in 1951, it is based on the story by Herman Melville on the theme of injustice: Billy, a British seaman, wrongly accused of treason by a ship's officer, kills his accuser and is himself executed. World premiere: Covent Garden, December 1, 1951.

*Blood Wedding*, by Sandor Szokolay. Composed in 1964, it is an operatic version of the García Lorca play of the same name. It is in the *verismo* tradition of *Cavalleria Rusticana*. World premiere: Budapest, 1964.

*Bluebeard's Castle*, by Béla Bartók. Based on the classic Bluebeard legend. World premiere: Budapest, May 24, 1918. First American production: concert version in English, Dallas, January 8, 1946. American stage premiere: New York City Opera, October 2, 1952 (in English).

*Bomarzo*, by Alberto Ginastera. A fantasy about the sixteenth-century Duke of Bomarzo and his "garden of monsters"—figures carved in stone. World premiere: Washington (D.C.) Opera Society, May 19, 1967. New York premiere: New York City Opera, March 14, 1968.

*Boulevard Solitude*, by Hans Werner Henze. Composed in 1952, it is a modern retelling of the Abbé Prévost's *Manon Lescaut*. American premiere: Santa Fe Opera Company, August 2, 1969.

*The Burning Fiery Furnace*, by Benjamin Britten. One of three church parables (others: *Curlew River, Prodigal Son*); about Shadrach, Meshach and Abednego, thrown into the fiery furnace by Nebuchadnezzar. World premiere: Aldeburgh (England) June Festival, 1966. American premiere: Caramoor Festival, Katonah, New York, June 25, 1967.

*Cardillac*, by Paul Hindemith. The story of a mad master jeweler who cannot bear to part with his creations, and destroys everyone who buys them. World premiere: Dresden Opera, November 9, 1926. American premiere: Santa Fe Opera Company, July 26, 1969.

*Carrie Nation*, by Douglas Moore. Based on the life of the famous woman temperance champion and "barroom smasher." New York premiere: New York City Opera, March 28, 1968.

*The Crucible*, by Robert Ward. Based on the play by Arthur Miller about the witchcraft trials in Salem, Massachusetts, in the 1690s. World premiere: New York City Opera, October 26, 1961.

*Curlew River*, by Benjamin Britten. Part Japanese Noh play, part English miracle play, part opera. American premiere: Caramoor Summer Festival, Katonah, New York, 1966.

*Danton's Tod*, by Gottfried von Einem. After the play of the same name by Georg Büchner. American premiere: New York City Opera, March 9, 1966.

*The Deadly Wishes*, (*Die Tödlichen Wünsche*) by Giselher Klebe. An opera based on the novel *Le Peau de Chagrin*, by Honoré de Balzac. The title of the novel (literally, "the skin of affliction") refers to the fragment of ass's hide which fulfills every wish of its possessor—but then shrinks and disappears, causing him to die. World premiere: Düsseldorf Opera, June 14, 1959.

*Delusion of the Fury,* by Harry Partch. Plotless. It is in the style of a Japanese Noh play, with accompaniment played on Partch's home-made esoteric instruments.

*Deseret,* by Leonard Kastle. Based on the life of the Mormon Brigham Young. World premiere (television): NBC Opera Company, January 1, 1961.

*The Devils of Loudon,* Krzysztof Penderecki. Based on John Whiting's play *The Devils* and Aldous Huxley's book *The Devils of Loudon.* World premiere: Hamburg Staatsoper, June 20, 1969. American premiere: Santa Fe Opera Company, August 14, 1969.

*Dialogues des Carmélites,* by Francis Poulenc. Opera based on the martyrdom of a group of Carmelite nuns during the French Revolution. New York premiere: New York City Opera, March 3, 1966.

*Don Rodrigo,* by Alberto Ginastera. An opera about an eighth-century Spanish king who loses his throne at the hands of a woman he betrayed. American premiere: New York City Opera, February 22, 1967.

*Down in the Valley,* by Kurt Weill. A one-act American folk opera first given by the School of Music of Indiana University on July 15, 1948. Subsequently it was given hundreds of times by amateur and professional groups throughout the United States, and was included in the repertoire of several European opera houses.

*Fiery Angel (Flaming Angel),* by Sergei Prokofiev. An opera about Renata, a nun, who is possessed by good and bad demons. To exorcise them, she seeks the aid of Madiel, the Fiery Angel, who first appeared to her when she was eight years old. Vienna premiere, 1955. American premiere: Chicago Lyric Opera, December 3, 1966.

*The Flowers of Hiroshima,* by Jean Kurt Forest. A "ban-the-bomb" opera based on a novella by Editta Morris, an American writer. Premiere: East Berlin Opera, October 10, 1969.

*The Good Soldier Schweik,* by Robert Kurka. The story of a simple but goodhearted soldier in the Austro-Hungarian army in World War I. He is made the target of ridicule but—like Wozzeck—he is no fool. American premiere: New York City Opera, April 23, 1958. Also produced by the Center Opera Company, Minneapolis.

*The Greek Passion,* by Bohuslav Martinu. Based on a novel by the Greek poet Nikos Kazantzakis, the plot is set in a Greek village and concerns the tragedy which overtakes a group of villagers chosen to act in a local passion play. World premiere: Stadttheater, Zurich, Switzerland, June 9, 1961.

*La Guerra,* by Renzo Rossellini (brother of film director Roberto). One-act opera about Italy at the time of the last air raid of World War II.

World premiere: Teatro San Carlo, Naples, February 25, 1956. American premiere: Baltimore Civic Opera, spring 1967.

*Hamlet,* by Humphrey Searle. Operatic version, in twelve-tone idiom, of Shakespeare's play. World premiere: Hamburg Staatsoper, March 5, 1968.

*Help! Help! the Globolinks!* by Gian-Carlo Menotti. An opera "for children and those who love children." Plot concerns invasion by beings from outer space whose touch turns earth people into electronic "Globolinks." Only defense against them is the sound of music. World premiere: Hamburg Staatsoper, December 1968. American premiere: Santa Fe Opera Company, August 1969. New York premiere: New York City Opera, December 22, 1969.

*Horspfal,* by Eric Stokes. An opera about the plight of the American Indian, epitomized by one with a name related to "Parsifal." Premiere: Center Opera Company, Minneapolis, February 15, 1969.

*I Am the Way,* by Jerome Hines, Metropolitan Opera basso. Sacred opera based on the life of Christ. Premiere, under the auspices of Bible societies, at the Metropolitan Opera House, April 7, 1968.

*Jacobowsky and the Colonel (Jacobowsky und der Oberst),* by Giselher Klebe. Based on the novel and play of the same name by Franz Werfel. American premiere: Hamburg Staatsoper, as part of the Lincoln Center Festival, New York, June 27, 1967.

*Jeppe,* by Geirr Tveitt. Opera based on Ludvig Holberg's comedy *Jeppe of the Hill,* a Scandinavian folk legend. World premiere: Bergen, Norway, June 10, 1966.

*The Journey (Die Reise),* by Lars Johan Werle. Details meaningless routine of typical "mass media" family. Uses back-projected slides, four percussion groups, rock combo. Mostly talking. World premiere: Hamburg, March 2, 1969.

*Katerina Ismailova,* by Dmitri Shostakovitch. Began as *Lady Macbeth of Mzensk* in 1932. Revised and retitled version presented in Moscow in 1963. American premiere (in English): San Francisco Opera Company, October 23, 1964.

*Die Kluge (The Wise Woman),* by Carl Orff. Story adapted from Grimm's *Fairy Tales.* A king marries a beautiful woman who answers his riddles. Bored with her, he tells her to leave, permitting her to take along anything she loves. One day in her travels she unlocks her trunk and lets out the king. He is delighted with her implied compliment—and her cleverness. She promises to stop being clever—because one cannot be clever and in love at the same time. First American performances by the Center Opera Company, Minneapolis, and by the New York City Opera Company at the Caramoor Festival, Katonah, New York, June 26, 1965.

*The Last Savage,* by Gian-Carlo Menotti. Satirical comedy about an American college girl on a scientific expedition to capture a primitive man. She ends up by falling in love with him. World premiere: Opéra-Comique, Paris, October 21, 1963. American premiere: Metropolitan Opera, January 23, 1964.

*The Leopard* (*Il Gattopardo*), by Angelo Musco. Operatic version of Giuseppe di Lampedusa's novel of people caught up in Italy's sociopolitical upheaval. World premiere: Palermo, December 19, 1967.

*Lizzie Borden,* by Jack Beeson. Operatic version of the notorious case of the New England spinster who murdered her father and step-mother during the 1880s. World premiere: New York City Opera, March 25, 1965.

*Louis Riel,* by Harry Somers. Opera based on the legend of Riel, leader of rebellion in Canada in 1869 and 1885. Canada's first major opera, with libretto in English, French, Latin and Cree Indian. World premiere: Canadian Opera Company, in celebration of Canada Centennial, Toronto, September 23, 1967.

*The Luck of Ginger Coffey,* by Raymond Pannell. Based on a novel by Brian Moore about the domestic troubles of an Irish immigrant in Canada. World premiere: Canadian Opera Company, Toronto, September 15, 1967.

*Luisella,* by Franco Mannino. Based on an early novel by Thomas Mann. Husband, to satisfy whim of sadistic wife, dresses in woman's clothes, sings at party, dies of shame. World premiere: Teatro Massimo, Palermo, Italy, February 28, 1969.

*Lulu,* by Alban Berg. The story of a femme fatale who destroyed all those who loved her—men and women alike—and who finally met her fate at the hands of Jack the Ripper. World premiere: Stadt-theater, Zurich, Switzerland, June 2, 1937. American premiere: Santa Fe Opera, August 7, 1963. New York premiere: Hamburg Staatsoper (in German), Lincoln Center Festival, New York, June 6, 1967.

*Madame Bovary,* by Heinrich Sutermeister. Based on the novel by Gustave Flaubert. Reverts to melodic style of the 1920s. Film projection used to illustrate thoughts of characters. World premiere: Zurich Opera, May 27, 1967.

*The Makropoulos Case,* by Leoš Janáček. A fantasy about a 342-year-old woman, kept in the prime of life by an elixir. She is looking for the formula in order to renew her life for another three centuries. American premiere: San Francisco Opera, November 19,

1966. New York premiere (in concert, sung in original Czech): Little Orchestra Society, December 11, 1967.

*Mathis der Maler,* by Paul Hindemith. Based on life of Mathias Grünewald, sixteenth-century painter and creator of the famous Isenheim altar triptych in Colmar, France. First uncut American performance: Opera Theater of University of Southern California, April 17, 1966.

*La Mère Coupable,* by Darius Milhaud. Described as a "sequel" to Mozart's *Le Nozze di Figaro.* Has the Count and Countess, twenty years later, plus son Leon and adopted daughter Florestine. World premiere: Grand Théâtre, Geneva, Switzerland, August 1966.

*The Mines of Sulphur,* by Richard Rodney Bennett. An opera about a troupe of actors stranded in an old English manor house on the moors. Titled after a line in *Othello.* World premiere: Sadler's Wells Opera, November 20, 1965. American premiere: Juilliard School of Music, New York City, January 17, 1968.

*Montezuma,* by Roger Sessions. An opera on the confrontation of Aztecs and Spanish during the Spanish conquest of Mexico in 1519. World premiere: Deutsche Oper, West Berlin, April 19, 1964; scheduled for production in May 1969 by the Opera Company of Boston, but at present writing it has not been performed.

*Moses and Aaron,* by Arnold Schönberg. An opera about the conflict between the two biblical patriarchs over the leadership of the Israelites. American premiere: Sarah Caldwell's Opera Company of Boston, in Boston, November 30, 1966.

*Mother of Us All,* by Virgil Thomson. Political fantasy about Susan B. Anthony, militant woman suffrage pioneer. Premiere: May 7, 1947, at Columbia University, New York, during American Music Festival.

*Mourning Becomes Electra,* by Marvin David Levy. Operatic version of the play of the same name by Eugene O'Neill. Commissioned by the Metropolitan Opera. World premiere: Metropolitan Opera, March 17, 1967.

*Murder in the Cathedral (Assassinio nella Cattedrale),* by Ildebrando Pizzetti. An opera about Thomas à Becket, Archbishop of Canterbury, and his struggle for power with King Henry II. American premiere: Carnegie Hall, New York, September 17, 1958, as part of the Empire State Music Festival.

*My Heart's in the Highlands,* by Jack Beeson. Based on William Saroyan's play of the same name. World premiere (television): National Educational Television, March 18, 1970.

*Nine Rivers from Jordan,* by Hugo Weisgall. Described as a fusion of dream and reality in the modern musical idiom, with the locale mostly in Italy during World War II. Central character is Lance

Corporal Don Hanwell, a battle casualty, whose life is shown in flashbacks. World premiere: New York City Opera, October 9, 1968.

*The Nose,* by Dmitri Shostakovitch. Satirical opera based on a story by Nikolai Gogol. Central character, Kovalyov, loses his nose, finds it on someone else's face, regains it. American premiere (in English): Santa Fe Opera Company, August 11, 1965.

*Of Mice and Men,* by Carlisle Floyd. Based on John Steinbeck's novel of the same name. World premiere: Seattle Opera Association, January 22, 1970.

*The Passion of Oedipus,* by Roy Travis. Composer's own adaptation of Sophocles' drama. Complex atonal score, brief bits of melody, contrapuntal choral writing. American premiere: University of California at Los Angeles, 1968.

*Penny for a Song,* by Richard Rodney Bennett. Based on the play of the same name by John Whiting. Satire on Britain's reaction to threat of war. Play set in 1804, with Napoleon as enemy. Action has balloon ascent and working fire engine. World premiere: Sadler's Wells Opera, October 31, 1967.

*Il Prigioniero,* by Luigi Dallapiccola. A twelve-tone opera about imprisonment and torture of a Flemish Protestant political prisoner during the reign of King Philip II. American premiere: Juilliard School of Music, March 15, 1951.

*Prometheus,* by Carl Orff. Based on the tragedy by Aeschylus. World premiere (staged): Stuttgart Opera, March 24, 1968. American premiere (concert): Little Orchestra Society, New York, October 14, 1969.

*Punch and Judy,* by Harrison Birtwhistle. Classic puppet characters brought to life in a tragicomic plot. American premiere: Center Opera Company, Minneapolis, February 12, 1970.

*Rape of Lucretia,* by Benjamin Britten. Story of the Roman beauty Lucretia, wife of the general Collatinus, who was ravished by the Etruscan Emperor Tarquinius. World premiere: Glyndebourne, July 12, 1946. American premiere: Chicago, June 1, 1947.

*The Servant of Two Masters,* by Vittorio Giannini. Operatic version of the comedy by Carlo Goldoni, in the style of *commedia dell'arte.* American premiere: New York City Opera, March 9, 1967.

*17 Days and 4 Minutes,* by Werner Egk. Burlesque opera, freely based on the *Odyssey.* Title refers to the time allowed those on Circe's island to escape before being turned by her into beasts. American premiere: Center Opera Company, Minneapolis, January 17, 1970.

*Die Soldaten,* by Bernd Alois Zimmermann. Based on Reinhold Lenz's play of the same name. Complex twelve-tone opera with jazz combos, Bach chorales, electronic effects and film projections. Composer originally planned its presentation on twelve small stages surrounding audience on swivel chairs. Called the most significant German opera since *Wozzeck*. World premiere: Cologne, Germany, 1965.

*Susannah*, by Carlisle Floyd. The story of a beautiful young girl in a Tennessee mountain village who becomes the target of vicious gossip as the result of being spied upon while bathing naked in a stream near her home. She is seduced by a lecherous itinerant evangelist, who is slain in revenge by her brother. World premiere: Florida State University, Tallahassee, February 24, 1955. New York premiere: New York City Opera, September 27, 1956.

*Taming of the Shrew*, by Vittorio Giannini. Based on Shakespeare's play. American premiere: Music Hall, Cincinnati, January 31,1953. New York premiere: New York City Opera, 1954 season.

*The Turn of the Screw*, by Benjamin Britten. Based on Henry James's novel of the same name, it is a Gothic horror tale of two small children menaced by two malevolent ghosts. World premiere: Teatro La Fenice, Venice Festival, September 14, 1954. American premiere: New York City Opera, March 25, 1962.

*Vanessa*, by Samuel Barber, with libretto by Gian-Carlo Menotti. The story, set in a Scandinavian country, concerns a somber love triangle involving Vanessa, her niece Erika and Anatol, the son of Vanessa's dead lover—for whom Vanessa has been waiting for twenty years. Anatol seduces Erika, marries Vanessa. Erika, in turn, is left waiting for a lover. World premiere: Metropolitan Opera, January 15, 1958.

*View from the Bridge*, by Renzo Rossellini. Adapted from Arthur Miller's play of the same name. World premiere: Teatro dell'Opera, Rome, March 11, 1961 (directed by Roberto Rossellini). American premiere: Philadelphia Lyric Opera, October 17, 1967.

*The Visitation*, by Gunther Schuller. Freely adapted from Franz Kafka's book *Der Prozess* (*The Trial*), the plot concerns the persecution of the Negro in the United States. American premiere (in English): Hamburg Staatsoper, at the Lincoln Center Festival, June 28, 1967.

*Volo di Notte* (*Night Flight*), by Luigi Dallapiccola. Based on Antoine de Saint-Exupéry's novel *Vol de Nuit*, the opera's locale is the office of an airline director in Buenos Aires. It concerns the death of a pilot on the first night flight, and the airline director's disregard of human life for the sake of technological progress. First performance in United States: Stanford University Opera Workshop, 1962. New York premiere: Opera Theater of the Manhattan School of Music, March 10, 1967.

*War and Peace*, by Sergei Prokofiev. Based on Tolstoy's novel and devoted to the Napoleonic invasion of Russia. Entire opera given in Leningrad, June 12, 1946. Final definitive version: Leningrad, April 1, 1955. First performance in the Western world: Florence May Music Festival, 1953. First American production: NBC-TV, 1957, in an English translation.

*Wings of the Dove,* by Douglas Moore. Based on Henry James's novel of the same name. Story of a young Englishwoman who plots to marry her lover off to a rich American girl—a semi-invalid doomed to die—to acquire her fortune. The scheme is revealed. When the girl bequeaths the young man her fortune, he, in shame, refuses it. World premiere: New York City Opera, October 21, 1961.

*The Young Lord (Der Junge Lord),* by Hans Werner Henze. Comic opera in which the central character is a trained ape. American premiere: San Diego Opera Company, February 17, 1966.

# OPERA ORGANIZATIONS IN THE UNITED STATES

## A REPRESENTATIVE LIST

Arundel Opera Theater, Kennebunkport, Maine.
Boston Opera Company.
Brooklyn (N.Y.) Opera Company.
Center Opera Company, Minneapolis.
Charlotte (N.C.) Opera Association.
Chattanooga Opera Association.
Civic Opera of the Palm Beaches.
Community Opera of New York in Westchester, Mount Vernon, N.Y.
    (repertoire of 32 standard and new operas; has given 450 perform-
    ances, 100 radio broadcasts).
Connecticut Opera Association.
Dallas Opera Company.
Dayton Opera Association.
Denver Lyric Theater.
Detroit Civic Opera.
Flint (Mich.) Civic Opera (has given one opera in English every year
    since 1932).
Fort Worth Opera Association.
Goldovsky Opera Theater.
Houston Grand Opera Company.
Indiana University Opera Theater, Bloomington.
Jackson (Miss.) Opera Guild.
Kansas City Lyric Theater.
Karamu Company, Cleveland, Ohio.
Kentucky Opera Association of Louisville.
Los Angeles Grand Opera Company.
Memphis Opera Theater.
Metropolitan Opera Company, New York City.
Milwaukee Florentine Opera Company.
Mobile (Ala.) Opera Guild.
New Orleans Opera Association.

New York City Opera Company.
Omaha Civic Opera Company.
Opera Guild of Greater Miami.
Opera Theater of New Jersey.
Philadelphia Grand Opera Company.
Philadelphia Lyric Opera Company.
Pittsburgh Opera Company.
Portland (Ore.) Theater Arts Association.
Riverside (Calif.) Civic Opera.
Rosa Ponselle's Civic Opera Company, Baltimore, Md.
San Diego Opera Company.
San Francisco Opera Company.
Santa Barbara Civic Opera.
Santa Fe Opera Company.
Santa Monica Civic Opera.
Seattle Civic Opera Association.
Seattle Opera Company.
Shreveport (Louisiana) Civic Opera Company.
St. Paul Civic Opera Association.
Sun State Opera Federation, Tampa, Florida.
Syracuse Symphony Opera.
Toledo Opera Association.
Tulsa (Okla.) Opera Company.
Turnau Opera Players, Woodstock, N.Y.
Washington, D.C., Opera Society.
Werner Wolff Opera Company, Chattanooga, Tenn. Founded 1943.

## "OPERA FESTIVAL" ORGANIZATIONS

Aspen (Colo.) Music Festival and Institute.
Berkshire Festival, Tanglewood, Mass.
Central City (Colo.) Opera Festival.
Chatauqua City (N.Y.) Summer Festival.
Colorado Springs Opera Association.
Empire State Festival, Ellenville, N.Y.
Hawaii Opera Festival, Honolulu.
Lake George (N.Y.) Opera Festival.
Musicarnival Tent, Cleveland, Ohio.
Oberlin (Ohio) Music Theater.
"Opera Under the Stars", Rochester, N.Y.
Ravinia Park, Chicago.

Redlands Bowl (Calif.), where Lotte Lehmann staged operas with singers
trained at her Music Academy of the West at Santa Barbara.
Red Rocks (Colo.) Theater.
San Antonio (Texas) Grand Opera Festival.
St. Louis Municipal Opera.

# INDEX